Sydney W. Head

Director of Broadcasting and Film Services

University of Miami

HOUGHTON MIFFLIN COMPANY

Boston • 𝔗𝔥𝔢 ℜ𝔦𝔳𝔢𝔯𝔰𝔦𝔡𝔢 𝔓𝔯𝔢𝔰𝔰 ℭ𝔞𝔪𝔟𝔯𝔦𝔡𝔤𝔢

Broadcasting
in America

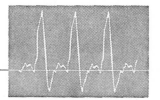

A Survey of Television and Radio

The Riverside Press
Cambridge · Massachusetts
Printed in the U.S.A.

To D. M. H.

Preface

Most wireless communication is essentially utilitarian. Ships receive navigational aid or send distress calls; airplanes follow radio beacons or exchange information with control towers; men transact business and relay news — in a thousand ways wireless facilitates the conduct of the world's business. None of this, however, is broadcasting. The relatively few stations devoted to the broadcasting service have an effect that is out of all proportion to their number, for broadcasting sets up a unique communication situation, one basically different from any other.

What is said or shown in broadcasting instantly becomes a part of the social environment. In consequence it becomes a subject of public concern and of social policy. For this reason broadcasting has never suffered from a lack of critics. It has, perhaps, suffered from a dearth of relevant, constructive criticism, for much of it has been based on assumptions and standards which apply to other media than broadcasting, other times than the present, and other places than America.

The purpose of this book is to provide a basis for appraising American broadcasting by standards relevant to the service as it exists here and now. Its basic assumption is that the system of broadcasting we have adopted in this country is fundamentally sound, is suited to our social, political, and economic philosophy, and is likely to remain in effect for some time to come. This assumption does not, however, imply blanket endorsement of the *status quo,* for it is also assumed that the interests both of the broadcasting industry and of society at large will be served by improvement of the quality of the broadcasting service within the framework of the present system.

In order to assess the need for improvement in the service and to form constructive opinions about the direction improvement should take, it should be helpful to consider where broadcasting is *now* and how it got there. What makes American broadcasting the way it is? That is the central question which this book tries to answer.

The present structure and character of American broadcasting are the products of several sets of interacting influences: the physical nature of the medium, the historical accidents of its origin and growth, the economic basis of its operation, and the social forces which modify its conduct. The first four parts of the book survey these four groups of factors. Finally, since broadcasting is not merely passive but has itself become a social influence, Part Five explores the social effects of the medium.

In making a survey such as this, one is struck by how little is new or unique about broadcasting when its several facets are considered separately. Nevertheless, broadcasting is a genuine innovation because it merges many older arts, technologies, skills, and bodies of information in a new combination. It is this new *synthesis* of elements which is unique. One of the special challenges in the study of broadcasting is the very fact that it does require the assimilation of material from many fields which in other contexts have only a nodding acquaintance with each other — if, indeed, they even know of each other's existence. In this survey the representatives of the various fields have been allowed to speak for themselves as much as possible. Each field has its own technical jargon and its own ways of conceptualizing, and an effort has been made to preserve these diverse flavorings, rather than to reduce them all to uniformity.

Anything factual that is said in print about as dynamic a field as broadcasting immediately becomes dated. Rather than avoid the presentation of relevant quantitative facts which necessarily change with time, I have tried to incorporate most of such material in tables and graphs and to cite readily available (even though sometimes secondary) serial sources, so that the reader can easily bring the tables and graphs up to date for himself.

Many publishers and other firms have been generous in allowing me to use quotations, data, and illustrations. Their contributions are gratefully acknowledged where they occur in the text. Another kind of help came from individuals who read and criticized parts of the manuscript. Among my colleagues at the University of Miami I should like to mention Virgil Barker, C. Henderson Beal, Clark Emery, Reinhold Wolff, and Charles Wurst; among practical broadcasters, John E. McCoy of the Storer Broadcasting Company; Eugene Rider of WQAM; John Allen, Lee Ruwitch, and Richard Wolfson of WTVJ; and George Thorpe of WVCG. Leo Martin, Chairman, Division of Communication Arts, Boston University, gave valuable advice on the manuscript as a whole. The author, however, assumes sole responsibility for any errors of fact or interpretation in the final content.

S.W.H.

Coral Gables, Florida

Contents

Part Two · The Origin and Growth of Broadcasting

Part Four • Social Control of Broadcasting

Part Five · Evaluating the Broadcasting Service

LIST OF PLATES

PART ONE

The Physical Bases
of Broadcasting

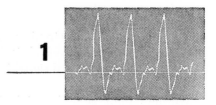

The Nature of Radio Energy

Most of us accept broadcasting as an end-result without pausing to consider what makes it physically possible. Yet in order to understand broadcasting in its broader implications it is necessary to consider its physical bases, since most of the really important problems associated with the operation of the broadcast media go back eventually to stubborn physical facts.

Fortunately, the theoretical principles involved are not hard to understand. It is a popular fallacy that theories are inherently recondite whereas practical applications are readily grasped by the layman. Actually quite the opposite is usually true: an Einstein can generally make more scientific sense to the layman than a radio repairman. The scientist sees through the tangle of wires and instruments to the general truth, but the technician's understanding is confined to the immediate complexities of specific practical application. The basic concepts and vocabulary necessary for an understanding of the theory of radio energy and its propagation are not difficult to grasp.

PRELIMINARY CONCEPTS

To start with, we must for the moment adopt a neutral view of the *meaning* of communications. From an engineering standpoint communication is a process of transferring *information,* which may consist of immediately significant material like words and pictures but also may consist of more remotely meaningful material such as arbitrarily coded sounds or pulses of energy, or even of entirely meaningless random elements. In wire and wireless communication the intentional components of information are usually called the "signal" and the unintended, spurious, accidental components are called "noise." Noise, in this special sense, provides information, but it is unintentional and, normally, unwanted information. Wire and wireless communications are always contaminated by a certain amount of noise, which may originate anywhere in the system — at the point of origin, along the transmission route, or at the receiving point. Common types of noise are hum from an electrical power source and static from atmospheric electricity. High-quality electronic equipment-components are rated in terms of "signal-to-noise ratio," which is a measure of the prominence of inherent noise in relation to wanted signal in the output of the given piece of equipment.

We must think of radio not in terms of programs but in terms of the transfer of energy from one point to another. This transfer involves processes of *transduction,* the transformation of energy from one form to another. The signal starts as sound energy or light energy; transducers (e.g., microphone and camera) change these forms of energy into electrical energy capable of being manipulated in wire circuits for amplification, mixing, and transport; at the transmitter, electrical energy, in turn, is transformed into electromagnetic energy and radiated into space. The heart of the matter is this last process, for the unique characteristic of radio communication is its ability to achieve a transfer of information through space without the aid of any intervening medium.

Radio energy bombards each of us every hour of the day. Hundreds of thousands of transmitters operate throughout the world, radiating invisible energy. At any given moment, if one could "tune in" on all the radio energy which is present in the environment, one would be overwhelmed with a stunning barrage of information. Fortunately, this ever-present deluge of information is not ordinarily perceived by the human senses until it has been detected and translated by an appropriate receiving device, although there are occasional weird instances of unplanned direct reception. An iron fence once spontaneously reproduced radio broadcasts; and a man who heard soap operas in his head thought he was going crazy until it was established that the fillings in his teeth were responsible.

Because radio energy is so impalpable we use figures of speech to describe it. We speak conventionally of the "air waves" much as we speak of the sun's going "down." It is no more accurate to imagine radio as energy carried by air than it is to imagine that the sun revolves around the earth. But we liken the unknown to the known and speak as though radio energy reached us in the same way that sound reaches us. Similarly, the term "wave" is based on analogy with the familiar movement of water, but this does not mean that radio energy actually consists of waves like those of the ocean. The fact is, no one has ever seen radio energy. All we know is that its behavior corresponds to a theoretical construct which is useful as a means of prediction and control.

Basically, we know that when energy in an electrical system is made to reverse its direction, so that it surges first in one direction and then in the opposite direction, some of the energy escapes to the space surrounding the system. All such alternating-current systems produce this radiation of energy, even the ordinary 60-cycle alternating current in the electrical systems in our houses. This leads to the concept of periodic or wave-like motion.

WAVE MOTION

Since periodicity is also characteristic of sound energy, it is convenient to explain the properties of such motion in terms of sound. In doing so, however, we must keep clearly in mind that this comparison is only an analogy; sound energy and radio energy are very different phenomena, having not only similarities but also important differences.

If we strike a tuning fork it produces a sound which has three obvious characteristics — pitch, loudness, and duration. Loudness varies with the amount of force or energy put into the stroke; but whether the sound is loud or soft its pitch remains the same, fixed by the size of the tuning fork. The duration of the sound is limited: unless new energy is supplied by another stroke, the sound gradually dies away. A tuning fork, like other sources of sound, produces its effect by means of physical vibrations. This fact can be readily demonstrated simply by touching the sounding prong with the finger or dipping it in water. However, the vibrations are so minute and so rapid that we cannot tell much about them by this simple test.

The classic device for demonstrating the detailed nature of such vibrations in slow motion is the pendulum. At rest the pendulum hangs straight down at what we will call the zero point. Given a push, it swings back and forth, both left and right of the zero point. How far it swings is determined by the amount of energy used to start it. If no further energy is supplied, it gradually runs down until it stops altogether at the zero point. The peculiarity of the pendulum's motion is that the rate at which it swings (the number of times it makes a complete left-and-right movement from the position of rest and back again in a given period of time) is constant. Whether it swings in a wide arc or barely moves, it takes just as long to complete each cycle of movement. In this it is like the tuning fork, whose pitch remains constant no matter how hard it is struck.

It would be helpful to be able to depict graphically the element of time (duration) involved in the pendulum's motion. Imagine a pendulum with a pen attached to the end so that it can trace its movement on a piece of paper. If the paper is moved horizontally past the penpoint at a constant speed, the pen will trace out a line something like that shown in Figure 1. Here we depict the time-factor by stretching out the action of the pendulum, showing each swing at a different place on the paper — i.e., at a different point in time. The resulting graphic representation of the pendulum's movement has several interesting things to tell.

One complete cycle of movement is seen to consist of two loops, one on each side of the point of rest. Thus a complete cycle consists of two opposites — an important fact to which we will return later on. Each complete cycle takes up an equal amount of space along the time dimension; this indicates that each cycle takes the same amount of time. Even though the pendulum is gradually running down, as indicated by the shortening dis-

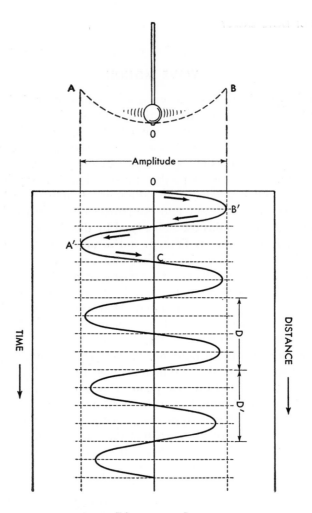

Figure 1

Concepts of Wave Motion

Assuming the pendulum moves from O, its position of rest, first in the direction B, a complete *cycle* of motion includes movement back past O to A and back again to O.

If as it moved the pendulum drew a line on a moving surface, its relative position from moment to moment would be depicted graphically as shown. The arrows indicate the direction of movement through a complete cycle, from O to B', back past O to A', and back to C, where it is ready to begin another cycle.

Turn the figure sideways to get the conventional graphic representation of a wave-train. The vertical line represents relative amplitude and the horizontal line both time and distance. Note that the time for the complete Cycle, D, is the same as that for the next cycle, D'. This is true for all four of the cycles depicted; it shows that the *frequency* and *wave length* of the pendulum are constant. The amplitude is shown to be decreasing, however, as the pendulum runs down.

tance that successive loops extend from the zero line, each cycle covers the same distance.

The graph of the pendulum's motion gives us the basic concepts associated with the behavior of radio energy. It is conceived of as being in periodic motion, like the pendulum. Each complete cycle of movement is conceived as a *wave*. Waves have a certain length, symbolized in Figure 1 by the distance covered during one cycle of movement. The waves are generated at a certain frequency, shown in Figure 1 by the number of cycles of motion completed in the time period depicted. Each wave has a certain *amplitude*, equivalent to the width of swing of the pendulum, which is dependent on the amount of energy supplied to the wave. As time passes, energy is used up and waves decrease in amplitude or run down, as illustrated by the pendulum. This is called *attenuation*. And finally, waves travel at a certain *velocity*, symbolized by the speed at which the drawing paper moved past the penpoint.

Let us now see how the concepts of cycle, wave, wave length, amplitude, attenuation, and velocity apply to sound energy. The amplitude of the pendulum's motion depends on how hard it is pushed, i.e., how much energy is applied to it; the amplitude of sound likewise depends on the amount of energy applied to the vibrating sound-source, and is perceived in terms of *loudness*. The frequency of the pendulum's motion (as also its wave length) is dependent on its physical dimensions. Obviously a long pendulum in a grandfather's clock would have a lower frequency (and a longer wave length) than a tiny pendulum in a small mantel clock. Similarly, the frequency and wave length of a sound are dependent on the size of the vibrating sound-source, and are perceived in terms of *pitch*. The low-pitched bass strings on a piano are long and heavy, suggesting low frequency and long wave length; by contrast the high-pitched strings are short and light, suggesting high frequency and short wave length. The farther away we are from the source of a sound, the more faintly it is heard; this diminution in loudness with distance from the source illustrates the concept of attenuation. Finally, we are conscious from many everyday experiences that sound travels at a finite velocity. We see the lightning before we hear the thunderclap, the flash of the gun before the report. These differences occur because sound travels much more slowly than light, with the result that we see the event perceptibly earlier than we hear the associated sound.

We have been speaking of frequency and wave length as being in some way equivalent to each other without explaining their relationship. Thus in Figure 1 the same dimension symbolizes both time and distance. Velocity is in fact a concept that involves *both* time and space, being a measurement of distance covered in a given unit of time, like miles-per-hour. A simple analogy will clarify the relationship. If a man marches at 100 steps per minute and each step is three feet long, in one minute he will travel 300 feet. Each step represents a wave, the step length represents wave length, and the distance traveled per minute represents velocity. If we keep velocity constant (300 feet per minute) and vary step-length, then step-frequency must change to meet the new condition. Thus if step-length is only two feet, the man will have to march at 150 steps-per-minute to cover the required 300 feet in a minute. Or conversely, if we change step-length to four feet, the frequency required to cover 300 feet in one minute is cut down to 75. As long as velocity remains constant, any given frequency has a corresponding wave length. Under the same condition, of course, any given wave length has a corresponding frequency. This condition is true of radio energy; its velocity in space is a constant. Hence if a frequency is given, the corresponding wave length can be always found by dividing the frequency into velocity; if a wave length is given, the corresponding frequency can be found by dividing the wave length into velocity. Thus, for practical purposes, wave length and frequency are different ways of measuring the same thing, and any given radio wave can be described in terms of either its frequency or its length.[1] The relationship is an inverse one: the longer the wave length the lower the frequency; the shorter the wave length, the higher the frequency.

SOUND v. RADIO ENERGY

So far we have been talking in analogies in order to show the essential simplicity and familiarity of the concepts involved. Although radio energy may seem a good deal more mysterious than the swinging of a pendulum or the sensation of hearing, it is mainly its impalpability that makes it seem so. Nevertheless, we must now emphasize again that radio differs in important respects from sound energy. One major difference is that radio energy travels through space at the rate of about 186,000 miles (300,000,000 meters) per second. This means that a radio wave can travel around the earth seven times in one second. Shakespeare's imagination stopped far short of this: Puck's boast was that he could "put a girdle about the earth in forty minutes." Sound, on the other hand, travels in air at only about one fifth of a mile per second, which means that radio waves travel over nine hundred thousand times as fast as sound waves.

Another important difference between the two forms of energy is the media in which they can travel. Sound, as usually perceived, travels in air, although of course it can also be conducted by other gases, by liquids, and by solids. In any event it has to have some physical medium in which to travel or it will not travel at all. This means sound cannot travel in a vacuum. The conventional demonstration of this fact is made by hanging an electric bell in a glass jar from which the air is slowly exhausted. As the air thins out the sound of the bell becomes fainter and fainter, and when the jar is nearly exhausted of air the bell cannot be heard at all, although the clapper can still be seen striking the bell. Radio waves differ radically:

---

[1] In the United States the term "frequency" is generally, though not always, used; in Europe it is more usual to designate a wave in terms of its length.

they require no ascertainable medium at all. They can go through a vacuum as easily as through air. One proof is the fact that radio waves have been sent to the moon and reflected back to earth; this clearly would be impossible if the waves needed an atmosphere as a vehicle. Radio waves can, under some circumstances, pass through liquids and solids as well as gases. On the other hand, under certain circumstances radio waves will be affected by such factors as the temperature, the density, and the water saturation of the atmosphere through which they pass. But their unique characteristic is that they need no physical matter of any kind as a medium in which to travel. Because it is hard for us to conceive of complete nothingness in space, or of energy traveling from place to place with no conductor whatever, one theory used to fill the emptiness with a word — "ether." But the word is as empty as the space it represents, because it means nothing that man has yet been able to explain.

THE ELECTROMAGNETIC SPECTRUM

It will be recalled that the velocity of radio energy in space is approximately 300,000,000 meters (or 186,000 miles) per second. This is a quantity of the greatest significance in modern physics, for it is the one absolute in the Einsteinian conception of the physical universe.[2] That 300,000,000 meters per second is also the speed of light is no mere coincidence, for light energy and radio energy are basically one and the same thing. The fact is that a tremendously varied range of physical phenomena is comprised under the single concept *electromagnetic energy*. This form of energy may manifest itself in very different ways — for instance, as light, as radio waves, as X-rays, as cosmic rays. But in back of this fantastic variety is a fundamental unity: all these forms of energy have that same significant velocity of 300,000,000 meters per second, all have the characteristics of periodic waves as previously described, all have the ability to radiate through space. The universe appears to be saturated with electromagnetic energy, which reaches the earth even from the depths of outer space in the form of cosmic rays.

The characteristic properties of the various forms of electromagnetic energy are determined by wave length (or, what is the same thing since velocity is constant, frequency). Wave lengths or frequencies laid out in numerical order are called a spectrum (see Figure 2). A spectrum is roughly analogous to the keyboard of a piano, which represents a spectrum of sound frequencies in ascending order, from low frequencies at the left end to high at the right. A visible example of a spectrum occurs when sunlight is broken up by a rainbow or a prism into its component colors.

---

[2] The expression c in the most famous equation of modern times, $E=Mc^2$, stands for the speed of light. This is the Einstein equation which predicts the tremendous energy released by atomic fission. The equation is so well known that it was used by CBS as the title of its program in memory of Einstein after his death in 1955.

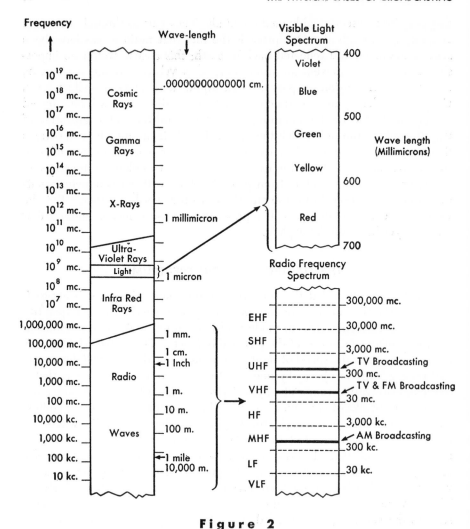

Figure 2

The Electromagnetic Spectrum

This color sequence is laid out in terms of frequency, the red end of the spectrum representing the lower frequencies, the blue end of the spectrum the higher frequencies. Beyond these limits of visible light are frequencies of invisible light — infra-red (below visible frequency) and ultra-violet (above visible frequency).

The electromagnetic spectrum begins with electrical energy, which has extremely low frequency and long waves. The radio part of the spectrum starts at a frequency of about 10,000 cycles per second, at which point each wave is 30,000 meters (over 18 miles) long. At the upper end of the radio part, waves have a frequency of 300,000,000,000 cycles and a length which is microscopic. Beyond this point the radio frequencies begin to blend into those of infra-red electromagnetic energy. Visible light begins at frequencies of about 375,000,000,000,000 cycles per second. Above the comparatively small part of the spectrum which yields visible light comes ultraviolet light, then X-rays, gamma rays, and cosmic rays. Just as the electromagnetic spectrum as a whole exhibits radically different behavior at different frequencies, so does the radio part of the spectrum have widely different characteristics in its various frequency ranges.

Waves of frequencies that are useful for radio communication lie, as has been pointed out, between 10,000 and 300,000,000,000 cycles per second in the electromagnetic spectrum. This vast range of frequencies has been classified into eight frequency ranges or bands by international agreement (Table 1).

It will be noted that the designation of these frequency ranges is peculiarly anticlimactic: after the progression from "very" to "ultra" to "super" we are rather let down by the mildness of "extremely." This terminology

Table 1

Subdivisions of the Radio Frequency Spectrum

Subdivision	Frequency Range
1. Very Low Frequency (VLF)	Below 30 kc.
2. Low Frequency (LF)	30-300 kc.
3. Medium Frequency (MF)	300-3,000 kc.
4. High Frequency (HF)	3,000-30,000 kc.
5. Very High Frequency (VHF)	30,000 kc.-300 mc.*
6. Ultra High Frequency (UHF)	300 mc.-3,000 mc.
7. Super High Frequency (SHF)	3,000-30,000 mc.
8. Extremely High Frequency (EHF)	30,000-300,000 mc.

* The term *kilocycle* (= 1,000 cycles) is used up to 30,000 kc.; thereafter the term *megacycle* (= 1,000,000 cycles or 1,000 kilocycles) is used. It is always to be understood that these terms refer to the number of cycles *per second*.

Source: International Telecommunications Union, *Final Acts of the International Telecommunication and Radio Conferences* (Atlantic City: ITU, 1947), Radio Regulations, Chapter II, Article 2, Section II.

reflects the way in which the utilization of the spectrum has developed. In the early days of radio communication it was supposed that frequencies above the MF range could not be usefully employed. By the outbreak of World War II the upper limits of the useful radio-frequency spectrum were in the neighborhood of 300 mc. During the war such high-frequency devices as radar led to tremendously accelerated development of technology in this area, and hence by the end of the war the ceiling had been raised to 30,000 mc. Further technological advancement has since pushed the limits of usability higher and higher. The problems of utilizing frequencies as high as 300,000 mc. are still acute, for properties of the atmosphere itself, such as the presence of rain, water vapor, and oxygen, extinguish waves at these frequencies almost as soon as they are launched. Nevertheless, previous events suggest that yet another range above EHF will ultimately be conquered.

WAVE PROPAGATION

The radiation of radio waves through space is referred to as *propagation*. Systematic study of the factors affecting efficiency of propagation at various frequencies is relatively new. In 1932 the essential knowledge of propagation could be gathered into a seven-page report; by 1950 the basic written material on the subject made a stack of documents over three feet high.[3] Theoretically, radio energy radiates from a transmitter into space equally in all directions, and the energy attenuates uniformly with distance from the transmitter. Attenuation occurs because as the signal travels straight out in all directions from the point of origination, it is progressively distributed over a larger and larger area; hence its energy becomes more and more thinly dispersed as it travels.

In practice, however, both the rate of attenuation and the geographical pattern of the coverage area are also affected by a number of highly variable factors, among them the nature of the terrain in the propagation path, the weather and atmospheric conditions encountered, the time of day and year, and even the condition of the sun and other extra-terrestrial phenomena. These factors produce discrepancies in the theoretical attenuation rate by causing refraction, reflection, diffraction, absorption, polarization, interference, and scattering of waves.

How much a given wave will be affected by given propagation conditions depends on the frequency of the wave. Take, for example, the phenomenon of refraction, which is a change in direction of a wave caused by its passage from one medium to another of differing density. This bending of the rays is due to the fact that a change of velocity[4] occurs in their passage from one medium to the next. The higher the frequency of a wave, the more markedly its velocity is changed by a new medium, and hence the more sharply its direction is changed. Therefore light is particularly subject to refraction. A familiar instance is the apparent displacement of underwater objects when observed at an angle from above the surface. The optical effects of lenses depend upon the phenomenon of refraction occurring in the passage of light from air to glass and glass to air. Radio waves may be affected even by changes in the density of the air along their propagation path; in the higher ranges of the radio frequencies and over long propagation paths, even very minute changes in velocity can have considerable bending effect.

[3] Joint Technical Advisory Committee of Institute of Radio Engineers—Radio-Television Manufacturers Association, *Radio Spectrum Conservation* (New York: McGraw-Hill, 1952), p. 21. Most of the material on propagation in this section is taken from this excellent summary of the problems of allocation in relation to propagation theory.

[4] The previously cited velocity-constant of 300,000,000 meters per second applies to electromagnetic energy *in a vacuum*.

To summarize, the study and prediction of radio wave propagation is tremendously complicated by the fact that the conditions affecting propagation are subject to constant change, while at the same time the influence of these conditions varies in accordance with the frequencies of the waves involved. In order to use the available radio frequencies efficiently for communication purposes, it is necessary so to allocate the various segments of the frequency spectrum that the peculiar characteristics of each group of frequencies will be suited to the requirements of the service assigned to them. For example, some services require long-distance communication, others only short distances; some require continuous, around-the-clock communication, others only occasional contacts; some can justify large, expensive transmitter installations and others must have lightweight, inexpensive transmitters; some require radiotelephony, others radiotelegraphy.

In the strategy of efficient frequency allocation, one of the basic considerations is the type of propagation path over which waves are capable of traveling. This is determined by frequency: waves of some frequencies travel in straight lines from transmitter to receiver; those of other frequencies tend to follow the curvature of the earth; waves of still other frequencies travel away from the earth and are reflected back. There are thus three basic types of waves in terms of transmission path: direct waves, ground waves, and sky waves (see Figures 3 and 4). Of particular importance to radio broadcasting are the sky waves, for long-distance reception is dependent upon them.

IONOSPHERE REFLECTION

Situated in several strata from about 30 to 250 miles above the surface of the earth is a layer of atmosphere called the *ionosphere*, or the Kennelly-Heaviside layer.[5] The ionosphere consists of ionized atmosphere, i.e., air which has a characteristic electrical property induced by the action of the sun's radiations. It is important to radio-wave propagation because at times it tends to reflect Medium- and High-Frequency waves back to earth. Waves of other frequencies pass through the ionosphere and dissipate their energy in space, but the waves reflected by the ionosphere can be usefully employed.

The ionosphere is not a fixed and constant reflector. It consists of several layers, not all of which are equally effective in reflecting a given radio frequency; moreover, it is subject to disturbances which are related to the sunspots and possibly to other extraterrestrial events. All this means that the service obtained from the sky waves is variable, subject to all sorts of changes. As far as the frequencies used for standard broadcasting are concerned, the most important consideration is time of day. During daylight

[5] The existence of the ionosphere was demonstrated in 1902 by two scientists working independently, Sir Oliver Heaviside in England and Arthur Kennelly in the United States.

hours the sky waves at broadcast frequencies cannot be used, but after the sun goes down the ionosphere gradually cools, until by two hours after sundown it is operating at maximum efficiency as a reflector. Reflected waves then may bounce back off the earth, be reflected a second time by the ionosphere, bounce back off the earth again, and so on. By this means tremendously long distance reception can be achieved, since relatively little

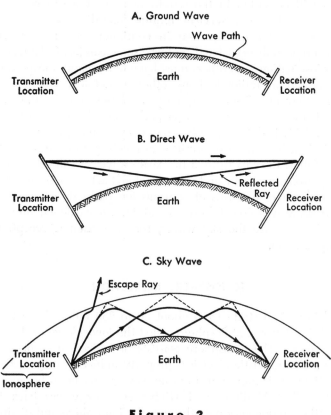

Figure 3

Types of Propagation Paths

A. The ground wave hugs the earth, following its curvature.

B. The direct wave behaves more like light. The height of sending and receiving antennas is important in compensating for the curvature of the earth.

C. Note that some energy may pass through the ionosphere and be lost. Actually, waves may be reflected from several different ionospheric layers. The rays are not thrown back sharply, as light rays are reflected by a mirror, but are bent back gradually.

Based on: President's Communications Policy Board, *Telecommunications: A Program for Progress* (Washington: Government Printing Office, 1951), p. 22.

attenuation from absorption is involved in the propagation of sky waves. However, in the process of bouncing back and forth sky waves leave some areas blank between bounces (skip distance). Another drawback is that a station's sky wave may interfere with its own ground wave. Self-interference results when ground wave and sky wave meet because the sky wave has traveled a much longer route and hence may arrive out of phase with the ground wave. The sky wave arrives at the receiving point with a fraction of a second's delay, and when two waves are not perfectly in step (i.e., in phase) they interfere with each other.[6] The ionosphere, then, makes possible long-distance nighttime reception of broadcast signals — albeit signals subject to fading and interference. At the same time, sky waves enormously complicate the problem of station allocation, because the service area of a station that uses frequencies capable of being reflected by the ionosphere expands greatly at night. The methods used to solve this problem will be discussed in the next chapter.

PROPAGATION CHARACTERISTICS AT VARIOUS FREQUENCIES

At the frequencies from 10 to 200 kc. good distance is achieved with ground waves (Figure 4). Atmospheric noise is high at these lower frequencies; it provides an effective barrier to the use of frequencies below 10 kc. The lower frequencies, then, are best suited to long-distance communications services which can afford to build very high-power stations (since power tends to override atmospheric noise) and very large antenna systems (since antenna size is related to wave length — the longer the wave, the larger the antenna).

In the next frequency range, 200-2,000 kc., sky waves begin to become effective (this range includes standard broadcasting). In the 2,000-kc.-to-30-megacycle range sky waves are of dominant importance; this range is useful for services requiring extremely long distance at relatively low cost in power. In this range, however, sky waves are increasingly subject to slight variations in the ionosphere, and hence services using them have to be ready to switch from one frequency to another as one ceases to be reflected and another comes into operation. As many as five different frequencies may have to be used by one transmitter during twenty-four hours' service. Ionosphere reflection affects waves up to 80 mc., but at the higher VHF frequencies the resulting sky waves are too unstable to be useful; however, these unstable reflections are still important, since they constitute a source of interference.

The 30-3,000-mc. group of frequencies is useful for short-distance transmission. Direct or line-of-sight waves work well in this range in place of sky waves and ground waves. This is the VHF and UHF range, to which FM and television broadcasting are allocated. In the highest range, 3,000-300,000 mc., the same considerations hold true, but now the waves begin

[6] Cf. the discussion of phase on pages 36-38.

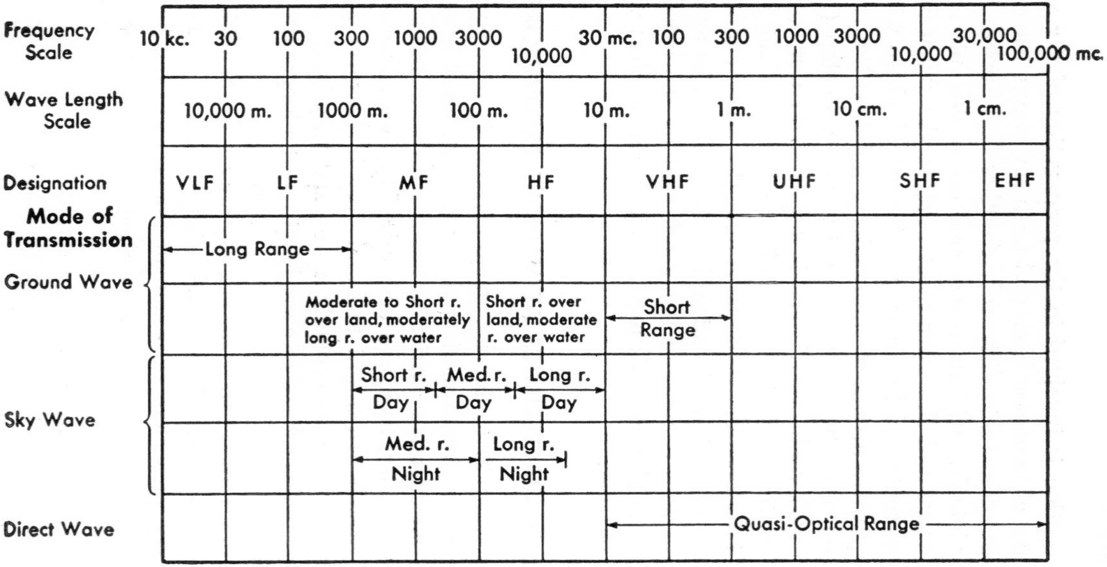

Frequency Scale	10 kc.	30	100	300	1000	3000	10,000	30 mc.	100	300	1000	3000	10,000	30,000	100,000 mc.
Wave Length Scale	10,000 m.		1000 m.		100 m.		10 m.		1 m.		10 cm.		1 cm.		
Designation	VLF		LF		MF		HF		VHF		UHF		SHF		EHF

Mode of Transmission

Ground Wave: Long Range — Moderate to Short r., over land, moderately long r. over water — Short r. over land, moderate r. over water — Short Range

Sky Wave: Short r. Day / Med. r. Day / Med. r. Night — Long r. Day / Long r. Night

Direct Wave: Quasi-Optical Range

Figure 4

Some Characteristics of the Radio Frequency Spectrum

Based on: President's Communications Policy Board, *Telecommunications: A Program for Progress* (Washington: Government Printing Office, 1951), p. 22.

to be subject to such atmospheric phenomena as rain and water vapor. Even the noise of electrons in motion in electron tubes becomes critical. This highest range of frequencies is particularly well adapted to directional propagation, which is achieved by constructing antennas which limit radiation to a desired direction. By concentrating the radiated energy into a narrow beam, antennas at these higher frequencies prevent the attenuation due to spreading of the signal over a wider and wider area as it travels. An important gain in efficiency results. The directive gain (ratio of effectiveness of power in a directional as compared with a non-directional antenna) is on the order of two, three, or four in the region of 2,000 kc. But at 30,000 mc. the gain can be as high as 100,000 and at still higher frequencies it can be as great as 100 million. This means that a directional antenna can be 100 million times as efficient as a nondirectional antenna. The principle is exactly the same as that of a spotlight, which instead of letting light dissipate in all directions concentrates it in a desired direction. Directive gain is employed in microwave relays, such as those used by a television station to pick up a sports event for relay back to the station's transmitter, or those used to relay network programs to affiliates. At frequencies used for standard broadcasting, directional antennas are important as a means of preventing interference between stations, as we shall see in Chapter 2.

This brief survey of the propagation characteristics of the various frequency ranges may be summarized by saying that ground waves are most useful at the lowest frequencies, sky waves in the middle frequencies, and direct waves at the highest frequencies (see Figure 4). The lowest frequencies are most subject to atmospheric noise, the highest frequencies to electron noise. The lower frequencies require very high power to overcome noise, whereas the higher frequencies need less power if directional antennas are used to increase the efficiency of propagation. In general it may be said that the higher the frequency of radio energy the more its behavior approximates that of light — for, indeed, the higher the frequency of radio energy the closer it comes to the frequency of light itself.

SPECTRUM UTILIZATION

The chief problem of allocation is that of employing the various frequencies to the best advantage by capitalizing on their strong points and avoiding degradation of service owing to their weak points. Unfortunately, the problem has been complicated by the fact that when the allocation of frequencies began there was no knowledge of the facts just outlined; by the time this knowledge had been developed, hundreds of thousands of transmitters were already in operation. It would have been prohibitively expensive and administratively difficult to change them all around to suit a master plan by the time the knowledge of how to construct a master plan was available. Furthermore, there are never enough frequencies to satisfy all the needs. New services are constantly developing and old services expanding; the demand for radio frequencies always exceeds the supply, and this condition grows steadily more acute. The allocation problem is a serious one on the international as well as the national level.[7]

To get some idea of the pressure on the frequency spectrum, let us look at the kinds of services and numbers of transmitters licensed by the United States (Table 2). The services are divided into three broad categories: (1) common carriers, (2) safety and special radio services, and (3) radio broadcast services. Common carriers are communications services which are available to the general public for the transmittal of private messages — i.e., the telephone and telegraph. Although these services are basically wire rather than wireless services, their communications networks include many radio links, e.g., television microwave relays and ship-to-shore telephones.[8]

Under the classification of safety and special radio services come eight major sub-classes of service: marine, aeronautical, public safety, amateur, disaster communications, industrial, land transportation, and citizens. Public safety services include police, fire, and forest conservation, among others.

Table 2

Radio Authorizations by Class of Service

Class of Service	Number of Authorizations as of June 30, 1954
Amateur	123,287
Marine	46,299
Aviation	40,154
Public Safety	15,697
Industrial	21,598
Land transportation	13,945
Broadcast	5,881
Experimental	586
Common carrier	1,635
Other	1,037
Subtotal	270,119
Operators	
Commercial	842,088
Amateur	120,535
Subtotal	962,623
Grand total	1,232,742

Source: FCC, *20th Annual Report* (Washington: Government Printing Office, 1955), p. 12.

Industrial services include radio communications networks used by power

---

[7] President's Communications Policy Board, *Telecommunications: A Program for Progress* (Washington: Government Printing Office, 1951), p. 7; Joint Technical Advisory Committee, IRE-RTMA, *op. cit.*, p. 17.

[8] In 1954, for example, the Bell System operated more than five million circuit-miles of microwave telephone facilities. FCC, *20th Annual Report* (Washington: Government Printing Office, 1955), p. 3.

companies, oil companies, motion-picture units on location, news agencies, etc. Land transportation services are used by railroads, taxicabs, buses, trucks, etc. The citizens' radio service is a special category which permits the private citizen to have his own personal radio communication facility between home and office, for instance, or for the control of model airplanes, boats, and even garage doors. This is quite apart from the amateur service in which private citizens operate stations for their own diversion to communicate with other amateurs. The amateur service has always been one of the largest classes (Table 2).

The broadcast services include, of course, television, standard (AM) radio, and FM radio. In addition, this category includes international broadcasting (short-wave), facsimile, and auxiliary broadcast services. The auxiliary services include remote pickup equipment, used occasionally to send programs from a remote point to the main transmitter; studio-transmitter links, used to relay programs from the studio to the transmitter by radio instead of wire; and developmental stations, used in research.

This greatly abbreviated list gives some idea of the tremendous variety of services which utilize the radio frequencies. Every one of these services must be allocated a block of frequencies, and in many cases each individual station (of which there may be thousands) within a service has to be assigned its own individual group of frequencies. Broadcasting is only one service among many whose claims to spectrum space must be considered.

These facts explain the background of some of the happenings in the field of broadcasting which often cause a good deal of impatience among the uninformed. For instance, the long delay from 1948 to 1952, when new television applications were frozen, was primarily caused by the need to assemble and interpret data on the propagation characteristics of television signals in the VHF and UHF regions. The continued delays, even after the freeze was lifted, in authorizing new stations in many communities were due to the fact that only a limited amount of spectrum space could be allocated to the television service without impairing other equally important and necessary services; hence in many localities there were many more applicants than available channels and a choice among mutually exclusive applications had to be made on the basis of detailed hearings.

Thus it is important to an understanding of broadcasting to realize that it is only one service among a great many. Although the other services come less often to the direct attention of the general public, they are of inestimable value to everyone — facilitating transportation and wire communication, increasing the safety of lives and property, aiding industrial development. Increasingly the non-broadcast services become an indispensable adjunct to the technological development of our times. The broadcasting services must work within a limited allocation of frequencies; and within these frequencies the many problems of propagation prediction and control both complicate and physically limit the ways in which the frequencies can be used to provide the nationwide, competitive program service which is our ideal objective.

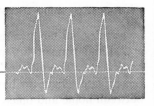

2

The AM and FM Broadcast Services

First among the broadcast services to develop was amplitude modulation (AM), officially designated as "standard broadcast." Modulation is the word for the process whereby the original information (e.g., sound in a radio studio) is translated into radio energy for transmission through space. Every broadcast transmitter radiates energy continuously as long as the station is in operation, whether or not a signal is being transmitted. When there is "dead air" in a radio program — a space of time in which no message is being sent — the transmitter nevertheless continues to transmit. This fact can be verified by tuning a receiver to a station during moments when it is not sending any signal. A slight hiss as the dial indicator passes the appropriate point indicates that energy is being received, even though it is not signal information. This basic and continuous emission of a station is known as its *carrier wave*. Figuratively speaking, at least, the function of the carrier wave is to "carry" the signal. This is accomplished by systematically altering the pattern of the carrier-wave energy in a way consistent with the pattern of energy in the original signal. This alteration of the carrier wave by superimposing an energy pattern on it is called modulation.

MODULATION

The concept of modulation is readily grasped from a consideration of the operation of an ordinary phonograph record. The record consists of a continuous groove in which a pickup stylus rides. Suppose a recording is made of "silence," i.e., no signal is recorded. On playback, the reproducing needle will ride in the smooth groove as the disc turns without producing any intentional sound. Nevertheless, a certain amount of noise — needle scratch, amplifier hum, etc. — will betray the fact that the phonograph is turned on and a record is being played. The "silent" recording is comparable to an unmodulated carrier wave, which sends no signal but nevertheless does transmit a certain amount of noise. After sound has been recorded on the disc, the sides of the groove are no longer smooth. A pattern of energy, originally in the form of sound, has now been translated into a corresponding pattern in the form of variations in the shape of the groove. The pickup stylus, responding to this pattern as the record spins, starts the process of re-translation back to sound.

Each radio transmitter has its own "groove," i.e., a group of frequencies to which it is assigned. These frequencies, known appropriately as a channel,[1] are identified in AM broadcasting by the central frequency in the group. Let us take as an example the standard broadcast channel located at 600 kc. (at 60 on most receiver dials). For reasons which are dealt with later in this chapter, all standard broadcast channels are ten kilocycles wide. Therefore the carrier frequency of 600 kc. is the midpoint of the channel, the full channel occupying the frequencies from 595 kc. to 605 kc. The station on this channel radiates a carrier wave which is 500 meters (1,640 feet) long. These large waves are radiated at the rate of 600,000 per second.

Radio waves can be modulated in several different ways, but in broadcasting two methods are used: amplitude modulation (AM) and frequency modulation (FM). Amplitude and frequency are the two most obvious choices among the variables which could be altered to provide modulation. If, as in the case of standard broadcasting, the original signal consists of sound, we are concerned with a form of energy that also has the two variables of amplitude (loudness) and frequency (pitch). Any sound can be fully described at a given moment in terms of its loudness and its pitch. Suppose, by way of example, that the sound to be transmitted from the studio has the pitch of middle C. Suppose further, to avoid complications, that this sound is a pure tone, i.e., one without overtones. That means that the sound-energy generated in the studio consists of a 264-cycles-per-second wave. The particles of air in the studio, agitated at this same frequency, cause a similar agitation in a delicately responsive component in the microphone. The actual physical movement in the microphone is, of course, extremely minute, but one can visualize its operation by recalling how a strong sound can produce sympathetic vibrations in a wall-panel or other physical objects. The pattern of vibration of the moving element is translated by the microphone into an identical pattern of electrical energy. Now we can no longer hear the signal. It travels, silent and invisible, along the microphone cable, through the wires and instruments of the control-room equipment, through more wires to the transmitter, where the unmodulated carrier wave is already being generated and radiated into space. At the transmitter the pattern of electrical energy, still vibrating at 264 cycles per second but by now amplified millions of times over what it was when the microphone started it on its way, is imposed on the carrier wave. Since this is an amplitude-modulated transmitter, the result is that the amplitude (amount of energy) of the carrier wave is altered 264 times per second.

[1] To avoid confusion it should be mentioned that the term "channel" is also used to designate an independently controlled input circuit to an amplifier. Examples: a three-channel amplifier is one to which three microphones can be fed, each with a separate control; in motion-picture recording it is usual to use separate channels for re-recording music, voice, and sound effects so that the several components can be properly mixed and blended.

Figure 5

Amplitude Modulation

Hypothetical sound, consisting of a single complete cycle of a pure tone. The reference line at the left represents relative amplitude.

Electrical wave having the same amplitude and frequency as the original sound.

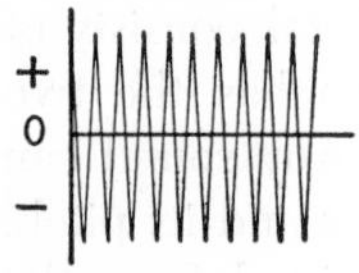

Sample of unmodulated carrier of a transmitter, consisting of many cycles in the time occupied by only one cycle of the signal.

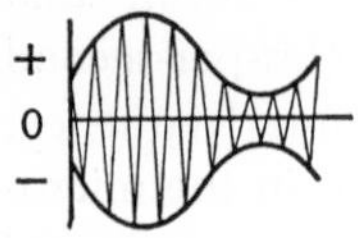

Amplitude of carrier modulated by the signal. Frequency of carrier remains constant. Note that both the plus and the minus phases of the carrier are modulated in patterns which are images of each other. Either pattern is sufficient to convey the signal.

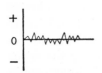

Erratic wave caused by static electricity.

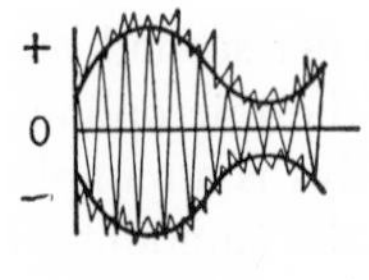

Energy from the static wave interacts with the amplitude of the carrier, distorting its modulation pattern.

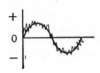

Resulting signal delivered by the loudspeaker. The receiver has stripped off the carrier wave but cannot remove distortion caused by static.

So far we have left out of this account the element of amplitude in the original sound. This component of the sound-energy pattern is accounted for by the amount (rather than the frequency) of change in the amplitude of the carrier wave. Thus if the loudness doubled, the average amplitude of the carrier wave would change proportionately, but the 264-cycle alternation in the amplitude would continue unchanged. In short, a single variable factor in the carrier wave can be used to do two things, since it can be varied independently as to both *rate* of change and *amount* of change.

One common source of confusion to avoid at this point is the assumption that there is any necessary connection between the frequency of the original sound to be transmitted and the frequency of the carrier wave on which it is transmitted. These two factors are independent. The 264-cycle sound can just as easily be transmitted by a carrier wave of 6,000,000 cycles as by one of 600,000 cycles. The 264-cycle energy pattern can be imposed on any broadcast-frequency carrier wave, irrespective of the carrier's own frequency (Figure 5).

Modulation, then, involves the transfer of a pattern of energy from one medium to another. Once the message, whether sound or any other kind of signal, is conceived as consisting essentially of an energy pattern, the possibility of translating the pattern from one medium to another becomes obvious. The air-waves in the studio, the electrical energy in the wired circuits, and finally the electromagnetic waves radiated by the transmitter all represent radically different media, yet each is capable of duplicating the pattern of amplitude and frequency of which sound consists.

THE AM BAND

Amplitude-modulated broadcasting is allocated to the frequency band 540-1,600 kilocycles. With each channel occupying 10 kilocycles, this band provides for 107 channels.[2] This band is allocated to broadcasting by international agreement. Receiver dials are generally calibrated in kilocycles, but for brevity the final zero is usually dropped; thus most home receiver dials read from 54 or 55 to 160 (the 540 kc. channel did not become available in the United States until 1952). Each standard broadcast station is assigned to a specific channel. The license stipulates the assigned channel, and the licensee must so equip his transmitter that it will not drift off frequency.[3] Frequency-monitoring equipment must be used by the station to keep a constant check on its frequency.

The designation of specific bands for the use of specific radio services is called *allocation*. The next step, permitting a station to provide service on a specific channel at a specific geographic location, is usually called *assignment*. The number of individual stations which can be assigned to the 107

[2] It should be recalled that the channels are identified by their mid-frequency; accordingly, the band actually extends down to 535 kc. and up to 1,605 kc.
[3] FCC rules permit a tolerance of only .02 kilocycles (20 cycles).

channels allocated to standard broadcasting depends upon the propagation characteristics of the frequency band within which these channels fall. The standard broadcast band of 540-1,600 kc. lies in the Medium Frequency range (Table 1). The propagation characteristics of these frequencies, it will be recalled, permit both ground waves and sky waves to be usefully employed. The former define a station's *primary* service area, the latter its *secondary* service area. Ground waves provide a relatively short-range (roughly 10 to 75 miles) service which is reliable at all times. Sky waves provide a long-range service which is available only at night when the ionosphere is effective in reflecting the waves. Since the atmosphere is subject to many vagaries of weather, sun-spot conditions and the like, even nighttime sky wave reception is not reliable all the time. Because sky waves can be a source of interference, they have to be taken into consideration even in places where sky wave service is not needed, or beyond the zone within which sky wave service is expected.

MUTUAL INTERFERENCE

Interference is at the heart of the assignment problem. When two or more signals are received at the same frequency, the receiver is unable to discriminate between them and to reject the unwanted signal.[4] Even though one of the conflicting signals may be relatively weak, it may be capable of distorting the stronger signal to the point of making it worthless. A wanted AM signal needs to be about twenty times as strong as an unwanted competing signal to overcome interference. Each station thus has a *nuisance* zone as well as a service zone. Furthermore, if two or more signals on *adjacent* frequencies are very strong, a receiver near the transmitters will not be able to keep them apart; the signals will spread to interfere with each other and spoil reception.

Mutual interference, then, may come from either co-channel or adjacent-channel stations. In the first instance, stations assigned to the same channel, if not sufficiently separated geographically, may interfere in the entire area covered by both signals. In the second instance, stations assigned to adjacent channels, if not sufficiently separated geographically, will interfere only in the area near the transmitters; with distance the signals become attenuated and receivers are then able to keep these weaker signals apart. This means that adjacent-channel interference is essentially a local problem. It has been found that a 30-kilocycle separation between the frequencies of transmitters in a given locality is desirable for preventing interference. The "30-kilocycle separation rule" requires that between any two AM broadcast stations assigned to a given locality there must intervene at least three channels (30 kc.) not used in that area. For instance, if the 600 kc. channel is assigned in a town, the nearest channels to that frequency which

---

[4] Technically, interference is signal distortion resulting from phase differences in two or more received signals.

could also be assigned in that town are 560 kc. and 640 kc. The practical effect of this rule is to limit to 27 the number of AM broadcast stations that can be assigned in a single limited area. Since few metropolitan areas have any need for this number of stations, avoiding adjacent-channel interference is merely a complicating factor in making assignments, not a serious limitation on the number of feasible assignments.

Co-channel interference creates a more serious problem. It occurs between stations assigned to the same frequency and arises from the fact that there is no way of absolutely limiting the extent or the shape of the area covered by an AM broadcast transmitter's signal. Coverage-area (especially of sky waves) is bound to vary as propagation conditions vary.

AM COVERAGE FACTORS

AM-station wave propagation is dependent primarily on frequency, conductivity of the soil, and power — although many other factors, as previously indicated, affect propagation, especially propagation of sky waves. Ground wave efficiency is highly dependent on conductivity of the soil. AM broadcast antenna towers consist of two parts, only one of which is visible to the casual observer. The visible tower structure itself is the radiating element. For efficient radiation, an antenna needs to be mathematically related to the length of the waves radiated. The longer the wave length, the taller the tower, as a rule.

The invisible part of the antenna is its ground system, a series of radially placed heavy copper wires buried in the earth surrounding the antenna. Ground wave strength depends upon the conductivity of the soil in which the ground system is buried. For this reason standard broadcast antennas are often found on swampy ground or even built over water. Salt water is one of the best conductors, and some AM antennas are actually built on artificial islands or pilings so that the ground system can be submerged in the water.[5] A dry, sandy soil is the least desirable location because of its low conductivity. Signal-strength measurements revealed that the signal from a 250-watt station's antenna located in highly conductive soil actually covered as large an area as that from a 50,000-watt station less favorably located.[6]

Frequency also has an inherently important influence on AM station efficiency. A given amount of power becomes progressively less effective as frequency increases. For instance, a 5,000-watt station at 550 kc. was found to cover a greater area than a 50,000-watt station located in the same city but operating on the 1,200 kc. channel.[7] Since Medium Frequency ground

[5] Salt water is estimated to be 5,000 times as conductive as the least conductive type of soil. FCC map, "Estimated Effective Ground Conductivity in the United States" (Washington: Government Printing Office, 1954).

[6] "New Way to Measure Coverage Told," *Broadcasting*, 8 September 1947, p. 16.

[7] *Loc. cit.*

waves tend to follow the contour of the earth, terrain features are less important in AM propagation than in the VHF and UHF bands of FM and television. Differential absorption of wave energy over the transmission path nevertheless plays a role in determining the coverage of an AM station.

A third major factor influencing coverage is power, which is expressed in watts or kilowatts. With given frequency and terrain conditions, power is the one variable which can be manipulated. However, since signal strength increases only as the square root of power, there is a point of diminishing returns when the gain from a power increase is offset by the cost. If a 1,000-watt station desired to double its signal strength it would have to quadruple its power; to get four times the signal strength its power would have to be increased from 1,000 watts to 16,000. After a certain point, increase in power does not affect ground-wave distance so much as sky-wave distance. Nevertheless, station operators are generally anxious to use as much power as the law and their pocketbooks allow, even when the need to protect co-channel stations requires them to use directional antennas which direct most of their signal energy away from the area they wish to cover. Not only does increased power enable the ground-wave signal to blank out possible nearby interference, but high power also has prestige value. Since most people do not understand the facts we have been discussing here, they are impressed by 50,000 watts (the maximum AM power permitted), even if the number is relatively meaningless in terms of useful physical coverage.

Because of the variety of factors affecting coverage, each station's service area is defined in terms of its *contour,* an irregular shape surrounding the transmitter which is determined by signal-strength measurements in the field. Relatively wide margins of distance must be allowed between stations operating on the same channel because in a station's fringe area its strength is too low or inconsistent for satisfactory service, yet may nevertheless be great enough to cause damaging interference (Figure 6).

Several methods are employed to deal with problems of co-channel interference. Of course the simplest solution would be to assign only one station to a channel — or at least to keep those stations which are assigned to the same channels two or three thousand miles apart. But with only 107 channels to work with, this solution would drastically limit the total number of stations that could be accommodated. One of the primary duties of the Federal Communications Commission is to provide as much broadcast service to the whole country as possible. The problem of completely equitable distribution of service, however, is impossible of perfect solution under a broadcast system which depends upon advertising revenue for its support. Economic necessity inevitably tends to create an overdemand for stations in densely populated areas and an underdemand in thinly populated areas. Thus an economic factor is added to the physical difficulties.

AM STATION AND CHANNEL CLASSIFICATIONS

The FCC has achieved, however, a considerable measure of success by means of a system of channel and station classification (Table 3). The 107 channels are divided into three classes: clear, regional, and local. Stations, in turn, are divided into Classes I, II, III and IV. Each class of station is

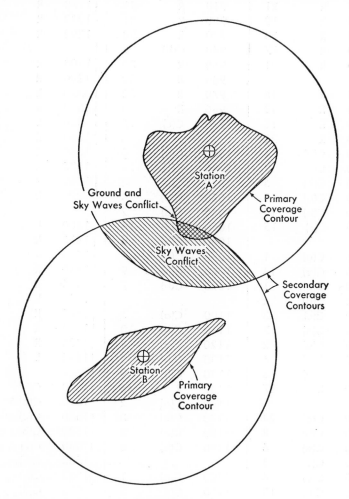

Figure 6

Co-Channel Interference (Idealized)

Station A and Station B are assigned to the same frequency. Their primary coverage (ground-wave) areas do not conflict, but their secondary coverage (sky-wave) areas overlap, so that during times of sky-wave propagation receivers located between the two stations would experience interference.

Table 3
Classification of AM Channels and Number of Stations on Each Channel

Channel (kc.)	Class	No. of Stations	Channel (kc.)	Class	No. of Stations	Channel (kc.)	Class	No. of Stations
540	C(c)	4	900	C(d)	33	1260	R	43
550	R	21	910	R	29	1270	R	29
560	R	19	920	R	31	1280	R	41
570	R	18	930	R	30	1290	R	37
580	R	17	940	C(b)	9			
590	R	21	950	R	30	1300	R	37
			960	R	32	1310	R	32
600	R	18	970	R	32	1320	R	35
610	R	18	980	R	23	1330	R	32
620	R	18	990	C(c)	27	1340	L	161
630	R	22				1350	R	30
640	C(a)	4	1000	C(b)	6	1360	R	42
650	C(a)	2	1010	C(c)	24	1370	R	41
660	C(a)	5	1020	C(a)	4	1380	R	36
670	C(a)	1	1030	C(b)	4	1390	R	32
680	C(b)	15	1040	C(a)	2			
690	C(c)	15	1050	C(d)	36	1400	L	157
			1060	C(b)	6	1410	R	33
700	C(a)	1	1070	C(b)	9	1420	R	33
710	C(b)	14	1080	C(b)	9	1430	R	31
720	C(a)	1	1090	C(b)	7	1440	R	32
730	C(d)	22				1450	L	160
740	C(c)	23	1100	C(a)	5	1460	R	28
750	C(a)	7	1110	C(b)	10	1470	R	31
760	C(a)	2	1120	C(a)	4	1480	R	31
770	C(a)	6	1130	C(b)	5	1490	L	155
780	C(a)	6	1140	C(b)	9			
790	R	27	1150	R	46	1500	C(b)	6
			1160	C(a)	2	1510	C(b)	11
800	C(d)	24	1170	C(b)	8	1520	C(b)	6
810	C(b)	8	1180	C(a)	2	1530	C(b)	3
820	C(a)	6	1190	C(b)	8	1540	C(c)	23
830	C(a)	3				1550	C(b)	6
840	C(a)	4	1200	C(a)	1	1560	C(b)	9
850	C(b)	13	1210	C(a)	5	1570	C(d)	32
860	C(c)	30	1220	C(d)	30	1580	C(c)	31
870	C(a)	7	1230	L	162	1590	R	33
880	C(a)	3	1240	L	147	1600	R	29
890	C(a)	3	1250	R	32			

Explanation of channel class symbols: R=Regional, L=Local, and C=Clear. (a)=unduplicated U.S. Clear Channels, (b)=other U.S. Clear Channels, (c)=Canadian Clear Channels, (d)=Mexican Clear Channels, (e)=Bahamian Clear Channels. The United States may assign only Class II stations to the foreign Clear Channels. The clear channels are popularly called "1-A," "1-B," etc.

Source: Station listings by frequency in *Broadcasting-Telecasting, 1955 Broadcasting Yearbook-Marketbook Issue.*

defined in terms of both channel and power. Class I stations use from 10,000 to 50,000 watts; Class II from 250 to 50,000 watts; Class III from 500 to 5,000 watts; and Class IV from 100 to 250 watts. Individual stations within a given class are licensed to operate at a specified wattage. With the exception of Class II, station classifications are in practice equivalent to channel classifications: Class I stations are assigned to clear channels, Class III stations to regional channels, and Class IV stations to local channels. A Class II station operates on a clear channel in a "secondary" capacity; it must defer to the Class I ("dominant") stations, and is tolerated on a clear channel only insofar as it avoids interference with the dominant station or stations on that channel. This circumstance has led to misunderstanding, sometimes deliberately fostered by Class II station operators. In the public mind the channel classifications are completely identified with station classifications. But a Class II station, though operating on a clear channel, is not a "clear-channel station" in the accepted sense of the term. The Class II stations are usually licensed to operate in the daytime only, so that they will create no skywave interference with the service of the dominant stations on their channels. For this reason it is well to bear in mind that, technically speaking, the terms "clear," "regional," and "local" are *channel* classifications, *not* station classifications.

Over half (59) of the channels are classified as clear channels. The purpose of this group is to provide interference-free sky-wave service to remote regions. Originally each clear channel was to be reserved for a single powerful station, but because of the pressure for more stations the clear channels were broken down into two subgroups. Twenty-four Clear Channels, popularly known as 1A channels, provide for the elite among broadcasting stations; to each 1A channel one and only one nighttime station is assigned. This group includes the oldest and best-known stations in the country — the network-owned-and-operated stations in New York; KDKA, the first licensed commercial broadcast station; WGY, the pioneer General Electric station, and so on. The only competition these stations have on their respective channels is from a few low-power Class II daytime-only stations. At night they operate in lordly isolation. Remote rural areas economically unable to support local stations can thus be assured at least of nighttime sky-wave service from distant clear-channel stations. It must be re-emphasized, however, that the vagaries of the ionosphere render this service subject to interruptions. It was estimated that in 1950 60 per cent of the geographical area (not population) of the United States depended on sky waves for nighttime radio service.[8]

The remaining clear channels have been "duplicated" by the assignment of two or more widely separated dominant (Class I) stations as well as a

[8] Testimony of the Chairman of the Engineering Committee, Clear Channel Broadcasting Service, in: Senate Committee on Foreign Relations Subcommittee, *Hearings on the North American Regional Broadcasting Agreement* (Washington: Government Printing Office, 1953), p. 54.

number of secondary (Class II) stations. An example of assignments on such a channel is shown in Figure 7. The regional and local channels are what the names imply — channels designed to serve relatively limited areas. There are 41 regional and six local channels. Class III and IV stations also produce sky waves, of course, but the fact that their secondary service areas are not protected from interference minimizes the usefulness of sky-wave emission from these classes of stations. In fact, the medium-power regional station may serve a smaller area at night than in the day because of sky-wave conflict from other regional stations.

In order to make the systems of channel and station classifications work, i.e., to maximize the number of stations operating without defeating the purpose of the clear channels or degrading the service of existing stations, the FCC uses several devices. To compensate for the difference between daytime and nighttime coverage, some stations are required to switch to lower power at night; others are required to go off the air entirely after dark; still others are required to use directional antennas (sometimes with different patterns at night than in daytime) to blank out the signal in a direction which might cause interference (Figure 7).[9] In a few towns two stations share time on one frequency.

STATIC INTERFERENCE

All the aforementioned devices are designed to prevent mutual interference between broadcast station signals. AM broadcasting is also subject to interference originating in other sources, both natural and man-made. From nature comes static — free electricity in the atmosphere which affects the amplitude of the carrier wave, adding random information which is received as noise — crackling, snapping sounds and signal distortions (Fig. 5). Static charges in the atmosphere are particularly common during stormy weather and during the summer. In some parts of the country, particularly the South, there are periods during the summer when static becomes so heavy as to preclude even ground-wave reception except over very short distances. In fact, the development of broadcasting in the southern states was seriously impeded before the advent of improved receivers which minimize the effect of static.

Interference also comes from a variety of electrical and electronic appliances and devices. Radio energy is radiated by many electrical devices as a by-product of normal operation; others actually use radio energy for industrial and medical purposes. Both atmospheric and man-made static tend to be blanked out by high transmission power, which improves the signal-to-noise ratio at the receiver; but attenuation of the ground wave in

[9] Directional patterns for standard broadcast stations are achieved by means of antenna "arrays," two or more separate antenna structures which set up interference and reinforcement patterns with each other. As many as ten antennas have been used in these arrays.

the vicinity of the transmitter is so rapid that this advantage is soon lost with distance. Only ground waves are strong enough to override static. This means that sky-wave service is chiefly useful in rural areas; man-made static generally prevents reliable sky-wave reception in large towns.

All the devices described tend in general to enable a more diversified standard broadcast service by permitting operation of the maximum number of stations that the economy can support. The system of assignment can

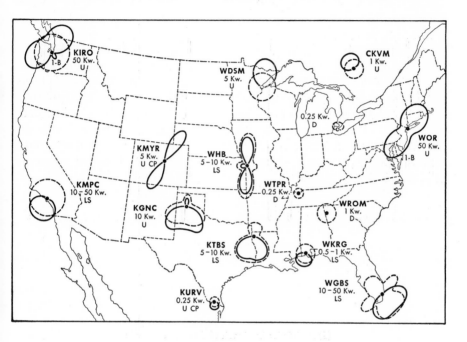

Figure 7

Geographical Distribution of Stations on an AM Clear Channel

Stations assigned to the 1-B Clear Channel 710 kc. Solid lines indicate the shape of nighttime coverage pattern, broken lines the daytime pattern (coverage patterns are symbolic only and do *not* show the actual area covered). The numbers indicate wattage in kilowatts. LS means "reduce power at the time of local sunset"; D means "daytime only"; U means "unlimited time"; CP means "Construction Permit." The two dominant (Class I) stations on this 1-B channel are WOR-New York and KIRO-Seattle. All other United States stations are Class II. A circular coverage pattern indicates no directional antenna; other shapes indicate directional patterns. Note how the nighttime patterns are designed to throw most of the signal energy in a direction which will not interfere with other stations on the frequency.

Source: Mutual Broadcasting System Engineering Department.

(1) Modulation by signals of different wave length

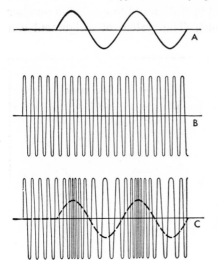

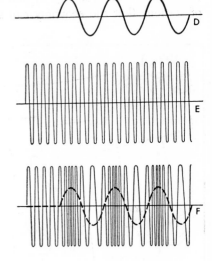

(2) Modulation by signals of different amplitude

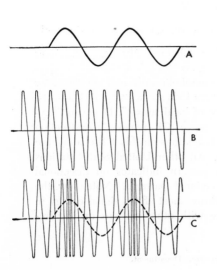

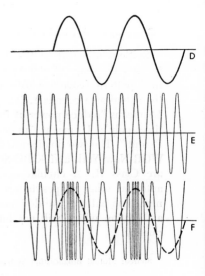

never be perfect, for both economic and technical reasons. Economics tends to force uneven distribution of stations, with high concentration in some areas and no stations at all in others. Technically, it is impossible to control radio-wave propagation in any absolute sense; limitations on power and directivity achieve only approximate control. There will always be freakish propagation phenomena to cause departures from desired coverage patterns.

FREQUENCY MODULATION

Although the techniques of modulating amplitude developed first, it was realized that, theoretically at least, the same result could be obtained by modulating frequency. It was believed, however, that frequency modulation presented technological problems which made practical application infeasible. In the 1930's a revival of interest in the possibilities of frequency modulation was led by Major Edwin Armstrong, an inventor who had already made important contributions to the early development of AM circuitry. Armstrong waged a virtual one-man crusade to secure recognition of the superiority of FM. One hundred 200-kc. FM channels have since been set up in the VHF region, running from 88 to 108 mc.

An important advantage of FM over AM[10] is the former's freedom from static interference. Static, it will be recalled, consists of free electrical charges present in the atmosphere, arising from either natural or man-made sources. Its effect is to distort the amplitude of the AM signal, adding or subtracting at random from the intended pattern of modulation (Figure 5).

---

[10] The terms "AM" and "FM" refer generically to types of modulation, not types of radio service. There are, of course, many non-broadcast services which also use both AM and FM. But in common usage, when the terms "AM" and "FM" are not otherwise qualified they refer to the radio broadcast services that use these forms of modulation.

Figure 8

Frequency Modulation of a Carrier by Various Signals

1) Two cycles of a signal are shown at A. At B is the unmodulated carrier. At C the carrier has been frequency-modulated by signal A (the original wave-form is superimposed on the carrier to show the relation more explicitly). Note that one phase of the signal-wave causes increase in carrier frequency and the other phase causes decrease. The amplitude of the carrier remains constant. D is a signal of the same amplitude as A but has a higher frequency. The difference between C and F consists in the number of times the frequency of the carrier changes in a given period of time.

(2) In this example the frequency of the two signals A and D is constant, but D has twice the amplitude of A. Modulating the same carrier (B and E) results in a more radical change in the frequency of the carrier at F than at C.

With FM, however, the wanted information is not dependent on signal amplitude but on signal frequency (Figure 8). Thus the intrusion of static does not contaminate the information in the FM signal. By eliminating static interference, FM provides undistorted reception in areas where — and at times when — satisfactory AM reception is impossible.

In order to find a frequency band for the new service, the FCC had to move FM up into the VHF region of the spectrum. The difference in frequency, of course, means difference in the propagation characteristics of the waves. In the VHF region, as previously pointed out, sky waves and ground waves are no longer usefully effective; in this region of the spectrum the propagation path is direct. This means elimination of the major problems of AM allocation created by the differential behavior of ground waves and sky waves. The direct radiation of FM signals from transmitter to receiver produces a relatively stable coverage pattern, its size depending upon transmitter power and the height of the transmitting antenna. It is true that at certain seasons of the year waves of the FM broadcast frequencies are affected by both the ionosphere and the troposphere (lower layers of atmosphere). Long-distance FM broadcast propagation, however, is sporadic and is not at all comparable to the useful sky-wave service that is possible at AM broadcast frequencies. The higher the antenna,[11] of course, the farther the station can "see." A high-powered FM transmitter cannot push its signal much beyond the horizon. Therefore "super-power" has no meaning for FM as it has for AM broadcasting.

This limitation on FM coverage simplifies the allocation problem. Since reception depends on direct waves rather than ground waves and sky waves, it is unnecessary to provide a wide "no-man's land" between stations on the same channel; hence FM enables more complete and uniform geographical coverage than does AM. Furthermore, the clear-channel concept, being based on the existence of sky waves for long-distance propagation, cannot be applied to FM; therefore the discrepancies in coverage between stations is not as great as in AM. The tremendous difference in the coverage of an AM station on a 1A Clear Channel and one on a local channel does not exist in FM broadcasting.

Still another factor which simplifies the FM assignment problem is the fact that the FM signal is better able to blank out interference from other signals than AM. A strong AM signal can be distorted by a relatively very weak competing AM signal, whereas an FM signal is better able to override a competing signal.[12]

---

11 The FM antenna proper is a physically small element, in keeping with the shortness of VHF waves. The antenna structure is merely a supporting device, not a radiator as it is in AM. Since FM does not depend on groundwave propagation, the elaborate ground system of the AM antenna is not required. Hence height rather than ground conductivity is the primary consideration in choosing an FM antenna site.

12 The AM signal-to-interference ratio is 20 to 1; the FM ratio is only 2 to 1.

THE HIGH COST OF HIGH FIDELITY

Another major advantage of the FM over the AM broadcast service is its ability to reproduce sound with higher fidelity than AM. This ability is not, however, inherent in FM. To explain this will require further discussion of modulation and of sound. It will be recalled that modulation of a broadcast carrier wave creates side bands, i.e., the involvement of frequencies adjacent to the carrier-wave frequency. A single cycle, of and by itself, is able to convey only a very limited amount of information at any instant. Since sound is relatively complex, consisting of a rather large amount of information, the communication of sound necessarily requires a number of side-band frequencies. The 10-kc. AM channel provides side bands of 5,000 cycles per second. This number defines the capacity of the channel. In effect, it limits AM sound reproduction to sounds of frequencies up to 5,000 cycles per second.

In any communication system it must be decided how much information is really necessary for the purposes of the system. The maximum amount of information desired must be balanced against the cost of communicating it — not only the expense of providing the necessary physical apparatus but also the expense in frequencies. Since there is always a shortage of spectrum space, the conservation of frequencies is of great importance; no service should use more than the minimum number of frequencies required to perform its necessary function. Rarely does a communication system attempt to reproduce information with absolute fidelity to the original, for rarely is such high fidelity necessary. The telegraph, for instance, strips the language of all the wealth of information which the speaking, rather than the printing, of messages conveys; the telephone restores a great deal of this information, but obviously much is still sacrificed. One does not attempt to communicate the aesthetic nuances of fine music or speech by telephone.

Radio broadcasting, unlike such utilitarian communication services as the telegraph and the telephone, *is* concerned with the aesthetic aspects of information. An adequate broadcast service should be capable of communicating the beauty of instrumental music, song, and speech; it should be capable of realistically recreating the sounds of actual events. These requirements call for a relatively high degree of fidelity to the original. Yet absolute fidelity, even if it could be achieved, would be prohibitively costly in both apparatus and frequencies. Therefore a compromise must be made at a point judged to be consistent with both economy and fidelity.

In the case of AM broadcasting, the choice of the specific 10-kilocycle channel width, then, is not dictated by either physical necessity or mere chance. It is the result of a decision: how high can we make fidelity without unduly reducing the number of available channels? How many channels can we make available without reducing fidelity below the point of toleration? The result, in AM broadcasting, has been a service which is far short of ideal sound reproduction but satisfies most people for most purposes. Sound reproduced on an AM radio contains less information than the original sound, but most of us are not conscious of the loss most of the time. However, if AM broadcasting were designed solely to serve a group of people to whom fidelity is very important — let us say orchestra conductors — the standard of AM broadcasting would be entirely inadequate.

SOUND QUALITY

To understand how broadcasting as a communication system can omit part of the original information we must consider again the nature of sound. A pure sound, consisting of a single frequency, such as the example previously used to illustrate the process of modulation, does not occur in nature. The sound of voices, musical instruments, the rustling of leaves, the burbling of brooks, the barking of dogs — all the sounds we normally hear — are complex. They consist of many different frequencies, each with its own amplitude, all combined in a way that gives a particular sound its particular character.

Previously we spoke of sound as having at least three variables: frequency (pitch), amplitude (loudness), and duration. But take the case of two sounds of exactly equal pitch, loudness, and duration — say a note played on a violin and the same note played on a clarinet. The ear detects a difference, a difference implied by such terms as "timbre," "quality," "color." The difference lies in the fact that pitch, or frequency, is not a simple, but a complex factor. We recognize the pitch of the two instruments as being apparently identical because in each case the psychologically dominant frequency is identical; we recognize the difference in quality between the two instruments because the other frequencies in the two sounds are not identical. These frequencies or pitches are not heard as such, but we perceive the *Gestalt*, the totality of the event, as a single, unified impression.

These secondary components of sounds are called overtones. They are usually multiples of the fundamental pitch. Thus the 264-cycle sound of middle C as played on the piano will have overtones at 528 cycles, 792 cycles, 1,056 cycles, and so on. The qualitative difference between sounds of the same fundamental pitch is due to differences in the distribution and amplitudes of the overtones (Figure 9).

In the graphic representation of the wave, the several frequencies are conceived as forming a composite wave. To understand this concept we must revert to the concept of phase, mentioned earlier in connection with the pendulum. It will be recalled that a complete cycle of motion of the pendulum requires a movement to one side and then to the other. These opposite phases of the cycle may be regarded as positive (plus) and negative (minus) aspects of the wave. If the positive aspects of two waves coincide, the energies of both will be combined to make a larger total amplitude at that point. If, however, a negative and a positive aspect of two

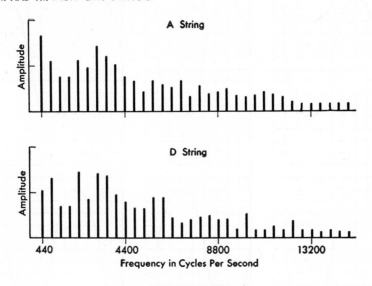

Figure 9

Overtones in Sounds

Two different strings on a violin playing a note at the same pitch (440 cycles per second) have recognizably different quality. The graphs show how the relative amplitudes of the fundamental pitch and the overtones account for this difference. Note, for example, that the first overtone is stronger than the fundamental in the D-string tone but weaker in the A-string tone.

Based on: Harry F. Olson, *Musical Engineering* (New York: McGraw-Hill, 1952), p. 255.

waves coincide, the smaller will subtract from the larger, making a smaller total amplitude at that point. When two waves of the same frequency exactly coincide they are "in phase." Let us assume that these two waves have exactly the same amplitude throughout the cycle. If now they are shifted exactly half a wave length *out* of phase, they will cancel each other completely, for one wave is advanced just as far in the negative direction as the other wave has advanced in the positive direction at any given moment throughout the cycle (Figure 10). The principle can be illustrated with two tuning forks of slightly different frequency. When both are struck the resulting composite sound will have a "beat"; at regular intervals the sounds will reinforce each other to a maximum amount and then cancel each other to a maximum amount. This beat can be heard in musical chords. Phase considerations are important in many practical ways throughout electrical and electronic systems. Two or more microphones fed to the same amplifier must be phased correctly; phase differences occur when a ground wave and a sky wave from the same transmitter meet, sometimes with results much

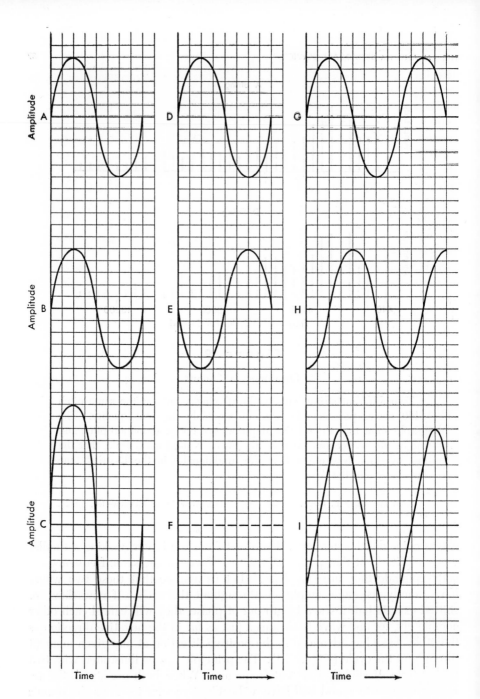

Figure 10

The Concept of Phase

A and B represent waves of equal amplitude and length which are *in phase*. The result of combining these two waves is shown at C.

D and E are two waves of equal amplitude and length which are exactly halfway *out of phase*. The result at F is complete cancellation.

G and H are the same waves one-quarter out of phase. The resultant, I, does not have the same amplitude or form as the resultant of the two waves when *in phase*, shown at C.

like the "beat" produced by the two tuning forks; color television makes important use of phase differences.

The relevance of overtones to the question of fidelity of reproduction of sound is this: Since overtones are of higher frequency than the fundamental tone, they tend to extend into the higher ranges of the audible frequency spectrum. A system of reproduction that is incapable of reproducing these higher frequencies therefore affects *quality* without necessarily affecting intelligibility. Standard broadcasting, with its 10-kilocycle channel, permits the reproduction of an audible frequency range of about 50-5,000 cycles per second. The total range of audible frequencies extends to about 20,000 cycles per second.[13] Thus AM broadcasting eliminates a very large segment of the audible frequency range. However, the frequencies above 5,000 cycles per second come into play as overtones rather than as fundamental pitches; hence the loss is in terms of overtones, which is to say quality. For purposes of speech reproduction, this loss is not important. The baritone singing voice, for instance, covers fundamental pitches only to about 400 cycles per second; the soprano singing voice goes only to about 1,200 c.p.s. But the fundamentals of the highest musical instruments reach into the 4,000-c.p.s. region, and the fundamental frequencies of certain high-pitched sounds reach even higher. It follows then, that the AM standard is adequate for the human voice, less adequate for instrumental music, and even less adequate for certain sound effects. The inadequacy of AM broadcast fidelity can easily be verified by listening to sound effects on the radio. We are accustomed to recognizing all sorts of sound effects in radio dramas, but we may not realize how much we depend on the context of the drama to tell us what to *expect*, and we unconsciously respond to this suggestion. When one listens deliberately to sound effects as isolated sounds it becomes clear that by themselves many of them are meaningless. The sound of applause is a good test, as are other sharp percussive sounds like rain, as well as scraping sounds such as striking a match.

In amplitude modulation, then, it was decided to provide sufficient radio frequencies per channel to enable *reasonably* faithful sound reproduction. But this standard is not high enough for realistic reproduction of many sounds, including many that are present in instrumental music. Since more frequencies are available in the VHF band, the FCC could set up a standard which permits a great improvement over AM. The channel width for FM stations is 200 kilocycles, and this channel width enables reproduction of sound frequencies up to 15,000 c.p.s. Since most people cannot hear sounds of higher frequency, this range permits almost "perfect" reproduction of sound. The word "perfect" is quoted because from the physical point of

[13] Sensitivity to higher sound frequencies varies widely among individuals; a characteristic hearing loss occurs in the upper frequencies with age. Some animals are known to be able to perceive frequencies beyond the range of human hearing. For instance, there is a dog whistle on the market which is so high-pitched that human beings cannot hear it.

view some frequency information is still being left out, but from the psychological point of view all the information which could be *useful* to most people is included.

Besides improved frequency range, FM also has the advantage of improved *dynamic* range over AM. This term refers to the range in degrees of loudness between the faintest reproducible sound and the loudest. The ear has an amazing capacity to adjust itself to extremes in this respect, whereas most sound-reproducing systems are very limited in dynamic range. Very faint sounds are lost in the noise of the system itself, and very loud sounds may overload the system and become distorted. AM broadcasting is particularly limited because, in order to get maximum average power from transmitters, the dynamic range is artificially compressed to eliminate extremes of loudness or softness.

THE DISADVANTAGES OF FM

With all these advantages over AM — stability of coverage area, freedom from static, increased frequency range — it would seem that FM should by now have surpassed AM in popularity. Instead, FM has actually been losing ground after its initial surge, and seems now permanently relegated to a minor role among the broadcasting services. The reasons for the failure of FM to compete more successfully against the older service are both physical and economic. The latter will be dealt with more fully in Chapter 9, but basically the economic weakness of FM is that it reduces all stations to relative equality of service area. The major AM stations, particularly the Class I stations on 1A clear channels, were naturally unwilling to surrender the great competitive advantage which their superiority of coverage gives them. For this reason the AM networks and the major AM stations, although paying lip service to FM by taking out FM licenses, have never really tried to develop FM as an independent service; instead they have kept it as a "slave" service, merely duplicating the programs already available on AM. Since network transmission lines are adapted to the limited frequency requirements of the AM service, duplication of AM network programs on FM nullifies all the advantages of FM's potentially superior fidelity (see Chapter 4).

A communication system is only as good as its weakest link. In FM the weakest link has been the inexpensive home receivers predominantly in use, which are not capable of reproducing the full range of frequencies available in the FM signal. Not enough listeners were sufficiently eager for increased fidelity to create a strong demand which could have forced manufacturers to produce better low-cost receivers. Indeed, some evidence suggests that the average listener actually prefers a limited to a full frequency response in sound reproduction.[14] Even those listeners who might

[14] Harry F. Olson, *Musical Engineering* (New York: McGraw-Hill, 1952), pp. 349-350. The recent enthusiasm for "hi-fi" suggests that tastes can be manipulated in this connection as in others.

have appreciated and wanted higher fidelity were not strongly motivated to embrace FM because not enough programming took advantage of FM's superiority. All these problems might have been solved in time had it not been for the fact that FM was just getting under way when television came along. Television, being an entirely new medium instead of an improvement of an existing medium, diverted attention from FM. The research laboratories, manufacturers, networks, and stations all focused their efforts on developing the newer, more exciting and potentially more profitable service, and FM found itself orphaned just when it needed solicitous care from all concerned.

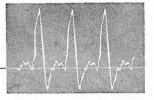

3

The Television Service

Before discussing the physical bases of the television service, it will be helpful to consider briefly some of the characteristics of human vision. To begin with, let us recollect that what we call visible light is a certain range of frequencies in the electromagnetic energy spectrum (Figure 2). These frequencies can be distinguished by the fact that the human eye is sensitive to them. In other words, the eye is a kind of transducer, transmuting electromagnetic energy into perceptions which we know as light, color, brightness, etc. Sights, like sounds, therefore, can be regarded as patterns of energy having certain characteristics of frequency and amplitude.

PICTURE DEFINITION

Essentially, the camera — whether still, motion-picture, or television — represents man's relatively crude attempt to build a mechanical eye, much as the microphone can be said to be a mechanical ear. Like the eye, the camera has an adjustable iris to control the amount of light admitted and a lens which concentrates the image on a light-sensitive screen or plate. The screen of the eye, the retina, consists of specialized nerve-endings (rods and cones) which respond to light. There are about 132,000,000 of these receptors in the normal human eye.[1] When an image falls on the retina, each of millions of active receptors responds independently in accordance with the amount of light which reaches it. The brain assembles the millions of resulting simultaneous impulses into a subjective "reproduction" of the object being seen. It is not, of course, a "perfect" reproduction. Visual acuity varies among individuals just as aural acuity varies. Even at best there are limits to the eye's ability to see detail, for which reason we use microscopes and telescopes to extend the normal limits of vision, as well as eyeglasses to correct abnormalities. The eye sees not "everything," but only as much as the nerve-endings in the retina permit. Obviously anything as small as or smaller than an individual nerve-end could not be distin-

[1] Ida Mann and Antoinette Pirie, *The Science of Seeing* (Harmondsworth-Middlesex: Penguin Books, 1950), p. 28. This little book is an excellent layman's introduction to a fascinating subject.

guished as a separate detail. An object that small could not be *resolved*. Resolution (definition) means the ability to recognize two adjacent objects as separate objects.

On the same principle as that of the eye, picture-reproducing devices depend on some method of breaking the total scene down into separate picture elements, each one of which takes care of one small area of the scene. The minuteness and the distribution of these picture elements, of course, govern the degree of definition, or resolution, that can be obtained. Even with the unaided eye it is possible to observe this piece-by-piece structure in some types of pictures. Newspaper pictures, for instance, have very low definition because of the coarseness of the dot-structure. The individual elements can easily be seen; clearly, this low resolution means inability to reproduce fine detail. An even more obvious example is the traveling headline on the *New York Times* building, in which each element is an electric light bulb (Plate I).

In film, the picture elements consist of tiny particles of light-sensitive chemical. Each particle responds proportionately to the amount of light to which it is exposed. When developed, the particles clump into grains of silver. Naturally, the ability of film to reproduce fine detail depends on the minuteness of these grains. "Graininess" in film means poor detail; "fine-grain" film is used where fine detail is important (see Plate I).

FILM FRAME FREQUENCY STANDARDS

Motion pictures add a time dimension to the process of reproduction: we see not a snapshot of frozen action but continuous action. The action is not in reality continuous in the film itself, but the eye experiences an *illusion* of continuity. This illusion depends on the fact that an image received by the eye persists briefly as a subjective (neural) image even after the original scene is no longer there. The eye cannot turn itself off, so to speak, instantaneously. A motion picture consists of a series of still pictures (frames) taken in rapid succession; each frame freezes the action at a slightly later moment than the preceding frame (see Plate II). Persistence of vision fills in the moments between pictures, achieving a smooth blending from one frame to another, and consequently an illusion of continuity of action. Silent motion pictures are standardized at 16 frames per second, which is adequate for achieving the illusion of continuity. Sound pictures, however, are standardized at 24 frames per second; this rate of travel for the film is desirable in order to get adequate sound quality from the sound track.[2]

Unfortunately, the eye is not completely satisfied with the illusion at this point. When a film is projected, the screen is not continuously illuminated, nor is the film continuously moving. After each frame is flashed on the screen there must be a moment of darkness while the next frame is pulled

[2] Cf. Chapter 4 for a discussion of sound tracks.

into position for projection. Even at 24 frames per second the eye detects the fact that the light on the screen is going on and off. Early movies were called "flickers" because of their slow rate of projection, which resulted in the eye's sensing systematic changes in over-all screen brightness, even though the illusion of continuity of motion may have been obtained. Since the eye is more sensitive to changes in over-all brightness than to changes in details of picture content, the rate of projection needed to give the illusion of brightness-continuity is higher than the rate needed to give the illusion of action-continuity. It is, of course, important from the point of view of film economy to use as few frames as possible per second; and since the 24-frames-per-second rate provides all the visual and aural information required, it would be wasteful to use a higher frame-rate just to avoid flicker. The problem is solved without increasing the amount of film by the simple expedient of projecting each frame *twice*.[3] In other words, when a given frame is pulled into place it is flashed upon the screen once, remains in place while the screen is blacked out momentarily, and then is flashed upon the screen a second time; during the next momentary blackout the next frame is pulled into place and the process repeated. The result is that although only 24 new frames are projected per second, the screen is illuminated by a picture (field) 48 times a second, which is sufficient to deceive the eye into accepting the illusion of continuous illumination of the screen. Thus motion pictures require two projection frequencies: one to achieve continuity of action (frame frequency), one to achieve continuity of illumination (field frequency). A similar double standard obtains in television.

FILM SIZE STANDARDS

It is essential that agreement be reached on such questions as standard frame-frequency so that film can be changed from one camera to another and from one projector to another. Two other film standards[4] require comment before we move on to television: film size and shape. The size of motion-picture film, like the size of a radio channel, must be based on a compromise between the need for economy and the need for communicating an adequate amount of information. It has been emphasized that a communication system is designed to carry not all the information available but only that portion of the total which answers the purpose of the particular system. The demands made of a moving picture (whether on film or television) are obviously different from the demands made of other kinds of pictures. A great deal of information which might be needed in a still photograph would be superfluous in a moving picture.

In the first place, since a motion picture normally shows objects in mo-

---

[3] Most modern projectors repeat each frame more frequently, but for purposes of comparison with television the example of two projections per frame is used throughout.
[4] All film standards are published by American Standards Association, Inc., 70 E. 45th St., New York 17, New York.

tion, it is impossible to study any one frame with the same attention to detail with which one might study a still photograph; the eye is constantly being hurried on to new perceptions and has no time to dwell on all the potential information in every frame. Again because of the factor of motion, the optimum viewing distance is different for motion pictures than for still pictures. One looks at moving pictures for a longer period of time than one normally looks at still pictures. To view a motion picture comfortably, without eyestrain and distortion, we sit at a distance from the screen. Thus, by the standards applied to some other types of photographic reproduction, motion pictures can be quite crude. There is deliberate omission of some information. The circumstances of normal viewing are such that this information would be quite superfluous: the eye would have no opportunity to see it under normal viewing conditions even if the information were there.[5] One has only to sit too near a motion-picture screen to become immediately conscious of the omissions; at this unaccustomed distance the eye becomes uncomfortably aware of the grainy structure of the picture and of the resulting lack of fine detail. One of the common sources of eyestrain in television viewing (especially among children) is sitting too close to the screen; the viewer then unconsciously strains to see detail which simply does not exist and would not be visible at a proper viewing distance even if it did exist.

The amount of information that a motion-picture film is capable of conveying depends on a number of factors, among them the size of the film itself, the speed at which it travels in the camera and projector, the physical make-up of the film stock, the developing and printing process, the precision of the various mechanisms involved in film handling, and the quality of the lenses used in cameras, projectors, and other devices. For certain highly specialized scientific applications, all these factors are brought to the optimum at great cost for relatively minute amounts of finished photography. But film for everyday use — for entertainment, documentation, and education — must be produced in great quantities at reasonable cost. Film is relatively quite expensive even when costs are kept at the minimum consistent with the communication of adequate information.

Since the definition of "adequate" varies widely, depending on the purpose of the communication, more than one set of standards has evolved for motion pictures. The highest standard (short of the costly special applications previously mentioned) has been developed for theatre exhibition and is represented by 35-mm. film practice. The measurement refers to the width of the film stock (Plate II), but it also connotes high standards of equipment (cameras, projectors, sound recorders, etc.), operating pro-

[5] Senate Advisory Committee on Color Television to the Committee on Interstate and Foreign Commerce, *The Present Status of Color Television* (Washington: Government Printing Office, 1950), p. 7. This Committee was chaired by the director of the National Bureau of Standards. The report is an excellent brief summary for the layman of the principles governing the establishment of television standards.

cedures, and production quality. With few exceptions, all film for regular commercial theatre exhibition conforms to these (or higher) standards.

Sixteen-millimeter film occupies a middle ground. It was developed originally in the 1920's as an amateur medium, but in recent years there has been such a tremendous increase in the use of non-theatrical film (including television use) that the best 16-mm. practice can now be regarded as on a professional level. The smaller size of this film makes it much more economical than 35-mm. For example, 16-mm. film runs at 36 feet per minute at sound speed (24 frames per second), whereas 35-mm. film runs at 90 feet per minute at the same frame speed. Along with the saving in costs for film stock go economies in equipment, processing, and production costs. Most television stations are equipped to use 16-mm. film only.

The third standard type of film is 8-mm., which nowadays is generally used instead of 16-mm. film for the purely amateur "home movie." In this medium the cost of film is minimized and the associated equipment designed for the utmost simplicity and economy.

ASPECT-RATIO STANDARDS

The fact that motion pictures consist of many frames in sequence means that it is also necessary to set up standards of picture *shape*. Still photos are standardized to a relatively few basic shapes and sizes for cameras, film stock, and related equipment, but the finished print itself can be trimmed to any size or shape required. A still picture of a skyscraper can conform to the vertical design of the subject; conversely, a panoramic view of a skyline can be cut to suit the horizontal orientation of the subject. The option of adapting the picture shape to the communication content is not available when the film must consist of many thousands of separate film frames and where the picture must be projected on ready-made screens of fixed shape and size. Hence early in the development of motion-picture photography it was necessary to standardize not only film size but also the shape of the frame. Logically a rectangular shape is the most practical; but what should be the aspect ratio, i.e., the proportion between the width and the height of the picture? The proportion selected is three units high by four units wide.[6] For example, a screen nine feet high must be twelve feet wide. This three-to-four ratio was chosen as being psychologically appropriate, as conforming to the normally horizontal field of view of the human eye, and as being adaptable to most subject matter. Actually, of course, no single shape is ideal for all subjects — otherwise all paintings would have the same aspect ratio. The fixed aspect ratio of the camera's field of view is a severe limitation; hence one of the major artistic problems of the cinema (and of television) is that of compensating for this rigidity

[6] The ASA standard for 16-mm. projector apertures is actually .284 by .380 inches, which is a ratio of 3 x 4.01. For comments on other aspect ratios used in wide-screen film systems, see Chapter 11.

of the medium. In early cinematography it was common practice to use masks to alter the shape of the scene; in order to focus attention on a particular object within a scene, for instance, a mask with a circular hole might be introduced to black out everything but the object of attention, which was then seen as through a peephole. Nowadays these problems are handled less crudely by means of ingeniously used camera angles, camera movement, perspective, light, and other devices.

TELEVISION STANDARDS

When the time came to set up standards for television, it was natural that previous experience with motion pictures should be used as a guide. In the television system the cost factor is computed not in film footage but in frequencies. By using a sufficiently wide channel, television theoretically could equal or surpass the quality of 35-mm. film. The question is, does television *need* to be as good as 35-mm. film? And as a corollary question, how good can television *afford* to be in terms of the frequencies available?

It was decided to approximate in television the quality expected in good 16-mm. film. It was reasoned that television is a home medium and should logically be adjusted to the standards of good home movies rather than those of theatrical exhibition.[7] This means that the standards adopted for television deliberately sacrifice a certain amount of visual information (just as the standards for AM broadcasting deliberately sacrifice a certain amount of aural information) in the interests of economical use of the available frequency space. The fewer frequencies needed for each television channel, the greater the number of channels that can be allocated and of stations that can operate.

TV IMAGE DISSECTION

Consideration of motion pictures as a communication system suggests that a system of television communication must include provision for (1) breaking the picture down into many separate picture elements; (2) securing a sequence of complete, independent pictures with sufficient frequency to achieve the illusion of action-continuity; and (3) securing a sequence of screen illuminations with sufficient frequency to achieve the illusion of brightness-continuity. It was recognized early in television experimentation (which goes back to the earliest days of radio experimentation), that the picture elements could not all be transmitted simultaneously. When light from a scene falls on a film negative, all the particles of light-sensitive material begin to respond at once. But a radio channel can only do one thing at a time; it cannot, like the film, respond simultaneously to a tremendous number of different pieces of information, each one potentially capable of being widely varied. The central problem in developing tele-

[7] Senate Advisory Committee on Color Television, *op. cit.*, p. 8.

vision, then, became the problem of devising a means of dissecting the picture into elements, transmitting each one separately, and reassembling all the parts in the correct order and in the correct places at the receiver — all of this happening so fast that the eye perceives all the picture elements simultaneously.

One experimental attempt at solving this problem used a bank of photo-electric cells. These cells convert light information into electrical informa-tion. By connecting the bank of cells to a mechanical device for discharging each cell in succession, it was possible to transmute the light information falling on the cells into a sequence of discrete electrical impulses; these impulses could then be used to activate a corresponding bank of lights in the reproducer. This remains the basic principle of television, although this early device was extremely crude. Photoelectric cells are too large to permit resolution of anything but the grossest detail, and any conceivable mechanical method of discharging the cells consecutively is too slow to achieve the necessary illusion of simultaneity. Television had to await the development of a subtler device to do the light-transforming job and of a non-mechanical device for dissecting the picture at extremely high speed. This development came about in 1923 with the invention of the *iconoscope,* the first electronic camera pickup tube. The successor of this type of tube is still in use, although for studio work an improved type, the *image orthicon,* is now standard (see Figure 11). These tubes have no moving parts; all operations are electronic. An entirely different method of image dissec-tion also is employed — at present to a lesser extent than the image orthicon — for dissecting the image. This is the "flying spot scanner," which illumi-nates the image one element at a time by means of a tiny spot of light which flies across the image.

PICKUP DEVICES

Light from the scene to be televised is concentrated by a lens on a small screen within the iconoscope pickup tube. The screen is covered with specks of light-sensitive material which has the property of converting light energy into electrical energy. Thus the screen translates the pattern of light which falls upon it into a pattern of electrical *potentials;* that is, each dot of light-sensitive material acquires and stores an electrical charge whose amplitude corresponds with the amount of light falling on that particular dot. The screen in the television pickup tube differs from film in that each image is not "fixed" but is replaced by each succeeding image.

The next problem is to discharge each of these thousands of picture ele-ments separately and systematically, so that they can be reassembled cor-rectly at the receiver. This is accomplished by directing toward the screen a narrow beam of electrons which triggers the electrical potentials of the picture elements. When the electron beam strikes one of the picture ele-ments, that element discharges the electrical energy it has stored. The elec-

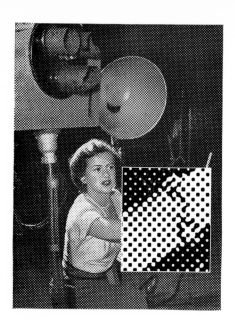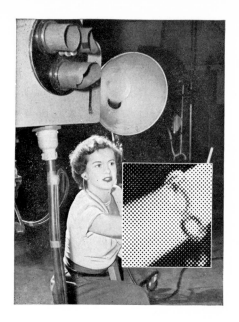

PLATE I
Picture Structure

Degrees of definition in picture reproduction. Right: Fine engraving, 133 lines per inch. The detail in the small rectangle superimposed on the 133 screen enlarged four times. Left: Same subject as reproduced in a newspaper, 55 lines per inch. The detail in the small rectangle superimposed on the 55 screen is the 55 screen enlarged four times.

WBZ-TV, Boston

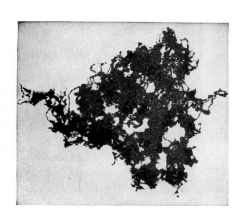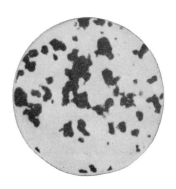

Grain structure in motion-picture film. Right: Under high magnification picture elements are seen to be distributed at random and to vary in size and shape. Left: a single "grain" under extreme magnification.

Eastman Kodak Company

PLATE II
Motion-Picture Sound Tracks
(actual size)

35-mm. variable-den-
sity optical track

35-mm. variable-area
optical track

Eastman Kodak Company

PLATE III

Motion-Picture Sound Tracks

(actual size)

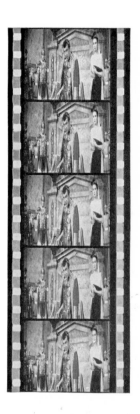

16-mm. variable-area optical track. Note that there is one sprocket hole per frame as compared to four per frame in 35-mm. film.

CinemaScope quadruple magnetic track. Note that sprocket holes have been reduced in size to provide more room for tracks and picture.

CinemaScope film courtesy of Twentieth Century-Fox Film Corporation

PLATE IV

Experimental motion-picture camera made by Edison in 1889. Note that the film travels horizontally instead of vertically, the orientation later adopted.

Photograph courtesy of The Thomas Alva Edison Foundation Museum, West Orange, New Jersey

Lee de Forest with a motion-picture camera converted for optical recording of sound (see p. 171) *Brown Brothers*

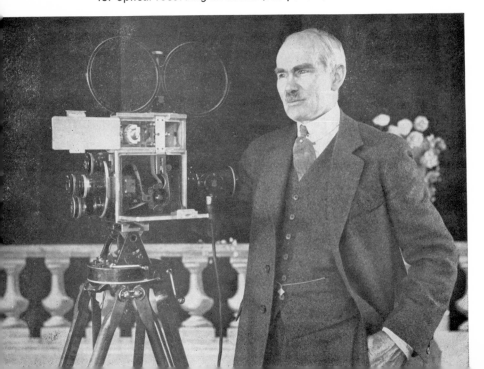

tron gun which generates the electron beam is often compared to a machine gun. The bullets (electrons) are sprayed back and forth across the screen. This scanning sequence follows the pattern of the eye in reading: it starts at the upper left, reads a line from left to right, drops down and reads another line, and so on until the whole page is finished. Then the electron beam returns and repeats the process from the top. It must be borne in mind that this complex series of movements occurs with such rapidity that no mechanically moving device could be designed to do the job. The electron gun itself is rigidly fixed in the tube. Electrons can be attracted or repelled by magnetic fields. The electron beam passes through magnetic fields on the way to the target; appropriate variations in the current in the magnetic fields cause the beam to make the back-and-forth and up-and-down movements involved in the scanning sequence.

Both the iconoscope and the image orthicon operate on the storage and scanning principle just described. They differ markedly, however, in the

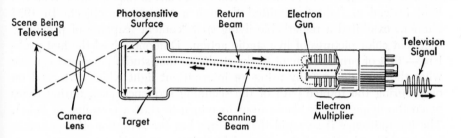

Figure 11

The Image Orthicon Tube

The image is focused on a sensitive plate which has the property of converting light energy into electrical energy. Electrons are emitted from the rear surface of this plate and reproduce an electronic equivalent of the image on the target plate. Each element in the image on the target plate holds a specific electrical charge. When the scanning beam strikes an element it reflects the beam back toward the gun in an amount proportionate to the charge on that element. The return beam is diverted around the electron gun and is amplified by the electron multiplier section of the tube before being fed out of the tube as the television signal. (The components which deflect the beam to produce the scanning pattern are external to the tube and are not shown.) The iconoscope tube differs in that the image is retained on a single plate (the mosaic); the scanning beam discharges each element in the mosaic immediately on contact, and the signal is fed directly from the mosaic. Not having the benefit of an electron multiplier section, the iconoscope produces a weaker signal (i.e., is less sensitive) than the image orthicon.

Source: RCA: *RCA Color Television* (New York: RCA, 1953), p. 24.

method of discharging the stored information (Figure 11). The flying spot scanner, on the other hand, has no need for storing the information, since it scans the image one element at a time by means of a spot of light, instead of illuminating the image completely and then breaking it down into elements. Transparent materials, such as films and slides, readily lend themselves to the flying-spot technique; the spot of light passes through the image and is picked up a photoelectric cell which converts light values into equivalent electrical values. As the spot of light moves across the image its intensity is modulated by the varying density of the transparent image, thereby causing variations in the light energy received by the photoelectric cell.

The use of the flying spot scanner for non-transparent subject matter, such as live programs in a studio, is more of a problem. In the first place, the subject matter has to be in *total darkness*, since only the single minute spot of light may fall on the subject. Secondly, the photoelectric cell which translates the light values into electrical values has to depend upon reflected light instead of light transmitted through a transparent object. In 1955 Dumont exhibited a remarkable flying spot "camera" capable of providing excellent color pictures of live studio action. Dumont solved the first problem — that of providing light in the studio so that studio personnel can see what they are doing — by using an intermittent light which is turned on only during the retrace path of the scanning sequence (i.e., during times when the flying spot is blacked out to return to start a new line or field). The intermittence is so rapid that the eye has the sensation of continuous low-level illumination of the scene. The flying spot itself also moves so rapidly that to the eye the "camera" seems to be projecting a rectangular block of very dim light on the scene. The "camera" contains, instead of a pickup device, a tube which is essentially like a receiver tube. It generates the spot of light and causes it to move through the standard scanning pattern. The camera is equipped with lenses for securing different apparent image-distances and can be manipulated like the ordinary image-orthicon camera. The pickup device in the Dumont system is a highly sensitive photoelectric cell which is hung in the same position in which lights would be hung to illuminate a scene for an image-orthicon camera. Several of these pickup devices are used; they receive reflections of the flying spot from the image and convert them into electrical values. Potentially the flying-spot studio camera is much cheaper than the image-orthicon camera. However, it can be used, of course, only in situations in which ambient light can be excluded from the scene.

THE SCANNING PATTERN

The rate of scansion selected for the United States standard is thirty frames per second. Frame frequency must be accurately standardized throughout the country if transmitters and receivers are to remain in step with each other. Since nearly all electrical house current throughout the United States has a frequency of 60 cycles, it was convenient to tie television in with this universally available standard. In the motion-picture projector, it will be recalled, frame frequency is 24 per second, but, in order to avoid flicker, field frequency is 48 per second. Repeating each whole film frame does not add to the information contained in the film; since film is a *permanent* record, the information in a frame is "remembered" and can be reused any number of times. However, the television information is momentary; it exists only very briefly, one dot at a time; therefore to repeat each frame would mean doubling the amount of information the system has to carry. Television avoids this burden by scanning each frame in two successive instalments, thus achieving 60 fields with only 30 frames. The method is to scan every other line for each field. The first field includes the first, third, fifth, seventh, etc., line; when the electron beam reaches the bottom of the picture it returns and picks up the second, fourth, sixth, eighth, etc., line. This is called interlace, or off-set, scanning. It ensures that the screen will be illuminated with sufficient frequency to prevent flicker, but minimizes the total amount of information per frame which the system has to transmit.

The television picture, then, is constructed of dots (elements), lines, fields, and frames. The last three are standardized in the United States at 525 lines per frame, 60 fields per second, and 30 frames per second. In practice each frame consists ideally of about 200,000 elements. Since 30 frames are transmitted per second, the number of elements transmitted per second is about 6,000,000.

At the receiving end, of course, the process must be reversed. Like the pickup tube, the receiver tube (kinescope) contains an electron beam which scans by interlace 30 frames per second. The electron stream is directed against the inner surface of the face of the tube, causing a phosphor coating on the inner face to glow as the electron beam reconstructs the picture, line by line. Theoretically only one element out of the 200,000 in a frame is visible on the screen at any given moment; in actuality the phosphor glows briefly even after the electron beam has passed a given position. Nevertheless, only a fragment of the total picture is ever on the screen at any given moment. Yet elements, fields, and frames succeed each other with such rapidity that persistence of vision gives the illusion of a continuous image. However, the number of lines in a frame is small enough to make the line-structure of the picture evident on close examination.

ACCESSORY SIGNALS

The television system is somewhat more complex than the foregoing description indicates. For one thing, what happens to the electron beam while it returns from the end of one line or field to the start of another? If the beam continued to read off the picture information along the fly-back path, the orderly picking up of picture elements would be destroyed. This dilemma is solved by a *blanking signal*, which is transmitted during fly-back periods. This signal is not apparent on the screen because it cuts off the electron beam. The video signal is negatively modulated; that is to say, a large amplitude of energy in a picture element (indicating whiteness at the corresponding point in the original scene) results in a low amplitude of energy in the transmitted signal. Conversely, a low amplitude in a picture element (indicating darkness at the corresponding point in the original scene) results in high amplitude in the transmitted signal. Therefore the amplitude of the transmitted signal can be artificially increased beyond the amplitude which produces visible black in the receiver. The boundary line is called the "cut-off" level. All accessory signals in the composite video signal are sent in this "blacker-than-black" region so that they do not interfere with picture information (Figure 12).

It can readily be imagined that if receiver and transmitter should get out of step the received picture would be ruined. Suppose, for instance, that the first picture element in the first line in the original image was received as an element in the middle of that line: half of the picture would be lost. In order to guarantee exact synchronization of scanning in the receiver with scanning in the camera, special synchronizing signals are included in the composite video signal. These signals, also sent in the blacker-than-black region (along with the blanking signals between frames), establish precise points of "registration," so that the picture in the receiver tube is scanned in exact synchronism with the picture in the camera tube (Figure 12).

Both these accessory signals — the blanking signal to eliminate evidence of retrace and the synchronizing signal to keep camera and receiver scansion in step — constitute part of the information being transmitted by the video system. It is not picture information, however, for it adds nothing to the amount of visual information received. In fact, it subtracts from the total amount of visual information that can be transmitted, since with a given number of frequencies in a channel only a given amount of information can be transmitted.

CHANNEL WIDTH AND INFORMATION CAPACITY

Essentially, it may be said that each cycle in a channel is capable of communicating two pieces of information per second.[8] Each United States television channel is six megacycles wide, but only about four megacycles are available for the video component. The rest of the channel is used for the audio component and for margins of isolation (guard-bands) between

---

[8] Note that the capacity of a channel is defined by the *difference* in frequency between the upper and lower limits of the channel, irrespective of where these points occur in the frequency spectrum. For example, television Channel 2 falls at 54-60 mc., whereas Channel 83 falls at 884-890 mc. The carrier frequency of one is tremendously higher than that of the other, yet each channel contains the same number of cycles — 6,000,000.

the audio and video signals and at the upper and lower edges of the channel. In short, the cycles available to carry the video signal number about 4,000,000, and since each can handle two pieces of information per second, this means that the whole video channel is capable of handling a maximum of 8,000,000 pieces of information per second (see Figure 13).

Let us see what has to take place during each second. There are 525 lines in each frame, and each frame is scanned at the rate of 30 times per second; therefore the total number of lines per second is 15,750. Dividing that

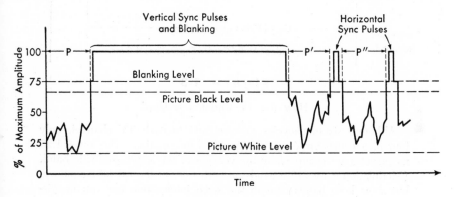

Figure 12

Composite Television Signal (Simplified)

The wave-form depicted is a simplified analysis of the picture, synchronizing, and blanking components of the composite video signal. During the interval P the last line of a field is being scanned. The uneven line at P represents the varying amplitudes generated by the scanning beam as it moves across one line of the picture, the higher amplitudes representing dark elements in the image and the lower amplitudes light elements. At the end of the line the signal is synthetically increased to an amplitude "blacker than black" (i.e., above the value which shows as "black" in the receiver), which cuts off the electron beam at the receiver. During the ensuing interval the electron beam is returning to the top of the frame to start another field; at the same time a complex series of pulses (not shown in detail) provide blanking and synchronizing information to the receiver. At the end of the vertical retrace interval the first line of the next field is scanned at P'. Then a very short time intervenes while horizontal retrace is taking place, during which a horizontal sync pulse is transmitted. At P" the second line of the field is scanned, and another retrace interval follows. Note that the "blanking level" is at a slightly higher amplitude than the blackest parts of the actual picture information. (Not drawn to scale.)

Based on: FCC signal specifications in Rules and Regulations.

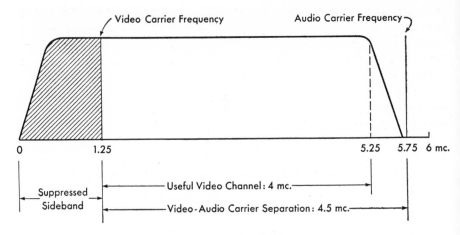

Figure 13

How the TV Channel Is Used

Although six megacycles are assigned to each TV channel, only four megacycles are available for video information. The lower 1.25 megacycles are occupied by the vestiges of the suppressed side band. (Modulation causes side bands on both sides of the carrier frequency, but since both bands contain the same information one can be discarded; however, the discarded side band cannot be cut off absolutely, and room has to be left for vestigial energy.) (Not drawn to scale.)

Based on: FCC Specifications in Rules and Regulations.

number into the 8,000,000 signal elements available per second discloses that ideally 508 signal elements are available for each line. But because some time is used up by the accessory signals, only 416 signal elements per line and 483 lines are available for useful picture information. This realizes 416 x 483, or 200,928 picture elements per frame. Multiplying the number of elements per frame by the number of frames per second, we arrive at 6,027,840 useful picture elements per second. Thus of the 6,000,000 cycles allocated to each television channel only 3,013,920 cycles are used for the picture proper, the rest for accessory signals, sound, and marginal spacing. Definition in the television picture is thus limited by the system itself to the amount of detail ideally resolvable by 200,928 picture elements. This standard provides a picture only a fraction as detailed as a fine engraving, but, as was previously pointed out, the circumstances of viewing pictures in motion make the rendering of finest details superfluous, since normally they could not be seen by the viewer in any event.[9] Magnifying the received

[9] A good 8 x 10″ photoengraving has about 2,000,000 dots; 35-mm. film, when projected, has the equivalent of about 1,000,000 halftone dots. Senate Advisory Committee on Color Television, *op. cit.*, p. 7. See Plate I.

picture adds no detail; a 12 x 16-foot theatre-television screen provides no more information than a 12 x 16-inch home-receiver screen. Larger screens simply make it possible to sit farther away from the screen and thus enable the accommodation of more viewers.

There is nothing absolute about the 525-line standard adopted in the United States. In Britain 405 lines are used, and in France 819 lines.[10] The standard adopted in the United States is a pragmatic one; it represents a compromise between the desire for a high-definition picture on the one hand and a limited channel-width on the other, and it takes into account the country's need for a commercial, competitive, nation-wide service permitting the maximum number of stations to operate.

TV SYSTEM SUMMARY

To summarize, the complete television signal contains four categories of information: picture, blanking, synchronizing, and audio. All four components are combined at the transmitter for radiation by the same antenna system. The video and audio components are handled separately, each with its own set of equipment, until they reach the diplexer in the transmitter (Figure 14). The function of the diplexer is to combine the two signals without mixing them so that they can be fed simultaneously to the antenna. The television-transmitting antenna elements are physically small, in keeping with the size of the waves to be radiated.[11] Direct waves are employed, so no ground-system comparable to that used in standard broadcasting is needed. The tower, instead of itself serving as the radiating element, is merely a support for the antenna proper.

In the studio the synchronizing generator originates the driving pulses for the scanning action of the camera, as well as the blanking and synchronizing information. The synchronizing information is added to the video signal only after the rest of the video information is developed, so that synchronization will not be lost in the course of switching the various video sources (Figure 14).

TV CHANNEL ALLOCATIONS

In 1952 the FCC adopted a table of allocations that made 82 television channels available, numbered 2 through 83.[12] As Table 4 shows, the first 12 channels are in the VHF band, the rest in the UHF band. Channels are not classified according to type of service in the manner of the standard-broadcast clear, regional, and local classifications, nor are stations classified

[10] Cf.: United Nations Educational, Scientific and Cultural Organization, *Television: A World Survey* (Paris: Author, 1953). Recent data are also found in *Television Factbook*.

[11] Channel 2 waves are roughly 18 feet long, Channel 83 waves only about one foot.

[12] The original Channel 1 had been re-allocated to other services in 1947, by which time it was inexpedient to re-number the remaining channels.

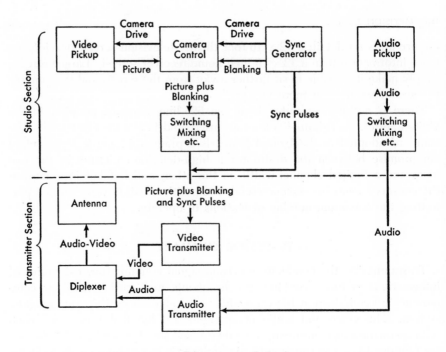

Figure 14

Block Diagram of TV System Components and Signals

This is a highly simplified diagram showing the basic components and their functions in originating and manipulating the signals. Each block represents a functional component (in practice this may consist of many different related components). The connecting lines indicate the signals delivered from one component to another. The picture information originates in a pickup device (e.g., a studio camera). The pickup device receives drive pulses from the sync generator; these pulses cause the scanning sequence to be performed. Picture information is then delivered to a control point where it is monitored, corrected, and amplified and the blanking information is added. This signal then goes to the control point where a number of such incoming signals (e.g., from several cameras, a film chain, a network) are selected in sequence or mixed to make up the program. Then the synchronizing information is added and the composite video signal is fed to the transmitter. Meanwhile the audio information has been handled simultaneously but separately. Pickup devices (microphones, records, film tracks) are fed to a control point for switching, mixing, and amplification. This signal is then fed to its own transmitter. The two transmitters feed the diplexer, which combines audio and video signals for delivery to the antenna. Finally the combined signal is fed to a single antenna system.

Based on a drawing in: Harold E. Ennes, *Principles and Practices of Telecasting Operations* (Indianapolis: Howard W. Sams & Co., Inc., 1953).

TABLE 4

Summary of Broadcast Channel Allocation

		Band	Channel Width	Number of Channels
AM		535-1,605 kc.	10 kc.	107
FM		88-108 mc.	200 kc.	100
TV	(Nos. 2- 4)	54- 72 mc.		
	(Nos. 5- 6)	76- 88 mc.	6 mc.	82
	(Nos. 7-13)	174-216 mc.		
	(Nos. 14-83)	470-890 mc.		

in categories of varying power. The FCC has attempted to give each station the opportunity to compete on a relatively equal physical basis with each other station, requiring only minimum standards of effective radiated power on the basis of the size of the population to be served.

Antenna height, as well as power, defines the effectiveness of the signal. Maximum permissible power, therefore, is related to antenna height. As with standard broadcasting, the lower the frequency the more effective a given amount of power can be because of progressively greater ground absorption as frequency rises. Hence, in order to make the channels approximately equal in coverage potentiality, a sliding scale is used to permit higher and higher power and antennas as the frequency rises.[13] For example, a station on a UHF channel with an antenna 2,000 feet or less above the average terrain may have a maximum power of 1,000 kilowatts. As antenna elevation increases there is a gradual reduction in permissible power until the curve stabilizes at about 7,500 feet, at which point maximum power is fixed at 100 kilowatts. Much less maximum power is permitted to Channels 7-13, and still less to Channels 2-6.

When modern regulation began, many standard AM broadcast stations were already in operation. It was not practicable to put them all off the air and start with a clean slate to make possible a "master plan" of channel allocations. With television, however, the fact that the government could control the growth of the medium from its inception has made such a master plan possible. Accordingly, the table of assignments allots one or more specific channels to each town of sufficient present or potential size to warrant an assignment. Assignments were made in the original table for 2,053 stations in 1,291 communities.[14] The table is set up with co-channel separations of from 155 to 220 miles, depending on the geographical zone and the frequencies involved. Adjacent-channel separations are 55 to 60 miles.

---

[13] *Cf.*: FCC, *Rules and Regulations,* Part 3, para. 3.614, for details.
[14] The table is found in: FCC, *Rules and Regulations,* Part 3, para. 3.606. It is subject to change as conditions require; about 50 changes were made during the first year of its operation. There are more than twice as many UHF as VHF assignments.

Further protection from co-channel interference is achieved by the requirement that certain assigned channels operate 10 kc. above or below the normal carrier frequency for those channels. This slight offset helps to prevent co-channel interference during occasional periods of extraordinarily long-distance propagation. Such periods occur seasonally and are due to both tropospheric and ionospheric reflection.[15] Distances of over a thousand miles are sometimes covered, but these freakish long-distance transmissions of television signals must be regarded as sources of interference rather than of service. Useful television service can generally be expected to reach between 20 and 70 miles from the transmitter. It is impossible, however, to be exact in this figure because of the many variables, such as frequency, power, antenna height, terrain, and interference conditions. Where set owners are willing to install expensive antennas, consistent service can be sometimes obtained over much greater distances than 70 miles.

Television station coverage can be extended and blank areas due to terrain can be filled in by the use of either booster or satellite ("slave") stations. The former rebroadcasts the signal of the mother station on the same frequency, whereas the latter usually operates on its own frequency. Communities too small to support their own stations and too far from stations in other communities to receive reliable signals are often served by community antennas. A community antenna system consists of a specially constructed receiving antenna, a sensitive receiver, and amplifiers; it picks up weak signals, amplifies them, and distributes the programs by wire to homes which pay an annual fee for the service.

UHF CHANNELS

Experience with commercial production and installation of VHF equipment was already a decade old in 1952, when the first commercial UHF station went on the air. Most UHF stations ran into difficulties because receivers had previously been built for the VHF channels (2 through 13). In markets already well served by VHF stations it was difficult to persuade set-owners to spend an additional twenty to fifty dollars or more to convert their sets and antennas for UHF reception. In this respect UHF television encountered somewhat the same kind of resistance which had greeted FM, and this circumstance has led to a widespread belief that UHF is doomed to a similar secondary status. There is little physical justification, however, for relegating UHF to an inferior status as compared with VHF.

In fact, UHF television has certain advantages over VHF. It is less subject to static interference. It is also less subject to "ghosts" — reflected signals which cause multiple images because of differing lengths of signal propagation paths. (This phenomenon is due to the fact that UHF antennas

15 Cf.: Ernest K. Smith, "The Effect of Sporadic E on Television Reception" (U.S. Department of Commerce, National Bureau of Standards Report #1907, mimeo., September 8, 1952).

are highly directive, and hence tend to reject all signals other than those they are adjusted to receive.) The quality of the picture received from UHF stations is as good as or better than that from VHF stations.

On the other hand, the high directivity of the UHF signal means that its coverage may be spotty because the signal can be cut off by buildings and terrain obstructions in the line-of-sight path between receiver and transmitter. UHF signals are more readily attenuated by absorption, and so require higher transmitting power and more sensitive receiving-antenna adjustment. When UHF television started commercially, transmitters capable of utilizing full permissible power had not been developed. In the present state of the technology of UHF and under the present antenna-height and power maximums set up by the FCC, VHF stations can secure greater coverage than their UHF competitors. This, of course, puts UHF at a serious, if not fatal, economic disadvantage. However, it is quite possible that improved equipment and adjustment of the rules on power and antenna height could substantially equalize the coverage of UHF and VHF stations in any given area.[16]

PERCEPTION OF COLOR

In order to understand color television, it will be helpful to go back once more to the human eye for a model. How the eye perceives color has never been fully explained, but a good deal is known about the physical nature of the stimuli which result in the subjective color sensations. Some of the more recent findings are of fundamental importance to color television. In the first place, it has been found that color sensation is not a single, unified perception. Instead, it involves three different perceptions: sensations not only of coloredness (hue) but also of brightness (luminance), and of color purity (saturation or chroma). Each of the three factors can vary independently.

The sensitivity of the eye is different for different colors, or light frequencies. For instance, the eye is about twice as sensitive to green as to red. Moreover, its sensitivity to color varies with the size of the object being observed. Relatively large objects are perceived in all three dimensions — i.e., in terms of hue, brightness, and purity, but as objects get smaller the eye loses its sensitivity to hue. The smallest details in an image are perceived only in terms of brightness. This loss of the ability to sense hues does not occur all at once; the colors to which the eye is least sensitive, such as blues, disappear first, and then as objects get smaller the colors to which the eye is more sensitive, such as greens, are finally lost. Eventually, in the smallest visible details of the scene, all that can be detected is the brightness factor. In other words, the normal eye is actually color-blind to small details.

Although these factors are relatively new discoveries, it has long been

[16] Economic and legal factors of the UHF-VHF problem are discussed in Chapter 10.

known that color sensation is trichromatic — i.e., that all color sensations can be reproduced by appropriate mixtures of only three primary colors. Any set of colors can be used as primaries as long as the three colors are such that no two can be mixed to match the third and a combination of all three in appropriate proportions results in the sensation of white.

The foregoing facts about color vision greatly simplify the problem of color reproduction. Nearly all color-reproducing systems depend upon the trichromatic nature of vision. The fortunate circumstance that all the thousands of hues can be derived from only three primaries enormously reduces the quantity of information contained in a color picture from what it would have to be if each hue were unique. The fact that the eye cannot detect hue and saturation information in small detail again relieves the reproducing system of the need for handling a vast amount of color information.

THE COLOR TV SYSTEM

Two arbitrary prior limitations were placed upon the color television system: it had to get along with the six-megacycle channel width already set up for black-and-white television; and it had to be compatible with existing black-and-white television receivers. Compatibility means the ability of a non-color receiver to pick up a color signal as a monochrome signal; it is necessary to avoid the possibility of outmoding millions of existing monochrome receivers.[17] These were severe limitations. Even with the savings previously indicated, it is obvious that color television represents a substantial increase in the quantity of information that must be handled by the system as compared to monochrome requirements; and the requirement of compatibility made any major changes in the monochrome scanning and other timing operations out of the question.

These problems were solved by the industry through its National Television System Committee (NTSC), whose recommendations were accepted by the Federal Communications Commission.[18] In setting up standards the Commission specified the basic composition of the signal but left to the manufacturers the choice of the means whereby the prescribed signal was to be achieved. Several methods of both pickup and reproduction have been developed; they differ in the details of method, but are sufficiently alike to permit any color receiver to respond to any color transmitter. We will not attempt here to discuss the rival systems, but merely to outline the basic specifications.

NTSC color standards retain the 525-line, 60-field standard of monochrome television. All the additional information needed must be packed

---

[17] *Reverse* compatibility is the ability of a color receiver to pick up a monochrome signal and to render it in black and white.

[18] FCC, *In the Matter of Amendment of the Commission's Rules Governing Color Television Transmissions,* Docket No. 10637. 18 Fed. Register 8649 (23 December 1953).

into the same four-megacycle channel used by monochrome television. To accomplish this, advantage is taken of the fact that in actual practice the energy of the monochrome signal is not distributed equally throughout the 4,000,000 cycles of the video channel. Instead, the energy clusters about certain frequencies, leaving others relatively unused. These unused frequencies, or blank spaces in the channel, are therefore available to carry extra information.

The image is picked up separately in each of the specified primary colors (red, blue, green). From each of these color signals is derived a brightness signal proportional in strength to the brightness value of that color. The brightness components of the three primaries when added together yield white, which (in terms of the specific primaries selected) consists of 59 per cent green, 30 per cent red, and 11 per cent blue. This mixed signal provides the brightness information for the color picture. Since brightness is *all* that can be perceived in the fine detail, the mixed signal provides all the fine detail in the color picture. This same signal provides the compatible monochrome picture for black-and-white receivers. Meantime, the three color signals (minus their respective brightness components) are transmitted on a separate carrier wave (the subcarrier) generated by the same transmitter. The resulting color picture suffers some loss in detail as compared to monochrome standards, but this is compensated for by the greater apparent detail which color provides.[19]

According to the foregoing description, the composite color signal consists of four different elements: the brightness component and the three primary colors. So far, however, provision has been made for only two signals within the video portion of the channel: the brightness signal on the main carrier, the color signal on a subcarrier. Since the color signal consists of three separate elements — the red, green, and blue values — it is necessary to devise a means of doing three things at once. The solution of this problem is the most ingenious part of the NTSC color system. First, the three color signals are reduced to two by a manipulation which mixes green with the other three signals (red, blue, and brightness) in such a way that the green information can be recovered at the receiver. This reduces to two the number of signals to be transmitted on the color subcarrier. The red and blue signals are then *multiplexed* on the subcarrier — i.e., both are sent in the same channel without mixture. There are a number of ways of multiplexing signals, the particular type used in this case depending on sending the two signals out of phase with each other. This operation requires extremely delicate timing, which necessitates an added synchronizing signal (the "color burst"), which is transmitted during the blanking period just after the regular synchronizing pulses. The purpose of the color burst is to provide the receiver with the reference timing signal needed to separate the multiplexed red and blue signals.

[19] FCC, *op. cit.*, para. 17.

At the receiving end, color is achieved by the use of three different types of phosphor on the face of the kinescope tube; each glows in one of the prescribed primary colors when struck by electrons. The color elements are separate but closely associated and very minute; hence the eye perceives all three simultaneously, although in fact each primary is displayed separately. In other words, the color mixing is done by the eye rather than by the tube. In one type of tri-color kinescope three separate electron guns are used, one for each primary. Another type uses only one electron gun; the electron beam "wobbles" as it scans a line, alternately touching on three thin stripes of phosphor in the three primary colors. The appropriate information modulates the beam as it touches each of the color-stripes in rapid succession.

The color system is so intricate and so precisely designed that it is extremely difficult to maintain the various components in proper adjustment. The fact is that it was still essentially in the laboratory stage of development in 1953, when it was authorized for commercial use. Color-television components must be fabricated with a precision never before attempted on a mass-production basis. For example, one type of tri-color kinescope tube uses a plate in which 400,000 holes must be accurately positioned. The timing operations involved in developing the color signal are so exact that compensation has to be provided for the minute delay caused by signals traveling through certain of the circuits. When three different pick-up tubes are used for the three primaries, a difficult problem in registration arises: the three separate images must be superimposed exactly or the type of blurred picture often seen in cheap color printing will result. The flying-spot scanner has a distinct advantage over storage-type pick-up tubes in this connection, since the same spot of light provides information for all three primaries, thereby making misregistration impossible.

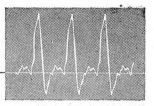

Relay and Reproducing Systems

An essential element in the economy of the mass media is the *syndication* of content. Individual outlets — newspapers, broadcast stations, theatres — are not themselves able to supply the raw materials in sufficient quantities and at a sufficient level of quality. At one extreme is the entertainment motion-picture industry, in which production is highly centralized and the retailer (exhibitor) has very little choice of product in general and none whatever of product in detail. The exhibitor is reduced to the position of providing the viewing facilities for a ready-made product. At the other extreme might be a newspaper like the *New York Times,* which, although it uses the syndicated materials of all the major news and picture agencies, itself has correspondents all over the world to supplement the syndicated materials. Broadcasting occupies a position between the extremes; as a whole it is absolutely dependent on syndication, but the individual station may exercise a good deal of choice both among syndicated offerings and between syndicated and self-produced materials.

Syndication depends on spreading the costs of a relatively very expensive product among a number of users. This in turn depends on high-speed mechanized methods of reproducing and distributing the materials. In broadcasting this means either networking or recording sound and pictures. Sound-recording methods in use include disc, tape, and film; picture-recording methods are kinescope-film and tape. In addition, regular motion-picture film produced for television use must be considered, even though it is not a "recording" in the sense of being a mechanical reproduction of materials picked up first by the television rather than the film camera. Network broadcasting as a type of syndication depends not on means of permanent recording but on the simultaneous delivery of program materials from the originating point to affiliated stations.

Network broadcasting, properly speaking, involves the simultaneous transmission of identical programs by a group of *connected* stations. The "net" of network broadcasting is the point-to-point relay system which passes the signal on from one station to another. Network programs normally originate from network "key" stations or special studios which are connected to the rest of the stations in the network either by wire or radio relay circuits

or by a combination of the two. Relaying is to be distinguished from rebroadcasting, as these terms are generally understood: the former means
the private (i.e., non-broadcast) communication of the signal from one
point to another, whereas rebroadcasting means that one station picks up
the broadcast signal of another station and in turn broadcasts that signal
on its own frequency (Figure 15).

The technical definition of network broadcasting has become somewhat
blurred in recent years owing to the fact that networks, which originally
regarded mechanical reproduction as inimical to the very existence of the
network method of distribution, have found it useful to combine both
methods — i.e., to record programs and then to distribute them simulta-

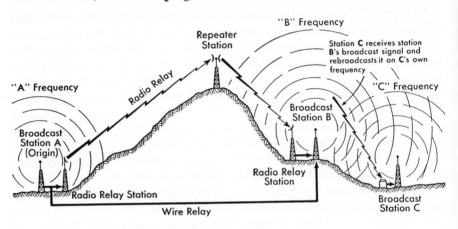

Figure 15

Comparison of Rebroadcasting and Relaying

Three broadcast stations, A, B, and C, operate on three different
frequencies. A program originates at Station A and is to be broadcast
simultaneously by Stations B and C. The program can be delivered
from A to B only by relay because B is too far away to pick up A's
broadcast signal. Normally all network broadcasts are relayed, either
by wire (including coaxial cable) or by microwave radio relay. If the
latter is used, the originating station feeds the program by wire to
a special transmitter which leap-frogs its signal through a series of
repeater stations, each of which consists of a receiver, an amplifier,
and a transmitter. In the illustration Station A's signal is beamed to a
repeater which retransmits the signal to a special receiving point
near Station B, which then feeds the signal to its broadcast transmitter.
(Normally the relay operations are handled by common carrier facilities, not by the stations themselves.) The relayed signal is on a band
of frequencies not picked up by broadcast receivers. Station C, however, is within the service area of Station B and hence can pick up B's
broadcast signal, feed it to its own transmitter, and rebroadcast it on
C frequency.

neously over the network relay system. The change in attitude was brought about by several circumstances. For one thing, the differences in time zones in a country of the size of the United States create a serious network scheduling problem, especially when summertime daylight saving is adopted by some states in the same time zone in which other states keep to standard time. "Delayed broadcasts" are now generally used in radio to solve these problems of time differentials, involving the necessity of mechanically recording network programs for network or local release in some parts of the country an hour or so later than the original live release. Another factor is the reluctance of some of the top-rank performers to continue submitting to the confinement of a live-broadcast schedule. The American Broadcasting Company first broke with tradition in 1946, establishing a trend followed by all the networks within three years. Finally, television networking began at a time when coaxial cable and microwave facilities were available to only a few cities; hence for some years a large number of major network affiliates were "non-interconnected," and had accordingly to depend upon kinescope recordings for network programs. Technically, of course, a "non-interconnected" affiliate is not part of a network at all, since the essential elements of simultaneity and connectedness are lacking when programs must be distributed to the stations as recordings for local release.

RELAY SYSTEMS

Relay systems use both wire and radio connecting links, and sometimes combinations of the two. Radio relay facilities suitable for broadcast signals are a later development than wire relay facilities, although from the start of broadcasting the potentiality of radio relay was recognized. Fortunately, a national wire network of telephone facilities already existed when broadcasting began, and hence national network operations could develop with relative ease and rapidity. The use of facilities originally designed only for telephonic use, however, posed a problem initially, since telephone standards of fidelity are considerably below radio broadcast standards. Characteristically, a wire circuit tends to act like a filter, self-limiting in the number of frequencies it will carry and becoming increasingly limited with the distance of the transmission. Special equalizing and booster, or repeater, equipment has to be used to maintain the signal for long-distance transmission. But even with the help of these devices an ordinary wire circuit is very limited in the frequency range it can carry; television, with its four-megacycle video signal, requires a much wider frequency capacity.[1] This need brought

[1] It will be recalled that although the television channel is six megacycles wide, two of these megacycles are used for the audio component and guard bands. When television programs are relayed the spacing is no longer necessary, and the audio and video components are handled on separate circuits, so as to reduce to the minimum the number of frequencies needed for any one circuit. This separate handling is the reason that the sound from one network program is occasionally matched to the picture from another program when an error in switching occurs.

about the development and installation of a specialized type of cable, called *coaxial* because it consists of two conductors, one inside the other and having a common axis. Each channel in a coaxial cable can accommodate a very wide range of frequencies, and each cable incorporates several channels.

Relay facilities, whether wire or radio, are classified as common carriers, which means that except for occasional remote pickups handled by a station's own equipment, the facilities must be rented from the American Telephone and Telegraph Company (see Figure 16). AT&T provides the long-distance telephone and relay facilities of the country as a public utility, subject to government regulation. Installation of coaxial cable, which is buried underground and requires amplifiers every eight miles, is very expensive. Fortunately, coaxial cable is useful for the telephone service as well as for relaying broadcasts. A single coaxial channel can accommodate hundreds of long-distance telephone calls simultaneously as against a single television program.

Coaxial cable was supplemented by microwave[2] relay facilities for the first transcontinental television network circuit, opened in 1951. Microwave relays take advantage of the propagation characteristics of the Ultra High Frequency waves, which can be focused into a narrow, concentrated beam for highly efficient short-range transmission. Stations are spaced about thirty miles apart to receive and re-transmit the line-of-sight signal. Microwave relays are, of course, almost indispensable for the transcontinental services, which have to contend with mountainous terrain in which it would be extremely difficult to lay coaxial cable. Microwave towers, erected on high spots in the terrain, provide a smooth radio highway through even the roughest mountain country. The repeater stations require no attendants; they operate automatically on information sent from control centers.

If wide-band relay facilities such as these had been available at the time, they might have brought about a fuller development for FM broadcasting. One of the major impediments to such development was the fact that network programs were distributed by relay facilities adapted to the limited frequency needs of AM, and hence network programs could not take advantage of FM's high fidelity. On the other hand, it is doubtful whether the added cost of wide-band relay circuits could have been justified. But television signals cannot be relayed at all over AM facilities; hence the development of this medium forced the development of appropriate relay facilities as well as acceptance of the added costs of network operations.

SOUND RECORDING

A lively disc-recording industry existed before radio broadcasting began. At the advent of broadcasting, discs were still dependent on acoustical methods of recording and reproduction. The pattern of sound energy to be

[2] Microwaves are extremely short waves at frequencies on the order of 1,000 mc. and higher.

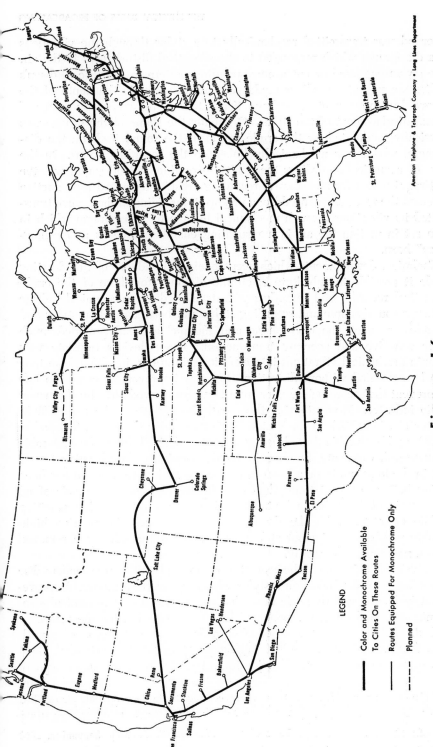

Figure 16

Coaxial Cable and Microwave Relay Routes

(As of 1 July 1955)

LEGEND

——— Color and Monochrome Available
To Cities On These Routes

——— Routes Equipped For Monochrome Only

– – – Planned

Source: Long Lines Department, American Telephone & Telegraph Co.

American Telephone & Telegraph Company • Long Lines Department

recorded was transmitted mechanically to a stylus through the vibrations of a diaphragm which responded to the acoustical disturbances in the air. The stylus engraved or cut a corresponding pattern in the disc. Edison's earliest acoustical recordings made vertical variations in the depth of the groove, but the current general practice is to vary the groove by means of lateral displacement of the stylus. Originally the shape of the groove was physically modulated by the crude action of the sound itself on the diaphragm, which was mechanically linked to the recording stylus. In the days of acoustical recordings the ability to produce a loud sound was the first requirement for a successful recording artist.[3] Acoustical reproduction reversed the recording procedure; a pickup stylus riding in the groove transmitted its vibrations through mechanical linkage to a diaphragm which in turn set in motion the air in a resonating chamber, such as a "morning-glory" horn.

Technical developments which accompanied the advent of broadcasting made it possible to substitute electronic methods for those of the crude acoustical recorder and reproducer. Instead of direct mechanical linkage between sound-source and recording stylus and between pickup stylus and sound-reproducer, the microphone and the pickup head provided much more sensitive and accurate transduction. These devices translate very minute mechanical vibrations into electrical vibrations, in which form they can be amplified without distortion. But this improvement came too late to prevent the recording industry from being swallowed alive by the newer radio industry. Mementoes of those early struggles are the names RCA Victor (harking back to the Victor Talking Machine Company, founded in 1898) and Columbia Broadcasting System (derived from the Columbia Phonograph Company, founded in 1888). Ironically, broadcasting turned out in the long run to be a boon to the recording industry, which has been doing better in recent times than ever before. Radio made music of all kinds universally available for the first time, educating as well as whetting public appetite. With the development of relatively inexpensive high-fidelity playback equipment and discs, the recording industry has moved into a new era of prosperity.

The simple principle of the acoustical recording is still in use; modern disc recordings still depend upon a stylus which modulates a groove. Improvement in fidelity and dynamic range has come with the refinement of electronic and mechanical components. In 1948 a new era for the recording industry began with the commercial introduction of "microgroove" recordings for home use.[4] These "LP" (long play) and "EP" (extended play) recordings represent several major improvements over the older type of

---

[3] The enormous popularity of Caruso as a recording star in the early 1900's is ascribed to his capacity for singing loudly without yelling. Cf. "Phonograph Records," *Fortune* (September, 1939), pp. 72 ff.

[4] Cf.: John M. Conly, "Five Years of LP," *The Atlantic Monthly*, September, 1953 (Vol. 192, No. 3), pp. 87-94.

disc recordings. The latter had been made on a shellac base which was thick, heavy, and brittle. Their speed was 78 revolutions per minute, a rate which appears to have no special significance except that it was fast enough to secure relatively uniform speed with inexpensive motors and turntables. The 33⅓-r.p.m. speed had been developed originally to suit the needs of sound motion pictures, which at first used discs rather than optical sound track integral with the film. This speed was adopted for the high-quality transcriptions developed in 1929 for use in broadcasting, permitting a full 15-minute program to be recorded on one side of a 16-inch disc. The 33⅓ and 45 r.p.m. microgroove recordings introduced in 1948 use vinyl plastic, a much lighter, more rugged base than the old shellac. Improved methods of recording make it possible to secure two to three times as many grooves to the inch. Rim-driven instead of axle-driven turntables make speeds under 78 r.p.m. possible without excessive cost. Improved pickup heads allow exceedingly light needle pressure with consequent reduction in noise and wear. These improvements together result in disc recordings that are longer-playing, of higher fidelity, smaller, more rugged and compact, and less expensive.

MAGNETIC RECORDING

Nevertheless, the use of discs for recording has many drawbacks from the point of view of securing the highest possible fidelity by the simplest possible means. One inherent disadvantage of the disc recording is the noise caused by the mechanical action of the stylus riding in a groove. Magnetic recording eliminates this factor altogether. Here the recording medium is any kind of flexible metallic substance, such as wire or tape, which can be passed rapidly over a recording or pickup head. A plastic-base tape with thin metallic coating has largely displaced all-metal media. The recording head consists essentially of an electromagnet whose magnetic properties can be modulated by electrical currrents supplied by a microphone. Tape passing over the recording head becomes magnetized in a corresponding pattern, which can be read off by a pickup head capable of translating the magnetic pattern back into electrical information for delivery to a loudspeaker. The amount of information that can be stored depends on the speed at which the tape passes the recording head. Sound tape for broadcast purposes has been standardized on a quarter-inch width, with speeds of 3¾, 7½ and 15 inches per second. When greater amounts of information must be handled, as in the case of tape-recorded television programs, greater speed must be used.

There are a growing number of specialized applications of tape-recording methods. In motion-picture applications, in which the picture and the sound track are usually handled on separate strips of film, coated film has been developed for sound recording. The sprocket holes ensure that the sound and picture will be kept in synchronism. A sound stripe can be added to a finished motion-picture film, and nonsynchronous sound can thus be added. Magnetic recording is now used in various intermediate steps in motion-picture production, even when release prints are to be optically recorded. Release prints can also carry magnetically-recorded sound (Plate II).

Since the television camera converts light information into electrical information, it is feasible to record on tape the video as well as the audio component of television programs. The difference between recording sound on tape and recording pictures on tape is the tremendous increase in the amount of information which must be handled. By 1953 this problem had been solved in principle to the extent of enabling public demonstrations of picture recording on magnetic tape.

These and other applications of magnetic recording methods take advantage of the important conveniences which the medium offers. Tape is economical, for it can readily be erased and used over and over again. It requires no processing, but can be played back immediately. Tape is easy to use: both recording and playback operations are so foolproof that virtually anyone can use a tape recorder after a few minutes of instruction — and, of course, tape is easy to edit by cutting and splicing.

OPTICAL RECORDING

Optical recording, the traditional method of cinematography, consists of photographing, in a narrow band beside the picture component of the film, a modulated beam of light. For playback, the resulting sound track modulates another beam of light which falls on a photoelectric (PE) cell, which has the property of converting light energy into equivalent electrical energy. Two basic methods of modulation are in use: one varies the width of the sound track; the other varies the density of exposure of the total width of the sound track (Plates II and III). Historically, the first method, variable area, was developed by RCA, and the second method, variable density, by Western Electric; these two methods are generally used in 35-mm. entertainment films, and one or the other company is usually credited in the opening titles of theatrical releases. A number of different sound-track subtypes have been evolved from these basic types to answer specific design problems. Just as in the case of magnetic tape, the amount of information that can be stored by optical recording depends on the speed at which the film travels past the recording head. The speed of 24 frames per second has been chosen as the standard sound-speed because it yields adequate quality. The standard is the same for both 16-mm. and 35-mm. film; this gives the latter a great advantage, for the linear speed of 35-mm. film at 24 frames per second is 90 feet per minute, whereas it is only 36 feet per minute for 16-mm. film.

Optically-recorded sound in motion pictures is handled in one of two ways: either the sound and the picture are recorded simultaneously on the same film strip (single-system) or the sound and the picture are recorded synchronously on separate film strips (double-system). Single-system is never used if sound quality is important, since it has so far proved impossible to devise a film stock which is equally well suited to both picture and sound. Single-system recording is confined almost entirely to newsreel work. Double-system photography involves not only processing the original films on which sound and picture are respectively recorded, but also printing and developing from these a single composite film which combines sound with picture. In the release print the part of the sound track that relates to any given picture frame is not located side by side with that frame. This is because in the projector the sound head must be located in a different place from the film gate where the actual projection takes place. It will be recalled that motion-picture film is not in motion when being projected; each frame must be pulled into place and held steady while being flashed upon the screen. This means that the movement of the film at this point is intermittent and therefore not suited for pickup of the sound track, which must move past the pickup head at a constant speed. The sound-pickup occurs after picture projection (20 frames later in 35-mm. film and 26 frames later in 16-mm. film).[5] The offset betrays itself when a release print has been broken and spliced, with the loss of a few frames. The observer will notice the resulting jump in the action a little before the corresponding jump in the dialogue occurs. This illustrates another major disadvantage of single-system photography: it is impossible to edit the composite sound-and-picture film freely, since every cut made at the right point in the picture will be at the wrong point in the sound track. Double-system photography avoids this problem, since the two components can be cut and edited separately.

KINESCOPE RECORDING

Film used in television may be divided into types made especially for television and types made originally for theatre exhibition Special television film includes film recordings of live television programs (kinescopes), "syndicated films,"[6] and miscellaneous material such as news footage, film inserts for live programs, filmed commercials, locally filmed subjects, and the like. Films made originally for theatre exhibition but subsequently used in television include feature films (regular full-length movies), short subjects, cartoons, and miscellaneous material such as travelogues. An increasingly important branch of the film industry is the non-entertainment branch, which includes business promotional, training, educational, and scientific films. Nowadays these types of film are nearly always made with an eye to

[5] From the film-handler's point of view the sound offset is toward the head of the film, and in that sense the sound precedes the picture.

[6] This term is misleading, since nearly all film is syndicated. Film is such an expensive medium that its cost can be justified only by dividing it among many different users. However, the term "syndicated film" has come to mean film subjects (typically half-hour dramatic programs) produced especially for multiple-station television release.

television release as well as release to schools, clubs, churches, and other non-theatrical outlets.

The film-recorded version of a television program is called a kinescope because the source of the picture is a kinescope tube, i.e., a television receiver tube. A kinescope recording is simply a motion picture of the images as they might be received on a home receiver. A special kinescope tube is used for kinescoping purposes, utilizing a phosphor especially suited to the needs of photography. The recording camera itself has to be specially designed to compensate for the fact that frame frequency in the television system is 30 per second whereas frame frequency in film is only 24 per second. If this precaution is not taken, horizontal traveling bars appear in the kinescope film.

A kinescope recording necessarily involves at least a double loss of information: to the inherent limitations of the television system are added the limitations of film. As a result, kinescope recordings do not yet approach the relative perfection of sound recordings, which can be virtually indistinguishable from live broadcasts. This being the case, the question arises why television recordings go through the indirect process of photographing the televised picture instead of simply photographing the original subject in the studio. There are a number of reasons why it is cheaper and easier to make a kinescope recording rather than a direct motion picture of a studio program. To begin with, the picture comes to the kinescope tube completely edited: all the sequences have been cut and joined by electronic means rather than by the tedious process of physically cementing together the desired sequences from separate strips of film. The television camera has the inestimable advantage over the film camera that the operator and the director know instantaneously and continuously what the finished picture looks like, without having to wait for film to be processed. This makes possible the simultaneous assembling and release of the finished product. Secondly, the lighting requirements for the two media are quite different. Moreover, there is never enough room for all the equipment and personnel needed to produce a television show; to add motion-picture cameras and crews would be to compound confusion. So by all odds it is cheaper and easier simply to make a film of the finished program as it is viewed on the kinescope tube, using equipment which operates virtually automatically once the necessary adjustments have been made.

SYNDICATED FILMS

However, the camera methods of live television have led to the development of motion-picture techniques which are a kind of compromise between the traditions of cinematography and the new methods of television. Traditional motion-picture production procedures are fantastically slow, inefficient, and expensive. In 35-mm. practice, each shot (sequence derived from a particular camera set-up) is usually separately staged and lighted, and is photographed a number of times. A good deal of creativeness usually enters into the process of assembling and editing which takes place after the actual photography.[7] In any event, the slow and expensive production methods of tradition do not fit the needs of television.

In consequence, hybrid production techniques have been developed, combining characteristic elements from both television and motion-picture practice. Dumont, for example, announced a system of dual-camera operation in 1955; the same taking-lens delivers an image to both a television and a film camera, and several such dual cameras are used simultaneously, as in the conventional television production method. The director uses the television version of the picture for monitoring and immediate editing; after development, the film version from the several cameras can be rapidly assembled into the finished product. Somewhat similar multi-camera motion-picture techniques had already been successfully used for rapid filming of half-hour syndicated dramas for television.

Such hybrid production methods seem at best to offer only a watered-down product which is neither as spontaneous as live television nor as flexible as motion pictures produced by more conventional methods. The unique capacity of film to transcend chronological sequence is sacrificed, and so is the unique capacity of television to report an event while it is actually taking place.[8]

THEATRICAL FILM

The motion pictures made originally for theatre exhibition offer a problem because of the fact that the capacity of the television system to reproduce a range of gray-scale values is only about half as great as that of film. When such films are transmitted by television the range of gray values in the original print is drastically compressed. This becomes evident when we observe large areas of a televised picture appear to be completely black or completely white, all detail in these areas being lost. In the original film these apparently uniform black or white areas turn out to be full of detail which is rendered in relatively subtle shades of gray. This problem can be solved when film is made especially for television by avoiding excessive contrasts in lighting; it can be only partially solved in films not made originally for television by making special television release prints which are developed in such a way as to limit the original contrast range.[9]

[7] Cf.: Karel Reisz, *The Technique of Film Editing* (New York: Farrar, Straus & Young, 1953).

[8] The relative advantages of the two media are discussed further on pp. 227-228. Albert Abramson's *Electronic Motion Pictures* (Berkeley: University of California Press, 1955) is an interesting exploration of the relations — present and prospective — between the film and the electronic picture technologies.

[9] Cf.: Eastman Kodak Co., *The Use of Motion Picture Films in Television* (Rochester: Eastman Kodak Co., 1949), in which the effects of excessive contrast are well illustrated photographically.

PART TWO

---

*The Origin and Growth
of Broadcasting*

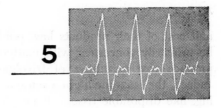

5

The Emergence of the Concept of

Mass Communication

Mass communication is a phenomenon distinctive of our age. Though used rather loosely, the term usually implies at least five things: (1) large audiences, (2) relatively undifferentiated audience composition, (3) some form of mechanical reproduction, (4) rapid distribution, and (5) low unit cost to the consumer. As a working definition, we might say that mass communication means the approximately simultaneous delivery of identical messages through mechanisms of high-speed reproduction and distribution to relatively large and undifferentiated numbers of people.

In former ages some publications — for example, the Bible or the works of Aristotle — certainly reached very large numbers of people in the course of time, but the elements of approximate simultaneity, low unit cost, and mass audience were lacking. A mass audience is not merely a large audience. It is an extremely heterogeneous audience, the members of which need have little in common beyond simultaneously receiving identical messages. A high degree of heterogeneity is possible because the members of the audience do not have to assemble in one place or otherwise engage in some common social act in order to participate as members. This heterogeneity is the basis of a great deal of misunderstanding about mass communication, for most of us do not have the opportunity to learn how "the other half" lives. Participating as an interviewer in a random personal survey concerning broadcast program preferences, for example, is always a salutary new experience. Most neophyte interviewers are astonished to discover how atypical their own tastes turn out to be. We unconsciously assume that the rest of the mass audience must be like *us* and hence that the content of the media should be tailored to *our* standards, needs, and tastes.

Before the development of cheap paper, high-speed printing machinery, rapid methods of distribution, and the concept of mass sales, a book was a thing of value. Books cost too much either to be wasted in great quantities on inconsequential matters or to come within the economic reach of most people. Because the output of the mass media must be great and the unit cost of their products low, public communications no longer need to be primarily concerned with matters of serious import. The mass media produce vast quantities of frivolous, trivial, highly ephemeral material. Indeed, the mass media in a sense *demand* a product which is self-liquidating, like disposable tissue. If people studied and pondered each message the system would soon become clogged, for the media depend upon a high rate of turnover. The motion-picture exhibitor tries to get his customer to leave the theatre after seeing the show once, so that he can usher another paying customer into the still-warm seat; the newspaper publisher hopes that yesterday's paper will line today's garbage pail, so that the reader will be ready to buy tomorrow's paper. Nothing could be more fatal to the operation of the mass media than to have their audiences pause and savor every message like so many sonnets or old masters.

Conditions which make mass communication possible include not only a highly developed technology for the inexpensive reproduction and distribution of messages but also an urbanized, relatively literate population, with buying power and leisure. An authoritarian state might limit these conditions to some extent, but essentially they are results of the Industrial Revolution rather than of political revolution. The Industrial Revolution brought about the changes in commerce, industry, transportation, and living conditions essential to the flourishing of mass communication. The groundwork was laid in the nineteenth century, but the mass media are essentially a twentieth-century phenomenon. The telegraph and telephone, forerunners of radio, were developed in the last half of the nineteenth century; so was the mass-circulation daily newspaper, the first of the mass media; the modern motion-picture industry is based on inventions first put to commercial use in the 1890's; broadcasting did not arrive upon the social scene until the third decade of the twentieth century. It achieved almost instant success.

By then, the communications field was already big business. The mass-distributed newspaper had established the precedents and developed the techniques for utilizing advertising for financial support, syndicating materials, and organizing its business on a large scale. The press, moreover, had developed philosophical and legal precedents of great value to broadcasting. The motion-picture industry had just gone through stages of development remarkably similar to those that faced broadcasting when it began. The telephone and telegraph, though not themselves mass media, had contributed vitally to the development of the newspaper; moreover, the wire communication systems had produced business empires whose prior existence profoundly affected the development of wireless communication, both economically and technologically. Thus the phenomenally rapid development of broadcasting can be ascribed in large measure to the fact that, although it was in some ways a completely new medium of mass communication, it profited considerably from the prior experience of the other mass media.

THE MASS NEWSPAPER

Newspaper publishing in the United States goes back to the start of the eighteenth century, but before the Industrial Revolution newspaper publishing was a small, low-investment business. Papers themselves, though numerous, were limited in circulation, each being addressed to a rather specific audience, usually one representing a political or other special interest. The shift from a predominantly agrarian to an industrial economy, with the consequent growth of great urban centers, created a new kind of audience. A new concept of the newspaper's function began to emerge in the 1830's, when the New York *Herald* and *Sun* broke the tradition of the small, specialized-audience paper. They developed a product intended to have mass appeal, free from the restraint of subsidization by special interests and priced to reach a market hitherto regarded as economically and educationally too depressed to be important to publishers. During the course of the century the technological means of realizing this aim were gradually achieved: cheap paper, typesetting machines, inexpensive engraving methods, high-speed presses. The result of these developments was an increase in the number of daily papers published as well as an increase in readership. A peak in the number of daily newspapers was reached just before World War I. Then began an opposite trend, a trend toward larger and larger producing units, reaching larger and larger audiences.[1]

We can discern in the history of newspaper publishing the evolution of the typical pattern of the mass media: a high degree of syndication of basic content material, mechanization of the means of production and distribution, the offsetting of increased costs of production by increased market penetration through consolidation of competing producers, a shifting of emphasis from a purely local, parochial outlook toward a regional or national outlook. Magazine publishing shows a parallel growth pattern. Economically, the trend is away from the highly individualized business operation toward the many-faceted corporate structure with economic interests in many related fields and with managers rather than entrepreneurs making the day-to-day decisions. In the early years of the twentieth century the trend was toward the building of personal empires through the acquisition of strings of newspapers and magazines, in the manner of William Randolph Hearst. The more recent ownership trend is toward fewer but larger units in any one medium and toward integration of several media in one corporate structure.

[1] Cf.: Raymond B. Nixon, "Implications of the Decreasing Numbers of Competitive Newspapers," in: University of Illinois Institute of Communication Research, *Communications in Modern Society* (Wilbur Schramm, ed.; Urbana: University of Illinois Press, 1948), pp. 43-57. Between 1930 and 1947 the number of United States daily newspapers decreased by 175, although circulation increased by over 12,000,000.

THE TELEGRAPH

Telegraphy, the first of the communication systems to utilize electrical energy, is a point-to-point system, adapted to the needs of private communication. However, the telegraph made an important contribution to the development of the mass media in that it soon became an essential tool in syndication of the news. The theoretical and experimental background of the utilization of electrical energy for communication can be traced back all the way to the Greeks, but the first practical applications came in the 1830's. In the United States we associate the telegraph with Samuel F. B. Morse, whose persistence led to the first successful telegraph line in this country, installed at government expense between Washington and Baltimore in 1844.

Morse's idea is remarkably simple, and it may seem surprising that it took him more than a dozen years to develop and install that first short link. We must bear in mind, however, that there were no precedents of any kind. Everything connected with the installation was an innovation. Since electrical theory itself was in a primitive state at the time, most decisions had to be made on the basis of trial and error; many wrong guesses were made before each workable expedient was evolved. The awe with which the achievement was regarded at the time is reflected in the first official message which Morse sent: "What hath God wrought!" Yet Morse and his contemporaries had no inkling in 1844 that the first breach in the wall of international isolation was being made. In less than a century the wall was to crumble completely.

The idea of the telegraph is based on the simple fact that wires conduct electrical energy. How to generate electricity in small amounts was already known. Morse's basic problem was to devise a way of making the energy convey information — i.e., a way of modulating the energy. The method of modulation is merely to turn the current on and off. In other words, the telegraph is fundamentally capable of sending two signals: "current on" and "current off." Even the most complex communication, however, can be built up out of such "bits" of information.[2] In telegraphy the problem resolves itself into that of inventing a code based on the signals "current on" and "current off" and a means of interpreting these signals at the receiving end. The Morse Code uses combinations of short and long pulses of energy (dots and dashes) to signify letters of the alphabet, numbers, and punctuation marks. For instance, the letter "e," being the letter most frequently used in English, is encoded as one dot. Less frequently used letters are assigned more complex code groups; for example, "q" is dash-dash-dot-dash.

---

[2] Information theory defines a *bit* as a binary digit, e.g., zero and one. Cf.: Claude E. Shannon and Warren Weaver, *The Mathematical Theory of Communication* (Urbana: University of Illinois Press, 1949) and Francis Bello, "The Information Theory," *Fortune* (December 1953), pp. 136 ff.

One disadvantage of this system of communication is that it requires intermediaries between the sender and the receiver of a message. Clerks must be trained in the special skill of encoding and decoding messages. Moreover, the maximum speed obtainable by manual operation is about 60 words per minute, although modern automatic devices now make higher rates of transmission possible.

THE ATLANTIC CABLE

It was relatively difficult to devise methods of installing wire connections overland, even after the feasibility of the system had been demonstrated.[3] A much more difficult problem was to insulate the conductors and to incorporate them into a cable strong and flexible enough to lay under the sea. The name of Cyrus W. Field is linked with the Atlantic Cable. After almost unbelievable difficulties, disappointments, and expense, transatlantic cable communication was finally established on a regular basis by 1868.[4] From then on it was only a matter of time before all the major commercial centers of the world were linked by a network of land and undersea wires.

The first messages sent over Morse's Washington-Baltimore telegraph link were news reports of political events. It is more than a coincidence that about eighty years later the first broadcast by the first regularly licensed commercial radio broadcasting station also should consist of news reports of a political event (see Chapter 7). Among the first commercial users of both wire and wireless communications were newspapers and news associations. Even before the days of the telegraph, newspapers had found it expedient to join forces in gathering the news so that the cost to the individual paper could be reduced. The high cost of telegraphic communication in the early days made joint action even more imperative. The rise of the news agencies, indispensable to modern world-wide news coverage, closely parallels the development of wire communication. Indeed, some of the early telegraph companies were actually organized by newspapers and news associations. Nowadays wire communication is used for the syndication of not only straight news stories but also news photos and many specialized types of written material. News agencies grew to national scope by about the turn of the century and to international scope after World War I. They now lease hundreds of thousands of miles of wire circuits for distribution of syndicated materials to thousands of subscribers or members.

[3] In the winter of 1847 a 30-mile stretch of a New York-to-Boston line was broken 170 times in a single night. Gleason L. Archer, *History of Radio to 1926* (New York: The American Historical Co., 1938), pp. 33-34.

[4] A cable laid in 1858 failed after a few months of intermittent operation. One of the factors in the final triumph over odds was a fantastic iron vessel, the *Great Eastern,* an enormous white elephant whose only practical use turned out to be in cable-laying. Cf.: James Dugan, *The Great Iron Ship* (New York: Harper & Bros., 1953).

THE TELEPHONE

Once the practical problems of communicating by simple electrical impulses over wire circuits were solved, the next step was to eliminate the awkward necessity of encoding and decoding messages. To send the human voice itself over the wires requires a transducer capable of modulating electrical current by converting the amplitude and frequency characteristics of sound into electrical equivalents. To send telegraphic signals requires no more than a simple "on-off" switching device. Sound signals require a much more complex switch, i.e., the microphone. Sound also requires wire with about forty times the minimum information capacity of telegraph conductors. Both Elisha Gray and Alexander Graham Bell solved the problem in the United States simultaneously. Bell applied for preliminary patents on the telephone in 1876, only a few hours before Gray. With this final basic development in wire communication, the stage was set for wireless.

However, the setting is more than technological. The telegraph had been a real innovation in human affairs. When Morse introduced telegraphy, its commercial possibilities were not even perceived. His own idea was that the instrument would be useful primarily to the government. At first it was regarded as a scientific curiosity even by legislators, rather than as a revolutionary means of speeding up the world's business. But by the time the telephone came along the commercial importance of the telegraph had already been established. Communication had become big business, with national and international ramifications. Before dealing with the advent of wireless, then, it will be helpful to look briefly at this economic background of that new medium.

INVENTION v. INNOVATION

Article I, Section 8, of the United States Constitution provides that "The Congress shall have the power . . . to promote the progress of science and useful arts, by securing for limited times to authors and inventors the exclusive right to their respective writings and discoveries." This is the constitutional authority for the laws of copyrights and patents. Copyrights are the source of a major economic burden to the broadcasting industry, and patents have been the pivotal points in the strategy of industrial control. A patent gives an inventor an exclusive property right in his invention for a period of seventeen years. During that time he has a legal monopoly. He can manufacture and sell the product himself, or he can sell or lease the patent rights to others. Our forefathers thought in terms of economic incentives to native genius at a time when this country was wholly dependent upon Europe for scientific knowledge. In creating patent rights they could hardly have foreseen that after the Industrial Revolution patents would become the cornerstones of great industrial monopolies from which the individual inventor often profited little if at all.

This circumstance arises from the fact that the qualities which make for inventive genius are rarely, if ever, combined in one man with the qualities which make for business genius. An invention is almost never a marketable product at its birth. Time, money, and business ingenuity must be liberally expended to develop the product, set up manufacturing facilities, create a market, secure distribution facilities, and defend the patent in the courts. The conversion of the raw invention into a marketable product has been called the work of the *innovator*, as distinguished from the work of the inventor:

> . . . the making of the invention and the carrying out of the corresponding innovation are, economically and sociologically, two entirely different things. They may, and often have been, performed by the same person; but this is merely a chance coincidence which does not affect the validity of the distinction. Personal aptitudes — primarily intellectual in the case of the inventor, primarily volitional in the case of the businessman who turns the invention into an innovation — and the methods by which the one and the other work, belong to different spheres.[5]

Business history is strewn with the wrecks of companies launched by optimistic inventors. In most cases they have ended either by losing control of their own companies and their own patents or by selling their rights for a flat fee.[6]

THE BUSINESS OF PATENTS

The difficulties of patent exploitation are much greater in some fields than others. In some fields important inventions have been successfully exploited by workers with no theoretical knowledge. This is true, for instance, of Mike Owens, inventor of the bottle-making machine. He had only a grammar-school education, yet he went on to become president of one of the great modern industrial enterprises. Radio, on the other hand, grew out of a scientific background which was inaccessible to the ordinary artisan. Edison was primarily an inventor, for instance, but he kept in very close touch with scientific developments. All of radio's inventors have similarly depended on science.

This means that inventions in the radio field tend to be not only complicated but also difficult to establish as unique, for any invention which depends upon another patented device for operation is automatically

---

[5] Joseph A. Schumpeter, *Business Cycles* (Copyright, 1939, McGraw-Hill Book Company, Inc.), I, 85-86. This concept has been applied with outstanding success to radio by W. Rupert Maclaurin in his *Invention and Innovation in the Radio Industry* (New York: The Macmillan Co., 1949). Maclaurin states: "No case has come to my attention in the history of the [radio] industry in which high inventive talent and the capacity for successful innovation were combined in one man" (p. 250). (Reprinted by permission of the Macmillan Co.)

[6] Lee de Forest, probably the most important American inventor in the radio field, is the classic example. (See Chapter 6.)

Figure 17

The Genealogy of an Invention

The flow chart shows graphically why no one man can be credited with "inventing" television, which synthesizes many scientific discoveries, inventions, and technological achievements.

Based on a diagram by Max Gschwind in: Edmund L. Van Deusen, "The Inventor in Eclipse," *Fortune* (December, 1954), pp. 134-135, © Time Inc.

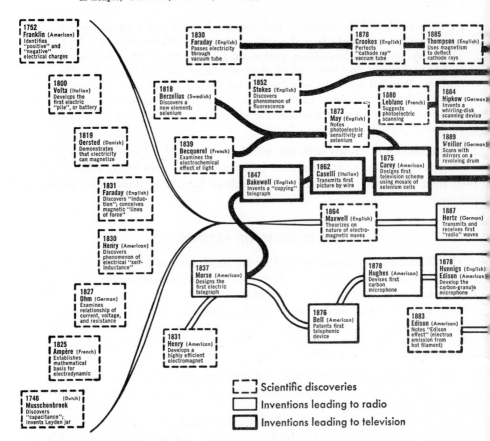

blocked by the prior patent. As a result, the whole history of radio has been marked by constant patent litigation, one of the most complicated of legal proceedings. It costs over $100,000 to take a patent suit through the Supreme Court. Edison himself is said to have spent more on litigation than he made in royalties.[7] In the highly developed technological fields it often takes millions of dollars and years of research to bring a product to

[7] Frank C. Waldrop and Joseph Borkin, *Television: A Struggle for Power* (New York: Wm. Morrow & Co., 1938), p. 206. See their chapter, "Patents and Power," for a somewhat alarmist view of patent monopolies.

the point at which it is marketable. The diesel engine took over thirty years to develop; nylon took thirteen years and an investment by one company of $27,000,000. Before television was ready for commercial exploitation, $30,000,000 had been spent in developmental work.[8]

Television was not "invented." Scores of individuals can be singled out as having made important contributions (Figure 17). Television as a commercial medium is essentially the result of teamwork, much of it in highly organized corporate research facilities. The great industrial laboratories which have made such miracles as nylon and television possible are all

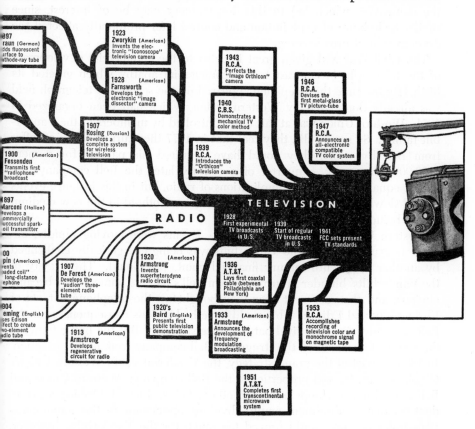

products of the twentieth century. The first modern industrial laboratory was set up by General Electric as recently as 1900, with a staff of only two men. A half century later nearly 3,000 industrial laboratories were in operation in the United States, employing a quarter of a million persons.[9]

[8] Frank Joseph Kottke, *Electrical Technology and the Public Interest* (Washington: American Council on Public Affairs, 1944), p. 158.
[9] David E. Lilienthal, *Big Business: A New Era* (New York: Harper & Bros., 1953), p. 71.

THE RISE OF AT&T

Because of these developments we must look to the history of the large industrial concerns in the communications field to understand the background of the development of radio. Patenting became inextricably involved with big business strategy in the latter half of the nineteenth century. Alexander Graham Bell's two basic patents on the telephone, taken out in 1876 and 1877, became the seeds of the world's greatest business enterprise, the American Telephone and Telegraph Company.[10] An account of the maneuvers which led to this development may be of interest, since similar techniques of exploitation and control later profoundly affected the development of broadcasting.

The Civil War had given great impetus to the commercial development of the telegraph, in contrast to the commercial apathy which greeted its birth. By the time the telephone appeared on the scene, the telegraph field was already dominated by Western Union, which had been organized in 1851. Western Union was at this time controlled by members of the Vanderbilt family. So secure did they feel that in 1877 they turned down an offer from Bell by which they could have acquired his patents for a mere $100,000. Ironically, a quarter of a century later the Bell company was almost equally blind to the implications of radio, but in this instance events moved slowly enough for the company to get a foothold in the new medium before being permanently frozen out.

Western Union was not so fortunate. Events were moving rapidly, because the supremacy of the Vanderbilts was being energetically challenged by another nineteenth-century financial giant, Jay Gould. The gravity of the Vanderbilts' blunder in turning down Bell's patents immediately became obvious, and the very next year they bought up the telephone patents of Elisha Gray and Edison. This could have had serious consequences for the Bell company, since the rival patents were superior. But the battle between the financial titans saved the struggling Bell company from early extinction. In 1879, as part of the grand strategy, the Vanderbilts sold Western Union's telephone patents and properties to the Bell company. Western Union and Bell agreed not to compete in each other's fields, thus establishing a precedent for many subsequent empire-dividing agreements in the communications industry. Jay Gould proved too much for the Vanderbilts, however, and by 1882 he had acquired control of Western Union and was master of the field. In the end the Bell company, once a mere pawn in the struggle for telegraphic supremacy, grew to the point where it was able to buy a controlling interest in the once invincible Western Union.[11]

[10] The first Bell patent, No. 174,465, issued March 7, 1876, may well be the most profitable single patent ever recorded. Litigation concerning it led to *The Telephone Cases*, 126 U.S. (1888), the only subject ever to occupy an entire volume of the Supreme Court reports.

[11] For details of the struggle for control, cf.: N. R. Danielian, *A.T.&T.: The Story of Industrial Conquest* (New York: The Vanguard Press, 1939).

Bell's original firm, the American Bell Telephone Company, was organized in Massachusetts in 1877, the year in which Bell secured the second of his two basic patents. The inventor and his friends could not raise enough capital to develop the company, and the control over the patents soon passed to others. Bell's name has been associated with the company ever since, but it ceased to be his company almost as soon as it was founded. The company went through a number of changes in organization and name as it expanded and brought in new investors, but it has had a continuous corporate history down to the present day. It now consists of a parent holding company and over a score of subsidiary companies which constitute the "Bell System" and provide over 80 per cent of the telephones in the United States. The parent company is the American Telephone and Telegraph Company (AT&T), often referred to simply as the Telephone Company or the American Company. The subsidiaries include Western Electric (a manufacturing company) and regional Bell System companies which stretch from coast to coast (Figure 18).

During its first seventeen years, while its patent monopoly lasted, the Telephone Company's strategy centered on keeping its patent position impregnable and vigorously suppressing infringements. During this period, the Bell Company brought 600 suits against competing firms for patent infringements. Rather than spread to ungainly proportions by seeking to supply service throughout the country, the Bell company adopted a policy of franchising independent regional operators to supply telephone service. The franchised companies received the exclusive and permanent right to use the Bell patents, and in turn gave the Bell company substantial stock holdings. By the time the patent monopoly period came to an end, the Bell Company had seen to it that it held controlling interests in these franchised companies. Expiration of the patents in 1893-4 brought an upsurge of competition, but in the long run the Bell company held a trump card: the long lines for connecting one area with another. Supremacy in this field was assured by the acquisition of patent rights to the audion (see Chapter 6) which made coast-to-coast long-distance service possible.

Even after the original Bell patents expired, the company retained a policy of not selling telephone equipment outright. In 1881 it had purchased Western Electric as its manufacturing subsidiary, thus making it possible to keep the whole process of manufacture, installation, and service within the Bell family. Nevertheless, the company felt the effect of competition after the expiration of the patents, and it was forced to expand its service and cut its rates to meet the threat. At the turn of the century nearly as many telephones were operated by independent companies as were operated by the Bell System. Once again new capital was needed, and once again new money brought new control. The Morgan banking interests now came to dominate the Telephone Company. It was during this period that the company acquired Western Union (1909), in a maneuver to combat Postal Telegraph, then a vigorous competitor in the telegraph field. Under pres-

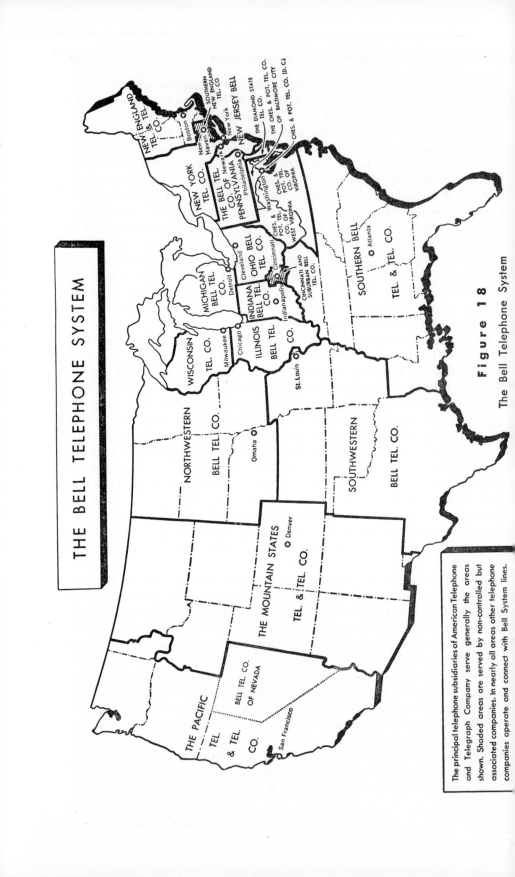

THE BELL TELEPHONE SYSTEM

NEW ENGLAND TEL. & TEL. CO.
Boston

SOUTHERN NEW ENGLAND TEL. CO.
New Haven
New York

NEW YORK TEL. CO.
Newark

NEW JERSEY BELL

THE DIAMOND STATE TEL. CO.
THE CHES. & POT. TEL. CO. OF BALTIMORE CITY
CHES. & POT. TEL. CO. (D. C.)

THE BELL TEL. CO. OF PENNSYLVANIA
Philadelphia
Washington

CHES. & POT. TEL. CO. OF VIRGINIA

CHES. & POT. TEL. CO. OF WEST VIRGINIA

MICHIGAN BELL TEL. CO.
Detroit
Cleveland

OHIO BELL TEL. CO.
Cincinnati

CINCINNATI AND SUBURBAN BELL TEL. CO.

SOUTHERN BELL TEL. & TEL. CO.
Atlanta

WISCONSIN TEL. CO.
Milwaukee
Chicago
Indianapolis

INDIANA BELL TEL. CO.

ILLINOIS BELL TEL. CO.
St. Louis

NORTHWESTERN BELL TEL. CO.
Omaha

SOUTHWESTERN BELL TEL. CO.
Denver

THE MOUNTAIN STATES TEL. & TEL. CO.

BELL TEL. CO. OF NEVADA
San Francisco

THE PACIFIC TEL. & TEL. CO.

Figure 18

The Bell Telephone System

The principal telephone subsidiaries of American Telephone and Telegraph Company serve generally the areas shown. Shaded areas are served by non-controlled but associated companies. In nearly all areas other telephone companies operate and connect with Bell System lines.

sure from the Department of Justice, the Telephone Company sold its Western Union stock in 1913. But in the meantime Postal Telegraph had been seriously weakened, and finally was itself absorbed by Western Union in 1934. In its century-long history Western Union had absorbed over 500 competitors. This last merger left it with a government-regulated monopoly on all telegraphic services (with some reservations in favor of AT&T). The government encouraged this consolidation in an effort to bolster the telegraphic service, which had been declining since World War I.[12]

Patents continued to play a major role in the strategy of the AT&T business empire. As we shall see, patents enabled the Telephone Company to dominate the infant broadcasting industry, and although the company ultimately withdrew from the operation of broadcast stations, it still plays an indispensable role in the broadcast industry through its monopoly of the facilities for station interconnection which are essential to network operations.

We have dealt at some length with the history of AT&T not only because it had a profound effect on the development of broadcasting but because the company in many ways typifies modern large-scale industrial organization, the role of patents in corporate strategy, and the whole complex of social problems resulting from bigness in business. Some social implications of these facts of modern business life are discussed in Chapter 24.

GE AND WESTINGHOUSE

Two other large companies which built industrial empires on nineteenth-century patents also played key roles in the development of radio: General Electric and Westinghouse. The foundation of the General Electric Company goes back to Edison's patent on the incandescent electric light. The present company was born of a merger between the Edison Electric Light Company and another manufacturing concern in 1892. The Westinghouse Manufacturing Company was founded by George Westinghouse, best known for the Westinghouse Air Brake and other important improvements in railroad equipment. GE and Westinghouse became embroiled in the usual patent litigation and in rivalry over the exploitation of competing electric power systems. Westinghouse installed the first alternating-current (AC) power system in 1886, and for ten years fought to establish it as the standard instead of the earlier direct-current (DC) system advocated by GE. The contest ended in 1896 when the two companies pooled their patents for their mutual benefit and agreed to standardize on the alternating-current system which we know today (though a few local DC power systems continue to operate).

[12] For a discussion of the problem of the decline in "record" communications cf.: President's Communications Policy Board, *Telecommunications: A Program for Progress* (Washington: Government Printing Office, 1951).

By the turn of the century, with electric power increasing in importance and with the demand for equipment high, both GE and Westinghouse had grown into very powerful concerns. With AT&T (including Western Electric) they were an invincible triumvirate in the field of communications and electrical manufacturing when radio came upon the scene. The existence of these powerful companies when the new medium arrived contrasts interestingly with the situation that obtained when the first of the electrical communication systems, the telegraph, began. Then there were no antecedent and powerful vested interests. Contrary to what one might expect, however, none of the companies took any immediate and major interest in radio.[13] But we must recollect that these companies were busy at the time trying to keep up with a rapidly expanding economy. Such research and development workers as they had concentrated their efforts on solving immediate problems of production and service. The failure of AT&T and the others to capitalize on wireless immediately is explained in more general terms as a lag between technological and scientific development. In the first half of the nineteenth century the opposite had been true: inventors made things work that could not yet be explained. In the twentieth century, at least in some fields, scientists know about many possibilities which have not yet been exploited by technologists. Industry and science have recognized this lag. The Bell Laboratories, for instance, have over a hundred scientists assigned exclusively to probe the implications of the most advanced scientific thought; their job is to foresee the implications of science for technology.[14]

By mid-twentieth century, the role of patents in business competition had changed considerably from what it had been in the period when radio was emerging from the laboratory. During that period the large companies we have been describing amassed patents by the thousands, many of which were never used but served to stave off competition. As we shall see in subsequent chapters, these companies used patent control as a means of dividing the communications fields among themselves. The Department of Justice has gradually weakened monopolistic agreements directly or indirectly based on patent pools by means of a series of consent decrees. Finally, in 1956, AT&T agreed to release, on a nondiscriminatory basis, over 8,000 patents on which it had pooling agreements with the other major firms, and to give up the last of those of its subsidiary activities that were not directly concerned with providing common carrier services, notably Westrex Corporation, a subsidiary for the manufacture of motion-picture sound equipment (see page 171).

---

13 "It is difficult today to conceive of the principal concerns in electrical communications being as oblivious to the possibilities of wireless telegraphy as most of them were in 1900." Maclaurin, op. cit., p. 22.

14 Morton M. Hunt, "Bell Labs' 230 Long-Range Planners," Fortune (May 1954), pp. 120 ff.

Wireless Communication

The most eminent men of the time were conscious of the problem, were interested in it, had sought for years the exactly right arrangement, always approaching more nearly but never quite reaching the stage of practical success. The invention was, so to speak, hovering in the general climate of science, momentarily awaiting birth. But just the right releasing touch had not been found. Marconi added it.   — JUSTICE WILEY RUTLEDGE

Despite a number of conflicting claims, Marconi is generally recognized as the inventor of wireless, and the date of his first British patent, 1896, is taken as the start of the wireless era.[1] But the *scientific* father of wireless was James Clerk Maxwell, the greatest theoretical physicist of the nineteenth century. Maxwell, a Scot, published in 1873 a basic theoretical work, *A Treatise on Electricity and Magnetism,* which put forward the modern concept of electromagnetic energy. This theory was taken up by another outstanding nineteenth-century scientist, Heinrich Hertz, who conducted research on it at several German universities between 1884 and 1893. In 1888 he published a paper, "Electro-magnetic Waves and their Reflection," in which he gave experimental confirmation of Maxwell's theory. Maxwell had used theory to generate certain predictions about the way radio waves should behave, based on the known behavior of light. Hertz devised the laboratory tests which fulfilled these predictions. To do this he in effect invented radio. He had to generate radio energy, transmit it, and detect it. In recognition of the fact that Hertz was the first man to create radio waves, they were for a time called "Hertzian waves." Hertz wanted,

[1] The terms *wireless* and *radio* are used interchangeably. *Radio* came into use in the United States Navy about 1912, since at that time the concept of wireless embraced certain non-radio methods of transmission. Sound broadcasting is an application of radio (or wireless) telephony. For a discussion of the origin of the term "radio," cf.: Gleason L. Archer, *History of Radio to 1926* (New York: The American Historical Company, 1938), p. 88.

however, to verify a scientific theory, not to invent a method of communication. Indeed, when asked if Hertzian waves could be used for communication, he advanced theoretical reasons to show that they could not — an interesting demonstration of how scientific theory can be used to block as well as to further progress.[2]

MARCONI THE INVENTOR

It remained for Guglielmo Marconi — more an inventor than a scientist — to make the practical application in defiance of theory. Stimulated by the reading of Hertz's paper, Marconi experimented with similar apparatus, first indoors and then on the grounds of his father's estate in Italy. Fortunately, Marconi had the leisure for experimentation and the money for equipment. Equally important was the fact that he had social entree to high official and business circles. This meant that he escaped the galling frustration, so familiar to inventors, of having to struggle against odds for recognition and financial support.

As soon as Marconi was convinced that wireless was more than a laboratory toy, he hurried to England, took out a patent in 1896, and in the next year formed a company there to exploit his invention. His objective was nothing less than the creation of a world monopoly in wireless communication. Had not the United States subsequently been particularly active in the development of wireless technology, and had not the national interest of this country become involved as a result of World War I, Marconi would very likely have succeeded in this objective.

Once Marconi had made the giant step from the laboratory to practical application, progress was rapid. By 1899 he had sent messages across the English channel; in 1901 he succeeded in sending a signal across the Atlantic; in the following year actual transatlantic intelligence was exchanged. Meanwhile, his example stimulated many others already working in the field to develop rival systems, and the rush to the patent offices began. The key to ultimate success was the ability to secure a set of patents covering a complete wireless communication system, so that a company could be set up without having to secure licenses from a rival. With each passing year, as the technology of wireless improved and grew more complicated, this objective became more difficult to attain. Before long, literally thousands of patents were involved, and the whole patent structure became so complex that no one was safe from patent-infringement suits. The growing complications of the patent situation made it inevitable that control of the new industry should gravitate toward the great corporations which had the resources to build up patent strength, to withstand the costly, long-drawn-out court battles, and to undertake the developmental work which patents always need. Eventually, as we shall see, a stalemate resulted: the largest

[2] W. Rupert Maclaurin, *Invention and Innovation in the Radio Industry* (New York: The Macmillan Co., 1949), pp. 15-16.

companies bought up patent rights as fast as they could, but none could carve out a self-contained system which would not at some points conflict with rival systems.

MARCONI THE INNOVATOR

Of all the pioneer inventors engaged in the struggle for self-sufficiency, Marconi alone succeeded. The others were overwhelmed by patent suits, business setbacks, and bankruptcies, for although the promise of eventual returns was great, immediate returns were small. American Marconi, the United States branch founded by British Marconi in 1899, lost money consistently for six years, and a whole decade passed before it realized substantial profits. The turning point came with the acquisition in 1913 of the assets of the rival de Forest company, United Wireless, which had succumbed to bankruptcy after the Marconi company won a patent-infringement suit against de Forest. This gave American Marconi 400 ship stations and 17 land stations and a virtual monopoly on commercial wireless in America.

Marconi succeeded because he was as much an innovator as an inventor. Although throughout his life he maintained a lively interest in the engineering aspects of radio, he produced no important inventions after 1902.[3] But he understood the importance of patents, and saw to it that his companies secured control of those it needed. He also understood the importance of business know-how, and saw to it that his companies were run by qualified business executives.

The Marconi company aggressively pursued its objective of a world monopoly. It used every device to freeze out competition. Not infrequently this policy created bad public relations. Prince Henry of Prussia, on his way home from a visit to the United States in 1902, tried to send a wireless thank-you note to President Theodore Roosevelt, but British Marconi refused to accept a message from a German ship. The failure of the international convention on wireless held in Berlin in 1903 is ascribed to the uncooperative attitude of the Marconi company.[4] The United States Navy at first adopted German equipment because of the restrictive terms insisted upon by the British company. The Navy continued its opposition to the Marconi company through World War I, as we shall see, and was finally instrumental in the losing of the American market by Marconi.

THE FIRST WIRELESS SERVICES

During the first two decades of wireless its commercial value consisted primarily in supplying communication *services*. The sale of equipment was secondary. It is true that money could be made in the sale of equipment

[3] MacLaurin, *op. cit.*, pp. 43, 48.
[4] Joint Technical Advisory Committee, IRE-RTMA, *Radio Spectrum Conservation* (New York: McGraw-Hill, 1952), p. 6.

to navies and to amateurs, but these were then relatively limited markets. There was nothing to compare with the tremendous mass market for receivers later created by broadcasting. The promise of riches at first lay mainly in the potentialities of world-wide communication networks in competition with the telegraph cables and secondarily with the telephone.

First to develop was the maritime mobile service, involving ship-borne stations and coastal land stations. Here no existing service was duplicated; wireless was unique. The relative efficiency of over-water propagation of radio made this service feasible even in the early days of the art, when equipment was still extremely crude. Long-distance transoceanic communication, however, was commercially the more promising field. Static was the great enemy of such a service. For two decades the major goal of inventors was a high-power generator capable of overriding the heavy static interference characteristic of the low frequencies employed. Marconi's 1901 demonstration of transatlantic reception proved that radio waves could travel great distances, but he was a long way from being able to set up a reliable transatlantic service capable of competing effectively with the cable service. In 1908 the Marconi company offered a transatlantic service from Nova Scotia to Ireland, but commercial development of long-distance radiotelegraphy was delayed by the outbreak of World War I in 1914.

A third service, overland wireless, competed with the telegraph and the telephone. This field was not extensively developed before 1920. In fact, the United States Navy still considered it of no consequence in planning postwar development of radio communication.[5]

The fourth service developed during the first two decades of wireless was the amateur service. Amateurs ("hams") were of peculiar importance during these pioneer days, when even the experts worked largely by rule of thumb. Relegated to high frequencies where they would not interfere with maritime traffic, the amateurs developed the techniques for employing this supposedly useless part of the spectrum. Their ranks included leading engineers and inventors, who could be called amateur only because they did not operate their stations for profit.

> . . . the amateur in many cases, had more money than some of the commercial companies. Moreover, both classes of wireless workers used apparatus almost equally crude. It is rather an unflattering commentary on the state of the art as it existed around 1903-1910, that the commercial concerns had to give jobs to the amateurs with the biggest sets around New York, in order to get a chance to receive their own messages.[6]

No explicit provision had been made for the amateurs as a recognized service in the Radio Act of 1912 (at that time there were 405 ship stations, 123

---

[5] House Committee on Merchant Marine and Fisheries, *Hearing on H.R. 13159, Government Control of Radio Communication* (Washington: Government Printing Office, 1919).

[6] Harold P. Westman (ed.), *Radio Pioneers, 1945* (New York: Institute of Radio Engineers, 1945), p. 30.

land stations, and 1,224 amateur stations). All subsequent legislation took cognizance of their rights, however, and the amateur class has continued to lead in number of stations to this day. Spokesmen for the amateurs appeared at all the important Congressional hearings on proposed new radio legislation in the postwar years,[7] and also at the four Radio Conferences held in Washington in 1922-1925.

Of all the early radio services, however, the maritime service was the most dramatic because of its unique value in times of emergency. As early as 1898 wireless had been used in a maritime disaster. A wireless-equipped British lightship was rammed in 1899, and wireless brought relief. In 1909 the S.S. *Republic* foundered off New York, and 1,500 passengers were saved by wireless-alerted rescue ships. A number of other maritime emergencies in these early years dramatized the unique capabilities of wireless communication.[8] The culminating event came in 1912, when the "unsinkable" luxury liner, the *Titanic*, struck an iceberg on her maiden voyage to the United States. The ship sank, with loss of many lives. The fact that its passenger list was studded with famous names in the arts, the sciences, the financial world, and diplomacy made the *Titanic* disaster the most dramatic tragedy of its kind in history. And the fact that for days the world's only thread of contact with the survivors was maintained by radiotelegraphy brought the new medium to public attention as nothing else had done. Subsequently, when it was discovered that a more rational use of wireless resources might have materially decreased the loss of life, the *Titanic* disaster had an important influence on the adoption of laws governing the use of wireless in maritime commerce.

Naturally, the naval powers of the world took an early interest in military applications of wireless. Pigeons had hitherto provided the only means of communication with ships beyond the range of sight. Both the British and American navies began experimenting with ship installations as early as 1899, and Germany followed the next year. The first naval use of radio in actual war occurred in the Russo-Japanese War in 1904-1905. The United States Navy became an important customer for the wireless equipment of American inventors. During and after World War I the United States Navy played a decisive role in freezing out the American branch of the Marconi company; the Navy regarded radio as its particular province, and after World War I it made a strong effort to secure complete control of United States radio (see Chapter 7).

Experimentally, both Hertz and Marconi had used relatively high frequen-

[7] Cf. the eloquent testimony of Hiram Percy Maxim, representing the amateurs' American Radio Relay League, in: Senate Committee on Interstate Commerce, *Hearings on S. 6, Commission on Communications* (Washington: Government Printing Office, 1930), pp. 2061-2074.

[8] A list appears in: House Merchant Marine and Fisheries Committee, *Hearings on H.R. 19350, To Regulate Radio Communication* (Washington: Government Printing Office, 1917), pp. 417-430. Until 1909 instances were sporadic. In 1909, however, 21 cases are listed, and in each succeeding year the list grows longer.

cies; but practical applications proved successful initially only at low frequencies. During the pre-World War I period the available equipment permitted efficient use of only a very small range of these frequencies. Moreover, the fact that the first commercial service involved ship-borne stations placed a practical limit on the frequencies that could be employed. It will be recalled that the optimal length of the transmitting antenna depends on the length of the waves it is designed to radiate. The size of the ocean-going vessels controlled the maximum size of antennas and hence determined what wave lengths were suitable for the maritime mobile service. Since 500-kc. waves represent a convenient average size for ships' antennas, that frequency was selected as the international distress frequency, and it is still so designated. Thus this earliest allocation of spectrum space came about more by chance than by design. Subsequently, when broadcasting began, the only frequencies available were those above the range already used by the maritime service. Ideally, broadcasting could have used the 300-550-kc. band,[9] but the lower limit of the broadcast frequencies is still determined by the necessity of protecting the 500-kc. distress frequency from interference.

It may be necessary at this point to remind ourselves that the four services we have been discussing in this chapter — maritime mobile, transoceanic, overland, and amateur — were radiotelegraphic services. Nowadays the word "radio" means intelligible sound to the average person, but we must remember that radio began, like the telegraph, as language encoded as dots and dashes of energy. Radiotelegraphy is still extensively used. However, the possibility of applying the principle of the telephone to wireless was apparent from the beginning, and experiments in this direction began as early as 1900. But the methods available in the pre-war period for generating carrier waves did not lend themselves to the complex modulation required for the reproduction of sound energy. Very crude apparatus can generate readable dot-dash code signals; the raw pulses of energy needed for code can survive a great deal of distortion and interference. But wireless telephony, as a commercially usable medium, had to await the development of the audion.

THE INVENTION OF THE AUDION

Marconi's gift to the world was a very imperfect instrument. To communicate across space with electromagnetic energy was in itself an achievement of great magnitude, of course, but the practical limitations of early wireless were very severe. All the major barriers to fuller exploitation of Marconi's invention were eventually to be broken by the audion and its numerous progeny (Figure 19). This device unlocked the realm of electronics. With it man can command "electricity itself, not just its manifestations."[10] Hence

9 Joint Technical Advisory Committee, *op. cit.*, p. 10.
10 Lee de Forest, *Father of Radio* (Chicago: Wilcox & Follett Co., 1950), p. 2. *Audion* is a word invented by one of de Forest's associates. In modern parlance it is the electronic (or vacuum, or thermionic) tube.

PLATE V

Marconi in the Newfoundland station where he received (see p. 92) the first transatlantic radio signal in 1901   *RCA*

David Sarnoff in 1908, working as a wireless operator on Nantucket Island, Massachusetts (see p. 113)   *RCA*

PLATE VI

Equipment of Frank Conrad's amateur ''broadcasting'' station, 8XK (see p. 106)

Crude microphone used in early radiotelephony (see p. 102)   *Brown Brothers*

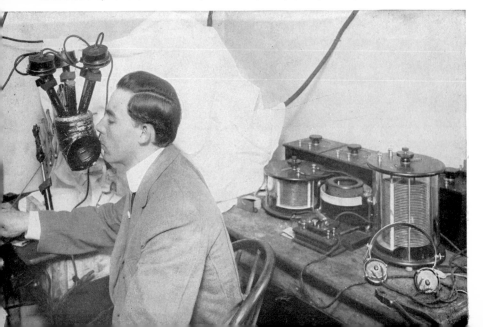

PLATE VII

Typical crystal set of the earliest days of broadcasting
(see p. 108) *The Bettmann Archive*

WWJ, Detroit, in 1920, showing crude method of
acoustical pickup of phonograph records *WWJ*

PLATE VIII

The Cliquot Club Eskimos, one of radio's first sponsored programs (see p. 122). The announcer is Graham McNamee.
Brown Brothers

KDKA's studio in 1922, showing early acoustic treatment
Westinghouse Photo

its importance extends far beyond its role in radio communication. It makes possible all of the thousands of devices which depend on electron manipulation — from guided missiles to automatic garage doors, from "thinking machines" to machines which automatically reject faulty units coming off a production line. As for radio, the vacuum tube is an essential tool in each of the basic operations: generating, modulating, amplifying, and detecting radio energy. The television pickup and kinescope tubes are, of course, examples of specialized applications. There are thousands of such specialized applications, and today millions of descendants of de Forest's audion are manufactured every year. By opening the field of electronics, vacuum tubes made possible a new industrial revolution. They freed technology from exclusive dependence on mechanical moving parts, with their inherent limitations. They make possible operations of such complexity, delicacy, and precision as were undreamed of before.[11]

The paternity of the audion, like that of radio itself, is complex, but history recognizes the claim of Lee de Forest, just as it recognizes the radio patent claim of Guglielmo Marconi. In 1883, while studying the problem of the tendency of electric lamps to blacken with use, Edison had discovered that current could be transferred through the space between the filament and a metal plate sealed inside the lamp. He patented a device for measuring this current, and that for the moment was the end of the matter. Two decades later Ambrose Fleming, a member of Marconi's research staff, studied the "Edison effect," and patented a radio detector based on this phenomenon (1904). The Fleming detector took advantage of the fact that a two-element tube (diode) can convert energy at radio frequencies into electrical currents. But the device was not a practical success, and when the more reliable crystal detector was developed (1906) the Fleming valve went out of use.

De Forest approached the work on thermionic tubes by another route. He had received a Ph.D. from Yale in 1899, and his first job was as an engineer with Western Electric. However, he found routine engineering research dull, and he soon began devoting full time to his own inventive bent. In 1903 he began experimenting with a radio detector, using an open gas flame. Since a flame has inherent practical disadvantages, he turned to the analogous idea of gas heated within an enclosed space by a glowing filament. He had such a device fabricated by a commercial electric-lamp maker in 1905.

The next and crucially important step was the addition of a third element in the tube, making it a three-element tube, or *triode;* this tube was the first to be called the "audion." The new element was a grid interposed between

[11] The transistor, announced by Bell Laboratories in 1948, may represent another decisive step forward in the electronic age. Whereas the audion deals with electrons in a vacuum, the transistor deals with electrons in a solid. It does most of the things vacuum tubes do but is much smaller, takes much less power, creates less heat, has longer life, and is more rugged. It is already extensively employed for miniaturization of electronic devices.

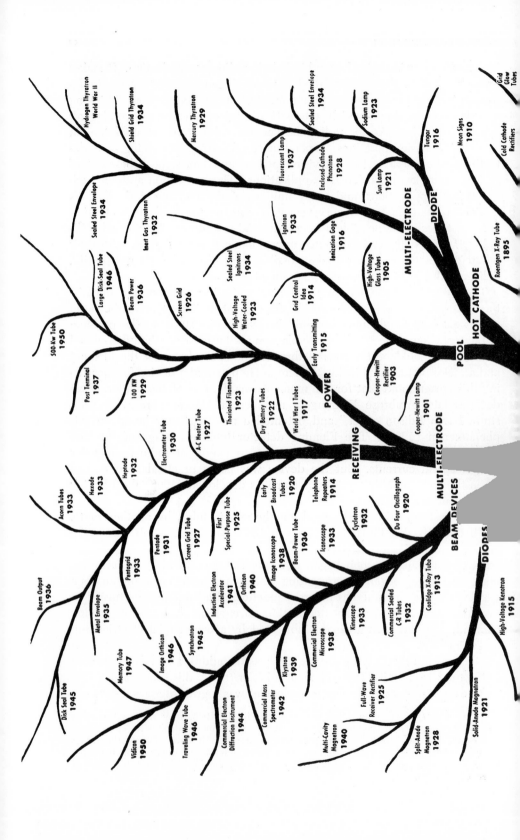

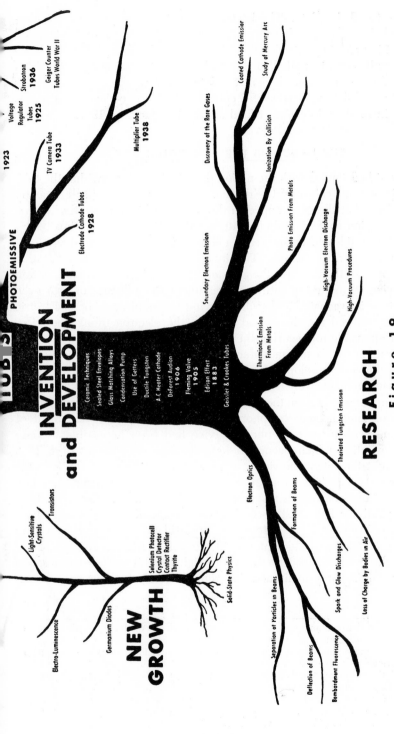

Figure 19

Family Tree of the Audion

More than a dozen fields of research combine to support the great technological growth which started with the audion in 1906. Note the new sapling which has produced the transistor; it may in time rival in size and complexity the "parent" tree, some of whose branches are likely to wither in the shade of the new growth.

Source: W. C. White in *Electronics* (September, 1952), p. 100.

the filament and the plate. The heated filament throws off clouds of electrons which, being negatively charged, are attracted to the positively charged
plate. But in order to get to the plate the electrons have to pass through the
grid. A small current applied to the grid can control with great precision
the flow of electrons from filament to plate. Very weak currents can thus
be used to modulate very powerful currents. This three-element tube was
first used in 1906, and de Forest filed a patent in January, 1907.

THE DAWN OF THE ELECTRONIC AGE

De Forest had started with the notion that the heated gas within the tube
was the important feature of the device. Had he realized, as subsequently
became clear, that the gas trapped in the tube is a hindrance rather than a
help, the ensuing confusion about patents might have been less involved.[12]
Electron tubes did not become really efficient until means were devised for
creating a near-perfect vacuum. This involves more than merely exhausting
the air trapped in the tube, for the glass envelope and the metal parts within
the tube give off minute quantities of gas under the influence of heat even
after the tube is evacuated and sealed. Irving Langmuir, a General Electric
scientist, recognized the theoretical basis of the electron tube's operation,
and was responsible for securing the high degree of vacuum needed. General Electric, as the major manufacturer of electric lamps, had a natural
interest in this new development.

Other improvements were made by Harold D. Arnold of AT&T. The Telephone Company's interest in the audion was based on its need for an efficient
amplifier for long-distance telephone circuits. Before the development of
the audion, coast-to-coast telephone service had been impossible because
of the attenuation which occurs in long-distance wire circuits. In 1913
AT&T bought the telephone rights to seven basic audion patents from de
Forest for $50,000.[13] This brought to bear on the many problems of audion
development the tremendous resources of the Bell System's research laboratories. By 1915 the first coast-to-coast telephone circuits, using vacuum tube
re-amplifiers (repeaters), were opened. In 1914 the Telephone Company
also began to take a belated interest in the possibilities of radiotelephony
and paid de Forest $90,000 for the radio rights to his audion patents, the
inventor retaining only manufacturing rights for sale to amateurs and ex-
perimenters.[14]

---

[12] The theory of thermionic emission is a branch of science distinct from the theory of
electromagnetic radiation.

[13] De Forest made this sale at a low point in the violent fluctuations of his financial
career. Obviously rights of such crucial importance to the Telephone Company were
worth more than a mere $50,000. De Forest claims that AT&T was willing to pay as
much as $500,000 but that he was hoodwinked by their agent into thinking he was sell-
ing the rights to a much less significant customer. Cf.: Lee de Forest, *op. cit.*, pp. 309-310.

[14] These radio rights were effectively paralyzed by a 1916 court decision (*Marconi
Wireless Telegraph Co. of America* v. *de Forest Radio Telephone & Telegraph Co.*, 236

The patent problems surrounding the development of the audion involved not only the tube itself but the electrical circuits which employed the tube as a basic component. One of the latter, the regenerative or feedback circuit, has been the subject of "the most controversial litigation in radio history."[15] This circuit uses the principle of feeding part of the received signal back on itself to build up the signal strength. It results in a tremendous increase in the sensitivity of radio receivers and hence represents a decisive development in the art. Four companies claimed to hold the controlling patent on this improvement: AT&T, with the de Forest patent; General Electric, with the Langmuir patent; American Marconi with a patent of Edwin Armstrong's; and the Telefunken Company with the German Meissner patent. This four-way battle was in and out of the courts for twenty years. After millions of dollars had been spent in legal fees, the Supreme Court finally decided in favor of de Forest in 1934.[16] Even the final court decision did not clear the atmosphere completely. Armstrong, who was stronger than de Forest on the theoretical side, seems to have understood the *principle* underlying the feedback circuit better than de Forest, who arrived at the invention by largely empirical methods.[17]

RADIOTELEPHONY

By 1934, however, de Forest had long since sold his radio patents and moved on to other fields. His feedback circuit and other radio patents had gone to the Telephone Company in 1917 for $250,000. By this time the great manufacturing and communications companies were actively engaged in research in the field after years of what de Forest considered "amazing indifference," and de Forest's pioneering interest had flagged.[18] He turned instead to a newer field, sound motion pictures. His adventure in this field is discussed in Chapter 11.

De Forest greatly enjoyed music, so it is natural that his attention should have turned to the possibilities of using radio for transmitting sound. The early commercial radiotelegraphic transmitters depended for the generation of radio energy first on a spark-gap, later on an arc. The problem of using the arc transmitter for radiotelephony was twofold: the frequency of the current used to activate the arc was so low that it fell in the audible range, and thus the tone of the arc itself tended to mask the intended signal. Sec-

---

F. 942) which left both litigants stalemated. The situation was not resolved until after World War I, when the assets of American Marconi passed to Radio Corporation of America, which also secured access to AT&T's patents through a cross-licensing agreement.

[15] Maclaurin, *op. cit.*, p. 78.

[16] *Radio Corporation of America, et al.* v. *Radio Engineering Laboratories, Inc.*, 293 U.S. 1 (1934). The decision is interesting for its review of the issues and some of the complex history of the litigation.

[17] Maclaurin, *op. cit.*, pp. 78-79.

[18] De Forest, *op. cit.*, p. 359.

ondly, there was the problem of modulating the powerful current fed to
the arc by the very weak current produced by a microphone. Early experimental microphones, closely coupled to arcs, had to be water-cooled. There
was even danger of singeing one's lips on the microphone.[19] Despite these
basic difficulties, de Forest and others persisted in their efforts. De Forest
broadcast phonograph music from the Eiffel Tower in 1908. In 1910 he
staged the first opera broadcast, from the Metropolitan, with Caruso in the
cast, but the voices were reported to be "hardly recognizable."[20] In 1916
he began work on the problem of adapting the audion as an oscillator, a
substitute for the arc. He set up an experimental radiotelephone station,
and beginning in 1916 broadcast phonograph records and announcements.
De Forest describes his personal announcements, crediting the Columbia
Gramophone Company for the recordings and mentioning the products of his
own firm, as the first commercial radio announcements.[21] He even broadcast
election returns in that year, four years before a similar broadcast over
KDKA which is usually credited as the historical beginning of broadcasting
(Chapter 7). In 1919, after the wartime shutdown, he resumed his informal
experimental broadcasts, but was forced off the air by a government radio
inspector who told him: "There is no room in the ether for entertainment."[22]

A great deal is owed to de Forest's imaginative and creative use of his
inventions as well as to the inventions themselves. His role in the early
history of radio is part inventor, part showman, and part businessman. As
an inventor he was prolific; he filed over 30 patents in the pioneer days of
1902-1906, and over the years has been granted more than 200. He has been
connected with a score of firms created to exploit his inventions. Much of
the time he carried on research and experimentation under the most adverse
financial conditions. He was victimized by the unscrupulousness and bad
judgment of business associates. His United Wireless Company went bank-
rupt in 1912, giving American Marconi a monopoly on wireless communications in the United States.[23] His fate symbolizes the problem of the
inventor-entrepreneur in a technological age.

> . . . although de Forest was perhaps the most imaginative inventor in the
> history of the radio industry, and had the opportunity to create a great radio
> enterprise, he failed entirely to do so. His career, when compared with
> Marconi's, effectively illustrates that an inventor, to achieve commercial
> success, must associate himself with men of exceptional business judgment.[24]

[19] Archer, *op. cit.*, p. 87.
[20] Cf.: de Forest, *op. cit.*, pp. 267-271, for details of this historic experiment.
[21] *Ibid.*, pp. 337-338.
[22] *Ibid.*, p. 351.
[23] American Marconi was later bought out by Radio Corporation of America; another
bankruptcy in 1926 resulted eventually in other de Forest assets finding their way to
RCA. This corporation thus owes a great deal, directly and indirectly, to the genius of
Lee de Forest.
[24] Maclaurin, *op. cit.*, p. 87.

OTHER PIONEERS

Another entrepreneur-inventor who pioneered in radiotelephony was Reginald Fessenden, who in 1893 became Professor of Electrical Engineering at the University of Pittsburgh. He has been called "the first important American inventor to experiment with wireless," having developed an invention second in importance only to the audion: the heterodyne circuit.[25] In his search for a means of practical radiotelephonic transmission, Fessenden also worked on the transmitting method. It will be recalled that alternating current is necessary to produce electromagnetic radiation. His object was to develop a high-frequency generator, or alternator, as it was called. In 1906 Fessenden made the first long-distance transmission of radiotelephony, using a 50,000-cycle alternator built for him by Ernst Alexanderson of General Electric.[26] In a sense this event could be said to represent the birth of broadcasting, at least from the technical point of view. But it was, of course, merely experimental, with an "audience" mainly of ships' operators. Fessenden, too, suffered disastrous financial setbacks in his attempts to exploit his own inventions.

Alexanderson, on the other hand, was not an inventor-entrepreneur like de Forest and Fessenden. He represents a later development, the approaching era of the great industrial research laboratory. In the General Electric laboratories he went on independently of Fessenden to develop alternators of higher and higher capacities. During World War I General Electric supplied the United States Government with 200-kilowatt Alexanderson alternators, by far the most powerful ever built up to that time. Alexanderson also developed the means of coupling the microphone to these powerful transmitters electronically, using electron tubes. These and other patents gave General Electric a very strong patent position in the field of radiotelephony by the end of World War I. The Alexanderson alternator was a huge, costly machine, described as "perhaps the most elegant machine ever known in the realm of Radio."[27] The fact that a United States firm owned the Alexanderson alternator contributed, as we shall see, to the breaking of the monopoly of American Marconi.

The final major link in the chain of inventions which made broadcasting commercially feasible was the superheterodyne circuit. This circuit, invented by Edwin Armstrong, increased the sensitivity of receivers so much that outdoor receiving antennas were no longer required. Nearly all modern radio receivers use the superheterodyne principle. It was patented in 1920, and by 1924 had come into general commercial use.

[25] *Ibid.*, pp. 59 and 61.
[26] Archer, *op. cit.*, pp. 86-87.
[27] George H. Clark in: Harold P. Westman (ed.), *Radio Pioneers, 1945* (New York: Institute of Radio Engineers, 1945), p. 42.

WORLD WAR I DEVELOPMENTS

World War I caused a great acceleration in the technological development of wireless communication. This was the first major war in which wireless had been used in naval operations, and by its close the new means of communication had taken its place as a vital military adjunct. Long-distance transoceanic wireless also was much improved during the war. Alarmed by the possibility that the Germans might cut off the United States from communication with its allies by the simple expedient of slashing the transatlantic cables, the United States government placed a high priority on the development of reliable alternative channels. The Alexanderson alternator came into use, and the wireless circuits to Europe played an important role both in military operations and in diplomatic communications during the peace conference.

The war contributed to radio development in other ways. The United States Navy took over the operation of all private stations that it could usefully employ, and required the shutting down and disassembling of all other transmitters. In order to capitalize fully on all United States patents, the Navy effected a kind of moratorium on patent suits. This resulted in a pooling of the country's total technical resources which previously had been quite impossible because of commercial rivalries.

In short, wireless advanced tremendously during the war, and came back to civilian life with materially altered status. The pre-war era had been dominated by the inventor-entrepreneurs. Now began the era of big business. AT&T had acquired the de Forest patents and built up an important interest in wireless telephony. General Electric, with the Alexanderson alternator and the family of related patents that went with it, held a commanding manufacturing position. American Marconi, though weakened by Navy inroads on its maritime business, still dominated the wireless communication service. Westinghouse, not at the moment deeply involved, was about to inject a new and dynamic element into the situation — a novel use of wireless telephony ultimately to be called "broadcasting."

At the close of World War I, however, the commercial utility of wireless telephony was by no means clear. In 1917 Lee de Forest had suggested that it might be used instead of wireless telegraphy on small ships to save the cost of skilled operators.[28] In 1919 David Sarnoff sweepingly predicted that radio could replace the telephone. The Navy, on the other hand, still regarded radio as essentially a maritime instrument which had no business competing with the telephone and telegraph wires.[29] The time was ripe for a business innovation: a practical, money-making use of radiotelephony that would not duplicate any existing service.

[28] House Merchant Marine and Fisheries Committee, *op. cit.*, p. 295.
[29] House Merchant Marine and Fisheries Committee, *Hearings on H.R. 13159, Government Control of Radio Communication* (Washington: Government Printing Office, 1919), pp. 204 *et passim*.

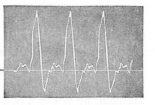

7

Broadcasting: A New
Communication Service

> "Broadcasting" means the dissemination of radio
> communications intended to be received by the
> public. . . .
> — COMMUNICATIONS ACT OF 1934, SECTION 3 (o)

"Intended" is the key word in the definition above. The nature of radio is such that it is impossible to prevent the general public, should it wish to invest in the necessary equipment, from receiving radio signals of any kind whatever. But most signals, though available to all, are *intended* only for specific recipients. Broadcasting alone is intended for any and all recipients.

This apparently simple concept represented a radical innovation in the communications business. The whole history and tradition, first of wire and then of wireless communication, had emphasized that commercial profit was to be derived from the exchange of *private* intelligence. The sender of the message rather than the receiver was the key man. The sender paid a fee for the use of the service, just as today one pays by the word to send a telegram or by the call to use a telephone. How else could a profit be made? What possible motive could a sender have for paying money to reach an unknown audience indiscriminately?

This is not to say that no one had visualized the desirability of bringing remote events to the ears of audiences. As early as 1890 the Telephone Company had experimented with wire "broadcasts" of public events to audiences at remote locations.[1] There was no lack of visionaries to imagine the performance of similar services by wireless. While radiotelephony was still in a primitive stage of development, de Forest set up a series of experimental and demonstrational transmissions to dramatize the possibilities

---

[1] William P. Banning, *Commercial Broadcasting Pioneer: The WEAF Experiment, 1922-1926* (Cambridge: Harvard University Press, 1946), pp. 4-5.

of broadcasting.[2] One of the visionaries is of particular interest because he not only saw his broadcasting predictions come true but has taken a prominent part in the development of commercial broadcasting down to the present day. In 1916, when he was assistant traffic manager of American Marconi, he wrote a memorandum to his chief, saying in part:

> I have in mind a plan of development which would make radio a "household utility" in the same sense as the piano or phonograph. The idea is to bring music into the house by wireless. . . . The receiver can be designed in the form of a simple "Radio Music Box" and arranged for several different wave lengths. . . . The main revenue to be derived will be from the sale of the "Radio Music Boxes" which if manufactured in lots of one hundred thousand or so could yield a handsome profit. . . . The Company would have to undertake the arrangements, I am sure, for music recitals, lectures, etc. . . . Aside from the profit to be derived from this proposition, the possibilities for advertising for the Company are tremendous; for its name would ultimately be brought into the household and wireless would receive national and universal attention.[3]

The writer was David Sarnoff. In the light of subsequent events this may not seem to have been a remarkable flight of imagination, but we must bear in mind that at the time of this memorandum Sarnoff was working for the largest of the United States firms dealing in radiotelegraphic communication. Radiotelephony was still in the experimental stage. The best evidence of the radical nature of his proposal is, of course, the fact that nothing was done about it. But he renewed his suggestion in 1920, by which time American Marconi had been taken over by the Radio Corporation of America and Sarnoff was in a better position to act on his own convictions. As we shall see, RCA later created the first national broadcasting network company.

The question was not so much whether broadcasting was ultimately possible or desirable, but whether and how broadcasting could make money. Not unnaturally, the companies which were making money out of precisely the opposite use of radio — private, rather than public, communication — failed to embrace the idea of broadcasting with enthusiasm.

THE FOUNDING OF KDKA

Finally, as was inevitable, an executive in a position to take decisive action saw commercial possibilities in this new concept of communication. In 1920 Dr. Frank Conrad, an engineer with the Westinghouse Corporation in Pittsburgh, was operating an amateur radiotelephone station, 8XK, in

[2] Speaking of transmissions made in the spring of 1907, de Forest writes: "I cannot, of course, claim that I originated the term 'broadcast,' but I think that I was the first one to apply so descriptive a term to this new art which I was then beginning to create. . . ." Lee de Forest, *Father of Radio* (Chicago: Wilcox & Follett Co., 1950), p. 226.

[3] Quoted in: Gleason L. Archer, *History of Radio to 1926* (New York: The American Historical Co., 1938), pp. 112-113.

connection with his work at the Westinghouse factory.[4] Conrad fell into the habit of transmitting recorded music, sports results, and the like on a more or less regular schedule in response to requests from other amateurs. His informal programs built up such an interest that they occasioned newspaper stories. He even began to receive requests for particular records from his amateur audience. These circumstances were not in themselves unique; similar amateur broadcasts had occurred in other parts of the country. What did distinguish the Conrad broadcasts was the chain of events that they set in motion.

Horne's department store in Pittsburgh, sensing an opportunity to capitalize on the growing public interest in wireless, installed a receiving set in the store. A small box in Horne's newspaper advertisements of September 29, 1920, advised: "Amateur Wireless Sets, made by the maker of the Set which is in operation in our store, are on sale here $10.00 up."[5]

Westinghouse had been casting about for a profitable entry into the communications field — in fact had already explored several possible new types of radio service. For this reason, no doubt, Westinghouse officials were particularly alert to the somewhat obscure hint contained in Horne's modest advertisement. Here they saw the possibility of a novel merchandising tie-up: Westinghouse could manufacture inexpensive radiotelephone receivers and create a new market for them by providing programs for the general public.

Once Conrad's superiors at Westinghouse realized that a new class of purchasers might be induced to buy radio sets in unprecedented numbers, it was a simple matter for them to try out the idea.[6] A radiotelegraphy transmitter was converted for radiotelephony at the Westinghouse East Pittsburgh factory, and went on the air as KDKA from a transmitter on the roof of the factory on November 2, 1920. The opening was timed to coincide with the presidential election, so that the inaugural broadcast could take advantage of public interest in the election returns. This first program by this first regularly licensed broadcast station consisted of the reading of the Harding-Cox election returns as they came in by telephone from a newspaper office to the announcer at the KDKA transmitter, interspersed with phonograph records and banjo music.

Broadcasting might have had a great deal more difficulty in getting started had it not been for the existence of a ready-made audience — the amateur set-builders. In order to understand the significance of KDKA's 1920 broadcasts we must reconstruct the circumstances of the time. It is hard for a push-button generation of radio listeners and television viewers to appre-

---

[4] Conrad's station had originally been licensed in 1916.

[5] The advertisement is reproduced in: E. P. J. Shurick, *The First Quarter-Century of American Broadcasting* (Kansas City: Midland Publishing Co., 1946), p. 18.

[6] The man who made the specific decision was Westinghouse Vice-President H. P. Davis. Cf. his "The Early History of Broadcasting in the United States," in: Harvard University Graduate School of Business Administration, *The Radio Industry* (New York: A. W. Shaw, 1928), pp. 189-225.

ciate the quality of interest such transmissions could arouse in 1920. Almost the only listeners were amateurs who had, in most cases, built their own sets. The advent of the crystal detector, an extremely simple and inexpensive rectifier of radio frequency energy, had brought radio within reach of almost everybody. The crystal set, the simplest form of radio receiver, consists basically of a tuning coil, a crystal detector, and a pair of earphones. The earphones are the only essential item which need cost more than a few cents. No battery or other electric power source is required. The crystal rectifier itself has the property of changing the high-frequency radio waves into weak electric currents, which are made audible by the headphones. Only certain spots on its surface are sensitive, and the listener painstakingly seeks out the spot that will yield the clearest reception by means of a "cat's whisker," a thin prong of wire used as a probe.[7]

Practically the only signals on the air in 1920 were in radiotelegraphic code. To hear news, music, and other entertainment instead of the monotonous drone of code in the earphones was an electrifying experience for any listener, amateur or professional. There was, too, a novel and unique satisfaction in the idea of hearing a program directed at the amateur listener himself; previously nearly all he had been able to do was to eavesdrop on messages intended for other people.[8] It is therefore not surprising that KDKA was an immediate and overwhelming success. Because there was as yet no crowding of the broadcast channels and hence no station interference, KDKA's sky wave could be picked up at great distances. Newspapers all over the country, and even in Canada, printed the station's program logs.

In its first year of operation KDKA pioneered in the broadcasting of many of the types of program which have since become standard radio fare: orchestra music, church services, public-service announcements, political addresses, sports events, drama, market reports. But one type of program material was conspicuously absent: there were no commercials. The expense of operation was being borne by Westinghouse, and it was no part of the Westinghouse plan to share with others the favorable publicity the station was bringing to the firm.

Although the Harding-Cox election program on KDKA in 1920 is usually cited as the historic beginning of broadcasting, there are a number of other claimants of the honor. KQW in San Jose, California, first broadcast in 1909 and ran a regular schedule in 1912; Station 2ZK, New Rochelle, New York, broadcast music regularly in 1916; a Detroit amateur station, 8MK (later WWJ), began regular broadcasting over two months before KDKA's maiden broadcast. Then, of course, there were the many experimental transmissions by de Forest and Fessenden previously mentioned. At least a dozen stations

---

[7] The crystal set went out of general use after 1922, when the regenerative vacuum-tube circuit, an immensely more sensitive detecting device, became available. However, small boys continue to build crystal sets to this day.

[8] Some inkling of the impact of broadcasting in the early days can be gained from reading the grateful letters of listeners. Cf.: William P. Banning, *op. cit.*, pp. 19-29, for examples.

still in operation date their beginnings from 1920 or earlier. But the fact remains that KDKA was the first commercially-licensed standard broadcast station listed in the Department of Commerce records.[9]

Westinghouse did not long have the field to itself, however. The other leading communication concerns — General Electric, AT&T, RCA — were watching with interest. Broadcasting had a strong appeal for other interests as well, such as department stores, newspapers, educational institutions, churches, and electric-supply dealers (Table 5). Increase in the number of stations was slow in 1920, with only 30 licenses issued by the end of that year. In the spring of 1922, however, the new industry began to gather

Table 5

Ownership of Broadcast Stations as of February 1, 1923

Type of Owner	% of All Stations Licensed
Communications manufacturers and dealers	39
Educational institutions	12
Publishers	12
Department stores	5
Religious institutions	2
Other	30

Adapted from: William P. Banning, *Commercial Broadcasting Pioneer* (Cambridge: Harvard University Press, 1946), pp. 132-133.

momentum. By May over 200 licenses had been issued, and the upward trend continued during the next twelve-month period, reaching a peak of 576 early in 1923. Mortality, however, was high among these early stations. Would-be broadcasters hastened to get licenses to be in on the ground floor of — they knew not quite what. Problems of financing and programming were left to improvisation as they arose. Stations not backed by adequate financing and planning soon fell by the wayside. Educational stations were particularly heavy losers in this respect. On the other hand, companies like Westinghouse, with a long-term interest and a high financial stake in the future of the medium, could afford to keep abreast of rapid improvements in technique, programming, and production.

THE TELEPHONE COMPANY STEPS IN

AT&T watched the sudden surge of activity in this new application of radiotelephony with the keenest interest. Telephony was its undisputed

[9] The detailed evidence is discussed in: Archer, *op. cit.*, pp. 207-208.

province, and its patent rights in radiotelephony were so extensive that, willy-nilly, broadcasting seemed to be its province, too. WEAF, the station built in New York by AT&T to experiment with the new medium, is of the greatest historical significance. As the showcase for the Telephone Company, WEAF had every financial, technical, and managerial advantage. The station went on the air August 16, 1922, replacing another AT&T station, WBAY, whose nearby location had proved unfavorable for good propagation. In this connection the technique of field-strength measurement was first developed. Other technical innovations of WEAF included the volume-indicator meter and the multiple-input control panel, or mixer, with independent control of microphone channels. The latter was developed because performers could not be depended upon to stay "on mike," so a multiple-microphone set-up was devised.[10] At WEAF the techniques of network broadcasting and commercial sponsorship were developed.

In order to understand the full historical significance of WEAF, however, we must look further into the background to explore the motivations of the Telephone Company in terms of the larger interests at stake. WEAF, after all, was but one manifestation of an epic struggle for the control of business empires, brought on by the opening up of a totally new field of business enterprise.

It may be useful at this point to review the conditions under which broadcasting began. First, it should be noted that the major communications companies all became active in broadcasting within its first two years. Second, broadcasting was a genuine innovation. No precedents existed to indicate how it should be financed and organized; the concepts of the sale of time to sponsors and the syndication of programs by networks did not at once emerge. Third, at that time the legal regulation of radio was based on a federal law of 1912; this law was intended to govern maritime communications, and could not possibly have anticipated the problems which such a radically different service as broadcasting might raise.

Each of these factors suddenly became critically important because broadcasting sprang into being almost overnight. Herbert Hoover, who as Secretary of Commerce was charged with the responsibility of administering the Radio Act of 1912, said early in 1922:

> We have witnessed in the last four or five months one of the most astounding things that has come under my observation of American life. [The Department of Commerce] estimates that today over 600,000 (one estimate being 1,000,000) persons possess wireless telephone receiving sets, whereas there were less than 50,000 such sets a year ago.[11]

This unprecedented growth of the new medium caught all concerned off guard, and precipitated several years of turmoil in the new industry. In

[10] Banning, *op. cit.*, p. 79. This history of WEAF is full of interesting details on early broadcasting.

[11] Department of Commerce, "Minutes of Open Meeting of Department of Commerce Conference on Radio Telephony" (1922, mimeo.), p. 2.

these critical years, from 1920 to 1927, the basic shape of broadcasting in America was hammered out.

GOVERNMENT MONOPOLY AVERTED

In April, 1917, the United States Navy had been given control of all private wireless facilities as a wartime measure. The war ended in November, 1918, yet the government did not relinquish control of these properties until February, 1920. During this delay of over a year extremely critical decisions were made that affected the whole future of radio in the United States, including the yet-unborn service of broadcasting. The war had demonstrated the vital importance of wireless communication facilities as a national asset.[12] Were they too vital to entrust again to private hands? The United States Navy thought they were. In fact, the Navy had always asserted jurisdiction over radio as a natural right on the mistaken assumption that radio was destined to remain primarily a marine service.

The Alexander Bill, introduced in Congress late in 1918, represented the Navy's point of view.[13] It proposed, in effect, to reduce radio to a government monopoly. The bill was badly drawn and was ineptly defended by the Navy witnesses at the hearings; yet it is by no means beyond the realm of possibility that eventually such a law could have been passed. After all, at that moment the Navy already had complete control, by virtue of its wartime powers. Other countries had long since made radio a government monopoly; and the United States radio law then on the books, the Radio Act of 1912, required little more than a registration procedure of private stations. That the Alexander Bill and other similar attempts to remove radio from the realm of private enterprise failed is due in large measure to an event which sharply changed the United States radio industry during the course of 1919 — the dissolution of American Marconi and the formation of the Radio Corporation of America.

It will be recalled (Chapter 6) that General Electric had developed the 200,000-watt Alexanderson alternator, the mechanism which made reliable long-distance radio communication possible. This machine had been successfully put into service by the Navy in 1918. Three years before this the potentialities of Alexanderson's experiments had been recognized by Guglielmo Marconi himself. At that time he had opened negotiations with GE for exclusive rights to the alternator, but these talks had been interrupted by the war. Now, in March of 1919, the negotiations were reopened. In

---

[12] Before the United States' entry into the war the German high-power station in Sayville, New York, violated United States neutrality by sending vital intelligence to German ships at sea. Later on a single message interception netted the United States alien property custodian $10,000,000. House Merchant Marine and Fisheries Committee, *Hearings on H.R. 13159, Government Control of Radio Communication* (Washington: Government Printing Office, 1919), p. 10.

[13] H.R. 13159 and S. 5036, 65th Congress, 2d Session. This bill was in fact a stronger version of a similar bill introduced in the 64th Congress, H.R. 19350.

this immediate postwar period, with the flow of government orders ceasing, no major United States market for wireless equipment existed. American Marconi was the only company in the United States with sufficient capital and commercial potential to qualify as a customer for the alternators. GE had spent a great deal on their development and justifiably expected substantial returns.

THE FOUNDING OF RCA

The prospect that American Marconi would consolidate its United States monopoly by capturing exclusive rights to the Alexanderson alternator was deeply disturbing to the Navy. The extent of its concern is measured by the fact that the Navy had already spent $1,600,000 to block American Marconi by securing in 1918 patent rights to the Poulsen arc, which was owned by the Federal Telegraph Company and was the next-best radio energy generator to the Alexanderson alternator.[14]

President Wilson himself is said to have taken an interest in the situation, even in the midst of the Peace Conference. He is said to have considered that international communication, together with oil and shipping, represented the key to the balance of power in international affairs.[15] In 1919 Britain led the world in maritime strength, and the United States led in petroleum production. Communication, then, was the critical factor. Britain already had a long lead in the field of worldwide cable facilities, and was now on the verge of obtaining the world monopoly on international wireless communication which for so long had been the objective of British Marconi. Thus what ordinarily would have been purely a matter of business and financial strategy was projected into the realm of international politics.

British Marconi found itself subjected to an international squeeze play. The American government made no overt move actually to expropriate British Marconi's American holdings; the international negotiations were carried out on a private level by Owen D. Young of General Electric. But it was made plain that British Marconi's position in the United States was untenable. The president of American Marconi told his stockholders in 1919:

> We have found that there exists on the part of the officials of the Government a very strong and irremovable objection to [American Marconi] because of the stock interest held therein by the British Company.[16]

We shall probably never know the full story of the behind-the-scenes maneuvers which led to the sale of American Marconi to American in-

[14] Senate Committee on Interstate Commerce, *Hearings on S. 6, Commission on Communications* (Washington: Government Printing Office, 1930), pp. 1013 ff. According to David Sarnoff, the Navy also pressured American Marconi into selling it 330 ship sets and 45 coastal stations for $1,450,000 in 1918 (House Merchant Marine and Fisheries Committee, *op. cit.*, pp. 195-201).

[15] Archer, *op. cit.*, p. 164.

[16] Quoted in: Archer, *op. cit.*, p. 178.

terests. There was obviously an admixture of patriotism and profit in the motivation of GE. Which incentive predominated became a matter of debate a few years later — a debate with strong political overtones. RCA, which was set up by GE to take over the American Marconi assets and operations, was accused of trying to justify RCA monopoly by claiming that it had come into being at the request of President Woodrow Wilson and therefore had a quasi-official status.[17]

RCA took over the operation of American Marconi's assets on November 20, 1919. It is significant that this antedates the opening of KDKA by a full year. Broadcasting was, therefore, not yet a tangible factor. Owen D. Young testified later, "We had no broadcasting in our minds in 1919 and 1920."[18] Investments in the new corporation were made by Westinghouse and AT&T as well as General Electric. In 1922 the stock distribution was approximately as follows:

> General Electric — 25 per cent
> Westinghouse — 20 per cent
> AT&T — 4 per cent
> Former American Marconi Stockholders and others — 51 per cent[19]

RCA was a unique corporate enterprise, "put together from the top" by Owen D. Young, the GE vice-president whose business statesmanship had successfully effected the complicated and delicate international negotiations. It remained for David Sarnoff in the years that followed to convert the abstract legal documents and high-level corporate policies into operational effectiveness. It took less than a year for Young to create RCA, but it took Sarnoff twenty years to make it into a completely integrated operating concern.[20] Sarnoff was the Marconi radiotelegraph operator who had maintained contact with the survivors of the *Titanic* disaster in 1912; in 1916, as Marconi traffic manager, he had argued for the "Radio Music Box." He typifies the American saga, the rise of the poor immigrant boy to leadership in the top ranks of industry. Sarnoff taught himself the Morse code while still in his 'teens. His entry into the communications industry was as an office boy with American Marconi, but his unusual skill with the key eventually won him the job of operator in the Marconi station located atop the Wanamaker building near Washington Square in New York, where he was working at the time of the *Titanic* disaster. Sarnoff foresaw the need

---

[17] Cf.: Senate Committee on Interstate Commerce, *op. cit.*, particularly the testimony of Owen D. Young, pp. 1081-1173 and 1176-1220. The origin of RCA was the subject of a number of inquiries; one of the earliest is to be found in: Federal Trade Commission, *Report on the Radio Industry* (Washington: Government Printing Office, 1924). The known story is reconstructed in: Archer, *op. cit.*, pp. 157-180.

[18] Senate Committee on Interstate Commerce, *op. cit.*, p. 1115.

[19] Federal Trade Commission, *op. cit.*, p. 20. American Marconi had had 1,800 American small stockholders. AT&T sold its interest in 1923. RCA remained under the control of General Electric and Westinghouse until it achieved independence in 1930.

[20] W. Rupert Maclaurin, *Invention and Innovation in the Radio Industry* (New York: The Macmillan Co., 1949), pp. 110, 248.

for industrial leadership which combined first-hand technical knowledge
with business ability; he is, in short, the true innovator. He became president of RCA in 1930 and also chairman of its board in 1947.

CROSS-LICENSING AGREEMENTS

RCA's real mission was not merely to take over and operate the half-dozen
American Marconi subsidiaries engaged in wireless communication. A
serious problem faced the parent companies. Young testified that "it was
utterly impossible for anybody to do anything in radio, any one person or
group or company at that time [1919] . . . Nobody had patents enough
to make a system. And so there was a complete stalemate."[21] RCA was to
be used to break this stalemate. It was Young's idea that the major patent
rivals could find a meeting ground in their commonly owned subsidiary.
Accordingly in 1919, 1920, and 1921 a series of cross-licensing agreements
were reached among General Electric, AT&T, Westinghouse, and RCA.[22]
Cross-licensing simply means the pooling of patent rights among participants
in the agreements. RCA participated as a cross-licensee because it had
inherited important patent rights from American Marconi. In the period
1919-1923 RCA entered into more than a score of licensing, traffic, and sales
agreements, both with its parent companies and with others.

But the purpose of the cross-licensing agreements was not solely to resolve patent conflicts. It was also to define and to hold free from intramural
competition the special area of interest of each company in the group.
Since RCA was not an independent entity, its role was to be a subordinate
one. General Electric and Westinghouse would use RCA's patents in the
manufacture of equipment, and RCA would act as a mere sales agent for the
other firms' products. AT&T's role was to maintain control over telephonic
communication, by wire and wireless. This control was to be ensured by
AT&T's exclusive right, under the cross-licensing agreements, to the manufacture and sale or lease of transmitters. General Electric and Westinghouse
could use the pooled patents to make transmitters for themselves but not
for sale to others. All these rights were exclusive among the parties to the
agreements.

Although the cross-licensing agreements in principle anticipated even
such technical developments as television, they did not take into account
the tremendous economic potential of broadcasting. The unexpected development of this new service almost immediately threw the carefully calculated plan for division of the communications empire out of balance. It
must again be emphasized that the market for receivers and components
was not of major economic importance before the advent of broadcasting.
In 1921 the retail value of all the receiving equipment sold in the United

---

[21] Senate Committee on Interstate Commerce, *op. cit.*, p. 1116.
[22] These agreements are printed in: Federal Trade Commission, *op. cit.*, pp. 122 ff.

States was about $5,000,000; by 1928 it had risen to $650,000,000.[23] The discovery of this rich mass market introduced a totally unexpected element into the business arrangements of the cross-licensees. Aside from the disturbing effect of this dazzling manufacturing bonanza, the advent of broadcasting also caused the cross-licensees difficulty in agreeing on the interpretation of certain provisions of their agreements. What were the Telephone Company's rights with respect to the use of telephone lines by broadcast stations, for instance? From the outset broadcasting had found wire facilities a necessary adjunct for remote pickups.[24] Soon wire facilities were also needed for network interconnection. Again, what were the Telephone Company's rights with respect to the use of transmitters for sponsored broadcasts?

DIVERGENT THEORIES OF BROADCASTING

As a result of these divisive forces within the ranks of the cross-licensees, a sharp cleavage developed. On one side was the Telephone Group, consisting of AT&T and its subsidiary, Western Electric; on the other side was the Radio Group, consisting of General Electric, Westinghouse, and their subsidiary, RCA. In the race for dominance in the new realm of broadcasting AT&T's entry was Station WEAF and the Radio Group's entry was WJZ. Each of these rival stations built up rival networks. In this competition WEAF had a distinct advantage: immediate access to AT&T's telephone lines and AT&T's telephonic know-how. Moreover, the Radio Group's stations, under AT&T's interpretation of cross-licensing agreements, were barred from operating stations for profit.

The split between the two groups carried over into the rationale of their early broadcast operations. The Radio Group started with the idea of operating broadcast stations as a means of stimulating the market for their manufactured products. Therefore the broadcast station assumed responsibility for supplying both the physical facilities and the messages sent over these facilities. The emphasis was on the public's interest in receiving a program service — at the price of investment in receiving equipment. According to this approach, each separate firm wishing to utilize broadcasting to create public good will for its products would operate a separate station for that purpose.

AT&T started with quite an opposite conception of the role of the broadcaster. It saw broadcasting as an extension of the telephone service, the main difference being that broadcasting was one-way instead of two-way telephony. This meant (1) that a relatively small number of stations would serve all users and (2) that the broadcast station assumed no responsibility for the messages sent over its facilities. Early in 1922, when the Telephone

[23] Testimony of David Sarnoff in: Senate Committee on Interstate Commerce, *op. cit.*, p. 1235.
[24] Note that even KDKA's inaugural broadcast utilized the telephone to relay election results from a newspaper office to an announcer at the transmitter.

Company was preparing to open WEAF, an official explained: "[the Company] . . . will furnish no programs whatsoever over that station. It will provide facilities over which the general public, one and all alike, may use those services."[25] This plan was based on a direct analogy with the Company's customary telephone services:

> Just as the company leases its long distance wire facilities for the use of newspapers, banks, and other concerns, so it will lease its radio telephone facilities and will not provide the matter which is sent out from this station.[26]

AT&T's broadcasting activities were accordingly placed under the long-lines department, and sponsored programs were called "toll" broadcasts, analogously with long-distance telephony. AT&T took the view that its exclusive jurisdiction over transmitters permitted it to restrain others from using them "for toll or hire, or for the rendition of any advertising or personal message service."[27]

As broadcasting finally evolved, elements from both the Telephone Group's concept of the medium and the Radio Group's concept were combined in a new synthesis. The Telephone Company was correct in assuming that the financial support of a limited number of broadcast stations would need to be distributed among many users, who would lease the facilities temporarily, as was done with the telephone. It miscalculated in placing the emphasis on the sender rather than on the receiver of the messages. Here the Radio Group's concept of service to the public, with emphasis on the public's program needs and wishes, is the one which finally prevailed.

TOLL BROADCASTING

WEAF was far from being one of the first stations on the air. More than two hundred stations were already licensed by the time WEAF was established, with fifteen already operating in the New York area. But WEAF has particular significance because of its role as AT&T's guinea pig in the new medium. The company spared no expense, investing a quarter of a million dollars during the first year's operation.[28] The two major practices which were to distinguish the American system of broadcasting — network syndication and commercial sponsorship — were first developed at WEAF. Even before the station went on the air, prospective advertisers themselves expressed an interest in hiring its facilities. Hitherto, as we have said, it had been assumed that each would-be advertiser would have to operate his own station to publicize his own wares, just as Westinghouse had done with KDKA. This concept led, of course, to the rapid multiplication of

[25] Department of Commerce, op. cit., p. 7.
[26] AT&T press announcement, 1922, quoted in: Banning, op. cit., p. 68.
[27] House Merchant Marine and Fisheries Committee, Hearings on H.R. 7357, To Regulate Radio Communication (Washington: Government Printing Office, 1924), p. 41.
[28] Testimony of W. E. Harkness in: House Committee on Merchant Marine and Fisheries, op. cit., p. 88.

stations. The Telephone Company received no less than 60 requests for transmitters in the New York area alone. AT&T conceived that such excessive numbers of stations could achieve nothing but interference and a general depreciation of the service. WEAF was built with the idea that a single station, operated as a common carrier by the Telephone Company, could serve many advertisers without leading to self-defeating congestion of the broadcast channels. The refusal to sell transmitters to all comers, based on this conception, led to charges that AT&T was attempting to monopolize broadcasting. Indeed, its intention seems to have been just that — and on perfectly logical grounds. Said the AT&T official in charge of radio:

> We have been very careful, up to the present time [1923], not to state to the public in any way, through the press or in any of our talks, the idea that the Bell System desires to monopolize broadcasting; but the fact remains that it is a telephone job, that we are the telephone people, that we can do it better than anybody else, and it seems to me that the clear, logical conclusion that must be reached is that, sooner or later, in one form or another, we have got to do the job.[29]

WEAF's facilities were first leased for a "toll" broadcast on August 28, 1922. A Long Island real-estate corporation supplied a "commercial" consisting of a ten-minute talk extolling in somewhat indirect terms the advantages of living in "Hawthorne Courts." The first commercial advertiser known to have provided entertainment along with the commercial on WEAF was Gimbel Brothers, which became a major advertiser on the station in its early days. However, WEAF was very circumspect in its handling of toll broadcasting. No direct advertising, such as the mention of prices, was permitted. There was earnest debate about whether such an intimate subject as toothpaste should even be mentioned on the air.[30]

Despite AT&T's restrictions on the sale of transmitters and its insistence that it alone had the right, under the cross-licensing agreements, to use transmitters for toll broadcasting, stations continued to multiply. Hundreds of stations operated in violation of the Telephone Company's rights. By February, 1923, 93 per cent of the 576 stations in operation were infringing on AT&T patent rights.[31] Although many of these stations were individually too short-lived or inconsequential to warrant serious concern, the Company nevertheless was unwilling to abandon its rights by default. Yet its refusal to sell transmitters to all comers had already evoked accusations of monopoly, so it was reluctant to adopt aggressive measures. It decided, therefore, to license toll stations that used transmitters involving its patent rights. A test case initiated by AT&T against WHN in New York in 1924 was settled out of court, with the license fee being paid by WHN.

[29] Quoted in: N. R. Danielian, *A.T.&T.: The Story of Industrial Conquest* (New York: The Vanguard Press, 1939), pp. 123-124. Copyright 1939 by The Vanguard Press.
[30] Banning, *op. cit.*, p. 150.
[31] *Ibid.*, p. 134.

NETWORK BROADCASTING

In the meantime another problem had arisen. As we have pointed out, the use of wire connections for picking up programs remote from the broad-cast-transmitter locations was a necessity from the outset — especially since the early transmitters were usually located in factories and other places relatively inaccessible to talent. AT&T interpreted the cross-licensing agreements as prohibiting the connection of broadcast equipment to telephone circuits. Naturally AT&T made its own lines available to its own station, WEAF. In fact, one of WEAF's primary purposes was to experiment with ways of integrating the Company's telephone facilities with its broadcast facilities. As early as 1921 the Telephone Company advanced the idea of a series of broadcast stations located at strategic points along its long-distance trunk lines which could occasionally broadcast identical programs, i.e., network programs. The Company conceived that these stations might be programmed by corporations set up in the various towns where the stations were located, representing the business and cultural interests of the communities involved. The Telephone Company would lease out the broadcast facilities and would have no hand in the programming — again an attempt to force the telephone concept on broadcasting.

The first actual test of the network principle occurred on January 4, 1923, when WEAF fed a program by wire for broadcast in Boston by WNAC, owned by Shepard Stores.[32] This was a five-minute broadcast of a saxophone solo, carried over lines especially adapted for the purpose. Telephone long lines normally were adjusted to carry a frequency band of 250-2,500 cycles per second. They had to be especially equalized for 100-5,000 c.p.s. to provide suitable broadcast fidelity.

Later in 1923 the first permanent network circuit (as distinguished from a one-time arrangement) was made between WEAF and WMAF in South Dartmouth, Mass. WMAF was the property of Col. E. H. Green, who operated it for his own amusement and had no means of programming the station. He persuaded WEAF to feed him both toll broadcasts and non-toll broadcasts. He paid a fee for the sustaining programs and broadcast the commercial programs without cost to the sponsor.[33]

AT&T continued experimenting with network broadcasts, gradually adding to the number of stations interconnected. In October, 1924, a special 22-station hookup carried a speech by President Coolidge from coast to coast. The regular WEAF network at that time consisted of six stations broadcasting three hours of network programs per day. The network still used regular telephone circuits temporarily equalized for broadcast purposes. In 1926,

---

[32] The Shepard family also was important in another, much later radio development when it gave the support of its Yankee Network in New England to Edwin Armstrong at a time when the major communications companies refused to support his attempts to promote FM broadcasting.

[33] WMAF was thus the first network "bonus station."

however, special circuits were set aside exclusively for broadcast purposes, and those for WEAF were differentiated from other circuits in the long-lines department charts by red tracing. This was the origin of the term "Red Network," which was applied to WEAF's own chain of stations. Other colors were used to identify other customers — hence later the term "Blue Network" for the WJZ chain.

THE RADIO GROUP

What of the Radio Group in the meantime? RCA's first station was WDY, located in a GE plant in Roselle Park, N. J. However, the location was not suitable for competition with WEAF, and in February, 1922, RCA took a half interest in a Westinghouse station, WJZ, which was located in Newark but had studios in the Waldorf-Astoria Hotel in New York. In the following year RCA bought out the Westinghouse interest, and thereafter WJZ became the chief rival of WEAF. RCA operated, however, at a considerable disadvantage. According to the cross-licensing agreements of which RCA was itself a signatory, it could neither use AT&T telephone lines for broadcast purposes nor sell time. WJZ cost RCA $100,000 a year to operate and brought in no income whatever, whereas WEAF was grossing three quarters of a million dollars annually by 1926.

WJZ tried using Western Union telegraph lines for network interconnection, but the requirements of telegraphic signals are so much lower than those of telephonic signals that the Western Union lines could not deliver broadcast quality. The Radio Group at this time seriously considered the possibility of radio-relay circuits for network interconnection, but suitable equipment was not yet developed for utilizing the microwaves which have since proved so useful for this purpose. Despite these difficulties, WJZ had succeeded in organizing a network of 14 stations by the end of 1925.

During these years of broadcast pioneering (1922-1926) continual behind-the-scenes negotiations had been in progress, with the purpose of resolving the conflicts produced by the cross-licensing agreements. By 1926 the Telephone Company had come to the conclusion that its original concept of broadcasting as just another branch of the telephone business was inadequate. Its excursion into broadcast operations, its repressive measures concerning the use of telephone lines for relay of competitive broadcast programs, its insistence on exclusive control of broadcast transmitters — all had resulted in taking the Telephone Company far afield from its primary business and in creating bad public relations for it. In sum, "as an experiment, broadcasting had been necessary; as a business, it was almost certain to be a liability."[34] Accordingly the signatories of the cross-licensing agreements finally arrived at a revised set of three agreements in July, 1926. The preamble to one of the new agreements frankly confessed:

[34] Banning, *op. cit.*, p. 272.

[Since] the art in certain of the fields dealt with in said [1920] agreement had not progressed to a point at which it was possible fully to comprehend the problems involved, disputes have arisen between the parties as to the meaning of various provisions of said agreement.[35]

THE EMERGENCE OF NBC

Some of the significant provisions of the new agreements were as follows: (1) The *license agreement* redefined the patent rights of each company in the light of the new developments. AT&T was granted exclusive control over wire telephony and two-way wireless telephony, both domestic and foreign. Wire-telegraphy rights also went to AT&T, but RCA retained rights in wireless telegraphy. Telephony was defined in such a way as to leave AT&T in control of network relays, whether wire or wireless, for radio or television. Broadcasting itself went to RCA. Western Electric was barred from competing with the Radio Group in the manufacture of home receivers and other devices for home use. AT&T surrendered its exclusive claims on transmitter manufacture, and thereafter RCA and Western Electric became competitors in this market. They also subsequently competed in the field of sound motion-picture equipment. (2) The *service agreement* required RCA to lease radio relay facilities from AT&T and to cease using Western Union wires for networking. (3) The *purchase agreement* provided for the sale of WEAF and its broadcast assets to the Radio Group for $1,000,000, with AT&T to be barred from reentering the field except under penalty.[36]

As far as broadcasting was concerned, the agreements of 1926 amounted to this: The Telephone Company would continue to profit from broadcasting as the source of all interconnection facilities for networks, and RCA would have a free hand in the development of commercial network broadcasting. RCA thus emerged as the overwhelmingly strongest force in the new business of broadcasting. David Sarnoff had long since recognized what had not been apparent to the officials of AT&T: that broadcasting was a genuine innovation in business which would require its own special organization, business methods, and personnel. He had no illusion that broadcasting could continue to be carried on as incidental to some other kind of business. Sarnoff had renewed the "Music Box" memo of 1916 immediately after the transfer of American Marconi to RCA. As early as 1922 he predicted the course broadcasting was to follow:

> When the novelty of radio will have worn off and the public [is] no longer interested in the means by which it is able to receive but rather, in the substance and quality of the material received, I think that the task of reasonably meeting the public's expectations and desires will be greater than any so far tackled by any newspaper, theater, opera, or other public information or

[35] Quoted in: N. R. Danielian, *op. cit.*, p. 127.
[36] Cf.: N. R. Danielian, *op. cit.*, pp. 126-132, for a more detailed description of the agreements. It should be borne in mind that the power and scope of these agreements derived from the patent rights of the parties concerned.

entertainment agency. . . . Let us organize a separate and distinct company, to be known as Public Service Broadcasting Company, or National Radio Broadcasting Company, or American Radio Broadcasting Company, or some similar name. . . .[37]

Herein Sarnoff anticipated what came to pass in 1926, with the withdrawal of AT&T from broadcasting. A few months after the settlement the Radio Group formed a new subsidiary, the National Broadcasting Company. At its inception NBC was owned 50 per cent by RCA, 20 per cent by GE, and 20 per cent by Westinghouse. It was the first company organized solely and specifically to conduct a broadcast network. A four-and-a-half-hour coast-to-coast inaugural broadcast took place on November 15, 1926. The program included Walter Damrosch conducting the New York Symphony Orchestra, with cut-ins from opera singer Mary Garden in Chicago and humorist Will Rogers in Independence, Kansas. It is estimated that the 25 stations in the network reached about five million listeners on that occasion. Not until 1927, however, did regular coast-to-coast network operations begin.

Starting with the new year in 1927, NBC was organized as two semi-independent networks, the Blue and the Red, with the Blue based on WJZ and the old Radio Group network and the Red based on WEAF and the old Telephone Group network.[38] The dual network operation was logical, since NBC now had duplicate outlets in New York and other cities, and there would have been no point in merely broadcasting the same programs on two stations in the same service area. As competitive networks developed, however, the dual-network operation took on a more significant character: by tying up not one but two of the best stations in each major city, and by playing one network against the other, NBC was later able to secure a significant competitive advantage over rival networks.[39]

CBS FOUNDED

The second national network followed closely on the heels of NBC. In 1927, the year after NBC began, over 700 stations were operating,[40] with

---

[37] Quoted in: Gleason L. Archer, *Big Business and Radio* (New York: American Historical Co., Inc., 1939), pp. 30-31.

[38] NBC changed the call letters of WEAF first to WNBC and then (in 1954) to WRCA.

[39] Coincidentally, RCA had earlier attempted a dual broadcast operation in planning a sister station for WJZ, to be called WJY. This station was to operate on a different frequency from WJZ and would specialize in classical music. The idea of two or more different specialized program services on different frequencies but under the same company has been adopted in several countries. This is the principle on which the British Broadcasting Corporation works, and in some countries even commercial operators are allowed two or more stations in the same service area.

[40] This number would be misleading if one assumed that all licensees were operating on the scale of modern broadcast stations. A great many stations existed more on paper than in fact. For example, the Federal Radio Commission finally cancelled the license of a New Jersey station whose studios consisted of the parlor of the owner's home, whose antenna was a wire on a pole nailed to a shed, and whose signal the Commission's monitors had been unable to pick up in an entire year [*Technical Radio Laboratory* v. *FRC*, 36 F. (2d) 111 (1929)].

only 7 per cent of the total affiliated with NBC. Stations were hard put to it to find program material to fill out their schedules. In January, 1927, United Independent Broadcasters was formed to supply program talent on a network basis. Having more ideas than money, the company sought financial backing and received an offer from the Columbia Phonograph Record Company. The record company, interested in publicizing its name and exploring the new field of broadcasting, set up a subsidiary, the Columbia Phonograph Broadcasting System, Inc., to work with UIB. The initial venture was a failure, and the record company withdrew. UIB, however, retained the subsidiary company, and the Columbia Broadcasting System's name derives from that fact.[41] In 1928 new financial backing was obtained, putting the firm on a sound basis. Since that time the controlling interest in CBS has been held by the William S. Paley family. Also in 1928, CBS purchased WABC, New York (call letters changed to WCBS in 1946), as its key station there. The company showed a profit by 1929, and it quickly developed to the point where it could offer NBC effective competition.

Thus, with competing national networks launched on a commercial basis, the basic evolution of the broadcasting concept was complete. In the few years between 1920 and 1927 a business revolution had taken place. Three major developments had occurred: AT&T, along with its common-carrier concept of broadcasting, had been removed from the field, thereby clearing the atmosphere of confusion about the type of service that broadcasting was to render; the technical facilities and business organization had been developed for successful national syndication of programs by means of competitive networks; and the sale of time to advertisers had proved a feasible method of financial support.

⌐ THE ACCEPTANCE OF COMMERCIALISM

Even after 1927, however, resistance to the full commercialization of broadcasting continued. At the First Radio Conference in Washington, in 1922, the sentiment against advertising had been almost universal. By the Fourth Conference, in 1925, the idea of advertising had been generally accepted, in principle, but the standards to be followed remained in doubt.[42] As late as 1929 the National Association of Broadcasters adopted a code limiting nighttime advertising to dignified identification of sponsors, reserving "direct" advertising for business hours of the day.[43] Even in 1930 a

[41] Ironically, CBS bought out the Columbia Phonograph Company itself a decade later.

[42] The Committee on Advertising and Publicity of the conference declared direct advertising objectionable and recommended good-will advertising only. Fourth National Radio Conference, *Proceedings and Recommendations for Regulation of Radio* (Washington: Government Printing Office, 1926), p. 18.

[43] "Time before 6 P.M. is included in the business day and therefore may be devoted in part, at least, to broadcasting programs of a business nature; while time after 6 P.M. is for recreation and relaxation, and commercial programs should be of the good-will type." Quoted in: Senate Committee on Interstate Commerce, *op. cit.*, p. 1735.

United States Senator could say, "Personally, I think [advertising] is going to be a disappearing part of the service," and the president of NBC could declare, "I am opposed to direct advertising on the air."[44] It was not until after advertising agencies began to play a larger part in the control of programming in the 1930's that all-out direct advertising became the generally accepted practice.[45]

Broadly speaking, however, the die had long since been cast, even before broadcasting began. When the United States government handed back the privately-owned radio facilities to private control in February, 1920, a decisive turning was taken. Thereafter it was almost inevitable that broadcasting, when it came along, should develop into a commercial medium. The various alternative expedients suggested in the early years of broadcasting — support by set manufacturers, public subscription, charitable foundations, government tax on receiving sets — were out of key with the destiny of the medium.

In the previously quoted 1922 memorandum of Sarnoff, proposing that RCA set up a network company, it was not contemplated that broadcasting would be a direct profit-making venture:

> I feel that with suitable publicity activities, such a company will ultimately be regarded as a public institution of great value in the same sense that a library, for example, is regarded today.[46]

When the National Broadcasting Company became a reality it seemed expedient to retain George F. McClelland, the key administrative man at WEAF, if he would consent to leave AT&T. When he was offered the vice-presidency, according to General James G. Harbord, then president of RCA, McClelland

> asked what was to be our aim — whether purely a money-making affair, or whether we aim to perform a big public service to which the income was somewhat incidental. I reassured him on this point, telling him we had the ambition to give a splendid public service, not unconscious of the fact, however, that if we did it, it would reflect itself to us in profits by that company and increased sales of radio apparatus by our own. He accepted the position without any understanding as to salary.[47]

[44] *Ibid.*, pp. 90, 1705.

[45] Of course, advertising as practiced in broadcasting never has been universally accepted. One of its most bitter critics has been Lee de Forest, who wrote: "As I look back today over the entire history of radio broadcasting since [1907] . . . I . . . am filled with a heartsickness. Throughout my long career I have lost no opportunity to cry out in earnest protest against the crass commercialism, the etheric vandalism of the vulgar hucksters, agencies, advertisers, station owners — all who, lacking awareness of their grand opportunities and moral responsibilities to make of radio an uplifting influence, continue to enslave and sell for quick cash the grandest medium which has yet been given to man to help upward his struggling spirit." Lee de Forest, *op. cit.*, pp. 442-443.

[46] Quoted in: Archer, *op. cit.*, p. 33.

[47] *Ibid.*, p. 281.

It is not necessary to conclude that such statements as these — which typify the attitude of many business leaders of the time — were simply hypocritical eyewash put out by cynical big-business men who in reality had every intention of exploiting radio broadcasting to the limit. The fact is that men in the position of Sarnoff, Harbord, and McClelland did not themselves realize what a social revolution was taking place. To them advertising on the radio, except during normal daytime business hours, was an unwarranted intrusion on the sacred privacy of the home. Their idea of the sanctity of the home and of the role of family life in society was essentially in the nineteenth-century tradition. But a profound social upheaval was under way in the '20's. We must recall that this was just after World War I. Victorian standards of taste, personal conduct, and morality were disintegrating. The temper of the times favored radio's commercial trend. A dignified broadcasting service, reflecting the hushed atmosphere of a great public library, would have been an anachronism. The advertising men, more conscious of the trend of the times than the network executives, took advantage of the jazzed-up tempo of the age. Almost before the broadcasters knew what had happened, the advertising agencies took over — and it was they who set the tone. Not until the advent of television did the networks have a chance to recapture control of their industry. By that time the advertising agencies had become so accustomed to controlling programming that they complained bitterly of the networks' presumption in hiring their own talent and producing their own programs.

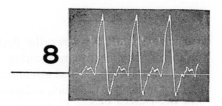

8

The Origin of Government
Regulation of Broadcasting

I think this is probably the only industry of the
United States that is unanimously in favor of having itself regulated.

— SECRETARY OF COMMERCE
HERBERT HOOVER (1924)

Experimentation and innovation in the technical and economic fields must
necessarily be paralleled in the field of jurisprudence. By their nature laws
tend to lag behind technical development, and the history of radio offers
many instances of legal absurdities brought about by the fact that this new
form of communication created novel situations which existing laws could
not have anticipated.

PRE-BROADCASTING LEGISLATION

The main precedent for the legal regulation of wireless was the prior
regulation of wire communications. As early as 1865 an international conference on telegraphs had been held in St. Petersburg. The first such
conference on wireless was held in Berlin in 1903. This conference accomplished nothing because of the Marconi Company's refusal to exchange
messages with other systems. However, humanitarian considerations soon
prevailed, for it was unthinkable that commercial self-interest should long
be allowed to stand in the way when human lives were clearly at stake, as
in maritime emergencies. The first effective international agreement in the
wireless field was reached at the Berlin Convention of 1906, which took
steps to ensure that the new medium would be available in times of emergency at sea. The provisions of this agreement were not, however, imple-
mented in the United States until 1912.

Two significant implications can be seen in these early international con-

ventions. First, it is noteworthy that the initial reason for establishing legal
control of wireless communication was a humanitarian one. Second, it is
significant that the earliest attempt at regulation was international in scope
— a fact indicative of radio's unique ability to transcend political boundaries.

In the United States, Congress amended the Interstate Commerce Act in
1910 by placing interstate and foreign wireless as well as wire communication under federal jurisdiction; in the same year the Wireless Ship Act
required large passenger vessels to carry radio equipment capable of ex-
changing messages at a distance of 100 miles. But the first comprehensive
piece of radio legislation in the United States was the Radio Act of 1912,
which remained in effect for fifteen years, all through the period of the basic
technical and economic evolution of the radio industry.

This law came belatedly (Great Britain had adopted its first radio laws
in 1904), as a direct result of the *Titanic* disaster. When the doomed ship
sent out the message "We've struck an iceberg. Sinking fast," another ship
was only fifteen miles away; but twenty-four-hour wireless watches were
not then required, and the other ship's operator had gone off duty fifteen
minutes earlier, thereby innocently condemning 1,517 people to freeze to
death in the Atlantic. The *Titanic's* own operator died at his transmitter.
Later, when the rescue ship *Carpathia* approached the United States with
the survivors, radio contact with the mainland was seriously impeded by
jamming from irrelevant signals.[1]

The *Titanic* disaster gripped the popular imagination, dramatizing as
nothing else had done the vital importance of the proper use of radio facilities on ships at sea. It was quickly followed, not only by the passage of the
Radio Act of 1912 in the United States, but also by another international
convention in London in the same year. The United States at last adopted
the recommendations of the Berlin Convention of 1906, which provided for
the use of the international "SOS" signal, for the prevention of unnecessary
interference with distress signals, and for the interchange of messages without regard to the commercial systems employed. The Radio Act empowered
the Secretary of Commerce and Labor,[2] among other things, to issue station
licenses to United States citizens and to specify the wave lengths to be used
(aside from the frequencies between 187 and 500 kc., which were reserved
for government use).

In the very year of its passage, however, the Radio Act of 1912 was found
to have a serious technical defect as an instrument of regulation. The Attorney General handed down the opinion that ". . . the Secretary of Commerce and Labor is only authorized to deal with the matter as provided in

---

[1] The story of the sinking of the *Titanic* is well told in: Karl Baarslag, *SOS To the
Rescue* (New York: Oxford University Press, 1935). David Sarnoff happened to be on
duty at the Marconi station in the Wanamaker Building in New York when wireless
contact with the *Carpathia* was established. He stayed at his post for three days and
nights and thus was the key figure in one of the most dramatic episodes in peacetime
history.

[2] Since 1913 the Secretary of Commerce.

the act and is given no general regulative power. . . ."[3] The Act provided that the Secretary of Commerce and Labor would grant licenses to United States citizens "upon application therefor." It did not provide any grounds on which the Secretary could exercise discretion in choosing licensees. In the light of the limited uses to which radio was put at the time, of course, there was no particular reason to anticipate that the Secretary would need to make any choice. It was presumed that all who wanted to and had a good reason to could be allowed to operate radio stations. Essentially the Act merely provided a registration procedure, somewhat analogous to the already-existing procedure for registering ships.

THE FAILURE OF THE RADIO ACT OF 1912

For a decade this concept of the role of government in relation to radio worked satisfactorily. The number of transmitters needed for the existing services was relatively small. Aside from amateurs, ships' stations formed the most numerous class; because of their mobility and the nature of their traffic, they could share a few frequencies without injurious conflict. But when broadcasting, an entirely new class of service, began to demand more and more stations in 1922-1923 a serious problem arose. Analogizing the broadcasting service to the maritime service, the Secretary at first required all broadcast stations to share time on the same frequency. But whereas a ship needs only intermittent exchange of specific messages, a broadcast station needs to transmit a continuing, uninterrupted program service. In 1921, 833.3 kc. was assigned to news and entertainment stations, and a second channel, 618.6 kc., to crop- and weather-report stations. The rapid increase in the number of broadcast stations soon created intolerable interference. Further increasing the number of frequencies assigned to broadcasting did not solve the problem, for the stations multiplied faster than ever.

To complicate matters, the engineering crudity of many early broadcast stations made them quite incapable of holding closely to an assigned frequency. Worse, some stations were portable, and the owners moved them from place to place, completely disrupting any orderly plan of service. An ever-increasing amount of interference resulted. This in turn led some station owners to take matters into their own hands. They began to change frequency, power, times of operation, and location — all in violation of their licenses. The unauthorized changes, of course, merely created worse interference, with the result that a vicious circle was set in motion whereby the broadcast service became more and more degraded.

An amusing side light on the kind of problems faced by the Secretary of Commerce in trying to control this obstreperous new medium is revealed by Herbert Hoover, the then Secretary. Aimee Semple McPherson, the phenomenally popular evangelist of the 1920's, operated a pioneer broadcast station from her "Temple" in Los Angeles. The station "wandered

[3] 29 *Ops. Atty. Gen.* 579, at 581 (22 November 1912).

all over the wave band," and after repeated warnings a government inspector ordered the station closed down. Secretary Hoover thereupon received the following telegram from Evangelist McPherson:

> PLEASE ORDER YOUR MINIONS OF SATAN TO LEAVE MY STATION
> ALONE. YOU CANNOT EXPECT THE ALMIGHTY TO ABIDE BY YOUR
> WAVELENGTH NONSENSE. WHEN I OFFER MY PRAYERS TO HIM
> I MUST FIT INTO HIS WAVE RECEPTION. OPEN THIS STATION
> AT ONCE.[4]

The conclusion was inescapable that the number of stations would have to be controlled in some way. Nevertheless, under the Radio Act of 1912 the Secretary of Commerce had no choice but to grant licenses to every applicant. In 1923 a court held that "the duty of naming a wave length is mandatory upon the Secretary. The only discretionary act is in selecting a wave length. . . ."[5] Unfortunately, there simply were no more usable frequencies for the Secretary to name. Finally, the Secretary's regulatory power was completely undermined by a court decision of 1926. WJAZ, Chicago (owned by Zenith Radio Corporation) had been licensed to share time with a Denver station. WJAZ had operated at times and on frequencies that were different from those authorized in the license. The Secretary brought suit under the Radio Act of 1912, but the court found in favor of the defendant, stating:

> If section 2 [of the Radio Act of 1912] is construed to give to the Secretary
> of Commerce power to restrict the operation of a station as [the Secretary]
> contends is done by this license, what is the test or standard established by
> Congress, by which the discretion of the Secretary is to be controlled? . . .
> Administrative rulings cannot add to the terms of an act of Congress and
> make conduct criminal which such laws leave untouched.[6]

This decision was followed by an opinion of the Attorney General, advising Secretary Hoover that there would be no point in pressing the case further — that under the Constitution he was indeed bereft of regulatory power. Said the Attorney General: "It is apparent . . . that the present legislation is inadequate to cover the art of broadcasting which has been almost entirely developed since the passage of the 1912 Act."[7] A basic American

[4] Herbert Hoover, Memoirs (New York: Macmillan Co., 1952), II, 142. Miss McPherson was persuaded to engage a competent engineer, and her station was allowed to reopen.
[5] Hoover, Secretary of Commerce v. Intercity Radio Co., Inc., 286 F. 1003, at 1007 (1923). Louis G. Caldwell, the first general counsel of the Federal Radio Commission, later pointed out that this decision "has frequently . . . been given a broader construction than the language of the opinion warrants. It did not hold that the Secretary of Commerce did not have power to restrict the power of a station or its hours of operation or its frequency." Testimony in: Senate Committee on Interstate Commerce, Hearings on S.6, Commission on Communications (Washington: Government Printing Office, 1930), p. 65.
[6] U.S. v. Zenith Radio Corp., 12 F. (2d) 614, at 618 (1926).
[7] 35 Ops. Atty. Gen. 126, at 132 (8 July 1926).

political concept is illuminated by this episode in the history of broadcast regulation. In a "government of laws, not men" it is essential to define the limits of the powers entrusted to those in authority. As the court remarked in the Zenith case, our system does not "leave room for the play and action of purely personal and arbitrary power."

THE ORIGIN OF THE RADIO ACT OF 1927

In leaving the Secretary's powers undefined, Congress in effect gave him no powers. What little restraint the Secretary had been able to impose on the industry evaporated with the Zenith decision. For three years Secretary Hoover and many of the broadcasters themselves had already been urging Congress to bring the Radio Act up to date. Each session of Congress considered bills proposing new legislation. But the nature of broadcasting had not yet been clearly defined, and it was difficult to pass a law to regulate an unknown quantity. The Zenith decision, however, made Congressional action imperative. In the period of less than a year that elapsed between this decision and the passage of the new Radio Act, 200 new broadcast stations took advantage of the moratorium on regulation and crowded on the air, compounding the bedlam that already existed. By this time it was impossible in most places to receive any kind of consistent broadcast signal. Thirty-eight stations operated in the New York area and 40 in the Chicago area alone. A marked drop in set-sales resulted from this vitiation of the service. In his message to Congress in December, 1926, President Coolidge said:

> . . . the whole service of this most important public function has drifted into such chaos as seems likely, if not remedied, to destroy its great value. I most urgently recommend that this legislation should be speedily enacted.[8]

Finally, on February 23, 1927, a new Radio Act was passed. Despite the urgency of the need for a new law, it can hardly be said that Congress rushed into this piece of new legislation. From 1923 on, radio bills had been continually under consideration. Nine Senate or House bills were prepared before a satisfactory measure was agreed upon.

The Radio Act of 1927, the first United States legislation to reflect the existence of broadcasting, was to a large extent the product of the radio industry itself. Secretary of Commerce Hoover, an ardent believer in free enterprise, had hoped that the industry would be able to discipline itself without government regulation. To this end he had called in Washington, in 1922, a conference of those interested in the field. Similar National Radio Conferences were held in 1923, 1924, and 1925. During those four years broadcasting emerged as a recognizably distinct service. Speaking at the Fourth Conference, Hoover said: "Four years ago we were dealing with a

[8] *68th Congressional Record* 32 (1926).

scientific toy; today we are dealing with a vital force in American life."[9]

Hoover bravely called the National Radio Conferences "experiments in industrial self government,"[10] but even at that time he must have suspected the hopelessness of the experiment. Repeatedly he commented on the indubitable fact that here was a case in which industry actually *wanted* government regulation. For example, at the very first National Conference in 1922 he said: "This is one of the few instances that I know of in this country where the public — all of the people interested — are unanimously for an extension of regulatory powers on the part of the Government."[11] From year to year the Radio Conferences grew more explicit in their recommendations for government control. The recommendations of the Fourth Conference (1925) were embodied in a bill (H.R. 5589) which eventually became the Radio Act of 1927. The only basic idea in the Act not already recommended by the Radio Conference was that of a permanent regulatory commission.

The Radio Act of 1927, approved on February 23, is essentially the same legislation under which broadcasting and all the other radio services operate today, although it has since been incorporated in the Communications Act of 1934. The Act brought to an end the era of doubt and confusion concerning the legal status of broadcasting, just as the withdrawal of AT&T from the operation of broadcast stations in 1926 ended doubt and confusion about the economic nature of the medium. A number of other circumstances contributed to the significance of this transitional point. The first network company was set up in 1926, the first competitive network operations and regular nationwide network service in 1927. In the same years a series of technical improvements occurred which encouraged the rapid growth of a mass audience: higher-powered transmitters, improved superheterodyne receiver circuits, the alternating-current power supply (eliminating batteries), the dynamic loudspeaker. We can thus establish the years 1926-1927 as a genuine turning point in the history of broadcasting. This was the transition from the era of tentative, trial-and-error growth of a new medium to the era in which the medium moved forward along a well-defined path of development.

THE PHILOSOPHY OF THE RADIO ACT

Senator Wallace H. White, who more than any other legislator was responsible for the Radio Act of 1927, summarized its significance for broadcasting by saying:

[9] Fourth National Radio Conference, *Proceedings and Recommendations for Regulation of Radio* (Washington: Government Printing Office, 1926), p. 1.

[10] Third National Radio Conference, *Recommendations for Regulation of Radio* (Washington: Government Printing Office, 1924), p. 2.

[11] Department of Commerce, "Minutes of Open Meeting of Department of Commerce Conference on Radio Telephony" (1922, mimeo.), p. 1.

We have reached the definite conclusion that the right of our people to enjoy this means of communication can be preserved only by the repudiation of the idea underlying the 1912 law that anyone who will may transmit and by the assertion in its stead of the doctrine that the right of the public to service is superior to the right of any individual to use the ether.[12]

The fundamental hypotheses of the Act may be summarized in the following assertions:

(1) *The radio waves or channels belong to the people.* The electromagnetic spectrum is a kind of natural resource of the nation, the value of which could be destroyed by uncontrolled private exploitation. No one has a right to "own" a frequency or channel; it can be used for private purposes only if by such use the public interest also will be served.

(2) *Broadcasting is a unique service.* Though similar in some respects to other types of communication services, broadcasting is nevertheless an innovation which requires separate recognition and treatment.

(3) *Service must be equitably distributed.* Since the radio frequencies belong to all the people, all the people have a right to expect to receive benefits from them.

(4) *Not everyone is eligible even to use a channel.* Licensees must qualify by meeting certain tests, both specific and general.

(5) *Radio broadcasting is a form of expression protected by the First Amendment.* The constitutional guarantee of freedom of speech and of the press extends to speech or publication through the medium of radio broadcasting, although broadcasting is subject to certain special limitations.

(6) *The government has discretionary regulatory powers.* The Act grants certain specific powers of regulation, but since not all situations can be anticipated the regulatory agency is also granted considerable freedom to use its own discretion. The limit on its discretion is defined by the "public interest, convenience and necessity."

(7) *The government's powers are not absolute.* Decisions must be made by due process of law, may not be arbitrary or capricious, and may be appealed to a court of law.[13]

Each of these principles has been tested in the courts and found to be consistent with the Constitution. They remain today as the conceptual foundation of the American system of radio regulation.

The Act contemplated that eventually most of the regulatory power would be vested in the Secretary of Commerce, as it had been under the Radio Act of 1912. Since the problems of putting the Act into effect were exceedingly complex and numerous, the Act provided for a five-man Federal Radio Commission (FRC), representing five zones of the United States, to do the

12 Quoted by Commissioner Robert T. Bartley in FCC mimeo. 1336 (29 January 1954).
13 Detailed discussion of the Act is found in Chapter 21.

initial job of putting things in order. The FRC was to have been reduced to a lesser role after the first year, but its task proved so much more difficult than Congress had anticipated that its original powers were extended for another year and then another. Finally it became apparent that the expanding realm of radio communication was so dynamic that it would continually raise difficult administrative problems, and the FRC was made a permanent body on December 18, 1929. Thus the FRC took its place as an independent regulatory agency, representing Congress in the day-to-day decisions required in the area of authority defined by the Radio Act of 1927.

THE FRC TAKES OVER

The FRC addressed itself to the monumental task before it on March 16, 1927. In its first year the Commission devoted itself "almost exclusively to clearing up the broadcast situation."[14] Among its first acts were: setting the broadcast license period for the time being at sixty days, defining the standard broadcast band as 550-1,500 kc.,[15] standardizing the designation of channels (by frequency rather than wave length), and eliminating portable broadcast stations. It failed to take really drastic action on the most pressing problem, however — the need to reduce sharply the number of stations in operation. The Commission chipped away at this problem over a number of years. From 1927 to 1932 the total number of broadcast authorizations was reduced only from 681 to 604. However, the number of stations authorized to operate at night (when sky wave interference becomes a factor) was reduced from 565 to 397.[16]

In its second year the FRC set up the classification system providing for local, regional, and clear channels. Its major project for that year and for some years to come was the effort to equalize the services in the country in accordance with the Davis Amendment to the Radio Act, approved March 28, 1928. This Amendment required the Commission to allocate broadcast services in proportion to the population in the five zones into which the United States was divided for the purposes of the Act. A unit quota system was put into effect, whereby the amount of service received by each zone could be calculated numerically. In order to fulfill the requirements of the Davis Amendment, the Commission had to change 164 authorizations. No less than 110 protesting licensees appeared at a mass hearing in Washington, bringing letters and affidavits by the hundreds of thousands.[17] But numerical quotas and arbitrary geographical zones are entirely at variance with the nature of radio. For example, a station near the border between two zones might be physically located in Zone 1, but the major audience in

---

[14] FRC, [First] Annual Report (Washington: Government Printing Office, 1927), p. 1.
[15] The band was extended to its present upper limit of 1,600 kc. in 1937 and to the present lower limit of 540 kc. in 1947.
[16] FRC, Sixth Annual Report (Washington: Government Printing Office, 1932), p. 25.
[17] Testimony of Louis G. Caldwell in: Senate Committee on Interstate Commerce, op. cit., p. 68.

its actual coverage area might be in Zone 2. Yet Zone 1 might be charged with the quota value of the station even though Zone 2 was getting most of the benefits of the station. The Commission struggled vainly with this absurd requirement until 1936, when the Davis Amendment was finally repealed. Since then the Commission has applied the *principle* of equitable distribution of service without having to abide by an arbitrary and essentially meaningless scheme of zoning and measurement.

By 1929 the FRC had been challenged on a number of its decisions, particularly with reference to the interpretation of the phrase "public interest, convenience, and necessity." The necessity of defending these decisions in court obliged the Commission to formulate its ideas concretely. Most of the basic concepts in this new area of jurisprudence had their origins in these early cases.[18]

At first the Commission had issued its rules in the form of sequentially numbered General Orders. By 1931 the number and complexity of its rules had increased to the point where the General Orders became unwieldy. Therefore the FRC adopted a method of codifying all standing orders in a systematic way as "Rules and Regulations." The first such set of Rules and Regulations became effective February 1, 1932. By this time, too, the technology of broadcasting had made many advances. The FRC had had the opportunity to make empirical tests and to collect expert opinion. Propagation theory was beginning to develop. During 1930 broadcasting experienced "almost a complete revolution in the type of equipment used."[19] All this enabled the Commission to adopt more stringent engineering standards aimed at reducing interference and improving signal quality. For example, where formerly stations had been required only to keep within 500 cycles of their assigned frequency, they were now limited to a 50-cycle tolerance. A set of "Standards of Good Engineering Practice" was issued by the Commission for the detailed guidance of engineers in carrying out the Rules and Regulations. Stations were now required to keep logs on both technical operations and programs. Also in 1930, the Commission adopted the practice of alleviating the pressure of its workload by delegating to Hearing Examiners the authority to conduct hearings. These time-consuming procedures are conducted much like a court, with all parties at interest submitting evidence and arguments with the aid of legal counsel. All these basic practices and procedures, devised during the first five years of the FRC, became a permanent part of the regulatory pattern.

THE COMMUNICATIONS ACT OF 1934

Even at the time that the Radio Act was passed some Congressmen had wanted to go a step further and place under one federal jurisdiction both wire and wireless communication, both interstate and foreign. By 1929 a

[18] FRC, *Third Annual Report* (Washington: Government Printing Office, 1929) extracts the pertinent material from the Commission's briefs of that year, pp. 31-43.
[19] FRC, *Fifth Annual Report* (Washington: Government Printing Office, 1931), p. 6.

bill had been introduced to revise the Radio Act by transferring from the
Department of Commerce and the Postmaster General their remaining duties
with respect to wireless and wire communications and to consolidate all
such powers under one law and one regulatory agency. Several variants of
this bill were considered in subsequent years. Finally, in 1934, President
Roosevelt forwarded an Interdepartmental Committee recommendation to
Congress, explaining:

> I have long felt that for the sake of clarity and effectiveness, the relationship
> of the Federal Government to certain services known as utilities should be
> divided into three fields: Transportation, power, and communications. The
> problems of transportation are vested in the Interstate Commerce Commis-
> sion, and the problems of power . . . in the Federal Power Commission.
> In the field of communications, however, there is today no single Government
> agency charged with broad authority.[20]

The result was the Communications Act of 1934. This law, still on the books,
simply re-enacted the Radio Act of 1927 as far as radio was concerned, but
it added new provisions for jurisdiction over interstate and foreign wire
communication. Two members were added to the Commission because of
the enlargement of its responsibilities, and its name became the Federal
Communications Commission (FCC).

In effect, then, the present law governing radio dates back to 1927. The
FCC took over from the FRC with no break in continuity. Every subsequent
session of Congress has seen numerous attempts to alter the Act; yet in the
years 1934 to 1952 the Communications Act was amended only 16 times.
Most of these amendments were of very minor consequence; the most important changes are embodied in the McFarland Bill, adopted in 1952.[21]
But even this amendment made no fundamental change in the law. That
the Radio Act has remained essentially intact since 1927 is significant in
view of the fact that it was the product of a Republican administration,
whereas the Communications Act was the product of the New Deal. That
Congress was satisfied with both the Act itself and the Commission's basic
interpretation is apparent from the fact that Congress made no major
changes when the opportunity arose in 1934 at the passage of the Communications Act. That the 1927 legislation has withstood the test of time and
attacks from every imaginable source attests to the remarkable soundness
of the work done by Congress (notably by the late Senator Wallace H.
White of Maine) back in 1927, when broadcasting was in its infancy. Both
wire and wireless communication have experienced enormous and revolutionary growth since then — witness FM, facsimile, television, radar, microwave relays, and coaxial cable, to mention only the most obvious
developments. Yet the Act has been flexible enough to foster and control
these innovations.

[20] Senate Document 144, 73d Congress, 2d Session (Washington: Government Printing
Office, 1934).
[21] Cf: House Committee on Interstate and Foreign Commerce, *Hearings on S. 658,
Amending Communications Act of 1934* (Washington: Government Printing Office,
1951).

9

The Radio Era: 1927-1948

From the transitional period of 1926-1927 emerged a national broadcasting system characterized by (1) competitive free enterprise dependent on advertising for economic support; (2) syndication of programs, primarily by means of national networks — without, however, complete sacrifice of local ownership and programming in favor of monopoly ownership or centralized program control; and (3) government regulation, based on a compromise between public and private interests. These characteristic traits of the American system of broadcasting did not, of course, emerge fully developed in 1927. The techniques of advertising, the functions of networks, and the concept of the dividing line between public and private interests in broadcasting are still evolving. But radio broadcasting advanced steadily for two decades on the basis of the fundamental charter, so to speak, which it received in 1926-1927.

This period came to an end about 1948. The year 1948 is selected as another critical turning point because of a number of television developments which culminated at that time (these will be discussed in Chapter 10). By then, sound broadcasting had reached its high water mark; thereafter it receded as it adjusted to the new competition of television. Many thought at the time that sound radio would very soon dry up almost entirely, but events have proved otherwise.

In broad outline, the history of radio broadcasting in these two decades might be subdivided as follows:

(1) 1927-1937. Developmental period in which the three factors — advertising, network operations, and government regulation — settled into a fairly well defined pattern of interrelationships. Relatively little change in total number of stations (Fig. 20).

(2) 1938-1945. Period of stability in which the medium was prosperous and even complacent, with gradual, orderly increase in station and network competition. Increased government surveillance. Artificial stimulation of profits and limitation on competition during the war years.

(3) 1946-1948. Period of rapid change. Sudden great increase in number of stations, with resulting sharper competition. FM introduced. Television imminent.

(4) 1948 and following. Period of adjustment to television, at first
accelerating to a panic, then settling down to a series of strategic
withdrawals and build-ups of strong points.

PROGRAM DEVELOPMENTS

In the first decade, 1927-1937, the initial problem was to resolve the tangle
which had resulted from the collapse of government regulation under the
Radio Act of 1912. The new law, the Radio Act of 1927, cleared the air by
defining the basic nature of the role the federal government was to play in
the regulation, not only of broadcasting, but of all forms of radio communication. By the time the FRC expanded into the FCC in 1934, the work of
clearing up the original technical confusion of the broadcast industry had
been completed. The FRC had already moved on to the next task, that of
cleaning up programming. This cleanup was not a matter of interference
by the Commission with programming in general. It was addressed rather
to a limited number of stations which had succumbed to the temptation —
always present in broadcasting and never resisted with entire success — to
use the medium to prey on the ills and misfortunes of mankind. Several
stations at this time were devoting much time to unethical medical-advice
programs, astrologers, fortune-tellers, quack psychologists, and the like.
There were also some relics from the earliest days of broadcasting, when
stations were erected as a hobby to become the mouthpieces for the personal
idiosyncracies of their owners. The Commission was sustained by the
courts in its moves to eliminate specific abuses of these kinds.[1]

SYNDICATION

Programming in general, however, developed along the lines familiar to
listeners today. The unique problem of broadcast programming is the unrelenting voracity of the medium. It eats up talent and program material
at an unprecedented rate. The only possible answer to this inexorable demand is syndication[2] of program material and repetitive patterning of programming. Very early in the history of broadcasting the need for networks
and recordings became apparent; and programming soon evolved formats
which lent themselves to repetition. Programming also adapted itself to
the cycle of habitual social activity of the household. Daytime programming developed formats which permitted daily ("across the board") scheduling; typical is the quarter-hour daytime serial drama, which spins out new
episodes day after day with a minimum of story development. Nighttime

[1] E.g., *Duncan* v. *U.S.*, 48 F. (2d) 128 (1931); *KFKB Broadcasting Assn., Inc.* v.
FRC, 47 F. (2d) 670 (1931); *Trinity Methodist Church, South,* v. *FRC*, 62 F. (2d) 850
(1932).
[2] See the discussion of syndication in Chapter 4.

programming developed half-hour series scheduled on a weekly basis, with the same basic ingredients being used week after week; a typical example is the half-hour comedy-variety program, with its permanent cast and recurring themes.

The need for syndication resulted in nearly all the major stations in the country affiliating with one of the two national networks, either NBC or CBS. By 1938 40 per cent of all 660 stations then in operation were network-affiliated. However, the importance of networks was much greater than this figure suggests, since the independent (i.e., non-affiliated) stations were mostly in the lower-wattage and part-time class. A more realistic measure is the fact that 98 per cent of the nighttime wattage represented network stations.[3]

Syndication is vitally important in music programming, radio's most fundamental program type, which in 1938 comprised over half of all radio programming.[4] Here broadcasters encountered difficulties almost from the first. Music, like other creative products, can be copyrighted, and the copyright owners not unnaturally expect to share in radio profits.[5] The question is: How much should a station or network be required to pay for the right to use copyrighted music? Considering the amount of music used — whether live or recorded, network or local — this is a question of some moment.

ASCAP

Since it is physically impossible for music composers, authors, and publishers personally to keep track of every performance affecting their rights, they formed an organization in 1914 to represent them, the American Society of Composers, Authors, and Publishers (ASCAP). This is a nonprofit association with thousands of members. Through the agency of ASCAP, royalties on performances are collected and distributed to the copyright holders. As early as 1922 ASCAP began to look askance at the radio performance of musical works in its catalogue. By the time of the Fourth National Radio Conference (1925) a committee of broadcasters was seeking

[3] FCC, *Report on Chain Broadcasting* (Washington: Government Printing Office, 1941), p. 31.
[4] FCC, *Fourth Annual Report* (Washington: Government Printing Office, 1938), p. 225.
[5] The law of copyrights, like that of patents, is derived from Article I, Section 8 of the Constitution. The basic statute now in effect dates back to 1909. It provides for copyrights of twenty-eight years' duration, renewable once. This law left a loophole as far as broadcasting was concerned, since it protected an author only with respect to the type of reproduction then normally anticipated. For instance, since novels are normally intended to be reproduced by means of printing, this kind of work could be read on the radio without violating copyright. This loophole was plugged in 1952 by an amendment to the statute. It should be noted that an author has a common-law right to his products, irrespective of the statute, but this right is surrendered when the product is either published or copyrighted under the statute.

ways of getting relief from the demands of ASCAP.[6] In fact, so universal was the problem for broadcasters that their trade association, the National Association of Broadcasters (NAB),[7] was formed in 1923 specifically to deal with the ASCAP problem.

As broadcasting grew, the fees collected by ASCAP from broadcasting amounted to the major share of the Society's income (85 per cent in 1954). When ASCAP proposed another increase in royalty fees in 1937, the broadcasters finally decided to stand and fight. By 1939 they had formed Broadcast Music, Incorporated (BMI) as a rival music-licensing organization in preparation for a showdown at midnight, December 31, when the old ASCAP contract expired. At about the same time ASCAP came under attack from the Department of Justice. As a result of both threats, ASCAP reduced its demands to a point where they were acceptable to the broadcasters. BMI continued in business, however, and has gradually built up a considerable catalogue. This was one of the few occasions on which the broadcast industry was able to muster a united front and to follow through an industry-wide issue to a successful conclusion. All stations are now licensed by one or more of several music-licensing organizations, for which they usually pay a percentage of their gross income; thus there is no necessity for the elaborate bookkeeping that a per-performance basis of payment requires.[8]

THE PRESS-RADIO WAR

Another important source of broadcast programming, and one also heavily dependent on syndication, caused difficulty in the 1930's. News had from the first been a radio staple. It will be recalled that the first broadcast of KDKA had been news of an election. Even earlier, back in the experimental days of radiotelegraphy, one of the first practical applications had been in reporting yacht races in 1901 and 1903. The *New York Times* had used radiotelegraphy in reporting the Russo-Japanese war. Newspapers are naturally interested in any means of transmitting information quickly and efficiently. However, they were interested in transmission to newspapers themselves rather than to the general public. Direct transmission of news by broadcasting seemed to threaten the well-entrenched vested interest of the press.

In 1933 the three major news agencies — Associated Press, United Press, and International News Service — cut off services to radio stations. The networks made some effort to establish an independent news-gathering

---

[6] Fourth National Radio Conference, *Proceedings and Recommendations for Regulation of Radio* (Washington: Government Printing Office, 1926), pp. 37-38. The committee complained that the terms offered by ASCAP were "prohibitive" and "unstable," and asked for equal treatment for all stations. Since this was a problem covered by existing law, the Conference took no action on the committee's recommendations.

[7] Since 1951, the National Association of Radio and Television Broadcasters (NARTB).

[8] Cf.: Bruce Robertson, "A New Harmony for an Old Discord," *Broadcasting-Telecasting* (25 October 1954), pp. 84-87, 103.

agency for broadcasting, but very quickly gave in to pressures which even included "subtle press agitation . . . for congressional legislation more strictly regulating the radio industry, accompanied by some kind words for the British system of government ownership and operation."[9] The result was the establishment of the Press Radio Bureau (1934-1940), which permitted stations to broadcast only ten minutes of news a day, and that only on a non-commercial basis and after the news had been published in newspapers. These terms are remarkable no less for what they reveal of the broadcasters' feelings of inferiority than for what they show of the ruthlessness of the press. They were called "tyrannical and indefensible" by a United States Senator, who likewise criticized the networks for having "surrendered radio's birthright."[10]

This inequitable arrangement, which so patently ignored the interest of the public, expired in 1940. After the press associations began to serve stations it became evident that radio news coverage, despite its ability to beat newspapers on spot news, actually did more to stimulate newspaper reading than to replace it. Nevertheless, it was not until the advent of television — and of the sense of responsibility and consequence which television brought to broadcasters — that the networks overcame their feelings of inferiority and fought with real vigor for equality with the older medium of news dissemination (Chapter 11).

FORMATS AND STARS

In other areas of radio programming an accomplishment of the 1930's was the development of special techniques for adapting program materials to the radio medium. Radio has introduced relatively little that is new. It is largely a synthetic or assimilative medium, which takes over and adapts the basic communication forms and products of other media. At first radio merely imitated, reproducing literally the products of the stage, screen, platform, press, pulpit, and concert hall. Later it became evident that these materials could often be made more effective on radio if adapted to its own potentialities and limitations. The first radio dramas, for example, were simply remote broadcasts of stage performances. Soon it was realized that plays could be more effective on radio when performed under studio conditions, with carefully coordinated music and sound effects; the loss of the visual element of drama could be offset by using suggestion, appealing to audience imagination, and capitalizing on the intimacy of the medium. In the early 1930's emerged serial dramatic formats suitable for strips — the

[9] Llewellyn White, *The American Radio* (Chicago: University of Chicago Press, 1947), p. 46. Copyright 1947 by the University of Chicago.

[10] Clarence C. Dill, "Radio and the Press: A Contrary View," in *The Annals of the American Academy of Political and Social Science* CLXXVII (January, 1935), pp. 170-175. The press side of the controversy is represented in the same publication by: E. H. Harris, "Radio and the Press," pp. 163-169.

familiar soap opera, which has been characterized as "the great invention of radio, its single notable contribution to the art of fiction."[11]

Radio discovered in the 1930's, as the cinema had discovered years before, that successful syndicated programming on a national scale depends in large measure on certain intangible assets possessed by star performers. These assets justify paying the star salaries which might seem entirely out of proportion to the intrinsic worth of his talents. Radio began to capitalize on the intangible assets of Hollywood stars as early as 1930, with *The First Nighter*. It later developed its own star performers. The control of talent was from the first an important factor in successful network operations, for which reason both NBC and CBS operated their own talent agencies until the practice was condemned by the FCC. In the strategy of network competition the ability of a network to command a lineup of top stars remains as important as its ability to muster a lineup of top stations as affiliates.

NETWORK DEVELOPMENTS

During this period of program evolution parallel developments in the business operations of national networks had been taking place. Since networks are limited by the Commission to ownership of relatively few stations, the basic network-affiliate relationship is a contractual rather than a proprietary one. From the rather loose, informal agreements in effect when NBC started, this contractual relationship had been elaborated, primarily by CBS, into a fairly standardized form. A network offers three basic services to the affiliate: It (1) provides network programs directly or indirectly; (2) arranges for the relay of programs from the source to the affiliate; and (3) sells the affiliate's time in the national market. In order for the network sales staff to have something definite to sell, affiliates contract to make certain hours of the day available to the network on an optional basis. That is, the network can count on certain hours' being available if it finds customers, but it is not saddled with the necessity of programming all these hours unless customers for them are found. In return for the network services the affiliate usually gives a stipulated number of hours to the network free of charge. All income from these free hours goes to the network. Income from the other hours optioned to the network is distributed among the affiliates according to agreed-upon time rates. In the late 1930's NBC and CBS were distributing about a quarter of their total income among their affiliates.[12]

As a natural outcome of these arrangements the network seeks to assure itself of as much stability of coverage as possible. This can be accomplished by such means as insisting on exclusive access to the affiliate as against

---

[11] Gilbert Seldes, *The Great Audience* (New York: The Viking Press, 1950), p. 113.

[12] FCC, *Report on Chain Broadcasting* (Washington: Government Printing Office, 1941), pp. 41-42. This report includes a wealth of data on network history and network practices; much of the latter had not hitherto been generally available.

other networks; long-term affiliation contracts; optioning all of the affiliate's best time; discouraging affiliates from cancelling or rejecting network programs. The power and prestige of the network and the great value of the affiliation make the affiliate particularly susceptible to domination by the network. Yet the licensee of each individual station, network-affiliated or independent, is equally and uniquely responsible under the Communications Act for his own station's programs and conduct.

That CBS- and NBC-affiliated stations were tied to these networks with peculiarly powerful bonds became evident when the Mutual Broadcasting System attempted to expand into a national operation in the late 1930's in competition with the older chains. The latter had tied up all but two of the 52 major stations on clear channels and nearly 75 per cent of the powerful stations on regional channels. In 1938 these two networks handled over half the business of the radio industry.[13] At this time there were only 660 stations in operation. Many sizable communities had fewer than four stations. This meant that CBS and NBC (Red and Blue) could effectively prevent competition from Mutual in such communities by means of exclusive affiliation contracts.

THE CHAIN-BROADCASTING INVESTIGATION

Mutual's complaints prompted the FCC to make a thorough investigation of network business practices in 1938. It concluded that the extent of control over the industry hitherto exercised by CBS and NBC was not in the public interest. The Communications Act empowers the FCC to "make special regulations applicable to radio stations engaged in chain [i.e., network] broadcasting."[14] Accordingly, the FCC adopted a set of "Chain Broadcasting Regulations" in 1941, aimed at relaxing the control of networks over their affiliates and opening the door to more competition from MBS. NBC and CBS fought the new rules bitterly, predicting that their adoption would mean the end of network broadcasting as it had been known and the negation of the achievements of the two pioneer networks. Not until 1942, four years after the investigation began, was the struggle finally settled by the Supreme Court, with a verdict in favor of the FCC rules.[15]

The most tangible outcome of the decision was the end of NBC's dual network operation. The Blue was sold in 1943 to a candy manufacturer, Edward Noble, who changed its name to American Broadcasting Company (ABC) in 1945. But the predicted collapse of the network system failed to

[13] *Ibid.*, p. 32.
[14] Section 303 (i). Note that the language of this provision confines the Commission to regulating individual stations, not networks as such. The FCC's only control over networks is thus indirect. Network organizations, as distinguished from stations, are neither licensed nor regulated directly by the FCC.
[15] *CBS* v. *U.S.*, 316 U.S. 407, and *NBC* v. *U.S.*, 316 U.S. 447. The Court voted 6 to 3 to uphold the FCC.

materialize. MBS expanded rapidly, although it never caught up with the three older companies. NBC and CBS continue to hold their lead.

THE DEVELOPMENT OF RCA

The *Report on Chain Broadcasting* called attention to the growth of RCA, whose story we left at the point where NBC was founded in 1926. By 1930 two of the co-owners of NBC, General Electric and Westinghouse, had withdrawn, making the network a wholly-owned subsidiary of RCA. In 1932 an antitrust suit caused Westinghouse and General Electric to sell their stock in RCA itself, which thus became entirely independent of its parent companies. Meanwhile, RCA had set up subsidiaries to handle the maritime and point-to-point radio communications business it had inherited from American Marconi. Radiomarine Corporation of America was incorporated in 1927 and RCA Communications in 1929. The class of business carried on by these subsidiaries, once the major business of RCA, has since come to represent only a minor source of income.

Also in 1929, RCA acquired control of the Victor Talking Machine Company, and in the following year it asserted its growing independence of GE and Westinghouse by going into the manufacture of receivers. RCA's manufacturing activities thereafter expanded into practically all fields of communication and electronics, including phonograph records and players, recording equipment, motion-picture projectors and sound equipment, public-address systems, aviation communication systems, electron microscopes, radio and television broadcast-station facilities, and many others. This branch of the RCA empire, representing the fusion of a number of specialized manufacturing companies acquired over the years, is now known as the RCA Victor Division. A special company exists to service RCA products in the field — the RCA Service Company. Since RCA is concerned with a field of technology in which research is all-important, it has set up elaborate industrial research facilities for exploring new fields, the RCA Laboratories Division. Another subsidiary, RCA Institutes, is a technical training school. RCA products are carried into the world market through the RCA International Division.

Aside from its own manufacturing activities, RCA had an important influence on manufacturing by others. Its patent position was such that no salable receivers could be built without licenses from RCA for the use of patents it owned or controlled. This near-monopoly had long been a matter of concern to Congress; as early as 1923 the Federal Trade Commission had been directed to investigate the radio-patent situation. Its thorough report[16] had a great deal of influence in subsequent Congressional hearings and even on the Radio Act of 1927. It indirectly brought about the antitrust suits of 1930 and 1932 which led to the withdrawal of GE and Westinghouse from

[16] Federal Trade Commission, *Report on the Radio Industry* (Washington: Government Printing Office, 1924)

ownership in RCA. The relaxation of RCA's licensing terms resulted in the successful development of a number of rival manufacturers in the 1930's, such as Zenith, Emerson, and Philco. Although paying royalties to RCA for patent rights, these companies were able to compete effectively against RCA, whose great size made it somewhat sluggish in competition with the lighter-weight but faster-moving newcomers.[17]

NBC, as a broadcasting network, therefore constitutes only one province in a great communications empire. At the time of the Chain Broadcasting Investigation, that empire even included a talent agency and concert-booking service. But the FCC pointed out that

> As agent for artists, NBC is under a fiduciary duty to procure the best terms possible *for* the artists. As employer of artists, NBC is interested in securing the best terms possible *from* the artists. NBC's dual role necessarily prevents arm's length bargaining and constitutes a serious conflict of interest.[18]

In summarizing the extent of NBC's and RCA's influence, the Commission concluded:

> It is significant that these numerous and, for the most part, critically important activities require a capital investment which, in other fields of enterprise, would not be regarded as staggering. The assets of RCA barely exceed $100,000,000; many a railroad, utility, bank, insurance company, or industrial establishment of relatively secondary importance has assets double or treble this amount. This tends to make RCA comparatively independent of the money market.
>
> RCA, like many other giant enterprises today, is a "management corporation." It has nearly 250,000 stockholders. No one owns as much as half of 1 percent of its stock. In such circumstances, stockholder control is practically nonexistent. RCA's funded debt is small, so there is no substantial creditor influence on the management. As a result, the management is essentially self-perpetuating, and the responsibility of the executives and directors is largely intramural.
>
> In short, RCA occupies a premier position in fields which are profoundly determinative of our way of life. Its diverse activities give it a peculiarly advantageous position in competition with enterprises less widely based. Its policies are determined by a management subject to little restraint other than self-imposed. Whether this ramified and powerful enterprise with its consistent tendency to grow and to expand into new fields at the expense of smaller independent concerns is desirable, is not to be decided here. We have thought it proper, however, to call the attention of Congress and the public to the broader problems raised by this concentration of power in the hands of a single group.[19]

[17] W. Rupert Maclaurin, *Invention and Innovation in the Radio Industry* (New York: The Macmillan Co., 1949), p. 248.

[18] FCC, *Report on Chain Broadcasting* (Washington: Government Printing Office, 1941), p. 17. (Italics added.)

[19] *Ibid.,* p. 20.

THE GROWTH OF CBS

Though not in the same corporate class with NBC, CBS also came in for a share of criticism in the Chain Broadcasting Investigation. Like NBC, Columbia had its own recording company and its own talent-booking agency. Columbia had taken the lead in evolving the restrictive network-affiliation contracts to which the FCC objected — contracts developed by Columbia in its efforts to compete with NBC. CBS had succeeded so well in these efforts that at the time of the investigation its net income was actually greater than that of NBC, despite the fact that NBC had both the Red and Blue networks.[20] The Blue, however, had been used by NBC more as a foil to the Red than as an all-out competitor with CBS. In 1938, 75 per cent of NBC's commercial programs were carried by the Red stations.[21] The fact is that during the easygoing years of the 1930's there was enough national business and enough high-caliber talent available to support two major networks (regarding NBC as one for the moment) without competition between the two becoming strident.

A new, more competitive era began in the 1940's, however, with four networks instead of two competing for the national advertisers' dollar. Moreover, by 1945 there were over 900 stations operating, as against fewer than 700 in the 1930's (Figure 20).

CBS challenged NBC, now shorn of its Blue network, to an all-out battle for the number-one network position. It might seem that in such a battle NBC would have insuperable advantages because of the enormous resources of its parent company, RCA. But just as in the case of the set manufacturers who competed successfully with RCA Victor, Columbia could take advantage of greater maneuverability. One Columbia maneuver was to capture the lead in programming. Another was to delay the coming of television as long as possible in order to give CBS time to develop its own television potentiality.

In 1948 CBS made a celebrated "talent raid" on NBC, by which it captured many of the top-ranking stars of radio, such as "Amos 'n' Andy," Jack Benny, Burns and Allen, Edgar Bergen, and Bing Crosby. The CBS program strategy was based on (1) recapturing control of network programming and talent from the advertising agencies and (2) building up an overwhelmingly strong radio talent position. By 1949 CBS could claim all ten of the top-rated radio programs and was well ahead of NBC in radio time sales (Fig. 24). These moves were designed to build up radio income for the developmental period during which network radio would have to support network television, as well as to provide a talent pool to draw on as television programming moved out of the experimental into the competitive phase.[22]

[20] *Ibid.*, pp. 17, 24.
[21] *Ibid.*, p. 70.
[22] Cf. "CBS Steals the Show," *Fortune* (July, 1953), pp. 79-82, 164-166.

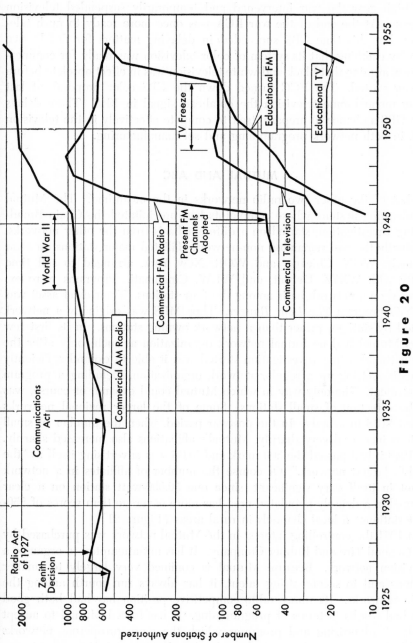

Figure 20

Trends in the Rate of Station Authorizations Since 1925

Authorizations include construction permits as well as licenses; hence their number exceeds the number of stations actually on the air.

Sources: Data since 1943, FCC *Annual Reports;* earlier data, *Broadcasting-Telecasting Yearbook,* 1955 *Broadcasting Yearbook—Marketbook Issue,* p. 437.

On the television front RCA had a head start on CBS and was ready for all-out exploitation of the market by 1940. But before RCA could move into high gear the war intervened and temporarily suspended television progress. At the end of the war RCA was once more ready to push television, but this time CBS succeeded in delaying matters for nearly two years by claiming that its system of color television was ready for commercial use, arguing that black-and-white television was in effect obsolete before it even started. The FCC turned down the CBS color proposal, at last giving monochrome television the go-ahead signal in 1948. These delays gave CBS a chance to prepare itself to compete effectively in the television field, in both network programming and set manufacturing.

MUTUAL AND ABC

What of the other two radio networks in the meantime? The Mutual Broadcasting System, whose complaints had precipitated the Chain Broadcasting Investigation, started on a different basis from the other networks. Originally the two remaining non-network-affiliated major stations on clear channels, WGN, Chicago, and WOR, New York, arranged to sell time jointly with WXYZ, Detroit, and WLW, Cincinnati. Programs were exchanged on a network basis among the four stations. Their chief asset was WXYZ's program *The Lone Ranger*. Thus MBS was originally a network owned by stations, rather than a network owning stations. In its first few years Mutual had no formal network organization as such; only after the Chain Broadcasting Investigation started was it able to expand sufficiently to justify setting up a regular network organization, including a program department. The only way in which Mutual could expand, of course, was in the direction of small stations. Some of the larger regional networks joined MBS in a body. In the postwar period, when the number of small stations increased very sharply, Mutual's affiliations also increased sharply. By 1948 it had passed the 500 mark and MBS was advertising itself as "the world's largest network." Of course the number of affiliates in a network is not in itself very significant, since one 50,000-watt station on a clear channel in a densely populated area has more coverage than scores of 250-watt stations on local channels in rural areas (Figure 21).

In 1951 the controlling interest in the Mutual network was purchased by the General Tire and Rubber Company. It has not attempted to organize a television network. Because Mutual is confined very largely to smaller stations and to second-string talent, it has always run fourth among the radio networks. Its unfavorable competitive position has had both good and bad results in terms of programming. It has forced Mutual to accept kinds of advertising and programs which the more prosperous networks could afford to turn down. It has also forced Mutual to try offbeat programs and ingenious sales methods which the older networks were too conservative to attempt.

The American Broadcasting Company automatically assumed the third rank among the networks upon its separation from NBC. The Blue had the advantage of bringing with it a respectable stable of strong affiliates, but it was weak commercially. Like Mutual, ABC had to seek new sources of advertising revenue and new program materials and talent. ABC plunged into television when the time came, but it lacked the financial staying power to compete in this most costly field and soon began to flounder. In 1953 the FCC approved a merger whereby ABC came under the control of United Paramount Theatres.

ABC and Mutual were forced to develop the means for tapping local advertisers for network revenue, since there were not enough national and regional advertisers to go around. MBS's *Kate Smith Show* was the first major program to be sold on a "co-op" basis, with over 200 local advertisers

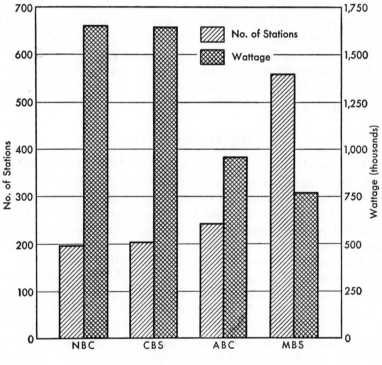

F i g u r e   2 1

Relative Size of Radio Networks: Affiliates and
Wattage (1955)

Based on aggregate nighttime wattage and all affiliates listed by the respective networks. At the time of this survey 53 per cent of AM stations on the air were not affiliated with a major network.

Sources: Network engineering departments.

sharing the bill. The first nighttime network program to be sold on a co-op basis was ABC's *Abbott and Costello,* in 1947. ABC and Mutual shattered another tradition by using recordings on network programs. In the earliest days of broadcasting, recordings had been frowned on as somewhat of a fraud on the public. The Department of Commerce actually forbade their use at one time, and one of the first rules of the FRC was the requirement that recordings be clearly announced as such.[23] From the point of view of NBC and CBS, of course, the most valuable asset of networks was the fact that they brought major *live-talent* programs to a national audience. ABC started using transcribed programs in 1946, quickly followed by MBS. CBS relaxed the long-standing ban as far as one-time playback of network programs was concerned in 1947. Not until 1949, however, did both NBC and CBS permit general use of recordings. The FCC, too, became more reasonable in view of the greatly increased fidelity of modern recordings and ruled in 1948 that stations could delay network programs by means of recordings in order to equalize the time differences incidental to the adoption of daylight saving time in some states and not in others; these recordings may be played without being identified as such except for one general announcement during the course of the broadcast day. The lifting of the self-imposed ban on the use of recordings on network programs resulted in a migration of the "disc-jockey" program format from the local to the network level.

THE ADVENT OF FM

Another new element in the radio picture of the 1940's was FM broadcasting. The principle of frequency modulation had long been recognized, the first United States patent on the principle dating back to 1905. But it was not until the patents of Edwin Armstrong improved the FM technique in 1933 that practical application became feasible. Armstrong made his findings public at an Institute of Radio Engineers convention in 1935, thereby precipitating the "biggest and bitterest behind-the-scenes fight in radio's career."[24] Armstrong, a man of singular persistence and conviction, fought against the skepticism (and even the concealed hostility) of the radio industry. During 1934-1935 he carried on tests, with the cooperation of RCA, from a transmitter site on the Empire State Building. Unfortunately for Armstrong and the cause of FM, RCA was by this time deeply committed to the future of television, and it later displaced Armstrong's transmitter in favor of television experiments. The inventor thereafter built W2XMN at Alpine, New Jersey (1937). Armstrong always contended that RCA had deliberately scuttled FM.[25]

[23] General Order No. 16, 9 August 1927.
[24] "Revolution in Radio," *Fortune* (October, 1939), p. 86.
[25] Senate Committee on Interstate and Foreign Commerce, *Hearings on Certain Charges Involving Development of FM Radio and RCA Patent Policies* (Washington: Government Printing Office, 1948). Cf. testimony of Edwin Armstrong, pp. 11-20 *et passim.*

The FCC first became interested in the new medium in 1935, and after hearings in 1936 assigned the first experimental channels to FM. But soon the interests of FM again conflicted with those of television, this time with respect to frequency allocation. The FCC assigned 19 channels to TV and 13 to FM in 1939, but the frequency and distribution of the FM channels were disadvantageous to FM.

> If the Commission and the industry had recognized the future importance of frequency modulation, the FM allocation would have been more generous. For it was FM rather than television which was on the verge of immediate commercial development. This initial mistake proved difficult to rectify.[26]

In 1940 the FCC assigned FM to channels in the 42-50 megacycle band and authorized commercial operation. By this time, of course, the war was imminent and the free development of FM was to be held up by the freeze on construction and manufacturing. Nevertheless, 30 FM stations were on the air by 1942. In 1945, however, after another extensive hearing and on the basis of highly controversial engineering evidence, the FCC moved FM up to the 88-108 megacycle band. This was a serious blow, since it outmoded all the sets built originally for the lower band. Nevertheless, most of the major AM stations felt obliged to take out FM licenses, as insurance against the possibility that FM really would outmode AM, as its enthusiasts predicted. FM licenses reached their high-water mark in 1948, when there were over 1,000 outstanding. But 1948 was also the year that television began to expand rapidly, and thereafter the number of FM stations decreased steadily (Figure 20). Most FM stations became relatively meaningless satellites of AM stations, dutifully duplicating AM programs. The few independently operated FM stations have, as a group, consistently lost money.

By 1948 FM broadcasting was turning to substitute sources of revenue. In that year Transit-FM, aimed at "captive audiences" in buses, began. Subsequently other captive audiences became targets in stores ("storecasting") and restaurants and other places of business. Specialized applications of this kind are known as "functional FM." Some public resistance was generated by the whole idea of the captive audience, but the courts sustained its legality.[27] The FCC objected to functional services, contending that they were a non-broadcast use of broadcast facilities. In 1955 the Commission set up a special class of authorization to permit limited functional operation in conjunction with regular FM broadcasting (see Chapter 21). The commercial value of functional FM, however, has proved negligible.

---

[26] Maclaurin, *op. cit.*, pp. 229-230. Cf. also testimony of Edwin Armstrong in: Senate Committee on Interstate and Foreign Commerce, *op. cit.*, p. 16.

[27] *Public Utilities Commission of the District of Columbia, et al. v. Pollak*, 343 U.S. 451 (1952).

POST WAR EXPANSION

The post-war era for broadcasting began officially on October 8, 1945, the date on which the FCC returned to peacetime licensing procedures. The years 1937-1944 had been extremely prosperous for the radio industry. Total annual revenue had more than doubled, and income had risen from twenty cents on the dollar of revenue to thirty-three cents. In 1944 alone the income of the industry amounted to more than a hundred per cent of the value of tangible broadcast property, computed at original cost.[28] Little wonder that the resumption of peacetime licensing found would-be licensees waiting in line to qualify for a share in so lucrative a business. In fact, so many new stations opened that the FCC felt it necessary to issue a cautionary report less than two years after the rush began, pointing out that, after all, there were limits to the number of stations the economy could support.

> While, on October 8, 1945, after a history of 24 years, there were 909 commercial standard broadcast stations authorized in the United States, by February 7, 1947, 16 months later, approximately 600 new stations were either on the air or under construction and more than 700 applications were still pending for new stations.[29]

Most of the new licensees were Class IV or Class II stations located in smaller cities. Whereas at the close of the war only 2 per cent of cities under 5,000 population and only 13 per cent of cities of 5,000-10,000 population had stations, by the end of the period under study 16 per cent and 43 per cent of these two classes of communities respectively had radio stations. The total number of radio communities nearly doubled in the sixteen-month period.[30]

Surprisingly enough, this great expansion, coming as it did on the eve of the advent of the television boom, did not completely disrupt the economy of the industry. One reason, of course, is that many of the new stations, being located in communities not hitherto served by local stations, opened up sources of local advertising revenue not previously available to radio. As competition grew more keen, means were devised to entice more and more small local businesses into using radio advertising. After all, only a limited number of companies are large enough to use national or regional advertising at the network level; the great unexploited potential lay in the tens of thousands of small, local merchants. Until 1945 network advertisers (i.e., national and regional advertisers) had contributed the largest share of radio's revenue. In 1947, for the first time, revenue from local advertisers surpassed that from network advertisers (see Figure 29). That trend in radio has continued.

28 FCC, *Public Service Responsibility of Broadcast Licensees* (Washington: Government Printing Office), pp. 48, 49.
29 FCC, "An Economic Study of Standard Broadcasting" (FCC mimeo., 1947), p. 1.
30 *Ibid.*, p. 27.

Increased radio competition made itself felt in the program field in forms both good and bad. The emphasis on selling led to an emphasis on program popularity ratings which amounted to a fetish. Reciprocally, there developed a tendency to devise programs which would "buy" audiences and thereby inflate ratings artificially, i.e., the "giveaway" program, which reached a zenith in radio in 1948. On the local level, the narrow margin of profit of the smaller, independent stations made it difficult to turn down advertising of doubtful ethical standing, and a resurgence of some of the pitchman and patent-medicine-show atmosphere of the earliest days of radio occurred.

On the other hand, competition shook the industry out of its complacency and stimulated networks and stations toward more imaginative, creative programming. For instance, the documentary program — the presentation of important factual matter in an effective semi-dramatic format — came into prominence in 1947. Many stations took the advice that the FCC offered in its 1946 study on the outlook for the industry and began to serve special minority groups which had hitherto not seemed important enough to merit more than passing attention:

> . . . increased attention should be given to the possibility of developing more listening by groups of potential listeners who do not now listen to the radio at any given hour of the day. The development of such "minority groups" into commercially feasible objects of local advertising efforts is the most obvious avenue for expansion. . . . A small segment of the listening audience, carefully selected as a minority group may, if it is loyally attached to the station, give it a unique attraction for advertisers.[31]

In communities served by all four networks, some kind of specialization by independent stations has become almost essential to survival. The result has been an extensive development of classical-music stations, foreign-language or racial-minority stations, sports stations, and the like.[32]

As the radio era drew to a close in 1948, two of the national radio networks had already taken out insurance against the future by getting a foothold in television. CBS and NBC were preparing to compete in television manufacturing as well as in the broadcast field. ABC's role was as yet doubtful. Mutual's radio position was precarious, for it depended largely on small stations, many of which might be expected eventually to founder as the television service penetrated more deeply into the country and made its effects known. Mutual's fate, however, was postponed by the fact that television did not grow as fast as its natural economic poten-

---

31 *Ibid.*, pp. 77, 85.

32 A *Sponsor* survey revealed interesting regional preferences for specialized services. For example, 40 per cent of the stations surveyed in New Jersey reported concert music as a specialized service; 48 per cent of Texas stations reported farm programs; 36 per cent of New York stations reported foreign-language programs; 60 per cent of Arizona stations reported Mexican programs; 66 per cent of Alabama stations reported Negro programs; 29 per cent of Georgia stations reported religious programs (*Sponsor*, 11 July 1955, p. 55).

tialities would have permitted; instead it was artificially limited and re-
tarded, first by World War II, later by the FCC.

Each national radio network had developed a fairly well-defined corporate personality of its own. NBC, as the oldest chain and the offspring of
a great corporation having its roots in government as well as industry, was
the most conservative and dignified, with a strong sense of the proprieties.
CBS, nearly as old as NBC and its only competitor in the same weight-class,
so to speak, had a brighter, more aggressive personality but also was
marked by considerable dignity and conservatism. Mutual was something of
a street Arab, picking up the leavings of its more fortunate rivals, surviving
by its wits. It had nothing like the prestige of NBC and CBS, and could
not afford to put on airs. ABC remained an anomaly. From RCA it inherited some of NBC's corporate conservatism, but circumstances forced
it into a different pattern. Its personality remained split and its future
doubtful until its financial underpinning was secured by its merger with
Paramount Theatres in 1953. All four of the networks have found it essential to ally themselves with larger economic units with diversified interests.
National network operations seem to require this alliance with big business
in order to have the financial resources and stability to compete effectively.

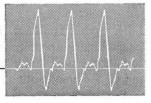

The Ascendancy of Television

A radio broadcast receiver built and sold in 1920 to receive KDKA would be capable of receiving KDKA's signal thirty years later. The same cannot be said of a television receiver built before about 1940. Herein lies a radical difference between the technologies of the two media which delayed the advent of full-scale commercial television service for years. This difference is due to what has been called the "lock-and-key" relationship of the television transmitter and receiver.[1] It will be recalled that the television receiver must do more than detect and amplify the television signal. It must also carry out the precisely-timed scanning sequence in exact synchronism with the camera. Unless both transmitter and receiver operate on the same line and field frequency standards, and unless the receiver is designed to receive and interpret specific synchronizing signals, the key will not fit the lock.

This fact presented the FCC with a nice problem of timing. The moment that standards were agreed upon for full-scale commercial operation, the technology of television might be frozen at that point of development. This follows from the fact that once a large number of receivers have been sold the public acquires a vested interest in the system on which those receivers operate. The difficulty experienced recently by UHF television is a case in point. Originally all sets had provision for VHF tuning only, since UHF stations did not yet exist. The only difference in the standards of UHF and VHF television transmission is the fact that the two groups of carrier frequencies are widely separated in the frequency spectrum. However, a given set of receiver tuning components can tune over only a limited band of frequencies; hence the tuning components built into VHF sets cannot receive UHF signals, and vice versa. To receive both groups of frequencies, a set must have two tuning components, either both built into the set originally or one attached to the set externally in the form of an adapter. UHF stations have had great difficulty in getting the public to make an additional investment in UHF adapters or in new receivers with built-in

[1] Testimony of FCC Chairman James Lawrence Fly in: Senate Committee on Interstate Commerce, *Hearings on S. Res. 251, Development of Television* (Washington: Government Printing Office, 1940), p. 7.

UHF tuning facilities. Had UHF been used along with VHF from the beginning, this problem would not have arisen. Now it may be impossible to take the next logical step, which is to delete the VHF channels and to put all TV broadcasting in the UHF band.[2]

A radical change of standards could wipe out a public investment of millions — and even billions — of dollars overnight. On the other hand, the longer the FCC delayed in permitting full-scale commercial development, the longer the public was denied the television service, the less opportunity manufacturers had to test their products in the market, and the less the free play of competition could contribute to the development of the medium.

THE DEVELOPMENT OF TV

Television, as a potentiality, has existed quite as long as radio itself (see Figure 17). It is rooted, like radio, in the prior art of wire transmission. Experiments in sending still and moving pictures by wire during the nineteenth century led to the subsequent development of the wire-photo service. All early attempts at devising a practical television system foundered, however, on the problem of achieving a method of sufficiently precise and rapid scansion of a large number of picture lines. Until the advent of the electronic system the most promising device was a rapidly revolving disk, pierced by a series of very small holes so arranged that one revolution of the disk scanned the scene in successive lines. The mechanical scanning disk could not, however, achieve high definition because of limits on the number of lines it could scan and on the amount of light that could get through the scanning holes.

Historically, the transition from the mechanical to the electronic era of television technology begins in 1923, when Vladimir Zworykin applied for his first patent on the iconoscope, an all-electric television tube. Zworykin worked at that time for Westinghouse; he eventually went to RCA. A dozen years elapsed before the iconoscope came out of the laboratory. In the meantime, hopes for the mechanical system reached their peak in the late 1920's. C. F. Jenkins, who made the first successful public demonstration of mechanically-scanned television, started a company to exploit his system commercially in 1930. But mechanical scansion proved not good enough, and Jenkins' premature efforts failed.

H. E. Ives, of AT&T's research laboratories, was responsible for pioneer work on a complete electronic television system in the 1920's. He was primarily interested in the problem of wire transmission of pictures. Ives sent a closed-circuit television picture of Secretary of Commerce Herbert Hoover from Washington to New York in 1927 in a public demonstration, and in 1929 he succeeded in reproducing a color picture. These experiments were important as the background to the development of AT&T's

[2] Proposed by Commissioner Hyde in: Senate Committee on Interstate Commerce Subcommittee, Hearings on S. 3095, *Status of UHF and Multiple Ownership of TV Stations* (Washington: Government Printing Office, 1954), p. 124.

coaxial cable and microwave relay facilities, essential components of a national television system.[3]

The Radio Group — General Electric, Westinghouse, and RCA — also began research in television during the 1920's. In 1930 RCA took over the research project from the others. Two individual inventors not connected with the major research laboratories also made important contributions — Philo Farnsworth and Allen B. Dumont. Farnsworth's inventions were so important that they blocked RCA's efforts to obtain patents on a completely independent system. The patent struggle of earlier radio days was revived. When Farnsworth won a longstanding patent suit against RCA in 1941, the contenders compromised by making a cross-licensing agreement.

Dumont had early experience in radio and television research through association with Westinghouse and de Forest as a specialist in vacuum tube design. In 1931 he went into business for himself in the manufacture of the oscilloscope (cathode-ray) tube, which is essentially similar to the television receiving tube, and is a basic tool of electronic research. The demand for these tubes increased rapidly during the 1930's, and Dumont was in a position to capitalize on the television market when it finally opened up in the 1940's. In fact, Dumont marketed the first home television receiver in 1939.[4]

Central among the many difficult technological problems which television presented in these formative years was the problem of getting a sufficiently high-definition picture to take television out of the curiosity class and make it a satisfactory medium of communication. The demonstrations of the 1920's all used very crude pictures of less than a hundred lines. During the 1930's the number of lines increased steadily; by the end of the decade 441-line pictures were being used with reasonably good results. Regular telecasting is regarded as having started at this point, with NBC's experimental station W2XBS, in 1939. In that year television was first seen by large numbers of the public at the New York World's Fair, and Dumont marketed the first home television receivers.

THE DEVELOPMENT OF TV STANDARDS

As far back as 1928 the FRC had made provision for experimental "picture broadcasting."[5] Not until 1940, however, was the FCC ready to hold

[3] In the period 1925-1935 AT&T spent over $2,000,000 in laboratory research on television and coaxial cables — a substantial investment, though representing only about 4 per cent of AT&T's total research bill for the period. FCC, *Investigation of the Telephone Industry in the United States* (Washington: Government Printing Office, 1939), p. 199.

[4] Dumont is remarkable for being "one of the very few inventors in the annals of American industry who have made more money from their inventions than anyone else has." Significantly, however, he had to sell a half interest in the Dumont Laboratories to Paramount Pictures in 1938 in order to finance expansion of the firm. Cf.: Robert Rice, "The Prudent Pioneer," *New Yorker* (27 January 1951), pp. 35-49.

[5] FRC, *Third Annual Report* (Washington: Government Printing Office, 1929), pp. 55-56.

hearings on proposals for the adoption of television standards looking toward full-scale commercial exploitation of the medium. The industry, through the Radio Manufacturers Association (RMA), proposed a 441-line picture at 30 frames per second, utilizing six-megacycle channels. But the companies chiefly concerned — RCA, CBS, Dumont, Zenith, and Philco — were by no means unanimously behind the RMA recommendations. RCA, with the biggest investment in research, was naturally anxious to start capitalizing on its premier patent position as soon as possible. The other companies were less eager. In view of the industry's lack of agreement, the FCC was unwilling to adopt the RMA standards; instead, it tried to compromise by permitting *limited* commercial operation for the sake of further experimentation and field testing, without the adoption of uniform standards.[6] These new rules, scheduled to go into effect September 1, were announced by the FCC at the end of February, 1940. They would have permitted at least three different and incompatible systems to operate — those proposed by RCA (the RMA standards), Philco, and Dumont.

RCA immediately began an all-out sales campaign to sell TV receivers. This was precisely what the FCC had tried to avoid in its compromise on "limited" commercial operation. The Commission had hoped that the manufacturers would proceed slowly, without attempting to develop the mass market for receivers before universal standards could be agreed upon. Television had been so long delayed and so heavily publicized that vigorous sales campaigns at this time could have eventually resulted in strong pressure to adopt the system used by that company which succeeded in selling the most sets.

The FCC acted decisively. On May 22 it withdrew the February decision and called a new hearing. This reversal put the Commission in a very bad light. Most people had no adequate idea of the magnitude of the problem and of the dangers inherent in freezing the standards at too low a level. To many the Commission's action seemed not only capricious but an attack on free enterprise. A Congressional investigation of the Commission ensued.[7]

To appreciate the pressures at work in this situation, we must recollect that millions of dollars had already been spent on research on electronic television systems — not to speak of the money that had gone into mechanical systems. RCA alone, in the years 1930-1939, had spent at least nine million.[8] Many more millions would have to be spent before stations, net-

---

[6] Many experimental television licenses had been issued before this, but experimental stations could not sell time; their purpose was to experiment with engineering rather than programming. Extensive development of programming necessarily had to wait until time could be sold commercially; by the same token, mass marketing of sets had to wait for development of programming. By "limited" commercial operation the FCC intended to open the door to experimentation in programming as well as in engineering.

[7] Senate Committee on Interstate Commerce, *Hearings on S. Res. 251, Development of Television* (Washington: Government Printing Office, 1940).

[8] W. Rupert Maclaurin, *Invention and Innovation in the Radio Industry* (New York: The Macmillan Co., 1949), p. 206.

works, and manufacturing facilities could be developed to the point where a profit would be made.

To eliminate the possibility that the standards might be influenced by one manufacturer more than another, a new industry-wide committee of engineers, the National Television System Committee (NTSC), was set up to recommend standards. By March, 1941, the NTSC was ready with a new proposal, and finally, in May, 1941, the FCC authorized full commercial operation on these standards on eighteen VHF channels, located between 50 and 294 mc.[9] The NTSC had changed the line-standard from 441 to 525, adopted FM rather than AM for the audio component of the signal, and left three different synchronizing methods to compete (RCA's finally won out). CBS pressed for the adoption of color television standards, but the NTSC believed that not enough was yet known about this art to adopt standards at that time.

Monochrome television standards as we know them today in the United States date from this FCC decision of 1941. After all the long years of research and experimentation, and after many false starts, television seemed at last ready to come into its own. But the end of delays had not come yet. Before manufacturers could tool up for mass production, and before new stations could be built and put into operation, the United States entered World War II. On April 22, 1942, all production on such civilian goods as radio and television sets came to a halt. Only six pioneer stations operated during the war years,[10] with only about 10,000 receivers in use.

THE COLOR CONTROVERSY

Nor did the resumption of licensing in 1945 lead to an immediate resumption of television activity. The postwar shortage of materials made it impossible to build stations or manufacture sets immediately. Before the shortages had been overcome, CBS once more raised the issue of color. During the war a great deal had been learned about the hitherto little-known possibilities of the Ultra High Frequency (300-3,000 mc.) band. Previously the upper limit of the usable radio spectrum had been considered to be at 300 megacycles; by the end of the war the limit had been extended to 30,000 megacycles. This encouraged CBS to contend that television should move into a higher frequency range, where there would be room for the wide channels presumably needed for color. Since the two systems — existing monochrome and proposed CBS color — were incompatible, a choice between them would ultimately have to be made. In the meantime manufacturers and potential station licensees, unwilling to risk betting on the wrong horse, preferred to wait for clarification of the issue. When the

[9] The number of channels was reduced to 13 in 1945.
[10] These included two network-owned stations, WNBT (NBC) and WCBS-TV (CBS), in New York; and two manufacturer-owned stations, WPTZ (Philco) in Philadelphia and WRGB (General Electric) in Schenectady.

war ended 158 applications for stations were on file, but half of them were withdrawn in view of this confused outlook.

CBS beat the drum for color with well-publicized demonstrations all through the spring and summer of 1946, and in September it petitioned the FCC to authorize commercial operation on the CBS color system in the UHF band. Hearings started in December. On March 18, 1947, the FCC gave its verdict: CBS color was not deemed ready for commercial use, and the monochrome standards were reaffirmed. Once more television was given the go-ahead.

By this time conditions were more favorable. The image-orthicon camera tube, introduced in 1945, had vastly improved the potentialities of the medium for live pickup; coaxial cables had been developed and installed; wartime shortages were about to end. During the summer and fall of 1947 the first television gold rush began.

1948: THE TURNING POINT

Thus 1948 became a crucial year in the history of television — the year in which it emerged as a mass medium. For the first time the expansion of the industry could go ahead on firm technical and economic grounds. During 1948 the number of stations on the air increased from 17 to 41, the number of cities served from 8 to 23. Set production increased more than 500 per cent over 1947 (Figure 23), the audience more than 4,000 per cent (Figure 22). Network relay facilities became available in the midwest as well as on the east coast. All four networks began regular service, and important advertisers began to try the new medium. Large-scale programming began — the national political conventions, Milton Berle's *Texaco Star Theatre*, Ed Sullivan's *Toast of the Town*, a telecast of the Metropolitan Opera.

Simultaneously with this explosive growth of television came the beginning of the decline of radio. Radio set production fell off after the postwar peak of 1947 (Figure 22). Radio broadcast earnings also reached a peak in 1947 which was never reached again (Figure 32). To be sure, radio did not go into the fatal decline which was freely predicted for it at the time; but 1948 was the pivotal year in which radio began to feel the impact of television and turn the corner into a new future.

THE FREEZE

Fortunately for the radio broadcast medium, however, the full impact of television was not to be felt for several more years. By the fall of 1948 the FCC became increasingly aware of the facts that (1) the current allocation plan, adopted before a great deal was known about VHF propagation characteristics, was resulting in interference between stations and (2) the

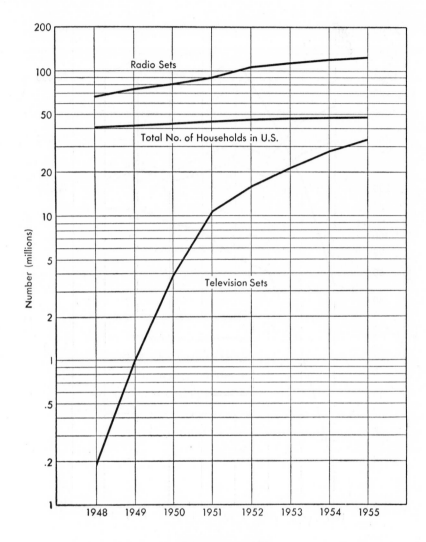

Figure 22

Rate of Growth of Broadcast Audience Since 1948
(Number of Sets in Use)

The radio audience has continued to grow, despite the rise of television. The curve for the number of U.S. households reveals the degree of saturation reached by each medium.

Sources: TV data, NBC estimates reported in *Television Factbook*, No. 21 (Fall-Winter 1955), p. 239; radio data, *Broadcasting-Telecasting*, *1955 Broadcasting Yearbook — Marketbook Issue*, p. 58; U.S. household data, Bureau of Census reports.

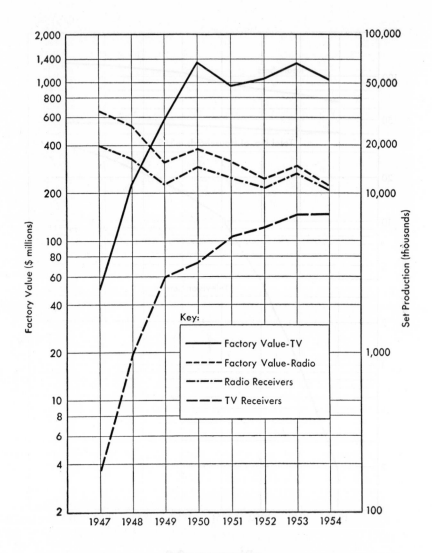

Figure 23

Rate of Broadcast Receiver Production Since 1947

The curves for radio are closer together than those for TV, because of the lower unit cost of radio receivers. The trend toward low-cost table models has caused the radio price and quantity curves to grow even closer together in recent years.

Source: *Television Factbook No. 21* (Fall-Winter, 1955), pp. 426-427.

PLATE IX

Large-screen TV receiver using mechanical scanning, designed by Bell Telephone Laboratories (1927). Left: Rear view, showing electric-motor-driven contact arm which sweeps over contacts leading to 2,500 wires connected to as many picture elements. Right: Viewing face of the "screen," with its grid of 2,500 lights, arranged in 50 lines (see p. 154) *All photos courtesy of Bell Telephone Laboratories*

Scanning-disc receiving apparatus of 1927. The wheel contains fifty spirally-placed apertures which scan the field with as many lines with each revolution. Note small size of image area as compared with size of scanning wheel (see p. 154)

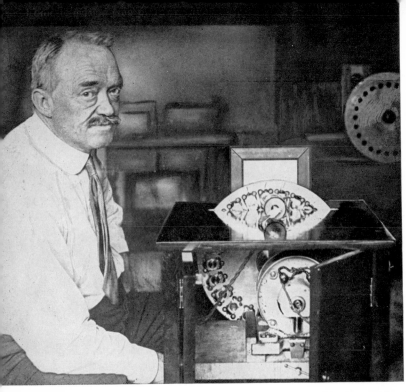

Charles Jenkins with the mechanical scanning-disc re
ceiver which he attempted to market in 1925 (see p. 154

PLATE X

Vladimir Zworykin and his iconoscope tube, the key invention
which opened the door to electronic television (see p. 154) *RCA*

PLATE XI

60 Scanning Lines

120 Scanning Lines

180 Scanning Lines

240 Scanning Lines

Improvement of definition with increase in the number of scanning lines (see p. 155)   *NBC*

PLATE XII

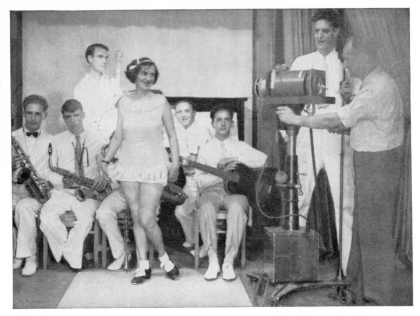

Farnsworth TV camera used in experimental productions in 1935 (see p. 155)   *International News Photo*

David Sarnoff at the 1939 World's Fair demonstration of electronic TV which approached modern standards (see p. 155)   *RCA*

12 channels then allocated to television[11] were going to be entirely inadequate to take care of the demand for stations. Furthermore, the color question which had beclouded the issue all along became more and more pressing as the technology of the medium progressed. Realizing that the existing rules were inadequate, the FCC suspended all pending applications on September 29, 1948. This was the start of the famous "freeze." It permitted already-authorized stations to go ahead with construction but froze all other applications. The result was that for nearly four years, until the end of the freeze on June 1, 1952, the maximum number of stations allowed to operate was arbitrarily limited to the 108 which had received authorization before October, 1948. Nevertheless, during this period television continued to expand phenomenally. The number of sets in use rose from a quarter of a million to fifteen million. After initial heavy losses, television broadcasters began to earn back their investment rapidly in 1951 (Figure 32, p. 269). The coaxial cable and microwave network joined the east coast to the west coast in 1951, thus inaugurating national network service.

Meanwhile, the FCC had been holding a long series of hearings to settle the engineering and policy questions which had precipitated the freeze. The long-awaited decision came April 14, 1952, with the FCC's historic *Sixth Report and Order.*[12] The new rules provided for 82 channels — 70 UHF channels in addition to the 12 VHF channels then currently in use by the freeze stations. The VHF channels retained the numbers 2-13; the new UHF channels became numbers 14-83. A table of 2,053 assignments awarded one or more channels to 1,291 communities, over 66 per cent being UHF assignments. About 10 per cent (242 assignments) were reserved for noncommercial educational use, some in the UHF band and some in the VHF band. Tremendous pressure for new stations had been built up during the freeze. Within less than a year all outstanding uncontested applications had been granted, and then the long-drawn-out process of deciding among competing applicants began. The number of stations authorized more than tripled in the first post-freeze year (Figure 20).

THE TWO COLOR DECISIONS

Meanwhile, after extensive comparative tests of the rival color systems, the FCC had adopted the CBS standards, effective November 20, 1950. This

[11] The 18 original VHF channels had been decreased to 13 by the FCC, effective early in 1946, as follows:

Channel	Frequency
1	44-50 mc.
2-4	54-72 mc.
5-6	76-88 mc.
7-13	174-216 mc.

Channel 1 was deleted August 14, 1947, but the old numbering system has been retained.

[12] Cf.: FCC, *In the Matters of Amendment of* § 3.606 *of the Commission's Rules and Regulations, Docket Nos. 8736 and 8975 . . .,* 17 *Fed. Register* 3905 (2 May 1952).

is one of the least comprehensible of the FCC's major decisions. True, the CBS system appears to have been capable of producing a slightly better color picture than its chief rival, the RCA system, at the time of the hearings. But the CBS color system had two defects which in the long run seemed fatal. First, it depended upon a mechanical device for constructing the color signal — a rotating color wheel, which exposed the pickup tube to the primary colors in sequence, field by field. In principle, any mechanical operation in a television system is a weakness; the great progress of monochrome television dated from the time when it became an all-electronic operation and mechanical devices could be abandoned. Second, the CBS system was not compatible with existing monochrome standards; therefore it implied the necessity of two separate systems, with their separate transmitters and receivers, existing side by side. One can only guess that the FCC, which was under strong pressure from Congress to "do something" about color, calculated that it could relieve the pressure by approving the CBS system, counting on the defects of the system to prove its own undoing.

Whether by the FCC's intention or not, that is substantially what happened. The industry generally looked askance at the risk of tooling up for a color system which might eventually go into the discard. CBS itself was in a difficult position. For a decade it had been urging adoption of its color system; now it had won at last, would the triumph turn out to be a Pyrrhic victory? "It would be difficult to find a more negative triumph — a championship dive with no water in the pool."[13] Conveniently, however, CBS was saved from the necessity of facing the final test of its color system in the market. First, RCA filed suit against adoption of the new FCC color rules. This delayed matters until the case reached the Supreme Court, which upheld the FCC on May 28, 1951, some six months after the original decision by the FCC.[14] Next, CBS and other manufacturers were asked by the Office of Defense Mobilization to suspend the manufacture of color receivers and equipment during the Korean war emergency.

During these delays a National Television System Committee went to work on an alternative proposal closer to the compatible, all-electronic system advocated by RCA and others. By the middle of 1953 the NTSC was ready to petition the FCC to reconsider color standards designed to meet these criteria. RCA, General Electric, Philco, Sylvania, Motorola, and eventually even CBS supported the NTSC proposals. Finally, on December 17, 1953, the FCC adopted new rules for color television based on the NTSC standards.[15] CBS had lost the battle, but in a sense it had won the war. At a crucial stage in TV development it had won time to prepare itself

---

[13] "CBS Steals the Show," *Fortune* (July, 1953), p. 164. © Time Inc.

[14] *RCA v. U.S.*, 341 U.S. 412.

[15] FCC, *In the Matter of Amendment of the Commission's Rules Governing Color Television Transmissions*, Docket No. 10637, 18 *Fed. Register* 8649 (23 December 1953).

for television competition with RCA and NBC in the manufacturing as well as in the network field.

NETWORK RIVALRIES

In 1951 CBS had bought Hytron, an old and established electronic manufacturing concern, for about twenty million dollars. This was CBS's entry into the manufacturing field, in which it immediately became a major competitor — though by no means in the same class as the old Radio Group (Table 6). In the same year the network was organized into six divisions: CBS Radio, CBS Television, Columbia Records, CBS-Hytron, CBS-Colum-

Table 6

Leading Manufacturers of Broadcast Receivers

Company	1954 Sales ($ millions)
General Electric Co.	2,959
Westinghouse Electric Corp.	1,631
Radio Corporation of America	941
Bendix Aviation Corp.	608
Avco Mfg. Corp. (Crosley)	375
Columbia Broadcasting System, Inc.	373
Philco Corp.	349
Sylvania Electric Products, Inc.	282
Admiral Corp.	219
Motorola, Inc.	205
Zenith Radio Corp.	139

Note: These are sales figures for all products; these firms all manufacture items other than receivers. (Source: *Television Factbook No. 21* [Fall-Winter, 1955], pp. 380-389.)

bia (sales and administration), and CBS Laboratories. One initial weakness of CBS in the television broadcasting field was its failure early to secure the maximum permissible number of owned stations, as NBC had done. This weakness was partially corrected in 1953, when the ABC–Paramount Theatres merger took place. The merger would have given the new company two television stations in Chicago, in violation of the FCC rule against duopoly. Paramount sold WBKB, one of the pioneer television stations, to CBS, thereby giving that network a coveted owned-and-operated station in another of the most important markets.

By 1953 the CBS networks were leading NBC in both radio and television, and the struggle for supremacy was becoming more vigorous. The two networks banked on differing concepts of television programming. The CBS trend was along traditional lines — big sponsors, big programs, regular scheduling. NBC, fearing that the traditional radio concept did not fit the economics of television, placed emphasis on (1) the "magazine concept" — multiple sponsorship of big programs like the highly successful and precedent-breaking morning show *Today* and (2) "spectaculars" — huge expensive programs scheduled periodically, temporarily displacing regularly scheduled programs.[16] In both the CBS and NBC plans a significant new note was the great extent to which the networks planned to control their own programming; the advertising agencies were not to be allowed to move in on television network programming to the same extent that they had moved in on radio network programming.

Mutual had not followed the other three radio chains into network television. A very weak fourth position in television was taken by a new television-only network built up by Dumont. In 1955 Dumont finally gave up the struggle to compete as a full-scale network. ABC, since 1953 a division of American Broadcasting–Paramount Theatres (AB-PT), continued in its third-place position (Figure 24).

THE PROBLEM OF TV RELAY FACILITIES

Network competition, however, had not encountered "normal" conditions, even with the end of the freeze and the final decision on color. Normal network competition, as it had evolved in radio, means a separate affiliate for each network in each important market. This condition cannot be met as long as (1) the number of stations in each market is limited to less than the number of national networks and (2) the number of relay channels available from AT&T is insufficient to provide each affiliate with separate programs from their several networks simultaneously in each market.

During the freeze, when the number of stations was arbitrarily limited, there were only four markets in the whole country in which each network could claim a separate affiliate. Elsewhere each station released programs of two, three, and often of all four networks. Hence each network could claim about the same number of affiliates. This claim was relatively meaningless, however, because the number of stations actually releasing a given network's programs at any given hour is dependent on a number of factors, among them the availability of network interconnection facilities, sponsors' coverage desires, the prestige and importance of the program, and the audience of the station (Table 13). In point of fact, Dumont and ABC had a desperate time assembling enough stations (aside from their owned-and-operated stations) to carry any but their most desirable prestige programs. Many programs on these theoretically national networks were carried by as few as half a dozen stations.

The availability of intercity relay facilities has lagged behind demand because of the enormous expense of coaxial cable and microwave installa-

---

[16] Cf.: Richard A. Smith, "TV: The Coming Showdown," *Fortune* (September, 1954), pp. 138-139, 164. The pioneer spectacular was the Ford 50th Anniversary Show in June, 1953.

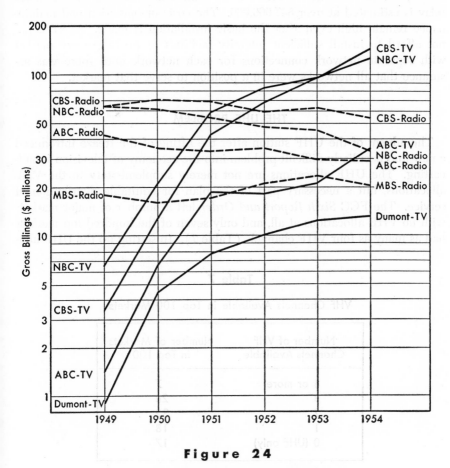

Gross Billings ($ millions)

CBS-TV
NBC-TV

CBS-Radio
NBC-Radio

ABC-Radio

CBS-Radio

ABC-TV
NBC-Radio
ABC-Radio

MBS-Radio

MBS-Radio

Dumont-TV

NBC-TV

CBS-TV

ABC-TV

Dumont-TV

1949   1950   1951   1952   1953   1954

Figure 24

Rate of Change in Gross Billings of Radio and TV Networks Since 1949

Note that CBS passed NBC in radio in 1949 and in TV in 1953 and that their TV billings did not exceed their radio billings until 1952.

Gross billings are computed at one-time rates and represent much more than the actual revenue received. They are considered valuable for purposes of comparison, however.

Based on: *Television Factbook No. 21* (Fall-Winter, 1955), p. 32 (from Publishers' Information Bureau data).

tions, the time it takes for installation, and the lack of stations to support the cost of the facilities.[17] The cost of completing the first coast-to-coast relay is estimated at over $37,000,000. The costs of operation and maintenance remain high even after the basic installation is made. AT&T could not afford to install sufficient intercity facilities to provide every market with separate network connections for each network until there was assurance that all networks were in a position to serve that market.

THE UHF PROBLEM

The advent of the UHF station after the lifting of the freeze introduced a new and peculiarly difficult problem into the economy of television broadcasting. The UHF allocations are not merely supplementary to the VHF allocations, but a necessary part of the plan for equitable distribution of service. The FCC *Sixth Report and Order* left a number of major markets with no VHF allocations at all, and only seven of the hundred top markets had as many as four VHF channels (Table 7). In setting up the UHF allo-

Table 7

VHF Channels Available in Top 100 Markets

Number of VHF Channels Available	Number of Markets in Top 100
4 or more	7
3	26
2	32
1	18
0 (UHF only)	17

Source: Harry M. Plotkin, *Television Network Regulation and the UHF Problem* (Memorandum prepared for the Senate Committee on Interstate and Foreign Commerce) (Washington: Government Printing Office, 1955), p. 6.

cations the FCC established rules about power and antenna height that were intended to give both UHF and VHF stations essential equality of coverage. In theory stations on higher frequencies would be enabled to compensate for the shorter range of those frequencies by using higher towers and higher power than stations on the more favorable lower frequencies. These rules initially failed of their purpose because the technology for the use of very high power at UHF frequencies had not yet been

[17] The economy of intercity relays is based on the fact that the more stations a network uses on a given relay route, the less the cost of reaching each station. The longer the jump between stations, the higher the per-station cost for network interconnection.

developed. The result is that the first[18] UHF stations began at a decided disadvantage. Not only were there no receivers in the hands of the public capable of tuning to the UHF band, but also the UHF transmitters were unable to get as wide a coverage as their VHF rivals. This made UHF stations in markets already reached by VHF service an undesirable buy from the sponsors' point of view and hence not attractive as prospective network affiliates. Lacking the attraction of high-prestige network programs, UHF stations had little to induce viewers to buy UHF converters. This in turn meant that they had little to offer local advertisers as compared with competitive network-affiliated stations.[19]

To make matters worse, the commercial possibilities of television stations as an investment had been so exaggerated by the artificial competitive situation that obtained during the freeze that many over-eager applicants rushed into UHF without realistically appraising the risks involved. As a result, UHF stations as a group lost fortunes instead of making them (Table 8) — chiefly owing to miscalculation of risks, inept management, and poor local programming. Still unwilling to face the facts, however, some UHF licensees

Table 8

Comparative Financial Status of 266 Post-Freeze VHF and UHF Television Stations

	Number of TV Stations		
	VHF	UHF	total
Reporting profit (January-October, 1955)	52	18	70
Reporting loss	91	73	164
Ceased operations by June 4, 1955	1	31	32
Total	144	122	266

Source: FCC, "Third Survey of Post-Freeze TV Stations" (August 19, 1955, mimeo.).

cast about for a scapegoat — the FCC, the networks, the VHF stations, AT&T. Ironically, after all the years in which the profitable radio industry

[18] The pioneer commercial UHF station was KPTV, which went on the air as the first station in Portland, Oregon, in September, 1952. No UHF transmitters were yet available from manufacturers at the time; KPTV purchased the experimental transmitter with which RCA had been developing UHF since 1949 at KC2XAK in Bridgeport, Connecticut.

[19] Cf.: Harry M. Plotkin (Memorandum prepared for the Senate Committee on Interstate and Foreign Commerce), *Television Network Regulation and the UHF Problem* (Washington: Government Printing Office, 1955).

had been castigating the FCC for interfering with the business of broad-casters, the unprofitable UHF television stations now begged for government intervention to pull their chestnuts out of the fire.

These circumstances combined to undermine the allocation plan of the FCC's *Sixth Report and Order,* which had not contemplated creating VHF stations as a favored group, with UHF stations occupying a secondary status. Late in 1955 the FCC turned down individual petitions from several markets for local "de-intermixture" — i.e., for making each market either all-UHF or all-VHF so that stations could compete on a basis of relative equality in their own areas. Instead, the FCC decided that the whole allo-cation plan would have to be reviewed once more.

Among the methods suggested for alleviating the UHF-VHF problem are (1) de-intermixture on a national scale and (2) deletion of VHF channels altogether, leaving television broadcasting to UHF channels only and at the same time encouraging the production of all-channel receivers. Any solution poses tremendously difficult problems because so many broadcasters and set-owners now have a vested interest in maintaining the *status quo.* De-intermixture can work ideally only in isolated markets, where signals from powerful VHF stations in neighboring markets cannot compete. If all new sets had to be equipped for UHF reception without extra cost, it might be possible in time to convert all the VHF channels to UHF without prohibitive expense to the public; even so, this would mean the loss of service to fringe areas now reached by VHF stations — and, of course, the cost of conversion (not to speak of the loss of competitive advantage) would place a con-siderable burden on the VHF licensees.

In the long run, it appears, a choice may have to be made between two different ideal concepts of the television broadcasting service. One is the ideal of maximum competition at the local level, which calls for as many stations as the economy can support, with provision for adding more sta-tions in growth-areas. The other ideal calls for fewer but larger primary stations, with less competition on the local level but a high quality of service from stations of regional scope. So far, the economy of the television in-dustry seems better suited to the latter approach (see p. 186). The ideal of maximum competition at the local level has worked out reasonably well for radio; however, because of the differences in the economic character of the two services, it may have been a mistake to use radio broadcasting too literally as the analogue of television. The allocation of over 2,000 channels for the television service in the *Sixth Report and Order* seems to have un-necessarily complicated the allocation plan, since it is estimated that the economy can support a maximum of only about 600 stations at the present time.[20]

[20] CBS, "How Many Stations Can the United States Support Economically?" (5 Octo-ber 1955, mimeo.).

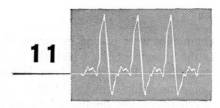

11

Some Inter-Media Relationships

In many ways broadcasting has assumed a pivotal position at which the currents of inter-media competition tend to intersect. As an advertising-supported medium with both local and national coverage, broadcasting competes directly with the newspaper and the popular magazine (Fig. 25). On the other hand, as a primarily entertainment medium, it also competes directly with the motion-picture industry. Yet broadcasting makes considerable use of the basic content material of all three of these competing media. Taking still another point of view, technologically radio contributed to the development of sound pictures, while pictures in turn contributed to the technological development of television.

Historically, the relationship between broadcasting and the competing media has been conditioned by the fact that it was the last to develop. To start with, the older media regarded radio (and later television) with condescension as upstarts and interlopers. An example is the cavalier treatment of radio by the press over the issue of news broadcasting (Chapter 9). Another is the smugness which led the motion-picture industry completely to misjudge the potentialities of television.

Having failed to dispose of broadcasting by ignoring it or making jokes about it, the older media have moved into the second stage, adopting the "if you can't lick 'em, join 'em" tactic. Carried to its extreme, this could result in the domination of broadcasting by the press and motion-picture interests through control of strategic necessities such as talent supply, networks and other agencies of syndication, programs, and key stations. Of the two, the motion-picture industry, a naturally monopoly-prone business, perhaps offers the more serious threat to the independence of broadcasting.

RADIO TECHNOLOGY AND SOUND FILM

An interesting parallelism exists between both the technical and the economic histories of the entertainment-film and broadcasting industries. Like broadcasting, the cinema was founded on technological improvements so numerous that no single company could control a complete system. In 1908 patents controlled by the Edison, Biograph, Essanay, and Vitagraph

companies were pooled by means of a cross-licensing agreement analogous
to the agreements by which the communication companies broke a similar
stalemate a dozen years later (Chapter 7). The Motion Picture Patents
Company, which emerged with a monopoly on film technology as a result
of cross-licensing, dominated the industry until 1915. Patents again became
a crucial battleground with the introduction of sound in 1927. At this point

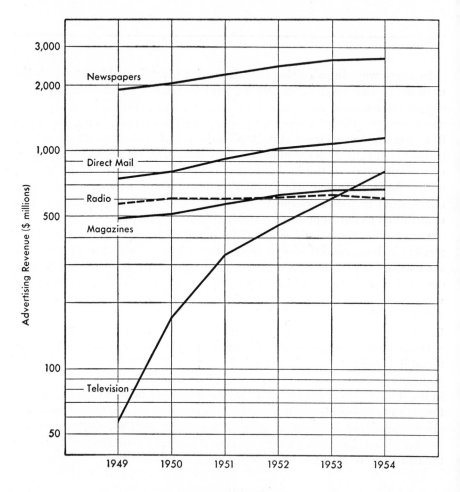

Figure 25

Comparative Growth Rate of TV Advertising Since 1949

Television exceeded both magazines and radio by 1954. Note,
however, that the competing media do not show a sharp decline,
despite the rapid rise of television.

Source: *Television Factbook No. 21* (Fall-Winter, 1955), p. 22.

the former radio rivals, AT&T and RCA, found themselves once more deeply involved in a battle for a new market.

Sound had been combined with pictures as early as the Edison experiments of the 1890's. But, as in the case of radiotelephony, commercial development of sound had to await the advent of the vacuum-tube amplifier. Significantly, Lee de Forest himself turned from radio to the new field of sound-on-film, and by 1924 was able to demonstrate publicly his "Phonofilm" method.[1] This preceded by four years the marketing of Western Electric's sound system, and was, moreover, a bona-fide sound-on-film system, whereas Western Electric at first depended on disc recordings. De Forest, however, was unable to persuade the motion-picture interests to risk money for commercial development of his invention. The habit of silence was hard to break: "What stone walls of indifference, stupidity, and solid negativity did we unearth among the dead bones and concrete skulls of motion picture 'magnates'!"[2] Despite many successful demonstrations of his system, de Forest failed to acquire the necessary capital in time to forestall AT&T and RCA.

In 1926 the former set up a subsidiary through Western Electric, Electrical Research Products, Incorporated (ERPI), with a working capital of forty million dollars. ERPI's primary purpose was to exploit Western Electric's sound system in the motion-picture field. By 1928, after a year's moratorium while the rival sound systems were investigated, all the major film producers had accepted licenses from ERPI. The license terms were calculated to freeze out competition: films made with WE recording equipment could be projected only on WE equipment; WE equipment could be serviced only by WE representatives; a double royalty had to be paid by WE licensees to project films made with non-WE equipment. In addition to leasing and maintaining the recording and projection equipment and collecting royalties on the use of sound film, ERPI cultivated the market for these services by lending financial assistance, through several subsidiaries, to film producers. In this way AT&T found itself once more in show business, a reminder of the WEAF days. In 1937 a court held that the restrictive provisions of the ERPI licenses, though not at first illegal, later became unlawful when competitive sound equipment was available.[3] In the meantime, however, ERPI had modified its practices under the threat of suit from RCA.[4]

AT&T's attempt to gain exclusive control of sound in the film industry was particularly galling to RCA, for part of AT&T's patent resources in the

[1] Lee de Forest, *Father of Radio* (Chicago: Wilcox & Follett Co., 1950), p. 392. De Forest registered 79 patents connected with sound-on-film.

[2] *Ibid.*, p. 370.

[3] *General Talking Pictures Corp.* v. *AT&T*, 18 F. Supp. 650 (1937).

[4] The rather involved history of ERPI's maneuvers in the early days of sound films is traced in: FCC, *Investigation of the Telephone Industry in the United States* (Washington: Government Printing Office, 1939), pp. 401-415. The contemporary successor to ERPI is Westrex Corporation.

field derived from the existing cross-licensing agreements between the two companies. In order to assure an outlet for its own products, RCA began purchasing motion-picture company stock in 1927, and by 1932 it held a controlling interest in Radio-Keith-Orpheum (RKO). RKO had an interest in about 150 concerns involved in motion-picture production, distribution, and exhibition. A few years later, after acquiring an assured place in the film-sound business, RCA sold its interest in RKO.[5]

Meanwhile, in 1928, RCA Photophone, Inc., had been set up by RCA to compete with ERPI. The latter captured an early lead, with installations in 90 per cent of the sound-equipped theatres by the end of 1928. The next year, as the number of theatres capable of exhibiting the new "talkies" rapidly increased, the extent of ERPI's lead fell off sharply. By 1936 resistance to ERPI's highly restrictive contracts had grown to a point where suits amounting to $175,000,000 had accumulated against the company. But ERPI had already begun to relax its contracts under pressure from RCA, and very little in damages was actually collected. Thereafter RCA and AT&T learned to live side by side competitively in this new field.

THE ORGANIZATION OF THE FILM INDUSTRY

Although the introduction of sound in 1927 caused a major upheaval and readjustment in the motion picture industry, the basic pattern of the industry had already been set by 1920, the time broadcasting began. Even in the nickelodeon days of the early 1900's it became obvious that the way to make money in motion pictures was (1) to syndicate the product, and (2) to combine theatres into chains. Syndication in this medium is even more essential than in other mass media. Local production analogous to local live broadcast programming or local news coverage is impossible in the motion-picture field because of the irreducibly high cost of picture production. Entertainment-film production facilities are highly centralized both physically and economically, the aggregate output is relatively small (Table 9), and the risks are considerable. Intervening between the producer and the exhibitor is the distributor. As the middleman he can exert great pressure on both producer and exhibitor. In order to gain economic efficiency and the strength to bargain effectively with the producer and distributor, the exhibitor tends to build up chains of theatres.

Since entertainment films are not a standardized product, the value of the producer's output is not highly predictable. For every hit film which brings in a tremendous profit there may be many mediocre successes and outright failures. In order to iron out the violent fluctuations in the value of the product, film producers and distributors early resorted to the practice of "block booking." This obliged the exhibitor to rent unproduced films in groups, sight unseen. The exhibitor thus found himself involuntarily

[5] FCC, *Report on Chain Broadcasting* (Washington: Government Printing Office, 1941), pp. 13-14.

Table 9

Feature Output of the Motion Picture Industry, Selected Years

Year	Number of Features	Estimated Production Costs	
		Total ($ thousands)	Per Picture ($ thousands)
1952	324	291,600	900
1948	366	376,336	1,028
1945	350	194,035	554
1942	588	197,921	337
1939	483	149,000	342

Source: Standard & Poor's *Industry Surveys*, March 3, 1955, "Motion Pictures," based on *Film Daily Yearbook* estimates.

saddled with a number of second-rate and third-rate releases. Another means of ironing out the erratic economy of motion-picture production is to combine the production, distribution, and exhibition functions under one economic unit. The producer then has an assured outlet for his product, and the risks of production can be offset by the relative stability of theatre income.

The practice of combining the production-distribution function with the exhibition function, together with block-booking and related restrictive distribution practices, have long been sources of contention within the industry. Antitrust suits dragged out for a decade before a Supreme Court decision in 1948 modified all these practices.[6] One result has been the "divorcement" of the leading companies, known as "The Big Five," by means of consent decrees. In 1950 Paramount Pictures, Inc., was dissolved to form Paramount Pictures Corporation (production and distribution) and United Paramount Theatres (exhibition). In 1950 Radio-Keith-Orpheum (RKO) became RKO Pictures and RKO Theatres, and the next year 20th-Century Fox's 385 theatres were transferred to a new company, National Theatres. In 1953 Warner Brothers became Warner Brothers Pictures and Stanley Warner Corporation (340 theatres). The last of the Big Five to undergo divorcement was Loew's, Inc. (MGM).

THE IMPACT OF TV ON THE FILM INDUSTRY

During World War II and the immediate postwar years the motion picture industry climbed almost to its peak of the pre-depression period (Table 10). By 1948 the impact of television began to make itself felt. The Su-

6 *U.S.* v. *Paramount Pictures, Inc.*, 334 U.S. 131 (1948).

Table 10

Average Weekly Attendance at Motion-Picture Theatres Since 1935

Selected Years	Average Weekly Attendance (millions)
1953	50
1952	45
1951*	54
1950*	60
1945	98
1940	80
1935	75

* Total number of seats in open and closed theatres — not comparable with other years.

Source: Standard & Poor's, *Industry Surveys*, March 3, 1955, "Motion Pictures," based on data from *Film Daily Yearbook* and *Motion Picture and Television Almanac.*

preme Court decision of the same year against block booking was another blow, especially to poor motion pictures, which television also hurt most. In the next four years several thousand marginal theatres closed, box-office receipts fell off alarmingly, production budgets were cut, studios closed down, and the whole motion-picture industry boiled in a ferment of uncertainty and doubt.[7] A symbol of television's effect on motion pictures was the demise of the Embassy Newsreel Theatre in New York. Established in 1929, the first of its kind, the Embassy had capitalized on public interest in pictorial news, particularly sports news. Television's first programming success came from on-the-spot coverage of sports events, and the newsreel theatres felt the competition immediately. The Embassy abandoned its news and sports policy on its twentieth anniversary as a newsreel theatre, in November, 1949. It was the end of an era.

One Hollywood reaction to the devastating inroads of television was to dust off some very old film tricks, on the theory that the sheer mechanical superiority of film could beat television at its own game. This theory is in line with the traditional Hollywood notion that mere size and mechanical ingenuity outweigh every other consideration in appealing to the mass public. It ignores the fact that for years the movie industry had been jeopardizing its own future by concentrating on an audience of teen-agers. As audiences matured, they matured away from the movies as a source of

[7] Cf. "Movies: End of an Era," *Fortune* (April, 1949), pp. 99 ff.; Robert Coughlan, "Now It Is Trouble That Is Supercolossal in Hollywood," *Life* (13 August 1951), pp. 102-115. Contrast, however: Freeman Lincoln, "The Comeback of the Movies," *Fortune* (February, 1955), pp. 127-131, 155-158.

entertainment. Instead of telling stories for people, movies had "degenerated into telling myths for children."[8]

Certainly the first efforts at weaning audiences back to the theatres typified this point of view. "Three-D," the first of the "gimmicks," had a brief vogue starting in 1952. Three-D pictures were almost universally condemned for their content as pictures, but the novelty factor caused a sensation. Based on "a simple optical illusion whose principle was known to Euclid and whose practice put grandfather to sleep on Sunday afternoons,"[9] Three-D achieved the illusion of three dimensions by the use of polaroid glasses. The camera takes a double picture through two lenses separated like the two eyes of normal human vision. The two slightly overlapping pictures are separated for the viewer by polaroid glasses. Although the illusion is rather novel, the system is fundamentally impracticable.

However, the unexpected temporary success of Three-D despite the low quality of the pictures set the major studios searching frantically for more practical "gimmicks." The sense of depth in human vision does not depend exclusively on the factor of binocular vision. A one-eyed person does not lose all depth perception. In life a number of different types of "cues" contribute to the perception of the depth dimension.[10] Theoretically, several different cueing devices could be employed, singly or in combination, to secure the depth-illusion.

The most successful system is Cinerama, invented in 1938 by Fred Waller and developed during World War II as a gunnery training device. Cinerama provides a convincing — in fact startling — sense of depth without the use of glasses. It uses the cues provided by peripheral vision — that sense of surrounding objects which the eye normally has even when focussed on a particular object directly in the foreground. The ordinary 3 to 4 aspect ratio of television and motion pictures narrows the width of field down to only about a sixth of the eye's normal arc of vision. Cinerama restores a large part of the scene which is normally seen "out of the corner of the eye." These peripheral cues are provided by a very wide, deeply curved screen. Three synchronized projectors with three separate film strips are required to fill the screen, and the major mechanical defect of the system is the difficulty of blending the three pictures without betraying the fact that they are, indeed, three different pictures. Economically, Cinerama is limited by the fact that it takes a large theatre to seat a small audience;

---

[8] Gilbert Seldes, *The Great Audience* (New York: The Viking Press, 1950), p. 88. "The relationship between age and movie attendance is probably one of the most spectacular findings in the whole field of communication behavior . . . confirmed in every study of movie going." Paul F. Lazarsfeld and Patricia Kendall, *Radio Listening in America* (Copyright, 1948, by Prentice-Hall, Inc., New York), p. 11. Reprinted by permission of the publisher.

[9] *Time* (8 June 1953), p. 66.

[10] Cf. Thaddeus R. Murroughs, "Depth Perception with Special Reference to Motion Pictures," *Journal of the Society of Motion Picture and Television Engineers* LX (June, 1953), pp. 656-670.

few existing theatres have both the physical dimensions and the necessary audience-turnover potential.

CinemaScope, developed by 20th-Century Fox, is a compromise system adaptable to most theatres. It provides a wide, slightly curved screen filled with a single picture. Anamorphic lenses are used, first to squeeze an image with about a 3 to 8 aspect ratio down to the 3 to 4 ratio of normal film stock, then to spread the image out again for projection on a wide screen. There is little, if any, depth illusion in CinemaScope, but the wide field of view is impressive. Other wide-screen systems introduced to compete with CinemaScope include VistaVision (Paramount) and Todd-AO (MGM) The latter is the first of the new systems to change the basic 35-mm. film size; it uses double-width film and an aspect ratio of 2 to 1.[11] All the wide-screen systems employ multiple sound tracks to obtain sound perspective, i.e., the illusion that sound is coming from the appropriate sector of the field of view.

Technical improvements mean little, of course, if the basic content is not entertaining or artistically sound. Experience has shown that a simple "flat" black-and-white film can be just as entertaining as one incorporating all the newer gadgets. Even the pre-wide-screen 35-mm. films provide a picture scale and a degree of definition which television cannot duplicate; therefore the competitive value of the various wide-screen processes has been more in terms of ballyhoo than in terms of basic improvement of the film product.

HYBRID SYSTEMS

Another approach to the problem of recapturing the theatre audience from television is to bring television into the theatre. Several companies have developed equipment for the projection of television images on theatre-size screens, so that televised events can be incorporated into motion-picture programs or substituted for film programs on special occasions. The Louis-Savold championship fight was televised in nine theatres in seven cities in 1951, and the next year the Marciano-Walcott bout was seen on screens in fifty theatres in thirty-one cities. In 1953, however, the FCC somewhat dimmed the prospects of a really major development of theatre television by refusing to allocate special wide-frequency channels to this service for use in relaying programs. Instead, the FCC ruled, theatres must lease relay facilities from AT&T, just as the broadcast networks do. When confined to the six-megacycle channel standard of broadcasting, theatre television

[11] It is an ironic commentary on the attitude of exhibitors that many of them, after installing wide screens, made it a common practice to project ordinary 3 to 4 ratio films to fit the new screens. This can only be accomplished by blowing up the size of the projected picture to fit the screen width and masking off the overlapping top and bottom of the frame. Thus the highly-skilled, highly-paid Hollywood cameramen spend a great deal of ingenuity and money in carefully composing pictures for the 3 to 4 ratio only to have their artistry nullified by the callousness of exhibitors.

cannot, of course, secure the detail which is desirable for theatrical exhibition. Theatre television seems to have possibilities for permanent but limited use.[12] As an essentially hybrid form of entertainment — combining the disadvantages of both film and television without capitalizing fully on the advantages of either — theatre television gives no promise of affecting either medium profoundly.

A second hybrid medium has been proposed in the form of subscription home television. This proposal envisions keeping television's advantages as a home medium while at the same time retaining the economic advantage of motion pictures as a box-office medium. Several systems of subscription television have been proposed. All involve the transmission of a scrambled television picture by an otherwise normal television broadcast transmitter. The picture is unscrambled for the paying customer by any of several unscrambling devices at the home receiver. The subscriber pays a moderate fee per program.[13] The theory of subscription television is that a relatively small fee collected from a relatively small audience (as network television audiences go) would amount to a relatively huge sum of money — much more money than sponsors can normally afford to pay for programs. Subscription television could thus theoretically afford to provide outstanding entertainment, such as first-run feature films, Broadway plays, and major sports events. Proponents originally envisioned an advertising-free service, but later began to waver on this promise.

Subscription television offers more of a threat, as a rival medium, than theatre television. It has been described as "probably the most complex — and the most important — new issue confronting the authorities, because it must inevitably evolve into a new determination of our entire philosophy of broadcasting."[14] Yet subscription television is by no means as simple an answer as might appear at first glance. It leans heavily on the delusion that broadcasting is "free." The fact is, of course, that audiences invest huge amounts in sets, service, power, and replacement parts (Table 24). Subscription television would add further to the set-owner's economic burdens, since he would have the expense of buying, maintaining, and operating a regular broadcast receiver in the first place even to become eligible to subscribe to the pay-see programs. It seems probable, too, that the proponents of subscription television (insofar as they propose to dispense with commercial announcements) overestimate the opposition of audiences to the advertising content of television programs. In radio at least, it was found that advertising was actually liked by a large proportion of the audience, that

[12] By 1953, 107 theatres were equipped for theatre television and eight producers and syndicates were in operation. *Television Factbook No. 18* (14 January 1954), pp. 276-277.

[13] Subscription television systems are to be distinguished from the coin-operated television sets used in hotels. In the latter case the viewer pays for the use of the *set* as such rather than for the reception of the program.

[14] "Pay-As-You-See Crossroads," *Broadcasting-Telecasting* (20 September 1954), p. 122.

only about 10 per cent was in fact aggressively opposed to advertising.[15] Further, subscription proponents are unduly optimistic about the quantity of talent available of a caliber acceptable to mass audiences. Regular broadcasters foresee that subscription-system operators would be in a position to outbid them, and that hence much of the top talent once available "free" to televiewers would become available only at a price.

CROSS-CHANNEL AFFILIATION

A third defensive maneuver by film interests against the competitive inroads of broadcasting is to enter broadcasting themselves. A standard gambit in any business venture, of course, is to buy into related fields as a hedge against possible technological obsolescence. Newspapers bought into radio from the very beginning of broadcasting; later AM radio bought FM on the same principle; still later AM radio bought television. "Cross-channel affiliation," as it has been called,[16] has resulted in complex interrelationships among the media. Early liaisons between the radio and film industries have already been reviewed in connection with the introduction of sound. Since the advent of television a new series of cross-channel affiliations has been made. The merger of the American Broadcasting Company and United Paramount Theatres in 1953, involving combined assets of 144 million dollars, was the biggest transaction of its kind. Paramount Pictures bought a substantial interest in the Dumont Television Network as early as 1939. Other Paramount television interests include Station KTLA in Los Angeles and half ownership of Chromatic Television Laboratories and of International Telemeter (subscription television system). The first major film company to come under the control of broadcasting interests was RKO Pictures, which was purchased for twenty-five million dollars by General Tire and Rubber Company, owner of General Teleradio, which in turn controls MBS. RKO thus came into the broadcasting orbit for the second time in its history. Newspaper interests are connected with about a fifth of all the radio stations in the country, and with an even higher proportion of television stations.

RADIO AND THE PRESS

During the 1930's, when radio was rapidly expanding, newspapers experienced a period of serious decline. The growth of commercial radio also coincided with the depression which followed the stock-market crash of 1929. Hence the difficulties of newspapers during the '30's may have been due as much to prevailing economic conditions as to the competition of radio. Certainly radio did not gain its increasing revenue merely at the

[15] Lazarsfeld and Kendall, op. cit., p. 61.
[16] Harvey J. Levin, "Economies in Cross Channel Affiliation of Media," *Journalism Quarterly* XXXI-2 (Spring, 1954), pp. 167-174.

SOME INTER-MEDIA RELATIONSHIPS

expense of the other media. It rode in on a changing economy which favored increased advertising budgets (Chapter 12). Moreover, radio created new advertisers, new advertising techniques, new advertising markets. An intensive study of competition among the media led to the conclusion that

> There is no evidence . . . that all or even most of radio's spectacular growth came at the expense of newspapers. Radio probably brought much new money into advertising and also took revenues from magazines, farm papers, car cards and the movies.[17]

The fact is that the economy of newspaper publishing has been undergoing a long-term readjustment ever since the turn of the century. Rising production costs and changing markets have led to a steady decrease in the number of daily papers published. In 1910, competitive daily newspapers were published in 689 cities, but by 1954 only 87 cities were served by competitive daily papers; in the meantime, however, aggregate circulation had gone up from 22 million to 54 million.[18] In short, the trend has been consistently toward fewer but larger newspapers.

Nevertheless, the direct rivalry between newspapers and radio for advertising budgets naturally tends to sharpen the sense of competition between the two media. For example, the broadcasters consider that radio and television station program logs are in the nature of news and should be published as such by the newspapers. Many newspapers, on the other hand, regard program logs as advertising for a rival medium and either charge substantial space rates or refuse to publish them altogether. This narrow view, however, seems to be on the wane, and the more enlightened publishers no longer fear the competition of radio to that extent.[19] Even so, newspapers occasionally resort to unfair tactics in their efforts to freeze out competitive broadcasting stations.[20]

Whatever commercial rivalries exist, the right and duty of broadcasting stations to broadcast the news is no longer questioned by the news services and newspapers. The broadcasters' main difficulty in this respect now comes from some of the sources of the news. Radio and television have long been fighting to establish the principle of "equal access," i.e., the right of radio and television to cover all news events to which reporters of any kind are admitted. The reporters for the radio and television services have secured an equal footing as reporters with those of the news services and print

[17] Harvey J. Levin, "Competition Among the Mass Media and the Public Interest," *Public Opinion Quarterly* XVIII-1 (Spring, 1954), p. 73.

[18] Raymond B. Nixon, "Trends in Newspaper Ownership since 1945," *Journalism Quarterly* XXXI-1 (Winter, 1954), p. 7.

[19] An NARTB survey found that in over half of the communities reporting, newspapers published program logs without charge and that most of the newspapers which do charge are in small communities. NARTB, "Newspaper Program Listing Practices" (mimeo., 1954).

[20] Cf. *Mansfield Journal Co. v. FCC*, 180 F. (2d) 28 (1950).

media; but direct radio and television reports by means of remote pickup or recordings have not yet been universally accepted. During the national political conventions and campaigns of 1952, television as an eyewitness reporter made important gains. When television was excluded initially from an important press conference held by General Eisenhower in Abilene, Kansas, in the summer of 1952, CBS forced the issue and won the argument.

Nevertheless, many thoughtful and impartial observers still fear that the presence of television cameras (whether live or newsfilm), microphones, lights, and the rest of the paraphernalia in such places as law courts, Congressional hearings, and important news conferences may do more harm than good. Difficult questions involving rights of privacy, due process of law, and orderly conduct of government arise. With such innovations as televised (though staged) Cabinet meetings and filmed (though edited) Presidential press conferences, broadcasting has recently taken a long step in the direction of equal access. It remains to be seen whether greater familiarity with television as a direct reporting medium will eventually make it more acceptable in more spontaneous situations.[21]

Two other printed products are of particular interest as mass media: comic books and paper-bound books. Comic books came into prominence in 1938, when *Superman* zoomed into print. It is impossible to secure an accurate estimate of the circulation of comic books, but it is believed to be at least as high as a billion per year. Some notion of the value of this output can be gained from the fact that in 1954, when the comic-book industry was under heavy attack because of the presumed bad effects of comics on children, the Comics Magazine Association set up a "czar" after the fashion of Hollywood with an annual budget of $100,000.[22]

Paper-back books represent an even more interesting mass-communication phenomenon, and to some extent offset the negative implications of the comic book. Here the methods of mass merchandising have been applied to a standard product to revolutionize its market.

> Paper-bound publishers say their market is made up mostly of people who used to read only magazines, who are intimidated by the forbidding air of a bookstore, and who can afford perhaps a small fraction of the price of most new hard-cover books. They buy and read on the move, picking books off a rack or newsstand to read while commuting or traveling or during a frenzied day of changing diapers and making meals. They are impulse buyers who pick books at point of sale, and after reading them throw them away or pass them on to someone else. Few paper-bound buyers, say the publishers, want to keep the books as personal possessions or "furniture."[23]

[21] The issue of equal access was the subject of the first editorial ever broadcast by a network. Cf.: Frank Stanton, *CBS Editorial* (New York: CBS, 1954).

[22] It is significant that the annual cost of comic books is estimated to be about four times the annual book budgets of all U.S. public libraries. "Comic Strips Down . . . ," *Time* (14 March 1955), p. 86.

[23] "The Boom in Paper-Bound Books," *Fortune* (September, 1953), pp. 123-124. © Time Inc.

In the "disposable" nature of the books, their adaptation to the tempo of everyday life, their low unit cost, and their method of distribution, we perceive the characteristic features of a mass medium. Their economic success depends on fast turnover; "packaging" aids sales by stressing typical mass appeals. Ludwig Lewisohn's *The Case of Mr. Crump* blossoms forth as *The Tyranny of Sex,* and Voltaire's *Candide* tells how "He chased a virtuous maiden through Europe's most bawdy age." If the merchandising methods are not always in keeping with the dignity of the product, it is significant that such titles as Plato's *Dialogues,* St. Augustine's *Confessions,* the *Iliad,* and the *Odyssey* have sold over half a million copies each.[24]

INTER-MEDIA STIMULATION

In the long run, and generally speaking, competition among the media seems to have resulted in mutual gains for all. Nevertheless, in order to meet competition the older media have had to make adjustments in their methods, their price, and the quality of their product. Newspapers have reacted to television competition by increasing production efficiency to reduce operating costs and space rates; the motion-picture industry has curbed some of its more conspicuously wasteful practices, cut back on the production of "Grade B" movies, aimed at fewer but better productions, developed technological improvements, and built 4,000 drive-in theatres since 1948; radio has begun to serve smaller audiences more generously with such limited-appeal programs as classical music.[25]

At the same time, media competition has been found to produce a good deal of cross-channel stimulation. For example, in 1922 there were five popular publications devoted to radio; the next year there were 25. More recently, television has produced a whole swarm of fan magazines, program guides, and the like, just as the motion pictures had done before. The *TV Guide* has become the top-selling publication on the newsstands nationally.[26] News about the doings of television stars, technical developments, and other items about broadcasting constitute a considerable fraction of the news material handled by the press associations and filling out the columns of the daily papers.

Television has tremendously stimulated the non-theatrical side of the motion-picture industry, since it uses far more film footage than the total output of Hollywood feature films. Two trends grow out of this circumstance. One is the conversion of Hollywood theatrical film facilities to the making of films for television. This type of production was pioneered by minor producers, but by 1955 the major film producers had become deeply involved in this new field, which by then represented several hundred mil-

[24] *Ibid.,* p. 124.
[25] Cf.: Harvey J. Levin, *op. cit.,* pp. 76-79.
[26] Cf. Earl A. Abrams, "Fan Magazines," *Broadcasting-Telecasting* (22 November 1954), p. 43.

lions of dollars annually. The second trend is the expansion of the non-theatrical film industry. During the late 1940's the number of non-theatrical film producers more than doubled.[27] Television created an entirely new demand for filmed commercials, besides creating a new outlet for industrial, public-relations, technical and scientific, travel, conservation and wild life, sports, educational and training, sales, and military films. Business and industrial film producers alone grossed fifty million dollars in 1953 and produced well over a thousand subjects.[28]

One of the most interesting examples of inter-media stimulation is the story of the near-demise and subsequent flowering of the phonograph-record industry. It will be recalled that the networks bought out the old-line phonograph companies at a time when radio seemed to have doomed home players to technological obsolescence. From a high of $100 million gross, Victor fell to $10 million in 1932. In the long run, however, radio popularized music and stimulated the urge to buy recordings; at the same time, radio provided the technological improvements which reduced the costs of home players and records while tremendously improving their quality. During the 1940's the traditional big three — Victor, Columbia, and Decca — were supplemented by Capitol, Mercury, MGM, and London (English Decca). With the introduction of long-playing records in 1948, still other, smaller companies sprang up rapidly. The classics achieved a hitherto unheard-of popularity.[29] By 1953 record sales had reached $250 million, a quarter of which was in the classical field — a remarkable tribute to both the technological and the aural influence of radio.

Similar inter-media stimulation occurs in the field of talent and programs. The radio program *Dragnet* led to a successful television series and from that to a successful motion picture. A television play, *Marty,* became a hit movie and won an international award. A steady flow of talent and material circulates from one medium to another. At the same time, one medium uses another for advertising purposes, both directly and indirectly. Television manufacturers became for a time one of the biggest radio advertisers; motion pictures use television advertising more and more (much of it donated for the sake of film program material). Walt Disney used inter-media stimulation with startling effect to snowball the "Davy Crockett" craze in 1955. All this emphasizes the fact that there is an essential unity underlying the diversity and competitive singularity of the media. Research has indicated that audiences are more selective with regard to the type of entertainment or information they desire than with regard to the channel by which it reaches them. A person who is a heavy consumer of the product of one mass medium is likely also to be a heavy consumer of the other mass media.

[27] This industry is not as concentrated geographically as the entertainment film industry. Cf. the annual directory of non-theatrical film producers in *Business Screen Magazine.*
[28] "Movies for Business," *Fortune* (August, 1954), pp. 94-98.
[29] Cf.: Dero A. Saunders, "Record Industry: The Classics are Hot," *Fortune* (December, 1952), pp. 128-131, 175-182.

Instead of one medium displacing another, one stimulates interest in the other.[30]

COMPETITION FOR SPECTRUM SPACE

One species of competition in broadcasting is often overlooked, although it is of vital importance — competition for frequencies in the electromagnetic spectrum. While the development of the broadcasting services was taking place, equally spectacular gains were being made in non-broadcast radio services. As the FCC has pointed out,

> Because it enters the home, broadcasting commands so much popular interest that the average person does not realize that there are now 45 times more non-broadcast than there are broadcast stations, and the former are equally important to the public interest and convenience.[31]

As has been previously indicated (Chapter 1), the allocation of services has not followed a rational over-all plan, simply because the practical need for allocation of services has kept ahead of our knowledge of the spectrum and of propagation theory. As a result we have such anomalies as the fragmented television allocation plan, with channels grouped in such widely separated portions of the spectrum that serious practical problems have arisen concerning efficient utilization of the space allotted. It has been estimated that a thorough program of analysis and control for allocations in the United States would cost $50 million a year,[32] which is several times as much as the FCC is allotted annually for its whole regulatory operation.

RADIO v. TELEVISION

Hitherto we have been speaking primarily of broadcasting in relation to other media. Although radio and television are in effect one medium from some points of view, they nevertheless compete sharply with each other for advertising revenue. While television was getting on its feet radio paid the bill, and hence network radio was placed in the unfortunate position of apparently presiding at its own immolation. Even the advertising power of radio became self-destructive as the means for promoting the sale of tele-

---

[30] Lazarsfeld and Kendall, *op. cit.*, p. 5. During the winter of 1953, an eleven-day strike stopped publication of all major daily newspapers in New York. The radio and television stations redoubled their news coverage, but the strike "resulted in what amounted to almost a physical hunger for the sight of type. The public denuded the newsstands of magazines and paper-back books, so intense was its yearning for print." Ben Gross, *I Looked and I Listened* (New York: Random House, 1954), p. 299. A very careful survey of readership of major national magazines such as *Life, Look,* and the *Saturday Evening Post* revealed higher readership in television homes than in non-television homes. Alfred Politz Research, Inc., *The Audience of Nine Magazines* (New York: Cowles Magazines, Inc., 1955), p. 50.

[31] FCC, *Eighteenth Annual Report* (Washington: Government Printing Office, 1953), p. 1.

[32] President's Communications Policy Board, *Telecommunications: A Program for Progress* (Washington: Government Printing Office, 1951), p. 27.

vision sets. By the end of the freeze, in 1952, the position of network radio had begun to deteriorate seriously. It was freely predicted by many observers that network radio was doomed. The networks tried various stratagems to stem the tide. A general overhauling of rates took place, with emphasis on reduction for the nighttime hours, when television has its greatest impact. New sources of business were sought through programming and scheduling devices intended to attract the smaller national and regional advertisers to network radio.

In August, 1953, David Sarnoff addressed a showdown meeting of NBC radio affiliates in Chicago.[33] NBC had run through several presidents who had been successively outmaneuvered by CBS. In the previous June Sarnoff himself had stepped down from his remote position as Chairman of the Board of both RCA and NBC to take over management of the network in person. His study of the radio network situation had convinced him that a reversal of policy was necessary. The trend had been toward integration of radio and television functions into a single network organization; he now realized that radio tended to be submerged and neglected in a joint operation.

A basic reorientation in the economics of the industry also seemed necessary to Sarnoff. The networks could no longer depend primarily on a limited group of major national advertisers able to spend a million or more dollars a year in the medium. Between 1948 and 1953 radio-network time sales decreased 22 per cent, whereas local sales had gone up 35 per cent. Obviously, as the major network sponsors deserted radio for television, radio networks would have to dip into the local market. This meant, for example, adapting network radio to an advertising technique which had become universal in local radio — participating sponsorship, which distributes program cost over a number of sponsors. Mutual, perforce, had already moved to tap local sources of revenue. The prospective competition in this field by NBC and CBS threatened the very existence of Mutual as a full-scale national radio network.

The new orientation in the economics of network operation calls for a corresponding change in programming. Sarnoff rejected the theory that the future role of radio will be reduced to the "music-and-news" format which has been successfully employed by some local stations. He pointed out that this format works only because such stations depend on a very limited audience. Most big stations have to make a wider appeal, and they depend on network programming for most of that appeal. On the other hand, the network cannot aim any longer for the great mass audience; it must seek relatively large, yet specialized audiences which, though perhaps small in a given market, add up to a respectable size when viewed as a national audience. This point of view opens the door to classes of "highbrow" programming previously regarded by the networks as too specialized in appeal.

[33] Text published in *Broadcasting-Telecasting*, 21 September 1953, pp. 108-112.

The tyranny of program ratings, the natural concomitant of the mass-audience point of view, may become less absolute with this new approach to network programming. "Our industry," said Sarnoff, "from the outset has been plagued by rating systems which do not say what they mean and do not mean what they say." Aside from the question of the validity of the ratings themselves as measurements of audience size, the significance of size itself is questionable, since, as is well known, audience size is not invariably directly related to effectiveness of advertising; it also may be questioned whether it is still appropriate to deal in the family as the unit of measurement, when in point of fact the television set has become the family entertainment, while radio has tended to become more personalized through portables, automobile sets, and small sets in the kitchen, bedroom, children's room, and bathroom. Since as far back as 1947 nearly 50 per cent of all radios sold had been in the small, portable categories. Sarnoff pointed out that the ubiquity of radio — one of its most most telling advantages over television — may well increase with the marketing of transistorized miniature pocket radio receivers.

Perhaps the most disturbing evidence of the impact of television on network radio as Sarnoff looked at it in the summer of 1953 was the prevalence of "rebates," which is a polite term for rate-cutting. This debilitating practice, in one form or another, has always been endemic in broadcasting, but the industry as a whole has fought against it, and hitherto the networks had been relatively successful in maintaining the integrity of the rate structure. The pretense of integrity was still maintained, but under the stress of increased competition the networks as well as individual stations had become prone to "deals" whereby the customer ended up by paying less for time than the published rate. In 1953 Sarnoff could go so far as to say that "deals and concessions are a blight on the radio network business."[34]

On balance, the prospect for network radio is not as hopeless as it seemed in the panicky days of 1952-1953, when the first sweeping cutbacks in network rates occurred. Network radio will find its own level, a level which may not support as many as four full-scale national networks. But television does not replace radio; it revises its scope and function. As a far less expensive medium (and hence one less rigidly committed to mass appeal) the national radio service may well become — in the hopeful slogan of the movies — "better than ever." By 1955 the downward spiral of radio, especially at the local level, seemed to have been halted and this prediction was already coming true.

THE EMERGENT ROLE OF TELEVISION

When television first expanded into a national medium, the industry naturally assumed that it would follow rather closely the pattern of radio with four national networks providing a generalized service and many small,

[34] For fuller discussion of networks, ratings, and rate structure, see Part Three.

local stations providing localized service. It now appears, however, that television may fall into a somewhat different pattern, a pattern which favors the continued health of radio. The expense of television is so great that the over-all trend seems to be toward a relatively limited number of major stations located in the larger population centers. Most smaller areas may be served either by small non-competitive television stations or, more probably, by various devices for the extension of service from large stations in the population centers. These devices include satellite and booster stations and community antennas, which at relatively modest cost can deliver a station's signal into areas beyond the range of the station's own antenna. This means that highly localized service (in terms of advertising outlets, programs, and community self-expression) may continue to be the peculiar province of radio, with television providing a primarily national and regional service.

Another interesting question is the extent to which film will come to dominate the television service. Hollywood takes an attitude somewhat comparable to that of the Telephone Company back in the early days of radio, i.e., that its prior monopoly of a related art makes it the logical master of the new art. This reasoning, like that of AT&T, is based on a misconception of the nature of the new art. To reduce television to a film medium would be a regrettable national loss. As Sylvester Weaver, President of NBC, has remarked, "We are not like the movies — merchants of dreams, salesmen of escape. We deal primarily with reality." This distinction is vital.[35]

---

[35] Cf. Table 30 for data on the present relative importance of film in TV programming.

The Economy
of the Broadcasting Industry

12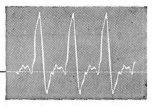

The Dynamics of the

Advertising Market

> If we seek an institution that was brought
> into being by abundance, without pre-
> vious existence in any form, and, more-
> over, an institution which is peculiarly
> identified with American abundance
> rather than with abundance throughout
> Western civilization, we will find it, I
> believe, in modern American advertising.
> — DAVID M. POTTER.*

Advertising is a multi-billion-dollar industry (Figure 26). Like mass communication itself, this industry is a typical by-product of the modern technological economy. Basically, the need for advertising arises when the sources of goods and services are removed from the immediate neighborhood of the consumer. When the housewife stopped making her own soap and buying shoes from the local craftsman she lost direct contact with the sources of supply. Advertising attempts to bridge the distance between the mass-producer and the individual user; in fact, it links up a whole series of economic entities which constitute the mechanism of mass distribution.

THE ECONOMIC ROLE OF ADVERTISING

A typical result of the separation of supplier and consumer has been the increase in importance of the branding of merchandise. Branding originated when medieval guilds compelled their members to mark their products so that inferior workmanship might be traced and corrected; but when the merchandise began to circulate beyond the geographic area controlled by

* *People of Plenty: Economic Abundance and the American Character* (Chicago: University of Chicago Press, 1954). Copyright 1954 by The University of Chicago.

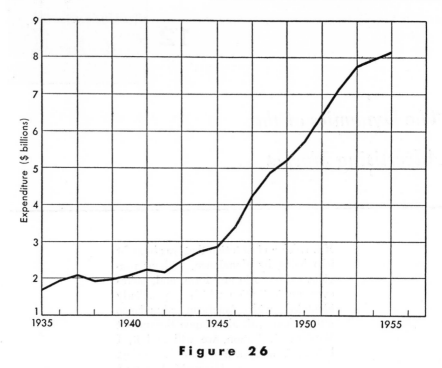

Figure 26

Growth of Total United States Advertising Expenditure Since 1935

Source: © *Printer's Ink* (19 August 1955), p. 21.

the guild, the brand became an asset as an assurance of good workmanship.[1]

In the contemporary American economy, however, the function of advertising is not merely to provide prosaic factual information about merchandise and services offered for sale.

> The purpose of advertisement is not to call your attention to the commodity and then to leave it to your judgment whether you will buy it or not, but to exercise some coercive force upon your judgment, to wheedle it, surprise it, overwhelm it, or at least, persuade it. . . .[2]

Much of the criticism of advertising as an institution and of the mass media in general is based on the assumption that this persuasive element is economically and morally wrong. Such criticism fails to grasp the contemporary function of advertising. David M. Potter, one of the few economic theorists to grapple with the significance of mass advertising in a broad social context, sees it as "the institution of abundance," the logical product of an economy of plenty. He reminds us that

[1] Neil H. Borden, *The Economic Effects of Advertising* (4th ed.; Chicago: Richard D. Irwin, Inc., 1947), pp. 22-23. Today trademarks are jealously guarded as an important asset, and are protected by a long tradition of common law.

[2] Max Radin, *The Lawful Pursuit of Gain* (Boston: Houghton Mifflin Co., 1931), p. 57.

advertising is not badly needed in an economy of scarcity, because total demand is usually equal to or in excess of total supply, and every producer can normally sell as much as he produces. It is when potential supply outstrips demand — that is, when abundance prevails — that advertising begins to fulfil a really essential economic function.[3]

Conditions of abundance are peculiarly favorable to the development of the typically American giant, semi-monopolistic corporations, a few of which may share the whole national market for a given product. Another commentator applies, instead of Potter's "abundance," the term "opulence:"

> The opportunity for product differentiation — for associating monopoly power with the brand or personality of a particular seller — is almost uniquely the result of opulence. A hungry man could never be persuaded that bread that is softened, sliced, wrapped and enriched is worth more than a cheaper and larger loaf that will fill his stomach. A southern cropper will not, as the result of advertising, develop a preference for one brand of cooked, spiced and canned ham over another. He will buy plain sidemeat. No one would advertise the sound-effects of processed breakfast foods striking the milk to Scottish crofters who have only the resources to buy oatmeal. In such communities all the commercial advantages lie with the producers of plain bread, sidemeat and oatmeal.[4]

The function of advertising in an economy of opulence or abundance is to create new needs, to educate for consumption. Price is no longer the sole, or even the primary, factor in competition. Most of the basic costs of manufacturing are stabilized; such items as labor, transportation, power, and taxes are likely to be pretty much the same for all competing firms in an established field. Therefore manufacturers seek competitive advantage in areas other than price — either in "marginal differentiation" among established products or in the development of new products.

> . . . competition more often than not centers on peculiar suitability to the user's needs (which producers have studied in detail), on engineering design, durability, low operating and maintenance cost, and scores of other similar considerations usually of more importance to the user's costs than purchase price. Much the same considerations now apply to consumer goods, in which superior packaging, style, color, flavor, durability, weigh heavily in the mind of the customers. It is here that advertising has served such a useful economic function.[5]

In the modern American economy the redistribution of income has created a vast new market in which the masses of consumers are able to employ

[3] David M. Potter, *op. cit.*, p. 172. Cf. particularly Chapter VIII, "The Institution of Abundance: Advertising."

[4] John Kenneth Galbraith, *American Capitalism: The Concept of Countervailing Power* (Boston: Houghton Mifflin Co., 1952), pp. 106-107. Cf. particularly Chapter VIII, "The Unseemly Economics of Opulence."

[5] David E. Lilienthal, *Big Business: A New Era* (New York: Harper & Bros., 1953), p. 52.

"discretionary purchasing." Formerly most purchasers had little choice but to buy those things they absolutely needed to clothe, feed, and house themselves. Nobody has to be persuaded to buy the necessities of life. Now, however, they have a margin of income which gives them the option of buying or not buying certain "extras." A decision is made between a second automobile and a power boat, a summer cottage and an outdoor patio, golf clubs and ski equipment, an automatic lawn-sprinkler system and a hi-fi phonograph system. Many products which were once the luxuries of the very rich have come, somewhat reduced in scale, within the command of the mass consumer. Pleasure-boats are a good example. The fabulous floating palaces of the extremely wealthy have become an anachronism; but a much larger market has been created for smaller but more numerous pleasure craft for the masses.

Only through mass advertising can such markets be created. Advertising develops new needs, standards, and tastes in consumption. Here is a role to which broadcasting is ideally suited. Radio and television, with their unique ability to enter the home and follow the prospective customer throughout the day can capitalize on discretionary purchasing power. As Potter says, "The older factual, prosy notice which focused upon the specifications of the commodity" has given way to "a more lyrical type of appeal" aimed at the wishes of the consumer.[6] Radio and television can be more lyrical — literally and figuratively — than other advertising media. There can be little doubt that the remarkable success of radio and television as advertising media (and hence their success as media of entertainment and information) in America must be attributed to their having come upon the scene at the right moment to participate in the American revolution in consumption. Had broadcasting been fully developed technologically in the 1890's when wireless itself first appeared, it would doubtless have developed in this country along entirely different lines than it has.

THE ADVERTISING MARKET

The advertising market is exceedingly complex and active. There are many media, and many ways of using each one. Ideas are burned up fast, and this causes a rapid personnel turnover at the top levels of the advertising industry. Tremendous ingenuity is required to restimulate attention dulled or distracted by a surfeit of advertising messages. The work of advertising is never done. A highly successful campaign to promote a new brand-name does not guarantee that the product is assured of sales thereafter. Brand-loyalty is shallow and easily diverted. It was found in one study, for instance, that about half the customers of one manufacturer switched brands in a three-month period, and only by attracting an equal number of new customers was the manufacturer able to keep the sales curve

[6] Potter, *op. cit.*, p. 171.

from sloping down abruptly.[7] A national soap manufacturer found that a brand of soap which had been its best seller before the war had lost all appeal when put back on the market after a short lapse.[8]

We have become so used to the ubiquity of advertising messages that we forget how many advertising channels are actually in use. Some readers may be surprised, for instance, to learn that one of the largest categories of advertising is direct mail (Figure 25). Most of us are probably far more conscious of billboards as an advertising medium, yet outdoor advertising represents a very small percentage of the total advertising expenditure. Furthermore, about 20 per cent of all advertising uses media other than the familiar channels of press, broadcasting, mail, and outdoor signs. Among the channels concealed in this "miscellaneous" category are such media as college newspapers, skywriting, handbills, trade shows and fairs, stickers, lapel buttons, and premiums. In fact, it is hard to find an object or an activity which is not at some time used as a vehicle of advertising.

Just as we are likely to overlook the diversity of existing advertising media, so also we may overlook the variety of kinds of advertising. Most of us probably think of advertising in terms of consumer goods (cigarettes, food, automobiles), and particularly in terms of branded merchandise. Actually, the field is considerably more complex, as the following breakdown reveals:

I. Manufacturers' advertising
   A. Of consumers' goods
      1. Directed to consumers
         a. To influence direct purchase
         b. To influence purchase through tradesmen
            (1) of branded merchandise
            (2) from maker or institution
      2. Directed to dealers
   B. Of industrial goods (equipment, material, supplies)
II. Dealers' advertising (consumer and industrial)
   A. For immediate sale
   B. For promoting brands
   C. For promoting institutions or departments[9]

This schema shows that advertising has a number of differing targets, differing economic relations between originator and target, and differing objectives.

When we take these facts into consideration, together with the fact previously pointed out — that advertising must constantly restimulate and recapture attention — we can better understand the assertion that the advertising industry is extremely mobile and complex. Because of this complexity, the devising and placing of advertising has become a highly specialized busi-

---

[7] NBC, "Why Sales Come in Curves" (1953, mimeo.), p. 6.
[8] "The Cleanup Man," *Time* (5 October 1953), pp. 92-100.
[9] Adapted from Borden, *op. cit.*, pp. 19-20.

ness which is carried on primarily by advertising *agencies* rather than by the advertisers themselves. Originally such agencies merely served as middlemen in the purchase of newspaper space. The modern concept of advertising-agency function developed after World War I; it has come to include not only the buying of space and time in the media but also the design and production of the advertising messages themselves, research on the effect of advertising and on the wants of the buyers, and many other services.

The research function of agencies has grown with that phase of advertising history which has been called the period of "scientific development."[10] From about 1925 on, advertising began to employ the techniques and findings of social science to take some of the guesswork out of its activities. This means, for example, the use of sampling and measuring techniques to find out within statistically defined limits of accuracy how many people a given advertising message reaches, what effect it has on sales, and what it costs in proportion to its effectiveness.

Broadcasting has, of course, grown up in this so-called scientific era of advertising; it has been the most dynamic of all the media because its whole history has been one of growth and innovation. From 1941 to 1951 the expense of radio and television to the public increased by over 300 per cent, as compared to an average increase in consumer expenditures of only 145 per cent. By contrast, expenditures for spectator amusements increased less than 100 per cent in that decade.[11] These data, of course, do not take into account the major growth of television, which should carry broadcasting through at least another decade of expansion.

ADVERTISING AS SUBSIDY

The value of advertising to the economy in facilitating the operation of the market is only one side of the coin. The other side is its value as an economic support of communications media that convey not only advertising messages but also much else of social value. It is estimated that about 70 per cent of the cost of producing metropolitan newspapers and 60 per cent of the cost of producing magazines and farm papers is met by revenue from the sale of advertising space.[12] This means, of course, radically reduced purchase prices for these publications. The trend seems to be toward increased advertising support, since the costs of production continue to rise more rapidly than publishers dare to raise the selling price of newspapers and magazines. *The Readers' Digest,* long the outstanding example of a mass-market periodical wholly supported by subscriptions and newsstand sales, finally conceded the need for additional income and in 1955 began to accept advertising.

[10] C. H. Sandage, *Advertising: Theory and Practice* (Homewood, Ill.: Richard D. Irwin, Inc., 1953), p. 24.
[11] Gilbert Burck and Sanford Parker, "The Changing American Market," *Fortune* (August, 1953), p. 104.
[12] *Printer's Ink Advertisers' Annual* (1954), p. 23.

Broadcasting, of course, is unique among the major media in that the cost of transmitting the service is almost entirely defrayed by advertising. The qualification implied by the word "transmitting" is often overlooked, and the blanket assertion is made that advertisers provide a *free* service to the public. Nothing could be farther from the fact. It may be said that in a sense the station operators get most programs gratis, since advertisers pay for programs as well as for station time. But the audience investment in sets is about three times the licensees' investment in all the broadcast stations in the country combined, and the annual cost to the audience of maintaining and operating these sets amounts to more than the combined payrolls of all the stations and equipment manufacturers as well (Table 23, p. 266). To receive communications through the channels of the press and motion pictures, the reader or moviegoer needs no special equipment; he merely pays his nickel at the newsstand or his dollar at the box office. The radio listener or televiewer, on the other hand, has to make an investment *in the medium itself*, since a transmitter is of no use without a receiver.

This fact significantly affects the psychological context in which the communications of the medium are received. To be sure, not every set owner pauses to calculate how much of his electric bill can be charged to Jackie Gleason or how many times he can watch *I Remember Mama* for the price of a new picture tube; but he does feel a certain proprietary interest — he considers that he has a stake in the medium, that he has a *right* to expect certain satisfactions from it.

PUBLICITY AND PROMOTION IN BROADCASTING

Advertising is generally distinguished from the related functions of publicity, promotion, and public relations.

> As contrasted with publicity and other forms of propaganda, advertising messages are identified with the advertiser either by signature or by oral statement. In further contrast to publicity, advertising is a commercial transaction involving pay to publishers or broadcasters and others whose media are employed.[13]

Broadcasting is much used for "publicity and other forms of propaganda." The motion-picture industry, for example, has found it useful to release excerpts from new feature films for insertion as part of the entertainment material in television programs; industrial films, made for promotional purposes, are widely used in television as a free source of sustaining program material; performers have been known to take advantage of their command of broadcast audiences to slip in favorable mentions of commercial products. This last practice, known in the industry as "the payola," is deliberately exploited as a form of publicity by some advertisers and as a source of extra income by some performers. There are, in fact, almost innumerable ways

[13] Borden, *op. cit.*, p. 17.

in which commercial exploitation can be tied in with broadcasting on a non-paying basis. Some of the methods are accepted as legitimate, as when an author of a new book appears for an interview on NBC's *Today*. The author gets "free" publicity for his book, and *Today* gets "free" program material; since the author is not a likely candidate for the purchase of a commercial spot on *Today*, a fair trade has been made from the broadcaster's point of view. On the other hand, the broadcaster does not welcome gratuitous commercial plugs inserted by performers or concealed in apparently non-commercial program material.[14]

[14] Cf. Rufus Crater, "Free Plugs Prove Fool's Gold," *Broadcasting-Telecasting* (9 June 1952), p. 23.

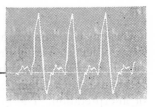

13

The Integration of Advertising
in the Program Structure

> Advertising messages should be presented with
> courtesy and good taste; disturbing or annoying
> material should be avoided; every effort should
> be made to keep the advertising message in har-
> mony with the content and general tone of the
> program in which it appears.— NARTB TELE-
> VISION CODE

Broadcast programs are transient, and programming involves a continuum, usually of about sixteen hours per day. This slavery to the clock is, of
course, another of the unique characteristics of the broadcast medium. Programming (which means both the sequence of individual programs and the
multitude of decisions which go into making up that sequence) must take
this unrelenting time-factor into consideration. It must, as well, consider
such factors as audience composition and expectations, circumstances of
reception, competition for audience attention, the sequence of activities in
the home, legal restraints, station policy, the financial and human resources
of the station, and many others.

Perhaps the most elementary structural feature of programming is the
fact that individual programs must be tailored to fit predetermined time-
segments. This arbitrary pattern in itself places serious restrictions on programming decisions. Yet it is a practical necessity, because advertising matter must be integrated in an orderly fashion, network schedules must be
met on the second, and audiences' expectations must be satisfied. Commercial broadcasting is often criticized for imposing arbitrary time-limits on
program matter, but the fact is that even in the absence of commercial com-
pulsions broadcasters would probably find that American audiences would
demand predictable program scheduling. In fact, non-commercial stations
usually follow the commercial pattern.

Custom, common sense, and a regard for the proprieties have standardized many other features of programming structure in varying degrees, but in no case have absolute and binding standards been set up. The legal requirements are, with minor exceptions, very general, permitting much freedom of interpretation. The radio and television codes adopted by the National Association of Radio and Television Broadcasters (NARTB) represent the consensus of the industry on these matters.[1] Even though observance of these codes is entirely voluntary (and is by no means universal or uniform), the codes show what standards the industry itself has accepted. They enable evaluation of station performance from the point of view of the *business* function of broadcasting as distinguished from its social, cultural, or political function.

THE CONCEPT OF PROGRAM SPONSORSHIP

When WEAF began to sell time on its facilities in 1922, the first purchaser bought a ten-minute segment. H. M. Blackwell, a representative of the Queensboro Corporation, used the ten minutes for an institutional talk about Hawthorne Courts, a cooperative apartment development in Jackson Heights, N. Y. Nowadays a ten-minute commercial talk would probably take the form of a "pitch," rising to a hard-selling climax, with great stress on low price, and ending with an urgent exhortation to "act now because this special offer will not last long." Mr. Blackwell's talk bore no resemblance to a pitch. It mentioned the Queensboro Corporation only once, and dealt chiefly with the healthfulness of living in the suburbs. It closed on a mild note of urgency, to be sure, but with no mention of price or of other commercial details: "Let me close by urging you to hurry to the apartment house near the green fields . . . the community life and friendly environment that Hawthorne advocated."[2] Indeed, Mr. Blackwell talked more about Hawthorne the writer than about Hawthorne the homesite.

Station policy of that period forbade direct selling, of course; radio was then regarded as a public-relations medium — a means of creating good will, not a direct means of making sales. The art of public relations has been defined as 90 per cent doing good and 10 per cent talking about it. The obvious way of doing good on the radio is to present a good program — to give the audience something outstanding to enjoy, such as music, drama, humor, or variety. In the 'twenties, however, station programming was rather haphazard. Norman Brokenshire, describing his experiences at WJZ in 1924, says: "If people dropped into the studio and could perform in any way, we had a program to put on the air; if no one dropped in, we were stuck." On one day when no one dropped in, Brokenshire had to improvise program material to fill one schedule blank after another; he finally resorted

---

[1] The codes are discussed in Chapter 25 and are reproduced in full in the Appendix.
[2] Gleason L. Archer, *The History of Radio to 1926* (New York: The American Historical Society, 1938), pp. 397-399.

to hanging the microphone out the studio window to broadcast the sounds of New York.[3]

Under such circumstances advertisers were in a good position to capitalize on the public hunger for professionally competent entertainment by assuming responsibility for programs as well as for advertising talk. The result was program sponsorship, which operates on the theory that it is permissible for the advertiser to subject the audience to a small amount of advertising talk if he returns a 90 per cent dividend of good entertainment. Accordingly, most of the largest early users of network radio advertising were sponsors who needed — and could afford — to spend money on institutional or general good-will advertising. In 1927 the leading product-group on network radio was naturally that of the radio manufacturers themselves, who obviously had everything to gain from improvement in programming. Radio manufacturers became much less important after 1929, by which time the burden had been taken up by other sponsors; but history began to repeat itself in 1948, when the manufacturers primed the television pump by sponsoring the kind of programming which would sell television sets. The second largest network sponsor-group in 1927 comprised insurance and finance companies — large corporations which use dignified institutional advertising primarily. Their number decreased in favor of such product-groups as foods and drugs after radio began to be used for direct selling.

Restrictions on direct selling on radio relaxed slowly and unevenly. The earliest network advertisers evaded rules against repeated mention of the sponsor's name by attaching it to the performers. Browning King's *Wednesday Night Dance* featured the "Browning King Orchestra," which of course was identified by name before each selection was played. Audiences of the 1920's were entertained by the Clicquot Club Eskimos, the A & P Gypsies, the Ipana Troubadours, and so on. Here is an example of an opening "commercial" from this period:

> Relax and smile, for Goldy and Dusty, the Gold Dust Twins, are *here* to send their *songs there*, and "brighten the corner where you are." The Gold Dust Corporation, manufacturer of Gold Dust Powder, engages the facilities of station WEAF, New York, WJAR, Providence, WCAE, Pittsburgh, WGR, Buffalo, WEEI, Boston, WFI, Philadelphia, and WEAR, Cleveland, so that the listeners-in may have the opportunity to chuckle and laugh with Goldy and Dusty. Let those Gold Dust Twins into your hearts and homes tonight, and you'll never regret it, for they *do* brighten the dull spots.[4]

As early as 1926 the La France Company (laundry aids) used commercial announcements not much different in length and content (though stilted in

[3] Norman Brokenshire, *This is Norman Brokenshire* (New York: David McKay Co., Inc., 1954), pp. 53-54.

[4] William P. Banning, *Commercial Broadcasting Pioneer: The WEAF Experiment 1922-1926* (Cambridge: Harvard University Press, 1946), p. 262.

style) from those which later became common. Nevertheless, the networks did not relax the ban against price-mentions until 1932.[5]

COMMERCIAL ANNOUNCEMENTS

Under the system of program sponsorship the advertiser undertakes a double expense: he pays not only for time on the facilities of the station or network but also for talent and other program ingredients. Not all advertisers want this polite but expensive way of utilizing radio. They reasoned: Why not save the expense of both program-time and the program itself by purchasing just enough time for a commercial announcement and no more? The fact that stations must periodically interrupt the sequence of programming to effect a transition from one program to another and to insert a station identification ("ID") announcement (required by law) creates a convenient niche into which such non-program-connected messages can be inserted. Thence has developed the station-break commercial.[6]

Not unnaturally, earlier program sponsors rather resented the introduction of these station-break announcements. After all, listeners were on hand to hear them only because they were tuned in to hear the preceding or following programs, and the spot announcement thus got a free ride, capitalizing on the popularity of sponsored programs but making no contribution to the entertainment of the audience. Nevertheless, spot announcements have become a major source of income for stations. They involve the minimum of time and the maximum of revenue for the station and a minimum of expense for the advertiser. Indeed, it has turned out that one of the chief values to a station of having a network affiliation is the fact that popular network programs make adjacent spots highly salable at a good price.

However, station-break announcements are, by their nature, limited in number — in many instances to only one every half-hour. Potentially, there are more advertisers who are able to buy spot announcements than there are advertisers able to stand the much greater expense of program sponsorship. In particular, broadcasting needs to be adapted to the use of the small local advertiser, who cannot afford to buy whole time segments, much less fill the time with program material. The answer to this need is the *participating* (or participation) spot announcement, made on a share-the-cost basis. In this case, the station rather than a sponsor provides the program material. The program is so designed that it can be interrupted periodically for the insertion of spot commercials. The participating advertiser

[5] The history of the development of commercial announcements, with a number of actual examples, is well summarized in: Herman S. Hettinger, *A Decade of Radio Advertising* (Chicago: University of Chicago Press, 1933), pp. 261-275. See also: Charles H. Wolfe, *Modern Radio Advertising* (2d ed.; New York: Funk & Wagnalls, 1953), pp. 617-650.
[6] Sometimes inaccurately called "chain-breaks," which are properly breaks in network programming filled by the network itself.

is not responsible for providing the program; he merely helps, with other advertisers, to defray the cost of the program. The disc-jockey show is the most obvious example. Popular records usually play for about three minutes; this makes it easy to insert participating spots at appropriate intervals. The format itself is the utmost in economy, since if necessary one man alone can select the records, play them, and read the participating spots. Other familiar types of participating programs are homemaking shows and, in recent years, network shows like NBC's *Today* and *Monitor* or CBS's *Morning Show.*

Finally, carrying the commercial trend to its logical conclusion, a type of program has emerged which consists of nothing but a sequence of commercial announcements. At this point the notion of giving the audience some sort of program fare in return for its attention to advertising material has been abandoned altogether, and the advertising material itself has become the program. This situation is justified by calling such programs "shopping guides," "market information," and so on, and presenting them as a service. The evolution of the industry's official justification of such programs is interesting:

1948 Radio Code	1952 Television Code	1954 Radio Code
Recognizing that such programs as shopping guides . . . render a definite service to the listening public; time standards for such programs may be waived for a total of one hour a broadcast day. . . .	Programs presenting women's services, features, shopping guides . . . provide a special service to the listening and viewing public in which advertising material is an informative and integral part of the program content . . . time standards set forth above may be waived to a reasonable extent. . . .	Programs of multiple sponsorship presenting commercial services, features, shopping guides . . . may include more material normally classified as "commercial" or "advertising," if it is of such nature as to serve the interests of the general public . . .

To summarize, the integration of advertising in the program structure eventually brought five basic forms into existence: (1) the *sponsored program,* which the sponsor supplies in its entirety, and which is traditionally 15, 30, or 60 minutes long (in each case minus 30 seconds for the station-break at the end of the time-segment); (2) the *station-break spot announcement* (either commercial or noncommercial), occurring at breaks between programs and having no relation to the preceding or following programs; (3) the *participation program,* which is supplied by the station or network but whose costs (for both time and talent) are defrayed jointly by several advertisers in return for participating spot announcements; (4) the *announcement program,* which consists of a series of commercial announcements purporting to have special value to the public as a shopping guide;

and (5) the *sustaining program,* which the station or network supplies, and for which it receives no revenue.[7]

SUSTAINING v. COMMERCIAL PROGRAMS

The distinction between sustaining and commercial programs is very important, since one of the quantitative criteria used by the FCC in programming evaluation is the balance between the two. Being somewhat of a hybrid, the participating program creates a problem in definition. The FCC arbitrarily classifies such a program as "commercial" if it is interrupted at intervals of less than 14½ minutes by commercial announcements.[8] For example, an hour-long participating program for which the station had been able to sell only one participating spot might be classified as 15 minutes commercial and 45 minutes sustaining.

There is thus no *intrinsic* difference between the two classes of programs; the same program may be classified as commercial one day and as sustaining the next, the only difference being the presence or absence of commercial announcements. This being the case, it may seem curious that the FCC considers the difference of such importance. The Commission places primary emphasis, however, on difference in *function* rather than on difference in content. If all programs were designed exclusively to function as vehicles for advertising messages, some types of program would never be produced at all, because certain kinds are not well adapted to functioning as advertising vehicles. Since this chapter deals primarily with the advertising function, discussion of other program functions is reserved for Part IV.

In any event, the broadcaster is generally faced with the practical necessity of producing sustaining programs, if only to fill in between commercial programs. Aside from questions of public policy, few stations would be able to sell all of their time, even if they tried to. The schedules of most solvent stations are probably 50 to 75 per cent commercial.[9] The relation is usually reported in terms of program-units rather than time-units. For example, an

---

[7] Terminology is not standardized, nor is practice. Programming situations not covered by the foregoing breakdown are generally known as "special features." The NARTB has proposed a standard terminology which makes a distinction between two types of program here combined for brevity under the term "participation program." The latter is defined by the NARTB as a program in which "the advertiser's message, along with other messages, is either prepared by the program conductor from material furnished by the advertiser or agency, or which is woven into the program as an integral part." As another classification, the NARTB defines "announcements" as "all messages that are independent of the station's program structure and are not scheduled in the station's breaks." NARTB, *Suggestions on Standardization of Rate Cards* (Washington: NARTB, N.D.), pp. 11-12.

[8] FCC, *Public Service Responsibility of Broadcast Licensees* (Washington: Government Printing Office, 1946), p. 1.

[9] In 1945 the FCC reported on the practices of 703 radio stations, which averaged 16 hours of programming per day. Fifty-four per cent of the programs reported were commercial, 46 per cent sustaining. The data admittedly were crude, and if the stations had used the definition of "sustaining" cited above the proportion of commercial programs would have been higher. *Ibid.*, p. 18.

hour-long sponsored program is counted as commercial in its entirety, even though it may comprise fifty-four minutes of non-commercial material and only six minutes of actual commercial announcements. Expense has prohibited more detailed analysis. However, such analyses have been made for television programming in certain cities over one-week periods in a series of studies sponsored by the National Association of Educational Broadcasters. During a test week in New York in 1954, for example, it was found that 13 per cent of all time of all television stations was devoted to commercial announcements.[10]

QUANTITY OF COMMERCIAL CONTENT

Balance between sustaining and commercial program time, by whatever yardstick measured, is only one of several ways of quantitatively defining the relative prominence of advertising in the program structure. Other indices are the length of individual commercial announcements, their placement in relation to each other and to other program material, their cumulative frequency, and their cumulative length within a given program.[11]

As to the length of individual announcements, no precise standards have yet been set up. Networks allow a 30-second lapse for local announcements between commercial network programs; this necessarily limits network station breaks to a 25-second spot plus station ID or a 20-second spot plus a 10-second spot integrated with the ID. However, when a sustaining network program is to follow, a full minute is allowed for local commercial announcements. Of course the non-affiliated station — or the affiliate when not carrying the network — can stretch the station-break time according to its own discretion. The NARTB *Television Code* speaks of participating announcements as "generally one minute in length."

Brevity is implicit in the very word "announcement." Generally speaking, a commercial announcement longer than about one minute begins to turn into a harangue, or pitch, and to lose its essential character as an announcement. The pitch is an extended high-pressure commercial talk which goes far beyond the concept of "announcement." It may run for five, ten, fifteen, or even thirty minutes. The pitchman's highly specialized skill enables him to hypnotize his victim with his voice much as the Indian fakir is said to hypnotize the cobra with his flute. The pitch has always been a minor irritation of the radio business, but it has come into more prominence with television. Traditionally, the pitch advertiser uses

[10] Purdue Opinion Panel, *Four Years of New York Television, 1951-1954* [NAEB Monitoring Study No. 7] (Urbana, Ill.: NAEB, 1954), p. 47.

[11] Another factor which apparently has not been studied objectively is the average *loudness* of commercial announcements in relation to that of adjacent program material. "Why advertising men confuse salesmanship with high decibels," says the columnist, Ben Gross, "is one of the mysteries of this age." Ben Gross, *I Looked and I Listened* (New York: Random House, 1954), p. 65.

ingredients which are timeless: a product which lends itself to demonstration, a pitchman who is glib enough to befuddle the average mind, a location to which a crowd can be attracted, and enough time for the pitchman to unload the contents of his duffle before the cops arrive.[12]

Typically, pitch advertising sells a product by mail, using a recorded or filmed pitch which is scheduled on many stations throughout the country. Curiously enough, the pitch can stimulate sales even when the product is grossly overpriced. For example, an item which died on the counter at 29 cents sold readily by mail for two dollars when given the benefit of the pitchman's persuasive talk.[13] A member of the FCC has said flatly that pitchmen "do not belong on the air."[14] They clearly violate both the spirit and the letter of the NARTB code. It is a measure of the immaturity of the medium that in 1954 70 per cent of the television stations were said to be willing to accept this type of advertising.[15]

THE PLACEMENT OF COMMERCIALS

With regard to the placement of commercial announcements in relation to each other, a tradition grew up in radio that station-break announcements should be limited to one spot plus a brief commercial "service" announcement, such as the well-known Bulova time signal. The NARTB 1948 radio code stipulated:

> The placement of more than one commercial announcement between two commercial programs should not be permitted except in those instances when one of the two announcements is a sponsored time signal, weather report, station promotion or location announcement of not to exceed a total of ten seconds in length.[16]

The tradition has weakened, however, as competition has increased; the 1954 radio and television codes contain no statements on this point, although

[12] John Osbon, "The Pitchman in the Parlor," *Broadcasting-Telecasting* (9 August 1954), p. 80.

[13] In 1953 the company which first capitalized on television as a medium for pitch advertising was ordered by the Federal Trade Commission to cease making false claims: "This order affected the advertising program of Charles Antell amounting to approximately $8,000,000 annually. Among other things the order forbade claims that Formula No. 9 would prevent baldness or loss of hair; restricted claims concerning its lanolin content; banned advertisements representing that the hormone content of Charles Antell Shampoo had any cleansing action on the hair; prohibited misrepresentation of the effectiveness of Hexachlorophene Soap; and outlawed misrepresentations of regular prices as 'reduced prices'." FTC, *Annual Report, 1954* (Washington: Government Printing Office, 1955), p. 38.

[14] Commissioner Robert E. Lee, "Comments of a Commissioner — One Year Old" (FCC Mimeo. 10915, 21 September 1954), p. 8.

[15] Osbon, *op. cit.*, p. 80. See also: Edwin H. James, "The Pitch on Radio and TV," *Broadcasting-Telecasting* (19 January 1953), pp. 80-82.

[16] NARTB, *Standards of Practice for American Broadcasters* (Washington. NARTB, 1948), p. 7. It should be borne in mind that the closing commercial of the preceding program and the opening commercial of the succeeding program add to the "pile-up" at station breaks.

the latter does imply that the station-break time should not exceed 30 seconds. Since, as has been pointed out, station-break spots are lucrative and easy to sell, stations are constantly tempted to squeeze more in. The FCC cited as a horrible example a radio station which regularly scheduled six spots in a row.[17] High costs of television operation have contributed to lessen the restriction on "double-spotting"; even triple- and quadruple-spotting are not uncommon.[18] One outcome of this trend is the clipping of network programs when the spots occur between network commercial shows. The practice has been condemned by the president of the NARTB as "just downright bad programming."[19]

The placement of commercial announcements in relation to other program material becomes a significant factor in advertising integration if the commercials inappropriately interrupt the program sequence. Research has established that audience attention usually drops when a program is interrupted by commercials; hence every effort is made to integrate commercials in such a way as to counteract this tendency. A standard device is to insert them after audience interest and expectations have already been built up. Breaking the continuity in this way is not always appropriate, especially if the program is a serious one, such as a news program. The Association of Radio News Analysts has always opposed the interruption of news analyses by commercial announcements.[20] The NARTB codes, although they devote whole sections to the treatment of news, contain no statements against the practice. The general trend at best seems to be toward a compromise: the newscaster introduces the program with a rundown of the "headlines," a commercial follows, and the body of the news is presented without interruption. Inserting a commercial in the midst of a newscast (or other comparable program) at a point not offering a natural break in continuity may be regarded as a substandard practice, though a very common one.

The cumulative frequency of commercials is likely to mount in participation programs. If the program is popular and advertisers eager to buy, the temptation to squeeze in a few more spots is strong. The NARTB Television Code suggests a cumulative frequency equivalent to no more than one minute of commercial to five minutes of program. This permits twice as much commercial time in an hour as the six minutes allowed by the Code for an hour-long sponsored program in Class A time (see Appendix). Significantly, the 1945 radio code contained a similar provision, but this does not appear

[17] FCC, *op. cit.*, p. 44.

[18] Television stations now apparently tend to shorten the program-time segments allotted to local programs in order to allow for more station-break announcements. For example, a 15-minute local sponsored program that was formerly assumed to be actually 14½ minutes in length might nowadays take only 13½ minutes (with the full knowledge of the sponsor, of course), allowing 1½ minutes for station-break announcements instead of only 30 seconds.

[19] "Fellows Attacks Spot Practices," *Broadcasting-Telecasting* (6 December 1954), p. 62.

[20] Cf. the ARNA Code of Ethics, para. IV, in ARNA, *History, Constitution, and Membership, 1942-1954* (New York: ARNA, 1954), p. 1.

in the 1954 revision. The fact is that many small radio stations are almost totally dependent on very low-cost participations for revenue.[21] Restrictions which would be entirely acceptable to the networks and to stations which operate on a safe margin of profit might at the same time be unrealistic for stations in less favorable economic circumstances.

QUANTITATIVE STANDARDS

As a practical matter, it appears that the most acceptable basis for setting up quantitative standards for commercial content is the cumulative time devoted to commercial announcements *per program*. This is the basis of the time standards in the radio and television codes of the NARTB (see Appendix). It is interesting that the original belief that advertising should be restricted to daytime hours (when retail business is normally conducted), leaving evening home life unintruded upon by business matters, persists in vestigial form in the television code's slight decrease in permissible length of commercials in Class A time.

Although no comprehensive data are available on observance of the time limits "suggested" in the television code and "established" in the radio code, it is probable that most network advertising adheres fairly well to these standards. However, even network single-sponsor programs have evaded the standards by adding simulated spot announcements outside the framework of the program proper yet within the over-all time segment allotted to the sponsored program. This device is known as a "cowcatcher" if the simulated spot precedes the purported opening of the program, or as a "hitchhike" or "trailer" if it follows the purported close of the program. A tobacco company, for instance, might use up the full allowable commercial time within the framework of a sponsored program which advertises a brand of cigarettes, but the program will close a minute early so that a trailer can be inserted that advertises the same company's brand of pipe tobacco. Both the NARTB codes explicitly oppose cowcatchers and hitch-hikes.

We may conclude from the foregoing that quantitative criteria governing the integration of commercial material in broadcast programming are by no means always clear-cut. Nevertheless, certain standards have evolved through actual practice that the industry itself considers reasonable. By these standards a station's performance can be evaluated fairly objectively in quantitative terms alone, without resort to more subjective criteria such as taste, artistic standards, or ideas about the social functions of broadcasting.

---

[21] The most extreme reported case is that of a radio station which scheduled a commercial announcement on an average of every three and one-half minutes throughout the broadcast week. FCC, *op. cit.*, p. 44.

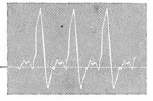

14

The Rate Structure
of Broadcasting

Commercial broadcasting is a business; it has something to sell. But what particular commodity is it selling? Superficially, of course, it is station *time*, just as page space is the commodity sold by newspapers and magazines. This is merely convenient shorthand, however. Station time has significance only because it represents viewer or listener time; this in turn has significance only as it represents viewer or listener attention. The FCC took this view of the merchandise of the broadcasting business in its 1949 effort to rule out "giveaway" programs on the ground that they were lotteries. A lottery is legally defined as "a chance for a prize for a price." The crucial question in that case was whether the listener or viewer paid a price merely by paying attention. The FCC thought he did, but the courts held otherwise.[1] In the strict technical sense, mere attention is not the kind of price contemplated by the lottery law as it has been interpreted. It might be argued, however, that this is another instance of the discrepancies that arise when laws that were enacted to regulate specific situations are applied to entirely novel problems, such as those created by the advent of broadcasting.

DETERMINING THE VALUE OF STATION TIME

A station's ability to command audience attention may be measured in several ways. In the first place, the physical reach of the station signal necessarily defines its scope. Next, the population contained within the geographical contours of its coverage area represents its maximum audience potential. These two factors can readily be measured: the first by an instrument which takes "field strength" readings at a sufficient number of geographical points near the transmitter to ascertain the area covered by a useful signal, and the second by census data. Quantitative data on populations can be evaluated qualitatively in terms of purchasing power. A number of standard "market indicators," such as retail sales, average in-

[1] *ABC* v. *U.S.*, 110 F. Supp. 374 (1953); affirmed, *FCC* v. *ABC*, 347 U.S. 284 (1954).

come, ownership of certain items, and the number of telephones in use, are used to judge the economic potential of a market. These signal, population, and market factors are relatively stable. The station must compete, however, minute by minute for audience attention — not only with every other broadcast station but with every other conceivable human activity. Of the total potential audience (everyone living within the coverage area of the station), only a fraction constitutes the total *available* audience (everyone who is awake and within reach of a receiver at any given moment). Only a fraction of the available audience, in turn, is an actual audience (i.e., watching television or listening to radio) at that moment. Finally, of that actual audience, a given station gets only a *share* of the total. The fact that this fractionating of the audience through three successive steps can leave the final audience-share of any one station big enough to be worth considering is an evidence of the universality of broadcasting. If the potential audience did not include very nearly everybody, the final station share would be minute indeed. The fact is that radio has reached close to 100 per cent saturation in most areas, and hence for practical purposes the *total population* is the base from which the station share is drawn. Television will probably reach a saturation very close to that of radio by the time set-distribution is stabilized (Figure 22).

The all-important variable, of course, is the programming which is responsible for the station's audience share. Here again that unique characteristic of broadcasting, its continuous character, is important. Programs should be thought of not as isolated experiences but as parts of a continuum. A station's service is more than a collection of programs. Programming builds up a certain institutional personality. The ability to develop this personality — to make it an attractive personality, one that is consistent and predictable, one that has meaning for its audience — is a key problem of station management. A certain economic leeway is required, for management cannot carry out a policy if its decisions are dictated by economic necessity. Management must be in a position to reject business which is contrary to policy and to control programming and advertising in terms of policy. If management either is unable to develop a practical policy or is forced to sacrifice policy for the sake of economic expediency, a vicious circle ensues. The more amorphous and characterless the programming becomes, the harder it is to hold an audience and to sell advertising; the harder it is to meet expenses, the more programming deteriorates.

Broadcasting's commodity, then, is fundamentally audience attention; this in turn is the product of programming; and the quality of programming in turn is affected by managerial skill and economic freedom. The inseparability of programming and economics is the factor most frequently misunderstood by the layman — and not infrequently by station management, as any tour of the dial is likely to demonstrate.

Determination of the costs of station operation, and hence of the value to the station of its own time, is relatively simple. It is a matter of adding

all the expenses involved — plant depreciation, amortization, and maintenance; costs of management, sales, engineering, and program departments;
charges for rent, utilities, and supplies; and so on — and dividing this sum
by the number of hours on the air. This yields a cost-per-hour figure which
represents the value of time to the licensee.

The value of the station's time to an advertiser is another matter, a much
harder value to establish. Newspapers can at least tell advertisers how
many papers of each edition are sold, but the fact that a family has bought
a television set is no guarantee that it will be tuned in to station "X" at any
given time. The necessity of demonstrating in some way the value of station
time in terms of audience attention has brought about an elaborate research
mechanism, which grinds out mountains of data. Broadcasting uses research
far more than any other medium. It has to, for in no other way can it establish the economic value of its commodity.

Leaving for the time being the question of how this research is carried
out (this subject is treated in Chapter 16), we can say that the licensee uses
whatever data he can collect on his station's ability to command attention
to justify adding a profit margin to the basic cost-per-hour of operation.
The resulting figure may be at first somewhat wide of the mark — he may
charge too much or too little — but competition and experience bring about
suitable adjustments. Whatever the figure, it is made public through a rate-
card, which is in effect the price-tag on broadcast time.

TIME-OF-DAY DIFFERENTIALS

Broadcast rates are a good deal more complicated than most price-tags,
however. For example, it requires no research to deduce that not all hours
of the day or week are equally valuable. Obviously people have to sleep,
work, and eat, and carrying out these and many other living functions affects
their availability as an audience. As a primarily *home* medium, broadcasting
is subject to the rhythm of daily life. Broadly speaking, the hours between
7 P.M. and 11 P.M. are the most valuable because the whole family is most
likely to be home, awake, and free to listen to the radio or watch television.
During the weekday daytime hours children are at school and employed
persons are at work; during the late-night and early-morning hours most
people are asleep (Figure 27).

In recognition of these conditions, broadcast time is generally classified
in two or more categories (Figure 28). Practice varies concerning the
number of time-classes used and the relative value assigned to each. The
following, used by the NARTB in constructing model rate-cards, will serve
to illustrate the common practice:

Class A (7 P.M.-10:30 P.M. all days) — Full rate (100%)
Class B (6 P.M.-7 P.M. weekdays; 1 P.M.-6 P.M. Sundays) — 67%
Class C (9 A.M.-6 P.M. and 10:30 P.M.-12 M. all days) — 50%
Class D (12 M.-9 A.M. all days) — 34%

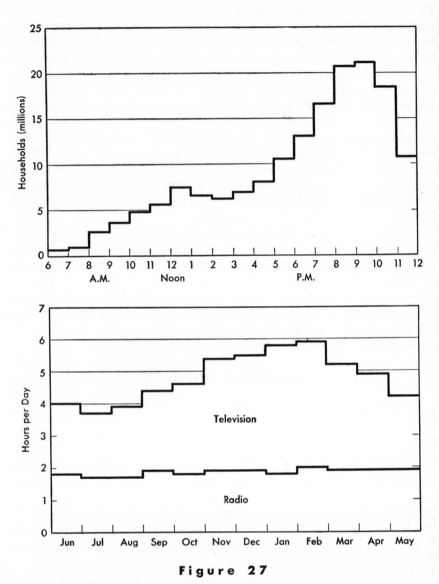

Figure 27

Relation of Time ‘to Size of Audience

Above: Total Number of United States Households Using TV, by Hours of the Day. Data as of March, 1955.

Below: Use of TV and Radio in TV-Equipped Houses, by Months of the Year. Based on Total Number of United States TV Households for the Period June, 1954-May, 1955.

Source: A. C. Nielsen Co.

The implication of these classifications is, for example, that the largest audience potential is expected to be available in the evenings after dinner but only about half that potential is expected to be available during working hours.

Since television took hold, the value of nighttime radio has decreased radically. But radio is better adapted to accompany the household chores or other working-hours activities; hence its daytime value has not decreased

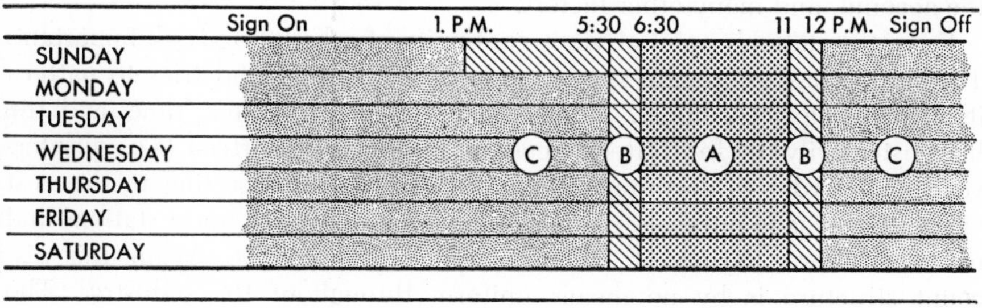

	Sign On	1. P.M.	5:30 6:30	11 12 P.M. Sign Off
SUNDAY				
MONDAY				
TUESDAY				
WEDNESDAY		(C) (B)	(A)	(B) (C)
THURSDAY				
FRIDAY				
SATURDAY				

Figure 28

Rate-Card Time Classifications

An example of time classifications in the local rate card of a television station.

Source: WTVJ, Miami, Florida.

proportionately (Figure 27). As a result there has been a trend toward reduction of radio time to a single class.[2] Television, on the other hand, has found itself better able to command audiences on Sunday and Saturday afternoons and late evenings than radio, and some stations have shifted time classifications accordingly.

Lack of uniformity in time classifications and in the relative values assigned to them inevitably arises out of local differences. Differences in living habits, competing attractions, weather conditions, population distribution, transportation facilities, school and working hours, average income, and many other factors affect the viewing and listening habits of audiences. Each station, therefore, must adapt to local conditions.

QUANTITY DISCOUNTS

Since the stuff of broadcasting is impermanent, and since audiences are constantly changing in composition, broadcast advertising relies heavily on repetition. Under most circumstances a single isolated commercial an-

[2] In a survey made in 1952, two-thirds of a group of stations queried believed that a single day-night rate for radio would be established. J. Frank Beatty, "Single Rate Card," *Broadcasting-Telecasting* (27 October 1952), p. 27.

nouncement or program would be of doubtful value to the advertiser. Broadcast advertising, even more than most other advertising media, typically operates on the principle of multiple exposure over a period of time. The design may take the form of a program series scheduled on one station at the same time week after week for many weeks, or of an intensive spot campaign on several stations in a single market several times a day for a few days or weeks; it may also take many other forms, depending on the advertiser's budget and objectives, the judgment of the agency handling the account, and many other factors.

From the station's point of view, continuity of scheduling is all-important. The station has to operate continuously in all seasons, and tries to pattern its advertising accordingly. Contracts for talent, programs, time, and the like customarily run for thirteen weeks, or multiples of thirteen (i.e., quarter-years). In order to encourage advertisers to use broadcasting to the best effect as well as to purchase the maximum amount of time, most stations and networks offer a variety of volume or quantity discounts. Again, this discount structure is by no means uniform throughout the industry. The NARTB recommendation will serve as an example, however. If we assume that the rate for one hour of time is the base, shorter segments cost proportionately more:

30 minutes — 60% of hour rate
15 minutes — 40% of hour rate
10 minutes — 30% of hour rate
5 minutes — 20% of hour rate

The various kinds of announcements are usually priced separately, with premium prices charged for spots in popular participation programs. Discounts are also allowed on such bases as annual dollar volume of time purchased and the number of consecutive days or weeks for which a time-segment is purchased.

LOCAL v. NATIONAL RATE

One further variable in rate determination remains to be considered. Broadcasting took over from newspapers the custom of charging national (or wholesale) advertisers a higher price for advertising than local (or retail) advertisers. The difference is ascribed mainly to the fact that advertising agencies usually handle national accounts and their commission has to be considered. Accordingly, most stations actually have two rate cards, one local and one national (or retail-wholesale, the terms being interchangeable). Not every station makes this distinction, and those that do offer varying markdowns for local (retail) advertising. Generally speaking, the local rate is from 50 to 20 per cent less than the national rate.

To summarize, we may say that the broadcast rate-structure is based on a charge per unit of time but the price per time-unit may vary depending on (1) who uses it, (2) when it is used, and (3) how much is used. This formulation, however, does not explain what "time" really means. Broadcast time is translated into a useful commodity only insofar as it represents audience time. The audience can be reached only insofar as both program material and the facilities for transmission are available. To what extent are these indispensables included in the price of broadcast time?

TIME RATES v. FACILITIES RATES

Unfortunately, industry practice varies so greatly that few generalizations can be made. It is safe to say that the time-charge invariably includes the use of the transmitter for the actual dissemination of the broadcast signal. In the program-sponsorship situation, it is established that the sponsor pays for the program, usually as a separate transaction, apart from the payment for time. But in other advertising situations the difference between program expense and time expense is less clear-cut.

These matters were much simpler before television. The expenses of maintaining and staffing radio studio facilities are relatively moderate; a flick of the switch by a control-room operator, and a studio is ready for use. On the other hand, a whole crew of men is required to prepare a television studio for use; cameras must be warmed up and adjusted (and camera pickup tubes are very expensive and have a limited life); settings and properties must be provided. Accordingly, television stations and networks have had to make special charges for facilities and service. Some stations do not include live studio facilities at all in their basic time-rate; others include them for the program-time plus a very limited rehearsal time. Each piece of extra equipment — an added camera, a special camera dolly — means an added facilities or service charge.

Participation programs are usually an exception, since it is possible for the station or network to establish a fixed price per participation which will include all expenses. Station-break announcements and participations in announcement programs may be handled the same way. But even in these cases, if the advertiser needs special equipment, personnel, art work, and so on, extra charges may be made.

Some of the common types of services, facilities, and program materials for which special charges (in addition to time charges) may be made include:

(1) *News* — for the use of national, state, or local news services
(2) *Music* — for the use of copyrighted music
(3) *Talent* — for the use of staff announcers, musicians, and the like
(4) *Music and film library* — for the use of stock footage or records and transcriptions
(5) *Remote control* — for picking up programs at points remote from the studio, such as sporting events

(6) *Art work* — for graphics (titles and the like), sets, properties
(7) *Studio facilities* — for crew and equipment for studio origination of programs
(8) *Film facilities* — for production of material on film

THE RATE CARD

All these cost factors are highly variable, and hence most stations do not attempt to quote prices for every contingency in the formal catalogue of prices which appears in the rate card. Because some degree of uniformity is desirable for business efficiency, the NARTB has drawn up model rate cards which contain basic information in a planned sequence. Even for these models, however, the NARTB found it necessary to draw up five different types, the differences arising from differing discount formulas.[3] All, however, include the following classes of information:

(1) Basic data identifying the station, location, power, key personnel, etc.
(2) A table of time-charges, showing discounts
(3) A statement of program policies concerning length of commercial copy, acceptability of advertising, etc.
(4) A statement of commercial policies covering items such as contract requirements, discount structure, and commissions on sales
(5) A description of facilities, services, and talent available and charges made for them

Since rate cards are constantly being revised, it would be impractical for national advertisers and their agencies to keep up to date on all the thousands of stations in the country by filing the rate cards themselves. This problem is solved by *Standard Rate and Data Service* (SRDS), a series of monthly publications which bring together the national rate cards of every station and network in the country.[4] SRDS has separate publications for radio stations, television stations, and networks. It also publishes separately rate information on films for television and on newspapers, magazines, business publications, and transportation media. Rates, therefore, are a matter of record. The fact that they are public information indicates equal treatment of all customers.

Ideally, at least, the rate card represents an honest evaluation of the commodity that a station offers for sale; it is the price tag. In most major forms of modern business enterprise price is not a figure picked out of the air but an amount representing production and distribution costs plus a fair

[3] Cf.: NARTB, *Suggestions on Standardization of Rate Cards* (Washington: NARTB, N.D.) and the accompanying model cards; Broadcast Advertising Bureau, *Standard Television Rate Cards* (New York: BAB, 1950).
[4] Published by Standard Rate and Data Service, Inc., 1740 Ridge Avenue, Evanston, Ill.

markup for profits. One does not expect to haggle over the price of a pair of shoes in a reliable department store or the price of a box of cereal in a grocery. If one wants cheaper shoes or cheaper cereal, he can usually find cheaper brands or retail stores which offer fewer customer services and hence lower prices. If the seller leaves the door open to bargaining over price, he also implies that his asking price may be unreasonably high.

It is true that there are many areas of the economy in which a certain amount of bargaining is more the rule than the exception — in real estate and second-hand automobile sales, for example. It is also true that standard-brand merchandise can sometimes be obtained at cut rates, and that in any city one can find merchants on the periphery of the business community whose price-tags are intended as invitations to negotiation rather than as bona-fide appraisals of worth. But broadcasting cannot properly be classi-fied with these forms of business enterprise. Legally it is not even primarily a business, but a service to the public (see Part IV). Broadcasting is some-thing more than inanimate merchandise; it is an institution, having a certain status by virtue of its access to the home, its importance to public policy, its frequent concern with matters of consequence as well as with the frivolous, and its favored position as the holder of a government franchise.

RATE CUTTING

Price cutting — failure to abide by the terms published in the rate card — is highly prejudicial to this special position of broadcasting. Rate cutting assumes many disguises. For instance, the advertiser may pay the full time rate but be charged less for talent and other essentials than their actual cost to the station or network. Or the station may give the client elaborate free merchandising services whose cost should normally be added to the time-rate. Whatever the device employed, however, rate-cutting implies one of two things: either the station does not even know its true worth as an advertising medium or it has misrepresented itself by overpricing. In either case the integrity of the medium is lessened.

Newspapers encountered this problem long before broadcasting did, and one reason for the relatively high standing of the press is the fact that it succeeded in building a tradition of integrity as an advertising medium by holding to its rates. The problem emerged in broadcasting as soon as broad-casting gained recognition as an advertising medium. Writing in 1933, a sympathetic critic noted:

> With regard to commercial practices, the principal problem affecting the future development of radio broadcast advertising is the maintenance of rates. . . . If this is not done, the progress of the industry will be greatly impeded. Since price-cutting brings with it the temptation to cut the quality of the program and to accept business of doubtful value, it tends to cheapen the entire industry and to cause broadcast advertising to lose prestige. Since advertising is founded upon respect for and confidence in the advertiser and

the medium, such a tendency would do tremendous harm to the development of broadcasting.[5]

Curiously enough, the self-defeating character of rate-cutting nearly always affects the guilty station adversely in the long run. It is virtually impossible to keep rate-cutting deals confidential. In fact, once the breach is made the station's own sales staff is forced into widening it. Eventually rates are cut for most customers, and the station might just as well have issued a rate card with lower rates in the first place. In the meantime the station has undermined advertisers' confidence in the medium, placed broadcast competitors at an unfair disadvantage, demoralized its own sales force, and started a downward spiral which may be impossible to stop. The economically marginal station is least likely to be able to resist rate-cutting. As was pointed out earlier, management cannot pursue an effective long-term policy if small day-to-day gains or losses mean the difference between failure and continued operation.

PER INQUIRY ADVERTISING

One of the conspicuous rate-cutting devices is a form of direct-mail sales known as "per inquiry" (PI) advertising. In the PI deal the station receives payment not for the time devoted to advertising but for the number of inquiries received or items sold. Often the station itself handles the transaction by telephone or mail, retaining its percentage of the purchase price and forwarding the rest to the dealer. The station's share may be as high as 50 per cent. Station income from a PI deal may actually total more than the station would have received from the sale of the equivalent time at the card rate, although it is more likely to be less. Per inquiry, in short, works on a piecework or commission basis, often converting the station into a retail distributor as well as an advertiser of the product.

This method of payment runs directly counter to the principle underlying the rate-card system. In a sense it implies that the rate-card method of time sales is essentially dishonest, since the station often receives more for its time at card rates than the advertiser earns back in sales directly attributable to his broadcast advertising. This is a basic fallacy in PI advertising — the assumption that the only valid function of advertising is to produce direct, immediate sales. The fact is, however, that some of the most important functions of broadcast advertising depend on its ability to create good will, to establish a brand name, to disseminate information about a product, and so forth. These are valid advertising functions, and their worth is not lessened when such activities do not yield equivalent value in direct, immediate, traceable sales.

Aside from these general considerations, however, the PI has specific

---

[5] Herman S. Hettinger, *A Decade of Radio Advertising* (Chicago: University of Chicago Press, 1933), p. 316. Copyright 1933 by The University of Chicago.

drawbacks. The product for which it is employed is usually a low-cost item of doubtful intrinsic value: patent medicines, how-to-do-it books, religious articles, household gadgets, and the like. In most cases the articles are greatly overpriced; sometimes they are out-and-out swindles. The method of advertising is comparable to the pitch, described previously. Commercials tend to be loud, over-long, delivered very rapidly in a tone of delirious urgency, highly repetitious, full of fantastic overstatement, nearly always emphasing low price ("two for the price of one," "special introductory price," "only a few left at this low price"), and concluding with strong urgings to immediate action ("act now," "while this offer lasts," "call at once," "don't wait," "the first twenty calls," etc.). On television, of course, PI's always include an impressive demonstration of the article. The conclusion is inescapable that most PI's are intended to confuse and paralyze the critical faculties of the audience. They prey on two widespread human weaknesses: avarice and ignorance.

All this means, of course, that the average PI is highly offensive to most critical and reasonably intelligent audiences; this in turn means that the station which persistently schedules PI's is systematically driving away the most valuable part of an audience — the part with buying power. Furthermore, since the PI merchandise is usually overpriced and sometimes actually worthless, even that part of the audience that is taken in by the PI is likely to become disaffected. On the other hand, if the merchandise is a useful product the station is setting itself up as a competitor of its own local retailers, who are losing business to the out-of-town PI dealer.

All this considered, it may seem remarkable that simple self-interest does not induce stations to refuse PI offers. Again, we must recall that the station operating on the verge of insolvency is not likely to take the long view; it must grasp at straws, and since PI offers are not accepted by the majority of stations they are a favorite means of keeping marginal stations in business. It must be added, however, that some highly profitable stations accept PI business. Their success can be attributed only to the fantastic scope of broadcasting, which makes it possible to capitalize commercially on the attention of tiny fractions of the total potential audience. When a medium can reach virtually every member of the population it is possible to assemble a sizeable number of people who are gullible enough even for the purposes of the PI.

Like rate-cutting in general, the PI has been with broadcasting from the beginning of its commercial success. Hettinger said of PI's in 1933: "Not only is the method of payment economically unjustifiable, but the questionable value of many of the products which companies are attempting to sell in this fashion raises a serious problem of public interest."[6]

The broadcast industry as a whole is strongly opposed to all forms of rate cutting and rate evading (the payola), including the PI. The more

[6] Hettinger, *op. cit.*, pp. 169-170.

enlightened segment of the industry is well aware that its long-term interest as a business lies in developing broadcasting into a medium of integrity. The higher its standing as an institution rises, the more effectively it can carry out its function as an advertising medium. So once again, as in the case of the standards discussed in the previous chapter, we find fairly objective criteria for evaluating station performance — criteria which the industry itself has accepted as reasonable.

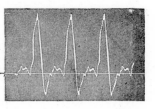

15

Mechanisms for Reaching the
Advertising Market

In the preceding chapter we pursued the analogy of broadcasting as a commodity offered for sale. It may be helpful now to look at this commodity from the point of view of the customer — i.e., the advertiser. For the small family-operated retail store or service business such as the neighborhood market or cobbler, advertising may consist of no more than the sign on the store-front. But nowadays business above this subsistence level is typically dynamic: the rule is "expand or perish;" there is no standing still. Most businesses actively seek to maintain, and if possible to expand, their market. This necessitates advertising.

A businessman therefore considers advertising a normal part of his operating budget, planning in advance to spend a certain amount, often calculated as a percentage of annual gross sales or net profit. At the level of the largest business enterprises advertising budgets reach many millions of dollars annually (Table 11). Decisions must be made about how best to expend the advertising budget — what media to use, what selling strategy, what timing, and so on. Normally this money is not spent on any one medium or type of activity but on several media and on a number of related activities, extending into the fields of promotion and publicity as well as of advertising proper.

SINGLE-MARKET v. MULTIPLE-MARKET ADVERTISING

Advertisers can be divided for practical purposes into two groups according to their scope of operations: single-market and multiple-market. This division is reflected in the dual rate card of broadcasting, local (retail) and national (wholesale). Multiple-market advertisers may be regional rather than national, but to simplify our exposition we will use the term "national" to include both.

Broadcasting needs some mechanism for selling time to both local and national advertisers. A broadcast station is, by its nature, limited to a single

Table 11

Advertising Budgets of Large Firms (Millions of Dollars)*

Company	Total Expenditures	Network TV	Network Radio	Newspaper Sections	Magazines
Procter & Gamble Co.	44	24	12	1	7
General Motors Corp.	37	10	4	2	21
Colgate-Palmolive Co.	27	14	5	4	4
General Foods Corp.	25	10	3	2	10
Gillette Co.	19	11	6	1	1
Chrysler Corp.	18	9	2	.4	7
General Electric Co.	18	7	.9	.4	10
Lever Brothers Co.	18	7	4	4	3
R. J. Reynolds Tobacco Co.	17	12	2	.3	3
General Mills, Inc.	16	8	4	1	3

* Amounts over a million rounded to nearest million.
Source: *Television Factbook No. 21* (Fall-Winter, 1955), p. 24, based on Publishers Information Bureau data.

market (or at most to one group of physically related markets). The station's own sales force can, of course, reach local advertisers within its own market area directly. But the central offices of national advertisers are concentrated in a few major cities; stations located elsewhere cannot afford to maintain salesmen in these centers as well as at home. By the same token, the national advertiser needs an efficient means of channeling advertising to many markets without having to deal separately with the local media in each market.

NETWORK ADVERTISING

One economic function of a broadcast network is meeting this dual need. From the advertiser's point of view a network converts broadcasting into a multi-market medium, comparable to a nationally-distributed magazine — which is the only other unitary medium that can reach all markets approximately simultaneously with identical messages. Network sales departments can offer the prospective advertiser nationwide coverage in a single transaction, and the advertiser can launch his advertising message from a single point at which it can easily be supervised and controlled. From the station's point of view the network is an extension of its sales staff, representing the station in the national field.

A second function of the network is to take care of the distribution of programs. This means providing the origination points for programs, making arrangements with AT&T for interconnection facilities, and handling program traffic on these facilities. The third function of the network is to produce programs — or at least to provide the facilities for the production or release of programs produced by others. Tremendous expense is involved in operating elaborate network sales departments, leasing interconnection facilities, and maintaining facilities for the production and origination of network programs. Such expense is justified only by the fact that a network reaches many markets at once; when total cost is divided by total markets, the cost per market becomes reasonable.

Even so, the traditional network method of securing national advertising coverage is relatively expensive. It is feasible only for a limited number of advertisers, essentially those in the "millionaire" class, i.e., those with annual advertising budgets of over a million dollars. For these companies the prestige attached to the sponsorship of outstanding network programs is a unique advantage. No other advertising medium offers a comparable opportunity for creating customer good will.

Besides the disadvantage of high cost, network advertising has the further disadvantage of relative inflexibility. A network provides one particular station to cover a given market, and that station is usually one of the larger and hence more expensive ones. That station may not be the one best suited to the advertiser's needs. To cite an obvious example, imagine a product which is primarily of interest to farmers. Networks tend to emphasize the rich metropolitan markets, which are very expensive for the advertiser yet may not include many farmers. Moreover, farm audiences are likely to be loyal to those stations which cater to their tastes and interests, and these particular stations may not be affiliated with the network. In such a situation the advertiser would do better to select only those stations which are (1) located in farm areas and (2) most attractive to farm audiences. He can bypass many major population centers and stations which do not meet these criteria. Furthermore, networks have relatively high program and advertising standards; some types of programs and advertising for which national sponsors exist are simply not acceptable to the networks.

NATIONAL SPOT ADVERTISING

To meet the need for such specially-tailored coverage, precisely adaptable to the pocketbook and the target-audience of the particular advertiser, some other avenue of national broadcast advertising is essential. Merely to select the individual stations which can best serve the needs of the advertiser is not as easy as appears. To begin with, the advertiser would usually prefer to have direct control over the program and advertising messages, as in the case of network broadcasting. Secondly, to negotiate scores of separate contracts for time on as many widely dispersed stations would be most inefficient and time-consuming. The first problem was solved in 1929, with the development of the electrical transcription (ET). The ET is simply a long-playing record of good fidelity; such records were regularly manufactured for broadcasting at a time when the ordinary phonograph record was still being made by the crude acoustical recording method and was limited to about four minutes of playing time. Transcriptions (and now, of course, films) made it possible for the advertiser to control program content and to deliver identical programs to all outlets. The program (or spot announcement) can be filmed or recorded at one time and one place under the direct supervision of the advertiser and then distributed by mail or express to the selected stations.

As to the second problem, there developed by 1932 a new form of middleman in the broadcast industry — the *station representative*. His function is to represent the station's sales interests in the national market. Each station-representative firm contracts to represent a number of stations and to seek the business of national advertisers for them on a non-network basis. The station keeps its representatives informed of its facilities, audience, and programs, and any facts which will help the representative in selling the station's time. A network-affiliated station, therefore, may be said to have three different sales forces at work: its own salesmen, covering the local market; the network sales department, covering the national market; and its station representative, covering the national market for non-network business. The non-affiliated station, of course, is entirely dependent on its station representative for access to national business.

The kind of national non-network advertising that is handled in this way is known as *national spot*. The term is unfortunate, since to most people it immediately suggests the idea of spot *announcement*. Actually, however, it refers to the fact that the national advertiser can "spot" his advertising anywhere on the map, instead of being confined to the fixed coverage pattern of a network. The fact is, any type of program or commercial announcement can be utilized in national spot advertising — with the one exception of network programs. For instance, as this branch of the business has developed, national spot advertisers have learned to capitalize on the fact that most stations have local talent on their staffs which has a loyal following — a newscaster, disc-jockey, women's commentator, cooking expert, musician, or weather reporter. For some spot advertisers this local flavor is desirable, and is something which cannot be duplicated by network advertising. National spot clients like to have their station-break announcements placed before or after the big network programs, because they can thus capitalize on the popularity of these programs without the expense of network program sponsorship. They also continue to use syndicated recorded program material — "package" programs, for example, which may offer complete recorded or filmed name-talent shows, equal in quality to many network programs.

Basically, then, broadcast advertising is divided into three classes: local, network (both national and regional), and national spot. Each has its own sales machinery and its own characteristic effect on programming. Historically, network advertising was the first of the three to develop fully. In the earliest days of broadcasting the problem of low-cost local programming was difficult to solve, whereas network programming developed rapidly because money was available at that level. Money was available, in turn, because large national advertisers — particularly those interested in broadcasting's unique public-relations potentialities — were willing to experiment with the new medium. Local advertisers, being more conservative, having less to spend, and needing direct selling rather than public-relations advertising, were slow to experiment. National spot, as we have pointed out, began to gain prominence as soon as electrical transcriptions solved the initial program-syndication problem in 1929.

THE INCREASE IN LOCAL BROADCAST ADVERTISING

It will be recalled that radio broadcasting remained relatively stable after its initial growth leveled off and the economy of the industry settled into a definite pattern (Chapter 9). During this period, which lasted until after World War II, network advertising accounted for the largest share of industry revenue, with local second and national spot third. The tremendous expansion of the industry after World War II, however, created a new situation. Network advertising, being, as we have pointed out, dependent on a relatively small number of major advertisers, reached a point beyond which it could not make any substantial advance. One great reservoir of potential advertising revenue was the class of advertisers who, though regional or national in scope, could not afford network advertising or could not use it efficiently; another promising resource was the small local advertiser, whose needs had never been fully studied and whose potential had never been intensively exploited. In every community many small businesses confined their advertising to routine newspaper insertions; indeed, many had never even advertised systematically at all. Furthermore, the explosive growth in the number of radio stations after World War II (see Figure 20) meant that many sizable communities which had never before had local radio outlets now for the first time had the opportunity to try this medium.

Intensified competition and wider distribution of facilities meant that the dormant local market now began to be systematically cultivated, along with the livelier national spot field. The result was that by 1947 the amount of local radio advertising surpassed the network share, and by 1950 national spot also surpassed network (Figure 29). Interestingly enough, television's early experience paralleled that of radio. Local programming developed slowly; stations were few in number, and national advertisers were eager to experiment with this new dimension in advertising. Not until local competition is maximized by the widest possible distribution of television stations can local advertising be fully and efficiently exploited.

The decrease in radio network advertising caused by increased competition both from non-network radio and from television has created serious problems for the chains. The increased use of recorded syndicated pro-

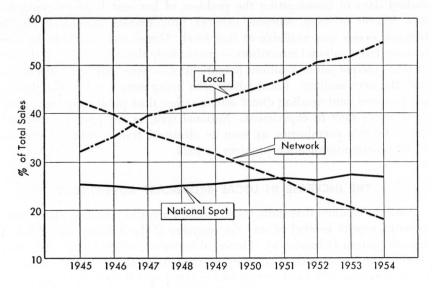

Figure 29

Trend in Relation of Radio Network to Spot and Local
Time Sales Since 1945

Note the consistent rise in importance of local sales.

Source: FCC reports.

grams also has contributed to the decline by partly undermining the net-works' advantage as a program syndication device.

One counter-measure adopted by the networks is competition for local advertising revenue by means of the cooperative network program,[1] whose emergence was discussed in Chapter 9. Another device, used particularly in television, is an adaptation to the network situation of the participation program, a format originally developed for the benefit of low-budget local advertisers. Since television generally costs the advertiser four or five times as much as radio, even major advertisers are likely to find it too rich for their blood. The network participation program provides for cost-sharing by several sponsors. It may be in the modified form of sponsorship of complete program segments (the CBS Arthur Godfrey program, for instance) or in the more literal participation form of NBC's "magazine format" series, *Today, Home,* and *Tonight.* So important has this source of revenue become that in 1954 NBC set up a special department to handle sales of

---

[1] This concept is to be distinguished from cooperative *advertising,* which refers to cost-sharing by the local dealer and the manufacturer or distributor. This type of co-operation is common, for instance, in the advertising of automobiles, with the Detroit manufacturer sharing the cost of locally-released advertising with the local authorized dealer.

advertising on these programs. The 40-hour weekend radio program, *Monitor*, introduced by NBC in 1955, represented an ingenious new achievement in network-program flexibility, with provision not only for network co-op, but also for national spot and local advertisers. This network invasion of a class of business traditionally regarded as the province of national spot has not been welcomed by the stations and station representatives.[2] The basis of the stations' objection is the fact that their income from spot advertising is higher than that from network advertising. However, this is not the only revision of established broadcast practice brought about by television; the higher cost of the new medium has brought about many such adjustments. Other examples are the practice of alternate weekly sponsorship of major television programs, the rotation of talent to provide more preparation time, and the scheduling of some program series at intervals of more than a single week. Nevertheless, the underlying pattern of sales, programming, and program distribution established by radio persists into the television era.

THE VALUE OF NETWORK AFFILIATION

In view of the economic predominance of non-network advertising (Figure 29 and Table 12) and the perfecting of non-network methods of program syndication, the interconnection of chains of stations for simultaneous broad-

Table 12

Relative Importance of Local, Network, and Spot
Advertising in Radio and TV, 1954

Medium	Source of Total Advertising Revenue		
	Local (%)	Network (%)	Spot (%)
Radio	55	18	27
Television	22	45	33

Based on: FCC, "Radio and TV Broadcast Financial Data — 1954"
(2 December 1955, mimeo.), Tables 2 and 12.

casts might appear to be an obsolescent feature of the American broadcast service. The fact is, however, that national networks remain one of the most characteristic and dynamic features of American broadcasting. Both local and national spot advertising realize vital indirect benefits from the

2 "Flanagan Says Network Pressure May Draw More Federal Legislation," *Broadcasting-Telecasting* (19 October 1953), p. 34.

existence of the networks, whose functioning is also an indispensable aid to the individual station's operation and to the public itself.[3]

What does a national network do for these three interests — advertisers, stations, and public? Advertisers, as we have pointed out, find in networks a unique means of reaching the national market. The sales function does not stop, however, at the point at which the network sales force persuades a sponsor to buy a segment of station time. The fact that network-sponsored programs form part of its schedule colors the station's whole institutional personality. One effect is to make the station's time more salable to local and national spot advertisers. In fact, a station's net income from network commercial time may be relatively small as compared with its local and national spot income. But these sources would yield much less income in the absence of the network affiliation.

From the point of view of local program operations, the fact that the network service comes to the station ready to take the air is of inestimable value. Broadcast stations operate under relentless pressure; the necessity of providing a continuous service, minute by minute, day by day, and week by week throughout the year profoundly affects the nature of that service. Gross simplifications result — elementary formats, repetitive patterns, standardized procedures, the minimum of innovation. When the station itself must be responsible for providing every minute of its programming these simplifications must be maximized, for there is no let-up of the pressure. The network-affiliate, on the other hand, can look forward to a number of hours each day when it is being fed by the network — hours during which it can devote thought and preparation to its own local programming. Of course the non-affiliated station could relieve the pressure simply by hiring more people to do the programming job. But the economics of the situation do not permit this form of relief. Economic necessity keeps the program staff at, or close to, the very minimum, and that minimum leaves little room for experimentation, originality, or wide variety. Thus the network-affiliate benefits not only directly from the basic fact that network programs enhance the value of its time but also indirectly from the fact that the network frees the affiliate's program staff from operational pressures, giving it more time to prepare local programming. Better local programming, in turn, brings in more money. So the network affiliation may be said to be part of a profitable cycle.

Of course, the public also is involved in the process. After all, the very fact that the network programs attract audiences sets the whole cycle in motion. The existence of national networks means that audiences on a national scale can see and hear events — significant or trivial — as they actually take place. It means that the creative talents of the entire nation

[3] The discussion is limited to national networks. Regional networks also exist, but they are of minor economic importance. Transcription, kinescope, or syndicated film "networks" are pseudo-networks, lacking the interconnection facilities of the true network.

(and to some extent of other nations) can be pooled and made available for the entertainment and information of all.

THE FUTURE OF NETWORKS

But the question naturally arises whether this process necessarily requires simultaneity and instantaneity, i.e., interconnection. Could not the same goal be achieved equally well and more cheaply, for all except a relatively few "actuality" programs, by means of mechanical reproduction? With regard to television, one school of thought replies affirmatively, on the theory that television is merely a new way of exhibiting motion-picture films. The fact that films — any kind of films — can be exhibited on television lends some strength to the contention. However, at least two fallacies are involved: One is the assumption that the creative techniques of the two media are identical; the other is that the sense of actuality is important only for real-life events, such as games or political ceremonies.

As for technique, the definitive element in the motion-picture art is the editing process. Motion pictures remained animated still photographs until the discovery of the one thing that sets the cinema apart from all other arts: its ability to transcend time and space relations in the cutting room. Television has no such cutting room. It is by nature a forgetful, not a remembering, medium. The pictures are there instantaneously — bound to the natural sequence of the time dimension. True, the cutting from one picture to another by switching from one camera to another seems analogous to the joining of one film scene to another; but the processes differ significantly in that the film scenes can be juggled without regard to time and the television scenes cannot.

This fact is basic to the second point: that the sense of actuality is important even in non-actuality (i.e., staged) television events. The proponents of the television-is-film theory argue that the use of film can ensure perfection, since mistakes can be corrected. Television, being time-bound, cannot call its mistakes back. Film does make possible a kind of mechanical excellence, a perfection of artifice that is sometimes valuable to television. (A sponsor, for example, may prefer the guaranteed perfection of a filmed commercial to the risks of live presentation.) But it does not follow that audiences are equally willing always to exchange the sense of spontaneity and actuality for the contrived correctness of film. Nothing can quite replace the satisfaction derived from seeing something that is taking place *now* and knowing that the future of the event has not already been irrevocably determined. This sense of the living event and of the unpredictable hazards of the future is broadcasting's unique dimension.[4]

It is no more reasonable to suppose that television as a medium of ex-

[4] Cf.: Martin Stone, "The Case for Live Television" and John L. Sinn, "The Case for Filmed Television," *Broadcasting-Telecasting* (19 and 26 January 1953), pp. 77-78.

pression should confine itself to the limitations of the film medium than it would have been to confine the novel as a literary form to the limitation of verse or newspapers to the limitations of literary prose. Like the newspaper, television is an assimilative medium, and film is just one of the many products which it digests. But a diet of film alone would be fatally out of balance and could only result in an anemic television service.

Network television, then, is not likely to succumb to kinescopes, nor is live television likely to be replaced by televised films.[5] This is not to say that current network practices will necessarily remain the same, or that all networks now operating can survive. The indications are that the present state of the economy justifies the existence of perhaps two radio networks of national scope and three television networks, supplemented by regional chains and quasi-network organizations.

Radio, of course, has been particularly hard hit at the network level by the emergence of television. In broadcasting a decline in sales not only cuts down income but also increases expense, because programming has to go on. The cost of radio-network sustaining programs on NBC increased fivefold from 1948 to 1953. Fixed costs also have been increasing: for example, line costs for interconnection to affiliates took 4 per cent of the network's revenue in 1948 and 9 per cent in 1953.[6]

NETWORK OWNERSHIP OF STATIONS

Turning now to the relationships between affiliated station and network, let us first recall that a network, as properly defined, involves simultaneous broadcasts of identical programs by connected stations, and that most stations in the national chains are related to the network organization on a contract rather than an ownership basis. Nevertheless, networks need the kind of control which ownership implies over at least a limited number of "key" stations. For one thing, owned and operated ("O and O") stations are an important source of income. The president of CBS Television told a Congressional committee that "without some owned and operated stations, the network is just not a profitable piece of business."[7] O and O stations are typically very powerful stations on desirable channels located in major markets.

Secondly, network O and O stations give the network basic production facilities which do not become merely costly overhead at hours when the network is not on the air; the facilities continue to earn income through

[5] See Table 31 for data on the proportion of live to filmed network television programs. It is noteworthy that most of the major programs — those in which networks try for the highest prestige — are live.

[6] David Sarnoff, "Address by David Sarnoff, Chairman of the Board, RCA-NBC, to NBC Radio Affiliates Committee in Chicago," *Broadcasting-Telecasting* (21 September 1953), p. 111.

[7] House Committee on Interstate and Foreign Commerce Subcommittee, *Hearings on H.R. 278, Investigation of Radio and Television Programs* (Washington: Government Printing Office, 1952), p. 310.

the local operation of the O and O stations. Thirdly, ownership of stations gives the network a licensee status, for networks as such are not licensed. They have no legal status under the Communications Act, and therefore appear in legal proceedings before the FCC primarily as licensees of stations rather than as networks *per se*.

The number of stations that a network (or for that matter any other licensee) may own is limited by FCC rulings to seven AM, seven FM, and seven television (of which no more than five may be VHF).[8] Therefore the majority of network affiliates have a contractual rather than a proprietary bond with the network organization. Since the network owns so proportionately small a number of its affiliates, its stability depends on the degree of control it can exercise by contractual means. The "Chain Broadcasting Regulations," adopted by the FCC after an investigation initiated in 1938 (see Chapter 9), place limits on the degree of such contractual control.

THE NETWORK AFFILIATION CONTRACT

The fundamental purpose of the affiliation contract is to give the network a commodity to sell. In order to enter the market to sell network time, the network organization must have assurance that (1) certain stipulated stations and (2) certain stipulated hours on those stations are available; otherwise, of course, the network salesman has nothing to offer the advertiser. From the business point of view, then, it would be desirable for the network to have exclusive, undisputed access to all of its affiliates' time all of the time. This would give the network maximum stability. Such an extreme, however, would reduce the affiliate to complete dependence on the network and would paralyze its ability to obtain local and national spot business, since the affiliate would have no control over its own time.

The particular devices employed by networks to assure themselves of having a commodity to sell and the limitations placed on these devices may be outlined by summarizing the FCC's chain-broadcasting regulations:[9]

1. *Contracts may not prevent an affiliate from receiving programs from a rival network.* This reflects the fact that a network would prefer to have "exclusivity of affiliation" — i.e., to prevent a rival network's having access to its affiliate, even if the affiliate's own network is not using the time.

2. *Contracts may not prevent the network from releasing a program to a station other than its own affiliate in that affiliate's service area.* This rules out "territorial exclusivity," which would give the station

---

[8] FCC, *Rules and Regulations*, Part 3, Secs. 3.35, 3.240, 3.636. See Chapter 22 for a discussion of the status of these rules.

[9] FCC, *Rules and Regulations*, Part 3, Secs. 3.101-3.108, 3.231-3.238, 3.658. The background to these regulations is thoroughly explored in the FCC's *Report on Chain Broadcasting* (Washington: Government Printing Office, 1941). The regulations apply equally to AM, FM and TV.

exclusive local control over programs of its network in return for the advantage which exclusivity of affiliation would give the network.

3. *Contracts may not run for longer than two years.* This reflects the fact that networks would generally prefer long-term contracts, because these would enable them to make long-term plans. Before the network contract regulations were adopted, both NBC and CBS contracts were binding on the affiliates for five years but on the networks for only one.

4. *Contracts may not require the affiliate to option more than a limited amount of time to the network, or to make this time available on less than fifty-six days' notice.* Option time is at the heart of the affiliation contract. It is that time which the station agrees in advance to make available for sale by the network. The network is not obliged, however, to program the time if it has not been sold on the network. Therefore the station may have to program this time on a sustaining basis; or, if the station tries to sell the time locally or to a national spot account, it has to keep in mind that the network may take up its option at any time. If this happens the station has to cancel the local or national spot advertising. The fifty-six-day notice requirement is intended to give the station the opportunity to sell network option time to non-network accounts with the assurance of being able to promise it for eight weeks at least. Since the network would tend to concentrate its option time at the best hours, the regulation limits option time to three hours from each of four time-segments, viz., 8 A.M. to 1 P.M., 1 P.M. to 6 P.M., 6 P.M. to 11 P.M., and 11 P.M. to 8 A.M.

5. *Contracts may not prevent affiliates from refusing to carry network programs.* Networks would naturally prefer to have positive assurance that all affiliates ordered by sponsors will carry commercial network programs. As a practical matter affiliates never have been obliged to carry all network *sustaining* programs, and rejection of such programs by many affiliates is not unusual. But since an affiliate wants neither to lose commercial business nor to alienate the affections of its network, rejection of commercial programs is comparatively rare. In some instances there are overruling considerations, however; the rule defines these as cases in which the affiliate believes the network program to be "contrary to the public interest," "unsatisfactory or unsuitable," or in conflict with another program of "outstanding local or national importance." Probably the most frequent occasion of cancellation of network commercial programs by an affiliate is the last of these, when local events of unusual importance or interest conflict with network commitments. Network sponsors are, of course, given rebates in such circumstances.

6. *Networks may not own more than one station covering the same service area.* Before this regulation was made, NBC's ownership of

both the Red and Blue networks gave it two O and O stations in each of four major cities.

7. *Dual networks are not permitted.* This too was aimed at NBC. It prevents dual networks only when they cover the same area at the same time.

8. *Contracts may not give networks control over affiliates' non-network rates.* This has particular reference to the possibility that the network will seek to influence its affiliates' national spot rates, since the network is competing with national spot representatives for the business of national advertisers.

NBC and CBS fought adoption of the chain-broadcasting regulations to the last ditch. They did succeed in obtaining three concessions from the FCC: (1) The provision against territorial exclusivity was softened to permit affiliates to have *first call* on their network's offerings; (2) option time, originally eliminated altogether, was restored with only moderate restrictions; and (3) the term of affiliation contracts was extended from one year to two years. Nevertheless, the networks continued in bitter opposition, and it was not until the Supreme Court upheld the FCC in 1943 that the rules finally went into effect. The networks' dire prediction that enforcement of the regulations would mean the end of the network system of broadcasting as it had been known was never fulfilled. It has often been said that such predictions were deliberately misleading, dictated entirely by the selfish interests of the chains. Yet even two dissenting FCC members feared that 'the revolutionary change proposed by the majority will result in the destruction of the present excellent program distribution system and the substitution therefor of some new kind of system, the effects of which the majority does not adequately visualize."[10]

If we assume that the carefully reasoned dissent of the FCC minority and the highly vocal opposition of the networks (which continued even after the original rules were moderated) had a basis in a genuine belief that the network regulations were radically destructive, it is of some interest to inquire why the predicted result did not come about. The basis of the prediction appears to have been the belief that the weakening of the networks' control over affiliates through the watering-down of the affiliation contract would undermine the stability of the network operation. If the network could not be assured of keeping its affiliate line-up intact, it could not make long-term plans or commitments. If affiliates could be easily pried loose from their networks and if the exclusive character of the network–affiliate relations were compromised, affiliates would be prone to "shop around":

. . . competition among competently managed networks would be replaced by an unwholesome conglomeration of opportunistic "time brokers" catering to an aggregation of local monopolies in the various towns and cities of the nation.[11]

[10] FCC, *op. cit.,* p. 116.
[11] FCC dissenting opinion, *loc. cit.*

Why, when the chain regulations finally became effective, did not these unhappy results materialize? Apparently because the simple self-interest of the individual station inclined it toward voluntary maintenance of the *status quo*. It was pointed out earlier that a station is not merely a collection of isolated programs; it develops an institutional personality, and its network affiliation becomes a most important part of that personality. It is *the* station of its network in its community; to all intents and purposes it is the network itself, for audiences have no contact with networks as such but only as they are represented by individual stations. Therefore the affiliated station is not likely either to change its affiliation often or to refuse to cooperate with its network at the risk of being dropped as an affiliate. The chain regulations prevent the networks from *forcing* unfavorable contract terms on the affiliate, but they do not prevent affiliates from accepting such terms as seem in their best interest. And so, for example, most affiliates continue to make option time available on only twenty-eight days' notice, preferring not to take advantage of the fifty-six days to which they are legally entitled.

That networks persisted and prospered despite the chain-broadcasting regulations attests to the fundamental vitality of the network principle. Competition was increased by the separation of the Blue network from NBC and the growth of Mutual, but not to the point at which it could become self-destructive.

NETWORK ORGANIZATION

As in all matters having to do with the business side of broadcasting, industry practice follows certain fairly well-defined lines but is not rigidly standardized. A good deal of improvisation has accompanied the rise of television, not only because of the innovations of the medium but also because there have not been enough stations to provide a separate affiliate in each market for each network. The problem of developing attractive local programming has been acute, and hence network programs have been in extraordinary demand as the only widely effective incentive to set purchasing. The following brief description of network organization and operations, though subject to exceptions, represents the general practice of the industry.

A network headquarters organization reflects its triple function. The several networks are variously organized, but they generally include under *sales* specific departments to handle research, advertising, promotion, and national spot sales for O and O stations. Under the program *distribution* function come departments of engineering, station relations, and traffic. Under the *program* function come departments for production, production services, continuity acceptance, news, and public affairs, as well as programs in general. These functions are supported by the activities common to any large business enterprise — departments to handle administration, finance and accounting, purchasing, labor relations and personnel, and legal matters. The O and O stations operate independently under a special administrative department. The headquarters offices of the networks are in New York, with major production centers also located in Hollywood. Offices are also maintained in other major cities, notably Chicago and Washington.

NETWORK OPERATION

Each network claims a certain number of affiliates, but this number can be misleading, for it does not necessarily represent the number of stations carrying any given program (Table 13). A national network needs strong outlets in about fifty major markets in order to survive economically. In order to meet the advertisers' needs for flexible coverage, the network offers various combinations or groups of stations. Generally a combination of the O and O stations and a group of the most important affiliates is offered as the *basic* network, a "must-buy" group necessary for the network's financial health. Other stations, either in regional groups or singly, can be used optionally by the sponsor. In order to extend the benefits of radio network programs to smaller stations whose locations do not make them desirable buys for sponsors, some outlets may be classed as "bonus" stations, in which case they get no pay for their time and, for their part, pay nothing for the programs. In television, however, "a bonus arrangement is impractical because television is too valuable an advertising medium to give away — no matter how small the market or how modest the station's operation."[12] The problem of the marginal station has been particularly acute since UHF television began. Advertising agencies do not value UHF stations highly, because their coverage is limited and it is difficult to get audiences to convert existing VHF sets. This in turn has made UHF stations unattractive to networks as affiliates. Unable to secure network affiliations, many UHF stations have lacked the one incentive to conversion which means anything to audiences, namely high-quality programming. Networks have received sharp criticism for their reluctance to break the deadlock by affiliating with UHF stations.[13] Yet a network cannot afford to affiliate at random. Its affiliation policy must be governed basically by the relative cost per thousand homes delivered by the station. A station which covers only part of a market or is located in a very small market is a relatively expensive investment for a network sponsor. CBS, for example, has set a circulation of 40,000 homes as the minimum which is economically feasible for a full-scale affiliate.[14] In 1954 CBS announced a modified form of affiliation contract for network "associates," stations of secondary commercial importance. This

[12] CBS, *CBS Television's Criteria in Affiliation Actions* (New York: CBS, 1954), p. 26.
[13] This problem is explored in: Senate Committee on Interstate Commerce Subcommittee, *Hearings on S. 3095, Status of UHF and Multiple Ownership of TV Stations* (Washington: Government Printing Office, 1954), *passim.*
[14] Cf. CBS, *op. cit.,* p. 7.

has the effect of securing sponsored network programs for these stations at merely token rates. For the sake of economy, programs are delivered by kinescope rather than direct relay, and hence these stations are not technically part of the network. Another television variant practice is to release network sponsored programs on a sustaining basis to stations in markets not purchased by the sponsor. In this case the station may pay for the program directly and cuts away from the network to substitute public-service announcements for the sponsor's announcements.

A television network's list of affiliates must also be qualified by the fact that during the period when many markets had only one station that station "affiliated" rather loosely with all four networks. For the time being the networks had to seek the stations' favor. As the number of stations increased, they began to form "primary" affiliations with one network, with looser affiliations continuing with one or more of the other networks, depending upon the number of stations in the market. Maximum competition and maximum service, of course, would require at least as many stations as there are networks in each market. Since it is doubtful that there will ever be as many television stations as radio stations in operation, it is probable that multiple affiliation will continue to be much more common in television than in radio.

Normally the sponsor pays the network at the affiliate's national card rate. The affiliated station generally pays the network for its sales, program distribution, and production services in terms of a stipulated number of "free" hours of time per week. The network keeps all the income from the sale of this time. This is another way of saying, of course, that the affiliate sells its time to the network at a greatly reduced rate. Seventy per cent or more of the income from network programming (depending on the bargaining position of the affiliate) goes to pay for the network overhead and the costs of program distribution. It is for this reason that network business does not usually represent a very large proportion of station income, particularly in television, where the network's distribution costs are so high.

Network sustaining programs may be either would-be commercial shows temporarily lacking a sponsor or shows conceived primarily as sustaining features for their prestige value. Networks are justly proud of the high quality and public-interest value of the latter, but unfortunately these outstanding examples of non-commercial broadcasting are frequently not carried by affiliates, or if carried are sometimes re-broadcast at less favorable times. Since the list of network sustaining programs has meaning only insofar as the programs are made available to the public, such lists can be rather misleading (Table 13).[15] The reason that affiliates reject network

---

[15] The FCC noted in 1946 some conspicuous examples of the small coverage achieved by radio network sustaining programs and the routine types of local commercial programs substituted. FCC, *Public Service Responsibilities of Broadcast Licensees* (Washington: Government Printing Office, 1946), pp. 32-46. About 24 per cent of NBC's and 13 per cent of CBS's programming was sustaining in 1954 according to: Robert F. Jones,

Table 13

The Amount of a Network's Programming Carried by Its Affiliates

Amount Carried (% of total CBS network offering)	Carried by (no. of stations)
91 - 100	8
75 - 90	35
50 - 74	19
25 - 49	51
10 - 24	33
Less than 10	50

Source: Robert F. Jones, Progress Report prepared for the Senate Committee on Interstate and Foreign Commerce, *Investigation of Television Networks and the UHF-VHF Problem* (Washington: Government Printing Office, 1955), pp. 42-45.

sustaining programs is, of course, that they bring no income, whereas if a sustaining network program is located in a good time segment the affiliate can instead sell the time locally or to a national spot account. Moreover, a sustaining program which interests only a small minority of the audience is likely to depress the value of adjacent time segments.

THE NON-AFFILIATED STATION

So much stress has been laid on the importance of the national network in this chapter that it may logically be asked whether a place is left for the independent, or non-affiliated, station. Certainly in radio the independent station has proved its value as an added source of variety. Networks, by their nature, must conform to the needs of very large, heterogeneous audiences. Independent stations can tailor their programming to local needs, and can even select from the total local audience potential a homogeneous minority whose interests it can serve. Hence the local, non-network-affiliated radio station has an important function, and many such stations have found specialized service remunerative.[16]

In television the independent station is currently facing a difficult problem. Radio has at its command highly developed sources of syndicated material — music, news, scripts, packaged programs — which make independent operation relatively easy. Television has not yet developed the syndication of visual materials to the same extent. Presumably, as the

Progress Report Prepared for the Committee on Interstate and Foreign Commerce, *Investigation of Television Networks and the UHF-VHF Problem* (Washington: Government Printing Office, 1955), pp. 42 and 46.

[16] Cf. "WNEW: Radio's Little David," *Fortune* (October, 1952), pp. 132-133, 222-232.

backlog of syndicated film is elaborated and improved in quality, and as techniques of low-cost local program production are evolved, independent television operation will become more practicable. In the meantime, television has had to rely heavily on highly unsatisfactory syndicated program material, such as the antiquated feature films which have become notorious. The natural growth of television was impeded by a series of technological and legal delays which artificially limited the number of stations in operation, so that initially there were virtually no independent stations. In only two markets — New York and Los Angeles — does independent television-station operation have a history, and in both cities the independents had a difficult time.

16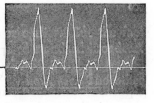

The Business of Measurement

and Evaluation

All advertisers need criteria for evaluating their investments in the various advertising media; by the same token, all media need yardsticks for measuring their own effectiveness. Both the medium (as seller) and the advertiser (as buyer) therefore become customers for market research. The advertiser asks two basic questions: Before making a decision he asks, "*How* shall I spend my advertising funds?"; after the decision he asks, "*What* did I get for my money?" In the one case prior data are needed as the basis of prediction; in the second case after-the-fact data are needed as the basis of evaluation.

In either case, great quantities of relevant objective data can be accumulated. But interpretation of all this information must be qualified by the fact that communication is a chain of events, one link of which is inaccessible to direct measurement. This intangible link lies between the message itself and the resulting behavior. Messages can be measured and behavior can be measured, but the subjective connection between them must be inferred (see Chapter 27). As far as the mass media are concerned, it is usually extremely difficult to demonstrate conclusively that Message "A" was directly and solely responsible for Behavior "B." This problem is common to all media. Broadcasting, however, presents the added difficulty that the *medium itself* is intangible. Its messages are fleeting sense impressions, not physical entities like space in a newspaper or on a billboard. As a result, the need for measurement and evaluation in broadcasting is both particularly acute and particularly difficult to meet. Every station, network, advertising agency, and station representative engages either directly or indirectly in some kind of market research. One of the broadcast-research mechanical devices alone is said to have cost more than $9 million to develop.[1] The annual expenditure for broadcast market research is estimated at ten million dollars.

[1] The Nielsen "audimeter," discussed below. Arthur C. Nielsen, *Evolution of Factual Techniques in Market Research* (New York: A. C. Nielsen, Inc., 1952), p. 18.

TYPES OF MEASUREMENT

Market research begins with the tabulation of relevant facts concerning populations and the economy. A basic market datum of broadcasting, of course, is the number of receivers in working order (Table 14 and Figure

Table 14

Basic Data on Radio and TV Receivers in United States Households

	Household Radio Sets	Auto Radio Sets	Household TV Sets
Total number of sets in working order	74,740,000	26,180,000	28,450,000
Total number of households having sets in working order	43,980,000	23,180,000	27,600,000
Percentage of all U.S. households	92.5	48.7	58.1

Source: Advertising Research Foundation, *National Survey of Radio and Television Sets Associated with U.S. Households, May, 1954* (New York: The Foundation, 1954), pp. 15-16, 18. Total number of U.S. households at time of survey (May, 1954): 47,560,000.

22). Further analysis reveals relations between sets of facts. For example, the Advertising Research Foundation, in cooperation with the national networks, made a nationwide study of set ownership which showed (among other things) how sets are distributed according to geographic areas and socio-economic status of owners, where sets are located in the households, and many interrelations between television-set households and radio-set households.[2]

Such a study reveals, for example, that the distribution of television sets according to the socio-economic level of households is almost exactly the same as the distribution of radios (Table 15). In the absence of such data one might have been inclined to guess that the much greater cost of television sets would have made them less common than radios in the lower-income groups.

But data of these kinds, based on simple listing of receiving sets as physical entities, tell us nothing about actual communication. Sets become significant only when people turn them on and attend to messages. As we have indicated, the crucial problem is to connect messages (e.g., advertising) with desired responses (e.g., purchasing). As a rule, only an indirect and highly inferential connection can be made. For example, it may be assumed that if a very large number of people are known merely to have been "exposed" to the message, a certain amount of purchasing response

[2] The Advertising Research Foundation, *National Survey of Radio and Television Sets Associated with U.S. Households, May, 1954* (New York: The Foundation, 1954).

Table 15

Distribution of Radio and TV Sets according to Socio-economic Quartiles

Socio-economic Rank (Quartiles)	Percentage of TV Sets	Percentage of Radio Sets
Upper	32.1	33.2
Upper-middle	27.6	27.5
Lower-middle	25.0	23.2
Lower	15.3	16.1

Source: Advertising Research Foundation, *National Survey of Radio and Television Sets Associated with U.S. Households, May, 1954* (New York: The Foundation, 1954), pp. 37, 80.

can safely be taken for granted; therefore a high program "rating" is desirable. But even "exposure" is difficult to measure. The researcher has the choice of (1) actually observing the exposure taking place; (2) inferring exposure from some related observable facts; (3) or asking the audience itself to testify. Since exposure to broadcasting takes place primarily in the privacy of the home, direct observation is not very practicable. Inferences can be drawn from the fact that people turn receiving sets on and off, so that set-tuning itself can often be used as a test of exposure. Or, finally, people can be interviewed or otherwise given an opportunity to testify about what they are now doing or have just done.[3] The researcher may, of course, try to break into the chain of events which constitutes the communication process at any point along the line. The foregoing examples tap the process at or near the point where the message is received, before any remote resultant response has taken place. Another method is to start the investigation nearer the end of the process — for example, by asking purchasers at the *point of sale* what influenced their choice of a given product. A still later point of entry is the *pantry check,* an actual physical inventory of the goods on the housewife's shelves. At an intermediate point the researcher can check on *sponsor identification,* ascertaining from the testimony of the viewer or listener whether the exposure to the advertising message has "taken," so to speak.

MEASUREMENT OF CIRCULATION

Whether the question is the prior one of how to advertise or the after-the-fact one of what the advertising accomplished, the most elementary quantitative datum to consider is *coverage* or *circulation.* This term means the number of people that can be reached by the advertising medium. It

[3] Letters, both voluntary and motivated, are of course the oldest and most obvious form of direct audience testimony. Letters are not generally regarded as having much value as a research tool for quantitative measurement.

is variously defined as the number of receiver-equipped homes in the signal area of the station as determined by physical measurements of the signal; as the number of homes which actually tune in the station at some time over a given period (usually a week); and as the number of homes which tune to the station a minimum percentage of the time during a week. Circulation is a measurement of a station's audience *potentiality*, therefore, rather than of its actual audience at a given time.

The prevalence of puffery or normal exaggerated "trade talk" in the realm of business discourse makes it axiomatic that the circulation claims of the medium itself cannot safely be accepted as fact by the buyer. Newspapers overcame the resulting confusion by surrendering the job of measuring their own circulation to an independent nonprofit organization set up for the purpose in 1914, the Audit Bureau of Circulation. The ABC reports of paid circulation, impartially audited and certified, are universally accepted.

Purchasers of broadcast time have no such single unimpeachable source of circulation information. Instead, a number of rival commercial measurement services compete for acceptance. Broadcasting would long ago have set up its own single audit bureau were it as easy to count audiences as it is to count newspaper sales, which are at least factual, even though their significance in terms of readership may be debatable. But broadcast audiences fluctuate from minute to minute throughout the day, from day to day, from season to season. It would be impossible constantly to follow these momentary fluctuations for millions of people and thousands of stations scattered from one end of the country to another. Drastic simplification is essential.

One simplification is to use a sample of the audience rather than the total audience as the basis of estimation. No one has even attempted to measure directly the listening or viewing behavior of everybody in the country. If it were possible at all, the task would be of such magnitude that it would probably introduce so many tabulating errors that it would actually be less accurate than a good sampling procedure anyway. The layman tends to be skeptical of a procedure which presumes to judge the behavior of an audience of many millions on the basis of a sample of only a few thousand; yet it has been well established in other fields that a properly chosen small sample can accurately show characteristics of a very large population. Most social surveys of the whole United States population use samples of only 2,000 to 5,000 individuals. Scientifically designed sampling is a routine research technique, used in a tremendous variety of measurement situations in which complete censuses would be either physically impossible or prohibitively expensive.[4]

Another simplification of broadcast audience research makes the test of membership or non-membership in the audience as uniform, clear-cut, and concrete as possible. Usually the test is simply whether or not a receiver is

[4] Cf.: Mildred Parten, *Surveys, Polls, and Samples* (New York: Harper & Bros., 1950).

turned on or a program being received. This set-use test obviously leaves out a great deal that might enable more refined measurement. We do not know how much attention is being paid to the program; whether the attitude toward it is favorable, indifferent, or hostile; whether the program was chosen after careful consideration of all programs available at that moment or whether the dial just happened to be set at that station, and so on.

A third simplification takes advantage of the fact that programming is repetitive. Since the same program series recur regularly in daily or weekly cycles, their relative popularity is likely to remain fairly stable. Similarly, audiences become habituated to patterns of listening or viewing in terms of stations as well as of programs, and hence a station's over-all audience also may be expected to remain relatively stable. Therefore it is not necessary to measure audiences every day of every week of the whole year. In other words, it is possible to draw inferences from samples of *time*, just as they are drawn from samples of the audience. "Continuous" measurement services are so called because they repeat the sampling procedure periodically, using the same methods each time; trends are revealed thereby because the data are comparable from one sample to the next.

METHODS OF MEASUREMENT

With these simplifications of the measurement situation in mind, we can turn next to the methods used for actually collecting data on audience behavior. Four methods are in most general use, either singly or in combination.

1. *The recall method.* This was the earliest to develop and is the most obvious — simply a matter of asking people to tell what programs they saw or heard in some past segment of time. Door-to-door ("personal") interviews are usually employed, although the information may also be secured by telephone. Often a list of the available programs is presented to the respondent to jog his memory, in which case the method is called "aided" or "roster" recall. The best-known practitioner of this method is The Pulse, Inc. Pulse uses door-to-door aided-recall interviews, with rosters for each of four day-parts. For example, to gather information on viewing-listening during the 8 A.M.-noon period, interviewers call on respondents from noon to 1 P.M. Late evening viewing-listening information is gathered the next morning. Interviews are conducted in a given market for several consecutive days in each month.[5]

---

[5] Cf.: The Pulse, Inc., *The Basic Deficiencies of the Telephone Coincidental Method of Broadcast Audience Measurement Compared to the Personal Interview-Aided Recall Technique* (New York: The Pulse, Inc., N.D.).

2. *The telephone coincidental method.* In this case the sample is interviewed by telephone and the respondent is asked to report on the program being seen or heard "now." The "now" is the reason for the term "coincidental," since in this method the asking of the question *coincides* with the actual viewing or listening reported. Of course coincidental personal interviews can also be employed, but this method is expensive and has been used only experimentally. The coincidental-telephone method is associated most notably with C. E. Hooper, Inc. One weakness is that it is confined to telephone homes, thereby making a truly representative sample impossible. Hooper has answered this objection by supplementing the coincidental telephone calls with diaries placed in non-telephone homes.[6]

3. *The diary method.* Members of the sample audience are asked to keep a record of their listening and viewing by filling in a form supplied by the research organization. Usually a small reward is offered as an incentive for keeping the "diary." American Research Bureau uses this method. It was also used for the important county-by-county national radio circulation surveys of Broadcast Measurement Bureau in 1946 and 1949.

4. *The automatic recorder.* A data-recording device, electrically attached to the receiving set, keeps a continuous record of when the set is turned on and off and which stations are tuned in. This device was developed by A. C. Nielsen and dubbed the "audimeter." Nielsen installs audimeters for every set in each sample home; set-owners are given free set-maintenance service and a small reward for mailing in the 16-mm. film record periodically.[7] This device has the unique advantage of providing a *continuous* record of set-use, thus revealing how long a given program is tuned in and the exact time when tuning in and tuning out take place. It can therefore continuously depict audience flow from one program to another.

Services which supply continuous circulation-measurement data use these four methods. Experiments also have been made on devices which would introduce a considerable degree of automation into the research procedure. Sets in sample homes would transmit tuning information directly to a headquarters point, where data would be automatically recorded and tabulated. Such a method, though very expensive, would have the extremely valuable advantage of providing almost instantaneous reports, whereas the present methods involve delays of two to five weeks for accumulation, tabulation, interpretation, and publication of the data.

---

[6] Matthew N. Chappell and C. E. Hooper, *Coincidental-Diary Method of Television Audience Measurement* (New York: C. E. Hooper, Inc., 1953). The same authors' book *Radio Audience Measurement* (New York: Stephen Daye, 1944), though now dated, is a useful introduction to the subject of audience measurement.

[7] Cf.: Arthur C. Nielsen, *op. cit.*

STATION COVERAGE v. PROGRAM COVERAGE

Basic audience information derived by the foregoing techniques is of two types: long-term station-coverage information and short-term program-popularity information. The first of these has to do with the basic ability of the station to reach an audience, without reference to specific fluctuations from program to program. The industry needs to be able to receive this kind of information on a standardized basis for all stations in the whole country. It was first supplied by Broadcast Measurement Bureau (BMB), founded in 1945 as a nonprofit cooperative service by the National Association of Broadcasters, the Association of National Advertisers, and the American Association of Advertising Agencies. BMB used a county-by-county diary method to sample the entire United States. Since its object was to secure useful data on every station in every locality, a relatively large sample of over 300,000 diaries was used. A survey of these dimensions is too expensive to make on a continuing basis. The first BMB report was issued in 1946, the second in 1949. With the expansion of private research services under the stimulus of television, BMB went out of existence in 1951. Its commercial successor, Standard Audit and Measurement Service, issued its first report in 1952. The only comparable source of information on basic station-circulation data for the whole country is provided by A. C. Nielsen's "Nielsen Coverage Service."

The other class of basic audience information is the one that is best known to the public because it produces the familiar "ratings" of network programs. Several companies compete in the rating field. A rating is a measurement of relative program popularity; it is dependent on the popularity of competing programs as well as the popularity of the program being rated; it may or may not be a measurement of audience size, depending on the method by which the rating is derived. If the rating is based on a sample which is numerically representative of the total audience, it may be "projected." Projection means extending a numerical characteristic of a sample to the total population from which the sample is drawn (see Figure 30).

The program rating is only one of several significant dimensions reported by the rating services. Generally speaking, it is useful also to know not only the number of homes ("households," "families") reached but also the number of individuals and something about their distribution in terms of sex, age, income level, and the like. The sum of all program ratings in a given market provides a "sets-in-use" rating, indicating the actual audience (as a proportion of the maximum potential audience) for the given program time-segment. Sets-in-use can be converted into "share-of-audience" by dividing the sets-in-use rating into the individual program rating (see Figure 30).

National ratings refer, of course, only to national network programs. The relative popularity of a network program can be properly determined only

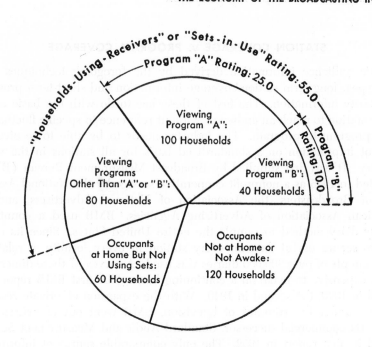

Sample: 400 Television Households
Universe: All Television Households in the Market

Figure 30

Rating Terminology

The pie represents a probability sample of 400 television households, out of the 100,000 television households in the market being surveyed. Note that the rating is derived from a percentage based upon the *total* sample, not just that part of the sample viewing programs at the time. In the example the universe (=100 per cent of the population being measured) is defined as all television households in the market. The universe could also be defined in other ways, for example, as *all households* in the market; this would lower the ratings (assuming that fewer than 100 per cent of the households in the market are television households).

The rating based upon a universe defined as all-households-using-receivers-at-the-time is called a "share-of-audience" rating. In this case there are 220 such households in the sample, and the share-of-audience of Program "A" would be 100/220, or .454, expressed as a rating of 45.4.

To project the rating of 25.0 for an estimate of the total number of households tuned to Program "A", take 25 per cent of 100,000 (=25,000 households). This figure might then be multiplied by the average household size of the community to find the estimated audience of Program "A" in terms of individual viewers.

if the data are drawn from markets in which each network is represented. In a market where only one network happens to be represented during a given time-segment, that network obviously would receive an inflated rating, since it has no competition from programming on the other networks. Network ratings are therefore based on a relatively few major markets in which all networks have outlets. Stations in other markets, however, also need rating information on their programs, whether network or local. Therefore the rating services also provide city, or individual market, reports as well as national reports.

RATING PROBLEMS

In recent years program ratings have come increasingly to be regarded by many in the industry as a liability rather than an asset.[8] To begin with, the several rating services do not always agree on their ratings of the same program, and this throws suspicion on the validity of the whole rating principle (Fig. 31).[9] Even assuming, however, that each rating service uses impeccable scientific procedures, it is still possible for them to obtain conflicting results as long as differences exist in their research methods and their underlying assumptions, as well as in their ways of defining and reporting data. For example, Nielsen assumes that the mere fact that a set is turned on (as recorded mechanically by the audimeter) means that someone is paying attention to the program; yet in one case a check on 500 homes is said to have shown that 36 per cent of the television sets turned on were not being watched.[10] Recall surveys assume that people will remember accurately what they have seen or heard; yet in some reported cases as high as 50 per cent of the respondents claimed to have seen or heard things that never happened.[11]

Differences in definition also cause much confusion and misinterpretation. For example, some reports are in terms of family units (homes, households), others in terms of individuals. Some reports are based on "average" audience per program, others on "total" audience per program; as an extreme example, imagine a 30-minute program which had an audience of 30 persons, each one for only one minute each. Its per-minute average audience would be only *one*, but its "total" audience would be 30.[12] Such discrepancies do not necessarily disprove the validity of ratings, as many

---

[8] Cf. "What's Wrong With the Rating Services?", in *Sponsor, All-Media Evaluation Study* (New York: Sponsor Services, Inc., 1954), pp. 91-96.

[9] Cf.: Matthew N. Chappell, *Comparisons of Ratings* (New York: C. E. Hooper, Inc., 1952). Chappell reports (pp. 4-5) that the correlation between Hooper and Nielsen national radio ratings on a given group of programs was .87 for daytime and .95 for evening programs. Since a perfect correlation would be 1.00, the average discrepancy in this case was not disastrously great, especially for evening programs.

[10] *Sponsor, op. cit.*, p. 92.

[11] Chappell and Hooper, *op. cit.*, pp. 10-11.

[12] Special Test Survey Committee, "A Plan for the Evaluation of Audience Measurement Methods" (1951, mimeo.), p. 10.

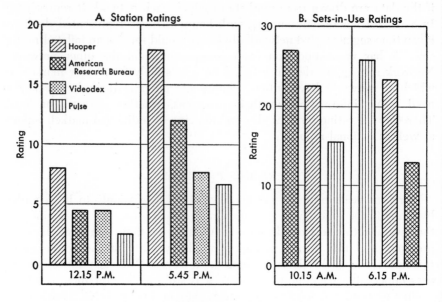

Figure 31

Discrepancies Among Rating Services

A. Ratings for the Same Two Time-Segments on KTTV in Los Angeles, by Four Different Major Rating Services.

B. Sets-in-Use Ratings for the Same Two Time-Segments in Columbus, Ohio, by Three Services.

Source: Ward Dorrell, "How the Different Rating Services Vary in the Same Market," in: Sponsor Services, *All Media Evaluation Study* (New York: Sponsor Services, 1954), p. 101.

contend; but they do prove the necessity of adopting standard definitions and methods of research and reporting and standard methods of compensating for any bias which may be characteristic of the method used.

In the meantime, however, the users of ratings shop around for the service that is most favorable to their particular interests; and the rival services attempt to discredit their competitors while defending their own methods. Furthermore, the users of ratings and other such data tend to abuse research information unconscionably, relying on it to support entirely unwarranted conclusions. Part of the abuse arises from ignorance of the meaning of statistical conclusions and of the limitations of research findings; more of it probably arises from deliberate misrepresentation.

One of the most common forms of abuse is the assumption that a small difference between two ratings is significant, irrespective of the size of the two ratings and their statistical basis. Yet it is axiomatic that all ratings are approximations, not absolute quantities. The significance of the difference between any two ratings can be specified; for the extent to which a rating could err as a result of pure chance can be calculated.[13] Many users of ratings, however, completely ignore the known limitations on their significance. Important decisions are constantly made on the basis of rating differences which are insignificant, i.e., meaningless.

Despite the fact that ratings are often misused; despite the fact that they are at best only crude approximations; despite the fact that they have no necessary correlation with sales effectiveness; and even despite rumblings of discontent from all quarters in the industry, ratings became more and more of a fetish during the increasingly competitive 1940's. Quite aside from the question of the reliability of the ratings, slavish surrender of independent judgment and all qualitative considerations to the rule of raw quantitative measurements is resisted by the more perceptive leaders in advertising. Progress is not likely to come from mob rule; as an executive in one of the largest advertising agencies has pointed out:

It is the great mass of people who stand by, chanting that the horseless carriage will never replace the horse, and that if God intended man to fly He would have given him wings. . . . If Christopher Columbus, the well-known sailor from Genoa, had applied modern advertising research methods to his proposed voyage, a consumer jury test would have told him in advance that the world was flat; depth interviews with expert seamen would have revealed the impressive monsters that awaited him hungrily at the end of the sea; motivational studies among his crew would have shown that they were only interested in money; Ferdinand and Isabella would have cancelled the appropriation; America would never have been discovered, and *you* would all be *Indians*.[14]

In 1950 a small pioneer San Francisco radio station, KJBS, published a full-page advertisement in a trade journal.[15] The advertisement cited the current discrepancies between reports of rating services in KJBS's area, and challenged the rating organizations and the industry to do something about it. The challenge aroused the industry, and a committee was formed to take it up. In 1951 the committee issued a report, analyzing the differences in results and recommending a decisive series of experiments to settle the debate between the rival methods once and for all.[16] Nothing came of the report. Subsequently the Advertising Research Foundation (ARF), a nonprofit organization supported by the advertising industry, took up the problem. The ARF has suggested, for instance, the standardization of a number of the most common procedures and measurement units used. Among other things, it recommends retaining set-tuning as the test of membership in the audience, using the household as the unit of measurement, measuring the use of all sets in sample households, and using minimum

[13] Cf.: J. Ward Dorrell, "The Reliability of the Ratings" (New York: Blair & Co., 1952, mimeo.), p. 2.

[14] Charles H. Brower, "The Growing Pains of Advertising," *Broadcasting-Telecasting* (17 January 1955), p. 37.

[15] *Broadcasting-Telecasting* (3 July 1950), p. 9.

[16] Special Test Survey Committee, *op. cit.*

samples of 400 households per quarter-hour for local surveys and of 1,200 for national surveys.[17]

TV v. RADIO

So much notoriety has attached to controversies over program ratings that one is likely to overlook the fact that a great deal of market research in broadcasting has other objectives. The more the advertising agency knows about audiences — their composition, habits, attitudes, motivations — the better it can plan an advertising campaign.[18] Moreover, the agency must think in terms of all the advertising media, and hence inter-media information must be expressed in measurements which apply with equal logic to two or more media; for example, the "share-of-audience" yardstick can be applied to both radio and television but not directly to other media. On the other hand, the "cost-per-thousand" concept can be applied to all media on the basis of individual "impressions." Of course, the psychological processes involved in receiving "impressions" from the several media are not identical; but this only brings us up against the underlying problem that all communications research finally has to face — that intangible link in the communicative process which cannot be measured objectively in any event.

One of the distinguishing features of broadcasting is the fact that, generally speaking, it is a *family* medium. This is why the ARF recommends the household as the unit of measurement for broadcasting research. The family is an economic unit; purchasing decisions tend to arise out of interaction between members of the group. For example, children's programs are known to influence the purchasing behavior of parents.

Inter-media competition between radio and television, however, has caused some revision of the research agency's concept of the family. The television set has taken over the role of focal point of family group participation, and the more mobile radio has been forced out of the living room into places where it is more likely to serve the family members as individuals — into kitchen, bedroom, automobile (Table 16). This change in role has, of course, important implications for the advertiser — not all of them adverse to radio.

A study of radio's changing role in television areas was made for one of the major station-representative firms by the Politz research organization in 1952-1953.[19] This study is interesting as an example of an inquiry into

[17] Advertising Research Foundation, *Recommended Standards for Radio and Television Program Audience Size Measurements* (New York: The Foundation, 1954).

[18] For a useful summary of types of commercial research and their applications, see: E. Lawrence Deckinger, "Conducting Research for TV Advertising," in: Irving Settel, Norman Glenn, and Associates, *Television Advertising and Production Handbook* (New York: Crowell, 1953), pp. 37-70.

[19] Alfred Politz Research, Inc., *The Importance of Radio in Television Areas Today* (New York: Henry I. Christal Co., 1953). Politz is a major commercial market-research firm. The study is based on about 5,000 interviews in television areas as of 1952, in which about 72 per cent of the population had television at that time.

Table 16

Location of Radio and TV Sets

Location	Percentage of TV Sets	Percentage of Radio Sets
Living room	85.3	25.1
Den, study, library	4.8	1.4
Bedroom	3.4	21.4
Dining room	3.2	4.4
Other	3.3	5.7
Kitchen	*	16.0
Automobile	*	25.9
Personal portable	*	0.1

* TV sets in these locations — if any — combined under heading "Other" in ARF report.
    Source: Advertising Research Foundation, *National Survey of Radio and Television Sets Associated with U. S. Households, May, 1954* (New York: The Foundation, 1954), pp. 31, 83.

qualitative as well as quantitative aspects of the audience. It is a *motivational* study, in the sense that the investigators not only listed particular types of behavior but also tried to find out the *why* of such behavior.

For example, why do people have radios? The Politz study found that two classes of reasons were by far the most important for most classes of people: for "entertainment, relaxation, enjoyment" and for "news." These reasons were almost equally predominant for both men and women, for all age groups, and for all economic classes. This finding confirms the fact that radio has a remarkable ability to override group differences.

What do audiences think are the advantages of radio over television and print? The most frequently cited advantage was that the listener can do other things while listening; the higher the educational level, the more frequently this advantage was cited.

Perhaps the most significant fact about radio in comparison with television is the trend toward multiple-set radio ownership, a trend which rose sharply in the 1940's.[20] The Politz study found that in areas served by television the middle- and upper-income groups averaged two or more radio sets per home; over 50 per cent of all homes had two or more sets. Furthermore, over 70 per cent of passenger-car owners had auto radios.

How do radio listening preferences vary with household activities throughout the day? The answers developed by the Politz study show how

[20] A regional study of multiple-set homes showed the following rate of increase in homes having two or more radios: 1940—17%, 1945—38%, 1950—48%, 1953—49%. Forest L. Whan, *1953 Iowa Radio-Television Audience Survey* (Des Moines: Central Broadcasting Co., 1953), p. 11.

Table 17

Why People Listen to Radio During Each Period of the Average Winter Day

Reason for Listening	Rank Importance Assigned to Reason for Listening						
	Between Waking & Break- fast	During Break- fast	Between Break- fast & Lunch	During Lunch	Between Lunch & Supper	During Supper	Between Supper & Going to Bed
News	1	1	*3	1	3	1	2
Music	3	2	*2	2	1	2	3
Programs, stories, etc.	4	4	*1	3	2	3	1
Weather, time, etc.	2	3	8	7	10	6	9

* Differences insignificantly small.
   Source: Adapted from: Alfred Politz Research, Inc., *The Importance of Radio in Television Areas Today* (New York: Henry I. Christal Co., 1953), Appendix, p. 24.

radio can adjust to the rhythm and pace of family life (Table 17). The marked differences in program preferences according to time of day (which is another way of saying according to the kind of home activities going on when the listening takes place) have obvious implications for radio pro-gramming, radio sales strategy, and the broader considerations of radio's ability to remain a competitive medium.

Broadcasting's proudest boast has long been that there are more radios in American homes than any other modern convenience, even bathtubs. The Politz study reaffirmed this well-known fact, but added an interesting dimension by asking people to rank radio with other conveniences as either a "necessity" or a "luxury." Answers to this question reveal some unex-pected subjective evaluations (Table 18). Nearly all the people had a radio, and yet 31 per cent considered it a luxury. One concludes that radio might be defined as America's "most necessary luxury."

TREND STUDIES

Another study which deals with the dynamics of inter-media competition for a place in the cycle of daily living is the "Videotown" series published by Cunningham and Walsh, an advertising agency.[21] This series is a unique annual appraisal of the effect of television on a particular community. It takes advantage of the unusual opportunity offered by the rise of television

---

[21] Cunningham and Walsh, Inc., *Videotown, 1948-1954* (7th edition; New York: Cunningham and Walsh, Inc., 1954). For the first five years the studies were based on complete censuses of the city, and during the first three years every set owner was in-terviewed.

Table 18

Ownership of Certain Household Items and Whether Considered
a Luxury or a Necessity*

Item	Percentage of All People in Sample		
	Have item in home	Consider it a necessity	Consider it a luxury
Radio	94	49	31
Refrigerator	93	85	5
Bathtub	85	82	6
Telephone	78	71	14
Television	72	23	66
Automobile	71	58	27

* No definition of "luxury" or "necessity" was given the respondents.
Adapted from: Alfred Politz Research, Inc., *The Importance of Radio in Television Areas Today* (New York: Henry I. Christal Co., 1953), Appendix, p. 34.

to study how an entirely new social institution is integrated into the existing pattern of living. "Videotown" is New Brunswick, N. J., "an independent, self-contained market of about 40,000 population." The series began with the expansion of the television service itself in 1948. Since New Brunswick is only 30 miles from New York City, it has been served longer and by more stations than most communities of its size. Television there has had the fullest opportunity to find its own level; by mid-1954 saturation (percentage of total homes having sets) had reached nearly 80 per cent. According to the evidence of "Videotown," it takes five years of maximum exposure for a community to adjust to the effect of television. The turning point in New Brunswick came in 1953:

Until then television had been cutting into normal daily routines more and more deeply at the expense of many other activities. The 1954 survey verified the prediction made last year that the public was rebudgeting its expenditure of time to permit the continued enjoyment of television and yet include more of other pleasures which had been curtailed . . . people were actually re-arranging their living habits. This change shows up most clearly in the time the average housewife devotes to running her home, taking care of and entertaining her children, preparing and eating meals, etc. The number of hours is about the same as before TV, between 10 and 11 hours on the average week day. However, before TV these hours were spread from early morning until bedtime. Today she concentrates more of her household chores in the morning and the early evening, leaving her evening hours relatively free for TV and other social relaxation.[22]

[22] Cunningham and Walsh, Inc., *op. cit.*, p. 1.

Table 19

Preferred Medium for Certain Types of Program

Radio Preferred over TV*			TV Preferred over Radio*		
Program Type	% Preferring†		Program Type	% Preferring†	
	Men	Women		Men	Women
News	23	23	Variety	20	28
Popular music	18	18	Complete drama	24	25
Serial drama	1	5	Featured comedians	18	16
			Sports	13	12
Market reports	17	8	Audience participation shows	5	14
Oldtime music	5	9			

* Based on Iowa homes having both radio and television receivers.
† Difference between percentages of sample reporting program types "best liked" on each medium. Read as follows: Of the men in the sample who liked news best, 23% more liked it on radio than on TV.
Adapted from: Forest L. Whan, *1953 Iowa Radio-Television Audience Survey* (Des Moines: Central Broadcasting Co., 1953).

The seventh "Videotown" survey reports other characteristics of a highly-saturated television community: Daytime viewing continues to rise, yet the amount of radio listening steadily recovers from the initial shock of television competition, and morning radio listening even increases from the pre-TV days; television is still distinctly a family affair, with one set per home, but 50 per cent of the TV homes have more than one radio. The only competitive medium not adversely affected by television (as far as attention is concerned) is the newspaper; in fact, increased newspaper reading goes along with television. Sets are found with equal frequency in upper- and in middle-class homes (80 per cent) but less frequently in lower-class homes (60 per cent).

An example of another trend-revealing series of studies — this one on a regional rather than a community base — is the annual Iowa audience survey conducted by Forest L. Whan, now of Kansas State College.[23] This series, which began in 1938 and has included television since 1950, has been based primarily on the interview method. A combination interview and diary technique was adopted for the 1953 study. Basically a report of station share-of-audience ratings for the region, the series has also developed information on a great many other facets of audience composition, characteristics, and behavior. For example, the 1953 survey ascertained how preferences vary between radio listening and television viewing in

[23] Cf. Forest L. Whan, *op. cit.*

accordance with the type of program (Table 19). News and popular music, in particular, appealed to more people on radio than on television.

EVALUATION OF BROADCASTING AS AN INSTITUTION

Probably the most frequently-cited surveys of broadcasting are two conducted by the National Association of Broadcasters (now the National Association of Radio and Television Broadcasters) in 1946 and 1948.[24] These surveys had a broader objective than most commercially sponsored research, and employed an outstanding research organization and a well-known social scientist to do the work. The objective was to provide the industry with useful ammunition to counteract the barrage of adverse criticism which bombarded broadcasters after World War II. They were designed not to support a specific commercial objective but rather to reveal the status of broadcasting as a social institution.

The 1946 study was believed to be the first "to record direct and comprehensive information on the public's attitude toward radio advertising".[25] It was found that, contrary to widespread belief, advertising was by no means universally resented by radio audiences. Indeed, only 35 per cent of the listeners preferred programs without advertising; similarly, only 29 per cent mentioned advertising when asked about ways in which radio annoyed them. Less than 10 per cent of the sample (in both studies) advocated outright elimination of advertising.[26]

Both NAB-NORC surveys revealed that people in general held radio in remarkably high esteem, believing it was doing a "better job" than such prestige institutions as schools, local governments, and newspapers. They also confirmed in some detail the fact, already well established, that in the long run the mass media "tend to complement, rather than compete with, each other."[27] The authors entered a *caveat* with respect to television, which was then still below the horizon. But subsequent experience (some of it cited earlier in this chapter) indicates that the same generalization applies

[24] Paul F. Lazarsfeld and Harry Field, *The People Look at Radio* (Chapel Hill: University of North Carolina, 1946); Paul F. Lazarsfeld and Patricia L. Kendall, *Radio Listening in America; the People Look at Radio — Again* (New York: Prentice-Hall, 1948). Data for both studies were based on interviews of a sample representative of the total population, gathered by the National Opinion Research Center, now located at the University of Chicago.

[25] Lazarsfeld and Field, *op. cit.,* p. 15.

[26] Of course the interpretation placed on such data as these depends on the interpreter's point of view. Here the view taken is that the NAB-NORC findings show a surprising degree of tolerance of radio advertising; others may put more emphasis on the anti-advertising data and draw the opposite conclusion. One commentator, for instance, reacted to these findings by asking: "How far can an industry dependent for its livelihood on advertising afford to be complacent over the evident resentment of almost a third of its customers?" and pointing out that the opponents of advertising were more emphatic than those who tolerated it. Charles A. Siepmann, *Radio, Television and Society* (New York: Oxford University Press, 1950), pp. 85-86.

[27] Lazarsfeld and Kendall, *op. cit.,* p. 5.

to television, despite the initial dislocations it has caused. The mass audience exhibits generally what Lazarsfeld has called "all or none behavior".[28] That is, people who are not heavy consumers of one medium are not likely to be consumers of another; and conversely, those who are the "fans" of one medium are likely to spread their consumption over all the media. The fact that, increasingly with television, there is a great deal of interchange of talent and program material among the media would naturally tend to bring about this result.

A third conclusion which the NAB studies supported in detail is that broadcasting differs from other media in the relatively greater uniformity of its appeal to all groups within the population. This uniformity obviously applies only generally; some programs are highly selective by their very nature — e.g., classical music *vs.* hillbilly music. The most universal program type is news, which is consistently the most preferred of all types, with remarkably small differences between the sexes or among educational, economic, and age levels. These group-differentiating factors do affect other program types. For example, the more educated are less likely to depend on radio for news, or to like daytime serials or religious programs; they are more likely to approve of classical music and information programs. Interest in popular music falls off sharply with age, but interest in religious programs and discussions of public issues rises.[29]

TESTING THE NEW

All the surveys mentioned so far have been based in varying degrees on sampling procedures and have sought to quantify audience characteristics. Their purpose is to describe audiences and their behavior so that the effects of mass communications can be measured, understood, and to some extent predicted. To return to our point of departure, the advertiser wants to know both *how* to invest his advertising budget and *what* was accomplished after the investment was made. But studies of the type so far described are all historical in character: they have to do with what has already happened, and therefore are confined to existing programs, media, and audiences. But what if the task is to try something *new* on which no historical record already exists? Several research techniques have been developed for trying out new ideas — notably the consumer panel or jury. On a wider scale, advertisers often try out new advertising campaigns in test cities, results in which are compared with those in matching control cities not involved in the campaign.

Panels are used at intermediate stages during the actual construction of the message. Motion pictures, for example, often use jury information in choosing plots, titles, and stars; later on, the finished picture may be re-

28 *Ibid.*, p. 9.
29 *Ibid.*, p. 136.

vised on the basis of the reactions of preview audiences.[30] New broadcast programs are tried out on studio audiences which are asked to register approval, disapproval, or indifference minute by minute throughout the program. The reactions can be recorded by simple pencil-and-paper methods. Averaging the results gives a minute-by-minute profile of the program, revealing at a glance the points of highest and lowest interest. In order to speed up the tabulating and to simplify the voting, mechanical devices (e.g., the Schwerin "reactocaster," the Lazarsfeld-Stanton "program analyzer")[31] have been developed. They require panel members to show their reactions by merely pushing buttons which activate an automatic tabulating device. Quick tabulation is desirable, since an important aspect of the panel technique is immediate discussion with the panel members to analyze their reactions.

Panel techniques have been used extensively by the Schwerin Research Corporation, particularly for the study of the effectiveness of commercials. What, for example, is the optimum length for a commercial? Schwerin research indicates that it varies with the circumstances but a longer commercial is not necessarily more effective than a shorter one; repetition may in fact merely weaken the impact of the message.[32] Schwerin conducted a study for NBC on the effectiveness of various methods of presenting television commercials; the resulting admonitions — such as "correlate audio and video," "demonstrate," and "keep it simple" — may seem obvious when baldly stated. Nevertheless, the study provided a quantitative basis for weighing the importance of various methods of presentation where only guesswork could be used before (Table 20).

Whether broadcasting market research is concerned with predictive problems (the "how" aspect of advertising) or with evaluative problems (the "what" aspect), its primary objective is to link cause with effect, stimulus with response, message with behavior. The advertiser's interest in this question is confined to a rather limited range of effects, responses, or behaviors. His messages are designed to stimulate either the specific response of purchasing or (in the case of institutional advertising) the more generalized response of favorable attention. He deals in most cases with a rather superficial level of human mental and behavioral processes. As we pointed out earlier, the "brand loyalty" induced by advertising is not lasting or deep-seated.

This chapter has been concerned with research primarily at the level demanded by the marketing function of broadcast advertising. In Part V

[30] Cf.: Leo A. Handel, *Hollywood Looks at Its Audience* (Urbana: University of Illinois Press, 1950).

[31] Cf.: Tore Hollonquist and Edward A. Suchman, "Listening to the Listener: Experiences with the Lazarsfeld-Stanton Program Analyzer," in: Paul F. Lazarsfeld and Frank N. Stanton, *Radio Research 1942-1943* (New York: Duell, Sloan and Pearce, 1944), pp. 265-334.

[32] Horace S. Schwerin, *Measuring Advertising's Power to Motivate* (New York: American Association of Advertising Agencies, 1954), pp. 17-18.

we consider research which deals with the effects of broadcasting on the
deeper human loyalties. For broadcasting is not merely an advertising
medium; it is also a social institution. From the social point of view, we
are interested in the effect of the service as a whole and its function in
society as a whole.

Table 20

Effectiveness Factors in Design of Commercials

Product Type	Method A (Less Effective)	Method B (More Effective)	Principle Illustrated	Ratio of Improvement (B over A)*
Cosmetic	Scantily dressed model demonstrates	Fully clothed model demonstrates	Avoid distracting presenter	6.5
Cleaning aid	Results of product use shown	Actual use of product shown as well as results	Demonstrate	4.7
Food-mix	Chef demonstrates use	Child demonstrates use	Misuse of authority	4.6
Food	Doctor advises use	Doctor advises use, patient shown following advice	Effective use of authority	3.0
Shaving aid	Presenter is a steelworker	Presenter is an office worker	Use the "right" authority	2.5
Food	Presenter identifies herself as a housewife verbally	Presenter shown doing a household chore	Use the right presenter, visually identified	1.7
Pancake mix	Mother brings product to table	Product shown being cooked	Enhance sensory impressions	1.6

* Commercials were scored by proportion of viewers remembering the points made in the presentations. Read the figures as follows: For the cosmetic commercial Method B was 6.5 times as effective as Method A. A ratio of "1" would mean no difference in effectiveness.

Adapted from: National Broadcasting Company, *How to Increase Effectiveness of Television Commercials* (New York: National Broadcasting Company, 1952). The research was conducted by the Schwerin Research Corporation.

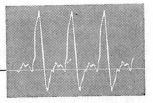

17

The Role of Advertising Agencies

in Broadcasting

When the trend toward national advertising set in, advertisers had no ready means of appraising circulation claims of magazines and newspapers. They could not personally investigate the status of publications in cities scattered from one end of the country to the other. To bridge this gap between the national advertiser and the advertising media, a class of middlemen began to act as brokers. Space brokers studied markets, appraised circulation data, and purchased space for resale to advertisers at a 15 per cent markup. As time went on, these brokers took over more and more of the increasingly technical details of designing the advertising itself and arranging for its placement. Eventually the brokerage aspect disappeared, and the advertising agency emerged. Agencies continued to collect a 15 per cent commission on sales, but now the commission was subtracted from the standard rate paid the media instead of being added to the purchase price of the space.

THE TIME BROKER

In the early days of commercial radio, history repeated itself. Time brokers began to act as intermediaries between national advertisers and individual radio stations. A story which typifies the atmosphere of early commercial radio is related by Ben Gross. In 1922 a would-be time broker bought time for resale from WEAF. The station, however, became alarmed at the resulting commercialism and refused to continue dealing with the broker. The broker thereupon purchased time from WAAM-Newark. But the station owner was so doubtful of the legality of the procedure that he insisted on receiving payment in cash rather than by check; moreover, he arranged to meet the broker clandestinely in a hotel, where the money could change hands secretly.[1]

[1] Ben Gross, *I Looked and I Listened* (New York: Random House, 1954), pp. 66-67. Time-brokerage has since become illegal, since it implies a surrender by the licensee of his legal responsibility for programming. It is still occasionally practiced in disguised form, however.

During the mid-1930's station-representative firms and the advertising agencies absorbed the time broker's functions.[2] N. W. Ayer and Son, one of the oldest advertising agencies in the print media, claims to have been the first major agency to take radio seriously as an advertising medium.[3] Ayer handled advertising for an optical company on WEAF as early as 1922, and introduced one of the most famous of early radio network-sponsored programs, the National Carbon Company's *Eveready Hour*, in December, 1923. In 1928 Ayer set up a separate radio department. Eventually all other major advertising agencies overcame their initial skepticism toward the new medium, and all large broadcasting accounts are now handled by agencies.

FUNCTIONS OF AGENCIES

To the casual observer it may seem curious that the advertising agency has come to play an indispensable role in negotiating the sale of broadcast time to large advertisers. Since all major advertisers have their own advertising departments, and all stations and networks have their own sales departments, it might appear that buyer and seller are well equipped to do business with each other without the aid of a middleman. Must we conclude, to paraphrase Fred Allen, that an agency executive is a man who comes to work in the morning to find a molehill on his desk and labors all day to make a mountain out of it? The fact is, of course, that large-scale advertising has become a very complex, specialized operation, and the peculiar resources of the advertising agency are really needed for efficient handling of a major advertising campaign.

To begin with, the national advertiser is faced with the existence of many thousands of advertising outlets — radio stations, television stations, daily newspapers, weekly newspapers, trade journals, magazines, and many other media. The mere task of intelligent selection is a difficult one, and time- and space-buying have become specialized occupations in themselves. Then the proper design of the advertising itself, in terms of the client's needs and the capabilities of the media, necessitates other difficult decisions. Besides advising clients in the selection of media and the design of advertising, the agency does the actual media-buying, creates the advertising proper, conducts necessary market research, negotiates contracts, handles accounting, and takes care of many other details connected with the advertising campaign.[4]

---

[2] For a contemporary account, cf.: Herman S. Hettinger, *A Decade of Radio Advertising* (Chicago: University of Chicago Press, 1933), "Middlemen Available for Spot Broadcasting," pp. 160-172.

[3] Ralph M. Hower, *The History of an Advertising Agency: N. W. Ayer & Son at Work, 1869-1949* (rev. ed.; Cambridge: Harvard University Press, 1949), p. 132.

[4] For a more detailed description of agency functions, cf.: E. F. Seehafer and J. W. Laemmar, *Successful Radio and Television Advertising* (New York: McGraw-Hill, 1951), "The Advertising Agency," pp. 276-291.

Major agencies maintain separate departments for radio and television. Ruthrauff and Ryan's radio department, for example, includes a vice-president in charge, a copy chief, production manager, a business manager, a production supervisor, four writers, a spot-buying manager, and three time buyers. Batten, Barton, Durstine and Osborn's television department includes a vice-president in charge, an executive in charge of new program development, a director of television producers, a production manager, a commercial supervisor, a manager of time buying, and a chief time buyer. Such agencies maintain offices in a number of major cities. BBD&O, for instance, has headquarters in New York and branches in Boston, Buffalo, Chicago, Cleveland, Detroit, Hollywood, Minneapolis, Pittsburgh, San Francisco, Syracuse, and Los Angeles.[5]

WHO FOOTS THE BILL?

Special services involving extra out-of-pocket expenses are billed by the agency to the client. But all of the agency's basic services are "non-billable." The client apparently pays nothing for these services. The agency bills the advertiser at the card rate for the time purchased, and then deducts its 15 per cent commission before passing on the payment to the station or network. This procedure parallels the usual practice of business agents. If you plan to take an extended vacation trip, a travel agent will plan an itinerary for you, purchase tickets, make reservations, and help you with many incidental services, all of which are paid for by commissions. You would pay the same price to the carriers and hotels if you made the purchases yourself directly. The experience, the up-to-date information, and the conveniences offered by the agency apparently cost you nothing.

In the final analysis, however, the consumer foots the bill. In the long run, rates must take into account the cost of commissions to agents. The higher rate usually charged for national (as distinguished from local) advertising reflects this fact. Therefore the advertising agency's position is somewhat dualistic. Where does its primary loyalty lie? The American Association of Advertising Agencies comments:

> It is important to note that the agency contracts with media in its own name, as an individual contractor. In its relations with media it is not legally the agent of its client, and the word "agent" or "agency" is, in a legal sense, a misnomer.[6]

Agency commissions are paid in one sense by the medium, in another by the advertiser. Before the advertiser has committed himself, the agency and the medium may team up to "sell" a client. Once the client is sold, how-

[5] *Broadcasting-Telecasting* radio and television yearbooks list all advertising agencies which handle national or regional accounts. The 1955 yearbooks list 554 agencies handling radio accounts and 512 handling television accounts.
[6] The American Association of Advertising Agencies, *The Structure of the Advertising Agency Business* (New York: The Association, 1954), p. 19.

ever, the agency naturally identifies itself with the advertiser, the direct source of revenue. If a conflict of interest develops between advertiser and medium, the agency is bound to argue for the advertiser and against the medium.

AGENCY CONTROL OVER PROGRAMMING

The close identification of the agency with the advertiser's interest becomes of peculiar importance in broadcasting because of the expanded function of the agency in this medium. In the space media, agencies customarily prepare the advertising copy and the advertising art work but have nothing to do with the publication's editorial content (i.e., non-advertising matter). In publishing, the editorial and advertising departments operate independently of each other, and no respectable newspaper or magazine would let advertisers or their agents control news stories or other basic editorial content. To be sure, this insulation between advertising and editorial content may not always be perfect. For example, many newspapers run certain "business" sections in which so-called news stories are actually little more than thinly-disguised advertisements. Again, a good deal of what passes for "news" in such areas as entertainment and sports is manufactured or planted by publicity agents. But in general it is fair to say that the basic editorial content of ethical newspapers and magazines is not directly influenced by advertisers, and certainly is not actually chosen and prepared by them.[7]

In broadcasting, on the other hand, quite an opposite tradition has been established. As we have seen, advertisers early moved into the program-production field as "sponsors," and advertising agencies took over the entire programming function for them. This result came about, not as a necessary condition of commercial radio operation[8] but as a practical expedient at a time when stations themselves were not prepared to offer advertisers effective programming of their own. The stations' own lack of program resources created a vacuum which sponsored programs filled. Indeed, the Ayer agency claims that its entry into program production was motivated by the desire to *protect the public* as well as its clients, in the belief that

> radio advertising was particularly open to abuse which might alienate public opinion. [Ayer] therefore adopted the policy that it would maintain direct control over the arrangement and production of all programs for which it was responsible, instead of leaving program production to the stations.[9]

[7] Leon Svirsky (ed.), *Your Newspaper: Blueprint for a Better Press, by Nine Nieman Fellows, 1945-46* (New York: Macmillan Co., 1949), pp. 128-129.

[8] Note that the commercial television service inaugurated in Great Britain in 1955 as a supplement to the non-commercial service of the British Broadcasting Corporation does not permit the advertiser to have anything to do with programs. In effect, British television advertisers cannot be "sponsors" as we use the term; they are confined to the equivalent of spot announcements, and are barred from either controlling program content or mixing advertising and non-advertising program material.

[9] Hower, *op. cit.*, p. 138.

Following this early precedent, nearly all commercial radio network programming eventually came under the direct control of advertising agencies, with the networks' own production activities being confined primarily to sustaining programs. "The agencies took all the good men away from the networks. They concentrated personnel and effort on a single show while the network had 18 hours a day, seven days a week to worry about."[10] Network and affiliates become a mere transmission mechanism for agency-produced programs; their control is the negative one of being able to veto anything which gets too far out of line with their policy. Since a few of the largest agencies handled a very large share of network advertising, this meant that control over a considerable fraction of the total radio service was concentrated in a very few hands.

CONSEQUENCES OF AGENCY INFLUENCE ON PROGRAMMING

This programming control by non-licensees creates an anomalous situation, for

> it enables men about whom the public knows nothing and whom the FCC is not required by law to investigate to enjoy franchises which the public grants to another, or "dummy," group for the use of the public's frequencies. It is rather like a householder who carefully investigates someone to whom he proposes to sublet his home, only to discover that quite another family, about which he knows nothing, and which is not bound by any lease to take care of the property, intended to occupy the premises all along . . . advertising men are not, in fact, ideal "tenants" of the airways. This is not to say that advertising men are not useful citizens and often very pleasant people to know, or to disparage the vital role that they play in the national economy. It concerns their point of view, their aim in life, their *raison d'être*.[11]

The point of view of the agency is necessarily narrow. The agency's basic obligation is clearly to its clients, the advertisers. It is not necessary to assume any conspiracy on the part of the agency — any lack of good faith or ethical standards — to see that this obligation inevitably produces a one-sided point of view. The agency depends for its existence on getting specific results for specific clients. Its viewpoint is consequently very narrow in comparison to that of the station or network, which has to think in terms not of just some advertisers but of all advertisers; not of just selected target-audiences but of all audiences; not of just some programs but of a complete program service.

This does not mean that the licensee operates his station as a charitable institution, or is any less interested in profit than the advertising agency.

---

[10] Sylvester Weaver, "Weaver Scans the Way Ahead," *Broadcasting-Telecasting* (28 February 1955), p. 40.

[11] Llewellyn White, *The American Radio* (Chicago: University of Chicago Press, 1947), p. 94. Copyright 1947 by The University of Chicago. Cf. pp. 93-98 for interesting documentation on the extent of agency control and the attitude of broadcasters toward it.

It does mean that for the licensee courses of action dictated by the profit motive must at least be moderated by general considerations of public welfare. It does mean that the licensee has to take into consideration the needs of the community in which he operates and of the medium of which he is a part.

One result of the agency's fiduciary position in relation to the advertiser is an ultra-conservative choice of programs. After all, the agency is spending someone else's money and does not wish to risk it unnecessarily. So the agency looks for the safe bet, and that generally means imitating already-successful programs rather than experimenting with something new.[12] Since the safest gamble is the one made on the largest possible audience (on the not-always-tenable assumption that sales results will be directly proportional to audience size), agencies tend to put great emphasis on program ratings and to prefer programs which appeal to the lowest common audience denominator.

Perhaps the contrast between the points of view of the agency and the broadcaster can best be shown by a small example which can serve to symbolize the difference. In the specialized world of the advertising agency the commercial takes on tremendous importance, of course. In an article on how to develop effective television commercials, the following advice appears:

> Don't abuse "medical authority" in commercials. Networks and stations have clamped down on this type of commercial, now require a disclaimer indicating such roles are staged with actors.[13]

Note that the networks and stations are here tacitly recognized as having points of view independent of other production agents. More significant, however, is the implication that the only reason for avoiding misrepresentation of medical authority in commercials is an arbitrary change of heart on the part of stations and networks. The real reason behind the clamp-down — the fact that such commercials are ethically indefensible — does not enter into the equation. In the equation as presented, the only reason for avoiding the unethical practice is the fact that one can no longer get away with it.

TELEVISION NETWORKS RECAPTURE PROGRAM PRODUCTION

It may be argued, of course, that networks and stations adopted the ruling in precisely the same spirit of expediency, and further, that no sub-

---

[12] A survey of station managers by *Broadcasting*, an industry trade journal, asked what they thought had "done the most to retard improvement in programming." Advertising agencies were cited as the leading cause by 47 per cent, sponsors by 44 per cent. All other causes — such as the FCC, the networks, and the rating services — were cited less than half as often as the agencies. "Who Does Most to Improve Radio?", *Broadcasting* (4 November 1946), pp. 16-17, 77.

[13] Harry W. McMahan, "7 Deadly Sins of TV Commercials," *Sponsor* (13 December 1954), p. 37.

stantial change in programming would result if agencies suddenly withdrew from the program field entirely. At least as far as the latter is concerned, experience proves otherwise. Broadcasters themselves have long chafed at the degree to which their programming had come under agency control. With the advent of television, broadcasters found themselves less at a loss for programs than they had been when radio began. Accordingly, the networks set out to recapture their own programming from the advertising agencies (see Table 21). It is indicative of the extent to which the idea of

Table 21

Sources of Network Programs

Source	Percentage of Programs on			
	ABC	CBS	NBC	All Networks
Package producer	60	53	59	57
Network itself	27	37	30	32
Advertising agencies	13	11	11	11

Source: *Ross Reports on Television.* 1955 data.

agency responsibility for programming had become established that agencies publicly showed indignation because the television networks presumed to want to produce and control their own programs.[14]

Aside from the natural desire to be master in their own house, networks were motivated by the fact that it was necessary to put television program sponsorship within the financial reach of the relatively small advertiser, since the traditional concept of network program sponsorship made network television too expensive for all but a limited number of top advertisers. A program like NBC's *Today* or CBS's *Morning Show* is offered to multiple sponsors on a participating basis; such a program would never have been developed by an advertising agency, whose program production activities are directed at creating programs exclusively for its own clients. By and large, the "best" network television programming — in terms of both originality of concept and quality of product — has come about as a direct result of the networks' own production efforts. Many of these programs originally represented the kind of gamble which an advertising agency could not possibly take. *Today*, for instance, represented a radical departure in network

[14] "'Editorial Control' by Networks Charged by Ellis," *Broadcasting-Telecasting* (15 January 1951), p. 23. The trade magazine replied editorially: "It seems to us that the more programs a network owns, the more it fulfills its fundamental responsibilities as a licensee of its owned-and-operated stations and as a program source for its affiliates. The responsibility to broadcast the best programs it can devise is one that no network can conscientiously abdicate in favor of an advertising agency or an advertiser." "TV's Talent Travail," *Broadcasting-Telecasting* (22 January 1951), p. 48.

television programming — an early-morning program supported by network participating sponsorship. Its chances of success were considered very small by many "experts." Such negative votes would have driven any advertising agency to substitute some sure-fire formula which had already proved its popularity. As Sylvester Weaver, president of NBC, expressed it, "We [networks] must gamble on shows, on talent, on projects; and we will lose in doing this all too often. But only a great network can afford the risk, and that is essentially why the great network service is so important to this country."[15]

15 Sylvester L. Weaver, "The Form of the Future," *Broadcasting-Telecasting* (30 May 1955), p. 56.

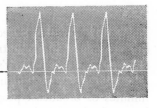

18

The Financial Organization
of the Broadcasting Industry

As measured by ordinary economic yardsticks — capital investment, revenue, payroll, income — broadcasting is not a big business (Table 22). Income from tobacco manufacturing is greater than that from broadcasting, and more people are employed in bowling alleys and billiard parlors than in radio and television stations. But the social role of broadcasting as a communications medium lends it an importance out of all proportion to its economic significance. Moreover, its full significance even in economic terms becomes apparent only when one considers that the broadcasting service creates a number of related economic activities — set manufacturing,

Table 22

National Income, Selected Industries

Industry	Income in 1953
Automobile	$7,698,000,000
Printing and publishing	4,389,000,000
Telephone and telegraph	4,118,000,000
Amusements and recreation	958,000,000
Motion pictures	835,000,000
Tobacco manufacture	615,000,000
Broadcasting	481,000,000

Source: *New York World-Telegram, The World Almanac and Book of Facts for 1955* (New York: *New York World-Telegram*, 1955), p. 756, based on U. S. Department of Commerce data.

sales, and servicing; electric power consumption; trade and consumer publications; advertising, talent, market research, engineering, and legal services (Table 23).

It is interesting to compare the financial structure of broadcasting with that of the motion-picture industry. Only a small part of its total investment and payroll are needed by the creative, or production, branch of the entertainment film industry; most of its investment is tied up in theatres, and most of the industry's employees work for exhibitors (Table 24). Yet the budget for a single major feature film (the equivalent of about ninety minutes of broadcast programming) represents enough capital to build a large television station or to operate such a station for a whole year. These

Table 23

Dimensions of the Broadcasting Industry

	Total Investment	Annual Gross Revenue	No. of Employees	Annual Payroll
		(For the year ended October 1, 1954)		
Manufacturers (4,100)	$ 400,000,000	$5,000,000,000	400,000	$ 800,000,000
Distributors, dealers, etc.	600,000,000	4,000,000,000	225,000	750,000,000
Stations (3,325), including talent costs	420,000,000	1,000,000,000	45,000*	550,000,000
Sets in use (160,000,000)	12,000,000,000			1,700,000,000†

* Regular staff employees.
† Operating expense.
Source: *New York World-Telegram, The World Almanac and Book of Facts for 1955* (New York: *New York World-Telegram*, 1955), p. 789, based on "Mart," Caldwell-Clements, Inc., data.

contrasts reflect the high degree of syndication in motion pictures, as well as the fact that broadcast stations to some extent combine the production-exhibition functions in a single organization.

INVESTMENT, REVENUE, AND INCOME

Nevertheless, there has been a marked shift in broadcasting toward larger economic entities as a result of television. In the days of radio-only, it was possible to establish stations with relatively small capital investments and reserve funds; in the early postwar years, for instance, the total outlay for technical equipment for a small radio station might amount to no more than the cost of a single television camera chain a few years later. The average construction cost of radio stations was well under $100,000 and the average annual revenue under $70,000.[1] Television has made such totals seem inconsequential. Average capital investment for television stations runs to over half a million dollars, and annual expenses to over a million (Table 25). Some idea of the revenue potential of the more favorably located stations

[1] FCC, *An Economic Study of Standard Broadcasting* (1947 mimeo.), pp. 44, 49.

Table 24

Economic Data on the United States Motion-Picture Industry

Industry Investment*	$2,688,700,000
Theatres	$2,500,000,000
Studios†	$ 142,000,000
Distribution	$ 25,700,000
Production	
Feature films released	344
Short subjects‡	415
Annual payroll	$ 251,000,000
Employed in production	11,900
Distribution	
Annual payroll	$ 45,000,000
Employed	12,500
Exhibition	
Theatres in operation	17,965
Average weekly attendance	50,000,000
Annual revenues§	$1,200,000,000
Annual Film Rentals	
Paid by theatres	$ 90,000,000
Annual payroll	$ 160,400,000
Employed in exhibition	122,500

* Includes non-theatrical.
† Hollywood only.
‡ Approved by the Production Code Authority.
§ Exclusive of Federal and state admission taxes.
Source: Standard & Poor's, *Industry Surveys,* March 3, 1955, "Motion Pictures," based on *Film Daily Yearbook* data for 1953.

can be gained from the fact that the sale prices of operating stations have risen from a third of a million dollars (the price of the first station to be sold, in 1949) to upwards of ten million for a particularly important station in 1954.

This trend toward a higher financial bracket has far-reaching consequences for the industry. Some of the more obvious are: restriction of ownership to fewer potential investors, with a trend toward corporate rather than individual ownership; altered managerial outlook when larger stakes are involved; dependence on large markets, capable of producing the necessary volume of revenue; more syndication to provide programs of a caliber capable of justifying these larger audiences. Of course, concentration of broadcast outlets in areas of dense population became inevitable from the moment that advertising was adopted as the source of broadcasting revenue. Yet radio can adapt itself to severe market limitations much more readily

Table 25

Investment in Tangible TV Broadcast Property, 1953

	Original Cost	Average Original Station Cost
4 networks and their owned and operated stations	$ 71,622,000	
309 other stations	161,512,000	$522,712
Total	$233,134,000	

Source: FCC, "Final TV Broadcast Financial Data — 1953" (20 October 1954, mimeo.), Table 8a.

than television. No parallel in television exists for the Class II or Class IV "coffeepot" radio station which can be operated successfully in a small community by an efficient owner-manager. Market size is the dominant variable factor in television operations: The larger the market the higher the salaries, the larger the staffs the longer the program day, the greater the number of network programs carried, the more remote programs originated — and the more lucrative the station. Over two thirds of the income from television broadcasting in 1953 was garnered in 16 large markets served by only 59 stations.[2]

Financial data on broadcasting are more readily available and more reliable than those on the other mass media. Data on the motion-picture industry, for instance, are notoriously unreliable. Broadcasters, however, are required by law to report regularly and in detail to the FCC. The Commission publishes data on the industry as a whole and provides various breakdowns by such categories as geographical area and station size, but does not release information on individual stations.

A general measure of the industry's economic health can be obtained by calculating the ratio of income to revenue or to investment. Both these indices rose very rapidly during the early 1940's until the glut of postwar radio stations began to lower the average income. In 1944 the ratio of income to original costs had reached 1.09, which means that radio stations as a whole were realizing over 100 per cent of their total investment in tangible property in the course of a single year, before deduction of Federal income taxes.[3] During the period of the freeze most television stations also began to experience great prosperity. Of course some stations operate at a

[2] Robert F. Jones, Progress Report Prepared for the Senate Committee on Interstate and Foreign Commerce, *Investigation of Television Networks and the UHF-VHF Problem* (Washington: Government Printing Office, 1955), p. 19.

[3] FCC, *Public Service Responsibility of Broadcast Licensees* (Washington: Government Printing Office, 1946), p. 49.

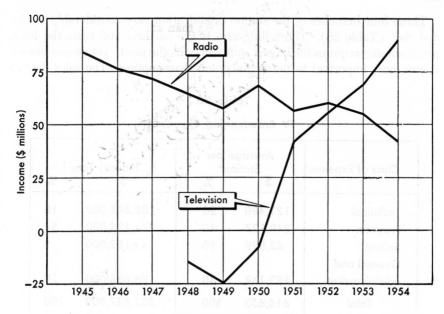

Figure 32

Radio and Television Income Trends Since 1945

Combined industry income (revenue minus expenses) before taxes. Note that the television industry as a whole broke out of the red in 1951 and exceeded radio income in 1953. (In terms of *revenue*, however, TV first surpassed radio in 1954.)

Sources: FCC annual financial data reports.

loss and some surrender their licenses each year; yet it can be said that broadcasting has been on the whole a remarkably lucrative industry for those who were fortunate enough to receive grants of desirable frequencies in sizable markets (Figure 32).

BROADCAST EXPENSES

Four categories of expense are recognized in the FCC's standardized breakdown of the broadcast financial structure: General and Administrative, Technical, Program, and Selling. These categories represent in a general way the basic functional organizational pattern of a station. The Administrative and General function is to provide the top policy-making nerve-center of the organization and the necessary accounting and housekeeping services for the other three branches. Selling, of course, is the income-producing function. The technical function is to provide and man the necessary gear for the specific broadcasting operation. All non-technical requirements of programming are included in the program function.

These four branches of the station organization vary considerably in size and cost (Table 26). The selling arm is the smallest and costs the least; programming requires the largest staff and costs the most. Yet no one branch is any more important to the organization than another. The sales depart-

Table 26

TV Broadcasting Expenses

Class of Expense	Average per Station*		Industry Total †	
	$	%	$	%
Technical	121,480	20	88,692,000	18
Program	249,127	40	274,125,000	54
Selling	62,899	10	41,182,000	8
General and administrative	183,147	30	98,638,000	20
Total	616,653	100	502,637,000	100

* Based on 377 stations; excludes 16 network-owned stations.
† Includes 4 networks and 393 stations.
Based on: FCC, "Radio and TV Broadcasting Financial Data — 1954" (2 December 1955, mimeo.), Table 3.

ment may consider itself the most vital, since without income the organization as a whole cannot survive. Yet the sales department cannot function without something to sell, and that something is the physical coverage provided by the technical department and the audiences attracted by the program department. And, of course, the whole operation has to be effectively coordinated and adequately housed.

In all four departments, salaries represent the largest expense item. The costs of syndicated radio program materials — wire services, transcriptions and records, and royalty and license fees — is relatively modest. A new category of program expense has been introduced by television, however, in the form of film rentals, which constitute a major expense item (Table 27). Film, whether in terms of the booking and handling of syndicated materials or of the creation of new materials for the station, represents such an important special activity that in practice it requires a department in itself. In recognition of this fact the NARTB in 1954 began reporting film as a separate category in its annual survey of employment and wages.[4]

EMPLOYMENT

Broadcasting as an occupation pays well above the national average, although staff salaries are not as high as the salaries of a few star performers

[4] NARTB, "TV Employment and Wage Survey" (1954, mimeo.).

Table 27

Average TV Station Program Expenses

Class of Program Expense	Average per Station	
	$	%
Salaries and wages	129,163	27.5
Talent	89,330	19.1
Royalties and license fees	55,569	11.9
Transcriptions and records	2,722	.6
Wire services	9,481	2.0
Film rentals	117,006	25.0
Film purchases	2,374	.5
Other film expenses	3,780	.8
Other	58,923	12.6
Total	468,348	100.0

Source: FCC, "Final TV Broadcast Financial Data — 1952" (31 July 1953, mimeo.), Table 6a.

might lead the uninitiated to expect (Table 28). About 25 per cent of the broadcast employees are women. Wage scales vary directly with size of market, which results in a good deal of mobility among broadcast employees, with constant effort to move on to a larger market and a higher wage bracket.

The casual observer of the industry sees and hears only the personnel who appear before the microphone and camera. He naturally tends to think of broadcasting in terms of its end product, which for him is programming. But every performer is backed by five or more employees who

Table 28

Broadcasting Wage Scales*

Class of Personnel	Weekly Wage Range
Program	$48 - 192
Film	50 - 114
Engineering	66 - 197
Sales	89 - 275
General and administrative	50 - 150

* Based on a sample of 16 typical staff jobs.
Source: NARTB, "TV Employment and Wage Survey" (1954, mimeo.).

make performance possible. The ratio of performers to non-performers is much higher than 5 to 1 for network programs; in fact, a single star may be the only visible member of a personal organization of a score or more persons.

The layman tends to form a highly inaccurate impression of the financial rewards of broadcast employment because of the notoriety received by those few top stars who command huge salaries. Such performers are no longer individuals in the usual sense. They become business enterprises or institutions; their salaries support a whole retinue of managers, agents, writers, producers, arrangers, secretaries, lawyers, and servants. Moreover, the star is projected into a realm in which the costs of the ordinary necessities of life, such as food, clothing, housing, transportation, recreation, and medical care become enormously inflated.

Star performers are in the category of "talent," which is distinguished from the category of "staff." The staff employee works for a salary and is identified with a particular station or network. He may receive certain bonuses (talent fees) over and above his base salary for specific chores on commercial programs. Staff jobs are primarily those specialized occupations which belong uniquely to broadcasting. No other job is quite like the job of staff announcer, commercial continuity writer, cameraman, floor manager, or broadcast "personality."

Talent, on the other hand, generally consists of people whose occupations are not uniquely a part of broadcasting. The actor, singer, juggler, dancer, or monologuist may find employment variously in night-clubs, hotels, vaudeville theatres, motion pictures, the legitimate stage, circuses, and the like, as well as in broadcasting. He is a free-lance entrepreneur who sells his services here and there according to demand and the conditions of the talent market. Talent is a commodity which is bought and sold, generally for particular programs or program series. Staff employees, on the other hand, work regularly at the same station, fulfilling the routine requirements of the programming schedule. About 50 per cent of the people who work in broadcasting are full-time staff employees, the other 50 per cent being in the category of part-time employees, or talent. Generally speaking, the salaries for staff employees are highest in the sales department (Table 28). Moreover, top management is usually recruited from this department. The program department, on the other hand, includes a larger number and a greater variety of personnel (Table 29). The income of talent cannot readily be calculated, because of the occasional nature of the work and the violent fluctuations of wage scales. Studies of the annual income of union members in various talent unions indicate that very few average a living wage from the sale of their talent; many are obliged to supplement their income through other kinds of work.

Like the sale of advertising, the sale of talent offers special problems which are best handled by agencies. Talent agencies occupy a strategic position because they are able to bid up the price of talent which is in great

Table 29

Number of TV Station Employees by Department

Department	Percentage of All Employees	Average Range in Number of Employees by Size of Station*
Technical	36	6 - 41
Program	31	8 - 41
Film	6	3 - 5
Sales and promotion	10	4 - 10
General and administrative	17	4 - 18
Total	100	25 - 115

* TV-AM combination employees are counted as one half. Averages are rounded to nearest whole number.
Based on: NARTB, "TV Employment and Wage Survey" (1954, mimeo.).

demand; this increases the cost of programming, which in turn affects the whole industry. As usually happens with agencies, there is a tendency toward domination of the market by a few firms.[5]

Unionization of talent has proceeded further than unionization of staff employees. This is because talent clusters at the large production centers. Union strategy in broadcasting has been to concentrate on the production centers, where network programs and package programs originate. At these strategic sources of supply, control can be obtained through contracts with relatively few organizations. Stations, on the other hand, are scattered throughout the country, some in places where the atmosphere is not favorable to strong unionization.

The most universally effective union is the American Federation of Musicians. This union asserted its strength early in the history of broadcasting because music forms such a major part of radio programming. The AFM has been able to enforce very broad controls on the broadcast industry on occasion, including such negative achievements as keeping network programs from release to FM stations for a considerable period. So notorious did the AFM's domination become that Congress amended the Communications Act in 1946 to outlaw "coercive practices affecting broadcasting" (Sec. 506 of the Act).

Performer unions, outside the motion-picture field, are grouped under the Associated Actors and Artistes of America; they include Actors Equity (legitimate theatre), the American Federation of Television and Radio Artists, the American Guild of Musical Artists, the American Guild of Variety Artists, and the Chorus Equity Association. Other types of creative

[5] "Talent Agencies: Have They Won Control Over TV Costs," *Sponsor* (24 January 1955), pp. 35-37, 116-120.

personnel usually belong to guilds — e.g., the Radio-Television Directors Guild and the Radio Writers Guild. The two major unions of technical personnel are the National Association of Broadcast Engineers and Technicians and the International Brotherhood of Electrical Workers.

Television has complicated the union situation in the broadcast industry by opening the door to the very powerful and tightly-knit motion-picture unions. Because television crosses so many boundaries among the various skills and performing arts, it has precipitated many jurisdictional squabbles among overlapping unions. Including the various motion-picture guilds and unions and those designed for office workers and building-maintenance personnel, about 50 different union organizations make claims on the broadcasting industry.[6]

Even with television, however, union discipline is not complete outside the major production centers. Motion-picture unions are all-powerful in the field of 35-mm. film; but 16-mm. production, having been devised originally as a home rather than a commercial medium, has not been so subject to unionization.

One of the major long-term problems of broadcasting is the systematic recruitment of well-educated personnel. Considering the importance of the industry, it is remarkable that it does so little to assure itself of continuingly improved education and methods of selection of staff employees. This condition is due, no doubt, to the fact that the broadcasting industry is so new that there has been no time to develop professional standards. Broadcasting started within the memory of many people still employed in the industry, and its workers were recruited from the widest possible variety of fields. Another problem is the fact that the station staff requires so many different types of personnel to carry out the four functions previously discussed. Still another difficulty is the fact that the industry has not generally developed a rational system for the induction and development of executive personnel. It therefore lacks attraction for the kind of recruit it needs — the most able, imaginative, creative, and ambitious of career-minded young people.[7]

PROGRAMMING ECONOMICS

The economic compulsion toward syndication of programs has been referred to in various connections in previous chapters. This is the most important generalization that can be made concerning the economy of broadcast programming. The only economic incentive countering the trend toward virtual disappearance of local, live programs is the value of such programs in enhancing a station's prestige and lending color to its institu-

---

[6] See *Broadcasting-Telecasting* yearbooks for complete lists. Interesting examples of jurisdictional hairsplitting are found in: Isidore Lindenbaum, "The Care and Feeding of TV Film Unions," *Broadcasting-Telecasting* (13 July 1953), pp. 88-94.

[7] The education of broadcast personnel is discussed further in Chapter 26.

Table 30
The Importance of Film in TV Programming

A. ACCORDING TO TYPE OF STATION AND OVER-ALL PROGRAMMING*

Program Classification	Amount Carried, by Type of Station			
	Interconnected Network Affiliates (%)	Non-Interconnected Network Affiliates (%)	Non-Network Stations (%)	All Stations (%)
Local				
Theatre film	15.7	30.6	30.2	16.6
Film made for TV	13.2	22.6	21.2	13.8
Total film	*28.9*	*53.2*	*51.4*	*30.4*
Local live	20.4	28.8	48.6	21.7
Total local	*49.3*	*82.0*	*100.0*	*52.1*
Network				
Network live	43.9	—	—	41.0
Kinescope film	6.8	18.0	—	6.9
Total network	*50.7*	*18.0*	—	*47.9*

B. LOCAL FILM PROGRAMMING ACCORDING TO TYPE OF FILM†

Type of Film	Percentage of all film hours	Percentage of stations using	Average cost per hour
Feature	53.5	100.0	$ 72.49
Syndicated	28.1	98.1	253.09
Short subjects	8.3	89.4	84.33
Film produced by station	1.4	36.5	278.13
Free film	8.7	91.3	—

* Source: *Broadcasting-Telecasting* (11 April 1955), pp. 66-67, based on a survey conducted March, 1955.
† Source: NARTB, *Film Manual, 1955* (Washington: NARTB, 1955), pp. 7-10.

tional personality.[8] The hard fact is that few local advertisers can afford to be program sponsors; hence there is little money for local programs, particularly in television. National spot advertisers can afford program sponsorship, but are likely to prefer using syndicated materials of their own choosing and devising.

For this reason local live programming is confined primarily to participation and announcement formats, which are inexpensive to produce and are suited to the needs of small advertisers. Distinctly localized materials

---

[8] Not considered at this point is the element of legal compulsion. The FCC puts considerable pressure on licensees to maintain a certain amount of local live programming and to reflect in some degree local interests and needs (see Chapter 22).

form the bulk of local live programming. Such programs must be simple enough in format and content to be produced without full scripts or rehearsals. The cost of more creative types of programming, such as drama, live music, or comedy-variety, is ordinarily far beyond the means of local advertisers, even if sufficient local talent and production facilities were available. Moreover, it is not easy to sell sponsors and audiences on home-grown talent when nationally-known performers in slickly finished productions are available at less cost on syndicated transcriptions or films.

In television the film buyer has accordingly come to occupy an important position. Indeed, for non-network-affiliated stations the film buyer may be the real key to successful operations. Sources include not only feature films, short subjects, and entertainment films made especially for television (the latter are usually referred to specifically as "syndicated films," although all entertainment film is in fact syndicated) but also promotional films made by industry and available free, which are invaluable for filling in sustaining chinks in the commercial schedule (see Table 30).

Local broadcasting has developed live program formats and staff talent suited to its peculiar needs and limitations. The "morning man," the afternoon disc jockey, the "personality," the cooking-fashions-interview expert, and other familiar types are the result. Talent for such programs may vary widely — from the disc jockey with an encyclopedic knowledge of popular music and an up-to-date vocabulary of teen-age slang to the trained home economist. But the successful performers all have one essential ability in common: along with their other skills goes ability to *sell*. A performer at the local staff level can rarely indulge in the luxury of devoting himself to art alone; he must do his share of the station's selling job.

At the local level television's unique ability to report real-life events directly as they happen can be exploited relatively infrequently (Table 31).

Table 31
Sources of Programs, by Size of Market

Size of Market	Sources of Programs			
	Network (%)	Local Film (%)	Local Studio (%)	Local Remote (%)
Below 25,000	40	37	23	*
25,000 - 100,000	33	44	22	*
100,000 - 250,000	51	31	18	*
250,000 - 500,000	52	28	19	*
500,000 - 1,000,00	49	30	21	*
Over 1,000,000	49	28	21	2

* Less than 1%.
Source: NARTB, "TV Employment and Wage Survey" (1954, mimeo.), p. 12.

The cost of setting up the equipment for a television "remote" (actuality broadcast from the scene of the event) prevents frequent use of this program resource. Moreover, special events (as such broadcasts are called) are difficult to absorb into the normal program pattern, since they come at their own time and in varying lengths and frequencies. Usually they necessitate cancellation of regularly-scheduled commercial programs, with consequent loss of revenue and disruption of schedule. In commercial television's pioneer days audiences were regaled with remote pickups of an extraordinary variety of events; but that was before studio programming and commercial schedules had been well developed. With more commercial prosperity has come more rigidity in programming. For example, in 1954 only Dumont and ABC carried the McCarthy–Army hearings live — not because they had any greater sense of public responsibility than CBS and NBC, but because the more prosperous networks could not well afford to cancel a heavy schedule of commercial programs for so long a period.

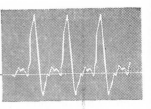

19

Economic Determinants of the Program
Service: Summary and Evaluation

In the previous seven chapters we have explored in some detail the economic aspects of broadcasting in America. It is now time to recall that the purpose of this exploration is to identify ways in which the economy of the system affects its end-product, the program service. The primary economic features of the system are (1) its dependence on advertising for revenue and (2) competition among stations (as well as media) for that revenue. That these economic factors profoundly and intimately affect the nature of the program service is quite evident. The question, therefore, is not whether the economy of the system affects the program service but rather how much and in what direction it affects it.

THE PROFIT MOTIVE

Some observers may conclude that the profit motive is in practice the only motive — that broadcasters merely pay lip service to considerations of public welfare and only reluctantly meet the letter of their legal obligations as licensees. According to this theory the profit motive would, for example, have the effect of increasing the commercial content of programming to the maximum salable amount, or the effect of channeling programming exclusively in the direction of certain types of program which have maximum value as advertising vehicles. This view, however, represents a naive and oversimplified conception of economic determinism. Any two station managers, equally motivated by the desire for profit, may arrive at entirely different decisions from the same set of facts. One manager may be more concerned with remote economic consequences than with immediate gain; he may reject a prospective client because of the adverse effect that client's advertising might have on the rest of the station's business. Furthermore, even these purely economic motivations shade off into non-economic considerations — standards of taste, of personal ethics and integrity, of social responsibility. Stations and networks very frequently turn down opportunities for profit for a variety of reasons, not all of them basically economic. In short, economic motivation is neither (1) a simple, unitary drive aiming always at the same immediate goal nor (2) free from coloration by other kinds of motivation. To paraphrase Oscar Wilde, economic motives are rarely pure and never simple.

If the profit motive were both pure and simple, the broadcaster would have only one standard to go by in making any decision: will it immediately make money? But the mixed character of the profit motive makes it possible to set up different standards of practice, still within the framework of commercial broadcasting. These standards represent a working compromise between extremes. For example, there is nothing absolute about the NARTB limit of three minutes of commercial copy in a half-hour nighttime sponsored program. From the programming point of view, no commercial at all might be preferable; from the sponsor's point of view a full half-hour commercial pitch might be preferable. The compromise of 90 per cent program and 10 per cent commercial seems reasonable to both sides.

REPRESENTING THE PUBLIC'S INTEREST

Compromise, to be fairly arrived at, must come about as a result of full and effective representation of all interests concerned. The problem in American broadcasting has always been to devise a practical means for securing full and effective representation of the public's interest. The FCC, of course, legally represents the public, but its prerogatives are rather stringently limited, and it cannot enter into many of the practical situations in which representation of the public's interest is most needed. It has been suggested that the public can secure representation through the formation of Listeners' Councils;[1] through professional criticism in the press; through individual letter writing; through boycotting of sponsors of objectionable programs; through a national Citizens' Advisory Board.[2]

Unfortunately, none of these devices does the job. Their main drawback is that they generally go into operation *after* decisions have been made and programs are already on the air. Furthermore, they tend to stress special-interest groups, rather than the general interest of the public at large.[3] To be effective, the public's interest must be represented in both policy-making and the day-to-day programming decisions of the station and network. The natural implement for this representation is, in general, the station's or network's program department itself.

In practical operations, the program department's proper concern is the

[1] Cf.: Charles A. Siepmann, *Radio, Television, and Society* (New York: Oxford University Press, 1950), Chapter V, "Rights and Duties of the Listener."
[2] Cf.: Senate Committee on Interstate and Foreign Commerce Subcommittee, *Hearings on S. Res. 127* (Washington: Government Printing Office, 1951).
[3] Among the registered Washington lobbyists interested in influencing broadcasting legislation, the Women's Christian Temperance Union spends the most. Cf. "Capitol Lobbyists Report Activities," *Broadcasting-Telecasting* (18 October 1954), p. 66.

achievement of quality and balance in the programming service. It should be professionally skilled in understanding and interpreting the public's interest. This outlook inevitably comes into conflict with the interests of the sales department. The individual salesman focuses with the utmost intensity on securing a client for a given program segment. He cannot allow his attention to be distracted by such larger issues as over-all program balance. His livelihood hinges on his ability to close transactions with individual clients for particular advertising vehicles. In this respect the station salesman's point of view has the same limitations as has that of the advertising agency, which was discussed previously. Unless held in check by an effectual policy rein, salesmen will cheerfully take over programming.

The sales department will tend to promise the client anything which will help to clinch the sale. The program department then finds itself in the position of having to produce an unproducible program, to displace a sustaining feature on short notice to accommodate a commercial show, to schedule material which throws the program structure out of balance, to accept material which does not meet its own professional standards.

Broadcast management's key problem is the resolution of this conflict between the interests of sales and the interests of programming. If management backs up sales and lets down programming, the only voice representing the interests of the public has been choked off and the programming service declines in quality. Examine the internal organization of any station whose standards of programming practice are below par and you will find dominance by sales, with the program function reduced to a subordinate role as a mere traffic department. The intelligent manager welcomes aggressive representation of both the programming and the sales points of view, so that

Table 32

Organizational Status of Executives in Charge of Program Functions at TV Stations

| Function | Number of Executives, by Rank in Organizational Hierarchy | | | | | |
	First	Second	Third	Fourth	Total No.	%
Administrative	364	192	53	23	632	43
Sales	11	116	120	99	346	24
Programs	2	50	134	153	339	23
Engineering	1	16	61	65	143	10

Explanation: The titles of the first four officers listed for all stations in the *Television Factbook No. 20* (Spring, 1955) were classified according to function and tabulated by rank. There is very little uniformity in titles; executives were classified under that function which appeared most likely to be represented by their titles.

issues can be fairly analyzed and equitable compromises worked out. Unfortunately, management is likely to weight the balance in favor of sales, since most top executives come up through the sales route. Most stations rank the program executive in third or fourth place in the organizational hierarchy, with the sales executive in second or third place (Table 32).

By and large, then, it may be said that the public's interest in programming can most effectively be represented in the broadcasting operation if (1) the program personnel have knowledge, taste, and professional integrity as individuals; and (2) the program department has an effective voice in the operation, both at the level of policy-making and in the day-to-day programming decisions. These conditions depend, in turn, on management's ability to select appropriate personnel initially, to maintain a power-balance within the organization, and to resolve conflicts equitably.

These desiderata are, of course, virtually impossible of achievement if many of the programs themselves are beyond the control of the program department by reason of ownership by sponsors or advertising agencies, or if the station's financial position is so shaky that its management cannot afford the luxury of following a policy which sometimes results in rejection of prospective customers.

CONTROL OF PROGRAMS

The conclusion is inescapable that the only way to keep the influence of the advertiser within bounds is to remove him from decisive control over the selection, production, and scheduling of programs. The ideal arm's-length relationship is not easy to achieve.

> It is almost impossible to explain to an advertiser why his particular program, which he is convinced is selling his product, is not acceptable to you, and yet unless this explanation is undertaken and followed by rejection, it is not long before the whole program standard of the station is lost, and your entire schedule becomes a heterogeneous hodgepodge of good, bad, and indifferent material . . . the owners of the facilities must cease to be merely renters and janitors, and must control by ownership or contract, a substantial portion of the program material which is used on their stations . . . the networks, realizing the fatal mistake they made in radio in this respect, are making every effort to hold the reins in television.[4]

Sylvester Weaver, NBC Board Chairman, was formerly an advertising-agency man, and as such advocated agency control of commercial programs. Despite this predisposition, he was obliged to admit, after joining NBC, that

> The programming just had no direction . . . there was no planned relationship of one program to another or to the competition, and no particular attempt to create a listening pattern for the people at home. I could see that the whole

[4] Robert D. Swezey, "Television and the Dirty Look" (NARTB, mimeo., 1954), p. 3.

programming service was running down hill, with sponsor and agencies seeking the cheap way of getting their messages across.[5]

On the national level, a conspicuous example of the type of programming which advertiser influence tends to emphasize is the "giveaway" quiz program, particularly that subspecies which capitalizes on the miseries of the participants to invest the proceedings with a morbid fascination. Ben Gross has characterized giveaways as "not entertainment, but incitements to human cupidity." *Broadcasting-Telecasting*, the trade journal of the industry (which is not noted for a "do-gooder" point of view), has editorialized against the giveaways in clear-cut terms:

> We are opposed to money and prize giveaway programs as parasitic and undesirable. We believe they are used artificially to stimulate audience and ratings. We believe, moreover, that as long as manufacturers can get free air credits by donating merchandise, they won't buy time. We believe these programs violate the commercial time limitations of the radio and tv codes.[6]

Giveaways like *Strike It Rich,* on which contestants tell heart-rending stories of poverty and suffering, have been singled out for attack from many quarters. *Life* editorialized that such programs "have sunk about as low as it is possible to sink," and John Crosby called them "the shame of television." But from the purely commercial point of view this is a good program — it draws audiences.

> The fact that the program commands an audience of commercially significant size is both a criticism of the morbidness that afflicts too many people and of the network and sponsor that pander to it. *Strike It Rich* exists only because it engages in that most depressing of all ways to make a buck — exploitation of human suffering. . . . The program is a classic example of pseudo-humanitarianism without excuse or merit.[7]

Another example of advertiser influence is provided by an absurd but symptomatic little incident which occurred near Christmastime on *This Is Show Business.* George S. Kaufman, the playwright, happened to say casually on the air, "Let's make this one program on which no one sings 'Silent Night'!" The sponsor received several hundred letters of protest and promptly took Kaufman off the program. Kaufman commented afterwards: "It's a fear-ridden industry, and that's the way it's ruled. When they get some letters they're afraid not to fire somebody."

Doubtless thousands of non-letter-writers heartily agreed with Kaufman's implication — that broadcasting tends to make the sacred seem trite by

[5] Quoted in: Thomas Whiteside, "The Communicator," *The New Yorker* (23 October, 1954), p. 59.

[6] "High Court Looks at 'Giveaways'," *Broadcasting-Telecasting* (19 October 1953), p. 130.

[7] "In Review," *Broadcasting-Telecasting* (31 August 1953), p. 16. For a spirited defense of *Strike It Rich,* cf.: Max Wylie, *Clear Channels: Television and the American People* (New York: Funk & Wagnalls Co., 1955), pp. 7-10, 227-235.

over-repetition. But the advertiser's intense dedication to the idea of offending no one quite overshadows any question of fact or principle. This particular instance is more amusing than alarming. But the same lack of principle was exposed in a more serious light when, starting in 1950, the industry came under the influence of the first of a series of privately-published blacklists of performers suspected of Communist affiliations. The *cause célèbre* was the Jean Muir case. Miss Muir performed on a program sponsored by General Foods. On the basis of a few calls (estimates of the number range from 20 to 200) Miss Muir's contract was summarily cancelled at a cost of $10,000 to the company. One of the charges against the actress was that she had sent a telegram of congratulation to the Moscow Art Theatre on the occasion of its anniversary. A number of other contract cancellations followed before the fury of fear died down.[8]

These incidents, whatever their importance in terms of the rights of the individuals involved, probably had little general effect on the broadcasting program service. Their significance in the present context lies in what they reveal of the advertiser's point of view and his power to control the details of program production. The full extent of this control — and the full extent of the advertiser's subservience to pressure groups — do not often come to the public's attention as they did in these cases.

It is of interest to compare an example of the reaction of the press to advertiser pressure. Arthur Hays Sulzberger, editor of the *New York Times*, reported that in 1936 the paper

unquestionably lost a large amount of advertising — and we wish we had it — because of the support of President Roosevelt during the campaign. We were accused of being traitors and Communists, and some advertisers were frank enough to tell us that they would not spend a dollar with a newspaper which represented such subversive interests.[9]

In the 1952 election campaign, when the *Times* supported Eisenhower, it sold space to Stevenson supporters in which these advertisers publicly challenged the *Times* to switch its support to Stevenson. The paper received 2,120 letters urging the change, and only 142 supporting its position. The *Times* reported this result and then reaffirmed its support of Eisenhower.[10] To be sure, it is doubtful that broadcasting will ever adopt editorial positions on political issues in the manner of newspapers; but these examples of adherence to principle in the face of controversy and even threats of economic reprisal from advertisers set a standard which serves as a challenge to the broadcasting medium. This challenge is made particularly urgent by the fact that broadcasting, more and more in recent years, has been claiming status as a news medium on a level with the newspaper.

[8] Cf.: Merle Miller, *The Judges and the Judged* (New York: Doubleday & Co., Inc., 1952).

[9] Arthur Hays Sulzberger, Address to the American Association of Advertising Agencies, *New York Times* (3 May 1941).

[10] *New York Times* (26 October 1952).

It should be added that when we speak of "advertiser" influence a great many different varieties and sources of influence are being summarily grouped under a single heading. No doubt what is called advertiser influence is often a subjective inclination of station management itself and unrelated to any direct pressure from advertisers. Certainly some of the commercial influence on programs is traceable to advertising agencies, talent agencies, production firms, station representatives, commercial research organizations, station salesmen and sales managers, the trade press, and trade associations.

THE LUXURY OF INTEGRITY

Broadcast stations as business enterprises have two peculiarities: (1) declining income cannot be countered by equivalent reductions in expenses, and (2) a money-losing station is slow to die. As to the first point, every commercial account that is lost not only subtracts that much revenue but also adds a certain expense, since the time has to be programmed whether sold or not. Therefore depreciation of the program service is likely to be rapid once income begins to lessen. On the other hand, even when a station has reached the lowest ebb it is likely to continue to operate, because there always seem to be people willing to work for nothing, to gamble on the future, to stall off the creditors for one more week in the hope of finding the magic formula for success without merit.

The general level of broadcasting could be much improved if it were possible, without violating the principle of free enterprise, to kill off quickly and painlessly hundreds of marginal stations whose income is insufficient to procure a reasonably high quality of program service. Unfortunately, the damage done by such marginal stations spreads wider than their own meagre audience coverage. For in their desperation they tend to abandon all standards, to resort to all the undesirable practices — rate-cutting, acceptance of questionable advertising, overloading their programming with bargain commercials, and the like. This brings pressure to bear on competing stations to lower their standards, too, in order not to be undercut.

In short, operation by the highest standards necessarily implies the freedom to make decisions. If acceptance or rejection of the next proffered account means the difference between survival and bankruptcy, the manager has no real freedom. He is governed by expediency; he cannot afford the luxury of integrity.

The range in degrees of freedom among stations is tremendous. The manager of a station on a favorable channel in a rich market without excessive competition can afford to set up statesmanlike long-term policies which look to the future as well as the present, which work toward the building of his station as an institution with a distinctive personality, good taste, and integrity. In practical terms, such policies will result in rejection of all advertising of doubtful ethical value, discrimination in the selection of program material and talent, strict adherence to time limitations on commercial copy, scheduling of well-produced sustaining features in salable time-segments, refusal to make deals in violation of published rates, and so on.

Consider, by contrast, the situation of the manager of a station on an unfavorable channel in an over-competitive, limited market. He is not sure he can meet his payroll at the end of the week. What happens when he tells a salesman that the client he has just succeeded in selling is unacceptable to the station? Can he turn down a good prospect because the time desired by the advertiser happens to have been promised to the P.T.A.? If a major sale hinges on an under-the-table rebate, can he afford to make a high-minded speech about the sanctity of rate cards?

This wide range in what we have called "degrees of freedom" means that broadcasting is in many ways not at all the same thing for all stations and networks. Because of such variations the NARTB has never been able to secure agreement on standards of practice which meet even the already-established standards of some stations and networks. It simply is not realistic to expect every network to be able to meet the same standards as NBC, or an unaffiliated UHF television station in a small market to meet the same standards as a network key station in New York.

Here, then, is a basic socio-economic problem created by the system of advertising support and competitive operation. It does not mean, of course, that all small, underprivileged stations are by definition unethical. Many in radio have found a *modus vivendi* by narrowing their service down to meet the needs of special groups; by skillful and efficient management many such stations offer a highly satisfactory service within the limitations they have marked out for themselves. (No such solution has yet been found, however, for the small-scale television operation.)

Nevertheless, there does remain the problem of the marginal station, hitherto described, which undermines the solidarity of the broadcasting industry. Such stations either cannot or will not meet even industry-sponsored standards of practice. As the editors of *Broadcasting-Telecasting* observed,

> A code serves only to express the attitudes of the majority that adopts it and practices its principles anyway, and in no way is it a deterrent to the minority whose excesses it is intended to cure. There is no evidence that the NAB code has changed the habits of any radio station that did not believe in its principles before they were formalized in a code.[11]

TASTE AND TRUTH IN ADVERTISING

Underlying the whole question of economic influences on programming, of course, is the basic issue of the social value of advertising itself. If one starts from the premise that advertising *per se* is economically wasteful and

[11] "TV Standards" (28 May 1951), p. 61.

socially detrimental, consideration of standards for its use becomes superfluous. But critics who start from this premise appear to be philosophically far removed from the main stream of American political and economic thinking. As one student of the economics of advertising has observed,

> Advertising has long been the subject of both criticism and praise. It is quite natural that this should be so since its very nature is such as to invite praise and censure. It is very conspicuous and seeks to call attention to itself. Because of this, advertising has been both blamed and lauded for its influence upon our social and economic life. A good deal of what has been said and written about advertising should be applied to our economic system rather than to one phase of it.[12]

In his very thorough and scholarly study of advertising's economic effects, Borden[13] concluded that in an expanding economy such as ours advertising does play a useful role. We have tried to describe this role briefly in Chapter 12.

In analyzing criticism of advertising based on ethical rather than economic grounds, Borden distinguishes: (1) the advertising of products which the critics consider undesirable as products; (2) advertising which critics find offensive to good taste; and (3) advertising which is false and misleading. As an example of the first of these, some people will always object to the advertising of liquor, irrespective of the quality of the advertising itself; they are opposed to liquor as such and hence to all liquor advertising. As to the second objection, some people may consider any advertisement for intimate toilet preparations in bad taste, though not objecting to the products themselves — or they may object merely to the way in which the subject is handled in the advertising message. Both these bases of objection to advertising are obviously subjective. It would be difficult to arrive at a consensus in any but the most extreme cases.

Deliberate factual error, on the other hand, might be more readily identified objectively. But as we have pointed out (Chapter 12), a great deal of modern advertising — and broadcast advertising in particular — is not highly factual. It deals in persuasion, in the manipulation of attitudes and feelings. How can one test the statement "L.S.M.F.T. — Lucky Strike means fine tobacco!" for factual content? This manipulative aspect of advertising has caused concern to some students of society.[14] But again, it is something which goes much deeper than advertising itself. Manipulation of opinion is a pervasive feature of modern societies — one that has international as well as national ramifications.

It is not difficult to find examples of false and misleading advertising.

---

[12] C. H. Sandage, *Advertising: Theory and Practice* (4th ed.; Homewood, Ill.: Richard D. Irwin, Inc., 1953), p. 29.

[13] Neil H. Borden, *The Economic Effects of Advertising* (4th ed.; Chicago: Richard D. Irwin, Inc., 1947).

[14] E.g., Robert Merton, *Mass Persuasion: The Social Psychology of a War Bond Drive* (New York: Harper and Bros., 1946), p. 10.

The Federal Trade Commission cites many cases every year, and doubtless only a fraction of the actual violations ever reaches official notice. But let us put aside the obviously and grossly unethical advertisers, advertising media, and advertising messages; let us consider only those which are unexceptional. Do we find that most such advertising is completely factual, objective, truthful, candid? A glance at any magazine or newspaper, a few minutes with any radio or television program, will uncover examples to the contrary. How many products are "best" or "better"? How many arguments are illogical, appeals irrational, assertions unprovable, allusions irrelevant, claims exaggerated?

In short, even "legitimate" advertising is "seller's talk" or "puffery." This kind of exaggeration is common to many contemporary realms of discourse. One learns to discount it, along with the thousands of other culturally approved devices which make things seem better or more desirable than they are. Ordinary advertising puffery is on a level with, for example, the many devices which women customarily use in our culture to make themselves seem better-shaped, better-colored, and better-smelling than nature made them. Puffery in advertising has been legally recognized, and the line of demarcation between what is permissible and what is fraudulent has been judicially defined.

> . . . the rule is well settled that mere general commendations . . . "trade talk", "dealer's talk", "seller's statements", or "puffing" do not amount to actionable misrepresentations where the parties deal at arm's length.[15]

People probably learn to handle the language of advertising just as they learn to handle the language of polite social intercourse (which is rarely candid). A study of the severity with which listeners criticized radio commercials developed the interesting fact that commercials were criticized almost twice as severely for being "noisy and distracting" as for "claiming too much for the product."[16] Borden conducted a rather elaborate study of consumer appraisal of magazine advertising and concluded:

> Examination of the data suggests that consumers have a considerable tolerance for exaggeration and puffery in advertising. Apparently they do not expect advertisements to be absolutely honest documents, just as absolute honesty is not expected in connection with most human activities. They undoubtedly expect advertisements to be biased and to present merchandise in an attractive light.[17]

FRAUDULENCE IN BROADCAST ADVERTISING

This is not, of course, to condone fraudulence in advertising. The media and the advertising fraternity as a whole at least make an effort to keep

[15] 23 Am. Jur., "Fraud and Deceit," §33.
[16] Paul F. Lazarsfeld and Patricia L. Kendall, *Radio Listening in America* (New York: Prentice-Hall, 1948), p. 71.
[17] Borden, *op. cit.*, p. 760.

fraud out of advertising through voluntary self-policing. The American Association of Advertising Agencies, for example, operates an opinion exchange through which the attention of its membership can be called to advertisements which transcend the limits of puffery. The president of Foote, Cone, and Belding, one of the largest advertising agencies, has said frankly:

> We have hucksters in our own association [the AAAA] and we should throw them out. We have hucksters among our advertisers and we should weed them out. We all know magazines that fail entirely to censor copy for the mealy, weasel words that make it at once both legally truthful and utterly dishonest . . . we all know radio and television stations that make a mockery of allowed commercial time on local programs.[18]

Broadcasting has offered a particularly fertile field for the fraudulent and near-fraudulent advertiser. It reaches a "sucker audience" which print hardly touches, and the potentialities for quick profits on the smallest investment are astonishing. It has been plagued recently, for example, by an outbreak of "bait-switch" advertising — a particularly ingenious type of high-pressure salesmanship which lures the prospect with the offer of a tremendous bargain (the "bait") and then persuades the victim that the bargain merchandise is in fact undesirable and substitutes a much higher-priced article (the "switch"). Objectionable types of per-inquiry advertising have already been discussed (Chapter 14). Mail-order selling by radio and television, though not necessarily either fraudulent or exploitative, seems in practice to be a constant source of embarrassment to the industry because of the character of the products frequently sold by this method as well as the character of the advertising used. Broadcasting might well gain in the long run by complete elimination of mail-order selling, although there seems no prospect of such a statesmanlike move in the near future. Referring to a rash of advertising of questionable medical products, one critic remarked: "If the radio and television stations are at all interested in cleaning up this mail order mess, they have shown little concrete evidence of that desire."[19] Over 200 radio stations are said to have been taken in by a fly-by-night advertising agency which a few years ago persuaded them to advertise a particularly crass mail-order deal which cruelly exploited the Christmas spirit to sell a worthless product.[20] Stations not only failed to collect from the agency but had to make refunds to their too-trusting listeners. These types of exploitation, which take advantage of audiences' trust in the broadcast medium and capitalize on the needs of low-income families, are extremely damaging to broadcasting. Much of it escapes critical notice because the worst examples are usually found not in the big cities, where

[18] Fairfax M. Cone, quoted in: Miles David, "Hucksters: What You Can Do About Them," *Sponsor* (31 May 1954), p. 28.

[19] E. B. Weiss, "Medicine Men are Back, on TV and Radio," *Printers Ink* (27 April 1951), p. 35.

[20] "Mail-Order Furor," *Broadcasting-Telecasting* (29 January 1951), p. 30.

audiences are more sophisticated and where the critics live, but in rural areas and small towns.

Although many such examples could be cited, broadcasting has made progress toward the status of an ethical medium. A reminder of what used to be, such as the following description by Ben Gross, the New York *Daily News* reviewer, is salutary:

> Tailors, preachers, loan sharks, swamis, and physical-culture men, merchants, nostrum dispensers and frenzied advocates of odd ideas, such as Colonel Henderson of Shreveport, Louisiana, who combined primitive theology with hatred of chain stores, indulged in a saturnalia of "free speech." . . . In a steady procession, there came before the microphones newscasters who merely read word-for-word items from the daily papers, owners of diploma mills, crystal-gazing fortunetellers, installment furniture men, conductors of matrimonial bureaus, fakers, nuts and dreamers making merry carnival.[21]

Broadcasting has certainly become more selective than it was in the 1920's. And even in the 1920's such programs were no doubt the exception rather than the rule. Nevertheless, broadcasting still has a long way to go before its advertising practices reach a level consistent with its potential status as a communications medium dedicated to serving the public. As the general manager of a major television station has said, "the industry is still too intent upon the quick buck and many bucks, and is still too subservient to advertiser pressure."[22] When each individual licensee (and it is he with whom the responsibility in a democratic system ultimately rests) lives up to the professions of the NARTB and the other trade associations, the cheap carnival atmosphere which still pervades much of broadcasting will disappear. The taint of the pitchman and the huckster remains today, but we must remind ourselves how immature the medium actually is. When we compare the great improvement that newspaper and magazine advertising has made in the last half-century, it seems evident that broadcasting has yet to find its proper level.

[21] Ben Gross, *I Looked and I Listened* (New York: Random House, 1954), pp. 68-69.
[22] Swezey, *op. cit.*, p. 2.

PART FOUR

Social Control
of Broadcasting

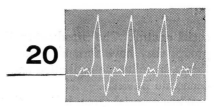

20

Agencies of Social Control

> ... the public arts cannot be escaped by turning
> off the radio or television set, by refusing to go
> to the movies; neither our indifference nor our
> contempt gives us immunity against them.
> — GILBERT SELDES

Everyone has an interest in the broadcasting service, including even those who never participate in it as members of an audience. We speak in this context of "interest" not in the sense of *being interested,* i.e., of having one's attention momentarily engaged, but in the sense of having an interest, i.e., standing to receive benefit or harm from the very existence of broadcasting.

Of course not everyone is necessarily conscious that his personal interests may be at stake, just as not everyone is aware that he has a personal interest in the proper operation of public health services, the judicial system, interstate commerce, and the many other institutions which determine the kind of social environment in which the individual must live.

THE ROLE OF SOCIAL GROUPS

No matter how conscious he may be of his interests, the lone individual — as such — has little opportunity for directly influencing the program service in order to shape it more nearly to his needs and tastes. In terms of the advertiser's interests, the individual becomes influential only by virtue of his membership in a group large enough to constitute a commercially worth-while audience. This form of influence, which is based on the individual's set-tuning behavior, exercises only a loose kind of control over the program service, as we shall see.

Another, and more positive, kind of influence can be exercised by the individual through his membership in organized social groups — a church, trade association, union, educational organization, political party, social or service club, or any of thousands of other associations which people form to implement their special interests. Such social groups function as agencies of social control. The broadcasters themselves, of course, constitute such a group; they have formed a trade association which seeks, among other things, to influence legislation and public opinion in the direction of their economic interests.

When a social group believes that its interests are affected, it may use a variety of techniques for bringing pressure to bear to change matters in the direction of its interests. It may use highly organized and sophisticated forms of pressure, such as lobbying, political action, or boycott, or crude forms, such as gang warfare or lynching; or it may merely contribute generally to the climate of opinion by communicating its views to others. Pressure may be focused where it will do the most good — on responsible individuals, business executives, government administrators, or lawmakers; or it may be diffused generally through speeches, resolutions, magazine articles, letters to the editor, and street-corner conversations.

Group interests, of course, are infinitely varied, and hence all degrees of conflict and concurrence appear in the social arena. Broadcasting as a subject of social control offers a conspicuous example. Each interest-group would like to remake the broadcasting service to suit its own goals and standards. One group wants more classical music, another less soap opera, another more religion, another less violence and crime. Prohibitionists think beer and wine advertising increases alcohol consumption and should be prohibited; trades and professions think unflattering portrayals of their occupations lower their collective prestige and should be prohibited; intellectuals think vulgar programs debase the public taste and should be prohibited; political extremists think that unslanted news programs misinform and should be prohibited, and so on. Each group sees broadcasting as a means of social control and seeks to use it to increase the scope of its own control. Whether or not broadcasting actually *has* the effects sought to be prevented or obtained is irrelevant as long as the group acts on the belief that it does.

THE CONCEPT OF "PUBLIC INTEREST"

Not all groups, of course, can be equally effective in promoting their particular interests. Some relatively small groups have disproportionately loud voices, because of unusual zeal, financial resources, or organizing skill. For this reason spokesmen for the broadcasting industry sometimes set up a false dichotomy: on the one hand stands "the public," the great mass of people, which is presumed to be perfectly satisfied with broadcasting as it is;[1]

---

[1] In answer to the question "Do you ever feel like criticizing when you listen to the radio?," 67 per cent of a national sample responded "Yes." Paul F. Lazarsfeld and Patricia L. Kendall, *Radio Listening in America* (Copyright, 1948, by Prentice-Hall, Inc., New York), p. 49. The authors assert that "we can safely say that *everyone* experiences [occasional dissatisfaction], but that only two-thirds bother to express it. The people who say that they never feel like criticizing radio, newspapers, or movies are relatively unsophisticated: They are less well educated, they read fewer books, and so on" (p. 50).

on the other hand stand a few malcontents and "do-gooders" — impractical reformers who want arbitrarily to impose their standards on everybody else. This oversimplification assumes that because "the public" does not, as such, maintain a lobby in Washington, write critical articles in newspapers and magazines, or send petitions to the FCC, it has no special interest in controlling the program service. The public, as such, cannot do any of these things for the simple reason that it does not exist. The public is not a vast, passive, homogeneous mass of people of identical interests, tastes, and needs. It consists of many groups, as we have pointed out. Do-gooders and reformers are just as much a part of the public as any other group; they merely happen to be more articulate and aggressive in the expression of their special interests than other groups. But the less articulate groups are just as ready to impose *their* standards on the rest of society as the reformers; they simply don't make a career of it.

Nevertheless, on some occasions we need to think and act in terms of society as a whole, arriving at some kind of balance among all the conflicting group interests. The law, as an agency of social control, represents such a compromise. Backed by the coercive power of government, the law expresses the general interests of society as a whole. Out of the many special interests emerges a broader, more inclusive interest — the *public* interest. This is not to say, of course, that the compromise is ever perfect. In actual practice the public interest has to be defined by someone (whether an individual or a group), and that someone cannot completely escape the influence of his own interests; hence the law may neglect some interests and favor others. A good deal depends on the political system under which a government operates and on the machinery provided to check the more aggressive interests and to make effective the voice of the less articulate interests. In our country, as far as broadcasting is concerned, that machinery is the FCC, whose task is to mediate between the private interests of the broadcaster and the other private interests of society and to effect an equilibrium among all these interests which can be interpreted as "the public interest."

THE CONCEPT OF "PUBLIC OPINION"

But the law covers no more than a small fraction of all the varieties of human behavior which are subject to social control. A much more detailed and exacting control guides each of us in our social conduct. This direct control of society itself works through the innumerable forms of human association, from the small family group through the larger groupings of neighborhood, occupation, church, region, and nation. The law itself avails nothing unless this pervasive social force lends it sanction. When laws run counter to the trend of social opinion they fall into disuse or become "interpreted" into something entirely different, something nearer the demands of society.

This agency of social control we may call *public opinion*. Again, as with the concept of the public interest, we must deal with an idea which is at once necessary and vague. In order to be perceived and acted upon, public opinion (like public interest) has to be interpreted by someone, and that someone may well confound his own opinion with public opinion. As it happens, the broadcasters provide us in practice with a convenient index of public opinion, as they interpret it. The program codes of the radio and television industry represent its effort to identify and codify public opinion on the subject of broadcast programs. Since the men who drew up the codes have had the benefit of a great deal of practical experience in the art of sensing and interpreting public opinion, we may assume that the codes furnish a reasonably accurate appraisal of the currently effective elements in the public's thinking about broadcasting — though colored, inevitably, by the private interests of the broadcasters themselves.

At first glance it might appear that the codes of practice adopted by the broadcasting industry itself might better be classified as an aspect of economic control, since these codes are controls exercised *within* the industry. A further look, however, makes it clear that the codes represent a curtailment of economic action.[2] They reveal the industry's estimate of the tolerance limits of existing public opinion; the industry follows the lead of public opinion, which is a force external to the industry. The validity of this interpretation can be specifically illustrated by the adoption by the NARTB Television Code Review Board of a resolution condemning bait-switch advertising. Not until public opinion had been aroused to the extent of stimulating legal intervention did this subject find its way into the Code. As an industry trade journal editorialized at the time, "A similar resolution, if adopted two or three years ago when public complaints against bait-switch frauds became widespread, would have suggested loftier motives and might have even corrected the situation before governments needed to intercede."[3] In other words, private incentives had not roused the broadcasters to control this particular economic practice. Only after public opinion had made itself felt as an external force did the industry take action.

To summarize the view of social control over broadcasting developed so far in this chapter, we can identify three agencies which tend to control the general character of the broadcasting service: (1) the internal economy of the medium, (2) the law, and (3) public opinion. The economic interests of those who operate the medium conflict in some respects with the interests of other social groups.[4] The general interests of society make themselves known through public opinion, as perceived and interpreted by the broadcasters and the government. The government acts as a mediator among con-

---

[2] For purposes of this discussion we may accept the codes at their face value. The question of how far they actually control programming is discussed in Chapter 25.

[3] "Snaring the Baiters," *Broadcasting-Telecasting* (28 February 1955), p. 118.

[4] This simplified analysis should not obscure the fact that the broadcaster himself is a social being and hence has acquired more than solely economic standards of value. This point is discussed in Chapter 19.

flicting interests by defining the public interest, a position of relative equilibrium among the relevant private interests.

BROADCASTING AND POLITICAL THEORY

The government's role is that of a referee, seeking to ensure a fair contest among the competing interests. Like most referees, the government receives its share of pop-bottles and catcalls, since no decision is likely to please every partisan. Indeed, the crucial controversial issue in the whole field of broadcast control is the nature and extent of the government's powers as a referee. The problem is to define the point at which the referee loses his impartial character and starts playing on one side or the other.

To begin with, laws to govern broadcasting are a political necessity, since broadcasting is itself an instrument of political control. Any concept of the role of government in the regulation of broadcasting necessarily reflects a particular political philosophy. Each country has adopted such laws in accordance with its own conceptions of public interest, of public opinion, and of private economic rights. Therefore many aspects of broadcasting can be understood only in a political context. To a marked degree broadcasting involves the basic political philosophy of a country, and we shall find that the study of the control of broadcasting will illuminate a number of concepts underlying our own system of government.

Speaking very generally, four theories of the function of public media of communication can be discerned.[5] During the era of absolute monarchs the authoritarian theory prevailed. According to this concept criticism of the government is treasonable; hence political ideas are subject to strict censorship, and publication can take place only under government license. Obviously the authoritarian theory persists in some countries to this day.

During the intellectual revolution of the eighteenth century an entirely different concept of government evolved, as typified in the origin of our own country. The basic assumption in this new concept is that people can and should govern themselves; they have no need for a specially ordained or gifted governing family or class. A necessary corollary of this idea is that in order to be fit for self-government people must have access to the knowledge necessary for making political judgments. Universal education and the free exchange of information follow logically from this proposition. It is likewise assumed that the utmost freedom of expression will in the long run be best for the individual and for society as a whole, for truth will ultimately prevail over falsehood if given the opportunity. This predicted outcome of the competition among ideas has been called the "self-righting" process. John Stuart Mill gave the classic exposition of this theory, the libertarian theory, in his eloquent *Essay on Liberty* in 1859.

[5] The formulation used here is that of Fred S. Siebert in "The Role of Mass Communication in American Society," National Society for the Study of Education, Fifty-third Yearbook, Part II, *Mass Media and Education* (Chicago: NSSE, 1954), pp. 13-29.

The libertarian theory is fundamental to American political ideology. The First Amendment to the Constitution places freedom of speech and press in the forefront of American civil rights. Libertarianism was one of Thomas Jefferson's most passionate attachments. Despite the fact that he was pilloried by the press with a viciousness unknown today, he never retreated from this belief:

> No experiment can be more interesting than that we are now trying, which we trust will end in establishing the fact that man may be governed by reason and truth. Our first object should therefore be to leave open to him all the avenues to truth. The most effectual hitherto found is the freedom of the press.
>
> * * * * *
>
> I have lent myself willingly as the subject of a great experiment, which was to prove that an administration, conducting itself with integrity and common understanding, cannot be battered down, even by the falsehoods of a licentious press . . . This experiment was wanting for the world to demonstrate the falsehood of the pretext that freedom of the press is incompatible with orderly government.[6]

Still later the Marxian view of government gave a new twist to the authoritarian theory. In the latter, government has an essentially negative effect on public communication, suppressing anything unfavorable to the existing regime. According to the Communist theory, however, the media of communication must undertake a positive role in furthering the revolutionary aims of the government. It is not enough for a Communist writer or broadcaster to avoid criticizing the regime; he must actively and affirmatively promote its policies. In fact, contrary to the authoritarian practice, the Communist press often does criticize those in power; such criticism is tolerated and even invited as long as it conforms to the current version of the Marxian ideology.[7]

Finally, as a result of the twentieth-century use of mass media, a fourth theory of public communication has emerged, the social-responsibility theory. This is really a modification or corollary of the libertarian theory; it grows out of doubts of the adequacy of the libertarian theory under modern social and economic conditions. The social-responsibility theory asserts that the modern mass media have become so powerful and so pervasive that they must accept a special responsibility for self-discipline. It asserts that the libertarian self-righting process cannot be depended upon to work automatically under modern conditions; the process must be helped along, either voluntarily by the media themselves or by some outside agency supported by the government.

[6] Letter to Judge Tyler, 1804; letter to Thomas Seymour, 1807. Quoted in: Saul K. Padover (ed.), *Thomas Jefferson on Democracy* (New York: New American Library, 1946), pp. 95-96. (Copyright, 1939, D. Appleton-Century Company, Inc., New York.)
[7] William Ernest Hocking, *Freedom of the Press* (Chicago: University of Chicago Press, 1947), pp. 27-28.

In this country broadcasting, more than the other mass media, illustrates the modification of the libertarian theory of mass communication by the social-responsibility theory. In setting up regulations Congress has followed well-established libertarian patterns. It has determined (1) that private economic rights should be protected and encouraged and (2) that the government's regulatory role should be limited, particularly with respect to freedom of speech; on the other hand, it has also determined (3) that economic freedom should be limited by considerations of public interest. This threefold conception parallels the triumvirate of control-agencies previously discussed.[8]

THE POSITION OF THE INDUSTRY ON GOVERNMENT CONTROL

In the course of broadcasting history in the United States, the industry itself has gone from one extreme to the other and part way back again in its attitude toward the government's role as an agency of social control of the medium. Originally, it will be recalled, the infant industry failed in its efforts at self-government, despite the sympathetic encouragement of the government itself (see Chapter 8). Therefore the industry urgently invited government intervention at the beginning. It could not, of course, predict the long-term results of such intervention. After the industry had reached an even keel under the Radio and Communications Acts it began to find government controls, as they had evolved, more and more irksome. The high point in resistance seems to have come during the period when Judge Justin Miller was President of the National Association of Broadcasters (1945-1951). Judge Miller was the admitted architect of a well-documented and systematic ideological attack on all FCC controls save those over purely technical matters of frequency, power, signal quality, and the like.

This campaign found its original stimulus in the Chain Broadcasting Regulations, adopted by the FCC in 1941 (see Chapters 8 and 15). The chain regulations grew out of the most intensive inquiry the Commission had ever made into the business practices of broadcasters, and the 1943 Supreme Court decision upholding the regulations focused attention on the basic issue of the FCC's jurisdiction over the program service. The broadcasters' case received its fullest and most vehement airing at the hearing of a Senate committee in 1947 on S. 1333, a bill to amend the Communications Act.[9] At this hearing Judge Miller and a number of other broadcasting executives joined forces in a frontal attack on the power of the FCC to exercise

---

[8] Some of the practical problems of applying the libertarian concept to broadcasting are discussed in Chapters 23 and 24.

[9] Senate Subcommittee on Interstate and Foreign Commerce, *Hearings on S. 1333, To Amend the Communications Act of 1934* (Washington: Government Printing Office, 1947). S. 1333 was almost identical with S. 814, an earlier bill which followed hard on the Supreme Court decision upholding the Chain Broadcasting Regulations; hearings on S. 814 were held in 1943.

discretionary control over programming. Again and again members of the
Senate subcommittee pinpointed the issue:

> *Senator McFarland:* Would the effect of your language be to prohibit the
> Federal Communications Commission from refusing to renew a license, no
> matter how poor the programs may have been over that station?
> *Mr. Miller:* If it is merely a matter of poor programming, it would; yes.
> *The Chairman* [Senator Wallace H. White]: I would like to have your view
> as to whether, in reaching a conclusion as to the public service or the want
> of public service being rendered, the regulatory body has a right to look at
> the programs and has any control whatsoever over the programs sent out.
> *Mr. Miller:* I think it has not.
> *The Chairman:* So you would say that the quality of the program has nothing
> to do with the question of whether a public service is being rendered or is
> not being rendered.
> *Mr. Miller:* I do . . .
> *The Chairman:* . . . Why, it seems to me that the quality of the program and
> the character of the program is the outstanding factor in determining whether
> the station is performing a public service or is not.

*   *   *   *   *

> *The Chairman:* You deny the right of the Government, I take it, from what
> I have heard of your statement, to look at the station program record of the
> station, in order to determine one of the considerations which would lead to
> a determination of whether that station should be relicensed or not?
> *Mr. Stanton* [President of CBS]: That is correct, Senator. That is my po-
> sition.

*   *   *   *   *

> *Mr. Trammell* [President of NBC]: . . . I do not believe that you would
> want to put into a Government agency the right to review the programs of
> the broadcaster . . .
> *The Chairman:* . . . so long as we have in the law that basic conception that
> an applicant has no absolute right to a license but must establish to the sat-
> isfaction of the Commission that he is serving a public interest or meeting a
> public necessity or a public convenience, something which seems to me
> basic in our law, I just do not see how there can be any judgment as to
> whether a station is serving a public interest or not unless there is a chance
> to view and review the programs which a station has been passing out . . .[10]

Put in the terms we have been using here, the broadcasters' argument was
that economic incentives, as modified by the broadcasters' own evaluation
of public opinion, provide a sufficient control over the program service, and
that any additional control exerted by the FCC is unnecessary, unwise, and
legally unjustifiable. Legislators on the Subcommittee challenged this view,
holding in effect that an independent evaluation of public opinion should
be made by an agency that had no financial interest in the outcome — i.e.,
the FCC.

[10] *Ibid.*, pp. 119, 122-123, 316, 409.

THE "QUANTITATIVE THEORY" OF CONTROL

How can the contention be justified that the broadcaster himself can adequately appraise public opinion and voluntarily submit to its dictates? The argument runs as follows: The commercial value of broadcasting depends on its ability to reach an audience; members of the audience are free to tune in or out, according to their liking; hence audiences control programming. This process is likened to democracy in action: tuning in a program is equivalent to a vote for that program; if a program receives but few votes it cannot survive, and a more popular candidate wins the election. Broadcasters, to put it another way, *give the public what it wants,* and the public makes its wants known through its tuning behavior. Typical examples at the network and local levels are the following: The then-president of NBC, Niles Trammell, is quoted as saying some years ago: "The broadcasting of any radio program which a substantial proportion of the available audience wants to listen to at the time it goes on the air is an example of broadcasting in the public interest."[11] The president of a small District of Columbia station, whose license renewal was recently approved over the dissent of three commissioners, declared that the "best answer" to allegations of objectionable advertising practices on his station was the fact that its audience had increased in size.[12]

For convenience we may call this theory of program control the *quantitative* theory. It regards programs merely as a means to an end, not as an end in themselves. The advertiser is essentially indifferent to program content, as long as the program attracts audiences. He would be just as happy to sponsor *Lucia di Lammermoor* as *Ma Perkins* if grand opera could sell as much detergent as soap opera. The index of success is a quantitative one — the number of "votes." The implications of this theory of program control are worth exploring in detail.

To begin with, it is axiomatic that broadcasting should serve *all* the people (the basis for this assertion appears in Chapter 21). Yet no program has ever proved universally popular. Only a very few — a fraction of 1 per cent of the total — attract even as much as a majority of the available audience. Most of the time group differences limit the audience of any given program to a relatively small minority of the total population. As has so often been pointed out, "*the* audience" or "*the* public" is a myth. No such thing exists operationally. Each program automatically selects a fraction of the potential audience. The service as a whole reaches an aggregation of minority publics. The quantitative approach to programming is almost bound to leave out some of these minority publics which are either too

[11] Quoted in "The Revolt Against Radio," *Fortune* (March, 1947), p. 103. In other words, said *Fortune,* "whatever sells is fine." © *Time* Inc.
[12] "Commissioners Hit WOL Ad Practices," *Broadcasting-Telecasting* (25 April 1955), p. 74.

small, too hard to please, too scattered, or too stubborn to be economically worth while.

In answer to this the proponent of the quantitative theory is likely to resort to the political analogy. In an election somebody has to lose; the majority rules. This analogy, however, overlooks the fact that even in a democracy elections do not decide everything; once elected, the people's representatives are expected to use responsible judgment on the issues that come before them. The losing side does not lose its rights. The non-voter is not penalized for his failure to vote. A system which makes the will of the majority the only standard and sacrifices the rights and interests of minorities is the opposite of a democratic system.

To continue the political analogy, it should be observed that a theory of control based on audience "votes" in terms of set-tuning gives the voter no opportunity to select candidates. He is offered a plebiscite, a "yes" or "no" vote on the programs offered. Possibly entirely different programs would please him even better, but the quantitative theory of control provides him no opportunity to learn about possible options. The economic motive un-alloyed does not, as we have pointed out, favor taking chances on untried programs.

The alleged democratic character of the quantitative theory is completely exploded when we consider that the quantity actually sought is only indi-rectly large numbers of listener-viewer "votes." Advertisers are ultimately interested in the number of *sales* resulting from their advertising, and if large numbers of sales can be obtained from audiences of small numbers, audience size is no longer the only quantity that counts. It happens that audience size and quantity of response usually parallel each other. But some programs deliberately and with foreknowledge sacrifice audience size for the sake of sales volume. This is the rationale of much per-inquiry adver-tising, which is pitched at such a level that it automatically eliminates most of the audience and holds only the least discriminating minority. This minority, by virtue of its lack of discrimination, is characteristically most susceptible to high-pressure salesmanship and therefore makes a high pur-chasing response despite its small size.

"GIVING THE PUBLIC WHAT IT WANTS"

Formulation of the quantitative theory of program control in terms of "giving the public what it wants" raises several interesting questions: (1) Is what the public wants necessarily what it should get? (2) Is it in fact possible to determine, by the available methods, what the public wants? (3) Is what the public now wants (or has wanted) necessarily the best guide to what it may want in the future? (4) Is any "giving" actually involved?[13]

The theory that any kind of program is justified if it commands a large

[13] Cf.: Edgar Dale, "Can You Give the Public What It Wants?" *The News Letter* XVI-4 (Bureau of Educational Research, Ohio State University, January, 1951).

audience has been specifically rejected in other areas of economic activity. The fact that many people will buy a product or service does not necessarily justify the sale of that product or service in the eyes of society. Pure food and drug laws and narcotics and gambling laws are familiar examples to the contrary.

> *Mr. [Neville] Miller* [NAB President]: With the economic competition which we have in this country and which we hope will continue to exist, that is the controlling force.
> *The Chairman* [Senator Burton K. Wheeler]: Now, if you say the economic thing should be controlling . . . most of the people of the country like to gamble, we will say, and the radio people say because of that fact they listen to our gambling programs. Supposing that a great many people like things that border on the obscene. Should radio companies put on that kind of a program? If they are going to be governed simply by the economics of the thing, that is what would happen.[14]

How does one determine what the public wants? In Chapter 16 we discussed at some length the expensive and elaborate machinery of measurement and evaluation employed by the industry. Because so much money and ingenuity go into this research activity, the assertion that the results tell the broadcaster just what the public wants often goes unchallenged. But let us recall that most of this research measures nothing more than *tuning behavior* — an overt response that can have infinite shades of meaning. That each individual who turns on a set to a given program actually *wants* that program in any psychologically significant sense is clearly an unwarranted assumption. A person may merely tolerate that program as the least of several evils. He may accept whatever comes first to hand, without even considering what alternatives are actually available. His reaction could be anything from intense pleasure to intense irritation, but as long as his set is turned on he is classified as "wanting" that program — wanting it, moreover, in preference to every other program available at the same time.

Not infrequently one hears the assertion that programs are literally controlled by the audience, that the switching off or on of receivers by some magic translates itself automatically into program fare. Even if we accept the current relatively crude research procedures as reliable ways of measuring wants, the measurement is not so accurate, so rapid, and so universally employed as to provide such robot-like control. Indeed, such a gross oversimplification is palpably absurd, since if station operators knew how to conduct programming with such precision no station would be likely to fail for lack of an audience, and an office boy could serve as program director. The facts that some stations do fail and that creative program directors command high salaries argue that operators are far from having unerring knowledge of audience wants.

[14] Senate Committee on Interstate Commerce, *Hearings on S. 814, To Amend the Communications Act of 1934* (Washington: Government Printing Office, 1944), p. 194.

What *do* people want? Essentially, that which they already have or see others enjoying. The social deviant, the exception, the genius, may want something different, but, as was pointed out in Chapter 6, invention does not automatically lead to innovation. New wants are created by the combined efforts of inventors and innovators to overcome social inertia. Had the world been ruled by plebiscites among the mass of people (who are neither inventors nor innovators), we should still be in the Stone Age (*"you would all be Indians!"*).[15]

Finally, the phrase "giving the public what it wants" denies the obvious and highly relevant fact that commercial broadcasting is not a matter of "giving" but a matter of selling. If any giving is involved, it is the giving of licenses to use the public's radio frequencies for commercial purposes, for which no charge is made. A broadcaster who insists, as some still do, that he is giving a service to the public simply does not face the facts, which are (1) that he is using public property for which the public is entitled to a return *as a matter of legal right* and (2) that he is using a medium which depends on the public's direct investment in receivers and payment of maintenance and operating costs (see Table 23).

We have gone to some length in this analysis of the quantitative theory of program control because it is so persistently used and because it so completely beclouds the issues involved. Since the quantitative theory patently does not account for what happens in American broadcasting, it remains to consider what actually *does* happen. Those who exercise economic control of the program service learn through experience with the medium and its publics to measure the climate of public opinion at the moment. They have no certain knowledge of public needs, tastes, or tolerance limits. Every program decision is a guess. Those whose decisions are guided entirely by quantitative considerations regard the public with contempt as a de-humanized mass. If the public consists of these hypothetical creatures, the broadcaster is relieved of any responsibility for its welfare. He is justified in taking the easiest way to a large audience — or to a highly susceptible small audience — irrespective of the kind of programming that results or the kind of effects produced.

On the other hand, the alternative point of view concedes that a human being is a thing of value and that a public consists of human beings for whose welfare the broadcaster has a degree of responsibility. On this theory the broadcaster will temper purely quantitative considerations with some thought of the outcome in human terms. Nevertheless, broadcasting in America is a business and cannot be divorced from business motivations. As long as broadcasting is conducted competitively for gain it cannot reasonably be expected to behave as though it were conducted as a non-profit service.

A balance must be struck somewhere between the extremes of complete

---

[15] *Supra,* p. 247.

irresponsibility toward the public welfare and complete irresponsibility toward commercial obligations. One function of the law is to help to define the nature and degree of public responsibility which the public interest must regard as minimal. Unfortunately, the law brings with it a burden of bureaucracy and a threat to freedom which may penalize the responsible along with the irresponsible. This fact accounts for the resistance that is offered to government encroachments by even highly ethical and responsible representatives of the industry.

CHANGING INDUSTRY OUTLOOK

In recent years, however, a good deal of evidence has appeared to suggest that the broadcasting industry as a whole has been withdrawing somewhat from the extreme opposition to government controls expressed in the S. 1333 hearings in 1947. By and large the industry seems to be tacitly recognizing that the excesses due to the quantitative theory may be a proper subject for legal sanctions. The following statement by NBC vice-president (and former FCC commissioner) Charles R. Denny is symptomatic:

> In planning our programs, we start with the conviction that broadcasting cannot do its job by meeting the lowest common denominator of taste . . . *We do not feel that the popularity of a program justifies departures from high standards of taste.* If the program is popular despite such departures from taste, we feel it would be even more popular if it conformed to proper standards of taste.

> Over and above that, we feel that broadcasting should provide for the cultivation of taste and the stimulation of interest, not for a few people, but for all of the people. We believe that if we offer the people opportunities to develop their tastes and broaden their interests, they will respond. And one of the ways we reach them is through their common interest in being entertained.[16]

And lest this be taken as mere window-dressing for the sake of impressing the Subcommittee, it should be added that NBC has actually done something to implement these ideas in both radio and television programs.

Another example is provided by J. L. Van Volkenburg, President of CBS Television:

> In the familiar debate between giving people what they want and giving them what we think they ought to have, we take the position of The American Library Association, which was stated at a recent convention: "It is inevitable in the give and take of the democratic process that the political, the moral, or the aesthetic concepts of an individual or group will occasionally collide with those of another individual or group. In a free society, each

[16] Testimony in: House of Representatives Subcommittee of Committee on Interstate and Foreign Commerce, *Hearings on H.Res. 278, Investigation of Radio and Television Programs* (Washington: Government Printing Office, 1952), pp. 241-242. Italics supplied.

individual is free to determine for himself what he wishes to read, and each
group is free to determine what it will recommend to its freely associated
members. But no group has the right to take the law into its own hands, and
to impose its own concepts of politics or morality or aesthetics upon other
members of a democratic society."

The most constructive solution to the problem seems to be to try to keep
ahead of changing patterns of taste.[17]

Another clue to the changed outlook of the industry is the contrast between the points of view implied by the radio code and the television code.[18]
The latter indicates a much more sophisticated concept of the social role
of the medium and also the explicit acceptance of a higher degree of responsibility by the industry. The tendency of the television networks to
reassert their control over programming (discussed in Chapters 15 and
17) is concrete evidence of change.

This shift in attitude can be ascribed to a number of possible causes. Of
course the process is still going on, and we cannot yet get a reliable perspective. With the fading of the New Deal the FCC may have grown less inclined to what Justin Miller called "ideological forays" against the industry,
more inclined to consider the business interests of broadcasters. However,
there has been no noticeable retreat on the part of more recent appointees
to the Commission under the Republican administration from the principles
and practices of the Commission under the previous administration.

Doubtless licensees have been deeply impressed — perhaps even a little
frightened — by the tremendous impact of television. The effect of the
Kefauver crime hearings, the Army-McCarthy hearings, and other such
events could not have failed to impress the industry with a sense of new-
found power. New television licensees, of course, have experienced no
previous regulatory conditions with which to compare present conditions.
It must be borne in mind that television started *after* the FCC had developed
a philosophy and a machinery of regulation. By and large new licensees
seem to have approached the programming promises they made in applications with less of the cynicism which characterized many radio applications
of earlier days, when many applicants apparently regarded the licensing
procedure as a meaningless ritual. The change may be partly due to the
fact that competitive applicants have been quick to expose unrealistic proposals, empty promises, and meaningless window-dressing. The public's
intense interest, probably coupled with an improved understanding of its
own rights, has made both industry and audience more conscious of program
standards: insofar as television represents a new instrument of social control
it becomes itself more subject to social control. It can be argued that television is a more effective medium for some kinds of desirable programs

[17] J. L. Van Volkenburg, *Television as an Extension School of Democracy* (New York:
CBS, 1953).

[18] The comparison is discussed in more detail in Chapter 25 below, and the codes
themselves appear in the Appendix.

which could not be so well handled by radio; greater program scope of television enhances its importance as a medium.

This apparent shift in attitude on the part of the industry does not mean either that the industry is any the more prone to accept enlargement of the government's sphere of control or that the government has sought such an enlargement. It means rather an easier, less contentious atmosphere, with the three agencies of control — economic, legal, and social — finding a more stable equilibrium.

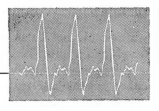

21

The Law of Broadcasting

> Underlying the whole law is recognition of the
> rapidly fluctuating factors characteristic of the
> evolution of broadcasting and of the correspond-
> ing requirement that the administrative process
> possess sufficient flexibility to adjust itself to these
> factors.   — JUSTICE FELIX FRANKFURTER

Historically, as we saw in tracing the origin of regulation in Chapter 8,
government intervention in radio affairs arose from the necessity of allocating frequencies in an orderly fashion. Secondarily, but no less significantly,
it arose out of the need to ensure efficient use of the frequencies for human
benefit. In the United States there is no single agency for over-all frequency
management. Authority is divided between the President and the Federal
Communications Commission. The former has control over allocation of all
government stations; the FCC's jurisdiction is confined to private stations, in
accordance with Section 305 of the Communications Act of 1934, which
specifically exempts government stations from licensing requirements. This
divided authority is regarded as antiquated, and should eventually give way
to a single coordinated frequency-management government agency.[1]

At present coordination depends on the Interdepartmental Radio Advisory
Committee (IRAC), on which the FCC is represented but which it cannot
actually control (Figure 33). Frequency allocation and other technical matters are also affected by international agreements, notably the International
Telecommunications Union (ITU) and the North American Regional Broadcast Agreement (NARBA). The ITU held its first international conference
in Madrid in 1932. Broadcasting in the United States is most affected by

---

[1] Cf.: President's Communications Policy Board, *Telecommunications: A Program for
Progress* (Washington: Government Printing Office, 1951). In 1950 53.3 per cent of
the spectrum space was assigned to non-government services and 28.2 per cent to government services, and 18.5 per cent was shared (p. 42). An example of the present
anomalous situation is the fact that the Armed Forces have set up broadcast stations
(both AM and television) in certain remote posts, using regular broadcast channels, yet
the FCC does not license these stations and cannot control them. The private broadcast
industry takes a dim view of government's invasion of the broadcast spectrum.

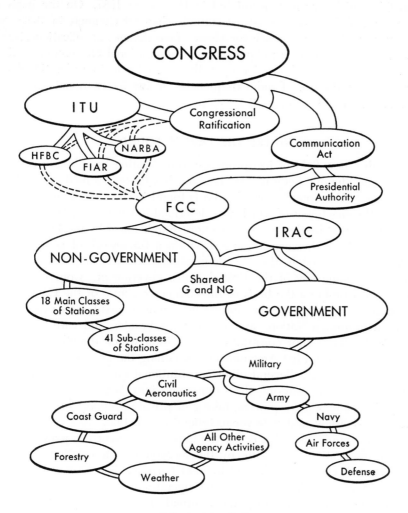

Figure 33

Government Agencies Affecting Frequency Allocations

The ITU (International Telecommunications Union) is the world-wide international control agency. The HFBC (High Frequency Broadcasting Conference) and NARBA (North American Regional Broadcast Agreement) are subsidiary agencies to ITU, having the status of treaties and therefore being as binding on the FCC as is the Communications Act itself. The FCC has complete jurisdiction over non-government services; it participates in the allocation of shared and government frequencies through IRAC (Interdepartmental Radio Advisory Committee).

Source: Forney A. Rankin, *Who Gets the Air* (Washington: NAB, 1949), p. 39.

NARBA, which was first negotiated in Havana in 1937. On the basis of NARBA, 777 American broadcast stations changed channels in 1941, primarily to create clear channels for Mexico (see channel classifications, Table 3). "NARBA occupies a unique place in international telecommunications law: It is the greatest limitation upon the age-old principle of national sovereignty over the use of radio frequencies of any international agreement ever formulated."[2]

WHERE THE LAW IS FOUND

Though a new field of jurisprudence, broadcasting has already accumulated a considerable body of case law and has become a field of legal specialization.[3] The organic law of radio is found in the Communications Act of 1934, the enactment of which was described in Chapter 8. It is a federal law, duly passed by the houses of Congress and signed by the President.

Congress itself, however, operates within a framework of constitutional law, so that ultimately the Communications Act may be said to derive from the organic law of the United States government. Congress asserts control over radio on the basis of the commerce clause of the Constitution (Section 8), which gives the federal government jurisdiction over "Commerce with foreign Nations, among the several States, and with the Indian tribes." Another major constitutional provision which directly affects the law of radio is the First Amendment, containing the guarantee of freedom of speech and press. Several other constitutional questions have arisen in the course of administering the Communications Act, such as the lawful delegation of legislative powers, taking of private property for public use, due process of law, and state versus federal jurisdiction.

The Communications Act is, for the most part, couched in general terms. Specific applications are made by the Federal Communications Commission, which is created by the Act for that purpose. The Commission is the agent through which the government operates in exercising control over communication by radio. In practice, broadcasters generally encounter the law in the form of the FCC Rules and Regulations. Every regulation promulgated by the FCC must, of course, have a justification in the Communications Act, from which the FCC derives its authority; therefore the Rules and Regulations have the full force of federal law, even though not directly enacted by Congress.

Not infrequently the FCC must make decisions in disputes among those who come before it. These decisions, though not in quite the same category as court decisions (since the FCC is not actually a judicial tribunal), tend to establish precedents and to provide a commentary by the FCC on the Communications Act and its own regulations.

---

[2] Forney A. Rankin, *Who Gets the Air?* (Washington: NAB, 1949), p. 10.

[3] Lawyers admitted to practice before the FCC are listed in *Broadcasting-Telecasting* yearbooks. In 1954 they numbered over 600.

The legality of both the rule-making and the decision-making of the FCC may be challenged in the courts. Appeal may be made to establish whether the Commission acted within the limits placed on it by the Communications Act and other applicable federal laws. Such right of appeal is, of course, a basic concept of American government; no official or group of officials may exercise unlimited power or undefined discretion. It will be recalled that the absence of limitation on the discretion of the Secretary of Commerce in the Radio Act of 1912 brought about its downfall (Chapter 8). Congress was careful, therefore, to avoid this pitfall in writing the Radio Act of 1927. Court decisions — whether supporting or reversing the FCC — contribute to the corpus of radio law by establishing legal precedents. Those few disputes which reach the Supreme Court become the leading cases.[4]

Radio regulation is the province of federal law; hence stations cannot be subjected to both federal and state controls in matters covered by the Communications Act. This does not remove stations entirely from state jurisdiction, however; for example, libel and slander are matters of state rather than federal law. Similarly, the Communications Act does not interfere with the application of relevant federal laws that are not a part of the Act. Copyright, obscenity, labor, and lottery laws are relevant instances.

To summarize, we may find the law of broadcasting embodied in the Communications Act of 1934, although the Act is subject to the Federal Constitution as the paramount authority. The Communications Act creates the FCC as the specific agent of government control of radio. We may find the operational but derivative law in the Rules and Regulations of the FCC. Other federal and state laws also apply to radio insofar as they deal with matters that are not regulated by the Communications Act. Finally, we may find interpretations of all these laws in the decisions of the FCC and of the courts.

GENERAL DESCRIPTION OF THE COMMUNICATIONS ACT

The body of our domestic radio law, the Communications Act of 1934, contains about a hundred sections, grouped into six "titles": (1) general provisions, (2) common carriers, (3) radio (in two parts, the first general, the second concerning shipboard radio), (4) procedure and administration, (5) penalties, and (6) miscellaneous. Section numbers conform to these groupings; for example, sections dealing with radio are numbered in the 300's. We are primarily concerned here with the general provisions which set up the Federal Communications Commission, the first part of the radio provisions, and some of the provisions related to administration and procedure. The present chapter will outline the essential content of the Act, organizing the material in terms of the seven principles previously men-

---

[4] Most appeals are brought to the United States Court of Appeals for the District of Columbia. See bibliographical notes to this chapter for information on where to find the materials discussed in this section.

tioned in Chapter 8. The practical application of these principles and the controversies which arise will be considered in succeeding chapters.

The purpose of the Act is set forth as follows:

> For the purpose of regulating interstate and foreign commerce in communication by wire and radio so as to make available, so far as possible, to all the people of the United States a rapid, efficient, Nation-wide, and world-wide wire and radio communication service with adequate facilities at reasonable charges, for the purpose of the national defense, for the purpose of promoting safety of life and property through the use of wire and radio communication, and for the purpose of securing a more effective execution of this policy by centralizing authority heretofore granted by law to several agencies and by granting additional authority with respect to interstate and foreign commerce in wire and radio communication, there is hereby created a commission to be known as the "Federal Communications Commission," which shall be constituted as hereinafter provided, and which shall execute and enforce the provisions of this Act (Sec. 1).

This first section reminds us that the purpose of repealing the Radio Act of 1927 and substituting the present Act was the centralization of authority; the 1934 legislation reenacted the 1927 radio laws with only minor changes. It should be noted that the jurisdiction of the FCC is defined as (1) both wire and radio communications, insofar as they are (2) either interstate or foreign.

PROVISION FOR THE FCC

Section 1 provides for a commission to execute and enforce the Act. Section 4 describes the commission. Its seven members are appointed by the President with the advice and consent of the Senate, one member being designated by the President as chairman. Commissioners must be citizens, may not have a financial interest in any type of communications business, must devote full time to the job, and are paid $15,000 a year.[5] No more than four of the seven commissioners may be of the same political party.

We perceive in these provisions that Congress sought to prevent economic and political prejudice on the part of the Commission. The term of seven years, contrasted with the presidential term of four years, makes it impossible for an incoming President to change the personnel of the Commission abruptly (the terms of the commissioners are staggered so that only one expires each year). On the other hand, the President can to some extent implement his administration's policies through exercising his right to appoint the chairman.

[5] Raised from $10,000 in 1949. The pay scale is still low as compared with that of private industry. It is not uncommon for an ex-commissioner to receive many times his federal salary on shifting to private employment. It is significant that a 1952 Amendment to the Act forbids commissioners who do not serve out their full seven-year term to practice before the Commission for one year after termination of their services as commissioners [Sec. 4 (b)].

The Commission is empowered to "perform any and all acts, make such rules and regulations, and issue such orders, not inconsistent with this Act, as may be necessary in the execution of its functions" [Sec. 4 (i)]. Elsewhere, throughout the Act, the Commission is given various instructions, most of which are couched in general terms. A few matters are not left to the discretion of the Commission; for example, the Act specifically requires that broadcast licenses may be granted for periods of no longer than three years [Sec. 307 (d)], but even here the Commission may use its discretion by issuing licenses for shorter periods. Most provisions of the Act give the Commission wide latitude for using its judgment on the basis of the particular set of facts it may be dealing with at the time. Nevertheless, since the Act would have met the same fate as the Radio Act of 1912 if the Commission had been given unqualified discretion, it was essential somehow to limit the Commission's powers in every case. Congress met this problem (wherever it did not wish to tie the Commission's hands with a specific, hard-and-fast directive) by introducing the matter with the phrase "if public convenience, interest, or necessity requires. . . ."[6] For example:

> Any station license or construction permit may be modified by the Commission either for a limited time or for the duration of the term thereof, if in the judgment of the Commission such action will promote the public interest, convenience, and necessity, or the provisions of this Act or of any treaty ratified by the United States will be more fully complied with [Sec. 316 (a)].

This gives the Commission the authority to modify a license (a vital power) even though no specific provision of the Act requires such modification, leaving to the Commission the determination of the "public interest, convenience, or necessity."

"OWNERSHIP" OF RADIO FREQUENCIES

All the powers of the Commission, as indeed the effectiveness of the Act itself, revolve around the licensing power.[7] This in turn derives from the fundamental assertion of the Communications Act — that electromagnetic frequencies used for communication cannot be privately "owned":

> It is the purpose of this Act, among other things, to maintain the control of the United States over all the channels of interstate and foreign radio transmission; and to provide for the use of such channels, but not the ownership thereof, by persons for limited periods of time, under licenses granted by

[6] The construction put on this phrase is discussed in Chapters 22 and 23.

[7] The reference here is to the licensing of *stations*. The Act also empowers the FCC to license *operators* of transmitters to ensure proper technical operation; such licenses (like station licenses) can be issued only to United States citizens [Secs. 318 and 303 (l) and (m)]. The FCC has set up several kinds of operators' licenses, which are classed according to the type of equipment for which the operator is to be responsible. Licenses are issued on the basis of examinations given by FCC regional offices. The law requires licensed operators at transmitters, but not in studios for the handling of studio equipment.

Federal authority, and no such license shall be construed to create any right beyond the terms, conditions, and periods of the license. No person shall use or operate any apparatus for the transmission of energy or communications or signals by radio . . . except under and in accordance with this Act and with a license in that behalf granted under the provisions of this Act (Sec. 301).

Congress was so emphatic on this point that it required that a licensee sign a waiver "of any claim to the use of any particular frequency or of the ether as against the regulatory power of the United States because of the previous use of the same" (Sec. 304). Furthermore, although the FCC may determine the form of the licenses it issues, one thing a license must include is the condition that it "shall not vest in the licensee any right to operate the station nor any right in the use of the frequencies designated in the license beyond the term thereof nor in any other manner than authorized therein" [Sec. 309 (d)(1)].

This emphasis reflects the experience of the period prior to 1927, when regulation broke down because the law did not give the government unequivocal control of the broadcast frequencies. Congress foresaw, moreover, that the introduction of effective control was bound to encounter the claim that prior use of frequencies had conferred a kind of squatter's right on pioneer broadcasters.

The licensing power is further safeguarded by the provision that a license cannot even be issued until after a station has been constructed and tested; it can then be determined empirically that its signal does in fact conform to the requirements of the license. Hence the first step toward acquiring a broadcast license is to obtain a Construction Permit (CP). The application for a CP requires a recital of all the information which will be required in the license itself.

Upon the completion of any station for the construction . . . of which a permit has been granted, and upon it being made to appear to the Commission that all the terms, conditions, and obligations set forth in the application and permit have been fully met, and that no cause or circumstance arising or first coming to the knowledge of the Commission since the granting of the permit would, in the judgment of the Commission, make the operation of such station against the public interest, the Commission shall issue a license to the lawful holder of said permit for the operation of said station . . . [Sec. 319 (c)].

Thus Congress made plain its intention of taking no chances on any misinterpretation: the radio frequencies are public property and accordingly must be operated in the public interest. The government may decide not only who shall be licensed to use this property in the first place but whether a licensee shall be entitled to continue to use it after the first grant is made, for license renewals are not automatic but are subject to the discretion of the FCC [Sec. 307 (d)]; moreover, a license can be revoked before the expiration of its term (Sec. 312). This circumstance places broadcasting in a unique situation; it is less free of government control than non-licensed businesses, yet more free than public utilities or common carriers.

Despite the care with which Congress spelled out its intention, the constitutionality of the licensing power has been challenged a number of times in the courts. Revoking licenses or deleting stations has been called taking private property for government use and taking property without due process of law, in violation of the Fifth Amendment to the Constitution. But the courts have consistently upheld the power of the government to control the frequencies:

> That the Congress had the power to give this authority to delete stations, in view of the limited radio facilities available and the confusion that would result from interferences, is not open to question. Those who operated broadcasting stations had no right superior to the exercise of this power of regulation. They necessarily made their investments and their contracts in the light of, and subject to, this paramount authority. This Court has had frequent occasion to observe that the power of Congress in the regulation of interstate commerce is not fettered by the necessity of maintaining existing arrangements which would conflict with the execution of its policy, as such a restriction would place the regulation in the hands of private individuals and withdraw from the control of Congress so much of the field as they might choose by prophetic discernment to bring within the range of their enterprises.[8]

This does not mean that the private enterprise based on the use of this public property, the radio frequencies, loses all claim to security. It is only when a conflict of interest occurs, when the broadcaster's private interest conflicts with the public interest in the effective use of the electromagnetic spectrum, that the private interest must give way. The classic instance of this kind of conflict is the resistance of an existing licensee to the addition of another station in his area, on the grounds that there is not enough business to support two stations. This question was adjudicated by the Supreme Court in one of the most frequently cited of all broadcast cases, the *Sanders Brothers Case:*

> Plainly it is not the purpose of the Act to protect a licensee against competition but to protect the public. Congress intended to leave competition in the business of broadcasting where it found it, to permit a licensee who was not interfering electrically with other broadcasters to survive or succumb according to his ability to make his programs attractive to the public.[9]

Another constitutional question raised by the establishment of government control is whether radio communication is (1) interstate and (2) commerce. It must qualify in both these respects in order to be subject to federal control under the interstate commerce clause of the Constitution. These questions were settled relatively early by the courts:

[8] *FRC* v. *Nelson Bros. Bond & Mortgage Co.*, 289 U.S. 266 at 282 (1933).
[9] *FCC* v. *Sanders Bros. Radio Station*, 309 U.S. 470 at 475 (1940).

It does not seem to be open to question that radio transmission and reception among the states are interstate commerce. To be sure it is a new species of commerce. Nothing visible and tangible is transported . . . The joint action of the transmitter owned by one person and the receiver owned by another is essential to the result. But that result is the transmission of intelligence, ideas, and entertainment. It is intercourse and that intercourse is commerce . . . The suggestion that broadcasting which is not for profit is not commerce may be put aside as imposing an unwarranted limitation upon the power of Congress.[10]

Broadcasting may be regarded as interstate in scope, even though the intended service area of a given station lies entirely within a state, for there is no way of controlling the interference area of a signal. As the failure of the Davis Amendment abundantly proved, it is impossible to stop radio waves at state lines.

"BROADCASTING IS UNIQUE"

In Chapter 7 we saw how broadcasting made a radical departure from previous forms of communication enterprise. Its peculiar and separate character is recognized in the Communications Act by three definitions:

"Radio communication" or "communication by radio" means the transmission by radio of writing, signs, signals, pictures, and sounds of all kinds, including all instrumentalities, facilities, apparatus, and services . . . incidental to such transmissions [Sec. 3 (b)].

*   *   *   *   *

"Common carrier" or "carrier" means any person engaged as a common carrier for hire, in interstate or foreign communication by wire or radio or in interstate or foreign radio transmission of energy, except where reference is made to common carriers not subject to this Act; but a person engaged in radio broadcasting shall not, insofar as such person is so engaged, be deemed a common carrier [Sec. 3 (h)].

*   *   *   *   *

"Broadcasting" means dissemination of radio communications intended to be received by the public, directly or by the intermediary of relay stations [Sec. 3 (o)].

Preliminarily, it should be observed that the legal definition includes television as well as sound transmission under the term "broadcasting." The most significant element in this series of definitions, however, is the fact that broadcasting is singled out for exclusion from the category "common carrier." This distinction is vital. The common-carrier concept (which extends to transportation systems such as railroads as well as to communication systems) applies to business enterprises of such character that public policy requires their services to be made available to all on a basis of equality.

v. *American Bond & Mortgage Co.,* 31 F. (2d) 448 at 454 (1929).

The Interstate Commerce Act provides that it shall be unlawful for a carrier subject to that Act to give "any undue or unreasonable preference or advantage" to one user of a carrier over another, or to subject any user to "any undue or unreasonable prejudice or disadvantage" (Chapter I, Sec. 3 [1] of the Act).

This means, among other things, that your dime is as good as mine in the pay-telephone and no one questions what we say when we place a call; all customers pay the same price for a railroad ticket for the same class of service, and all are entitled to buy a ticket as long as space remains. In short, a carrier is supposed to concern itself not with the nature of the traffic it carries but merely with supplying the facilities for carrying — always assuming lawful kinds of traffic, of course.

Carriers occupy a position of limited monopoly, since public policy forbids duplication of services where deterioration of service might result. One cannot build a railroad, start a busline, inaugurate an air route, or install a telephone system for public hire without a license, from either a state or a federal agency, depending on whether the proposed service is intrastate or interstate in scope. Such a license carries with it some protection from competition, in return for which the business of the licensee is closely supervised by the licensing agency. AT&T, for example, cannot change long-distance telephone rates without the permission of the FCC; an interstate rail line cannot alter its service schedule without the permission of the Interstate Commerce Commission.

Let us consider what would have been the consequences of applying the common-carrier concept to broadcasting. The licensee would have had to accept all buyers of time on a first-come-first-served basis. The licensee could not concern himself with what the purchasers of time did with that time, so long as nothing unlawful was done. The result would be programming chaos; the licensee would have no control whatever over what was said or shown on his facilities, and hence could not be held responsible for the character of the broadcasting service rendered.

All this would completely reverse the primary emphasis of broadcasting, which is on the interests of the *recipients* of the messages, not the *senders*. This emphasis is appropriate because the senders are using a facility (i.e., the electromagnetic spectrum) belonging to the recipients. Those who directly profit economically through the broadcasting service — the advertisers and licensees — do so only in consideration of a service rendered to the general public. The hardheaded business man often finds this secondary position of the private economic interests of the licensee difficult to accept; he simply cannot see how voluntary investment and risk-taking can fail to entitle him to freedom in his quest for profits. As long as a licensee clings to this point of view he remains at odds with the basic philosophy of the Communications Act. No broadcast application which explicitly placed the interest of the licensee ahead of that of the public would receive serious consideration

One further point needs to be emphasized in connection with the definition of broadcasting. It is a form of communication *intended* to be received by the public. This phrase automatically excludes from broadcasting all forms of communication which, though perhaps *receivable* by the public, are aimed at specific recipients. On this basis direct communication to individuals in the audience by broadcast performers is forbidden. Such a communication is a common-carrier use of broadcasting and hence a violation of the law. The FCC does not make an issue of the casual "hellos," waves of the hand, anniversary greetings, etc., which frequently occur. However, there have been cases where direct communications have been more substantial. For example, a station received license renewal only after discontinuing programs of direct personal advice by an astrologer and a "spiritual psychologist." The Commission remarked that

> their practices involved the transmission of point-to-point or individual messages that could not reasonably be said to have any general interest for the public. Broadcasting is by definition and essential characteristics a service for the general public. The use of a broadcast station for point-to-point delivery of messages is inconsistent with the terms of the station license and the regulations under which licenses are issued.[11]

An illustration of the practical significance of the definition of broadcasting is provided by the case of "functional" FM operation, i.e., the providing of special programs for stores, busses, and other locations (see p. 149). The FCC found this type of service to be non-broadcast in character, and has provided a special class of license to permit FM stations to offer this service, a Subsidiary Communications Authorization.

> . . . in so far as the programming is directed to the special interests of the industrial, mercantile, transportation, or other subscribers and is not primarily intended for reception by the general public, [functional FM] must be characterized *predominantly* non-broadcast in nature. The fact that a large portion of these transmissions — including most of the program material — may be received by the general public on home receivers as an incidental by-product of the primary intent of the transmissions does not change this rationale.[12]

Since transmissions under a Subsidiary Communications Authorization are not broadcasting, they come under the protection of Section 605 of the Communications Act, which forbids the unauthorized divulgence or publication of communications subject to the Act. Broadcasting is, necessarily, made an exception to this rule. The applicability of Section 605 to func-

---

[11] *In re Scroggin & Co. Bank* (*KFEQ*), 1 FCC 194 at 196 (1935). Other similar cases have involved programs of financial advice, horse-racing information, and medical advice. The concept of broadcasting as "a service for the public" does not rule out the special-interest station which aims the bulk of its programming to a particular public, such as a specific ethnic or cultural group.

[12] FCC, *In the Matter of Amendment of Parts 2 and 3 of the Commission's Rules and Regulations* . . . Docket No. 10382, 20 *Fed. Register* 1821 (25 March 1955).

tional FM stations, however, empowers the stations to prevent unauthorized persons from installing receivers to take advantage of their service. As long as the service was "broadcasting" they could not prevent this form of piracy.

EQUITABLE DISTRIBUTION OF SERVICE

It follows from the principle of public ownership of the frequencies and the definition of broadcasting that *all* the people are entitled to service. Section 1 of the Act, it will be recalled, speaks of "all the people of the United States." With more specific reference to broadcasting:

> In considering applications for licenses, and modifications and renewals thereof, when and insofar as there is demand for the same, the Commission shall make such distribution of licenses, frequencies, hours of operation, and of power among the several States and communities as to provide a fair, efficient, and equitable distribution of radio service to each of the same [Sec. 307 (b)].

It will be recalled that the original attempt to equalize distribution of service mathematically proved impracticable (Chapter 8). Section 307 (b) leaves the matter to the judgment of the FCC on a case-to-case basis. Since the Commission is limited by the element of "demand" (from would-be licensees), it cannot arrive at an ideal distribution of facilities. The demand will naturally tend to exceed the supply in areas of highly concentrated population and commercial activity.

The Commission has, however, been successful to some extent in arriving at a compromise between the two kinds of distribution of facilities implied by demand on the one hand and by equity on the other. By setting up nation-wide allocation tables of FM and television channels in advance of authorizing the services, the Commission prevented inequalities which would undoubtedly have arisen if allocations had been governed by random economic demands. The Commission's authority to make such advance allocation tables has been sustained in the courts.[13]

"Fair, efficient, and equitable distribution of radio service" has been interpreted to mean more than simply providing a local program service for the benefit of set owners. Both the FRC and the FCC have considered that an important aspect of radio "service" is providing local *access* to broadcast facilities for the benefit of originators of communications as well as for the benefit of receivers of communications. This interpretation has been supported by the Supreme Court: "Fairness to communities is furthered by a recognition of local needs for a community radio mouthpiece."[14] This means an opportunity for local businesses to use the medium for advertising, for local candidates to appeal for political support, for local public-service agencies to promote their objectives, for representatives of local

[13] E.g., *Logansport Broadcasting Corp.* v. *U.S.*, 210 F. (2d) 24 (1954).
[14] *FCC* v. *Allentown Broadcasting Corp.*, 349 U.S. 358 at 363 (1955).

controversial issues to air their points of view, for local governments to inform the electorate, for local educational and cultural institutions to broaden their community service, for local newsmen to report on community happenings, for local talent to have an outlet, and so on. In short, a station serves its area as a means of community self-expression, giving it a broadcast voice as well as a broadcast ear.

LIMITATIONS ON ELIGIBILITY OF LICENSEES

Under the principle of public ownership of frequencies, the Act establishes that no private individual can own a frequency allocation. Furthermore, even temporary, licensed use of a frequency allocation is not open to all comers. Licensees must meet certain criteria of eligibility:

> All applications for station licenses, or modifications or renewals thereof, shall set forth such facts as the Commission by regulation may prescribe as to citizenship, character, and financial, technical, and other qualifications of the applicant to operate the station; the ownership and location of the proposed station . . . the frequencies and the power desired to be used; the hours of the day or other periods of time during which it is proposed to operate the station; the purposes for which the station is to be used; and such other information as it may require . . . [Sec. 308 (b)].

Of these the citizenship qualification is the most specific, since Sec. 310 (a) goes on to deny licenses to aliens. An applicant's financial qualifications can be expressed quantitatively; he is expected to have enough money at his disposal not only to build a proposed station but to operate it at a loss for a time. Character qualifications can hardly be measured quantitatively. They are revealed by past and present conduct; on the negative side, for example, prior conviction of a crime or misrepresentation of facts to the Commission would be very damaging. Technical qualifications include knowledge and understanding of the law of broadcasting, of station operations, of programming, and engineering. The applicant is not expected to be a lawyer, a program director, or an engineer; but he should show that he has expert counsel in those matters in which he is not himself an expert.

If a broadcast license is revoked by a court for violation of anti-monopoly laws the FCC must comply with the court decree (Sec. 311). Congress was particularly sensitive to the possibility of monopoly in the communications field, having ample precedent to consider. In fact, Section 311 originally also forbade the licensing of persons who had been found guilty of monopoly or unfair competition in the field of radio communication or manufacturing. This part of the Section was repealed in 1952 because of its "double jeopardy" character. Another section permits the revocation of licenses held by a person found guilty of violating antitrust laws in addition to other penalties provided by the antitrust laws themselves (Sec. 313).

THE APPLICABILITY OF THE FIRST AMENDMENT

Aware of broadcasting's significance as a means of public enlightenment, Congress emphasized that in adopting legislation to govern broadcasting it did not intend to exclude it from the protection against government interference with freedom of the press that is provided by the First Amendment to the Constitution:

> Nothing in this Act shall be understood or construed to give the Commission the power of censorship over the radio communications or signals transmitted by any radio station, and no regulation or condition shall be promulgated or fixed by the Commission which shall interfere with the right of free speech by means of radio communication (Sec. 326).

Very little else in the Act makes specific reference to the content of the program service. Section 317 requires that commercial matter be announced as paid for and attributed to the source. This rule is intended to prevent anonymous propaganda or advertising in disguise, and is analogous to the publishing practice of printing the word "advertisement" above matter which might otherwise be mistaken as part of the publication's editorial content. Practically all regular commercial advertising, of course, identifies the sponsor automatically. No formal announcement that matter is paid for is required unless the material might otherwise be misinterpreted as station editorializing or news copy.

From the political point of view perhaps the most vital function of broadcasting is as an instrument of information and persuasion in connection with the election of public officials. Congress would not be likely to overlook this factor; accordingly, it made a special provision for candidates for public office:

> (a) If any licensee shall permit any person who is a legally qualified candidate for any public office to use a broadcasting station, he shall afford equal opportunities to all other such candidates for that office in the use of such broadcasting station: *Provided,* That such licensee shall have no power of censorship over the material broadcast under the provisions of this section. No obligation is hereby imposed upon any licensee to allow the use of its station by any such candidate.
>
> (b) The charges made for the use of any broadcasting station for any of the purposes set forth in this section shall not exceed the charges made for comparable use of such station for other purposes.
>
> (c) The Commission shall prescribe appropriate rules and regulations to carry out the provisions of this section (Sec. 315).

It should be noted that this provision applies *only* to candidates while they are candidates, not to political officials once they are elected. Moreover, it applies only to the candidates themselves, not to other persons speaking in their behalf. Section 315 imposes no obligation on the licensee to make his facilities available to candidates in the first place, but once he opens the door to one he must keep it open for other candidates for the same office. Paragraph (b) is an amendment adopted in 1952; it reflects the fact that many stations had made a practice of charging higher rates to candidates than to commercial advertisers.

Section 315 has been one of the most troublesome provisions of the Communications Act, not only because of the inherently controversial nature of politics but also because of a conflict of laws. In prohibiting the licensee from censoring speeches of political candidates, Congress had in mind the possibility that the intention of the law could be circumvented by licensees who wished to favor one candidate simply by emasculating the speeches of his opponents. However, the laws governing defamation come under state jurisdiction; hence the licensee is prohibited under the Federal law from avoiding the commission of what may be an actionable wrong under state law.[15]

Nothing further in the Act refers *directly* to programs.[16] The layman generally supposes that the Communications Act contains a great deal of regulation concerning programming on which, in fact, the Act is completely silent. It says nothing about sustaining programs, unethical advertising, controversial issues, religion, public-service programs, and the many other program matters which are associated with the notion of government regulation.

Indirectly, however, the Act gives the Commission much latitude in program matters. From the beginning the Commission has assumed that this latitude permits consideration of the character of the program service provided by licensees. This assumption may seem to run directly counter to Section 326, which explicitly withholds the power of censorship from the Commission. The Commission will not, to be sure, substitute its judgment for that of the licensee by approving or disapproving *in advance* any program that may be proposed; this would indeed fit the classic definition of censorship, i.e., "prior restraint." The Commission will, however, consider the *over-all* program service of the licensee. The courts have repeatedly upheld this procedure. Even aside from the question of prior restraint, however, the law assumes that the licensee, with his intimate knowledge of local conditions and needs, is far better qualified than distant bureaucrats to determine what is in the public interest for his locality.[17]

[15] The FCC pinpointed the issue in the *Port Huron* case (12 FCC 1069, 1948), and inasmuch as Congress took no action to solve the problem the Commission has since insisted on enforcement of Sec. 315 even when stations might be penalized by state laws. A majority of the states have amended their libel and slander laws in recent years to exempt stations from suit when unable, under Sec. 315, to prevent libelous statements by political candidates.

[16] Originally the Act contained prohibitions against obscenity and lotteries. These provisions have been removed from the Communications Act and recodified in the United States Code under "Crime and Criminal Procedure."

[17] The FCC on request will give advance declaratory opinions on purely legal questions such as whether a proposed program constitutes a lottery.

An important consequence of the prohibition of censorship, and of the previously outlined principles embodied in the Communications Act, is that unqualified responsibility is placed on the licensee. Neither the FCC nor the courts, neither the purchaser of time nor his agents, can relieve the licensee of his personal responsibility to maintain control of his station and its program service. The government, not the licensee, is prohibited from censoring. To prohibit the licensee from controlling program content would transform broadcasting into a common carrier. That, as we have pointed out, would completely subvert the intention of the Communications Act.

Licensee responsibility is a positive duty. The licensee may not sell a station without permission, and the purchaser must apply for the license and must satisfy all the criteria of an applicant for an original license (Sec. 310[b]). By the same token, a licensee may not legally turn over the management of a station to another or sell time to a time broker for resale.

DISCRETIONARY POWERS OF GOVERNMENT

Congress was well aware of the impossibility of writing a really definitive or comprehensive law to govern radio. It therefore left all but a few fundamental matters open to the application of the discretion of the moment. The FCC was created as an arm of Congress to exercise this discretion, and the standard of "public interest, convenience, and necessity" was set up as the limiting factor. With respect to the licensing power the following instructions appear:

The Commission, *if public convenience, interest, or necessity will be served thereby,* subject to the limitations of this Act, shall grant to any applicant therefor a station license provided for by this act [Sec. 307 (a)].

* * * * *

Upon the expiration of any license, upon application therefor, a renewal of such license may be granted from time to time for a term of not to exceed three years in the case of broadcasting licenses, and not to exceed five years in the case of other licenses, *if the Commission finds that public interest, convenience, and necessity would be served thereby* . . . [Sec. 307 (d)].

* * * * *

If upon examination of any application [for construction permit, license, or modification or renewal thereof] *the Commission shall find that public interest, convenience, and necessity would be served* by the granting thereof, it shall grant such application [Sec. 309 (a)].

* * * * *

No construction permit or station license, or any rights thereunder, shall be transferred, assigned, or disposed of in any manner, voluntarily or involuntarily, directly or indirectly, or by transfer of control of any corporation holding such permit or license, to any person *except* upon application to the

Commission and *upon finding by the Commission that the public interest, convenience, and necessity will be served thereby* . . . [Sec. 310 (b)].

❋   ❋   ❋   ❋   ❋

Any station license or construction permit may be modified by the Commission either for a limited time or for the duration of the term thereof, *if* in the judgment of the Commission *such action will promote the public interest, convenience, and necessity* . . . [Sec. 316 (a)].

❋   ❋   ❋   ❋   ❋

. . . changes in the frequencies, authorized power, or in the times of operation, of any station, shall not be made without the consent of the station licensee *unless,* after a public hearing, the Commission shall determine that *such changes will promote public convenience or interest or will serve public necessity* . . . [Sec. 303 (f)].[18]

Thus the Commission must consult the public interest, convenience, and necessity in making every major decision about licensing.

Section 303 of the Act lists a number of rather specific powers of the FCC, including the power to: (a) classify stations, (b) prescribe the nature of the service to be rendered, (c) assign frequencies, (d) determine station location, (e) regulate the kind of apparatus used, (f) prevent interference, (g) study new uses for radio and provide for experimental uses of frequencies, (i) make special regulations for network stations, (j) require the keeping of records, (l) prescribe qualifications for station operators and issue them licenses, (o) designate call letters, and (p) publish necessary information. This entire list, however, is preceded by the admonition to do these things *"as public convenience, interest or necessity requires."*

All this gives the Commission wide latitude, since very few significant provisions fail to leave the door open for the exercise of its discretion. The phrase "public interest, convenience, and necessity," or any variant thereof, therefore takes on critical importance; in effect, it determines the practical results of the application of the generalities contained in the law. The function of the public-interest concept has been well summarized in a court decision:

> The Congress of the United States, which has plenary power to regulate the radio industry, has designated the Commission as its administrative agent, because it is desired to have the regulatory work done by technically trained experts, skilled and experienced in the technical duties of radio regulation. The Congress defined the scope of the authority of its agent or, as is sometimes said, it established the standard according to which the agent should act. The broad scope of authority, or standard of action, established by the Communications Act is that public interest, convenience and necessity must be served. Within that framework the administrative agent is free to exercise its expert judgment; it cannot act unconstitutionally, for neither could its principal, the Congress, and the stream cannot rise higher than the source; it must proceed within the scope of the authority granted to it, that is to say,

[18] Italics supplied.

it must observe the standard established; and it cannot act arbitrarily or capriciously . . . The doctrine is that the act of the administrative agent is the act of Congress itself; as long as the agent stays within the boundaries of the standard and does not act arbitrarily or capriciously . . . It would be difficult, if not impossible, to formulate a precise and comprehensive definition of the term "public interest, convenience, or necessity", and it has been said often and properly by the courts that the facts of each case must be examined and must govern its determination.[19]

As the Court remarked, the Commission may not act arbitrarily or capriciously in its decisions or rule-making. In the first place, it cannot take any important action involving opposing interests without first holding a hearing and considering the points of view of the persons involved. If the Commission decides not to grant a license request, it must advise the applicant and others concerned of its objections; the applicant then has an opportunity to reply, and if the Commission still decides against the applicant, it must set the matter for hearing, "specifying with particularity the matters and things in issue" (Sec. 309 [b]). If the Commission proposes to change a station's power, frequency, or time of operation, the licensee is automatically entitled to a hearing (Sec. 303 [f]).

On the other hand, if the Commission grants an application *without* a hearing, the grant is subject for thirty days to protest from "any party in interest"; if the protest shows the protestant to be a real party in interest raising specific issues, the Commission must hold a hearing on the matter and postpone the effective date of its decision (Sec. 309 [c]).[20]

After hearings are held, the hearing officers (either Commissioners or hearing examiners delegated for the purpose) must file an initial decision. Exceptions may then be filed by the parties involved, pointing out objections to the conclusions reached in the decision. If requested, the Commission must then consider oral arguments on the exceptions before issuing a final decision or order (Sec. 409 [b]). If the Commission wishes to revoke a license or issue a cease-and-desist order, it must first invite the licensee to appear at a hearing to show cause why such action should not be taken (Sec. 312 [c]). In all these proceedings the Commission is governed by the Administrative Procedures Act, which applies in general to agencies of the federal government. Finally, a "person aggrieved or whose interests are adversely affected" by a decision or order which grows out of a hearing may also petition for a rehearing, although the Commission may use its own discretion in granting such requests (Sec. 405).

[19] *WOKO, Inc.* v. *FCC*, 153 F. (2d) 623 at 628-629 (1946). FCC interpretations of the public interest, convenience, and necessity standard are discussed in Chapters 22 and 23.

[20] Section 309 (c) was added as one of the 1952 Amendments to the Act. It was intended to protect the rights of licensees who might sustain real injury through the granting of a new license; in practice, however, it also opened the doors of hearings to irrelevant intervenors whose main purpose was to delay and harass legitimate applicants. In 1956 Sec. 309 (c) was amended to give the FCC more freedom to screen protests.

These safeguards ensure that persons affected by a Commission action have ample opportunity to be heard; they cannot be subjected to summary or arbitrary decisions. Although the FCC is only quasi-judicial (i.e., is not strictly speaking a court of law), its procedures must conform in general to judicial standards and it must, of course, observe the safeguards provided by the Constitution. On occasion judges have reminded the FCC of these obligations:

> . . . it will be helpful to spell out the process which a commission properly follows in reaching a decision. The process necessarily includes at least four parts: (1) Evidence must be taken and weighed, both as to its accuracy and credibility; (2) from attentive consideration of this evidence a determination of facts of a basic or underlying nature must be reached; (3) from these basic facts the ultimate facts, usually in the language of statute, are to be inferred, or not, as the case may be; (4) from this finding the decision will follow by the application of the statutory criterion.

> ✿   ✿   ✿   ✿   ✿

> Administrative orders, quasi-judicial in character, are void, if a hearing was denied, if that granted was inadequate or manifestly unfair, if the finding is contrary to the indisputable character of the evidence, or if the facts found do not as a matter of law support the order made. The commission may not capriciously make findings by administrative fiat. Such authority, however beneficently exercised in one case, could be injuriously exercised in another, is inconsistent with rational justice, and comes within the Constitution's condemnation of all arbitrary exercise of power.[21]

THE RIGHT OF APPEAL

Even after all the safeguards of hearings, rehearings, initial decision, exceptions, and oral arguments have been exhausted, a person adversely affected by Commission rules or decisions still has a further recourse. Section 402 provides for appeals to the courts to enjoin, set aside, annul, or suspend Commission actions. Most appeals go to the United States Court of Appeals for the District of Columbia, which is open to: (1) a person whose application for a CP or license has been denied; (2) a person whose application for renewal or modification has been denied; (3) a person whose application for transfer of ownership of CP or license has been denied; (4) a person whose CP has been modified or revoked; (5) "any other person who is aggrieved or whose interests are adversely affected by any order of the Commission" granting or denying an application; (6) a person who has received a cease-and-desist order; or (7) an operator whose license has been suspended. If the Court of Appeals fails to satisfy a litigant, he can petition the Supreme Court of the United States to review the decision of the lower court. The Supreme Court is not bound to accept the case if in

[21] *Saginaw Broadcasting Co.* v. *FCC*, 96 F. (2d) 554 at 559 (1938); *White* v. *FRC*, 29 F. (2d) 113 at 115 (1928).

its opinion no substantial Federal question is involved. In such a case the decision of the lower court becomes final.

All the materials developed at hearings and the other procedures prior to an appeal become part of the record for consideration by the courts. Generally speaking, the courts have taken the position that they should not substitute their judgment for that of the FCC, which is the body set up by Congress for the purpose of bringing expert judgment to bear on regulatory problems. The court usually confines its actions to determining whether the Commission has followed proper procedure, whether it has acted within its lawful powers, and whether it has been arbitrary or capricious in its conclusions. As Supreme Court Justice Frankfurter has said,

> Congress has charged the courts with the responsibility of saying whether the Commission has fairly exercised its discretion within the vaguish, penumbral bounds expressed by the standard of "public interest." It is our responsibility to say whether the Commission has been guided by proper considerations in bringing the deposit of its experience, the disciplined feel of the expert, to bear on applications for licenses in the public interest.[22]

---

[22] *FCC* v. *RCA Communications, Inc.,* 346 U.S. 86 at 91 (1953).

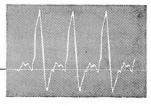

Administration of the Law

Congress . . . did not frustrate the purposes for which the Communications Act of 1934 was brought into being by attempting an itemized catalogue of the specific manifestations of the general problems for the solution of which it was establishing a regulatory agency.

— Justice Felix Frankfurter

The FCC is one of nine independent regulatory commissions of the federal government. Other examples are the Interstate Commerce Commission (the first, set up in 1887) and the Federal Trade Commission. These agencies supervise private activities in commerce, utilities, transportation, labor, finance, and communication — dynamic fields of enterprise over which Congress could not maintain effective supervision without administrative intermediaries. A relatively new, hybrid governmental organization results, one which blurs the traditional lines of demarcation between the legislative, executive, and judicial branches of government. The primary function of the FCC is executive: the carrying out of laws enacted by the legislative branch. Insofar as it makes rules and regulations, which have the force of law, the FCC also has a legislative function; and insofar as it makes decisions in controversies it has a quasi-judicial function.

This mixed responsibility is reflected in the method of setting up the Commission. It comes into existence at the instance of Congress, which created the FCC and defined its scope of operation. On the other hand, it serves as an arm of the executive branch. The American system of checks and balances is well exemplified here, for although the President appoints the commissioners his choice must be approved by the Senate. Approval is not automatic. Not infrequently the Senate holds extensive hearings on appointments by way of reminding appointees of their responsibility to Congress.[1] Moreover, Congress constantly looks over the shoulder of the

[1] For an example see: Senate Committee on Interstate Commerce, *Hearings, Confirmation of the Members of the Federal Communications Commission* (Washington: Government Printing Office, 1935). These hearings concerned six of the original ap-

Commission. It is one of the most often investigated of all government agencies. Every major question that comes before it is likely to be looked into by the Senate Interstate Commerce Committee, the House Interstate and Foreign Commerce Committee, a special Select Committee, and occasionally one of the other standing committees of Congress. Finally Congress can always have the last word in the long run, since it approves the FCC budget and has the power to change the Communications Act itself.

THE ORGANIZATION AND THE WORKLOAD OF THE FCC

Broadcasting itself is the concern of only one of the dozen bureaus and offices of the FCC (Fig. 34), the largest of which is the Field Engineering and Monitoring Bureau. Over a thousand employees are needed to staff not only the Washington headquarters but also 24 district offices and 18 monitoring stations. Decisions concerning licenses are at the core of the Commission's work, but it has many other important functions, among them participation in international conferences, commenting or testifying on domestic legislative proposals, investigating interference complaints, detecting and locating illegal stations, inspecting stations, conducting technical research, and approving new communications-equipment models.

Although common-carrier and safety and special radio services involve a much larger number of licenses than the broadcasting services (Table 2), the work of the Broadcast Bureau is the most complex and difficult. Nonbroadcast problems do not often involve highly controversial questions and highly competitive, mutually exclusive applications, nor do they involve the general public to the same extent as broadcasting. Broadcasting is everybody's business, so everybody wants to tell the FCC how to regulate it.

THE RULES AND REGULATIONS

The origin of the FCC Rules and Regulations has been previously described (Chapter 8). They convert the generalities of the Communications Act into applicable form. Each service is governed by a separate part of the rules, and other parts cover administrative procedures, organization of the Commission, delegations of authority, and the like. Broadcast services are covered by Part 3, which includes subparts for standard broadcast, FM, noncommercial FM, television, and international broadcast stations.

New rules are first issued in the form of proposals, so that interested parties may have an opportunity to comment. On complex matters (such, for example, as the rules governing chain broadcasting or color television) extensive hearings or fact-gathering investigations may be conducted. When

---

pointees: Thad H. Brown and Eugene O. Sykes, previously members of the FRC; Norman Case, former Governor of Rhode Island; George H. Payne, an editor; Irvin Stewart, formerly a communications specialist with the Department of State; and Paul Walker, formerly a state utilities commissioner.

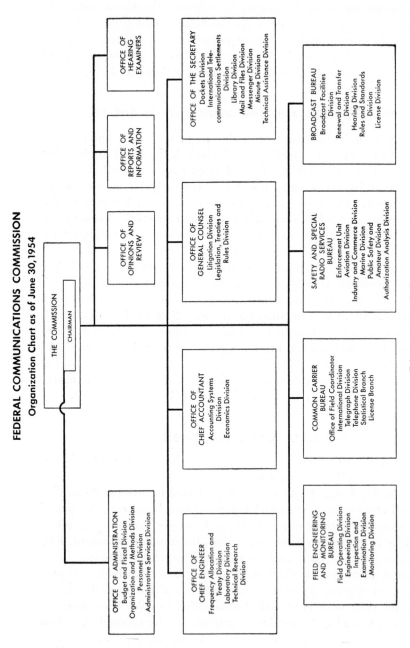

FEDERAL COMMUNICATIONS COMMISSION
Organization Chart as of June 30, 1954

THE COMMISSION

CHAIRMAN

OFFICE OF HEARING EXAMINERS

OFFICE OF REPORTS AND INFORMATION

OFFICE OF OPINIONS AND REVIEW

OFFICE OF THE SECRETARY
Dockets Division
International Tele-
communications Settlements
Division
Library Division
Mail and Files Division
Messenger Division
Minute Division
Technical Assistance Division

OFFICE OF GENERAL COUNSEL
Litigation Division
Legislation, Treaties and
Rules Division

OFFICE OF CHIEF ACCOUNTANT
Accounting Systems
Division
Economics Division

OFFICE OF ADMINISTRATION
Budget and Fiscal Division
Organization and Methods Division
Personnel Division
Administrative Services Division

OFFICE OF CHIEF ENGINEER
Frequency Allocation and
Treaty Division
Laboratory Division
Technical Research
Division

FIELD ENGINEERING AND MONITORING BUREAU
Field Operating Division
Engineering Division
Inspection and
Examination Division
Monitoring Division

COMMON CARRIER BUREAU
Office of Field Coordinator
International Division
Telegraph Division
Telephone Division
Statistical Branch
License Branch

SAFETY AND SPECIAL RADIO SERVICES BUREAU
Enforcement Unit
Aviation Division
Industry and Commerce Division
Marine Division
Public Safety and
Amateur Division
Authorization Analysis Division

BROADCAST BUREAU
Broadcast Facilities
Division
Renewal and Transfer
Division
Hearing Division
Rules and Standards
Division
License Division

Figure 34

FCC Organization Chart

This chart graphically points up the fact that the Broadcast Bureau of the FCC represents only a part of the Commission's responsibility and workload.

finally adopted, rules must be published in the *Federal Register* in order to go into official effect.

Examples comparing the way the Communications Act treats a topic with the way the FCC rules enlarge upon it will serve to clarify the relationship between the two. The Communications Act provides as follows:

> All matter broadcast by any radio station for which service, money, or any other valuable consideration is directly or indirectly paid, or promised to or charged or accepted by, the station so broadcasting, from any person, shall, at the time the same is so broadcast, be announced as paid for or furnished, as the case may be, by such person (Sec. 317).

The Rules and Regulations governing television (for example) expand this brief statement to:

§3.654. *Sponsored programs, announcement.* (a) In the case of each program for the broadcasting of which money, services, or other valuable consideration is either directly or indirectly paid or promised to, or charged or received by, any television broadcast station, the station broadcasting such program shall make, or cause to be made, an appropriate announcement that the program is sponsored, paid for, or furnished, either in whole or in part.

(b) In the case of any political program or any program involving the discussion of public controversial issues for which any films, records, transcriptions, talent, scripts, or other material or services of any kind are furnished, either directly or indirectly, to a station as an inducement to the broadcasting of such program, an announcement shall be made both at the beginning and conclusion of such program on which such material or services are used that such films, records, transcriptions, talent, scripts, or other material or services have been furnished to such station in connection with the broadcasting of such program: *Provided, however,* That only one such announcement need be made in the case of any such program of 5 minutes' duration or less, which announcement may be made either at the beginning or conclusion of the program.

(c) The announcement required by this section shall fully and fairly disclose the true identity of the person or persons by whom or in whose behalf such payment is made or promised, or from whom or in whose behalf such services or other valuable consideration is received, or by whom the material or services referred to in paragraph (b) of this section are furnished. Where an agent or other person contracts or otherwise makes arrangements with a station on behalf of another, and such fact is known to the station, the announcement shall disclose the identity of the person or persons in whose behalf such agent is acting instead of the name of such agent.

(d) In the case of any program, other than a program advertising commercial products or services, which is sponsored, paid for or furnished, either in whole or in part, or for which material or services referred to in paragraph (b) of this section are furnished, by a corporation, committee, association or other unincorporated group, the announcement required by this section shall disclose the name of such corporation, committee, association or other unincorporated group. In each such case the station shall require that a list of the chief executive officers or members of the executive committee or of the board of directors of the corporation, committee, association or other unincorporated group shall be made available for public inspection at one of the television broadcast stations carrying the program.

(e) In the case of programs advertising commercial products or services, an announcement stating the sponsor's corporate or trade name or the name of the sponsor's product, shall be deemed sufficient for the purposes of this section and only one such announcement need be made at any time during the course of the program.

In the foregoing example, the rules clarify and expand a mandatory provision of the Act, with due recognition of several practical questions which arise in the application of the provision. The next example illustrates more extensive improvisation by the FCC on a permissive, rather than mandatory, provision of the Act. The Communications Act provides:

Sec. 303. Except as otherwise provided in this Act, the Commission from time to time, as public convenience, interest, or necessity requires shall —

*   *   *   *   *

(j) Have authority to make general rules and regulations requiring stations to keep such records of programs, transmissions of energy, communications, or signals as it may deem desirable.

This leaves the Commission with the option of requiring anything from no records at all to as detailed and extensive records as it may "deem desirable." In practice the Commission has concluded that it needs two types of records: one covering the technical operation of transmitters, the other covering the content of programming.

§3.663. *Logs; maintenance of.* The licensee or permittee of each television station shall maintain program and operating logs and shall require entries to be made as follows:

(a) In the program log:

(1) An entry of the time each station identification announcement (call letters and location) is made.

(2) An entry briefly describing each program broadcast, such as "music," "drama," "speech," etc., together with the name or title thereof and the sponsor's name, with the time of the beginning and ending of the complete program. If a mechanical reproduction, either visual or aural, is used, the entry shall show the exact nature thereof and the time it is announced as a mechanical reproduction. If a speech is made by a political candidate, the name and political affiliations of such speaker shall be entered.

(3) An entry showing that each sponsored program broadcast has been announced as sponsored, paid for, or furnished by the sponsor; or that the broadcast is under the auspices of a nonprofit educational organization other than the licensee or permittee.

(4) An entry showing, for each program of network origin, the name of the network originating the program.

(b) In the operating log:

(1) An entry of the time the station begins to supply power to the antenna, and the time it stops.

(2) An entry of the time the program begins and ends.

(3) An entry of each interruption to the carrier wave, its cause, and duration.

(4) An entry of the following each 30 minutes:

(i) Operating constants of last radio stage of the aural transmitter (total plate current and plate voltage).

(ii) Transmission line meter readings for both transmitters.

(iii) Frequency monitor readings.[2]

*   *   *   *   *

A further section provides rules on how long logs must be retained (two years), who must keep them (persons having actual knowledge of the facts), the form of logs ("suitable"), how logs may be corrected (only by original keeper), and the use of rough logs (must be kept on file).

A final example will illustrate a rule for which there is no specific authority in the Act but which is generally authorized under Sec. 303 (r), which empowers the Commission to make "such rules and regulations and prescribe such restrictions and conditions . . . as may be necessary to carry out the provisions of this Act . . ." No specific mention is made in the Act concerning station identification announcements; yet it is desirable to be able readily to identify the source of all radio signals. Accordingly, the Commission's rules include such provisions as these:

§3.652. *Station identification.* (a) A licensee of a television broadcast station shall make station identification announcement (call letters and location) at the beginning and ending of each time of operation and during the operation on the hour. The announcement at the beginning and ending of each time of operation shall be by both aural and visual means. Other announcements may be by either aural or visual means.

(b) Identification announcements during operation need not be made when to make such announcement would interrupt a single consecutive speech, play, religious service, symphony concert, or any type of production. In such cases, the identification announcement shall be made at the first interruption of the entertainment continuity and at the conclusion thereof.

MUTUALLY EXCLUSIVE APPLICATIONS

It will be helpful to an understanding of the FCC's operation in the broadcast field to adopt the point of view of a license applicant. In most cases nowadays an application for a new license is likely to be contested by one or more rival applicants. Such mutually exclusive applications provide the most revealing test of the FCC's interpretation of public interest, convenience, and necessity, for each applicant usually meets the statutory requirements for a license; therefore the Commission must fall back on the

[2] Note that the station is not required to keep actual *recordings* of programs. Such a requirement has often been suggested, at least for certain types of programs, but it would impose a heavy financial burden on the licensee.

issue of which will best serve the public interest to find a basis of differentiation.

The specific statutory requirements are relatively simple: a licensee must be a citizen of the United States, and must have suitable "character," financial, and technical qualifications.[3] Most applicants are equally able to meet these requirements. That is, each will be a citizen and have a good character, enough money to build a station and operate it at a loss for a reasonable length of time, competent engineering advice on all technical requirements, and experienced program personnel capable of planning a diversified service.

At this point the applicant (or, more accurately, his legal counsel) consults prior decisions of the FCC for either refinements of these grounds or additional grounds on which to claim superiority. A survey of the FCC's first year of decisions, for example, reveals that it considered the following facts favorably:

1. Commercial support for the station was shown to be probable (1 FCC 267).
2. Local talent and program material were shown to be available (1 FCC 259).
3. Previous experience in broadcasting indicated applicant was able to render a meritorious service (1 FCC 253).
4. Applicant had engaged an experienced staff (1 FCC 244).
5. Programs proposed were suited to local needs and would constitute a complete and diversified service (1 FCC 212).

Over the years such refinements as these have become well established as criteria of selection. These elements of fine differentiation are usually found in (1) the character of the program service proposed (together with the assurances that proposals will really be carried out); and in (2) the implications of the ownership with respect to monopoly and integration with the local community to be served.

PROGRAM CRITERIA

As to the program service, the Commission stresses the need for a "balanced" or "well-rounded" service, with emphasis on local needs. The meaning of "balanced" in this context has been defined by the Commission in the *Blue Book*.[4] According to this interpretation, a responsible broadcast service

[3] An applicant for an AM license must be able to show that the proposed station will not create objectionable interference with other stations; in a competitive hearing he may also have to show that the proposed location is desirable from the point of view of equitable distribution of service. FM and TV applicants do not ordinarily encounter these issues, since the FCC has already set up tables of allocation for these services in advance.

[4] Popular name for: FCC, *Public Service Responsibility of Broadcast Licensees* (Washington: Government Printing Office, 1946). This publication is not part of the Commission's Rules and Regulations; it is an expression of the Commission's philosophy on program matters, at least as of 1946. The *Blue Book* has not been repudiated by subsequent commissioners and presumably still reflects Commission thinking in the main.

should include (1) sustaining programs, (2) local live programs, (3) discussions of public issues. At the same time, programming should avoid advertising excesses, both quantitative (e.g., the piling up of commercials) and qualitative (commercial exploitation of patriotic feelings, commercials of doubtful taste concerning bodily functions, commercials which propagandize on social issues instead of selling goods and services).[5]

According to the *Blue Book,* sustaining programs are essential for several reasons: Some types of desirable programs are not appropriate for commercial sponsorship; significant minorities should be served and yet may not be attractive advertising targets; non-profit organizations should have an opportunity to use broadcast facilities; and there should be experimentation in programming (advertisers being notoriously averse to risking untried program formulas). But perhaps the most significant role of sustaining programs is what the FCC called their "balance-wheel function." This often-misunderstood concept merely takes into account the fact that purely commercial considerations tend to limit program choice. It does not assume that commercial programs are necessarily crass, vulgar, and lacking in public-interest value or that sustaining programs are, by the same token, necessarily uplifting and impeccably artistic. This would be a patently absurd conclusion. The balance-wheel function of sustaining programs simply means that commercial criteria of choice should not be the only criteria, irrespective of the kind of programs which may result from commercial motivations. Conceivably every sponsor might want classical music, in which case counterbalancing sustaining programs might be designed to serve those who are interested in popular music, folk music, or no music at all.[6]

Local live programs derive their importance, in the FCC's view, from the Communications Act requirement of equitable distribution of service.

[5] Although the Commission's opposition to such commercial excesses as these has not changed substantially since the *Blue Book* was issued, it obviously has not been preventing them. The patriotic motif was a temporary wartime phenomenon, but other excesses of both quantity and quality are still evident. An association of electric-power companies sponsoring *You Are There* on CBS offered a conspicuous example of the propaganda commercial. The program was designed to sell not power but the idea of private as opposed to government-operated power companies. For instance, a program on "The Sailing of the Mayflower" yielded, according to the commercial, the "lesson" that "government ownership does not work." The other types of commercial excess are too familiar to need illustration.

[6] The right of the Commission to inquire into the amount of sustaining time proposed by an applicant has been emphatically supported by the Court of Appeals: "To argue that the Commission may not in the performance of its plain duty inquire into the amount of sustaining time a prospective licensee purports to reserve if granted a license, and to further argue that if it does, such inquiry is in excess of its authority, contravenes the First Amendment and constitutes censorship prohibited by Sec. 326 of the Act, is to suggest that Congress intended to create the Commission and then by the very act of its creation, stultify and immobilize it in the performance of the specific functions that called it into being. Congress obviously intended no such thing. The test laid down for the guidance of the Commission is as practical as any that could be devised for a body functioning as it does in the field of delegated authority. . . ." *Bay State Beacon, Inc.* v. *FCC,* 171 F. (2d) 826 at 827 (1948).

"Service" is interpreted to mean not merely the availability of a broadcast signal to receivers in a community but also the availability of a broadcast station for the local self-expression of a community. The FCC emphasizes the *use of* local facilities as well as *reception from* local facilities.

Discussions of public issues, the third major aspect of public service mentioned in the *Blue Book*, reflect the Commission's concern that broadcasting should be utilized as a medium for disseminating ideas and opinions as well as facts and entertainment. This concern has its roots, of course, in the libertarian philosophy of communication discussed in Chapter 20. Licensees are expected not merely to accept programs dealing with public issues but to seek out such programs actively.

Another clue to the Commission's concept of program balance can be inferred from the content categories used in application forms for construction permits and license renewals. Proposed or actual programs must be classified as follows:

1. Entertainment (programs intended primarily as entertainment, such as music, drama, variety, comedy, quiz, breakfast, children's)
2. Religious (sermons, religious news, music and drama, etc.)
3. Agricultural (farm or market reports and other information addressed directly to the agricultural population)
4. Educational (programs prepared by or in behalf of educational organizations, exclusive of discussion programs)
5. News (including commentaries)
6. Discussion (including forum, panel, and round-table programs)
7. Talks (conversation programs not previously classified; includes sports)
8. Miscellaneous.

This breakdown has several points of interest: (1) The FCC's choice of non-entertainment categories reveals the types of program it considers to be important for appraisal of programming balance; (2) no distinction is made between commercial and sustaining programs; (3) educational programs are so defined as to require participation by educational organizations; and (4) no norms for relative amounts of each program type are suggested.

Another tabulation requires a breakdown of total programming into the following categories:

	Network	*Recorded*	*Wire*[7]	*Live*
Commercial	%	%	%	%
Sustaining	%	%	%	%

Again, it should be noted that this analysis does not reveal the extent to which any particular type of program is commercialized, nor does the FCC say what percentage of each type must be broadcast. In none of the quanti-

[7] Refers to press-service news received by teletype.

tative tests of programming is the licensee told to meet a predetermined standard. The criterion in each case is what is "reasonable" under the circumstances. A rural station which supplies the only daytime service to its community, for example, might reasonably be expected to offer a very different kind of programming from that of a station which is one of fifteen or twenty operating in a metropolitan area.

The program analyses called for by the FCC do not include a category identified as "public service" programs; nor do they invidiously separate programs of any given content-category into sustaining sheep and commercial goats. The term "public service" is used ambiguously in the industry; it is sometimes applied to all types of non-entertainment programs, sometimes to all non-commercial programs, sometimes to only some of each type. In any case the phrase is unfortunate, for it implies that only *some* programs are intended to serve the public. Programs of pure entertainment surely serve the public just as importantly in their way as do programs of pure information, instruction, or uplift in theirs. The legitimate and valuable recreational function of broadcasting has been relegated, by implication, to an inferior position.

In any event, our hypothetical applicant should submit a proposed program schedule with due regard to over-all balance and to serving local interests. He can further bolster his case by including assurances that these proposals actually reflect the needs of the community in which he plans to operate and actually have a chance of realization. Appropriate evidence might include surveys of community needs and resources; letters showing that local talent, community leaders, educational authorities, and others have agreed to cooperate; specific formats, descriptions, and budgets for the proposed programs.

OWNERSHIP CRITERIA

Emphasis on availability of local broadcast facilities for reception and for use naturally leads to consideration of certain ownership factors. For example, an applicant has an advantage if he can demonstrate that he has participated actively and personally in the life of the community; a past history of service in charitable drives, social welfare organizations, community betterment enterprises, and similar projects argues that he will be likely to understand and serve the needs of the locality.

Similarly, an applicant who can show that he is going to participate directly and personally in station management has an advantage over one who plans merely to sit back and collect profits earned by hired hands. Integration of ownership and management tends to assure the Commission that the professed objectives of the owner will be carried out conscientiously in day-to-day operation. If the applicant is a corporation it is advantageous to show that the stockholders are local residents and represent diversified interests in the community. Local ownership integrated with management suggests that the licensee will have a real, personal stake in the community he proposes to serve and therefore will be more willing and better able to render a genuine public service to that particular community than owners for whom the station is simply an impersonal investment.

Another aspect of ownership involves the question of monopoly. There is no prospect of any single owner's establishing a national monopoly in broadcasting, since the FCC can limit ownership. Monopoly on a national scale could arise, however, from ownership and control of syndicating agencies (e.g., networks) rather than ownership of stations. Of course each station license grants the licensee a *local* monopoly on a particular channel; where the local economy can support only one station or where only one broadcast channel is available for allocation, the licensee obtains a complete local monopoly. This is a "natural" monopoly situation; the FCC forestalls the artificial creation of these situations through the "duopoly" rule, which prevents a single licensee from controlling more than one station in any given service area.

The monopoly issue becomes more complex when the applicant for a broadcast license is already the owner of other communications media. The owner of the only daily newspaper in a community would be at a great disadvantage in a competitive hearing for the only broadcasting channel allocated to that community. If he applied for one of several available channels his newspaper monopoly would still be a point against him, but its significance would depend on his other qualifications and on the strength of the opposing applicants on other issues. All this arises from the doctrine of "diversification of control of the mass media," which is derived from the libertarian theory.

Diversification of control does not, however, override all other considerations. Experience in broadcasting or in newspaper operation can be cited to the advantage of an applicant; a good record of public service is better than no record at all.

OBTAINING A LICENSE [8]

Our hypothetical applicant's first formal step would be to submit an application for a Construction Permit. The application (Form 301) requires a recital of the facilities applied for, the qualifications of the applicant, proposed financing, proposed programming, and engineering data.

Although the form itself is relatively brief, the supporting exhibits may reach formidable proportions. Television applications not uncommonly grow to a stack of documents four or five feet high, since the applicant who faces cross examination from rival applicants can expect to be quizzed in the minutest detail. He must show that every inch of his studios has been

---

[8] Detailed information on applications and their processing, hearings, and related matters is found in Part 1 of the FCC's Rules and Regulations, "Rules Relating to Practice and Procedure."

properly designed, every iota of necessary equipment listed, every minute of programming provided with the necessary space, equipment, personnel, and content material. Once the hearing stage has been reached, it is too late to correct mistakes; the application must stand or fall on its merits. Opposing legal, engineering, and program experts study it from every possible angle, seeking even the smallest oversight which may serve to embarrass a witness on the stand.

Both the applicant himself and the key personnel he may have already engaged are subjected to searching examination. The applicant, in particular, must expect that any flaw in his character or past conduct may be produced to support the contention that he is not the one best fitted to operate in the public interest, convenience, and necessity. In short, the broadcast applicant in a competitive hearing must be prepared to have his whole life laid bare, his character examined, his financial position analyzed, his motives appraised, his plans minutely dissected, his technical competence challenged.

If our hypothetical applicant survives the hearings, the initial decision, the exceptions, the oral argument before the Commission, and the final decision (barring a rehearing or a court appeal on the decision), he is ready to begin construction. He pays no license fee, either for the CP or the station license,[9] but the costs of preparing an application and participating in all the proceedings connected with a competitive hearing run to many thousands of dollars. In fact, the amount of money and time consumed in hearings has been investigated by Congress, and a number of steps have been taken to simplify the proceedings.[10] Nevertheless, an applicant must still be prepared to risk a very considerable outlay for legal and engineering consultants' fees, preparing and duplicating elaborate exhibits, purchasing transcripts of hearings, and transporting and maintaining witnesses in Washington. He must also be prepared to face delays which may run into years.[11]

The would-be licensee (or applicant for a change in an existing license) may have to face competition from still another source. An existing licensee who can claim that his interests would be adversely affected by a decision or rule of the FCC may appeal the Commission's action. One form of adverse effect, economic injury, has already been mentioned in connection with the Sanders Brothers case in Chapter 21. In this case the Supreme Court ruled that the Commission has to consider the economic injury that

[9] The Fourth Radio Conference, in 1925, proposed station license fees ranging from $25 to $5,000 (p. 20), but this proposal was not made part of the Radio Act of 1927. In 1954 the idea was revived as part of the Republican economy drive in several proposed Congressional bills.

[10] Senate Committee on Interstate and Foreign Commerce, *Hearings on Workload of the Federal Communications Commission* (Washington: Government Printing Office, 1953). The hearing procedure and its problems are discussed in detail on pp. 13-35.

[11] As of June 30, 1954, the FCC reported 1,635 broadcast applications pending, of which 17 per cent dated back a year or more. FCC, *Twentieth Annual Report* (Washington: Government Printing Office, 1955), pp. 108-9.

the granting of a new license might cause to a current licensee only insofar as public interest, convenience, and necessity may be involved.

Another type of injury that an existing station may anticipate from a new station is loss of coverage due to signal interference. The issue involved in such a circumstance has produced more litigation and legal quibbling than any other single issue in broadcasting law. The classic example, the KOA case, resulted in seventeen judges' writing ten different opinions, of which five were on one side and five on the other. KOA is a Class I-A clear-channel station in Denver that was once owned by NBC. The Commission, by a bare majority, proposed to grant a modification of license for WHDH on the same channel in Boston, changing it from one kilowatt daytime to five kilowatts unlimited time. This move was fought with particular intensity, despite the wide separation of the two stations, because it represented an encroachment on the clear-channel principle. The Commission was finally allowed to make the change, and subsequently granted WHDH fifty kilowatts.[12]

KEEPING A LICENSE

Assuming our imaginary applicant has surmounted all obstacles and finally become a full-fledged broadcast licensee, what must he do to keep his hard-won privilege? Fundamentally, of course, he must operate in the public interest, convenience, and necessity. More specifically, he must abide by the operating rules of the FCC, submit required periodic reports on ownership, finances, and programming, and remember to apply for a renewal of license every three years.

In 1952 an amendment to the Communications Act gave the FCC a new method of dealing with violations by licensees, the cease-and-desist order (Sec. 312 [b]). Before that time the Commission's only way of penalizing a station had been to jeopardize the license itself, by either a revocation or a renewal proceeding. This meant, in effect, that there was no punishment available short of capital punishment. The Commission was naturally reluctant to invoke this penalty:

> . . . we go through long hearings, but when you get right down to it the penalty is so severe that the Commission is not inclined to do anything about it. The upshot of it is that ultimately they try to get the thing straightened out and let it go right ahead, and I don't know whether that is a healthy thing.[13]

        ✲   ✲   ✲   ✲   ✲

The record of the Commission shows that there are very few revocations and very few denials of licenses since it does not wish to impose this harsh remedy.

---

[12] *In re Matheson Radio Co.* (*WHDH*), 8 FCC 397 (1940); *NBC v. FCC*, 132 F. (2d) 545 (1942); *FCC v. NBC*, 319 U.S. 239 (1943).

[13] Testimony of James L. Fly, FCC Chairman, in: Senate Committee on Interstate Commerce, *Hearings on S. 814, To Amend the Communications Act of 1934* (Washington: Government Printing Office, 1944), p. 44.

The Commission is of the opinion that the Broadcasting industry believes it can get away with almost anything because the Commission will not revoke their licenses or deny an application for renewal.[14]

The cease-and-desist order provides an intermediate step. Such more substantial penalties as fines or temporary suspensions of operations are not feasible, since they would tend to penalize the public (in terms of deterioration or loss of program service) as much as the broadcaster. It seems likely, however, that the Commission will continue to favor the renewal hearing as a corrective device, since the cease-and-desist orders (like revocations) can issue only for specific violations, whereas renewals can be set for hearing on the general question of whether public interest, convenience, or necessity would be served by renewal.

Information or evidence on which the FCC might set a renewal application for hearing could come from (1) citations for infractions of the rules or (2) the logs of the station, which may reveal violations of the law or suggest failure to operate in the public interest. In addition, (3) the program and financial reports of the station, which the FCC requires to be filed regularly, may contain similar revelations; (4) complaints may have been lodged against the station by individuals or organizations; or (5) the licensee may have been found guilty of some kind of unlawful conduct that is not under the immediate jurisdiction of the FCC but diminishes his ability to operate in the public interest.

The FCC does not itself monitor programs to evaluate their content. The chief duty of its monitoring stations is checking on technical matters, such as unauthorized radiations or signals, or failure to maintain assigned frequency and prescribed signal characteristics. Inspections of stations also are primarily concerned with compliance with technical rules. Questions of program content usually come to the attention of the Commission as the result of complaints or local legal actions incidental to programming. Audience members may either write directly to the FCC or seek action through their Congressmen. Many complaints can be classified as crank letters and given routine answers; others can be handled informally by correspondence between the FCC and the station involved; if complaints seem substantial and serious, they can lead to punitive action.[15] Section 309 of the Act requires the Commission first to notify the licensee of the reasons for questioning renewal and then to consider the licensee's reply to this notice. If the reply does not satisfy the Commission, it may then set the matter for

---

[14] Testimony of Wayne Coy, FCC Chairman, in: House Committee on Interstate and Foreign Commerce, *Hearings on S. 658, Amending Communications Act of 1934* (Washington: Government Printing Office, 1951), p. 137.

[15] In a period of 75 days in 1951 the FCC received 967 complaints of which the most numerous were against the advertising of alcoholic beverages (26 per cent); indecency, obscenity, or profanity (23 per cent); false or misleading advertising (13 per cent); lotteries and giveaways (11 per cent). Robert D. Swezey, "Give the Television Code a Chance," *Quarterly of Film, Radio, and Television* VII-1 (Fall, 1952), p. 15.

hearing, at which the burden of proof is upon the applicant (rather than upon the Commission, as in revocation proceedings).

In most cases renewal hearings have resulted in the licensee's promising to mend his ways, whereupon the Commission has granted renewal. This procedure has been criticized because the licensee, in order not to risk losing his license altogether, tends to accept the Commission's ruling without submitting it to a court test. Thus, conceivably, the licensee's legal rights could be lost by default. As long as the licensee knuckles under and agrees to change his ways he tacitly admits he was wrong and therefore has no grounds for appeal. Only when he refuses to change his ways and invites the FCC to deny license renewal does the licensee have a case. Most licensees do not want to undertake the expense of an appeal to the courts at the risk of losing their cases and with them their licenses.

Probably the most notable instance of this sort of "judicial legislation" by the FCC is the Mayflower case. A Boston station, WAAB, owned by the Yankee Network, adopted a policy of "editorializing," i.e., expressing views on political candidacies and other controversial public questions in the name of the station itself. This practice is to be distinguished from expression of such views by commentators; it corresponds to editorializing in newspapers, where the editorials represent the views of the publisher. The Commission took the view that such editorializing was not in the public interest, holding that "a truly free radio cannot be used to advocate the causes of the licensee. It cannot be used to support the candidacies of his friends. It cannot be devoted to the support of principles he happens to regard most favorably. In brief, the broadcaster cannot be an advocate."[16] The Yankee Network submitted affidavits showing that it had discontinued its editorializing practices and would never revive them in the future, in consideration of which the Commission renewed the license. This established that the FCC had the power to prevent a licensee from editorializing. That "the broadcaster cannot be an advocate" became, in effect, the law without ever having been challenged. The decision caused so much resentment throughout the industry that the Commission voluntarily revised it in 1949 to permit advocacy by the licensee, provided that the licensee allows opposing points of view an opportunity to be expressed.[17]

LOSING A LICENSE

Renewal has been denied only in rather extreme cases, usually those involving specific violations rather than failures in the "vagueish" area of

[16] *In re The Yankee Network, Inc.*, 8 FCC 333 at 340 (1941). The case derives its name from the Mayflower Broadcasting Corp., which applied for the channel occupied by WAAB. The Mayflower application was rejected on other grounds.

[17] However, the risk of being charged with unfairness even when it is not intended prevents most licensees from taking advantage of their opportunities for editorializing under the revised Mayflower ruling. See Daniel W. Kops, "Radio Needs to Editorialize," *Broadcasting-Telecasting* (19 September 1955), pp. 140-141.

public interest, convenience, and necessity. The following examples of decisions made after renewal hearings illustrate the difference:

RENEWAL GRANTED	RENEWAL DENIED
Inspector found transmitter being operated by unlicensed operator (2 FCC 51).	Licensee had surrendered control over programming, programs included objectionable one by a marriage broker, technical equipment was in very poor repair, management's financial affairs were in very poor condition, station had engaged in unethical business practice (2 FCC 209).
Station discontinued objectionable programs in one of which analyses of dreams and advice on love, marriage, business, and various other subjects were given; technical flaws had been due to transmitter repairs; evidence of failure to identify transcriptions according to rule was conflicting (4 FCC 125).	Station's service had been interrupted owing to faulty equipment; time brokerage was permitted; misrepresentation in advertising was condoned (4 FCC 521).
Broadcast of alleged lottery advertising discontinued after few days (4 FCC 186).	Licensee transferred control of station in violation of law, made false representations to the Commission, was not financially qualified to continue operation (8 FCC 434).
Station had been cited a number of times for violation of technical rules and failure to keep log properly; it had briefly carried a program by an astrologer (7 FCC 219).	

Out-and-out revocation of the license under Section 312 of the Communications Act is rare. This section specifies the grounds for revocation as: (1) false statements in an application, (2) "conditions coming to the attention of the Commission which would warrant it in refusing to grant a license or permit on an original application"; (3) "wilful or repeated failure to operate substantially as set forth in the license," (4) similar violation of the Act, Rules and Regulations, or treaties; (5) violation of cease-and-desist orders. Broad as these grounds are, they do not encompass everything the Commission has included under "public interest, convenience, and necessity." Moreover, Section 312 places the burden of proof on the Commission. Hence licenses have more frequently been jeopardized and actually lost under Section 307, which provides for renewal of licenses.

TRANSFERRING A LICENSE

In the event that our imaginary licensee decides to withdraw from the broadcasting business, an interesting question arises: Since the licensee does not *own* the license, how can he sell it? Of course he may own the technical equipment, buildings, and land necessary to the operation of the station, but all this property greatly enhances in value by virtue of its use in a broadcasting business. The station as a going concern is worth much more than the aggregate value of its individual parts. The actual sale prices of stations often amount to ten and even twenty and more times the value of the inventory of the physical property involved. Part of the difference may be chargeable to "good will," but obviously most of it is due to the value of the license itself, or, more accurately, the right to use a particular broadcast channel which the license confers. In a large market with a limited number of VHF television channels, the right to use a particular channel may be worth literally millions of dollars.

The fact that licenses have cash value on the market, even though they do not represent "ownership" of a broadcast channel, has led to applications for CP's and erection of stations as pure business speculations. This "trafficking in licenses" presents a problem to the FCC, for although it is not illegal it directly contravenes the theory of the Communications Act. The Act assumes that a man who applies for a broadcast license does so with the thought of rendering a public service; it makes no acknowledgment of the fact that a man might build a station for the sake of a quick and profitable sale, with no real intention of serving the public. Nor does it contemplate that broadcast stations might become mere incidental chattels in changes of ownership of large corporations.

The problem was pointed up by a hearing on the transfer of WLW, Cincinnati, to the Aviation Corporation (Avco). WLW was licensed to Crosley Corporation, an old-line electronics manufacturing concern. Avco, a large holding company with many subsidiaries, was buying the Crosley Corporation, and the broadcast properties of Crosley were mere incidentals in the $22,000,000 transaction. The transfer was approved by a bare majority of the FCC, which took occasion to remark that more than 50 per cent of the existing licensees at that time (1945) had been selected not by the Commission but by transferors.

The FCC minority dissent pointed out that Avco's officers demonstrated serene and unblushing ignorance of the most elementary facts about broadcasting, the Communications Act, and the obligations they were proposing to undertake; the Commissioners added that even an applicant for the lowest grade of operator's license has to pass a test to show that he understands his duties and responsibilities under the Act.

> Programming is the essence of broadcasting and yet not a single witness for the transferee demonstrated more than the vaguest idea about the kind of program service which would be rendered, the availability of program talent and sources, the needs of the people in WLW's service area, or even about the type of program service being rendered under the previous management. They did not even know how much they were paying for the broadcasting facilities being purchased.[18]

[18] *In re Powel Crosley, Jr.,* 11 FCC 3 at 37 (1945).

This case led to the adoption by the FCC of the "Avco rule," which required that stations offered for sale be advertised and competing bids solicited, so that the FCC could choose the best qualified applicant. In the four years of the Avco Rule relatively few competing bids were entered and usually the original purchaser was approved anyway. In 1949 the Commission repealed the rule. It now requires filing of application for transfer sixty days in advance of the proposed transfer date.[19]

Such extreme cases as the Avco transfer can be more readily prevented by the Commission under a 1952 amendment to Sec. 310 (b) of the Communications Act. Previously the licensee had merely to secure written consent for a transfer from the FCC, which could decide whether public interest would be served by the proposed transfer. The amended section requires the same action on an application for transfer as on an original application for a license. This amendment prevents the consequence complained of by the majority in the Avco decision — the choice of licensees by transferors instead of by the Commission.

CONSISTENCY IN FCC DECISIONS

Applicants and their lawyers wish the FCC would be more consistent in its interpretations and hence more predictable in its decisions. In his analysis of broadcast law Harry P. Warner reverts again and again to the same theme — "irreconcilable conflict in the decisions on this topic . . .," "patent inconsistency throughout the decisions on this topic . . .," "Commission's decisions are in hopeless confusion. . . ."[20] He concludes:

> The standard of performance [of the FCC] in dealing with the social, economic and political phases of broadcasting does not measure up to the Commission's *expertise* on technical matters. This can be attributed for the most part to the broad gaps in statute, the vagueness and indefiniteness of the statutory standard of public interest, convenience and necessity, and the failure of Congress to provide definite policies which can be interpreted and applied by the Commission.[21]

The failure of Congress to fill in gaps and provide policies can only be interpreted as deliberate, for Congress has amended the Communications Act many times yet has never chosen either to define public interest, convenience, and necessity or to inhibit the Commission with more rigid policies. The Commission, in turn, has been reluctant to set up hard-and-fast standards. To do so would almost certainly hamper the development of the media of communication in the long run. A standard which is reasonable

[19] See: Rufus Crater, "Avco Repeal," *Broadcasting-Telecasting* (13 June 1949), pp. 23, 88. A 1952 Amendment to Sec. 310 (b) of the Communications Act prevents the FCC from instituting any procedure comparable to that required by the Avco Rule.
[20] Harry P. Warner, *Radio and Television Law* (Rev. ed.; New York: Matthew Bender & Co., 1953), pp. 176, 182, 190.
[21] *Ibid.*, pp. 796-797.

and appropriate here today might be unreasonable or inappropriate either elsewhere today or here tomorrow; therefore the Commission has proceeded largely on a case-by-case basis.

Take newspaper ownership and the doctrine of diversification of mass-media control as an example. What weight should the fact of newspaper ownership have in a comparative hearing? Should it count for or against an applicant? Study of the hearings in which newspaper ownership has been an issue produces no clear-cut answers. In some cases newspaper ownership was the controlling factor, in others an incidental factor; in some cases it counted against the applicant, in others for the applicant. These apparent inconsistencies arise because, as one Commission Chairman has said, "to get at the question of what public interest is, you must have before you a set of facts in a particular case; because all of the aspects of the public interest that may have arisen in a particular case before the Commission will probably not arise in any other single case."[22]

This case-by-case method seems the most workable one available in a dynamic field such as that governed by the FCC. It is not a method which appeals to the legal mind. However, the FCC, though quasi-judicial in function, is not a court of law; it is not bound to the same extent as a court by the rule of *stare decisis,* which constrains courts to harmonize new decisions with those that went before.

However, the Commission's freedom from the restraints of formal consistency does not at the same time free it from the restraints of fact and logic. The Court of Appeals has described the essentials for a legally valid decision in a comparative hearing as follows:

(1) The bases or reasons for the final conclusion must be clearly stated.
(2) That conclusion must be a rational result from the findings of ultimate facts, and those findings must be sufficient in number and substance to support the conclusions.
(3) The ultimate facts as found must appear as rational inferences from the findings of basic facts.
(4) The findings of the basic facts must be supported by substantial evidence.
(5) Findings must be made in respect to every difference, except those which are frivolous or wholly unsubstantial, between the applicants indicated by the evidence and advanced by one of the parties as effective.
(6) The final conclusion must be upon a composite consideration of the findings as to the several differences, pro and con each applicant.[23]

HOW IMPARTIAL IS THE FCC?

It will be recalled that the Communications Act seeks to ensure the impartiality of the FCC by limiting any political party to a bare majority of

---

[22] Testimony of Wayne Coy in: House Committee on Interstate and Foreign Commerce, *op. cit.,* p. 108.
[23] *Johnston Broadcasting Co.* v. *FCC,* 175 F. (2d) 351 at 357 (1949).

the Commissioners and by prohibiting Commissioners from having any financial interest in the industry which they regulate. Nevertheless, any political appointee whose decisions affect the disposal of privileges worth many millions of dollars cannot escape a multitude of pressures:

> . . . in their own interest as well as in the interest of their constituents, Congressmen themselves form a pressure group, or rather a number of small but intensive pressure groups, influencing, cajoling, threatening, or entreating the regulatory Commission which they have created.[24]

Congressmen are themselves under constant pressure not only to enlarge the scope of the Communications Act by converting public opinion into law but also to influence specific decisions of the Commission.

The broadcasting industry is probably less grateful than it should be for the fact that the Commission has on the whole steadfastly advised against the statutory enlargement of government power, which could easily lead to much more rigid controls than those improvised by the FCC on the basis of existing legislation. The chairman of the House Committee on Interstate and Foreign Commerce, which has jurisdiction over radio regulation, has asserted that if the Communications Act were to come before Congress today as a new piece of legislation, Congress would be likely to impose far more restrictive regulations on the industry than it did in 1934.[25]

An intensive study of the political connections of Commissioners and licensees that was made before the era of television failed to uncover evidence of political favoritism:

> Most of the criticism levelled against the present Commission has been founded on the charge that political considerations have motivated its actions. A study of the actual record does not appear to sustain this charge . . . Neither party, despite its most energetic efforts when out of office, has been able to uncover any concrete evidence of narrow partisanship in the Commission's decisions . . . Even after twelve years of the New Deal, a check of the political sympathies of station owners reveals that the most powerful stations are about equally divided between Republicans and Democrats.[26]

More recently the pressures and temptations have mounted because the value of television channels is so much greater than that of radio channels. The change from a Democratic to a Republican administration in 1952 led to a shift in the balance of power in the Commission. Presumably a Republican-controlled Commission would tend to favor business interests more than one controlled by Democrats. Yet in 1954 a Republican appointee to

---

[24] Carl J. Friedrich and Evelyn Sternberg, "Congress and the Control of Radio-Broadcasting," *American Political Science Review* XXXVII-5 & 6 (October and December, 1943), pp. 797-798. The authors are highly critical of Congressional handling of radio regulation.

[25] Percy J. Priest, "Communications Legislation Under Congress" (24 May 1955, mimeo.).

[26] Rolf Kaltenborn, *Radio and Politics* (Unpublished Ph.D. dissertation, Yale University, 1944), p. 183.

the Commission, Robert E. Lee, gave the industry "one of the soundest governmental spankings broadcasters could recall."[27]

AN APPRAISAL

The most vociferous criticism of the Commission has naturally come from those whose financial interests have been adversely affected by its decisions. Ironically, a disinterested study of the history of the FRC and the FCC leads to the conclusion that, from an idealistic point of view, their major weakness has been a tendency to compromise principle by making practical concessions to vested economic interests. This compromise began at the very outset, when the FRC failed to wipe the slate clean and start afresh, as it was entitled to do under the Radio Act of 1927. This would have meant arbitrarily putting hundreds of stations off the air and redistributing the service equitably throughout the country. It could have been done only at the expense of many of the pioneer broadcasters, who, though having no legal right to retain their advantageous position, had a certain moral right by virtue of their priority. The FRC chose to avoid taking drastic measures, with the result that the clear-channel problem has plagued the Commission ever since. There have been many subsequent instances in which the Commission recognized desirable policies in principle but temporized in their application.

> In every case the striking departures from declared policy have occurred with respect to policies which, if rigorously enforced, might reduce somewhat the profitability of broadcast operation. It is highly unlikely that commissioners have permitted this consideration to enter into decisions in individual cases. It is rather the belief of the writer that at the root of the difficulty is the milieu in which the Commission operates. The Commission is brought into contact largely with the industry it regulates and very little with representatives of the listening public, whose interests it has declared to be synonymous with the public interest in the broadcasting field. At a public hearing it is the "regulated" who appear and offer argument — regularly, forcefully, and with a show of massed strength. The industrial giants in this field have, moreover, shown marked ability and determination to organize pressure on Capitol Hill, on the Commission, in the press, and over the radio whenever it has appeared to them that a proposed or promulgated Commission policy would affect their interests adversely. Groups that represent listeners are rare, and those that do arise have become impotent with impressive regularity. Under these circumstances it would be remarkable if there were not a disposition on the part of the Commission to overlook, in concrete cases, what common sense dictates as constituting the public interest in the abstract. Perspective is likely to become distorted. The listener is likely to seem as abstract as the principles which announce his rights.[28]

[27] "FCC Comr. Lee Advises Broadcasters to Clean Own House to Avoid Controls," *Broadcasting-Telecasting* (27 September 1954), p. 40.
[28] *Ibid.*, pp. 220-221. Similar views are expressed by Robert E. Cushman in *The*

In appraising the work of the FRC and the FCC we must bear in mind, on the other hand, the extraordinary complexity and difficulty of the tasks they faced.

Here was an attempt to entrust to a body of legal and engineering experts the task of meeting the problem of the disparity between technical advance and its social control that has so consistently plagued modern man. Until the establishment of the Atomic Energy Commission, the Communications Commission's program constituted our only significant venture of this kind.[29]

Under the circumstances some mistakes were inevitable, errors in judgment unavoidable, injustices likely. Taking the long view of the whole development of broadcasting under the FRC and the FCC, an objective appraiser must conclude that the results in terms of the general public interest have been on the whole good. To be sure, the advantage of hindsight enables us now to see mistakes. If the Commission had had foreknowledge of the outcome would it willingly have created the muddled television post-freeze allocation plan? Now that we know the results it is easy to find fault; but a reading of the numerous hearings and reports which led up to the plan reveals such conflicting testimony, such evidence of intense and contradictory pressures on the Commission, that the wonder is that we have a reasonably workable and technically acceptable television system at all. It would have been all too easy for the Commission to yield to the impatient clamor of ill-informed Congressmen and self-seeking industrialists and to saddle the country with an inflexible set of regulations and inferior technical standards.

Independent Regulatory Commissions (New York: Oxford University Press, 1941): "The two commissions have followed the line of least resistance and have assumed that what is best for the radio industry as a business enterprise must also be best for the country" (pp. 730-731).

[29] Murray Edelman, *The Licensing of Radio Services in the United States, 1927 to 1947: A Study in Administrative Formulation of Policy* (Illinois Studies in the Social Sciences, XXXI-4; Urbana: University of Illinois Press, 1950), p. 14.

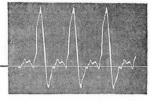

23

Regulation: Enemy of Freedom

Most of the significant controversies surrounding the regulation of broadcasting involve in one way or another the principle of free speech and press. Interference with this fundamental liberty is interdicted by the First Amendment to the Constitution:

Congress shall make no law respecting an establishment of religion, or prohibiting the free exercise thereof; or abridging the freedom of speech, or of the press; or the right of the people peaceably to assemble, and to petition the Government for a redress of grievances.[1]

Generally regarded as the most precious article of the American Bill of Rights, the First Amendment occupies a preferred position which gives it "a sanctity and a sanction not permitting dubious intrusions."[2] As Justice Holmes put it, ". . . if there is any principle of the Constitution that more imperatively calls for attachment than any other it is the principle of free thought — not free thought for those who agree with us but freedom for the thought we hate."[3]

THE THEORY OF THE FIRST AMENDMENT

Justice Douglas, in an eloquently argued dissent, has recently restated the rationale of the First Amendment:

Free speech has occupied an exalted position because of the high service it has given our society. Its protection is essential to the very existence of a democracy. The airing of ideas releases pressures which otherwise might become destructive. When ideas compete in the market for acceptance, full and free discussion exposes the false and they gain few adherents. Full and free discussion even of ideas we hate encourages the testing of our own prejudices and preconceptions. Full and free discussion keeps a society

---

[1] The First Amendment restricts only the federal government, but the Fourteenth Amendment extends the prohibitions of the federal Constitution to the state governments. In addition, all the state constitutions contain provisions similar to those of the First Amendment.

[2] *Thomas* v. *Collins*, 323 U.S. 516 at 530 (1945).

[3] *U.S.* v. *Schwimmer*, 279 U.S. 644 at 654-655 (1929).

from becoming stagnant and unprepared for the stresses and strains that work to tear all civilizations apart.

Full and free discussion has indeed been the first article of our faith. We have founded our political system on it. It has been the safeguard of every religious, political, philosophical, economic, and racial group amongst us. We have counted on it to keep us from embracing what is cheap and false; we have trusted the common sense of our people to choose the doctrine true to our genius and to reject the rest. This has been the one single outstanding tenet that has made our institutions the symbol of freedom and equality. We have deemed it more costly to liberty to suppress a despised minority than to let them vent their spleen. We have above all else feared the political censor. We have wanted a land where our people can be exposed to all the diverse creeds and cultures of the world.[4]

No writer in the libertarian tradition has been more persuasive than the English philosopher John Stuart Mill. "If all mankind minus one," he wrote, "were of one opinion, and only one person were of the contrary opinion, mankind would be no more justified in silencing that one person, than he, if he had the power, would be justified in silencing mankind." He goes on:

> . . . the peculiar evil of silencing the expression of an opinion is, that it is robbing the human race; posterity as well as the existing generation; those who dissent from the opinion, still more than those who hold it. If the opinion is right, they are deprived of the opportunity of exchanging error for truth: if wrong, they lose, what is almost as great a benefit, the clearer perception and livelier impression of truth, produced by its collision with error.[5]

Living up to this ideal is not easy: no one has difficulty in recognizing the importance of freedom for himself, but it requires an unusual measure of self-restraint and tolerance always to grant the importance of that same freedom to those with whom we violently disagree. "The last acquisition of civilized man," Justice Learned Hand has remarked, "is forbearance in judgment and to it is necessary one of the highest efforts of the will."[6] We tend to assume that we have already arrived at our destination, to "think that new truths may have been desirable once, but that we have had enough of them now."[7] Our natural egocentricity (not to speak of ethnocentricity) persuades us that we in *our* time and *our* place have reached the pinnacle. From this conviction arises the presumption that it is necessary to maintain the *status quo* at all costs and the fatal delusion that it is possible to attain total security. But, as Justice Holmes has said, "all life is an experiment":

> . . . when men have realized that time has upset many fighting faiths, they may come to believe even more than they believe the very foundations of their own conduct that the ultimate good desired is better reached by free

---

[4] *Dennis* v. *U.S.*, 341 U.S. 494 at 584-585 (1951).
[5] John Stuart Mill, *On Liberty* (Oxford: Basil Blackwell, 1946), pp. 14-15.
[6] Learned Hand, *The Spirit of Liberty* (New York: Alfred A. Knopf, 1952), p. 27.
[7] Mill, *op. cit.*, p. 24.

trade in ideas — that the best test of truth is the power of the thought to get itself accepted in the competition of the market, and that truth is the only ground upon which their wishes safely can be carried out. That at any rate is the theory of the constitution. It is an experiment, as all life is an experiment.[8]

CENSORABLE FORMS OF EXPRESSION

The constitutional prohibition on censorship leaves room for no exceptions: "Congress shall make no law . . ." The admonition is absolute. Yet it cannot be taken with complete literalness, for some modes of expression are properly subject to penalty, notably obscenity, defamation, and treason. This paradox is resolved by considering that the benefits of free speech can be realized only in an organized society. "The hermit is free to sing, but not to sing in a chorus or an opera."[9] It follows that the use of freedom to destroy the conditions necessary to its enjoyment is self-defeating. Words which have this destructive effect are not exempt from punishment: "The very utterance of such words is considered to inflict a present injury upon listeners, readers, or those defamed, or else to render highly probable an immediate breach of the peace. This is a very different matter from punishing words because they express ideas which are thought to cause a future danger to the State."[10]

Let us take the case of obscenity. It is presumed to have an immediate and harmful effect on society. Legally defined, obscenity means "tending to stir sex impulses or lead to sexually impure and lustful thoughts."[11] The test is that of the effect on a normal, reasonable man. In a given instance opinions could differ, but the courts have held that obscenity is not unconstitutionally vague and that its suppression is proper exercise of the police powers of the government.

Nevertheless, the subjectivity of the concept of obscenity leaves a loophole for the unwarranted censorship of literature and art. The supporters of individual liberties fight a constant battle against those who profess to find obscenity in the nudity in paintings by the masters and in the realism of literary classics.[12] An important decision in this connection was made in 1933 in the case of James Joyce's *Ulysses*. It established the principle that a literary work must be judged *as a whole* and in terms of the intentions of the author.[13] Without this safeguard the censor can take a word, phrase, sentence, or passage out of context, declare it obscene, and suppress the

---

[8] *Abrams* v. *U.S.*, 250 U.S. 616 at 630 (1919).

[9] William Ernest Hocking, *Freedom of the Press: A Framework of Principle* (Chicago: University of Chicago Press, 1947), p. 67.

[10] Zechariah Chafee, Jr., *Free Speech in the United States* (Cambridge: Harvard University Press, 1942), p. 149.

[11] *U.S.* v. *One Book Called "Ulysses,"* 5 F. Supp. 182 at 184 (1933).

[12] Cf.: Morris L. Ernst and Alexander Lindey, *The Censor Marches On* (New York: Doubleday, Doran & Co., Inc., 1940).

[13] *U.S.* v. *One Book Called "Ulysses,"* op. cit., p. 185.

whole work. A similar technique is often used to condemn books as subversive or Communistic on the basis of isolated passages torn out of context.

Like obscenity, speech which is grossly defamatory or likely to lead to an immediate breach of the peace is legally preventable because of the immediate and lasting harm it can cause. If there were no way of punishing slander or libel, no man would be safe from false defamations which could easily cause loss of job and social standing. If there were no way for the state to protect itself, seditious utterances could precipitate riots and revolution. These examples of admittedly proper and necessary exceptions to the First Amendment might lead to the conclusion that the distinction between the kinds of speech it protects and the kinds it does not protect hinges on whether or not a given utterance will cause harm to others. In other words, a man could say anything whatever with impunity as long as he caused no injury to other persons; he would be subject to punishment only for saying anything which hurt others.

THE RIGHT TO DEFAME

This test, however, oversimplifies the problem. Indeed, it tends to abolish freedom of speech at the very times when it may be most necessary. One of the most effective ways of ascertaining whether or not genuine freedom of speech exists is to criticize those in power — if necessary, to criticize them harshly and vociferously. Is an office-holder believed to be dishonest, incompetent, ignorant, lazy, unprincipled? If so, there must be an opportunity for publicly exposing him. Even if the accusations are false, there should at least be an opportunity to bring them into the light and test them. It is significant that the first act of a dictator on seizing power is forcibly to suppress freedom of the opposition to criticize his regime. The right to censure is inseparable from a democratic system. In fact, one commentator goes so far as to assert that "the right to censure is the *right to defame*."[14]

Those who closely identify their interests with the *status quo* usually interpret any criticism of the *status quo* as an injury. History is replete with examples of ideas which when first introduced seemed to those in power intolerably wrong, radical, subversive, or impious — in short, dangerously injurious; yet in the course of time these same ideas have turned out to be none of these things and have come, indeed, to be accepted with perfect equanimity. These are the occasions, says Mill,

on which the men of one generation commit those dreadful mistakes which excite the astonishment and horror of posterity. It is among such that we find the instances memorable in history, when the arm of the law has been employed to root out the best men and the noblest doctrines; with deplorable success as to the men, though some of the doctrines have survived to be (as

[14] Louis G. Caldwell, "Freedom of Speech and Radio Broadcasting," *Annals of the American Academy of Political and Social Science* CLXXVII (January, 1935), p. 183.

if in mockery) invoked in defence of similar conduct towards those who dissent from *them,* or from their received interpretation.[15]

So we must conclude that it is not enough merely to tolerate those ideas
which at the moment seem safe and harmless and to suppress those which
seem dangerous and harmful. This theory of the First Amendment could
only defeat its real purpose. Freedom of speech is not an unloaded gun; it
must aim at securing results, and those results may well be painful to the
target. If a malicious or unwarranted injury occurs, laws such as those of
slander or libel provide redress; but this remedy must follow after, not come
before to prevent the very utterance; and if truth can be proved the injury
is warranted.

THE "CLEAR AND PRESENT DANGER" TEST

Two methods have been proposed for distinguishing forms of speech protected by the First Amendment from those not so protected. One is based
on the consequences of speech, the other on the content of speech. The
former theory, developed explicitly by Holmes and Brandeis in a series of
notable Supreme Court cases which followed the first World War, is the
"clear and present danger" principle. It first appeared in an opinion written
by Holmes in 1919. The case involved a wartime attempt to obstruct the
military draft by means of a circular intended to incite direct resistance.
Said Holmes:

> We admit that in many places and in ordinary times the defendants in saying
> all that was said in the circular would have been within their constitutional
> rights. But the character of every act depends upon the circumstances in
> which it is done . . . The question in every case is whether the words used
> are used in such circumstances and are of such a nature as to create a clear
> and present danger that they will bring about the substantive evils that
> Congress has a right to prevent. It is a question of proximity and degree.[16]

In subsequent cases Holmes and Brandeis elaborated on this principle, emphasizing repeatedly that in order to justify suppression a danger must be
both very apparent and very immediate. In 1927 Brandeis expressed it
this way:

> Those who won our independence by revolution were not cowards. They did
> not fear political change. They did not exalt order at the cost of liberty. To
> courageous, self-reliant men, with confidence in the power of free and fear-
> less reasoning applied through the processes of popular government, no
> danger flowing from speech can be deemed clear and present, *unless the
> incidence of the evil apprehended is so imminent that it may befall before
> there is opportunity for full discussion.* If there be time to expose through

[15] John Stuart Mill, *op. cit.,* p. 21.
[16] *Schenck* v. *U.S.,* 249 U.S. 47 at 52 (1919).

discussion the falsehood and fallacies, to avert the evil by the processes of education, the remedy to be applied is more speech, not enforced silence.[17]

The "clear and present danger" theory gained ground until after World War II. The security-conscious, fear-ridden atmosphere of the subsequent "cold war" period, however, was not hospitable to this interpretation of the First Amendment. Many Americans grew less confident of the outcome of full discussion, more apprehensive that evil would befall before discussion could take place. An important Supreme Court decision in 1951 seems to retreat from the Holmes-Brandeis position. In the Dennis case the Court upheld the Smith Anti-Subversive Act, under which Communist party leaders in this country have been jailed.[18] Justices Black and Douglas wrote vigorous dissents to the majority opinion. The Dennis case brought into sharp focus the outstanding political problem of our times — that of how Democracy can combat Communism without sacrificing the very things sought to be preserved. The freedom-of-speech issue in this case was whether the accused could be found guilty on the basis of things said which did not represent a clear and present danger to the country, as this phrase had been generally understood, but instead an indirect and relatively remote danger. Justice Douglas remarked that the tendency of the majority opinion was "to make freedom of speech turn not on *what is said,* but on the *intent* with which it is said. Once we start down that road we enter territory dangerous to the liberties of every citizen."[19] Justice Black said flatly: "No matter how it is worded, this is a virulent form of prior censorship of speech and press, which I believe the First Amendment forbids . . . the only way to affirm these convictions is to repudiate directly or indirectly the established 'clear and present danger' rule."[20] Justice Douglas used the occasion to restate the underlying libertarian concepts quoted earlier in this chapter.

It might be argued, in opposition to Justice Black, that the majority decision in the Dennis case represents not so much a repudiation of the clear-and-present-danger test as a new conception of how "clear" and how "present" the danger has to be. This, at any event, points up a theoretical weakness of the Holmes test: its susceptibility to varying interpretations. Moreover, it admits that under *some* circumstances *no* utterance would be exempt from government censorship, despite the unequivocal wording of the First Amendment. The purist position on freedom of speech, on the other hand, insists that there must be some areas which are inviolable, some forms of speech which, no matter what the circumstances, are inherently and *inalienably* free.

[17] *Whitney* v. *California,* 274 U.S. 357 at 377 (1927). Italics supplied.

[18] *Dennis* v. *U.S.,* 341 U.S. 494 (1951).

[19] *Ibid.,* p. 583.

[20] *Ibid.,* pp. 579-580. Justice Frankfurter, in a separate opinion concurring with the majority, gives a scholarly analysis of the origin and history of the clear-and-present-danger principle. The intensity of conviction and persuasiveness of the arguments on both sides of the issue presented in the Dennis case demonstrate the acuteness of this problem.

THE INALIENABLE RIGHT TO SPEAK

This position is skillfully upheld by Alexander Meiklejohn in a series of lectures on free speech in relation to self-government.[21] Meiklejohn makes a distinction between those forms of speech which serve purely personal and selfish purposes and those which serve the needs of a self-governing society. The former he included under the "liberty" mentioned in the Fifth Amendment rather than in the First. The Fifth Amendment prohibits the government from depriving any person of life, liberty, or property without due process of law (the "due process" clause); "liberty" in this context has been interpreted to include the liberties enumerated in the First Amendment. The Supreme Court has said:

> The difference between the two amendments is an emphatic one and readily apparent. Deprivation of a liberty not embraced by the First Amendment, as for example the liberty of contract, is qualified by the phrase "without due process of law"; but those liberties enumerated in the First Amendment are guaranteed without qualification, the object and effect of which is to put them in a category apart and make them *incapable of abridgement by any process of law.*[22]

Meiklejohn contends that speech which serves private ends can be legally censored in accordance with due process; only that speech which serves public ends qualifies for the protection of the First Amendment. The latter is the kind of utterance which has to do with the individual's functions *as a citizen.* When the First Amendment says "Congress shall make no law abridging the freedom of speech," it means that the government may pass a law abridging some forms of *speech* but the *freedom* implied cannot be abridged under any circumstances. In Meiklejohn's view there are two sets of civil liberties, only one of which is abridgeable by due process of law; the other is beyond the reach of the law, belonging to those "inalienable rights" of life, liberty, and the pursuit of happiness of which the Declaration of Independence speaks.

Like the Holmes doctrine, the doctrine of Meiklejohn stands or falls in practical applications on a question of definition. In the one case someone must say of a specific publication, speech, or other communication: how clear and how present is the danger it presents to the community? In the other case, given that same communication, someone must say: how positively can it be classified as belonging either to the area of private, alienable, permissive rights or to the area of public, inalienable, transcendent rights? Either test will work satisfactorily some of the time; neither will work to everyone's satisfaction all of the time.

[21] Alexander Meiklejohn, *Free Speech and Its Relation to Self Government* (New York: Harper & Bros., 1948).
[22] *Associated Press* v. *National Labor Relations Board,* 301 U.S. 103 at 135 (1937). Italics supplied.

That some forms of speech do not rise in importance to the level of deserving the protection of the First Amendment has been judicially noted. Advertising matter, for example, being intended entirely for the private profit of the advertiser, has been held to be a form of expression not entitled to protection from censorship under the First Amendment. An interesting case in point established that an advertiser using an illegal advertisement could not claim immunity through the device of printing the advertisement in conjunction with a discussion of a public issue which of itself would be protected by the First Amendment.[23]

WHAT IS INCLUDED IN "THE PRESS"?

On the other hand, this does not mean that the only communications protected by the First Amendment are serious discussions of social or political issues. The modern mass media have introduced means and types of expression not contemplated by the authors of the Constitution. At first there was doubt whether motion pictures, for example, should be considered a form of "the press" and therefore entitled to the protection of the First Amendment. In a significant decision made in 1915, the Supreme Court upheld an Ohio court in excluding motion pictures from the concept of "the press." The Ohio court held motion pictures to be mere "spectacles," saying:

> It cannot be put out of view that the exhibition of moving pictures is a business pure and simple, originated and conducted for profit, like other spectacles, not to be regarded, nor intended to be regarded by the Ohio constitution, we think, as part of the press of the country or as organs of public opinion.[24]

The opinion of the court is understandable, considering that it was written at a time when motion pictures were in their infancy. Significantly, however, this litigation coincided with the release of the first motion picture to deal with a social question, *The Birth of a Nation*.

The Mutual Film case left motion pictures vulnerable to government censorship. Attempts to enact federal film-censorship laws failed, but a number of states and many municipalities adopted local censorship measures, the earliest of which was the Pennsylvania law of 1908.[25] In 1952, however, in the *Miracle* case, the Supreme Court reversed its position of

---

[23] *Valentine v. Chrestensen*, 316 U.S. 52 (1942). The case involved a municipal ordinance against the distribution of advertising handbills in the streets. The Court pointed out that "if that evasion were successful, every merchant who desires to broadcast advertising leaflets in the streets need only append a civic appeal, or a moral platitude, to achieve immunity from the law's command" (p. 55).

[24] *Mutual Film Corp. v. Industrial Commission of Ohio*, 236 U.S. 230 at 244 (1915).

[25] An attempt under the Pennsylvania law to censor films shown over television was overthrown on the grounds that broadcasting is interstate commerce. The provision of the Communications Act forbidding censorship (Sec. 326) was interpreted as removing this subject from state jurisdiction. *Allen B. Dumont Laboratories v. Carroll*, 184 F. (2d) 153 (1950).

1915. *The Miracle* is an Italian film which many Catholics in this country found offensive (although the Catholic church did not ban the film in Italy). It was banned in New York under a statute permitting censorship by the state on the grounds of sacrilege. The Supreme Court ruled against that part of the statute, holding: "It is not the business of government in our nation to suppress real or imagined attacks upon a particular religious doctrine, whether they appear in publications, speeches, or motion pictures."[26] Although the *Miracle* case was decided on the narrow grounds of the adequacy of "sacrilege" as a basis for censorship and did not therefore rule out existing state and local censorship laws, its importance cannot be overestimated. It finally established that motion pictures are to be included under the term "press" in the First Amendment, thereby putting future attacks on film censorship laws on a sound constitutional footing. It was shortly followed by Supreme Court reversals of instances of censorship based on "immorality," "harmfulness," and "contribution to racial misunderstanding."[27]

By now it is generally established that all the modern media of communication are to be understood as "the press" as that term is used in the First Amendment. Moreover, the fact that mere entertainment or fiction can be instrumental in conveying ideas has been judicially noted:

> We do not accede to appellee's suggestion that the constitutional protection for a free press applies only to the exposition of ideas. The line between the informing and the entertaining is too elusive for the protection of that basic right. Everyone is familiar with instances of propaganda through fiction. What is one man's amusement, teaches another's doctrine. Though we can see nothing of any possible value to society in these magazines, they are as much entitled to the protection of free speech as the best of literature.[28]

As this decision indicates, a publication or utterance does not have to demonstrate an intrinsic value to society in order to qualify for the protection of the First Amendment. The same doctrine has been applied specifically to broadcasting: the "fact that radio and television 'giveaway' programs might have little possible value to society does not deprive the producers of such programs of their constitutional protections of free speech."[29] In other words, it is the *principle* of free speech, not merely particular instances of speech, which is protected.

[26] *Joseph Burstyn, Inc.* v. *Wilson, Commissioner of Education of New York*, 343 U.S. 495 at 505 (1952).

[27] *Commercial Pictures Corp.* v. *Regents of the University of the State of N.Y.* and *Superior Films* v. *Ohio Department of Education*, 346 U.S. 587 (1954). The films involved were *La Ronde, M*, and *Native Son*.

[28] *Winters* v. *New York*, 333 U.S. 507 at 510 (1948). Of course the realization that fiction can be used to disseminate political ideas is not new. In Shakespeare's day plays were suppressed for veiled political commentary. Soviet Russia has long since drafted not only fiction but even music and the graphic arts as propaganda media in the service of its revolutionary aims.

[29] *ABC* v. *U.S.*, 110 F. Supp. 374 at 375 (1953).

This doctrine results in a situation very familiar in our jurisprudence: not infrequently the guilty go free because we place primary emphasis on protection of the innocent. The presumption of innocence necessarily places all the devices of due process of law (the right of public trial, protection from self-incrimination, etc.) at the disposal of the guilty as well. To do otherwise, however, would require presumption of guilt. Similarly, to give the courts the power to prejudge the social value of communications would defeat the purpose of the First Amendment, which is to leave that judgment to each individual recipient of communications. In the Near case the Supreme Court upheld the right of publication of a scandalmongering Minneapolis newspaper which most people would probably agree was hardly deserving, aside from the question of principle, of the protection of the First Amendment. But the Court said that "the fact that the liberty of the press may be abused by miscreant purveyors of scandal does not make any the less necessary the immunity of the press from previous restraints in dealing with official misconduct," and quoted the well-known words of Madison:

> Some degree of abuse is inseparable from the proper use of everything, and in no instance is this more true than in that of the press. It has accordingly been decided by the practice of the States, that it is better to leave a few of its noxious branches to their luxurious growth, than by pruning them away, to injure the vigour of those yielding the proper fruits.[30]

The refusal of courts to pass qualitative judgment on the contents of communications (outside the recognized areas of illegal utterance such as obscenity) points up the weakness of the Meiklejohn theory of the First Amendment. Some forms of communications (like commercial advertising) are admittedly private in character and some (like speeches in a political campaign) are obviously public. But in the wide middle ground between such extremes it is often impossible to make clear-cut distinctions. Whoever set himself the task of making such distinctions — the consequence of which would be either to expose utterances to legal censorship or to protect them from such censorship — would himself become a censor.

BROADCASTING DISTINGUISHED FROM "THE PRESS"

Turning now to specific consideration of broadcasting in relation to the theory of the First Amendment, let us recall that this medium is explicitly brought within the ambit of the Amendment in the Communications Act itself (Chapter 21). According to the interpretation of the Amendment discussed in the foregoing pages, this fact should mean that the government

---

[30] *Near* v. *Minnesota*, 283 U.S. 697 at 718 (1931). The paper charged, among other things, that a "Jewish gangster was in control of gambling, bootlegging and racketeering in Minneapolis, and that law enforcing officers and agencies were not energetically performing their duties" (p. 704).

(i.e., the FCC) is positively forbidden to interfere with the freedom of broadcasters to say anything they like over their stations, with very few exceptions. These exceptions permit the government (as long as it does not act arbitrarily or capriciously) to prevent or to modify the broadcasting of (1) certain specific types of intrinsically injurious material such as obscenity; (2) materials presenting a clear and present danger to the state; and (3) materials of a purely private nature, i.e., advertising matter.

In actual practice, government regulation goes a long way beyond these limits. As the previous chapters have indicated, the FCC asserts the right to review the whole program service of stations and to take that service into consideration when deciding on license renewals. Moreover, the FCC sets up standards of public interest, convenience, and necessity with reference to specific types of programs and to the balance among the various types. The FCC's contention that it avoids censorship because it avoids prior restraint does not hold water, for the Supreme Court has pointed out that post-publication penalties can censor just as effectively as prior restraint. The threat of punishment (in this case, loss of license) can hamper freedom of speech almost as rigorously as the censor's blue pencil. "Immunity [from prior restraint] . . . cannot be deemed to exhaust the conception of the liberty guaranteed by state and federal constitutions."[31]

Government regulation of broadcast programming under the FRC and FCC, had it been applied to newspapers instead of broadcast stations, could never have been successfully defended in the courts. It would certainly have been found unconstitutional at many points. As Caldwell has suggested, broadcasters have lost their licenses for programs far less intemperate and scandalous than the articles in the Minneapolis newspaper which was granted a cloak of immunity by the Supreme Court in the Near case.[32]

Paradoxically, the courts have nevertheless consistently upheld the Commission's right to control various important aspects of broadcast programming. On the one hand broadcasting is recognized as a form of "the press" that is protected from government interference by the First Amendment; on the other hand the government interferes with the freedom of the broadcaster to say what he chooses. This contradiction becomes understandable only when it is recognized that the inclusion of broadcasting in the phrase "the press" cannot be taken quite literally. For want of another word "press" must do, but this does not mean that broadcasting really is exactly like the press. To be sure, broadcasters have long argued that as far as the First Amendment is concerned they are literally the same thing (see Chapter 20). The fact remains, however, that broadcasting is inherently different from the printed media and always will be; mere words cannot erase the differences.

These distinguishing characteristics of broadcasting have been discussed

[31] Ibid., pp. 714-715.
[32] Caldwell, op. cit., p. 203.

hitherto. It will suffice merely to recapitulate them here, together with their implications:

(1) Broadcasting uses the publicly-owned frequency spectrum (Chapter 21); therefore all the people are entitled to a broadcasting service.

(2) There is a limited number of channels available in the spectrum (Chapter 2); therefore not everyone who wants to can operate a broadcast station where he wants to, and some basis of choice among applicants is necessary.[33]

(3) The public makes a huge investment in the medium itself (Chapter 19); therefore the public as well as the licensee has a property interest to be considered.

(4) Broadcasting is a home medium; therefore it must observe certain restraints not expected of a medium which is not so intimately a part of home life.

(5) Broadcasting is more accessible to children than any other medium; therefore it must observe certain restraints not required of other media.[34]

THE ORIGIN OF THE CONCEPT OF THE PUBLIC INTEREST

Clearly, broadcasting has special social responsibility, not quite like that of any other medium. This responsibility is implied in the Communications Act by the phrase "public interest, convenience, and necessity." Neither the term nor the concept originated with broadcasting legislation, however. The term was borrowed from public-utilities law — a fact which explains the words "convenience" and "necessity." It is easy to find literal applications of these words in the public-utilities field: a water supply for fighting fires is a public necessity; considerations of public convenience may dictate the route a transportation line should take. In the field of broadcasting the phrase is taken as a whole for its general implications, but the word "interest" applies most aptly to the broadcasting situation.[35]

The concept of the public interest cropped up almost from the very be-

[33] It should be emphasized again that the contention that the shortage of channels has been alleviated since the Radio Act was written is a specious argument. It is true that many channel-assignments in the television table of allocations, for example, are not being put to use; that, however, is because their use is at present economically impracticable. The shortage of *desirable* channels persists, and, with the pressure on spectrum space from other services continuing to mount, will no doubt continue to persist.

[34] It should be noted that the libertarian concept of freedom of speech applies to the mentally adult: "It is, perhaps, hardly necessary to say that this doctrine is meant to apply to human beings in the maturity of their faculties. We are not speaking of children, or of young persons below the age which the law may fix as that of manhood or womanhood." Mill, *op. cit.*, p. 9.

[35] The phrase "public service" is equated with "public interest" by the FCC in its *Public Service Responsibility of Broadcast Licensees* (Washington: Government Printing Office, 1946). It discusses "four major issues currently involved in the application of the 'public interest' standard to program service policy" (p. 12).

ginning of discussions of the nature of broadcasting. At the First Radio Conference, in 1922, Herbert Hoover remarked that ". . . this large mass of subscribers need protection as to the noises which fill their instruments [i.e., radio receivers]."[36] Two years later Hoover testified at a Congressional hearing:

> Radio communication is not to be considered as merely a business carried on for private gain, for private advertisement, or for entertainment of the curious. It is a public concern impressed with the public trust and to be considered primarily from the standpoint of public interest to the same extent and upon the basis of the same general principles as our other public utilities.[37]

At the Fourth Conference, in 1925, the National Association of Broadcasters presented a resolution recommending that a law should be enacted making public "convenience and necessity" the basis of choice among competing applications; a Committee on Operating Regulations mentioned "public interest" as a guide.[38] At that conference Hoover remarked: "We can surely agree that no one can raise a cry of deprivation of free speech if he is compelled to prove that there is something more than naked commercial selfishness in his purpose."[39] The legislative history of the Radio Act of 1927 makes it apparent that Congress adopted essentially the same point of view. In answer to the NAB's later contention that the Commission was created merely to regulate technical aspects rather than program aspects of broadcasting, Senator Burton K. Wheeler replied:

> Well, I was on the committee that considered the matter at that time, and I do not agree with you that that was the entire idea, just to regulate the physical aspects of radio broadcasting stations. That was not the intention of the Senate. I went through all those hearings at that time, sat as a member of the committee, and it was not the intention of the committee, nor of the Senate, just to regulate these physical things.[40]

From the outset the FRC assumed that its supervisory duty definitely included consideration of program service. In its 1929 *Annual Report* the FRC said:

> Many programs are still of doubtful value. Offensive sales talks are too common. The attitude of the listening public will tend ultimately to cause the correction of such defects.

[36] Department of Commerce, "Minutes of Open Meeting of Department of Commerce Conference on Radiotelephony" (1922, mimeo.), p. 3.

[37] Testimony of Herbert Hoover in: House Merchant Marine and Fisheries Committee, *Hearings on H.R. 7357, To Regulate Radio Communication* (Washington: Government Printing Office, 1924), p. 10.

[38] Fourth National Radio Conference, *Proceedings and Recommendations for Regulation of Radio* (Washington: Government Printing Office, 1926), pp. 10, 23.

[39] *Ibid.*, p. 7.

[40] Testimony of Senator Burton K. Wheeler in: Senate Committee on Interstate Commerce, *Hearings on S. 814, To Amend the Communications Act of 1934* (Washington: Government Printing Office, 1944), p. 238.

The radio act specifies that the commission shall exercise no censorship over programs. Nevertheless, the kind of service rendered by a station must be a means of appraising its relative standing and must be considered by the commission in making assignments.[41]

JUDICIAL ACCEPTANCE OF THE CONCEPT OF THE PUBLIC INTEREST

This assumption — that Commission appraisal of programming is not a prohibited form of censorship — has been converted over the years to a judicially accepted fact. Some examples of the specific requirements of the Commission concerning programming which have been challenged as violations of the First Amendment but upheld in the courts will illustrate.

Requirement of balance between commercial and sustaining time. Bay State Beacon, Inc., lost in a competitive hearing for a Brockton, Mass., radio channel because, among other things, it proposed to devote less time to sustaining programs than the successful applicant. Bay State proposed to make 80 per cent of its time available for regular commercial sponsorship, 15 per cent for "institutional sponsorship" (public service agencies charged at half-rates), and only 5 per cent for sustaining programs.[42]

Requirement that licensee affirmatively seek out discussions of controversial public issues. Johnston Broadcasting Company and a rival applicant for a radio channel in Birmingham, Ala., were substantially equal except that Johnston did not show that "an affirmative effort" to encourage programs dealing with controversial issues would be made, whereas the opposing applicant provided for "positive action" on this score. Johnston lost primarily on this ground.[43] On appeal the Commission was sustained on this point (though reversed on other grounds). The court remarked that

> . . . in a comparative consideration, it is well recognized that comparative service to the listening public is the vital element, and programs are the essence of that service. So, while the Commission cannot prescribe any type of program (except for prohibitions against obscenity, profanity, etc.), it can make a comparison on the basis of public interest and, therefore, of public service. Such a comparison of proposals is not a form of censorship within the meaning of the statute.[44]

Requirement that programming be tailored to the local community. Allen T. Simmons (WADC) and another station each applied for a mutually exclusive change to a more desirable frequency and higher power. The Simmons application was rejected because it proposed to carry nothing but network programs from 8 A.M. to 11 P.M. This, said the Commission,

---

[41] FRC, *Third Annual Report* (Washington: Government Printing Office, 1929), p. 3.
[42] 12 FCC 567 at 569 (1948). Affirmed in a decision previously quoted, 171 F. (2d) 826 (1948).
[43] 12 FCC 517 at 524 (1947).
[44] *Johnston Broadcasting Co.* v. *FCC*, 175 F. (2d) 351 at 359 (1949).

. . . is not only tantamount to a voluntary abdication to the network of the duty and responsibility of a broadcast station licensee to determine for itself the nature and character of a program service which will best meet the needs of listeners in its area, but is an abdication to an organization which makes no pretense to scheduling its programs with the particular needs and desires of any one service area in mind.[45]

Requirement that certain network business practices affecting programs must be changed. This followed from the FCC's investigation of chain broadcasting, which has been previously cited in several different connections, notably in Chapter 15. The Supreme Court decision affirming the right of the FCC to regulate contracts between networks and affiliates is the leading case in point and therefore is quoted at length:

> The Regulations, even if valid in all other respects, must fall because they abridge, say the appellants, their right of free speech. If that be so, it would follow that every person whose application for a license to operate a station is denied by the Commission is thereby denied his constitutional right of free speech. Freedom of utterance is abridged to many who wish to use the limited facilities of radio. Unlike other modes of expression, radio inherently is not available to all. That is its unique characteristic, and that is why, unlike other modes of expression, it is subject to governmental regulation. Because it cannot be used by all, some who wish to use it must be denied. But Congress did not authorize the Commission to choose among applicants upon the basis of their political, economic or social views, or upon any other capricious basis. If it did, or if the Commission by these regulations proposed a choice among applicants upon some such basis, the issue before us would be wholly different. The question here is simply whether the Commission, by announcing that it will refuse licenses to persons who engage in specified network practices (a basis for choice which we hold is comprehended within the statutory criterion of "public interest"), is thereby denying such persons the constitutional right of free speech. The right of free speech does not include, however, the right to use the facilities of radio without a license. The licensing system established by Congress in the Communications Act of 1934 was a proper exercise of its power over commerce. The standard it provided for the licensing of stations was the "public interest, convenience or necessity." Denial of a station license on that ground, if valid under the Act, is not a denial of free speech.[46]

The Network case requires further comment, because in it the Supreme Court settled a number of important controversial questions about the regulation of broadcasting but in doing so raised a new problem — the significance of the phrase "the composition of the traffic" as used by the Court in its decision:

> The [Communications] Act itself establishes that the Commission's powers are not limited to the engineering and technical aspects of regulation of radio

[45] 12 FCC 1160 at 1173 (1947); affirmed 169 F. (2d) 670 (1948).
[46] *NBC v. U.S.*, 319 U.S. 190 at 226-227 (1943).

communication. Yet we are asked to regard the Commission as a kind of traffic officer, policing the wave lengths to prevent stations from interfering with each other. *But the Act does not restrict the Commission merely to supervision of the traffic. It puts upon the Commission the burden of determining the composition of that traffic.* The facilities of radio are not large enough to accommodate all who wish to use them. Methods must be devised for choosing from among the many who apply. And since Congress itself could not do this, it committed the task to the commission.[47]

The issue hinges on the meaning of the word "traffic." It has been widely interpreted to mean "programs," in which case the Court seems to be saying that the FCC has the responsibility of determining what programs shall be broadcast. This proposition so obviously conflicts with the First Amendment that it seems doubtful that such an interpretation can have been intended by the Supreme Court. A more acceptable interpretation is that "traffic," in the context, means "stations," or more accurately "licensees": the FCC has the responsibility not only of regulating the signals from stations to prevent interference but also of determining *who* shall be licensed. Commission Chairman Fly put it: "the traffic officer simply guides and controls the traffic which comes along on the highway, but the licensing authority determines what cars shall compose the traffic, or what cars shall be permitted upon the highways."[48] Giving the Commission the right to determine who shall be licensed admittedly means that it can exercise an indirect control over programs in general, but does not mean that it can directly censor programs. This type of indirect control seems to have been accepted by the courts as a legitimate form of governmental restriction of freedom of speech in broadcasting.

TWO CRUCIAL PUBLIC INTEREST CASES

In most cases, as we have already pointed out, when the Commission cites a given program or practice as contrary to the public interest, the station involved voluntarily changes the program or practice and continues in operation. Two cases in which the programs of stations were so extreme as to be directly responsible for loss of licenses may be regarded as particularly significant tests of the Commission's powers. In both these cases the Com-

[47] *Ibid.*, pp. 215-216. Italics supplied.
[48] Testimony of James L. Fly in: Senate Interstate Commerce Committee, *op. cit.*, p. 937. Fly analyzes the implications of the passage in detail, pp. 933-938. He accuses the industry of deliberately misinterpreting the phrase to becloud the issue. On the other hand, it must be confessed that the Court's analogy is singularly misleading, since the term "traffic" as used in the telecommunications field has long meant the *messages themselves*, not the channels over which they are sent, the transmitting facilities, or the licensees. Curiously enough, Herbert Hoover used the term "traffic policeman" with reference to radio regulation as early as 1925 (Fourth Radio Conference, *op. cit.*, p. 8); but the previously quoted opinions of Hoover demonstrate that he must have had in mind a concept similar to that expressed by the Court in the Network Case.

mision was upheld by the Court of Appeals, and the Supreme Court refused to review the lower court's decision.

KFKB in Milford, Kansas, was owned by one Dr. J. R. Brinkley, who won national notoriety for a "goat-gland" operation which purported to restore flagging vitality. The station was used to advertise Brinkley's hospital and certain drugs, which Brinkley packaged and retailed through hundreds of outlets. Three daily half-hours on the station were devoted to a "Medical Question Box" program on which Brinkley would diagnose the ailments of correspondents and prescribe his packaged remedies. Excerpts from actual broadcasts illustrate the technique:

> Here's one from Tillie. She says she had an operation, had some trouble 10 years ago. I think the operation was unnecessary, and it isn't very good sense to have an ovary removed with the expectation of motherhood resulting therefrom. My advice to you is to use Women's Tonic No. 50, 67, and 61. This combination will do for you what you desire if any combination will, after three months persistent use.
>
>   *   *   *   *   *
>
> Sunflower State, from Dresden, Kansas. Probably he has gallstones. No, I don't mean that, I mean kidney stones. My advice to you is to put him on Prescription No. 80 and 50 for men, also 64. I think that he will be a whole lot better. Also drink a lot of water.[49]

The last prescription is interesting in view of the fact that the drugs prescribed were medicaments for *both* kidney stones and gallstones. The highly unethical procedure of diagnosing ailments and prescribing medicines on the basis of letters from patients naturally embroiled Brinkley with the American Medical Association, which found that he possessed no recognized medical degree. The FRC refused to renew his license. In upholding the FRC the Court remarked: "In considering the question whether the public interest, convenience or necessity will be served by a renewal of appellant's license, the commission has merely exercised its undoubted right to take note of appellant's past conduct, which is not censorship."[50]

The second case involved an entirely different class of objectionable programs. KGEF was licensed to the Trinity Methodist Church, South, in Los Angeles, but in fact was owned by one Reverend Dr. Shuler. A large number of local residents protested the renewal of KGEF's license, with some 90 witnesses appearing at the FRC hearing. Shuler had used the station for highly personal attacks, and had twice been convicted of using it to obstruct the orderly administration of justice.

> On one occasion he announced over the radio that he had certain damaging information against a prominent unnamed man which, unless a contribution

---

[49] *KFKB Broadcasting Association, Inc.* v. *FRC*, 47 F. (2d) 670 at 671 (1931).

[50] *Ibid.*, p. 672. Brinkley almost succeeded in becoming Governor of Kansas, being one of the first to use radio effectively in a political campaign. His colorful history is related in Chapter 4 ("Early Medicine Men of Radio") of Francis Chase, Jr.'s, *Sound and Fury* (New York: Harper and Bros., 1942), pp. 56-79.

(presumably to the church) of a hundred dollars was forthcoming, he would disclose. As a result, he received contributions from several persons. He freely spoke of "pimps" and prostitutes. He alluded slightingly to the Jews as a race, and made frequent and bitter attacks on the Roman Catholic religion and its relations to government.[51]

In upholding the FRC's decision to deny renewal of the license, the Court said:

Appellant [Shuler] may continue to indulge his strictures upon the characters of men in public office. He may just as freely as ever criticize religious practices of which he does not approve. He may even indulge private malice or personal slander — subject, of course, to be required to answer for the abuse thereof — but he may not, as we think, demand, of right, the continued use of an instrumentality of commerce for such purposes, or any other, except in subordination to all reasonable rules and regulations Congress, acting through the Commission, may prescribe.[52]

The implication of these two cases, and of others which have been previously cited, makes it clear that the courts have adopted the views that (1) those who choose to become broadcast licensees thereby voluntarily subject themselves to certain restrictions of their freedom of utterance and (2) although the First Amendment applies to broadcasting, it does not apply to the same degree that it does to the medium of print. Some thoughtful commentators believe that these qualifications of the positive mandate of the First Amendment constitute a serious violation of the Constitution. Louis A. Caldwell has vigorously attacked the Commission and the court interpretations: "The phrase 'public interest, convenience or necessity' has proved to be the Achilles' heel by which a serious wound has been inflicted on the First Amendment to the Constitution."[53] Harry P. Warner holds that broadcasting and print can be treated precisely alike and that the only control over programs should be that of the listener who chooses or rejects.[54] These commentators would have allowed Brinkley and Shuler to continue operating their stations despite the character of their programs. Theirs is the traditional view of government regulation as the enemy of freedom. The contrary view, that of the government as the ally of freedom, will be developed in the next chapter.

[51] *Trinity Methodist Church, South v. FRC*, 62 F. (2d) 850 at 852 (1932).
[52] *Ibid.*, p. 853.
[53] Caldwell, *op. cit.*, p. 206.
[54] Harry P. Warner, *Radio and Television Law* (Rev. ed.; New York: Matthew Bender & Co., 1953), pp. 460-461.

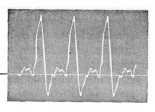

24

Regulation: Ally of Freedom

> The disposition of mankind, whether as rulers or
> as fellow-citizens, to impose their own opinions
> and inclinations as a rule of conduct on others, is
> so energetically supported by some of the best
> and by some of the worst feelings incident to
> human nature, that it is hardly ever kept under
> restraint by anything but want of power . . .
> — JOHN STUART MILL

Fear of the absolute power of government dominated the thinking of the statesmen who "brought forth a new nation" in 1776. All political experience had led to the conclusion that the state, unless held in check, inevitably uses its collective force to restrict the individual liberties of its citizens. The state's coercive resources of the law, the police, and the army prevail against the puny strength of the private individual. The Constitution, and in particular the Bill of Rights (the first ten amendments being essentially a part of the original document), arms the individual citizen with a counterbalancing power. The First Amendment therefore views the *government* as the source of power from which suppression of freedoms may be expected, and hence forbids *Congress* to abridge those freedoms.

Suppression, however, can likewise come from private, nongovernmental sources of power. Mill was particularly conscious of the "despotism of custom" and the intolerance of majorities. He realized that protection against the government is not enough:

There needs protection also against the tyranny of the prevailing opinion and feeling; against the tendency of society to impose, by other means than civil penalties, its own ideas and practices as rules of conduct on those who dissent from them; to fetter the development, and, if possible, prevent the formation, of any individuality not in harmony with its ways, and compels all characters to fashion themselves upon the model of its own. There is a limit to the legitimate interference of collective opinion with individual independence: and to find that limit, and maintain it against encroachment, is as in-

REGULATION: ALLY OF FREEDOM

dispensable to a good condition of human affairs, as protection against political despotism.[1]

Closely linked to the despotic potentialities of "prevailing opinion and feeling" is the coercive power of large economic concentrations. The technological revolution of the nineteenth century and its twentieth-century economic consequences have given rise to private domestic empires far more powerful than any conceivable by the eighteenth-century standards of the Constitution's authors. General Motors for example, with more than half a million employees and annual sales of nine billions of dollars, is larger and in ways more powerful than many a sovereign state or nation.

CURBING THE FREEDOM TO DESTROY FREEDOM

Economic developments which make such colossal business enterprises possible have exploded the eighteenth-century economic doctrine of *laissez-faire*. According to this doctrine, unrestricted economic competition will *automatically and inevitably* result in the greatest social good for the greatest number. It was based on conditions of communication, transportation, merchandising, purchasing power, and business organization which tended to keep domestic industries localized and to impose limits on growth. Under modern conditions of distribution and growth potential, competition can produce (and often has produced) results quite opposite to those predicted by the *laissez-faire* theory. The passage in 1890 of the Sherman Act, the first United States antitrust law, constituted formal recognition of the fact that under modern conditions an unregulated competitive economic system is not necessarily self-perpetuating. The purpose of the Sherman Act and of subsequent legislation in the field of business regulation is not to curb economic freedom but to preserve it. Government regulation of this kind seeks to limit the freedom to destroy freedom.

These developments in the economic realm have their parallel in the realm of the free trade in ideas. The two are, in fact, inseparable.[2] The great business corporations of today are more than businesses; they are social institutions. The following appraisal, coming as it does from an editorial in *Fortune* (the very symbol of modern corporate enterprise), has particular significance:

---

[1] John Stuart Mill, *On Liberty* (Oxford: Basil Blackwell, 1946), p. 4.
[2] The broadcasting industry has been correct in its contention (e.g., in the Network case) that control of the business affairs of broadcast stations is tantamount to control of programs. On the other hand, the industry has overlooked the corollary that FCC regulation of purely technical matters has a similar potential for influencing programming. Regulation of power, frequency, time of operation, and the like profoundly affects the economy, and hence the programming, of a station. Even such trivia as the requirement that mechanical reproductions be identified as such have economic effects. Broadly considered, regulation of technical and business matters is likewise regulation of program matters.

The ideas and philosophies of the men who are coming to power in the big corporations carry national interest and significance; they are true public characters, their policies and decisions often having more direct influence on the daily lives of our citizens than those of state governors or even Cabinet officers.[3]

If private citizens, unsupported by such official sanctions as police power, can exert this influence, it is evident that government is not the only potential threat to individual freedoms.

With this growth of private economic and social sources of power, the government has taken on a new role. In the eighteenth century the government was regarded negatively, as possessing a dangerous degree of power which must be curbed to preserve the individual liberties of its citizens. In the twentieth century the government is regarded as no less dangerously powerful and in need of restraint, but it is also regarded more positively, as a means of protecting its citizens from private sources of potentially oppressive power. The government's role is thus a dual one, as both the enemy and the ally of individual freedoms.

This principle is hardly open to debate, having become deeply imbedded in our law and national policy. Antitrust laws, fair-trade laws, labor laws, and the Communications Act are but a few examples. On the other hand, lively debate continues on the subject of the *degree* to which the government should emphasize the paternal aspect of its dual role. Certainly there is danger to individual freedoms at either extreme; there is room for wide differences of opinion about where the balance should be struck.

It will have been recognized by now that the principle we have been discussing is an aspect of the "social responsibility" theory, mentioned in Chapter 20. Those who manage the great corporations and the kinds of business which have peculiar social importance, such as communications, have a special responsibility to society. "Modern inventions have enormously extended the power of the few over the many. There is no safety for our society without a comparable extension of the sense of responsibility."[4]

In some measure the law defines private responsibility and makes its acceptance mandatory. In larger measure, unless the government is to assume more authority than is safe in a free society, responsibility must be privately defined and voluntarily accepted. It has been accepted — probably more fully than many critics are willing to admit — by individual businessmen. Unfortunately, American industry has been particularly inept in stating its own case.[5]

Broadcasting offers perhaps the best example of the type of business to

---

[3] "Fortune's Wheel," *Fortune* (June, 1953), p. 3. © *Time*, Inc.

[4] Charles A. Siepmann, "Scramble for Air Time," *The Nation* CLXXVIII (15 May 1954), p. 423.

[5] Cf.: William H. Whyte, Jr., *Is Anybody Listening? How and Why U.S. Business Fumbles When It Talks with Human Beings* (New York: Simon and Schuster, Inc., 1952).

which the social-responsibility concept applies. Here is a business that is profoundly involved in considerations of public interest. In the first place, its function as a public communications medium gives it a special significance in a democracy (see Justice Douglas's summary of the political role of free communication, quoted in the previous chapter). In the second place, it has the unique physical, economic, social, and legal characteristics previously described. The government, through the FCC, exercises a supervisory control, defining the nature of the public interest involved and to some extent compelling fulfilment of the responsibilities implied. Nevertheless, the major responsibility remains that of the broadcaster himself, freely and conscientiously accepted. Mere enforcement of rules, mere mechanical compliance with the letter of the law, cannot ensure socially responsible use of broadcast facilities; nothing short of intelligent understanding and discerning application of the spirit of the law can bring about the desired result.

THE LETTER v. THE SPIRIT OF THE FIRST AMENDMENT

We return now to the paradox mentioned at the close of the previous chapter — the fact that the courts have upheld the FCC's imposition of program regulations which appear to be clear violations of the First Amendment, which (in other contexts) has been so jealously guarded by those same courts. These regulations have the purpose of enabling the realization of the objectives of the First Amendment. They curb some freedoms in order to enlarge others. They violate the spirit of the First Amendment to the same extent that anti-monopoly laws violate the spirit of a free, competitive economic system. We need not argue, for the moment, the question whether the particular techniques, standards, or judgments of the FCC have been the best possible ones for the purpose; at this point let us consider the principle rather than the specific applications.

What are the objectives of the First Amendment? They do not include, we may surely presume, giving license to worthless communications, such as those involved in the Near case; the abuses incidental to the use of a freedom are not its goal. Nor do they include the use of the letter of the law to evade compliance with the spirit of the law. That the First Amendment is to be interpreted in terms of its spirit was established by the Supreme Court in a question involving alleged conflict between the First Amendment and the antimonopoly laws. The Associated Press contended that the finding that certain of its business practices were monopolistic amounted to interference by the government with the freedom of the press. But the Court pointed out that the purpose of the First Amendment is to secure "the widest possible dissemination of information from diverse and antagonistic sources." Therefore "freedom of the press from government interference under the First Amendment *does not sanction repression of that freedom by private interests.*"[6] In this decision the Supreme Court implicitly recognizes the social-responsibility theory.

Bearing in mind the Court's definition of the purpose of the First Amendment — to secure "the widest possible dissemination of information from diverse and antagonistic sources" — let us examine some of the ways in which this purpose might be frustrated by private (as contrasted with governmental) power. These fall essentially into two groups of practices: (1) monopolistic practices and (2) unfair practices. Either of these could reduce the diversity of sources of information. Monopolistic factors in broadcasting include (1) control over patents, (2) possession of superior facilities (frequency, power, location, etc.), (3) multiple ownership (either of broadcasting facilities or of broadcasting facilities in combination with those of other mass media), and (4) surrender by the individual licensee of control of his facilities to some central agency such as a program-syndication organization.

BIGNESS IN BUSINESS

Monopoly means approximately exclusive possession or control, i.e., the relative absence of competition. It is a desirable condition in some fields, such as utilities or common carriers, in which competition would not be in the public interest because economically unsound. To duplicate the vast communications network of AT&T, for example, would be colossally wasteful, even if economically feasible. Wherever a legal monopoly such as that of AT&T exists, it is stringently regulated in order to prevent abuse of the favored position of the monopolist. Regulation supplies the checks which otherwise would be supplied by competition.

In competitive fields monopolies or quasi-monopolies can take many forms. They can be local or regional as well as national; they can be achieved by means of patent licensing, interlocking directorates, trade association agreements, mergers, cutthroat competition, discriminatory legislation, and many other devices. The line between legally preventable monopoly and non-monopoly is hard to define. Does mere size and "unexerted power" constitute monopoly? How few firms may control a field before it begins to be monopolized? Are conditions which might eventually lead to monopoly a sufficient cause for taking antimonopoly action now?

By the same token, competition has many facets: in broadcasting there is competition between stations, between networks, between network-stations and non-network stations, between radio and television, between radio-television and newspapers, and so on. The individual aligns himself with different groups at different times, depending upon the nature of the interest momentarily involved. Individual stations which under most circumstances are strongly competitive may partially forego competition to protect them-

---

[6] *Associated Press* v. *U.S.*, 326 U.S. 1 at 20 (1945). Italics supplied. The AP contended that it had the right to grant local monopolies on its news wire service.

selves as a group against another medium or against government interference. It is characteristic of American society that groupings of interest are rather fluid. Instead of monolithic interest-groups, like the three estates of pre-revolutionary France, we tend to form many temporary or partial alliances. This means more give-and-take, better adaptability, and less danger of serious internal strife.

Americans are devoted to the idea of competition. Ours is a free-enterprise system, and an enduring American symbol is the poor boy who makes good, the inventor who rises from humble beginnings to the heights of industrial power. Our understanding of the economic role of bigness in business and our legal criteria for control of monopoly are still emergent. The problem is complicated by emotionalism. "The belief that Bigness is, in itself, something evil is a theme that runs through the political thinking of this country."[7] The cry of "monopoly" has been a popular political slogan, but a crudely simplified antithesis between "big business" and "free enterprise" confuses the issue. An ironic commentary on the discrepancy between the facts of modern business technology and the theory of economic legislation was provided in 1952 when one branch of the government turned to DuPont as the only private firm with the colossal resources needed for the development of the H-bomb at the very moment that another branch of the government was suing DuPont for being too big.

Bigness is a contemporary economic necessity. The basic technology of modern commercial broadcasting, for instance, is essentially the product of big business; only the corporate giants like RCA and AT&T have the resources for the commercial development of a product like television. On the other hand, the phenomenal growth of broadcasting has been materially aided by smaller manufacturers who have developed inexpensive receivers and vigorous merchandising methods. In justification of the tremendous concentration of power in such corporations as General Motors, AT&T, RCA, General Electric, and Westinghouse it must be considered first that their very size forces them to take the public interest into consideration. The robber-baron type of individualistic, public-be-damned industrial leader is a thing of the past. The modern corporate executive has to think in terms of public opinion, and increasingly the emphasis among such business leaders is on a socially responsible outlook. Secondly, the corporate giant has developed new kinds of competition. For example, intracorporate rivalry can sometimes be as intense as it would be if the sub-units were actually under separate ownership. Another example is high-level competition between interchangeable products, such as soap and detergents, coal and petroleum, steel and lighter alloys.[8] Further, the large manufacturers find it economical to job out the manufacture of many components to small specialty firms.

---

[7] David E. Lilienthal, *Big Business: A New Era* (New York: Harper & Bros., 1935), p. 38.

[8] Cf. "How Big is Too Big," *Time* (25 October 1954), p. 80.

Moreover, the economic advantages are not all on the side of bigness. An industrial giant is hampered by its own bureaucratic structure. Smaller, nimbler competitors can often respond more quickly to public demand and technological change. A case in point is the great success of smaller radio and television manufacturers, such as Philco and Zenith, in the face of RCA's advantages of patent strength, research facilities, and sheer size. Even in the realm of invention it took an independent like de Forest to conceive the audion and another like Armstrong to develop FM.

We have dealt at some length with the general question of bigness in industry and its relation to monopoly in order to provide a context in which to discuss the existence and the regulation of monopolistic tendencies in broadcasting. The economy of broadcasting, no less than that of other industries, favors the development of large economic units.[9] Bigness, no less in broadcasting than in other industries, has its uses. However, it is more important also to ensure the viability of small local firms in the broadcasting industry than in industries not similarly charged with public responsibility. There is no social detriment in the standardization of consumer goods, but a similar regimentation of ideas would be fatal to a democratic political system. Whether cigarettes are manufactured locally or shipped in from the other end of the country makes no difference, since there is no particular need for a local flavor in tobacco; but there is need for local flavor in ideas, opinions, and information. It follows that concentration of ownership may be more socially desirable in the manufacture of such items as cigarettes, automobiles, or steel than in the operation of the mass-communication media. Because of the strategic social importance of mass communication the question of monopoly in this field is peculiarly sensitive.

MONOPOLISTIC PRACTICES IN BROADCASTING

Having decided in 1920 not to keep radio a government monopoly, Congress was almost immediately faced with the possibility that it would become a private monopoly (Chapter 7). The 1923 Federal Trade Commission's report on the radio industry[10] indicated that a monopolistic patent situation existed. This report directly influenced Congress to include antimonopoly provisions in all subsequent radio legislation. Antitrust suits resulted eventually in the outlawing of various coercive practices by which the Radio Group capitalized on its patent monopoly, as well as in the release of patents to rival manufacturers on reasonable royalty terms. Although RCA

[9] Economic stability in a national network, for example, seems to require both size and diversification. NBC is one of a number of corporations under RCA; CBS has branched out into manufacturing and related fields through the acquisition of subsidiaries; ABC, after operating at a loss for a time, merged with Paramount Theatres; MBS is now controlled by one of a dozen subsidiaries of General Tire and Rubber Company.

[10] FTC, *Report on the Radio Industry* (Washington: Government Printing Office, 1924).

still retains control of the majority of the important patents necessary for the manufacture of modern receivers, there is little expectation that this power will be used in restraint of trade. Both the anti-monopoly laws and the changing philosophy of corporate leadership must be credited with creating this optimistic outlook.

The monopolistic potentialities of unusually favorable broadcast facilities were demonstrated in 1934 when the FRC granted WLW, Cincinnati, a Special Temporary Authorization to operate at 500,000 watts, ten times the prevailing maximum. Hitherto the power maximum had been subject to technological limitations. When the FRC began, about 30,000 watts was the maximum power obtainable; 50,000 had been reached by 1931. Next "super-power" of 500,000 watts became feasible. The advantage over competitive stations which the tenfold increase gave WLW is evidenced by the fact that, according to an FCC survey, WLW became the station of first choice among the listeners of thirteen states.[11] The outcry from other stations against WLW's power-advantage resulted in a "sense of the Senate" resolution to the effect that 50,000 watts should be the maximum power permitted.[12] Accordingly WLW, despite its protests, was reduced to 50,000 watts, which has since remained the maximum power permitted AM stations in the United States.

A similar problem, but one not so easily disposed of, is that of the AM clear channels. A Senate subcommittee has called the clear-channel problem "the most important question from a policy standpoint in the field of AM radio broadcasting."[13] It will be recalled (Chapter 2) that twenty-four of the original fifty-odd AM clear channels, known as 1-A channels, have been kept free of nighttime competition. Assignment to one of these channels confers a complete nighttime monopoly of the channel — a competitive advantage of incalculable worth. The stations on these twenty-four favored channels have long argued against even daytime assignments on their frequencies both because such assignments compromise the clear-channel theory in principle and also because of sky-wave interference, which was not anticipated when daytime-only stations were first assigned to the 1-A channels. On the other hand, interests outside the clear-channel group of stations argue for further breakdown of the clear channels to achieve more equitable distribution of facilities. The Clear Channel Group's case rests on the need of clear channels to serve rural populations.[14] The fact remains, however, that the stations on the twenty-four 1-A channels possess an eco-

[11] FCC, *Second Annual Report* (Washington: Government Printing Office, 1936), p. 61.

[12] S. Res. 294, 75th Cong. (13 June 1938).

[13] Senate Committee on Interstate and Foreign Commerce Subcommittee, *Communications Study Interim Report* (Washington: Government Printing Office, 1949), p. 5. The Subcommittee criticized the FCC for not going further in "duplicating" the 1-A clear channels (p. 6).

[14] Cf.: Senate Committee on Foreign Relations Subcommittee, *Hearings on North American Regional Broadcasting Agreement* (Washington: Government Printing Office, 1953). The NARBA is closely linked with the clear-channel problem because it affects both power limits and channel assignments.

nomic advantage which is hard to justify to the two-thousand-odd other AM stations not so favorably situated in terms of facilities. It appears to be only a question of time before the 1-A channels are "duplicated" just as are the rest of the clear channels.

A related monopoly problem is that of multiple station ownership. It will be recalled (Chapter 15) that the Chain Broadcasting Regulations introduced the ruling that a network organization might not operate dual networks in such a manner as to provide affiliation with two of the available stations in a given service area. At the same time the "duopoly" rule forbade ownership of more than one station serving the same area; thirty-three instances of such dual ownership existed at the time. These rules affecting diversification of ownership or program sources in a given service area were not seriously questioned, once the pain of separation subsided, for it can hardly be denied that control over two of the several stations in an area gives an unfair competitive advantage.

More debatable are rules establishing the maximum number of non-overlapping stations that may function under common ownership. There can be no doubt that multiple ownership has powerful arguments in its favor. As in other businesses, large size has economic advantages; it puts the owner in a good bargaining position in relation to networks and other program sources, permits saving through quantity buying of supplies, makes it feasible to employ high-caliber supervisory personnel, and so on. All this can result (though not automatically) in a better program service from all of the stations under common ownership than any one of them could render independently.

On the other hand, to allow a single owner to accumulate an unlimited number of stations would invite monopoly. The problem is where and how to draw the line. The Commission has chosen to draw it in terms of number of stations. Currently the limit is seven stations in each of the three services, AM, FM, and television. Television ownership, however, is limited to a maximum of five VHF stations, the remaining two being UHF.[15] This, however, is a highly arbitrary, essentially meaningless criterion. The owner of seven Class IV (250-watt) small-market AM stations would not have a fraction of the influence exerted by the owner of a single Class 1-A (50,000-watt) station. The same contrast applies to seven UHF television stations in small markets as against a single VHF station in a major metropolitan market. Doubt has been cast on the legality of the FCC's multiple-ownership rules, but on the basis of a procedural technicality rather than on the basis of their logic.[16]

[15] Cf. "Lamentable Limitation," *Broadcasting-Telecasting* (7 December 1953), p. 138.
[16] *Storer Broadcasting Co.* v. *U.S.*, 220 F. (2d) 204 (1955). The basis of the reversal is the fact that the multiple-ownership rules can result in denial of an application without a hearing, whereas the Communications Act requires a hearing before denial, Sec. 309 (a) and (b). The decision is significant in that it is "the first time within recollection" that the Court of Appeals has ruled against specific language in the FCC's rules. Cf. "Multiple Rule Goes Out the Window," *Broadcasting-Telecasting* (28 February 1955), p. 118. The FCC appealed the decision to the Supreme Court.

CROSS-CHANNEL AFFILIATION

"Cross-channel affiliation," another aspect of multiple ownership, involves control of outlets in more than one medium by a single owner. This is one of the most controversial and involved problems in current broadcasting regulation.[17] The problem arises frequently because of the natural tendency of newspapers to become broadcast licensees.[18] On the one hand, newspapers are the most direct competitors of broadcast stations, and hence every newspaper–broadcasting combination necessarily reduces potential competition among the media. On the other hand, newspaper owners are often particularly well fitted to operate stations because of their experience, resources, and knowledge of the community to be served. In 1941 the Commission conducted the "Newspaper-Radio Inquiry" to determine the extent to which common ownership of press and broadcasting facilities might be reducing competition. It found that in over ninety communities the only local newspaper owned the only local radio station and that 150 stations were related to newspaper chains.[19] The inquiry did not result in the adoption of specific rules, but the Commission does take cross-channel associations and the prior conduct of newspaper applicants into consideration on a case-to-case basis in competitive hearings. Two appealed cases are of particular significance:

The Scripps Howard case is the leading case on the diversification issue. In a mutually exclusive hearing the FCC found against Scripps Howard Radio, Inc., although it had some points of superiority to the successful applicant. The fact that greater diversification of ownership of the mass media would result from denying the Scripps Howard application was one of the major bases of the decision. The Court of Appeals adverted to the Associated Press case in its opinion supporting the FCC, recalling that the Supreme Court had emphasized there that "the widest possible dissemination of information from diverse and antagonistic sources" is the objective of the First Amendment. The court concluded:

> In considering the public interest the Commission is well within the law when, in choosing between two applications, it attaches significance to the fact that one, in contrast with the other, is disassociated from existing media of mass communication in the area affected.[20]

In the *Mansfield Journal* case the Commission was supported in its use of evidence of unfair competitive practices by a newspaper as a basis for the

[17] Cf.: Earl B. Abrams, "Diversification: Its Case History," *Broadcasting-Telecasting* (1 November 1954), pp. 86-92.

[18] As of 1954, 30 per cent of the commercial television stations in operation were connected with newspapers.

[19] FCC, *Seventh Annual Report* (Washington: Government Printing Office, 1941), p. 26.

[20] *Scripps Howard Radio, Inc.* v. *FCC*, 189 F. (2d) 677 at 683 (1951). The Supreme Court refused to review the decision, 342 U.S. 830 (1951).

denial of an application. The Court of Appeals found that the FCC need not wait for an applicant to be found technically guilty of violating anti-trust laws but could use its own judgment on the basis of the evidence presented.

> . . . whether Mansfield's competitive practices were legal or illegal, in the strict sense, is not conclusive here. Monopoly in the mass communication of news and advertising is contrary to the public interest, even if not in terms proscribed by the anti-trust laws.

> ❋   ❋   ❋   ❋   ❋

> The ultimate matter in question was not whether Mansfield was innocent or guilty, but whether qualified or unqualified and the appellant's conduct was considered only in that regard . . . The Commission did not deny the license merely because the newspaper refused to print certain items or because it refused to serve certain advertisers, but rather because the Commission concluded that those practices were followed for the purpose of suppressing competition. Similarly, it would appear that Mansfield was not denied a license because it was a newspaper, but because it used its position as sole newspaper in the community to achieve a monopoly in advertising and news dissemination. Such a denial does not constitute a violation of the First Amendment.[21]

The Court further extended the principle established in the Associated Press case — that the First Amendment should be interpreted according to its spirit:

> Just as the First Amendment does not provide the press with immunity from the commands of the anti-trust laws, so a newspaper, when it stands as an applicant for a radio license, may not rely on the First Amendment to compel the Federal Communications Commission to disregard public interest in considering its application.[22]

Finally, monopolistic restraints can arise from licensees' surrender of individual autonomy to some central organization. As a matter of fact, all network affiliates make such a surrender to their network in some degree. It would be impossible for the network to supply — or for the affiliate to review — all program material in advance. By and large, the affiliate accepts the network's offerings on faith, sight unseen. The network's past conduct is sufficiently reliable indication of its practice to make this procedure perfectly acceptable to the affiliate. In the interest of consolidating its competitive position, however, the network may be inclined to encroach further and further upon the autonomy of its affiliates until they come completely under network domination. This was the trend which the FCC perceived in the network practices revealed by its chain-broadcasting investigation (Chapter 15).[23] The resulting regulations governing network-

21 *Mansfield Journal Co.* v. *FCC*, 180 F. (2d) 28 at 33 and 35 (1950).
22 *Ibid.*, p. 35.
23 Cf.: FCC, *Report on Chain Broadcasting* (Washington: Government Printing Office, 1941).

affiliate contracts are designed to preserve the autonomy of the affiliate and to encourage competition among networks.

UNFAIR PRACTICES

The second kind of broadcasting practices which may tend to frustrate the purposes of the First Amendment come under the general heading of "unfairness." The typical examples of unfairness are: (1) distortion of factual (news) information through slanting, suppression, and the like; (2) emasculation of the medium through avoidance of serious program content and submission to prevailing opinion or feeling; (3) one-sided presentation of controversial matters; and (4) economic exploitation of the public.

Of these practices the first occurs infrequently. Even the least conscientious and responsible broadcaster is likely to have some sense of the gravity of tampering with the news. The one conspicuous case of alleged tampering ended inconclusively with the death of the accused licensee.[24]

Emasculation of the medium through avoidance of serious content, such as discussions of controversial issues, on the other hand, is an ever-present likelihood. In fact, it would have been easy for broadcasting as a whole to become an almost purely escapist entertainment medium, after the pattern of the entertainment motion-picture industry. Advertisers have an understandable aversion to giving offense; therefore commercial programs usually avoid material which might cause controversy, and advertisers are usually hypersensitive to the views of pressure groups (Chapter 17). Similarly, most licensees have an understandable desire to shun program material that is likely to invite criticism from socially, economically, and politically influential groups or individuals in their community. These motivations tend to reduce programs to harmless banalities, inhibiting full use of the broadcasting medium for the exchange of information and opinion on serious issues. Broadcasting, in short, is highly susceptible to the "tyranny of the prevailing opinion and feeling" of which Mill spoke.

The surrender of broadcasting to these pressures is treated by the FCC as a kind of unfairness, in the sense that it is unfair to the public to deny it the benefit of broadcasting as a forum for the exchange of opinion on the vital issues of the day:

> The problems involved in making time available for the discussion of public issues are admittedly complex. Any vigorous presentation of a point of view will of necessity annoy or offend at least some listeners. There may be a

---

[24] The Richards case, involving the license of three stations in Detroit, Cleveland, and Los Angeles. Richards, the licensee, was accused of ordering newscasters on his stations to slant the news in keeping with his own prejudices. Hearings on the charges occupied seven months, 280 witnesses were heard, and the transcript of the record ran into many thousands of pages. The hearing is said to have cost Richards upwards of a million dollars. On Richards' death in 1951 the FCC dropped the charges. Cf. "Richards' Renewals," *Broadcasting-Telecasting* (3 December 1951), pp. 23, 104-105.

temptation, accordingly, for broadcasters to avoid as much as possible any discussion over their stations, and to limit their broadcasts to entertainment programs which offend no one.

To operate in this manner, obviously, is to thwart the effectiveness of broadcasting in a democracy.

❋   ❋   ❋   ❋   ❋

The carrying of any particular public discussion, of course, is a problem for the individual broadcaster. But the public interest clearly requires that an adequate amount of time be made available for the discussion of public issues. . . .[25]

At one time the NAB recommended a policy of refusing to sell time for solicitation of memberships, discussion of controversial subjects (including race, religion, politics), or a number of other emotionally-charged topics. On its face this policy leaves room, of course, for the giving of free time for such subjects; in practice, however, the policy appears to have been used as a device for enabling the licensee to screen out program material which might annoy advertisers or create uncomfortable public relations for the station. The policy was directly challenged by the UAW-CIO when it petitioned the FCC not to renew the license of WHKC, Columbus, alleging discrimination and censorship. The FCC in effect ruled out the NAB policy, saying that it is the

> duty of each station licensee to be sensitive to the problems of public concern in the community and to make sufficient time available, on a nondiscriminatory basis, for full discussion thereof, without any type of censorship which would undertake to impose the views of the licensee upon the material to be broadcast . . . the operation of any station under the extreme principles that no time shall be sold for the discussion of controversial public issues and that only charitable organizations and certain commercial interests may solicit memberships is inconsistent with the concept of public interest established by the Communications Act as the criterion of radio regulations.[26]

Two points are worth noting here. First, the FCC extends the principle of the Associated Press case previously discussed: literally, the First Amendment forbids censorship by the government, not by private agents. In fact, broadcast licensees must have the right to censor in order to fulfill their duty to maintain control over programs.[27] But where communications

---

[25] FCC, *Public Service Responsibility of Broadcast Licensees* (Washington: Government Printing Office, 1946), p. 40.

[26] *In re United Broadcasting Co.* (*WHKC*), 10 FCC 515 at 517-518 (1945). The station agreed to modify the objectionable policy and the petition was accordingly dropped.

[27] This point was made in a case in which a clergyman complained to the FCC because station WPEN cancelled a religious program. Supporting the FCC's rejection of the complaint, the Court of Appeals pointed out that "the First Amendment was intended to operate as a limitation to the actions of Congress and of the federal government. The [station] is not an instrumentality of the federal government but a privately owned corporation. The plaintiffs seek to endow WPEN with the quality of an agency of the federal government and endeavor to employ a kind of 'trustee-of-public interest' doctrine to that end." *McIntire* v. *Wm. Penn Broadcasting Co.*, 151 F. (2d) 597 at 601 (1945).

involving the public aspect of speech (as Meiklejohn defined it) are concerned, censorship even by a private agency violates the spirit of the First Amendment. Secondly, it should be noted that the FCC here adopts the positive role of government in ensuring that the opportunity for the exercise of freedom of speech exists; in doing so it curbs the freedom of the licensee to inhibit that freedom by excluding certain material from his facilities on the basis of his own personal fears, prejudices, or indifference.

ACCESS TO THE MEANS OF EXPRESSION

This position reflects an important aspect of the social-responsibility theory, which holds that those who control the means of communication have a responsibility to make them available to others:

> . . . since freedom is for action, and action is for an end, the positive kernel of freedom lies in the ability to achieve the end; to be free means to be free *for* some accomplishment. This implies *command of the means* to achieve the end.[28]

To put it in the FCC's words, "freedom of speech can be as effectively denied by denying access to the public means of making expression effective — whether public streets, parks, meeting halls, or the radio — as by legal restraints or punishment of the speaker."[29] Against this view it may be argued that no one forces a newspaper publisher to open his editorial columns to those who do not happen to have a newspaper at their disposal as a personal organ of expression. It should be noted, however, that the FCC here refers to *public* means of expression, placing broadcasting in the same context as public streets and parks. In other words, we arrive once more at a reminder that broadcasting, however much it may be comparable to the press in some ways, differs significantly in others — in this instance, in that ownership of the channels is public.

Access to broadcasting facilities cannot be extended to everyone. A nice question is therefore raised concerning which subjects and persons shall be granted access and which denied. This question arose in the Scott case. Scott, an atheist, petitioned the FCC not to renew the licenses of three California stations, KQW, KPO, and KFRC, because they had refused to give him an opportunity to reply to attacks on atheism contained in religious programs. The Commission dismissed Scott's petition, leaving the burden of responsibility on the stations. In doing so, however, the Commission apparently feared that its decision might be misinterpreted as giving stations *carte blanche* to prevent the broadcasting of all minority points of view. "If freedom of speech is to have meaning," the FCC pointed out, "it cannot be predicated on the mere popularity or public acceptance of the

[28] William Ernest Hocking, *Freedom of the Press: A Framework of Principle* (Chicago: University of Chicago Press, 1947), p. 54.
[29] *In re Robert Harold Scott*, 11 FCC 372 at 374 (1946). Essentially the same position is adopted in the Mayflower case, discussed in Chapter 22.

ideas sought to be advanced. It must be extended as readily to ideas which we disapprove or abhor as to ideas which we approve."[30] At the same time the Commission recognized the quandary in which the licensee finds himself:

> In making a selection with fairness, the licensee must, of course, consider the extent of the interest of the people in his service area in a particular subject to be discussed, as well as the qualifications of the person selected to discuss it. Every idea does not rise to the dignity of a "public controversy," and every organization, regardless of membership or the seriousness of its purpose, is not per se entitled to time on the air. But an organization or idea may be projected into the realm of controversy by virtue of being attacked. The holders of a belief should not be denied the right to answer attacks upon them or their belief solely because they are few in number.[31]

The Commission's reasoning in this opinion clearly echoes Mill. Nevertheless, the FCC retreats somewhat from Mill's militant individualism. If in fact "all mankind minus one were of one opinion," in such a case the majority must surely prevail as far as broadcasting is concerned; the lone dissident could not reasonably expect to use broadcasting facilities to argue his case. Again we encounter a circumstance peculiar to broadcasting which requires special consideration. Broadcasting is a mass medium, and as such necessarily deals in program material adapted to the needs and interests of *relatively* large numbers of people (though not necessarily the majority). Mill's lonely intransigent might talk on a street corner, circulate pamphlets, make a documentary film, or use many other private avenues of expression; but he could not reasonably assert a right to use the public facilities of broadcasting.

"EQUAL OPPORTUNITIES"

Section 315 of the Communications Act, it will be recalled, requires that candidates for public office be afforded "equal opportunities" at rates no higher than those charged to others for comparable time periods. This apparently straightforward and simple requirement leads to unexpected complications. The FCC has found it necessary to issue an advisory bulletin answering more than forty questions which the application of these simple rules has raised.[32]

---

[30] *Loc. cit.*

[31] *Ibid.*, p. 376. Despite the fact that the FCC rejected Scott's petition, using the occasion merely to restate the traditional libertarian position on freedom of speech, the decision has been severely attacked. The President of the NAB called it a "masterpiece of confused thinking," and quoted a House Select Committee's opinion that "the Commission in the Scott decision demonstrated a dangerous and unwarranted policy of 'thought policing' that has no basis in law." House Committee on Interstate and Foreign Commerce, *Hearings on S. 658, Amending Communications Act of 1934* (Washington: Government Printing Office, 1951), p. 375.

[32] FCC, "Use of Broadcast Facilities by Candidates for Public Office" (Public Notice, 8 September 1954). Sample question: "May a station with both 'national' and 'local' rates charge a candidate for local office its 'national' rate?" Answer, No (p. 4).

According to Section 315, "no obligation is hereby imposed upon any licensee to allow the use of its station by any such candidate." The Commission has held that a station may not arbitrarily limit the amount of time made available, once some time is made available. WDSU, New Orleans, had a policy of not cancelling any regularly scheduled commercial programs for paid political programs. The FCC declared:

> This statement of policy reflects such a complete failure on the part of [the licensees] to appreciate their obligations as station licensees (to operate in the public interest) as to require severe censure of such policy . . . a station licensee has both the right and the duty to cancel such previously scheduled programs as may be necessary in order to clear time for broadcasts of programs in the public interest.[33]

Unfortunately, the "equal opportunities" doctrine often makes it virtually impossible for stations to give free time to political candidates, because of the large number of candidates involved when every party, even the most inconsequential, must be given equal time. This means that in a national election, for example, the networks cannot invite the Democratic and Republican presidential candidates to appear on a discussion program without committing themselves to making the same invitation to the representatives of from fifteen to twenty minor parties who also are "legally qualified candidates for public office." The sale of time, on the other hand, usually has the effect of screening out all but the major parties, since only they are likely to have sufficient funds for the purpose.

The "equal opportunities" doctrine has been extended to the broader fields of political controversy not directly involving candidates for public office. In practice the doctrine has led to abuses which tend to obscure rather than clarify the controversies involved. For example, on the basis of a highly incidental allusion to Senator J. R. McCarthy in a 1953 network speech of Ex-President Truman, McCarthy claimed the "right" of a full-dress reply over the same facilities. Edward R. Murrow, the CBS commentator, presented a critical program on McCarthy in the same year on *See It Now*, permitting the Senator to reply on the same program the following week. *Broadcasting-Telecasting's* editorial comment on the resulting performance was that

> The irresponsible attack made by Sen. Joseph R. McCarthy against Edward R. Murrow on Mr. Murrow's own show last Tuesday demonstrated the utter futility of the "equal time" policy now prevailing in U.S. radio and television.
>
> The only justification for the principle of equal time is that it assures the public of receiving well-reasoned arguments representing diverse views on controversial subjects. How hopeless it is to make this principle work by

---

[33] *In re Stephens Broadcasting Co.* (WDSU), 11 FCC 61 at 65 (1945). Cf. also *In re Homer P. Rainey*, 11 FCC 898 (1947).

simply handing out facilities and time without retaining the right of editorial judgment was clearly shown on last week's *See It Now.*[34]

A set of "ground rules" proposed by Charles A. Siepmann for the handling of such "equal opportunities" problems might go a long way toward resolving the inequities and confusions resulting from the ambiguities of present methods: (1) The licensee alone should decide who shall be the parties to a broadcast on a controversial subject — no one has the inherent "right" to reply irrespective of circumstances; (2) speakers should be confined to the issues; and (3) personal abuse, innuendo, and the like should be prohibited.[35]

ECONOMIC EXPLOITATION

As was pointed out previously, broadcasting lends itself peculiarily well to high-pressure selling of unethical or marginally ethical products and services. Its psychological impact and its accessibility to the illiterate and near-illiterate make broadcasting an efficient means of capitalizing on the gullibility of the uninformed or uneducated listener-viewer. Thus broadcasting is in a position to exploit those who are economically the least able to afford exploitation and intellectually the least able to defend themselves against exploitation.

The previous examples of unfairness impinge on the First Amendment because they tend to frustrate its purpose. The present example is in a different category, harking back again to the Associated Press case. The use of a medium of communication for unfair economic exploitation is not immune from legal restraint because the medium of communication is protected by the First Amendment. The FCC has taken the position that it must stand between the credulity of audiences and the advertiser who would exploit it. Typical of the advertising condemned is that of the fraudulent scientific expert. The advertising of a man purporting to be an astrologer-psychologist-doctor-scientist and that of another billed as a "world famed spiritual psychologist" dealt with

> . . . questions purporting to come from their audience, these selections usually including a wide variety of material with a liberal allowance of matter bordering on indelicacy and scandalousness, if not actually scandalous. Even a cursory examination of the discussions broadcast would seem to have been enough to convince the management of the station that they were intended to exploit and victimize the credulous, to capitalize the troubles and distress of questioners and in some instances even to draw upon the public by appeal to religious instincts.[36]

[34] "Is the Sky the Limit?" *Broadcasting-Telecasting* (12 April 1954), p. 134. Cf. also: "Murrow Wins the Nation's Applause," *Broadcasting-Telecasting* (15 March 1954), p. 33.

[35] Charles A. Siepmann, *op. cit.*, pp. 422-424.

[36] *In re Scroggin & Co. Bank (KFEQ)*, 1 FCC 194 at 196 (1935). The station's license was renewed.

License renewals of five stations were set for hearing on the basis of advertising containing such continuity as the following:

> Here is good news for all those people who are sick or in ill health. The Alhambra Electronic Institute has installed the latest Scientific Invention — the Electron-o-meter — a machine that shows you definitely the cause of your illness, the condition of your internal organs, the severity of the ailment, and how to correct the faulty condition.[37]

This miraculous instrument was made available at one dollar per examination, although the announcement went on fraudulently to claim that ten dollars was the regular fee, with the one-dollar fee available only to the first ten applicants. The licensees had so little sense of responsibility as to argue that it was not their job to evaluate advertising, to which the FCC replied: "The contention that licensees should not have the duty of examining into the propriety of advertising to be broadcast is manifestly contrary to the law."[38] Nor does the FCC accept the evasive excuse that other stations have carried the same advertising: licensees "have the positive unqualified responsibility of serving the public interest as a matter of law, and it will not avail one licensee that some other station . . . has placed upon others the responsibility which is his, as licensee of a station."[39]

By 1940 such extreme types of exploitative advertising as these had been eliminated from broadcasting. In more recent years the forms of exploitation have been somewhat less obvious — bait-switch advertising, shoddy per-inquiry merchandise, exaggerated and misleading claims for otherwise legitimate products, such as cigarettes and drugs. It is difficult to say where puffery or trader's talk ends and downright fraudulence begins. Often advertising which would be condemned by common-sense application of ordinary moral standards cannot be banned by legal means because there is no technical violation of law — a circumstance which again points up the inadequacy of legislated responsibility in the absence of personal acceptance of such responsibility.

A good example is the giveaway programs in their various forms — adaptations of bingo, "lucky bucks," *Stop the Music, What's My Name, Sing It Again*, and so on. Here the content of the programs themselves, rather than advertising, is at issue, but the element of exploitation is present. Some giveaways border on lotteries, which are forbidden by a provision of the United States Code that was formerly part of the Communications Act. Technically, however, they do not conform to the legal definition of a lottery, and the FCC's attempt to set up rules restricting such programs was defeated by the Supreme Court. The FCC contended that the giveaway programs were "nothing but age old lotteries in a slightly new form. The

[37] *In re Ben S. McGlashan (KGFJ) et al.*, 2 FCC 145 at 149 (1935). All five licenses were renewed.
[38] *Ibid.*, p. 147.
[39] *In re The Farmers & Bankers Life Ins. Co. (KFBI)*, 2 FCC 455 at 459 (1936).

new form results from the fact that the schemes here are illicit appendages to legitimate advertising . . . the gambling spirit — the lure of obtaining something for nothing or almost nothing — is exploited for the benefit of the promoter of the scheme."[40] The Supreme Court remarked that the enforcement of laws against lotteries is complicated by the fact that there are "as many types of lotteries as the seemingly inexhaustible ingenuity of their promoters could devise in their efforts to circumvent the law."[41] The Court found no exact precedent for the broadcast giveaway programs, but it concluded that the element of consideration (necessary to the legal definition of lottery) was missing, inasmuch as "the only effort required for participation is listening."[42] The Court seems to have been considerably influenced in its decision by the fact that neither the Department of Justice nor the Post Office Department had joined the attack on the giveaways.

This points up the existence of multiple jurisdiction in the field of illegal broadcast advertising and programming. The FCC is reluctant to take action when the other government agencies do not support its view. These agencies include the Federal Trade Commission, the Post Office Department, the Food and Drug Administration, and the Department of Justice. They are more likely than the FCC to adopt a legalistic point of view, less likely to appreciate the peculiar fiduciary status of broadcasting.

THE FEDERAL TRADE COMMISSION

Of these agencies, the Federal Trade Commission has the most to do with broadcast advertising. The FTC was set up in 1914 to supplement the Sherman Antitrust Act. Among other things it is concerned with "the use of false and misleading advertising concerning, and the misbranding of, commodities, respecting the materials and ingredients of which they are composed, their quality, purity, origin, source, attributes, or properties or nature of manufacture, and selling them under such name and circumstances as to deceive the public."[43] As an aspect of fair trade, the FTC also has jurisdiction over the making of "false and disparaging statements respecting a competitor's products and business." The FTC examines samples of radio and television continuities as well as other advertising. In 1951-1952, 228,051 radio and 84,325 television commercials were scanned; about three per cent of the radio and four per cent of the television samples were set aside as questionable.[44]

Most allegations of illegal advertising by the FTC are settled by "stipulation"; i.e., the advertiser changes the questionable practice voluntarily. If

---

[40] *FCC* v. *ABC*, 347 U.S. 284 at 291 (1954).

[41] *Ibid.*, p. 292.

[42] *Ibid.*, p. 294.

[43] FTC, *Annual Report for the Fiscal Year Ended June 30, 1953* (Washington: Government Printing Office, 1953), p. 81.

[44] FTC, *Annual Report for the Fiscal Year Ended June 30, 1952* (Washington: Government Printing Office, 1952), p. 49.

the advertiser chooses not to accede, the FTC can issue a cease-and-desist order and secure compliance through the courts. FTC complaints have not been confined to the fly-by-night advertisers of unethical products and services; a great many of the well-known major advertisers have been cited as well. That sales can flourish on advertising misrepresentation and that the FTC has a salutary effect is illustrated by the reported fact that the sale of a "miracle drug" dropped from two million to a half million dollars after an FTC injunction stopped fraudulent advertising.[45]

This case also illustrates a weakness of the whole machinery for controlling unfair advertising: the public can be bilked of millions of dollars before the legal machinery goes into action. The kind of fly-by-night product which capitalizes on the power of hard-sell broadcast advertising typically runs its course in a year or two, and hence by the time the FTC catches up with it the company may already have gleaned its profit and be ready to go out of business anyway.

As the carrier of unfair advertising the station is relatively immune from legal punishment other than FCC action. Under the Wheeler-Lea Act of 1938 (amending the FTC Act) a station is held responsible for fraudulent advertising only if it prepares the broadcast material itself; if it did not prepare the material it can absolve itself by naming the source. Licensees are responsible, however, for violations of the Food and Drug Administration standards, and the Post Office Department can bar the use of the mails to stations engaged in fraudulent advertising. A "fraud by radio" provision of the United States Criminal Code enables the Department of Justice to attack the source of advertising directly; the broadcaster is at fault only insofar as he "knowingly permits" transmission of the material.

There can be no doubt that unethical broadcast advertising, though not representative of the great majority of advertising in the medium, swindles the public out of millions of dollars every year. More rapid and efficient enforcement of the existing laws would be highly desirable, but the dimensions of the problem of detection alone are staggering when one considers the number of stations in operation and the quantity of their output. In the final analysis, the best that can be expected of legal restraints is correction of the most flagrant and persistent abuses. Many borderline programs, advertising practices, and advertised products and services, though technically legal, violate the spirit of the law. The presence of such material tends to degrade the broadcast service as a whole by creating an atmosphere of hucksterism and an impression of irresponsibility. In order for broadcasting to grow in stature as an ethical, highly responsible medium there must be voluntary elimination of shoddy mail-order "deals," pitchman tactics, bait-switch come-ons, quasi-lotteries, and other such legal but exploitative practices. To expect such a growth from the broadcasting industry is by no means naive. A good deal of progress has already been made toward better standards, as the following chapter will show.

[45] *Ibid.*, p. 16.

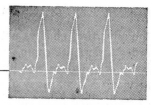

25

Self-Regulation

> The television broadcaster . . . is obligated to
> bring his positive responsibility for excellence and
> good taste in programming to bear upon all who
> have a hand in the production of programs.
> — NARTB TELEVISION CODE

Most self-regulation by businesses and industries arises from the need to cultivate good public relations and to forestall official regulation by the government. It does not necessarily follow, however, that self-regulation always remains at this level. Many self-regulating codes are undoubtedly adopted for purely practical reasons; many probably never rise above this level. On the other hand, the very mental discipline of developing a well-thought-out code, the very existence of the code as an explicit statement of principles, objectives, and standards, can have a long-term ameliorative ethical effect. Unconsciously the members of an industry may begin to acquire in fact and practice a sense of responsibility to which at first they may have paid mere lip service.[1]

THE MOTION-PICTURE CODE

Codes for broadcasting find their precedent and archetype in the motion-picture production code.[2] The content of films, the advertising of films, and the conduct of people associated with films came under increasingly severe criticism during the early 1920's, accelerating the trend toward official censorship by municipalities and states. In short, the motion-picture industry found its public relations deteriorating to the point of crisis. In 1922 the

[1] When the National Association of Broadcasters first asked radio stations for copies of their local policy statements as a basis for drawing up the NAB radio code, few licensees had gone to the trouble of thinking through a statement of policy and reducing it to writing. — Testimony of NAB President Neville Miller, Senate Committee on Interstate Commerce, *Hearings on S. 814, To Amend the Communications Act of 1934* (Washington: Government Printing Office, 1944), p. 176.

[2] The three codes — television, radio, and motion-picture — are reproduced in parallel columns for easy comparison in the Appendix.

major producing companies set up an organization to restore the industry's reputation. Will H. Hays resigned as United States Postmaster General to head the new film organization, which became popularly known as the Hays office.[3] Hays was paid an annual salary of $100,000.

By 1930 the Hays office had evolved a formal Production Code to govern the details of motion-picture content. At first the code had relatively little effect, but in 1934 the Catholic Legion of Decency organized a nation-wide boycott of objectionable films. This direct action resulted in the setting up of an enforcement mechanism, the Production Code Administration, with provisions for issuing official certificates of approval and for a $25,000 fine for the release of a film without approval. The Code Administration passes on both scripts and finished pictures. Virtually all entertainment feature films released today carry the MPAA seal of approval and certificate number.

The MPAA Production Code had its substantive origin in an earlier document which reflected the producers' accumulated experience with touchy picture content, and which consisted of a bare list of "Don't's" and "Be Careful's." To this list was appended a set of "reasons why," a rationale which purports to explain and justify the admonitions of the code proper. The language of these added sections has an obvious theological ring, and in fact appears to have been written by a Catholic priest.

> Fundamentally, the complete Code is a moralistic document. The word "moral" or its derivatives appears in it twenty-six times. Valuative terms like "sin," "evil," "bad," "right," and "good," appear frequently. Although divine law is mentioned only once, the language and reasoning of the Code belong to moral philosophy rather than to social science.[4]

CRITICISM OF THE MPAA CODE

The MPAA Code is often criticized, and on several grounds. To begin with, it is much easier to construct a code in negative terms than in positive terms (significantly, the Code grew out of a list of "Don't's" and "Be Careful's"). Despite the "reasons supporting" and the "reasons underlying" which are appended to the Code proper, the MPAA Code remains essentially dogmatic and negative in tone. There is little likelihood that the Code could positively inspire a producer to make a good film; at best it prevents him from using certain words, scenes, and implications, irrespective of whether he is making a good film or a bad one. It has often been pointed out that this approach results in a kind of sly evasion of the spirit of the Code through the use of indirect language and methods of presentation which avoid explicit code violations. Inglis recognizes this as a fundamental

[3] In 1945 the Hays Office became the Johnston Office when Eric Johnston succeeded to the post. In that year the producers changed the official name of their organization to its present form, the Motion Picture Association of America (MPAA).

[4] Ruth Inglis, *Freedom of the Movies* (Chicago: University of Chicago Press, 1947), pp. 116-117, 128. (Copyright 1947 by The University of Chicago.) Most of the material on the MPAA code in this chapter is based on Inglis's excellent analysis.

criticism but believes that adequate supporting evidence is wanting.[5] Nevertheless, it is easy to recall MPAA-approved films far more morally questionable than, for example, *The Moon Is Blue* (characterized by *Life* as "on the whole ingratiating, witty, and 100% on the side of conventional morality"), which was refused the MPAA seal and condemned by the Legion of Decency.

Another charge brought against the Code is that its administration is dominated by Catholics. After a careful analysis of this charge Inglis rejects it, although Catholics have certainly been closely connected with its origin and operation. Inglis points out, however, that the Code contains "metaphysical reasoning compatible not only with Catholic but with Protestant and Jewish theology," and all three churches have cooperated with the Legion of Decency.[6]

The significance of the close association of Catholicism with the MPAA Code rests not on rivalry among religious faiths but on the question of principle involved when any highly organized religious group asserts supervisory control over a medium of communication. This question of principle was raised in the *Miracle* case (Chapter 23), in which the Supreme Court decided that a church could not use the coercive powers of government to censor films on the grounds of alleged sacrilegious content. Of course a distinction must be made between the boycotting technique of the Legion of Decency and the technique of official censorship involved in the *Miracle* case. In the former a church exacts pledges from its members *voluntarily* to refrain from seeing certain films; in the latter a church seeks to use the police power of the state *forcibly* to prevent all persons from seeing certain films.

Essentially this same result may be obtained, however, if a church membership is well enough disciplined and sufficiently numerous or influential to use the economic coercion of the boycott to deny a film to others as well as to themselves. Even some Catholics question the desirability of a church's dictating to its members (and indirectly perhaps to the rest of society) in such matters. Walter Kerr, a Catholic layman writing in a Catholic journal, declared that dogmatic application of the MPAA Code is "moving closer and closer to the sort of stand which might well be described as vulgarity for God's sake."[7] Libertarians will agree that the mentally mature should be left to make their own decisions in such matters. *The Miracle*, in fact, provides an apt illustration of the danger in the "assumption of infallibility," as Mill expressed it, for even Catholics could not agree among themselves concerning whether or not the film was sacrilegious.

The third and most telling criticism of the MPAA Code is that it confuses superficial moralizing with genuine morality. Gilbert Seldes, for example,

[5] *Ibid.*, p. 184.

[6] *Ibid.*, p. 181.

[7] Walter Kerr, "Catholics and Hollywood," *Commonweal* LVII-11 (19 December 1952), p. 277.

believes that the Code, "as it operates today, does actual, demonstrable harm to the community." He contends that

> It is a self-defeating document because if its premises are true, if the movies are responsible for moral standards . . . if like other works of art they are "the presentation of human thought, emotion, and experience, in terms of an appeal to the soul through the senses," then they cannot possibly function under an imposed Code; only movies made purely for distraction, appealing to the mass minority, can be made this way.[8]

Essentially, the rationale of the MPAA Code is based on the assumptions (1) that films are primarily a mass medium and therefore subject to certain limitations not imposed on other media and (2) that the medium is responsible for the teaching of conventional moral values, specifically those contained in the Code. This point of view inevitably conflicts with the concept of films as primarily an art form. Artists and works of art are noted neither for their mass appeal nor for their concern with conventional morality. Shakespeare cannot be transferred to the screen without expurgation, and innumerable instances could be cited in which the screen adaptation of a play or novel of acknowledged artistic merit has been accomplished only at the expense of precisely that quality.[9]

The Code itself acknowledges the problem of Art vs. Morals. In the section of "Reasons Supporting Preamble of Code" it asserts that since motion pictures, unlike other arts, appeal to every age and class and penetrate to every place, they cannot be judged by the standards applicable to books, newspapers, or plays:

> It has often been argued that art in itself is unmoral, neither good nor bad. This is perhaps true of the THING which is music, painting, poetry, etc. But the thing is the PRODUCT of some person's mind, and the intention of that mind was either good or bad morally when it produced the thing. Besides, the thing has its EFFECT upon those who come into contact with it. In both these ways, that is, as a product of a mind and as the cause of definite effects, it has a deep moral significance and an unmistakable moral quality.[10]

We need not be diverted here by such interesting questions as the relation of an artist's intention to the ultimate effect of his work or the complex philosophical subject of the relation between ethics and aesthetics. Let us grant that art does have "deep moral significance and unmistakable moral quality." Moreover, let us grant that art has ascertainable moral effects (although this postulate, too, could lead to an involved debate). The issue

---

[8] Gilbert Seldes, *The Great Audience* (New York: The Viking Press, 1950), p. 73. Cf. Seldes' devastating analysis of the Code, pp. 64-87.

[9] Seldes cites striking examples of this adaptive process, which he calls "The Art of Licking." *Ibid.*, pp. 50-54.

[10] MPAA, *A Code to Govern the Making of Motion Pictures* (New York: MPAA, 1954), p. 10.

then becomes whether it is possible arbitrarily to classify the intrinsic morality of a work of art under one of the two categories of "good" and "bad" on the basis of the Code's list of "Don't's" and "Be Careful's." Many would argue that on the contrary it is perfectly possible to fulfill all the superficial moral requirements of the Code and at the same time produce a work which is in a deeper sense thoroughly immoral.

THE RADIO CODE [11]

Broadcasters formed their own trade association, analogous to the MPAA, in 1923. The National Association of Broadcasters, like the MPAA, adopted its radio code in an effort to restore deteriorating public relations (although broadcasting never sank to the level of films at their worst). Membership in the NAB (since 1951 the NARTB) is voluntary, and only about 50 per cent of the radio stations belong. Code-making is but one of many functions of the broadcasters' trade organization, which aids its members in a variety of ways, e.g., providing statistical information, aiding in labor-relations problems, and representing broadcasting interests at Congressional hearings. A very brief radio code was adopted in 1929, but the present code stems from one developed in 1937.

In the highly concentrated film industry, a few major producer-distributor-exhibitor firms could impose an effective code on the whole industry. The monolithic character of the film industry made it possible to secure almost complete compliance, even without resorting to the $25,000 fine (which is of doubtful legality in any event). Broadcasting, however, is not sufficiently homogeneous to arrive at such unanimity. Moreover, it is much easier to control the content of a few hundred film productions per year, each of which takes anywhere from several weeks to many months to complete, than to control the content of many thousands of programs continuously produced by many hundreds of radio stations scattered throughout the country. Observance of the radio code is entirely voluntary. There is no "seal of approval," such as that of the MPAA, nor is there any penalty for violation.[12]

The history of the radio code has been one of struggle between the "haves" and the "have-nots." The more prosperous stations and networks advocated standards far higher than their less prosperous colleagues would tolerate. Significantly, the smaller stations revolted against even a comparatively mild set of standards (which to the outsider seems perfectly reason-

---

[11] The term "code" is used here for convenience. Actually the current published statement is called *Standards of Practice for Radio Broadcasters of the United States of America,* and it presumably differs from a code in the sense that there is no mechanism of enforcement (although at one time the term "code" was used and there did exist a "Code Compliance Committee").

[12] Trade associations are barred by antitrust laws from the restraint of trade which could arise from the exercise of coercive control over the business practices of their members. The legality of the MPAA $25,000 fine has never been put to the test.

able and desirable) on the grounds that observance of such standards would drive them out of business.[13] Therefore the radio code emerged as a rather weak compromise.

A comparison of the broadcasting codes with the MPAA code (see Appendix) points up the differences between the media. The advertising content of programming — a major concern of the broadcasting codes — has, of course, no equivalent in films.[14] The many implications arising from the fact that broadcasting is (1) a home medium, (2) a news and information medium, and (3) a medium of local self-expression also are lacking in the film code. Parallelism between the codes occurs in the area of dramatic presentation; here, it will be noted, the film code goes into more specific detail than do the broadcasting codes, especially on such subjects as the treatment of sex, crime, and brutality.

But the most significant contrast lies in the fact that both the broadcasting codes are completely devoid of the dogmatic theological reasoning which is appended to the MPAA code. Such terms as "sin," "evil," and "soul" do not occur in the broadcasting codes. Moreover, the explanation accompanying the film code is essentially in the nature of an afterthought — an *a posteriori* justification; but the reasoning in support of the broadcasting codes is integrated with the substance of the rules.

THE TELEVISION CODE

Television presented a somewhat different code-making problem than did radio. At the time the television code was adopted (1952) the freeze was still in effect. Only about a hundred stations were in operation, nearly all of them in sound financial condition; their standards could not be watered down by the anguished outcry of hundreds of small marginal operators who could not afford the price of relatively high standards. The television broadcasters had behind them all the experience of the MPAA and the radio codes. They were not, as were the other media, reacting defensively after a long period of half-measures and compromises. They were setting up a code only four years after television had become a going concern commercially, before public opinion had crystallized (though by no means before public criticism had been voiced). They were pioneering in a tremendously exciting new medium, a medium with almost awesome potentialities.

Generally speaking, the radio code, as compared with the television code, is more on the defensive, emphasizing radio's commercialism and freedom from external control as "rights" rather than broadcasters' responsibilities. The radio code is more general and more permissive; it shows less consciousness of the informational function of the medium, as compared with

[13] For details of the radio code's evolution see: Llewellyn White, *The American Radio* (Chicago: University of Chicago Press, 1947), pp. 68-100.

[14] Note, however, that the MPAA does have a separate advertising code, applicable to the advertising *of* films, not to advertising *in* films. Film advertising has posed almost as serious a problem as the content of films themselves.

the entertainment function; it is negative where the television code is positive.

The key word in the television code is *responsibility;* in a sense this takes the place of the key word *moral* in the MPAA code. The word is used explicitly more than a dozen times, and the whole document rests squarely on an assumption of licensee responsibility. In short, the television code represents an overt expression of the responsibility theory of a mass medium. It requires broadcasters to acknowledge the implications of the fact that television is a home medium and an information medium; they must accept responsibility for controlling all aspects and sources of production — i.e., they may not surrender program responsibility to the advertiser, the network, the package producer, the salesman, or the advertising agency; they must accept responsibility for all types of programs, implicitly rejecting the pejorative concept of "public service" programs previously discussed (see p. 337); they accept responsibility as organs of community self-expression.

Whereas the radio code tends to accept responsibility passively, the television code is emphatic in making responsibility positive, affirmative, and active. Television broadcasters are expected to *seek out* programs of a controversial nature, important public events, factual and informational program material, opportunities for cooperation with educational and cultural institutions. They are even expected to *invite* criticism. Symptomatic of the sociological (rather than theological) orientation of the code is its definition of education: "that process by which the individual is brought toward informed adjustment to his society." The radio code does not even attempt to state what it means by education; this is understandable, since in the past this has been one of the most abused terms in the broadcasting lexicon (see Chapter 26). Whereas the radio code tells licensees that they "should cooperate with responsible and accountable educational and cultural entities of the community to provide enlightenment of listeners," the television code tells them they should *affirmatively seek out* such institutions, and should provide opportunity for *instruction* as well as enlightenment.

Naturally the visual element of television calls for a number of specific rules not relevant to radio (for instance, the whole section on "Decency and Decorum" in the television code). Even in matters of common application, however, the television code tends to be more specific and more detailed than the radio code. For example, it goes into much detail on the nature of broadcasting's responsibility to children, on the handling of advertising in news programs, on courtesy and good taste in advertising. The television code rules against a number of specific practices not mentioned in the radio code at all, e.g., particular proscribed words and expressions, advertising claims intended to disparage competitors, paid religious advertising, the advertising of fortune-telling, racetrack publications, and the like.

Unlike the radio code, the television code provides for enforcement machinery. Following the example of the MPAA, the NARTB grants to code subscribers a Seal of Good Practice; but whereas the MPAA seal appears in the opening credits of each individual film subject, the NARTB seal is shown only occasionally by the member station, without being associated with any particular program.[15] The Seal of Good Practice is granted upon subscription to the Code (open to non-NARTB members), and the right to use it can be suspended or revoked.[16] A five-man Code Review Board of NARTB members monitors programming, receives and processes complaints, and prefers charges when breaches of the Code are detected.[17]

APPRAISAL OF THE TV CODE

The adoption of a code for television somewhat comparable to the MPAA film code was viewed with misgivings in some quarters. The American Civil Liberties Union, for example, regarded the code as requiring an improper surrender of licensee responsibility. Said the ACLU:

. . . we believe that it is stultifying and illegal censorship which must be abrogated in its entirety . . . the code would completely prohibit the production of any adult, mature programs dealing with issues of a serious nature, except that in some cases treatment of such problems would be permitted if the solutions thereof conformed to certain requirements laid down by the code.[18]

One of the formulators of the Television Code, Robert Swezey, attempted to dispose of this class of criticism as follows:

I regard it an unwarranted indictment of the creative mind that in order to make its fullest contribution in the public service, it must work in areas generally considered unwholesome, obscene, or otherwise contrary to accepted moral standards.[19]

---

[15] If the NARTB seal were to be entirely analogous to that of the MPAA it would be attached to each individual program *at the source*. To show the seal as representative of the practice of the station is analogous to awarding the MPAA seal to the film *exhibitor* rather than the film *producer*. This contrast points up the difference in the way in which the production–exhibition functions are related within the two media.

[16] As of July, 1955, 55 per cent of the TV stations in operation had subscribed to the code.

[17] As of 1955 no such suspension or revocation had taken place, nor would the Code Review Board release any quantitative data on the number or type of complaints processed or the extent of compliance or non-compliance. Some general comments on the first year's experience of the Code Review Board and some specific examples are contained in: NARTB Television Code Review Board, *First Report to the People of the United States* (Washington: NARTB, 1953).

[18] ACLU letter to FCC, quoted in: House Committee on Interstate and Foreign Commerce Subcommittee, *Hearings on H. Res. 278, Investigation of Radio and Television Programs* (Washington: Government Printing Office, 1952), pp. 134-135.

[19] Robert D. Swezey, "Give the Television Code a Chance." Reprinted from the *Quarterly of Film, Radio, and Television*, VII-1 (Fall, 1952), published by the University of California Press. Pp. 20-21.

Both the foregoing arguments are based on questionable assumptions: the ACLU argument assumes that the Code alone could be responsible for excluding "adult, mature programs dealing with issues of a serious nature" from the television service; the Swezey argument assumes that the Code excludes nothing of merit from the television service. As for the first assumption, the plain fact is that the determination of what is acceptable and what unacceptable in the mass media is made, in a broad sense, by society itself; codes only reflect, with varying degrees of distortion, prevailing social standards. As for the second assumption, it is based on a naive view of morality, as though it consisted of certain relatively superficial actions and attitudes which had universal and permanent moral significance. In actuality the moral significance of many specific behaviors and attitudes varies considerably, not only from one country to another but also from one class or group to another within a country.

Let us examine this last assumption in detail. William Faulkner, for example, is one of the three or four great American novelists of the present era, internationally recognized, winner of a Nobel prize. It is no "indictment of the creative mind," surely, that nearly all Faulkner's novels contain quantities of material which could not possibly meet the standards of motion-picture, radio, and television codes.

Again, take the previously mentioned example of the film *The Moon Is Blue*, which was generally agreed to be a fairly accurate presentation of the stage version of the play. The film version was refused approval by the MPAA Production Administration and condemned by the Legion of Decency; yet the stage version ran for two years on Broadway and toured over thirty cities throughout the country (including Boston) without being either censored or condemned. Paperback books have offered many striking examples of a similar double standard. Works which have long since been accepted as standard literature by those who read them in hard covers and which have never caused the slightest stir of criticism (though available to all in the regular libraries and book stores) suddenly come under attack for obscenity, immorality, or subversiveness when introduced to a less sophisticated readership through 100,000 pocket-book stands in such places as drugstores, bus stations, and supermarkets. In short, people get accustomed to different things, depending on their social environment. Most people have little awareness — or tolerance — of these differences because most people are class-bound.

Returning now to the other assumption — that codes rather than society itself are responsible for limitations on the kind of content the mass media will accept — let us recall that the nature of the mass media heavily commits them to prevailing opinion. In one sense codes represent the attempt of one man (or a small group of men) to assay public opinion and predict what it will tolerate and what it will reject. The relatively sophisticated and articulate members of the audience demand presentations that according to their standards are "mature," "adult," "realistic," "original," "experimental," "artistic," "intelligent," and so on. On the other hand, presentations that meet these criteria are likely either to bore or offend large numbers of people whose standards are different.

In other words, with or without codes the mass media are going to lean in the direction of the tastes, opinions, and standards which are most prevalent in society. The basic problem, then, is to make sure that adherence to these tastes, opinions, and standards is not so rigid and dogmatic as to stifle completely those of other classes. This latitude should work in both directions: it would be just as unfair for the devotees of Bach to deny the devotees of hillbilly music all chance to indulge their taste as the other way around.

The rigidity and dogmatism with which codified standards are applied are likely to depend upon the spirit in which they are applied, which in turn depends upon their conceptual background, their rationale. If, as in the case of the MPAA Code, the "Don't's" and "Be Careful's" are conceived as reflecting basic theological issues, the effect is to transmute relatively superficial, conservative, middle-to-upper-lower-class standards into eternal verities. That this conception leads to dogmatic application of the rules is amply demonstrated by the practical results of the MPAA Code.

Fortunately for the television service, the broadcasters completely rejected the MPAA's moralizing approach in constructing a rationale for the television code. They do not discuss "sin," "evil," "correct standards of life," "the lower and baser emotions," "the criminal classes," "the love which society has always regarded as wrong," but talk in terms of social customs. This less rigid approach offers at least the possibility of an application which will recognize the facts of changing standards and the differences among social groups.

Granting the premises of the Television Code, what of its effectiveness? Any viewer can probably find at least minor violations any day, even among Code subscribers. On the evidence some critics conclude that the Code is indeed a mere public-relations expedient:

> The utility of any code is questionable, particularly if the code is written for the cynical purpose of having something to show when criticism of prevailing practices becomes significant. . . .

❋ ❋ ❋ ❋ ❋

> It hardly seems desirable that stations be allowed indefinitely to show the public a Seal of Good Practice at one moment and clutter up the air with obvious violations of the code at another.[20]

The problem of monitoring literally all programs on all stations and correcting all abuses would be staggering. The Code Review Board obviously cannot undertake such a herculean task. Its attention must be confined essentially to those stations, programs, and violations which are specifically

---

[20] "Ornaments or Implements," *Broadcasting-Telecasting* (1 February 1954), p. 106.

brought to its notice, either by chance or by reason of notorious transgressions. Nor would a giant monitoring organization serve any useful purpose, for the effectiveness of the Code depends ultimately on the good will and sincerity of subscribers. Even the loss of the Seal of Good Practice, after all, is hardly a grave enough penalty to deter a licensee bent on transgressing the Code. The Code rests squarely on the concept of responsibility: responsibility voluntarily accepted by the licensee for using his facilities in the public interest.

According to the Code Review Board, the broadcasters are responding in this spirit. "In no instance," it declares, "has a question been raised with a station or network without subsequent full cooperation in terms of corrective action." The Board points out that

> . . . progress in improving program content and advertising is an evolutionary one and seldom dramatic. We can only point out progress in a general way and in terms of broad areas of endeavor. We believe, for example, that during the past several years there has been marked improvement in such areas as costuming, production decorum in general, the presentation of advertising and the length of commercials.[21]

NETWORK SELF-REGULATION

Networks maintain "continuity acceptance" departments, whose job is to check all network material (whether network-produced or from other sources) for compliance with network policies. NBC had developed its own code as early as 1934,[22] and with CBS was instrumental in the formulation of the NAB radio code. NBC had already incorporated television into its code by the time the NARTB met to formulate the industry television code. Stockton Helffrich, manager of NBC's Continuity Acceptance Department, describes his work as "a sort of cross between public relations advisors, common sense censors and umpires for enforcing such rules as exist on what constitutes good taste." The care with which scripts are examined, and the amount of serious notice given even to individual letters of criticism by such a department would probably surprise most laymen. Networks are under constant pressure from every conceivable commercial interest, each of which is likely to find invidious allusions in the most unlikely places. Helffrich lists a few:

> We are looked to for fair treatment of and consideration for the gas interests (if a death was caused by same), the meat interests (if a high cost of living reference or adlib suggests that rising prices pertain only to lamb chops), florists (if a line admonishes "Please omit flowers"), the bowling and billiard people (if gangsters are depicted as collecting only in poolrooms), the warehouse interests (if clichéd writing suggests that night watchmen are invariably eighty years old, invariably sleepy, invariably assigned to dirty and

---

21 Personal communication from the Code Board, 29 July 1955.
22 Cf.: NBC, *Radio and Television Broadcast Standards* (New York: NBC, 1951).

abandoned warehouses in the worst section of towns where murders invariably occur). Some of our duties out of context seem amusing, but we find ourselves taking them just as seriously as we do problems everybody admits are important.[23]

Continuity acceptance by no means confines itself to special economic interests: every imaginable question of taste and morality which captious human ingenuity can devise has to be considered. Here, for example, is a list of a few deletions from old cartoons made at NBC's Chicago office (ironically, a great deal of film material previously used without comment in theatres has to be cleaned up for television): a dancing hippo doing a shimmy and grind; a cat magician glamorizing whiskey in a bottle trick; a farmer and his cat getting drunk on cider at a mill, followed by "leering it up" over some female apparitions brought on by their inebriation; racial stereotyping in the form of a Mammy portrayal in which the "chillun" are told how mules got to be so ornery; humorous treatment of a drunk navigating a hallway and a flight of stairs; a nauseated woman clapping her hand over her mouth.[24]

[23] Personal communication from Stockton Helffrich, 24 May 1955.
[24] NBC, "Continuity Acceptance Report" (April, 1955, mimeo.), p. 1.

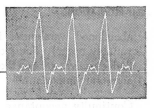

26

Higher Education as a Factor

in Social Control

In considering higher education as a factor in the control of broadcasting, we are here concerned with the influence of education as an institution. It is true, of course, that formal education of the individual has a great deal to do with control of the medium in the long run, since it is well established that programming preferences vary markedly with degree of formal schooling. If, say, 95 per cent of the broadcast audience consisted of college graduates, doubtless the program service would be very different from what it is now (considering that less than 5 per cent of the present population has had four or more years of college education).

Institutionally, higher education can influence the program service through two quite different avenues: (1) It can provide an educational program service, primarily by supplementing the commercial service through the operation of noncommercial, institutionally-owned stations; or, more indirectly, (2) it can influence the commercial service itself through the professional education of broadcast personnel. These two approaches may be called education *by* radio and television and education *for* radio and television.

EDUCATION BY COMMERCIAL RADIO

From the very first, broadcasting was believed to be a potentially effective instrument of direct education. Accordingly, educational institutions were one of the most numerous classes of early AM radio licensees (see Table 5). Most of these early educational stations, however, were short-lived. Educational institutions were not prepared to indulge the pioneer enthusiasm of a few faculty members when developing standards of engineering and programming and increased commercial demand for frequencies made substantial financial support essential.[1] A few stations survived by changing

[1] Of over 200 licenses granted to educational institutions through 1936, only 38 remained in force in 1937. S. E. Frost, Jr., *Education's Own Stations* (Chicago: University of Chicago Press, 1937), p. 3. Frost recounts revealing case histories of many of these stations.

to a commercial basis of operation. Of the few which continued the struggle as noncommercial operations, most belong to the tax-supported land-grant colleges of the Middle West, such as Iowa State College; these schools have specific statewide educational responsibilities, and hence broadcasting can be justified as a legitimate public expense for extension education.

Given sufficient time to develop financial resources and to overcome the conservatism of educational administrations, the proponents of noncommercial AM stations might have been able to coax life into the moribund educational broadcast service. Unfortunately, however, no AM channels had been set aside or reserved for a noncommercial service. Noncommercial stations as a class did not exist; educational stations were licensed on the same basis as commercial stations, and operated noncommercially as a matter of deliberate choice. Forfeited assignments were snapped up by commercial interests, and hence opportunities once lost could in most cases never be regained. During the Congressional debate on the Communications Act of 1934, a proposal to reserve channel assignments for education became a major issue. Opponents of the proposal were inspired by the realization that the only way to make such reservations would be to take back assignments already made to commercial operators, since there were no desirable unused assignments to be had. In order not to delay passage of the Act, the supporters of educational reservations agreed to a compromise: a provision in the Act [Sec. 307 (c)] requiring the FCC to report to Congress on the advisability of allocating "fixed percentages of radio broadcasting facilities to particular types or kinds of non-profit radio programs or to persons identified with particular types or kinds of non-profit activities."

The FCC duly reported in January, 1935, that in its opinion existing commercial facilities gave ample opportunity for educational programming and that no special allocation of frequencies for this purpose was needed. In order to bring about the fullest educational use of existing facilities, however, the FCC encouraged the formation of a tripartite industry-government-education committee. Accordingly, the Federal Radio Education Committee (FREC) was set up, comprising over forty leading educators and industry representatives. In the next few years funds were secured from the industry and from such sources as the Rockefeller Foundation, the Payne Fund, and the Kellogg Fund. National conferences were held, studies made, reports published. For example, the First National Conference on Educational Broadcasting in 1936 was attended by over 700 people, 25 of them from foreign countries, 59 from the industry. High government officials such as the Secretary of the Interior, the United States Commissioner of Education, and the Chairman of the FCC addressed the Conference. Many high-minded things were said, and everyone agreed that the educational potential of radio was incalculable; in fact, the general atmosphere of enthusiasm and optimism was very similar to the atmosphere that was to surround the advent of educational television twenty years later. Even some of the phrases used were identical. Said the FCC Chairman in 1936: "Radio, properly used, can become an even greater instrument of instruction than the printing press . . ."[2] Recently television was similarly compared in educational significance to the printing press.

In the subsequent years, however, the high hopes held out for educational radio faded. The activities of the FREC dwindled until by the 1950's they had ceased altogether, though without any formal announcement of dissolution. Networks abandoned their educational showpieces, such as the CBS daily "American School of the Air" (1930-1948). Educators and commercial broadcasters withdrew to different camps. The Institute for Education by Radio (now Radio-Television), which has met annually at The Ohio State University at Columbus since 1929, used to be a meeting ground for the executives of the industry and the educators. The commercial executives, however, eventually came to feel that the educators were more interested in setting up a rival noncommercial service than in helping to improve the commercial service. Rightly or wrongly, the leaders in commercial broadcasting dropped out.

A CASE OF INCOMPATIBILITY

The failure of educational radio to flourish on the basis proposed by the FCC in 1935 has been tacitly accepted but never fully analyzed. No doubt some day — when the information is far less accessible than it is now — a thorough study of this interesting social experiment will be made. Several reasons are apparent on casual inspection, however. To begin with, there was a tendency on all sides to assess the educational potentialities of radio with too much uncritical enthusiasm, with consequent underestimation of the limitations of the medium: "Learning from radio required more motivation and more mental training than had been anticipated."[3] This misjudgment might have been avoided if more of the leading educational institutions had participated in the movement. Llewellyn White sums up his critique of educational radio (which he entitles "The Light That Failed") by declaring: "The leaders have not led." The major privately-financed institutions with the highest educational prestige like Harvard, Yale, and Chicago remained aloof.[4] Apparently such institutions, lacking the broad responsibilities of the land-grant colleges for providing extension-education to all the taxpayers of whole regions, chose to devote their resources to more immediate educational responsibilities.

There seems also to have been a good deal of confusion concerning what the various interests meant by "education by radio" operationally. Com-

---

[2] C. S. Marsh (ed.), *Educational Broadcasting, 1936: Proceedings of the First National Conference on Educational Broadcasting* (Chicago: University of Chicago Press, 1937), p. 18. See this volume for more details on the origins of the FREC.

[3] Paul F. Lazarsfeld and Patricia L. Kendall, *Radio Listening in America* (Copyright, 1948, by Prentice-Hall, Inc., New York), p. 41.

[4] Llewellyn White, *The American Radio* (Chicago: University of Chicago Press, 1947), p. 111. (Copyright 1947 by The University of Chicago.)

mercial broadcasters are naturally inclined to broaden the term "educational" to include as much of their normal commercial programming as possible. It is true, of course, that

> Anything from which we learn something is, in a broad sense, educational. But "education" and "learning" lose any vestige of meaning when interpreted too broadly. We reach the farcical, for instance, when (as actually happened in radio's early days) a network offered, as evidence of its educational endeavor, a live performance by Amos and Andy before the Federal Radio Commission! If this is education, so is the braying of an ass.[5]

The FCC's sensible evasion of the dilemma of definition is to pass it on to the educators themselves: licensees may classify as "educational" only those programs which are "prepared by or in behalf of educational organizations, exclusive of discussion programs."

Finally (and this is fundamental), there seems to be a basic incompatibility between the objectives of commercial stations and those of formal education. Educators and broadcasters have been inclined to blame each other for this circumstance, when in fact it appears to lie deeper than either the intellectual's scorn for commercialism or the broadcaster's impatience with academicism.

Educational broadcasting can obviously mean many things, but most educators would probably agree that it should usually be delimited at least by the following considerations: Most educational programming should have (1) a definite educational goal, (2) an organization of subject matter consistent with its goal, (3) skillful presentation effectively employing broadcasting techniques without sacrificing educational integrity, (4) a chance to be seen or heard at convenient times when the target audience is available, (5) sufficient frequency of scheduling and individual program length to make the educational goal obtainable, (6) sufficient stability of scheduling and audience promotion to give audiences a chance to learn of its existence and to build cumulatively, and (7) a target audience for each program sufficiently homogeneous (and hence limited in size) for the program to achieve its purpose.

In practice it has been found that commercial stations cannot reasonably be expected to provide these conditions. In the first place, they require substantial investment in the programming itself. To achieve their goal educational programs should be designed and produced by professionals with specialized training, adequate production resources, and supporting promotion. Many station managers, however, consider that in giving *time* to education they have discharged their obligation, despite the fact that time has value only in terms of program service. Time, without the means of filling it with suitable program content, is worthless. The more enlightened broadcast executives, of course, recognize this fact; but since

[5] Charles A. Siepmann, *Radio, Television, and Society* (New York: Oxford University Press, 1950), p. 254.

they are accustomed to passing on program costs to sponsors they do not often find it easy to give substantial financial support to programs which produce no income. The few prestige programs which are conspicuous exceptions do not invalidate the general rule. Educational programming on commercial facilities, then, is too often inadequately planned (in educational terms) and ineffectively produced (in broadcasting terms) simply because these jobs are left to volunteers or to the least capable and lowest paid.

The other criteria for educational programming concern scheduling. No responsible commercial-program director willingly schedules a program with a low audience rating (which an educational program is by definition) between two programs with potentially high audience ratings. The problem is not, as the layman usually supposes, merely the loss of revenue from the educational program (assuming it to be sustaining); its low rating also seriously diminishes the value of adjacent time-segments. Few commercial managers can justify to themselves — or to their owners or stockholders — this double loss of revenue due to what, in commercial terms, is downright bad programming practice. Educational programs on commercial stations are therefore usually relegated to the less salable times of the day when all audience ratings are low. Even then, if a conflict arises concerning whether to move an educational program or lose a prospective account or a popular entertainment feature, the educational program usually loses. Educational programs on commercial stations therefore tend to be migratory.

In other words, good educational programming conflicts with some of the basic principles of good commercial programming: it aims at relatively small audiences, often harms adjacent programs, and produces no revenue; yet it is expensive to produce and requires stable scheduling in time-periods in which it displaces large-audience, revenue-producing entertainment programs.

THE SECOND SERVICE

One answer to this dilemma is to abandon the attempt to enforce an incompatible union between commercial and educational interests, and to allocate each interest separate facilities for providing separate broadcast services. This solution was turned down by the FCC in 1935, but a decade later the Commission reversed its previous thinking by reserving 20 of the 100 FM channels for noncommercial broadcasting.

Since the audience for FM has remained small, the reservation of FM channels for education has not turned out to be as successful as its proponents hoped. In 1948, in order to encourage educational institutions to take advantage of these channels, the FCC liberalized its rules to permit the informal operation of very low-power (10-watt) noncommercial stations under the most economical conditions possible. Syracuse University, which had cooperated with General Electric in the development of low-cost transmitter facilities for the 10-watt FM stations, received the first grant under the revised rules, in October, 1948. This expedient has made it possible for about fifty institutions which otherwise had little chance of doing so to set up their own broadcast facilities (see Fig. 20). Educational FM broadcasting can now be considered mildly successful; it at least has continued slowly growing, whereas the commercial FM service has been shrinking.

Television, as we have said, revived all the enthusiastic hopes for educational broadcasting which flourished in the first ten or fifteen years of AM radio. In 1950 the Joint Committee on Educational Television (JCET) was formed, representing eight national educational organizations, to press the educators' case for a second service in the field of television. By the time the hearings came (1951), educational broadcasters were well organized and in a position to present their case effectively. Since in this instance the allocation of channels was to be made in advance of full commercialization of the medium, there was no prospect that reservations for education would mean actual deletion of existing stations; so the commercial broadcasters' opposition to the plan was not as highly motivated as it had been in 1935. Educational interests were virtually unopposed at the FCC hearings. In fact, existing (pre-freeze) television stations generally welcomed the prospect of lessened commercial competition, which would result if some channels were to be classified as noncommercial. Indeed, many commercial stations have given their noncommercial colleagues very substantial financial assistance. The *Sixth Report and Order,* ending the freeze, earmarked 242 channels (80 VHF and 162 UHF) as noncommercial.

Noncommercial educational stations may be licensed only to "non-profit educational organizations upon a showing that the proposed stations will be used primarily to serve the educational needs of the community; for the advancement of educational programs; and to furnish a nonprofit and noncommercial television broadcast service."[6] They may transmit "educational, cultural and entertainment programs, and programs designed for use by schools and school systems in connection with regular school courses, as well as routine and administrative material pertaining thereto." Noncommercial stations may not be paid for broadcasting programs; however, they may use "programs produced by or at the expense of or furnished by others than the licensee for which no other consideration than the furnishing of the program is received by the licensee." Programs supplied by a commercial source may be identified as from that source; moreover, "where a sponsor's name or product appears on the visual image during the course of a simultaneous or rebroadcast program either on the backdrop or similar form, the portions of the program showing such information need not be deleted."

Upon issuance of the FCC's *Sixth Report and Order,* JCET, the National Citizens' Committee for Educational Television, and other interested organizations instituted a nationwide drive to persuade educational institutions

[6] FCC *Rules and Regulations,* 3.621 (a). Under certain circumstances municipalities also may be licensees.

(or, in many cases, special nonprofit organizations formed to combine the educational interests of a community into a single entity to operate a station) to take advantage of the reservations. Although the FCC has fixed no terminal date for the reservations, the presumption is that the channels will not be held idle forever if educators show no interest in using them. Those of the educational channels which are VHF and are located in large markets have tremendous potential commercial value, and commercial interests will have a persuasive argument for reclassification of such channels if they continue to lie idle.

Television, as we have repeatedly stressed, poses a different economic problem than radio. There is no equivalent of the very low-cost 10-watt FM token operation. The lowest costs of television station installation and operation are very large in contrast with the kind of money that educational institutions have been accustomed to spending for radio. Nevertheless, the JCET and others believe that the importance of a second service is such that the expense could legitimately be defrayed by educational interests. In the first two years following the start of educational-station licensing, ten such stations started broadcasting. The first to start operation was KUHT, licensed to the University of Houston and the Houston public schools and operated by the University, which began operations in May, 1953 (see Fig. 20).[7]

During the same two-year period, according to a JCET estimate, about $25,000,000 in funds for educational television had been made available, nearly half of it from foundations and about a quarter from taxes.[8] Financing of the second service so far has come from four major sources: (1) foundations, (2) taxes, (3) business and industry (notably broadcasting), and (4) the audience. There seems little prospect, on the basis of experience, that educational television stations can be supported entirely by voluntary contributions from their audiences; the foundations are chiefly interested in priming the pump, not in supplying operating funds; industry support is spotty, depending particularly upon the profit-and-loss position of commercial stations which would be affected by the conversion of educational channel assignments in their own areas to commercial use. With the exception of a few stations in the largest markets, it seems probable that the long-term support of the second service will have to come from taxes in one form or another.

Estimates of educational television station construction and operating costs vary wildly, primarily because the FCC does not require such stations to operate on a minimum schedule and because there are so many ways of either exaggerating or minimizing expense items. It appears, however, that even under circumstances favoring the utmost in economy an educational

---

[7] WOI, Iowa State College, has been in operation since February, 1950, but this station is licensed and operated commercially.

[8] JCET, "Two Years of Progress in Educational Television" (mimeo., September, 1954).

television station's operating expenses will run to $100,000 per year; consistently outstanding programming costs a great deal more. This year-in-year-out expense (which should, in fact, increase each year if the educational station is going to keep pace with the developing television art) is the real problem. It is not difficult, in a metropolitan community at least, to drum up a high pitch of enthusiasm for educational television and to secure the necessary gifts of materials and money to put a station on the air. But then the annual operating budget stretches into the indefinite future, and it is for this long-term commitment that tax-money seems the only answer in most communities.

THE NATURE OF THE SECOND SERVICE

The potential thus exists in both FM and television for an expanding second service — a broadcasting service to supplement that of the commercial system, free of the programming limitations imposed on commercial broadcasters by the economics of a competitive, profit-seeking, advertising-supported operation. The second service is not necessarily confined, however, to formal education. It will be recalled that the FCC definition of a noncommercial television station's service includes not only educational programs as such but also "cultural and entertainment programs." This opens the door in educational programming to virtually every type of program (other than commercial announcement programs) seen on commercial stations. On the other hand, it should be noted that the existence of the educational stations does not relieve commercial licensees of the educational obligations which are part of their public-service responsibility. Therefore some of the types of specifically educational programs seen on the noncommercial stations will also be seen on commercial stations. In other words, the two services are not completely different; a certain amount of overlap can occur.

Educational programming as such can be roughly divided into two types: in-school broadcasting and adult education. The former consists of programs, usually of a formal and overtly instructional nature, so scheduled and integrated with a public-school curriculum as to supplement regular classroom instruction. This is known, in the jargon of education, as curriculum "enrichment." Adult education may vary from formal instructional material such as "telecourses" (which may even be offered for college credit to those qualified) to popularized culture and information not basically very different from the "public service" programming of commercial stations.

The noncommercial educational station, no less than the commercial station, has to depend primarily on syndicated materials. No educational station has the financial resources to handle its own programming on a purely local-live basis. This poses a problem for educational broadcasting, since American education is not standardized on a national basis but is committed to the theory of local autonomy. To be successful, however, syndication always calls for a certain degree of generalization and popularization, since syndicated programs have to be acceptable to many different audiences in many different localities. Syndication on a true national basis seems in any event too expensive for educational broadcasting, although some states have succeeded in setting up state networks.

Pseudo-network (non-interconnected) services have been developed for radio by the National Association of Educational Broadcasters (NAEB) and for television by the Educational Television and Radio Center (ETRC). The NAEB grew out of the association of a small group of pioneer educational station operators, primarily in the Middle West, formed during the 1920's. For many years it was no more than a relatively informal association providing an opportunity for the discussion of mutual problems of the small band of struggling educational station directors. In 1949 some members of the NAEB met for a seminar at Allerton House, at the University of Illinois, with the financial aid of the Rockefeller Foundation. This turned out to be a germinal occasion, and the participants emerged from the experience with a new orientation; thereafter the NAEB was imbued with a sense of mission.[9] That mission is a renewed and re-energized dedication to the philosophy of the second service, of which the NAEB is the professional spokesman. Financial aid from the Kellogg Foundation, the Fund for Adult Education, and other sources has enabled the NAEB to set up permanent headquarters with a paid staff at the University of Illinois, to develop its tape network, to engage in research, to publish many reports and studies, to award scholarships and fellowships, to offer workshops, to make grants for the production of program series, and in many other ways to further the cause of educational broadcasting as a separate service.

Funds from the Fund for Adult Education have also been allocated to create the ETRC, which is set up at the University of Michigan. ETRC provides a television programming service comparable to the NAEB tape network. It aids institutional production centers in the production of program series (some on kinescope, some filmed directly) and secures program material on film from other sources to support the programming of educational television stations. The FAE also has made grants to a limited number of educational stations for capital expenditures, one condition being that part of the money shall be spent for kinescope equipment, in order to enable each station to record program material for the Center to distribute.

PROBLEMS OF THE SECOND SERVICE

The theory of a second service rests on the assumptions (1) that the commercial broadcasting service is necessarily self-limiting and cannot provide

[9] Harold E. Hill, "The National Association of Educational Broadcasters: A History" (NAEB, 1954, mimeo.); Robert B. Hudson, "Allerton House 1949, 1950," *Hollywood Quarterly* V-3 (Spring, 1951), pp. 237-250.

the completely-rounded broadcasting service the country needs and (2) that educational interests must operate their own noncommercial stations to supplement the commercial service with a service able to compensate for the omissions of commercial broadcasting. These assumptions require that educational broadcasting offer a service which is recognizably different from the existing (and even from the potential) programming of commercial stations.

> Educational broadcasting is foredoomed to failure as it attempts to ape or rival the commercial broadcaster. Its real opportunity is to provide those services (and they are many) that commercial broadcasting either does not provide at all or offers in inadequate amount and quality.[10]

At first blush this may not seem a very difficult requirement to fulfill. Educational stations, however, face many problems which are little different from those faced by their commercial colleagues. Even educational broadcasting is a mass medium, at least to this extent: when it costs more per audience member to maintain the service than it would cost to communicate the same material by more conventional means (e.g., films, visiting lecturers, house visits by teachers, radio rather than television), the educational station operation can no longer be justified economically. It would be difficult, perhaps, to reduce relative costs to a formula which would permit an accurate comparison, but it is obvious that an educational television station which cost up to a half-million dollars to construct and in addition costs several hundred thousand dollars a year to operate cannot justify its existence by appealing to only a few hundred people at a time. Even taking into consideration the *cumulative* size of audiences (which educational broadcasting must do), the audience for each program must be relatively large. This necessity of keeping sizable audiences interested presents a constant temptation to compromise educational objectives and ideals by resorting to the same kind of mass-audience-building devices as the commercial broadcasters.

Although educational programming should certainly not compete in the sense of *aping* commercial broadcasting, it *must* compete in the sense that every viewer or listener makes some kind of choice among the various offerings of all the stations in his vicinity. Commercial broadcasting spends huge sums on every conceivable device to attract audiences simply to gain their attention in the face of a multitude of competing stimuli. Educational television will not have in its arsenal the stellar talent, the fan magazines, the newspaper advertisements, the thousand and one merchandising and promotional devices by which national attention is attracted to commercial programs. Nor can an educational station be satisfied with appealing only to those who heroically refuse to watch commercial television at all (most of them will not have sets, in any event). Essentially it must deal with the

10 Siepmann, *op. cit.*, p. 286.

same audience as that for commercial broadcasting, because commercial broadcasting created the audience in the first place.

Again, it seems probable that many worthwhile program resources will not be exploited by educational stations any more than by commercial stations, for precisely the same reason: the cost would be excessive. For example, one of the best things educational stations could do would be to schedule a great many actuality (remote) broadcasts, which would capitalize on television's unique capacity for instantaneous reporting of real events. It seems likely, however, that the cost of such broadcasts (as compared to the cost of syndicated film programs and simple live studio formats) will prevent educational stations from exploiting this potentiality to the full. At the same time it should be borne in mind that the commercial stations *will* carry as remotes those events which are of the most outstanding interest and importance.

A great deal has been made of the presumed potentiality of educational stations for providing high-level cultural programs in greater quantity than commercial stations — opera, drama, ballet, symphony. Such productions, however, are extremely expensive and will probably continue to appear more frequently in the commercial than in the educational service. Another presumed potentiality of educational stations is program experimentation — new formats and program devices which the freedom from commercial stereotyping will encourage. The fact is, however, that commercial interests gather creative talent from the ends of the country for precisely this purpose, and are constantly experimenting with new program ideas.[11] Educational programs have to be stereotyped for precisely the same reason that commercial programs are stereotyped: because it is impossible to be original every broadcast hour of every day every year on a cue from the studio clock. In the main it is broadcasting — not commercialism in broadcasting — which necessitates the stereotyped program formats.

A related problem is that of talent. Educational stations are bound to uncover new creative personalities — directors, writers, performers, designers, and the like. As soon as these persons develop enough distinction to command unusual attention they begin to receive offers from commercial interests. Few will be able to resist the attraction of salaries which, compared to those obtainable in noncommercial operations, will seem astronomical.[12] The same thing happens with programs. If an educational station

---

[11] It is instructive to consider the history of the academic theater, which also is theoretically free to experiment because it is not bound by commercial conventions. A candid comparison, however, will show that the commercial theater nowadays does more experimentation than the noncommercial theater, which in the main simply follows the lead of Broadway.

[12] The experience of Dr. Frank C. Baxter is both an exception and a case in point. Dr. Baxter made a phenomenal hit with educational programs on Shakespeare (initially, as it happens, on a commercial station). He immediately became the target of fabulous offers (by academic standards) from commercial motion-picture and television interests. Although he has performed on commercial programs, Dr. Baxter appears to have been

discovered that a telecourse in elementary Greek, to use an unlikely example, touched some hidden need in modern man and attracted audiences in the hundreds of thousands, elementary Greek would soon be selling soaps and cereals.

Finally, it is sometimes alleged that educational stations will be able to surmount many of the taboos of commercial broadcasting which prevent it from handling certain touchy subjects. It is true that an educational station does not have to cater to the sponsor's hypersensitive desire to offend no one and to please all, but college presidents, boards of regents, school superintendents, and school trustees have their own hypersensitivities. Although individual teachers (especially college teachers) may be able to afford unconventional opinions, educational institutions as such tend to be very conservative. So far, educational stations have not been notably less wedded to conservative values than commercial stations. In fact, there is a strong possibility that noncommercial stations may turn out to be on the whole even more timid than their commercial colleagues.[13]

All these problems may seem to add up to a pessimistic outlook for the prospect of educational broadcasting's achieving a genuine second television service. That there is a need for such a second service cannot be doubted, but in the light of the prior experience with educational radio it seems important to appraise realistically the problems which stand in its way. To summarize the foregoing list of problems in more positive terms, we may say that educational broadcasting must: (1) be well-enough founded financially to secure audiences sufficiently large to justify the service — which means among other things employing competent, creative personnel and having adequate facilities and program budgets; (2) develop the procedures for finding and training creative talent to replace that drawn off by commercial interests; (3) achieve sufficient independence of political and social pressures to make up for the omissions of the commercial service. On the more optimistic side, educational television, as compared to educational AM radio, has in its favor the facts that channels are reserved, that specialists in the field are already experienced and well organized, that it is much easier to teach by television than by radio, and that certain of the large foundations that have a strong interest in adult education see in television a worthwhile instrument.

---

philosophically predisposed to turn down most of these offers. Such fortitude is unusual, however, and is hardly to be expected of younger men lacking in Dr. Baxter's amused detachment.

[13] A study made in 1951 indicated a very conservative policy on the part of educational radio stations, particularly those associated with public school systems. One station confessed: "Controversial subjects and political opinion programs are not permitted under our broadcast policy. This same policy has been in effect since the establishment of the station beginning December 1, 1924." Cf.: Irving Rodgers Merrill, "Broadcasting by Political Candidates on Educational Stations" (M.S. thesis, University of Illinois, 1952, mimeo.).

EDUCATION FOR BROADCASTING

Education *by* broadcasting has received a great deal more attention than education *for* broadcasting. This relative emphasis is natural. Educators at first thought of using broadcasting as another device for furthering existing educational aims. Moreover, until the broadcasting industry took shape and became stabilized there was nothing definable to educate people *for* in broadcasting. Although the emphasis (particularly as measured by foundation grants) remains on the use of broadcasting as another audio-visual teaching device, in recent years there has been an increasing realization that higher education has an important responsibility in another direction — providing professional education for those who are going to enter the broadcasting industry.

The importance of this responsibility lies in the fact that in the foreseeable future commercial broadcasting will continue to reach vastly more people with vastly more hours of programming than noncommercial broadcasting. The social influence of several thousand commercial stations with unlimited funds to employ the cream of the country's creative and technical talent is very likely to be more pervasive than the influence of a few hundred (at the most) educational stations operating on limited budgets. If colleges and universities can indirectly influence the programming of commercial stations by educating the people who make the program decisions so that they will make those decisions wisely and conscientiously in terms of social needs, education will have accomplished a very great service to society.

It is only recently that it has become possible to talk intelligently about a specific academic discipline for broadcasters. After all, the industry is still so young that some of the very people who started it are still actively engaged in it. Many generations of broadcasters will come and go before a solid tradition emerges. In the meantime, however, enough is known to make it possible to plan at least an interim curriculum for professional training in broadcasting.

It is instructive to compare the academic history of journalism with that of broadcasting, since journalism is the academic field which is most analogous to the emergent field of broadcasting. The first college course in journalism was introduced in 1869, a course in "Typography and Stenography," taught by the editor of a local newspaper. The University of Missouri started a course in the history of journalism in 1878, and established a School of Journalism in 1909. The Columbia University School of Journalism was started in 1912.[14] The first journalism courses were practical inductions into the mysteries of the trade — typography, reporting, editing, and so on. Then came courses with more intellectual content — the history, economics, and ethics of the field. Next came research and evaluation. At first practical

[14] Cf.: UNESCO, *Reports on the Facilities of Mass Communication; Press, Radio, Film,* IV (Paris, 1950), pp. 183-186.

newspapermen scorned the notion of a college education in journalism. *They* hadn't needed college training for their profession, so why should the new generation? Gradually this attitude changed as employers realized that higher education could indeed enhance the value of new employees — and in the long run the status of the profession as well.

Substantially the same kind of progress is being made in education for broadcasting, except that in most respects this field is still back where journalism was in about 1900. Aside from its novelty, one reason that broadcasting education has not advanced faster is the fact that it impinges on so many different existing academic disciplines. Journalism teaching was introduced before college curricula had ramified into many specialized departments; its only logical rival was English. Broadcasting, however, touches the domains of many different academic specialties — speech, drama, journalism, advertising, public relations, English, psychology, sociology, audio-visual education, etc.[15] Speech departments (which often also include drama) were the most active in introducing the early radio courses, no doubt because announcing is one of the most basic functions in radio. This more or less accidental linking of broadcasting with speech and drama training was unfortunate, because it tended to produce undue emphasis on the artistic aspects of broadcasting and to neglect its economic, social, and technical aspects. This inappropriate emphasis was a major cause of industry suspicion of and dissatisfaction with college training programs in its field. The average station manager regards his announcers as salesmen, and was understandably baffled by a college-graduate applicant for employment with specialized broadcast training who had no background in sales and regarded announcing as a form of dramatic art. This kind of misunderstanding was often compounded by educators who insisted on judging American broadcasting as though it were governed by the laws of aesthetics rather than by the laws of economics.

The fact is that broadcasting is academically much closer to the social sciences than to the arts. It does not, however, conform to any prior academic discipline, for the simple reason that broadcasting is not quite like any pre-existing medium. As we have said, journalism is probably the most analogous field. Like broadcasting, journalism is assimilative; it employs, in one way or another, practically all skills, arts, and disciplines. The fact that broadcasting is the most significant economic rival of the press, however, can make a journalism curriculum a somewhat prejudiced host.

Another barrier to an independent academic status for broadcasting is the fact that many educational administrators view with alarm the tendency of college curricula to become fragmented into ever narrower specialties, with an increased emphasis on vocational training. Since many of the arts, skills, facts, and theories involved in broadcasting are specialized applica-

---

[15] Broadcast instruction comes under 29 different department titles in 78 colleges and universities offering degree programs in the field, according to an NAEB survey (unpublished at the time this was written).

tions of pre-existing disciplines, there is a certain logic in scattering the broadcasting curriculum among existing departments, with the result that the student goes to Business Administration for courses in advertising and management, for example, to Journalism for courses in news, and to the various fine and applied arts departments for courses in these fields. This dispersal of the broadcasting curriculum, however, almost inevitably means that it cannot be integrated into a cohesive pattern. A more satisfactory approach is to draw upon existing departments for the basic knowledge and skills-training in their fields, and to incorporate in the broadcasting curriculum proper the particular applications of these knowledges and skills. This procedure has analogies in many other fields. For example, statistics is taught as a basic mathematical discipline but also as an applied discipline in such fields as psychology, education, business, and engineering. Writing is taught basically as a field of English, but specialized forms of writing are also often taught in such fields as journalism, drama, science, and engineering.

In the final analysis, broadcasting needs to stand on its own academic feet. It cannot logically be classed as a subsidiary or derivative subject of any other subject; wherever it is so classed, the treatment of broadcasting is likely to be one-sided, incomplete, or inadequate. It matters little, of course, what academic name is given to the administrative entity under which broadcasting instruction falls, as long as its unique character is recognized. At Boston University it is taught in a Division of Communication Arts under a School of Public Relations and Communication; at Northwestern University in a department of the School of Speech; at the University of Illinois in the School of Journalism and Communication; at Southern California in a Department of Telecommunications, and so on. The important thing is that the broadcasting curriculum should have the freedom to develop along lines appropriate to broadcasting, instead of being forced into a pattern appropriate to some other medium or field of study.

TOWARD PROFESSIONALIZATION

Our discussion of the development, economy, and regulation of commercial broadcasting makes it clear that in the final analysis the progress of broadcasting toward a higher status depends upon the intelligence, good will, social insight, and conscientiousness of the people responsible for its conduct (see page 371). The forces of legal regulation, self-regulation, and public opinion can prevent the worst, but they cannot achieve the best. The best must come ultimately from the individual integrity of those who work in the medium. That in turn can best come from a sense of *professional responsibility*. If broadcasting has as profound an effect on the individual and the society as it is usually believed to have, it is not too much to expect that its practitioners should attain the status of a profession. What that means was explained by Harold Lasswell, speaking in another connection at the 1951 NAEB annual convention:

> What are the distinctive marks of a skill group that deserves to be called a profession? The essential mark is not only the acquisition of skill, not only the development of literate theories of these skills, but the demand to serve the public interest. The mark of a profession from this point of view is whether its members will turn down jobs. A rough-and-ready way to decide whether you have a profession is to find out if people will turn down jobs in the field because the jobs would be against the public interest.
>
> How do you develop a profession? A profession is always developed slowly, as people who perform specialized operations begin to develop elaborate theories about what they do. Also, many of them become alert to the aggregate impact on society of what they do and begin to feel they should themselves take responsibility for deciding the extent to which the skill benefits society in concrete situations. Hence they evolve standards of professional conduct.[16]

If to expect this kind of integrity of broadcasters seems naive and utopian, it should be remembered that professions emerge slowly from the gradual accretion of tradition, whereas broadcasting is still in its infancy. Moreover, despite the cynicism which the huckstering aspects of broadcasting engender, the fact is that the more responsible stations and networks actually do "turn down jobs," in the sense that they reject a great deal of business which is perfectly legal but would work against the public interest. So far, however, this sense of responsibility is more institutional than personal. The great need of the industry is for the extension of the concept of responsibility to every individual whose decisions could affect the quality of the service.

The task of professionalization is a communal task for the industry, the public, the government, the individual critic, and education. Education cannot reach the goal unaided. Nor can it succeed either by ignoring or by weakly deploring the present broadcasting service. Education should look at the broadcasting industry first for what it is as well as for what it may be and should be. Secondly, it should look at broadcasting in the context of the other mass media, for, as we have pointed out, its position is strategic as an intersecting point in the currents of inter-media competition. Thirdly, it should regard broadcasting primarily as a social science rather than as a fine art.

This last is not to advocate the elimination of the arts and skills involved in broadcasting from the broadcasting curriculum. These *as ends in themselves,* however, are not appropriate subject matter for college-level broadcasting education. There are many trade schools, some of which teach the broadcasting skills very rapidly and efficiently. The college is concerned with

[16] Harold Lasswell, "Educational Broadcasters as Social Scientists." Reprinted from the *Quarterly of Film, Radio, and Television,* VII-2 (Winter, 1952), published by the University of California Press. Pp. 160-161.

training the mind rather than the hand; yet it must train the hand along with the mind, for the very practical reason that otherwise its graduates will not be able to compete in the job market for the opportunity to *use* their minds.

Professional broadcasting education might well include, in addition to the general courses of the normal liberal education, thorough specialized study of the political and social concepts involved in the theory and practice of freedom of speech; of relations between economic and political theories, with special reference to problems of monopoly, public opinion, and propaganda; of the growing body of theory and data on the mass-communication media — their content, their control, their effects; of not merely the contemporary practical applications of communications law but also the social and political theories which underlie it, with special reference to their significance to our own political system; of not merely the contemporary commercial practices of broadcasting but also the broader context of the American economy and its dynamics.

Broadcasting as an industry has hitherto paid remarkably little attention to its own personnel-recruitment needs, as was pointed out in Chapter 18. Generally speaking, the relations between the industry as a whole (there have been conspicuous local exceptions) and education as a whole have been strained. A possible indication of a changing view on both sides was the formation in 1955 of a joint industry–education organization, the Association for Professional Broadcasting Education, in which broadcasters (through the NARTB) and educators are equally represented, and to the support of which broadcasters contribute financially (a significant measure of their seriousness). The formation of APBE may be an indication of the allaying of old fears and prejudices and a step toward mutually beneficial relations between higher education and commercial broadcasting as a professional field.

PART FIVE

Evaluating the
Broadcasting Service

27

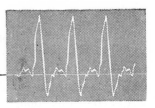

The Communication Process

and Its Effects

It is 5:25 P.M. — you have just finished broadcasting; you have also practically finished breaking up a happy home. Our set was installed last evening. Today, my wife has not left her chair, listening all day. Our apartment has not been cleaned — the beds not made —the baby [not] bathed — and no dinner ready for me.
— FAN-LETTER TO WEAF, 1922*

Broadcasting undoubtedly has an effect on people, and it is for this reason that broadcasting becomes a subject of serious concern to society. It is generally believed that the effects of the mass media are both widespread and profound. Opinions on the subject are likely to be very positive, but since they are also likely to be contradictory, it is apparent that the cause–effect relation of communication content to human behavior is not a simple one. The presumed "bad" effects of the mass media receive more stress than the presumed "good" effects.

> The belief that the vulgar arts have some kind of social significance, normally evil but potentially good, has generally been acted upon without much discussion, perhaps because those who enjoy the vulgar arts are not, by and large, those who write and talk about art.[1]

Walter Lippmann introduces his valuable pioneer study of public opinion with a chapter on "The World Outside and the Picture in our Heads." The pictures in one head do not always agree with the pictures in another head; nor does either group of pictures necessarily agree with reality, even when we have immediate access to the outside facts. Yet the problem of securing

* William P. Banning, *Commercial Broadcasting Pioneer* (Cambridge, Mass.: Harvard University Press, 1946), p. 90.

[1] Richard T. La Piere, *Sociology* (New York: McGraw-Hill, 1946), p. 326.

a reasonably accurate picture of reality is even further complicated because most of us never directly experience much of the world outside. Our real environment is limited to our own living space, and the only means we have of knowing anything at all about the world beyond this narrow home territory is communication. Vicariously we can learn a good deal of this world outside by reading, listening, and looking at pictures. The significance of television as a communications medium is that it can make vicarious experience more "real" to us than any other medium. As Lippmann pointed out long before television,

> Photographs have the kind of authority over imagination today, which the printed word had yesterday, and the spoken word before that. They seem utterly real. They come, we imagine, directly to us without human meddling, and they are the most effortless food of the mind conceivable.[2]

This is at once the great virtue and the great hazard of television: its seeming reality and its effortlessness make it a wonderful instrument for providing us with data for improving the fidelity of the picture in our heads; but at the same time those very qualities make it equally capable of distorting our picture of reality. It is sometimes asserted that the television camera, when reporting actual events directly, cannot "editorialize," that the pictures come to us "without human meddling." Nothing could be further from the truth. In the first place, someone has to select those events which will be televised and those which will not; in the second place, either consciously or unconsciously, those responsible for "taking" the television pictures exercise editorial judgment in their selection. It is perfectly possible for a direct telecast of a real event to be so contrived as to produce a completely misleading "picture in our heads."

TYPES OF "BAD" EFFECTS

Criticism of the social effects of the mass media, with particular reference to the effects of broadcasting, may be roughly classified for purposes of discussion into six categories. Broadcasting is alleged to (1) debase the arts and audience taste, (2) encourage escapism, (3) engage in economic exploitation, (4) undermine moral standards, (5) set up false images of reality, (6) and distort reality through omission.

The first three of these criticisms come typically from the intellectual. We may take as an example the indictment of Roger Manvell, an English commentator on the popular arts. According to Manvell, television "degrades and sensationalizes everything educational it touches, out of fear of losing its hold on the public mind"; moreover, as a result of the "invasion of the privacy of the home by crude values, low humor and low necklines . . . virtues of concentration and contemplation are being lost to the world."[3]

---

[2] Walter Lippmann, *Public Opinion* (New York: Macmillan & Co., 1922), p. 92. Reprinted by permission of Macmillan Co.
[3] Roger Manvell, *The Crowded Air* (New York: Channel Press, 1953), pp. 42-43.

According to this view, the popularization of knowledge and of the arts which is presumably necessary to make them palatable to mass audiences results only in their degradation, with like effects on the tastes of audiences.

The second criticism — that the mass media encourage escapism — is implied by Manvell in the comment that television "encourages in adults and children alike a craving for continuous visual excitement. . . . The desire for personal activity slowly atrophies."[4] This view deplores the fact that the time spent in watching television is necessarily time taken from other, presumably more beneficial, activities. The point is made in Robert Hutchins's sally that a mysterious kind of moss discovered on Mars has finally been identified as the vestigial remains of a race of human beings — reduced by passive television watching to vegetable form.

On the third point Manvell asserts that television "persuades people to buy things they don't need with money they don't possess."[5] This is based on the valid inference that in the absence of mass advertising people would want fewer things and hence buy fewer things. Advertising deliberately sets out to create "needs" which were not previously felt, and to use all the arts of persuasion to induce people to satisfy these newly-felt needs irrespective of their ability to pay.

Fourth, television is alleged to undermine moral standards. This opinion is more widely held than the three previously mentioned. It is the assumption underlying most of the negative rules of the production codes. These rules are based on the belief that the presentation in the mass media of actions and attitudes which do not conform to the moral code will incite audience members to imitate these immoral actions or to adopt these immoral attitudes. The dramatic exposition of a technique for committing a crime, for example, is believed to be likely to cause viewers to imitate that technique in real life. Presentations in which criminals escape without punishment are believed to teach the lesson that "crime *does* pay" and hence to encourage (or at least not to discourage) the commission of real crimes. This category of criticism is based not on what actually happens in society (crime obviously does pay sometimes) but on what *should* happen according to a set code of conduct. In other words, it represents a point of view that is essentially dogmatic and moralistic.

The fifth criticism — that television sets up false images of reality — is based on the belief that it would be beneficial if the content of the medium more accurately reflected what really does happen in society. It is the antithesis, in fact, of the dogmatically moralistic viewpoint. The mass media tend to present human relationships in stereotyped forms; by constant repetition these stereotypes are presumed to become the misleading "pictures in our heads" which falsely reflect the "world outside." Gilbert Seldes has made a game of reducing some of these stereotypes as they appear in the movies (he believes that they largely owe their existence to the super-

[4] *Loc. cit.*
[5] *Loc. cit.*

ficial moralizing of the MPAA Code) to social "laws" of the mythical world
that the movies project:

> Pure love, as the Code calls it, is not sexual; it may have what the phys-
> iologists call "secondary sexual characteristics," but it's not physical.

> Divorce occurs for trivial reasons only; it is the consequence of hasty tem-
> pers or misunderstandings or a desire to rise in the world of society and
> finance.

> A man and a woman, destined to fall in love, always loathe each other when
> they first meet.

> Women are always wiser than men in the conduct of life, shrewder in busi-
> ness, and craftier in statesmanship; also, often, handier around the house.

> There are no economic forces; there are a few unscrupulous manipulators
> who may bring disaster on many people.[6]

Critics with a psychoanalytic frame of reference go further and see hidden
significance in the "latent" meaning of such stereotypes. Such meanings are
concealed in symbolic terms, like the meanings of dreams. Frederic Wertham has analyzed comic books from this point of view, and finds themes
of homosexuality, sexual sadism, and the like in recurrent scenes of the
torturing of women, injury to the eye, and other forms of brutality.[7]

MASS-MEDIA CONSERVATISM

The sixth allegation — that the mass media distort reality by omitting
certain categories of content — is one of the most common criticisms of the
mass media made by social scientists. These critics are concerned not about
abundance (frequency of presentation) but about deprivation (absence of
alternative presentations). In their view, the fact that the mass media tend
toward conservatism and avoidance of controversial or unpopular ideas
automatically reinforces the social and economic *status quo*: "By leading
toward conformism and by providing little basis for a critical appraisal of
society, the commercially sponsored mass media indirectly but effectively
restrain cogent development of a genuinely critical outlook."[8] A similar
view has been expressed with specific regard to the advertising content of
the mass media:

[6] Gilbert Seldes, *The Great Audience* (New York: The Viking Press, 1950), pp. 74-84
passim. A serious study of this sort of stereotyping is found in: Martha Wolfenstein and
Nathan Leites, *Movies: A Psychological Study* (Glencoe, Ill.: The Free Press, 1950).

[7] Cf.: Frederic Wertham, *Seduction of the Innocent* (New York: Rinehart, 1954).
Wertham includes a chapter on television, "Homicide at Home," pp. 353-383. Cf. also:
T. W. Adorno, "How to Look at Television," *Quarterly of Film, Radio, and Television*,
VII-3 (Spring, 1954), pp. 213-235.

[8] Paul F. Lazarsfeld and Robert K. Merton, "Mass Communication, Popular Taste and
Organized Social Action," in: Lyman Bryson (ed.), *The Communication of Ideas* (New
York: Harper & Bros., 1948), p. 107.

. . . the most important effects of this powerful institution [advertising] are not upon the economics of our distributive system; they are upon the values of our society. If the economic effect is to make the purchaser like what he buys, the social effect is, in a parallel but broader sense, to make the individual like what he gets — to enforce already existing attitudes, to diminish the range and variety of choices, and, in terms of abundance, to exalt the materialistic virtues of consumption.[9]

What are these conservative, *status quo* values? They are not necessarily the values by which society actually governs itself, but the values which have the sanction of tradition. They are often the standards to which people pay lip service, and by which they expect everybody to be ruled but themselves.

The curse of modern mass culture seems to be its adherence to the almost unchanged ideology of early middle-class society, whereas the lives of its consumers are completely out of phase with this ideology. This is probably the reason for the gap between the overt and the hidden "message" of modern popular art. Although on the overt level the traditional values of English Puritan middle-class society are promulgated, the hidden message aims at a frame of mind which is no longer bound by these values.[10]

It may well be asked, what is wrong with conservatism? If it is true that the mass media primarily reflect *status quo* values, is there any harm in this emphasis? From the social theorist's point of view, the harm is not in the nature of the values themselves but in the absence of alternative presentations. A function of communications, especially mass communications, is believed to be the facilitation of harmonious social change. Whether we like it or not, changes take place, and a society which becomes deeply divided by a static, anachronistic system of values may find itself eventually torn apart by violence. "Unless the communication process allows us to maintain a certain consensus on how we want . . . change to take place and to identify the goals of social change, we have a complete breakdown of social organization. . . ."[11]

THE COMMUNICATION PROCESS

These six categories of criticism will bear further examination, but it will be helpful first to look into the known facts about the mass communication process and to see how the effects of communications are related to their

---

[9] David M. Potter, *People of Plenty: Economic Abundance and the American Character* (Chicago: University of Chicago Press, 1954), p. 188. Copyright 1954 by The University of Chicago.

[10] T. W. Adorno, "How to Look at Television," reprinted from the *Quarterly of Film, Radio, and Television,* VII-3 (Spring, 1954), published by the University of California Press. P. 219.

[11] John E. Ivey, Jr., "Communications as a Social Instrument," in: University of Illinois Institute for Communications Research, *Communications in Modern Society* (Urbana, Ill.: University of Illinois Press, 1948), p. 148.

content. Scientific study of the mass-communication process is relatively new, having developed primarily from an interest in propaganda and opinion formation. Mass-media propaganda was first used extensively in World War I. In the postwar years the revelation of the important role that propaganda had played as an instrument of wartime policy led to a serious study of the social and psychological processes involved. For a time it was believed that this new weapon was all-powerful, that all of us were helplessly manipulated by a few sinister leaders in the "manufacture of consent." Subsequent study, however, revealed that propaganda — and hence the predictability of mass-communication effects — is a far less universally effective weapon than had at first been supposed.

The study of propaganda and opinion formation has brought together several different disciplines, requiring as it does a variety of research techniques and theoretical constructs. Mass-media research and theory use basic material from psychology, social psychology, and sociology. They impinge on the interests of such fields of study as political science, journalism, broadcasting, and economics. They are of special interest in such specific areas of study as juvenile delinquency, rumor, panic, social control, literary history, popular culture and the sociology of knowledge. A recognizably distinct field of mass communications research and theory appears to be evolving, representing a new synthesis of previous fields of study.[12]

The study of mass communication deals with the implications of the question "Who says what through what channel to whom with what effect?"[13] This simple statement reminds us that the effect of a communication is the end result of a sequence of events. The sequence starts with the communicator himself — his character, motivations, skills. He must submit his message to the limitations of a given channel, or medium, of communication. The message itself is thus affected by both the intention of the communicator and the characteristics of the medium employed. The message is received by an audience, consisting of a person or persons in a certain environment which affects the way in which the message will be perceived. Finally, the message is interpreted with varying degrees of accuracy (in terms of the communicator's intention), and then perhaps is acted upon in some way. The overt acts eventuating from this chain of events are generally what is meant by effects, although logically such subjective acts as paying

[12] An interesting illustration is the research tool known as "content analysis," i.e., the techniques for describing significant aspects of bodies of communications material, primarily in quantitative terms. A surprisingly wide variety of communications have been subjected to content analysis, including such materials as letters, psychoanalytic data, and paintings, as well as newspapers, magazines, and broadcasts. Many of these analyses could have been materially aided if researchers had been aware of the previous work of others in apparently unrelated fields. This information was brought together and made generally available for the first time in: Bernard Berelson, Content Analysis in Communication Research (Glencoe, Ill.: The Free Press, 1952).

[13] Adapted from: Bruce L. Smith, Harold D. Lasswell, and Ralph D. Casey, Propaganda, Communication, and Public Opinion (Princeton, N. J.: Princeton University Press, 1946), p. 121.

attention to the message, perceiving it, and interpreting it are also effects. The process does not necessarily end here, however. If the communication does have effect, the members of the audience may take some action which eventually gets back to the communicator and in turn has some effect on him. A familiar example is the audience reactions in a face-to-face communication situation which the speaker perceives and uses to modify his speech. This process is known, in analogy with engineering communication systems, as *feedback*.[14] Feedback in mass communications is necessarily delayed and indirect, since the communicator cannot receive cues from his audience simultaneously with the delivery of the message as can the speaker in face-to-face communications.

To particularize on this description of the whole communication process, let us suppose that the "who" is a political speaker, the "what" a speech against a pending piece of legislation, the "channel" a television program, the "whom" a businessman and his wife, and the "effect" a telegram which the businessman sends to the speaker. Dynamic relationships among these elements can be imagined. The speaker is conscious that he represents business interests in his constituency, and is arguing against a bill which would adversely affect these interests. The fact that he is using television causes him to pitch his address at the level of an intimate talk with a small family group and to use charts and graphs to illustrate his points visually. The medium also affects the message directly because the station's policy has prevented the speaker from making certain libelous statements he had planned to use (he is not now a candidate for office). The businessman and his wife emphatically agree with the talk, and the man promptly picks up the telephone and sends a telegram of congratulation and support to the speaker.

LEVELS OF RESPONSE

Unfortunately, the outcome of mass communications is not usually as clear-cut and measurable as this overt act. Harold Lasswell, one of the pioneer students of mass communication, has defined five stages or levels of response, four of which precede such direct action as the example of the telegram.[15] The first level is that of *attention;* obviously no further response can occur if the audience does not direct attention to the message in the first place. But attention does not necessarily involve cognition; so the next level is the response of comprehension. This is a highly variable response; any person who works in the communication fields soon learns that recipients of his message are likely to interpret his intention with many different shades of meaning. Next come the stages of *enjoyment* (like-

14 ". . . feedback is the control of a system by reinserting into the system the result of its performance." Norbert Wiener, *The Human Use of Human Beings* (Boston: Houghton Mifflin Co., 1950), p. 71.
15 Smith, Lasswell, and Casey, *op. cit.*, p. 80.

dislike, etc.), *evaluation* (approve-disapprove, etc.), and finally *action*. Each of these levels of response can be measured. For example, evaluation responses can be measured by means of tests for attitude change after exposure to a persuasive argument. Note, however, that responses do not emerge as objective events until after the terminal stage of action is reached. Attention, comprehension, enjoyment, and evaluation are *subjective* responses and therefore can be measured only indirectly.

Even at the level of action, however, the precise measurement of response is difficult, for most communications aim at producing post-exposure responses. This means that the subject is exposed to other stimuli between the time of the original communication stimulus and the time when the action is taken. It is therefore difficult rigorously to define the response as due *solely* to the communication itself. In the hypothetical example of the telegram previously cited we had the man telegraph *immediately* to obviate this problem. If, however, he had telegraphed the next day, other stimuli might have been responsible for the act. For example, he might have discussed the talk with his wife the next day over breakfast, and she might have persuaded him to send the message. Conversely, the next day the man might have been distracted by business problems and have forgotten to send the telegram at all.[16]

Most commercial research on the effects of broadcasting necessarily deals with the preliminary stages of response. Set-tuning, for example, is antecedent even to the level of attention, and must be ascribed to previous stimuli, such as memory of earlier programs in a series, recommendation from a friend, an advertisement in the newspaper, habit, and so on. Set-tuning data do not even reveal conclusively whether the level of attention is eventually reached in every instance, although set-tuning is generally assumed to be significant at the level of enjoyment. At the level of action, the available data are also generally inferential, depending, for example, on a comparison of the sales graphs between a test city in which an advertising campaign is conducted and a matching city where the campaign is not scheduled (see Chapter 16).

NON-CONTENT FACTORS IN RESPONSE

A study of responses to actual mass communications and also of responses in situations artificially created for research purposes indicates that the result of a message depends only in part on the content of the message itself. Non-content factors in the dynamics of the communication situation include: (1) the channel, or medium, by which the message is sent; (2) personality

---

[16] Note that the technique of per-inquiry advertising is designed to link stimulus and response directly, and hence the cause–effect relationship is evident. The message is not necessarily the only, or sufficient, cause, however, as the further analysis of the communication process below demonstrates.

factors in the recipient; and (3) situational factors present at the time of reception.[17]

As for the medium employed, it has been well established, for example, that a given medium enjoys a certain status in the eyes of audiences. This status affects their attitude toward the medium and hence toward its content. Radio as a medium for news, for instance, is known to have a relatively high status, in that people tend to place more confidence in news heard over the radio than in news received from other sources. How this status can affect the results of communications was well illustrated by the panic which was caused by the famous Orson Welles broadcast *The Invasion from Mars*. Many of those who were panic-stricken by the broadcast gave as their reason for believing that the dramatization was a real event their belief in the credibility of radio news.[18]

Personality factors determine the way in which communications are *perceived*. Mass media deliver *identical* messages to large numbers of people; all are exposed to precisely the same content stimulus, yet people "see" different things. Research has established that perception involves not a simple one-way stimulus–response sequence but a two-way *interaction* between the stimulus and the responder.

> . . . the individual reacts *on* the stimulus material (content) rather than passively responding *to* it . . . the perceiver structures the situation (stimulus material, content) in a manner which makes it meaningful to him. . . .
> In general, we want to be disturbed as little as possible and to continue to perceive the world in ways that confirm our existing frame of reference. We become skillful in avoiding stimulus material (for example, communications content), which is likely to seriously challenge our established value systems.[19]

The mass media are thus at a disadvantage when attempting to communicate content which the target-audience is likely unconsciously to evade or "misunderstand," for the communicator cannot immediately know of these perceptual difficulties and adjust his message to them. The mass media provide at any given moment only *one-way* communication, lacking in the two-way give and take (feedback) of face-to-face communication.

Hadley Cantril's study of *The Invasion from Mars* again provides striking illustrations of the way in which audiences fit their perceptions into existing frames of reference. Many people who were panic-stricken by the broadcast tried unsuccessfully to check its authenticity. When confronted with evi-

---

[17] This analysis is that of Franklin Fearing. Cf. his "Social Impact of the Mass Media of Communication," in: National Society for the Study of Education, *Fifty-Third Yearbook, Part II, Mass Media and Education* (Chicago: University of Chicago Press, 1954), pp. 165-191.

[18] Hadley Cantril, *The Invasion from Mars* (Princeton, N. J.: Princeton University Press, 1947), pp. 68-70.

[19] Fearing, *op. cit.*, p. 173.

dence which at the very least should have raised doubts of the broadcast's authenticity, they unconsciously twisted the significance of the evidence so that it would *support* their misconception:

> "I looked out of the window and everything looked the same as usual *so I thought it hadn't reached our section yet.*"

> "We looked out of the window and Wyoming Avenue was black with cars. *People were rushing away, I figured.*"

> "My husband tried to calm me and said, 'If this were really so, it would be on all stations' and he turned to one of the other stations and there was music. *I retorted, 'Nero fiddled while Rome burned.'* "[20]

SITUATIONAL FACTORS

Situational factors in the receipt of communications are manifold. The influence of the immediate physical situation should be apparent — the degree of comfort–discomfort of the situation, the presence of distracting stimuli, the mechanical quality of message reproduction, and so on. The immediate situation also has social aspects: the receiver perceives the message alone or with other persons; if with others, they may be many or few, peer-group, parents, strangers, and so on. For example, a few people in a large theatre make a "cold" audience; they do not respond in the same way or in the same degree as when the house is crowded. The difference is apparent to both performers and audience.

More remote but nonetheless significant situational factors are the social class and the usual social environment of the perceiver. A person still "belongs" to a certain social group even when not actually among members of the group; he carries with him the "internalized" standards, predispositions, attitudes of his own group. The stereotype of the Empire-conscious Englishman who meticulously dresses for dinner alone in the depths of the jungle is a trite example.

CONDITIONS FOR EFFECTIVENESS

These circumstances of the process of receiving and interpreting communications suggest caution in drawing hasty conclusions about the effects of communication content. They suggest that the ability of messages to produce a predicted effect depends on how well the messages fit into the frame of reference and value system of the target-audience. Propaganda which fails to take these factors into account falls on barren soil. It has been found, in fact, that propaganda which collides head-on with highly-structured opposing convictions may even backfire and produce the opposite of the intended result, an even more stubborn adherence to the existing

[20] Statements of participants in the panic, quoted in Cantril, *op. cit.*, pp. 93-94 *passim.*

viewpoint. This well-recognized phenomenon has been called the "boom-erang effect."[21]

Mass communication is most effective when either one of two conditions prevails: (1) the target-audience is so confused about its own needs and values that it becomes susceptible to any persuasive argument which promises security and order or (2) the communication conforms (or seems to conform) with the needs and value system of the audience. The former condition can be artificially created, and the way thus paved for successful propaganda, by a totalitarian regime which can control not only the content and the channels of communication but also to a large extent the psycho-logical and situational factors of reception. The second alternative is the only one available when the communicator does not have at his disposal totalitarian methods of "softening up" the audience. At best he may "canal-ize" existing audience attitudes in the direction of his goal.[22]

It is often asserted that because Americans are so highly successful in using the mass media for selling goods and services they should be able to use their skills with equal success in selling ideas. This is a naive assump-tion; persuading a person to switch brands of soap is by no means the same thing as persuading him to change his deepest convictions on such subjects as religion, race, politics, or economics.

. . . the leap from the efficacy of advertising to the assumed efficacy of propaganda aimed at deeprooted attitudes and ego-involved behavior is as unwarranted as it is dangerous. Advertising is typically directed toward canalizing preexisting behavior patterns and attitudes.[23]

Another common assumption is that the mass media alone can be respon-sible for the outcome of political campaigns. A good deal of research has gone into the problem of political opinion-formation because of the obvious importance of the subject in a country in which public opinion is held to be the ultimate source of political power. A very careful study of the effects of various avenues of political persuasion in a particular community and a particular election led to the conclusion that the mass media did relatively little to shift votes from one party to another. Voting behavior was found to be firmly linked to socio-economic status of the individual, and was not much affected by sources of persuasion external to the immediate social environment.[24]

REFERENCE-GROUP THEORY

This finding fits a theory of social control known as "reference-group theory." According to this theory, the most important of the forces which

21 Interesting examples can be found in: Eunice Cooper and Marie Jahoda, "The Evasion of Propaganda: How Prejudiced People Respond to Antiprejudice Propaganda," *Journal of Psychology*, XXIII (January 1947), pp. 15-25.
22 Lazarsfeld and Merton, *op. cit.*, p. 117.
23 *Ibid.*, p. 114.
24 Paul Lazarsfeld, Bernard Berelson, and Hazel Gaudet, *The People's Choice* (New York: Duell, Sloan & Pearce, 1944), *passim*.

cause the individual to modify his behavior in keeping with social requirements is the influence of the small primary social group to which the individual belongs. The reference-group theory of social control minimizes the influence of the mass media as models for behavior and attitude formation. Two of the leading social scientists specializing in the field of mass-communications research and theory have concluded, in fact, that "the present role of mass media is largely confined to peripheral social concerns and the media do not exhibit the degree of social power commonly attributed to them."[25]

One of the most persuasive proponents of reference-group theory, Richard T. La Piere, is of a skeptical, rigorously scientific turn of mind, and the logic of his theory carries him to complete rejection of the notion that the mass media have socially significant effects.

> Current concern over the effects on contemporary society of the mass media is initial in character and should not be taken as a measure of either the current or the eventual consequences to social life of the newspaper, the radio, the motion picture, television, and other relatively recent developments in communication technology or uses. In sum, much of the literature — and it is quantitatively impressive — on advertising, political and other propaganda, psychological warfare, and the effects of motion pictures, comic books, etc., is by and large about as meaningful as the small child's excited prattle over the new puppy.[26]

La Piere's position, though somewhat extreme, serves as a useful antidote both to the alarmist school of critics who fear the mass media as the ruin of modern society and to the visionary school of critics who believe that if only the mass media could be reformed they might transform society. More conservative judgment indicates that it is unlikely that television and the other mass media can either reduce the human race to a vegetable existence or convert it into a community of wise men and scholars.

MEASURABLE EFFECTS

In order to recover perspective after the foregoing exploration of divergent estimates and interpretations of broadcasting's effects, it may be helpful to review some of the effects which are objectively measurable. We know that the existence of broadcasting has motivated people to spend billions of dollars to receive the service — more money, in fact, than they spend for any other form of recreation.[27] We know that broadcasting motivates people to spend several hours a day watching and listening. We know that people

[25] Lazarsfeld and Merton, *op. cit.*, p. 117.

[26] Richard T. La Piere, *A Theory of Social Control* (Copyright, 1948, McGraw-Hill Book Company, Inc.), pp. 518-519. Reprinted by permission of the publishers.

[27] Department of Commerce, Bureau of Labor Statistics, "Consumer Price Index: Relative Importance of Components in Revised Index, December, 1952" (July, 1953, mimeo.).

respond by consistently selecting some programs in preference to others. We know that responses reach the level of action in terms of purchasing, letter-writing, donating money, and various other actions which can be measured. Quantitative research on effects is beset with so many technical difficulties that few scholarly studies have been carried out on this most important aspect of mass communications. A few such studies have been made of striking instances of massive response to particular broadcasts.[28] Of course, commercially-sponsored research on effects goes forward continually, but this has limited objectives. Commercial interests are concerned with effects in terms of such responses as brand recognition and purchasing behavior (see Chapter 16). An example of a carefully-designed piece of such commercial research is a before-and-after study of the effect of television on the Fort Wayne, Indiana, market made by NBC in 1953-1954. Typical findings are the following: people in the sample increased the average time devoted to the advertising mass media by 40 per cent after television came; brand awareness of six television-advertised brands increased from 51 to 74 per cent; brand preferences between two competing condensed-milk products reversed themselves when one of the products was advertised on television, with the non-television-advertised milk leading by 6 percentage points before television and trailing by 15 percentage points after television.[29]

Aside from formal research on effects, all of us make our own observations on what happens in our own households and among our own friends. Some people rearrange their living habits to conform to the demands of the television schedule so that they will not miss their favorite programs. Arguments over television have been the proximate cause of family quarrels, assault and battery, divorce, and even homicide. Parents see their children pick up the catch-phrases of popular comedians ("One of these days — pow! Right in the kisser!"), shoot it out with Lone Ranger pistols, garb themselves in Davy Crockett hats. Children learn to recognize brand names before they can even read. When not sitting mesmerized before the television set, they collect box tops, join fan clubs, and browbeat parents into purchasing advertised products.

All these data about effects taken together are certainly impressive, but they do not necessarily tell us about other effects which have long-term

[28] E.g., broadcasts which caused panic (Cantril, *op. cit.*); raised money (Robert K. Merton, *Mass Persuasion* [New York: Harper & Bros., 1946] and Charles N. Winslow, "Sympathetic Pennies: A Radio Case Study," *Journal of Abnormal and Social Psychology* XXXIX-1 [January, 1944], pp. 174-179); and influenced voters (Lazarsfeld, Berelson, and Gaudet, *op. cit.*). A summary of mass-media effects, known and presumed, is found in: Joseph T. Klapper, "The Effects of Mass Media" (New York: Columbia University Bureau of Applied Social Research, 1949, mimeo.). An excellent summary of research on specific television effects is: Thomas E. Coffin, "Television's Impact on Society," (*American Psychologist* X-10 [October, 1955], p. 630), which has a bibliography of 60 items.

[29] NBC, *How Television Changes Strangers into Customers* (New York: NBC, 1955).

importance to society. Does the fact that the mass media mushroomed the Davy Crockett craze into a hundred-million-dollar merchandising spree in the course of a single year also mean that millions of children will be permanently affected by the system of values associated with Davy Crockett? We know that most people spend from three to five hours a day listening to the radio and watching television; does this also tell us that in the absence of broadcasting these hours would be spent in more beneficial ways? We know that programs about crime are very popular, and that these programs are required by the codes to teach the "lesson" that crime does not pay. Is the lesson of such programs any more likely to be "don't commit crimes" than "don't make these mistakes or you will get caught"? Is there, in fact, any effective lesson at all in these modern morality plays?

Questions like these can be answered positively only by making a hazardous leap from the known facts about effects to presumed facts. Our knowledge of the communication process and the many factors which enter into the determination of its outcome give us every reason to be cautious in making predictions and generalizations. On the other hand, it must be noted that people who are concerned about what they believe to be the bad effects of the mass media act on their convictions, irrespective of the facts. We have laws, codes, boycotts, Congressional investigations, magazine articles, books, newspaper columns, letters to the editor, speeches, manifestos, resolutions — all based on assumptions of varying degrees of validity about the effects of the mass media. The mass media are obliged largely to conform to these assumptions, and they therefore act *as though* such effects took place, whether or not they do take place in fact.

28

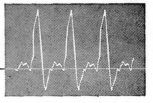

Standards of Evaluation

> It is possible that standards for art forms produced
> by a small band of creative talents for a small and
> selective audience are not applicable to art forms
> produced by a gigantic industry for the popula-
> tion at large.
>
> — PAUL F. LAZARSFELD AND
> ROBERT K. MERTON

One purpose of this book has been to establish a basis for arriving at
reasonable critical standards for the broadcasting system as it actually operates in this country. We have seen in earlier chapters that many pressures,
both internal and external, have a part in determining the content of the
mass media. To recapitulate: The technology of the media requires large
investments which can be justified only by mass marketing of their product.
This in turn requires syndication, which involves making the product of the
media attractive to large and heterogeneous audiences. Insofar as content
is dependent upon advertisers it tends to be determined by their economic
interests rather than by artistic or intellectual considerations. The wide
reach and influence of the media subject them to social pressures which,
though often conflicting, tend to restrict them to content which reflects the
prevailing standards of middle and upper-lower classes of society.

These circumstances should not be ignored in setting up critical standards. If criticism is to have a useful influence, it must be relevant to the
object being appraised. One does not judge automobiles by the criteria
developed for the judgment of horses, nor does one judge horses by the
standards applicable to automobiles. It is as futile to castigate the horse
for not having chromium trim, upholstered seats, and power steering as to
blame the automobile for consuming gasoline instead of hay and running
on tires instead of shoes. Because broadcasting is an innovation it has so
far been judged by criteria developed for other modes of communication.
Eventually, however, standards must be developed which are logically
applicable to the unique mode of communication which is broadcasting.

The basic implement for effective criticism of American broadcasting is understanding of the role that advertising plays in the American system. To ignore this factor is to overlook the most elementary fact about the system. To discuss American broadcasting as though advertising did not (or should not) have any function is to be irrelevant. On the other hand, it is relevant to discuss the standards by which advertising is selected, composed, and inserted in the programming, or its influence on the choice, tone, and structure of programming. It is relevant to discuss the character and comparative merits of advertising-supported broadcasting and tax-supported broadcasting. But if the discussion centers on American broadcasting, advertising is a necessary part of the context.

> Students of the radio and of the mass-circulation magazines frequently condemn advertising for its conspicuous role, as if it were a mere interloper in a separate, pre-existing, self-contained aesthetic world of actors, musicians, authors, and script-writers; they hardly recognize that advertising created modern American radio and television, transformed the modern newspaper, evoked the modern slick periodical, and remains the vital essence of each of them at the present time. Marconi may have invented the wireless and Henry Luce may have invented the news magazine but it is advertising that has made both wireless and news magazines what they are in America today. It is as impossible to understand a modern popular writer without understanding advertising as it would be to understand a medieval troubadour without understanding the cult of chivalry, or a nineteenth-century revivalist without understanding evangelical religion.[1]

CREATIVE INNOVATION AND MASS MEDIA

One of the most frequent sources of confusion about critical standards for mass-media content is the assumption that the creative artist or intellect has, or can have, the same kind of freedom for personal creativity in these media as he has in other media. The fact is that the mass media are unable to provide a hospitable environment for the germinal artist or thinker in which to work out his private vision. Creative work in the mass media is essentially public — a group rather than a private enterprise. In this enterprise the individual has little autonomy; he must often compromise, accommodating himself not only to the physical nature of the medium but also to its economic and institutional nature. One might at first glance suppose that in broadcasting the writer is relatively autonomous — an individual creative agent, somewhat removed from the hurly-burly of the mechanism of production. Before his work can reach the public, however, it passes through the hands of producers, directors, actors, technicians, agency and client

[1] David M. Potter, *People of Plenty: Economic Abundance and the American Character* (Chicago: University of Chicago Press, 1954), pp. 167-168. (Copyright 1954 by The University of Chicago.)

representatives, and continuity-acceptance personnel. It must be brought into conformity with the NARTB code, network or station policy, and the interests of organized pressure groups. As one successful television writer has said, "There are more people getting into the act every day. For a commercial show the story first has to be cleared with Madison Avenue, then maybe Detroit and goodness knows where else. Finally . . . it develops that the sponsor's wife doesn't like a story about railroads. So you start all over again."[2] The "industrialized" writer, according to Elmer Rice, must even conform in his personal life: "You not only have to write right, you have to think right, perhaps even prove that you don't think wrong."[3]

Under these conditions the sharp, individualistic edges of the creative product are dulled with much handling. A characteristic blandness and slickness results. This quality is particularly noticeable in Hollywood movies, which often have a sophisticated manner and a mechanical perfection that are strangely at odds with the banality of their content. The many satirical stories about the frustrations of writers enticed to Hollywood from other media are more than jokes; they reflect the undeniable fact that the mass media use artists instead of artists using the mass media.[4]

Mass media on the whole seem mainly to *reflect* society as it is, leaving little scope for the innovator, whose imagination takes him on from the present stage of development of an idea or an art form to a new frontier. Eventually, to be sure, the mass media seize innovations and convert them to their own use, but only after the pioneering work has been done.[5] It is not surprising that artists and innovators often resent the fact that the mass media are inhospitable to their work in the first instance, only to welcome it after it has already found acceptance elsewhere. Speaking long before the television era, Walter Lippmann observed:

> The men who do alter the stereotypes, the pioneering artists and critics, are naturally depressed and angered at managers and editors who protect their investments. . . . They have forgotten that they are measuring their own success by standards that artists and wise men of the past would never have dreamed of invoking. They are asking for circulations and audiences that were never considered by any artist until the last few generations. And when they do not get them they are disappointed.[6]

[2] Thomas W. Phipps, quoted by Val Adams in "Report on a Video Script Writer," *New York Times* (16 December 1951).

[3] Elmer Rice, "The Industrialization of the Writer," *Saturday Review of Literature* (12 April 1952), p. 63.

[4] The distinction is well made in Lillian Ross's *Picture,* a perceptive study of Hollywood movie-making (New York: Rinehart & Co., Inc., 1952).

[5] An interesting study could be made of the way in which the mass media (e.g., film cartoons and magazine advertising) have adapted and absorbed some of the conceptions of "modernistic," non-objective art, thirty to forty years after these innovations were introduced in the realm of the fine arts.

[6] Walter Lippmann, *Public Opinion* (New York: Macmillan & Co., 1922), p. 167. Reprinted by permission of Macmillan Co.

"THE EGGHEADS" AND "THE OTHERS"

In appraising the mass media we must constantly remind ourselves of the fact of audience size and its consequences. Never before have the *whole people* of a country as vast as the United States been showered with such attention and deference as the mass media provide. The dimensions and heterogeneity of the audience for even a moderately popular network broadcast program are not easy for the mind to grasp. Here is a new communication situation, significantly different from those which the traditional rules have concerned.

Nevertheless, broadcasting is often criticized because it fails to live up to the rules pertaining to books, literary dramas, paintings, or concert-hall programs. Although broadcasting uses these products in its own ways, it differs fundamentally from book publishing, the legitimate theatre, the art gallery and museum, the concert hall. Broadcasting requires popularization of the arts on an unprecedented scale. Lyman Bryson has asserted:

> Critics who were trained to talk about pictures in frames, and books in private libraries or in school classrooms, and music made by visible and present musicians, trained to describe situations which still exist and are more than ever important but which have little to do with mass communications, have done the arts great disservice by chatter about what they call popular arts without knowing in any precise way what they are talking about.[7]

Bryson points out, moreover, that such critics tend to condemn broadcasting as a whole rather than to select for criticism those programs which merit critical attention. Book reviewers have never proposed to make such sweeping judgments about "print." "The new art is carelessly judged as a whole; the old arts are carefully judged by the only parts of their performance good enough to demand judgment."[8] Some people expect to be able to turn on the radio or television set at any hour of the day or night to be greeted immediately with a program suited to their particular tastes and interests. These same critics would not, one presumes, expect to enter the stacks of a library and be satisfied with the first book that came to hand. Print-minded critics, however, are used to being able to enjoy a printed work at their own leisure and in their own time, and do not adjust easily to the fact that in broadcasting the desired program may be available only at a certain hour of a certain day and hence be enjoyed only by adjusting to the demands of the broadcast schedule.

Such critics are the object of an anecdote which had wide currency at the time when television first began to reach the dimensions of a mass medium. Two intellectuals were discussing the state of the arts. One of them launched into a long catalogue of the sins of television, citing many instances of its

---

[7] Lyman Bryson, *The Next America* (New York: Harper & Bros., 1952), p. 134.
[8] *Ibid.*, p. 135.

debasing effects, whereupon the other replied, "You're absolutely right. I don't have a set either."

The element of snobbishness here adverted to is not a novelty in broadcasting. In the earliest days of radio, for example, the Metropolitan Opera opposed the idea of broadcasting its productions on the grounds that such an innovation would "cheapen" opera.[9] The sensitive critic is scandalized by the fact that broadcasting shows so little discrimination in its appetite for all the arts, all ideas, and all happenings. The Metropolitan Opera, the New York Philharmonic, or Shakespeare may be sandwiched in what strikes the critic as hideous juxtaposition with moronic chatter.[10] The whole catalogue of prejudices betrayed by the intellectual snob when faced with the monstrous advent of television has been neatly exposed by Donley Feddersen (a professor of broadcasting) in a gem of satire, *The Egghead and the Others*.[11] In Feddersen's parable the Egghead finally capitulates and allows a television set in the house, but only to gather firsthand material for lectures on such subjects as "The Opiate of the 'Others'," "The 'Thing-Men' Take Over," and "The Rape of Culture."

Behind much of the impatience with the mass media and the resentment of their profane encroachments on the fine arts there also seems to lurk an attitude based on unconsciously projected moral considerations. There exists the implication of something morally wrong in wasting time with the trashy output of mass media when people could be occupied with more constructive activities. Paul Lazarsfeld has sensed this attitude: "[Social reformers] have fought for several generations to give people three more hours of free time each day. Now that their old battle is won, they find that people spend this time listening to . . . radio programs."[12] The next step in reform becomes the reformation of leisure time.

The intellectual finds it hard to accept a medium of communication which, as Bryson has said, treats communication content as "essentially merchandise, like food or clothing sold in the market place."[13]

American popular culture, so roundly condemned by its critics at home and abroad, is essentially and unashamedly a machine-age art. A product of the machine — like most of the content of American civilization today — American popular culture is likewise mediated by the machine and organized

[9] William P. Banning, *Commercial Broadcasting Pioneer: The WEAF Experiment, 1922-1926* (Cambridge: Harvard University Press, 1946), p. 114. Ironically, broadcast audiences have since made vital contributions to keeping the Met alive.

[10] It will be recalled that British opponents of commercial television used as a horrible example the fact that Dave Garroway juxtaposed the coronation of Queen Elizabeth with the antics of Muggs, the chimpanzee.

[11] Donley Feddersen, *The Egghead and the Others* (Chicago: The Coach House Press, Inc., 1955).

[12] Paul F. Lazarsfeld and Patricia L. Kendall, *Radio Listening In America* (copyright, 1948, by Prentice-Hall, Inc., New York), p. 85.

[13] Bryson, *op. cit.*, p. 132. It is perhaps significant that, as was pointed out in Chapter 26, radio was at first accepted into higher education on the assumption that broadcasting was an art rather than a business.

institutionally. . . . *To understand popular culture in America today* . . .
*it is necessary to accept the centrality of machine technology in the American
way.*[14]

This understanding should make the critic of broadcasting conscious of
the fact that there are some things it can reasonably be expected to do and
others which fall outside its limitations. All media have their characteristic
limitations — "one cannot whistle an algebraic formula."[15] For example,
the physical limitations of the television system make it incapable of reproducing works of art with sufficient fidelity to make the reproductions even
nearly equivalent to the originals. The economic limitations of the television
system prevent it from confining itself to the needs and tastes of a small
minority of its potential audience. The social limitations of the television
medium prevent it from transmitting material which large numbers of
people believe to be immoral, subversive, or otherwise socially harmful,
whether or not such harm would actually result.

In pointing out the irrelevance of some of the criticisms of broadcasting,
we have by no means intended to imply that the broadcasting service is
above criticism. Even by the most tolerant standards the service deserves
and needs criticism. Our point has been that standards, in order to be useful
in improving the service, should take into consideration the nature of the
medium, its capabilities and its limitations.

In previous chapters many relevant critical points have been raised concerning such subjects as frequency management, broadcasting's obligation
as a news medium, television's need to resist the encroachments of film, the
importance of keeping control of programming in the hands of licensees,
types of economic exploitation to which broadcasting is liable, the possible
adverse effects of monopoly and unfairness, the need for professionalism in
the industry, the role of the second service, and above all the importance of
responsibility on the part of licensees. Each of these matters has its influence, direct or remote, upon the character of the program service.

"BAD" EFFECTS RECONSIDERED

In the previous chapter six categories of alleged bad effects of the mass
media, and of television in particular, were discussed. It is time now to
re-examine these allegations in the light of the intervening discussion of the
nature of the mass communication process, the factors influencing the
outcome of communications, and the relevance of critical standards.

1. As for the allegation that television debases taste, the fact is that very

[14] Paul Meadows, *The Culture of Industrial Man* (Lincoln: University of Nebraska
Press, 1950), pp. 114-115 (emphasis supplied).
[15] Whitney J. Oates, "Classic Theories of Communication," in: Lyman Bryson (ed.),
The Communication of Ideas (New York: Harper & Bros., 1948), p. 28. Of course
you *can* whistle an algebraic formula if you and at least one other person agree on a set
of whistled symbols; the point is, however, that the medium of whistling is not well
adapted to this purpose.

little is known on this subject. A study of various beliefs concerning the effects of the mass media yielded the conclusion that "The paucity of empirical data bearing directly upon the questions [of effects on taste] is perhaps the most conspicuous, if disappointing, finding of the entire research."[16] Existing tastes do not seem to be changed by mass-media consumption. The same study concluded that tastes "seem so fixed that mass media have little chance to do anything about them. For it now appears that a given kind of material, distributed through the mass media, reaches only those persons who already like such material."[17]

On the other hand, it may be retorted that tastes have to be formed initially in some way, and the accessibility of the mass media to children argues that the media will strongly influence their early standards. That the media have some influence in the formative years seems certain, but according to reference-group theory it may be questioned whether this influence actually prevails over that of family, social class, and other aspects of social environment.

2. Concerning the statement that the mass media provide an avenue of escape and hence prevent audiences from participating in more beneficial activities (the "vegetable" theory), the question arises whether people actually do give up golf, tennis, reading, writing, conversation, travel, concert-going, or whatever other activities may be considered beneficial, for the sake of watching television. The evidence seems to indicate the contrary. Participant sports are on the increase. Such activities as boating, skiing, bowling, and fishing have skyrocketed in popularity during the years of television's distractions. Moreover, concert-going, museum attendance, and book-reading also are on the increase. As the president of CBS Television has pointed out, television seems to affect the rival forms of entertainment more than traditional areas of culture.[18] It also seems apparent that television does not necessarily rob viewers of time, since there is evidence that they tend to rebudget their time in order to fit their viewing schedule into their accustomed patterns of activity (Chapter 16).

3. The broad allegation of economic exploitation concerns our economic system as a whole rather than broadcasting alone. Other forms of advertising are often far more exploitative than radio and television advertising. In any event, as was pointed out in Chapter 12, a good case can be made for the economic necessity of the kind of turnover in goods and services which mass advertising alone can bring about. However, a legitimate criticism can be made on the score of economic exploitation. As we have indicated, the broadcasting industry has yet to achieve the highest integrity as an advertising medium; we have shown, indeed, that this criticism comes

[16] Joseph T. Klapper, "The Effects of Mass Media" (New York: Columbia University Bureau of Applied Social Research, 1949, mimeo.), Introduction, p. 13.

[17] Ibid., Introduction, p. 12.

[18] J. L. Van Volkenburg, Television as an Extension School of Democracy (New York: CBS, 1953).

from within the industry as well as from without. Insofar as broadcast advertising is in spirit fraudulent (irrespective of its technical legality) it is indefensible.

CULTURAL MEDIATION

4, 5. Both the criticisms that concern the alleged use of the mass media as models for behavior and attitude formation are based on the belief that the mass media have the function of *cultural mediation*. Human beings are not born as social beings. They have to learn, as they mature, the exceedingly complex sets of behavior and of values which their particular society expects of them. At first all these requirements are foreign to the individual, but normally he gradually *internalizes* them — makes them a part of himself — so that he automatically does the "right" thing. This process of *acculturation* is a learning process, and since it begins at the moment of birth it is initially a responsibility of the child's immediate family. Later on the peer group (children of the same age group and social status) and the more formal educational agencies supplement the family as agents of acculturation.

The mass media seem to have had at least a secondary influence in this all-important process of acculturation. They have taken on to some extent the job of mediating the culture, i.e., teaching it to the neophyte member of society. The family, the peer group, and the schools no doubt still play the chief role in mediating the culture, with the mass media playing a supplementary role. Through the mass media the child learns about how people dress, talk, and conduct themselves in situations that he does not directly experience in his own social environment. If the things learned in this way conflict with what the child learns through his own environment, the parents are likely to become alarmed about the "bad" effects of television.

Since parents have more opportunity to observe their children's contact with television than the other mass media, they are likely to be more critical of television than of the other media. At the same time, since the child is more likely to experience television with its family than alone or with peer groups, the impact of television is modified by established family-sanctioned standards (bearing in mind the role of situational factors in determining the effects of communications).[19]

The fact that television is received directly in the home and therefore is easily accessible to all ages naturally enhances its role in cultural mediation. It can capture the attention of children too young to be taken often to the movies or to enjoy comic books. Moreover, the distinctions between what is

[19] A rather limited pilot study revealed that for young children the usual social situations involving contact with the mass media are: comics, alone; movies, with peers; television, with family. The children's preferred situation is the family situation in the lowest age group, but this preference decreases with age. At the kindergarten age television is 100 per cent the preferred medium, but by sixth-grade age television is preferred by only 37 per cent and movies by 63 per cent. (Eliot Freidson, "The Relation of the Social Situation of Contact to the Media of Mass Communication," *Public Opinion Quarterly* XVII-2 [Summer, 1953], pp. 230-238.)

appropriate to childhood and what appropriate to maturity become somewhat blurred, for the child has ready access to materials intended primarily for adults.[20]

This close association of television with the primary agent of acculturation (the family), together with its own role in that process, indisputably places it in a position of great social responsibility.[21] This is a type of responsibility alien to the fine arts as communication media, and is therefore another factor which must be kept in mind when the mass media are subjected to criticism on the level of aesthetic criteria.

There is so far no convincing evidence, however, that the mass media produce the simple one-for-one effects sometimes attributed to them. That is, children are not likely to manifest criminal or otherwise antisocial behavior grossly foreign to the standards of their own social group merely because crimes are depicted. Nor does the number of crimes committed in television per hour or per week seem to be a valid measure of the number of children who are going to turn out to be criminals. At worst, it appears, the media can occasionally have a trigger effect on a personality already deeply disoriented. Such personalities are destined to clash with society in any event; the ideas they may get from watching television or reading comic books are not the *cause* of their anti-social behavior but merely the *cue* for setting it off, and such cues might be innocently provided by any number of stimuli.[22]

OMISSIONS IN MASS-MEDIA CONTENT

6. We come now to the final criticism — that the mass media offend by omission rather than by commission. This seems to be a valid statement, especially if the content of the medium is considered in terms of its categories. For example, there can be little doubt that the dramatic fare offered on television (one of television's most popular types of program, and one which accounts for nearly half of the total service) avoids many legitimate dramatic themes, characters, plots, situations, and outcomes.[23] In the category of discussion there are doubtless many ideas about politics, religion, economics, race, and other sensitive subjects which never receive adequate representation in the broadcast service, even though supported by respectable numbers of responsible people. Insofar as these and other kinds

[20] Cf.: David Riesman, et al., *The Lonely Crowd* (New Haven: Yale University Press, 1950), "Changes in the Agents of Character Formation," Chapters II, III, and IV.

[21] Note the way in which the Television Code specifically acknowledges this responsibility (*Appendix*, p. 462).

[22] After examining available data and hearing testimony from many of the country's leading experts on the subject, a Senate subcommittee was unable to reach a definite conclusion about the influence of television on juvenile delinquency — except that the subject needed more study. Cf.: Senate Subcommittee of the Committee on the Judiciary, *Interim Report, Television and Juvenile Delinquency* (Washington: Government Printing Office, 1955).

[23] Cf.: Sydney W. Head, "Content Analysis of Television Drama Programs," *Quarterly of Film, Radio, and Television* IX-2 (Winter, 1954), pp. 175-194.

of content may be excluded through the influence of advertisers, broadcasting invites and deserves adverse criticism. Broadcasting will never attain the status it should have until its editorial content is at least as free of advertiser-control as the editorial content of the most respected newspapers.

On the other hand, it would be unfair to say that broadcasting has completely surrendered its autonomy to expediency, although this is sometimes alleged. Broadcasters do in fact often resist undue economic and social pressures — probably not as much as they should, but enough to show progress. For example, Edward R. Murrow of CBS has provided conspicuous examples of independence of thinking at a time when considerable risk was entailed.[24] One need not be persuaded of the correctness of his position to recognize that Murrow has been an important influence in the maintenance of the principle of free discussion at a time when it would have been easier and safer to remain silent. As long as there are Murrows highly placed in the industry (he is a member of the board of directors of CBS) and willing to base even a few programs on conviction rather than on expediency or salability, broadcasting is not completely the creature of the conformists.

CONCLUSION

We have described broadcasting in America as a primarily private-enterprise, competitive, advertising-supported nationwide system, highly dependent on syndication of program materials. It is a licensed medium, regulated by an agency of government whose task is to represent the public interest. The potentiality for a second, complementary service exists in noncommercial educational stations.

Three preliminary assumptions have been made in describing and analyzing the American system of broadcasting. First, it has been assumed that the basic elements of the system are sound and relatively stable; therefore adverse criticisms or suggestions for improvement have been made within the framework of the existing system rather than being posited on any essential change in the system.

Second, it has been assumed that mass advertising, from which commercial broadcasting receives its support, is a useful and necessary element in the American economy. Therefore criticism of advertising has been concerned with abuse rather than use, and it has been shown that many of these criticisms come from within the industry as well as from without.

Third, it has been assumed that the interests of the industry as well as those of society at large will be served by improving the broadcasting service — heightening its social usefulness, its integrity, and its sense of responsibility.

On the basis of these assumptions we have surveyed the technology, the history, the economy, and the control of American broadcasting with a view to enabling a fair appraisal of the service and of the conduct of the industry.

[24] See p. 383, *supra.*

The implications of these four factors may be summarized as follows:

Technology. The channels assigned to broadcasting have a limited information capacity. The choice of channel capacity has been pragmatic — based on a compromise between the objective of securing equitable distribution of service on a commercially competitive basis and the objective of providing a high standard of fidelity in the reproduction of information. The propagation characteristics of the radio frequencies place physical limitations on the number, distribution, and coverage of broadcasting stations. Broadcasting is further limited by the fact that many non-broadcast services also require frequency-spectrum space.

History. Broadcasting is a unique form of communication. As a mass medium it resembles the other mass media in many respects, but it has certain characteristics which have no direct analogues in other media. The development of American broadcasting coincided with profound social changes by which it has been affected and which it in turn has affected.

Economics. Critical problems of conduct and standards arise in connection with the extent to which purely economic motives dominate programming, the integration of advertising into the program structure, and the standards by which advertising is accepted or rejected. The industry itself has set up standards of conduct and criteria for evaluation in most of these connections. A major unsolved problem is how to deal with stations which because of economic instability cannot meet reasonable standards.

Control. American broadcasting must be responsive to the demands of a political philosophy which places the highest value on an informed electorate and on the libertarian concept of the social value of free speech. Monopolistic concentrations and unfairness in the conduct of the service endanger these values. The FCC's function is to mediate between the private interests of broadcasters and the public interest, but its success depends upon the voluntary assumption of social responsibility by the licensees. Higher education can aid the industry in developing the professionalism it needs in order to fulfill this responsibility. Control from whatever source is potentially dangerous to society insofar as it may dogmatically eliminate alternative attitudes to that which is currently the popular, the official, or the institutionally-sanctioned point of view.

Finally, relevant criteria for broadcasting must keep in mind that it has all the inherent limitations of a mass medium. Though itself an innovation, broadcasting is not primarily an innovator. It is therefore not well adapted to the role of reformer or of aesthetic and intellectual pioneer. Its social effects are probably not as massive, as direct, or as obvious as its more alarmist critics suppose. Nevertheless, it no doubt does have effects as a secondary agent of cultural mediation, and this function gives it a particularly sensitive social responsibility. Under modern conditions of highly-developed technology and large concentrations of economic power, the traditional American balance between the ideals of individual freedom and of social order seems most likely to be preserved if private enterprise freely accepts and intelligently carries out this responsibility.

---

*Comparison of the Television, Radio,
and Motion-Picture Codes*

Bibliographical Notes

COMPARISON OF THE TELEVISION, RADIO, AND MOTION-PICTURE CODES

An item-by-item comparison of the three trade-association codes for radio, television, and films reveals significant differences. In the following compilation the *Television Code* is used as the standard of comparison. It is reproduced in full and in its original sequence, with all headings. A major difference in form between the broadcasting codes and the motion-picture code is that the former integrate the reasoning behind the regulations into the statements of the regulations themselves, whereas the body of the motion-picture code is in the form of bare categorical statements, the rationale being reserved for a section at the end (here omitted). Provisions of the radio and motion-picture codes have in some instances been moved out of sequence to match them with comparable provisions of the television code.

The Television Code of the National Association of Radio and Television Broadcasters (2d ed.; Washington: The Association, 1954) went into effect March 1, 1952. The version presented here is revised to March, 1954. *The Standards of Practice for Radio Broadcasters of the United States of America* (Washington: NARTB, 1955) were adopted in 1937 and were revised in 1945, 1948, 1954, and 1955. *A Code to Govern the Making of Motion Pictures* (New York: Motion Picture Association of America, Inc., 1954) was adopted in 1930, with occasional revisions and amendments having been made at various times since then.

THE TELEVISION CODE

Preamble

Television is seen and heard in every type of American home. These homes include children and adults of all ages, embrace all races and all varieties of religious faith, and reach those of every educational background. It is the responsibility of television to bear constantly in mind that the audience is primarily a home audience and consequently that television's relationship to the viewers is that between guest and host.

THE RADIO CODE

Preamble

The growth of broadcasting as a medium of entertainment, education, and information has been made possible by its force as an instrument of commerce.

This philosophy of commercial broadcasting as it is known in the United States has enabled the industry to develop as a free medium in the tradition of American enterprise.

The extent of this freedom is implicit in the fact that no one censors broadcasting in the United States.

Those who own the nation's radio broadcasting stations operate them — pursuant to these self-adopted Standards of Practice — in recognition of the interest of the American people.

The Radio Broadcaster's Creed

We Believe:

That Radio Broadcasting in the United States of America is a living symbol of democracy; a significant and necessary instrument for maintaining freedom of expression, as established by the First Amendment to the Constitution of the United States;

That its influence in the arts, in science, in education, in commerce and upon the public welfare is of such magnitude that the

THE MOTION-PICTURE CODE

Preamble

Motion picture producers recognize the high trust and confidence which have been placed in them by the people of the world and which have made motion pictures a universal form of entertainment.

They recognize their responsibility to the public because of this trust and because entertainment and art are important influences in the life of a nation.

Hence, though regarding motion pictures primarily as entertainment without any explicit purpose of teaching or propaganda, they know that the motion picture within its own field of entertainment may be directly responsible for spiritual or moral progress, for higher types of social life, and for much correct thinking.

During the rapid transition from silent to talking pictures they realized the necessity and the opportunity of subscribing to a Code to govern the production of talking pictures and of reacknowledging this responsibility.

On their part, they ask from the public and from public leaders a sympathetic understanding of their purposes and problems and a spirit of cooperation that will allow them the freedom and opportunity necessary to bring the motion picture to a still higher level of wholesome entertainment for all the people.

★ ★ ★

only proper measure of its responsibility is the common good of the whole people;

That it is our obligation to serve the people in such manner as to reflect credit upon our profession and to encourage aspiration toward a better estate for all mankind; by making available to every person in America, such programs as will perpetuate the traditional leadership of the United States in all phases of the broadcasting art. . . .

★ ★ ★

The revenues from advertising support the free, competitive American system of telecasting, and make available to the eyes and ears of the American people the finest programs of information, education, culture and entertainment. By law the television broadcaster is responsible for the programming of his station. He, however, is obligated to bring his positive responsibility for excellence and good taste in programming to bear upon all who have a hand in the production of programs, including networks, sponsors, producers of film and of live programs, advertising agencies, and talent agencies.

The American businesses which utilize television for conveying their advertising messages to the home by pictures with sound, seen free-of-charge on the home screen, are reminded that their responsibili-

Advertising is the principal source of revenue of the free, competitive American system of radio broadcasting. It makes possible the presentation to all American people of the finest programs of entertainment, education and information. Since the great strength of American radio broadcasting derives from the public respect for and the public approval of its programs, it must be the purpose of each broadcaster to establish and maintain high standards of performance, not only in the selection and production of all programs, but also in the presentation of advertising.

★ ★ ★

ties are not limited to the sale of goods and the creation of a favorable attitude toward the sponsor by the presentation of entertainment. They include, as well, responsibility for utilizing television to bring the best programs, regardless of kind, into American homes.

Television, and all who participate in it are jointly accountable to the American public for respect for the special needs of children, for community responsibility, for the advancement of education and culture, for the acceptability of the program materials chosen, for decency and decorum in production, and for propriety in advertising. This responsibility cannot be discharged by any given group of programs, but can be discharged only through the highest standards of respect for the American home, applied to every moment of every program presented by television.

[*We Believe:*] That we should make full and ingenious use of man's store of knowledge, his talents and his skills and exercise critical and discerning judgment concerning all broadcasting operations to the end that we may, intelligently and sympathetically:

Observe the proprieties and customs of civilized society;

Respect the rights and sensitivities of all people;

Honor the sanctity of marriage and the home;

Protect and uphold the dignity and brotherhood of all mankind;

Enrich the daily life of the people through the factual reporting and analysis of news, and through programs of education, entertainment, and information;

Provide for the fair discussion of matters of general public concern; engage in works directed toward the common good; and volunteer our aid and comfort in times of stress and emergency;

Contribute to the economic welfare of

all, by expanding the channels of trade; by encouraging the development and conservation of natural resources; and by bringing together the buyer and seller through the broadcasting of information pertaining to goods and services.

★ ★ ★

In order that television programming may best serve the public interest, viewers should be encouraged to make their criticisms and positive suggestions known to the television broadcasters. Parents in particular should be urged to see to it that out of the richness of television fare, the best programs are brought to the attention of their children.

Advancement of Education and Culture

1. Commercial television provides a valuable means of augmenting the educational and cultural influences of schools, institutions of higher learning, the home, the church, museums, foundations, and other institutions devoted to education and culture.

2. It is the responsibility of a television broadcaster to call upon such institutions for counsel and cooperation and to work with them on the best methods of presenting educational and cultural materials by television. It is further the responsibility of

Advancement of Education and Culture

Because radio is an integral part of American life, there is inherent in radio broadcasting a continuing opportunity to enrich the experience of living through the advancement of education and culture. The radio broadcaster in augmenting the educational and cultural influences of the home, the Church, schools, institutions of higher learning, and other entities devoted to education and culture:

THE TELEVISION CODE

stations, networks, advertising agencies and sponsors consciously to seek opportunities for introducing into telecasts factual materials which will aid in the enlightenment of the American public.

3. Education via television may be taken to mean that process by which the individual is brought toward informed adjustment to his society. Television is also responsible for the presentation of overtly instructional and cultural programs, scheduled so as to reach the viewers who are naturally drawn to such programs, and produced so as to attract the largest possible audience.

4. In furthering this realization, the television broadcaster:

a) Should be thoroughly conversant with the educational and cultural needs and desires of the community served.

b) Should affirmatively seek out responsible and accountable educational and cultural institutions of the community with a view toward providing opportunities for the instruction and enlightenment of the viewers.

c) Should provide for reasonable experimentation in the development of programs specifically directed to the advancement of the community's culture and education.

THE RADIO CODE

Should be thoroughly conversant with the educational and cultural needs and aspirations of the community served.

Should cooperate with the responsible and accountable educational and cultural entities of the community to provide enlightenment of listeners.

Should engage in experimental efforts designed to advance the community's cultural and educational interests.

★ ★ ★

THE MOTION-PICTURE CODE

Acceptability of Program Material

Program materials should enlarge the horizons of the viewer, provide him with wholesome entertainment, afford helpful stimulation, and remind him of the responsibilities which the citizen has towards his society. Furthermore:

a) (i) Profanity, obscenity, smut and vulgarity are forbidden, even when likely to be understood only by part of the audience. From time to time, words which have been acceptable, acquire undesirable meanings, and telecasters should be alert to eliminate such words.
(ii) Words (especially slang) derisive of any race, color, creed, nationality or national derivation, except wherein such usage would be for the specific purpose of effective dramatization such as combating prejudice, are forbidden, even when likely to be understood only by part of the audience. From time to time, words which have been acceptable, acquire undesirable meanings,

Dramatic Programs

In determining the acceptability of any dramatic program containing any element of crime, mystery, or horror, proper consideration should be given to the possible effect on all members of the family.

Radio should reflect realistically the experience of living, in both its pleasant and tragic aspects, if it is to serve the listener honestly. Nevertheless it holds a concurrent obligation to provide programs which will encourage better adjustments to life.

This obligation is apparent in the area of dramatic programs particularly. Without sacrificing integrity of presentation, dramatic programs on radio should avoid:

★ ★ ★

Obscenity in word, gesture, reference, song, joke, or by suggestion (even when likely to be understood only by part of the audience) is forbidden.

Pointed profanity and every other profane or vulgar expression, however used, are forbidden.

No approval by the Production Code Administration shall be given to the use of words and phrases in motion pictures including, but not limited to, the following: Bronx cheer (the sound); chippie; God, Lord, Jesus, Christ (unless used reverently); cripes; fairy (in a vulgar sense); finger (the); fire, cries of; Gawd; goose (in a vulgar sense); hot (applied to a woman); "in

THE TELEVISION CODE

and telecasters should be alert to eliminate such words.

iii) The Television Code Review Board shall maintain and issue to subscribers from time to time, a continuing list of specific words and phrases which should not be used in keeping with this subsection. This list, however, shall not be considered as all-inclusive. *

* The NARTB refuses to release this list.

b) (i) Attacks on religion and religious faiths are not allowed.

(ii) Reverence is to mark any mention of the name of God, His attributes and powers.

(iii) When religious rites are included in other than religious programs, the rites are accurately presented, and the ministers, priests and rabbis portrayed in their callings are vested with the dignity of their office and under no circumstances are to be held up to ridicule.

c) (i) Contests may not constitute a lottery.

THE RADIO CODE

THE MOTION-PICTURE CODE

your hat"; Madam (relating to prostitution); nance; nuts (except when meaning crazy); pansy; razzberry (the sound); S.O.B.; son-of-a; tart; toilet gags; whore.

It should also be noted that the words "hell" and "damn", if used without moderation, will be considered offensive by many members of the audience. Their use, therefore, should be governed by the discretion and the prudent advice of the Code Administration.

★ ★ ★

The treatment of low, disgusting, unpleasant, though not necessarily evil, subjects should be guided always by the dictates of good taste and a proper regard for the sensibilities of the audience.

★ ★ ★

No film or episode may throw *ridicule* on any religious faith.

★ ★ ★

Ministers of religion in their character as ministers of religion should not be used as comic characters or as villains.

Ceremonies of any definite religion should be carefully handled.

★ ★ ★

(ii) Any telecasting designed to "buy" the television audience by requiring it to listen and/or view in hope of reward, rather than for the quality of the program, should be avoided.

d) Respect is maintained for the sanctity of marriage and the value of the home. Divorce is not treated casually nor justified as a solution for marital problems.

e) Illicit sex relations are not treated as commendable.

f) Sex crimes and abnormalities are generally unacceptable as program material.

[Any broadcasting designed to "buy" the radio audience, by requiring it to listen in hope of reward, rather than for the quality of its entertainment should be avoided.]*

* Deleted in 1955 revision.

The sanctity of the institution of marriage and the home shall be upheld.

Pictures shall not infer that low forms of sex relationship are the accepted or common thing.

Adultery and Illicit Sex, sometimes necessary plot material, must not be explicitly treated or justified, or presented attractively.

Scenes of Passion:

a. These should not be introduced except where they are definitely essential to the plot.

b. Excessive and lustful kissing, lustful embraces, suggestive postures and gestures are not to be shown.

c. In general, passion should be treated in such manner as not to stimulate the lower and baser emotions.

Seduction or Rape:

a. These should never be more than suggested, and then only when essential for the plot. They must never be shown by explicit method.

THE TELEVISION CODE

g) Drunkenness and narcotic addiction are never presented as desirable or prevalent. h) The administration of illegal drugs will not be displayed.

i) The use of liquor in program content shall be de-emphasized. The consumption of liquor in American life, when not required by the plot or for proper characterization shall not be shown.

j) The use of gambling devices or scenes necessary to the development of plot or as appropriate background is acceptable only when presented with discretion and in moderation, and in a manner which would not excite interest in, or foster, betting nor be instructional in nature. Telecasts of actual sports programs at which on-the-scene betting is permitted by law should be

THE RADIO CODE

Stations should avoid broadcasting program material which would tend to encourage illegal gambling or other violations of Federal, State and local laws, ordinances, and regulations.

★ ★ ★

THE MOTION-PICTURE CODE

b. They are never the proper subject for comedy.

Sex perversion or any inference of it is forbidden.

White slavery shall not be treated.

Abortion, sex hygiene, and venereal diseases are not proper subjects for theatrical motion pictures.

Scenes of *actual child birth*, in fact or in silhouette, are never to be presented.

Children's sex organs are never to be exposed.

★ ★ ★

The illegal drug traffic, and drug addiction, must never be presented.

★ ★ ★

The following subjects must be treated within the careful limits of good taste:

★ ★ ★

Liquor and drinking

presented in a manner in keeping with Federal, state and local laws, and should concentrate on the subject as a public sporting event.

k) In reference to physical or mental afflictions and deformities, special precautions must be taken to avoid ridiculing sufferers from similar ailments and offending them or members of their families.

l) Exhibitions of fortune-telling, astrology, phrenology, palm-reading, and numerology are acceptable only when required by a plot or the theme of a program, and then the presentation should be developed in a manner designed not to foster superstition or excite interest or belief in these subjects.

m) Televised drama shall not simulate news or special events in such a way as to mislead or alarm.

n) Legal, medical and other professional advice, diagnosis and treatment will be permitted only in conformity with law and recognized ethical and professional standards.

o) The presentation of cruelty, greed and selfishness as worthy motivations is to be avoided.

p) Excessive or unfair exploitation of others or of their physical or mental afflictions shall not be presented as praiseworthy.

q) Criminality shall be presented as undesirable and unsympathetic. The condoning

When plot development requires the use of material which depends upon physical or mental handicaps care should be taken to spare the sensibilities of sufferers from similar defects.

★ ★ ★

[Dramatic Programs on Radio Should Avoid]

Sound effects calculated to mislead, shock, or unduly alarm the listener. . . .

★ ★ ★

No picture shall be produced which will lower the moral standards of those who see

THE TELEVISION CODE

of crime and the treatment of the commission of crime in a frivolous, cynical or callous manner is unacceptable.

r) The presentation of techniques of crime in such detail as to invite imitation shall be avoided.

THE RADIO CODE

Techniques and methods of crime presented in such a manner as to encourage imitation, or to make the commission of crime attractive, or to suggest that criminals can escape punishment . . .

★ ★ ★

THE MOTION-PICTURE CODE

it. Hence the sympathy of the audience shall never be thrown to the side of crime, wrongdoing, evil or sin.

Correct standards of life, subject only to the requirements of drama and entertainment shall be presented.

★

[Crimes against the law] shall never be presented in such a way as to throw sympathy with the crime as against law and justice or to inspire others with a desire for imitation.

★ ★ ★

Details of crime must never be shown and care should be exercised at all times in discussing such details.

★

The technique of murder must be presented in a way that will not inspire imitation.

★

There must be no display, at any time, of machine guns, sub-machine guns or other weapons generally classified as illegal weapons in the hands of gangsters, or other criminals, and there are to be no off-stage sounds of the repercussions of these guns.

There must be no new, unique or trick methods shown for concealing guns.

The flaunting of weapons by gangsters, or other criminals, will not be allowed.

All discussions and dialogue on the part of gangsters regarding guns should be cut to the minimum.

★

Methods of Crime should not be explicitly presented:

a) Theft, robbery, safe-cracking, and dynamiting of trains, mines, buildings, etc., should not be detailed in method.

b) Arson must be subject to the same safeguards.

c) The use of firearms should be restricted to essentials.

★ ★

★ There must be no suggestion at any time, of excessive brutality.

★

The following subjects must be treated within the careful limits of good taste:

Actual hangings or electrocutions as legal punishments for crime.

Third degree methods.

Brutality and possible gruesomeness.

The sale of women, or a woman selling her virtue.

Surgical operations.

Miscegenation.

★ ★

★ Brutal killings are not to be presented in detail.

★

Detailed presentation of brutal killings, torture, or physical agony, horror, the use of supernatural or climactic incidents likely to terrify or excite unduly . . .

★ ★

★

s) The use of horror for its own sake will be eliminated; the use of visual or aural effects which would shock or alarm the viewer, and the detailed presentation of brutality or physical agony by sight or by sound are not permissible.

THE TELEVISION CODE

t) Law enforcement shall be upheld, and the officers of the law are to be portrayed with respect and dignity.

u) The presentation of murder or revenge as a motive for murder shall not be presented as justifiable.

v) Suicide as an acceptable solution for human problems is prohibited.

THE RADIO CODE

Disrespectful portrayal of law enforcement.

★ ★ ★

The portrayal of suicide as a satisfactory solution to any problem.

★ ★

THE MOTION-PICTURE CODE

Action suggestive of wholesale slaughter of human beings, either by criminals in conflict with police, or as between warring factions of criminals, or in public disorder of any kind, will not be allowed.

★

Because of the increase in the number of films in which murder is frequently committed, action showing the taking of human life, even in the mystery stories, is to be cut to the minimum. These frequent presentations of murder tend to lessen regard for the sacredness of life.

★

★

Law, natural or human, shall not be ridiculed, nor shall sympathy be created for its violation.

★

★

There must be no scenes, at any time, showing law-enforcing officers dying at the hands of criminals, unless such scenes are absolutely necessary to the development of the plot. This includes private detectives and guards for banks, motor trucks, etc.

★

★

Revenge in modern times shall not be justified.

★

★

Suicide as a solution of problems occurring in the development of screen drama, is to be discouraged as morally questionable and as bad theatre — unless absolutely necessary for the development of the plot. It should never be justified or glorified, or used to defeat due processes of law.

* * *

No picture shall be approved dealing with the life of a notorious criminal of current or recent times which uses the name, nickname or alias of such notorious criminal in the film, nor shall a picture be approved if based upon the life of such a notorious criminal unless the character shown in the film be punished for crimes shown in the film as committed by him.

* * *

* * *

. . . there shall be no . . . apparent cruelty to animals.

* * *

w) The exposition of sex crimes will be avoided.

x) The appearances or dramatization of persons featured in actual crime news will be permitted only in such light as to aid law enforcement or to report the news event.

y) Treatment of Animals. The use of animals, both in the production of television programs and as a part of television program content, shall, at all times, be in conformity with accepted standards of humane treatment.

Simulation of court atmosphere or use of the term "Court" in a program title should be done only in such manner as to eliminate the possibility of creating the false impression that the proceedings broadcast are vested with judicial or official authority.

* * *

* * *

THE TELEVISION CODE

Responsibility Toward Children

1. The education of children involves giving them a sense of the world at large. Crime, violence and sex are a part of the world they will be called upon to meet, and a certain amount of proper presentation of such is helpful in orienting the child to his social surroundings. However, violence and illicit sex shall not be presented in an attractive manner, nor to an extent such as will lead a child to believe that they play a greater part in life than they do. They should not be presented without indications of the resultant retribution and punishment.

2. It is not enough that only those programs which are intended for viewing by children shall be suitable to the young and immature. (*Attention is called to the general items listed under Acceptability of Program Materials.*) Television is responsible for insuring that programs of all sorts which occur during the times of day when children may normally be expected to have the opportunity of viewing television shall exercise care in the following regards:

a) In affording opportunities for cultural growth as well as for wholesome entertainment.

THE RADIO CODE

THE MOTION-PICTURE CODE

[Children's programs] should contribute to the healthy development of personality and character.

[Children's programs] should afford opportunities for cultural growth as well as for wholesome entertainment.

b) In developing programs to foster and promote the commonly accepted moral, social and ethical ideals characteristic of American life.

c) In reflecting respect for parents, for honorable behavior, and for the constituted authorities of the American community.

d) In eliminating reference to kidnapping of children or threats of kidnapping.

e) In avoiding material which is excessively violent or would create morbid suspense, or other undesirable reactions in children.

★ ★ ★

[Children's programs] should convey the commonly accepted moral, social, and ethical ideals characteristic of American life.

★ ★ ★

Programs specifically designed for listening by children should be based upon sound social concepts and should reflect respect for parents, law and order, clean living, high morals, fair play, and honorable behavior.

★ ★ ★

[Dramatic Programs on Radio Should Avoid]

Episodes involving the kidnapping of children.

★ ★ ★

[Children's programs] should be consistent with integrity of realistic production but should avoid material of an extreme nature which might create undesirable emotional reaction in children.

With special reference to the crime of kidnapping — or illegal abduction — such stories are acceptable under the Code only when (a) the kidnapping or abduction is not the main theme of the story; (b) the person kidnapped is not a child; (c) there are no details of the crime of kidnapping; (d) no profit accrues to the abductors or kidnappers; and (e) where the kidnappers are punished. It is understood, and agreed, that the word kidnapping, as used in these Regulations, is intended to mean abduction, or illegal detention, in modern times, by criminals for ransom.

THE TELEVISION CODE

f) In exercising particular restraint and care in crime or mystery episodes involving children or minors.

Decency and Decorum in Production

1. The costuming of all performers shall be within the bounds of propriety, and shall avoid such exposure or such emphasis on anatomical detail as would embarrass or offend home viewers.

2. The movements of dancers, actors, or other performers shall be kept within the bounds of decency, and lewdness and impropriety shall not be suggested in the positions assumed by performers.
3. Camera angles shall avoid such views of performers as to emphasize anatomical details indecently.

THE RADIO CODE

[Children's programs] should avoid appeals urging children to purchase the product specifically for the purpose of keeping the program on the air, or which for any reason encourage children to enter inappropriate places.

★ ★ ★

THE MOTION-PICTURE CODE

Pictures dealing with criminal activities, in which minors participate, or to which minors are related, shall not be approved if they incite demoralizing imitation on the part of youth.

Complete nudity is never permitted. This includes nudity in fact or in silhouette, or any licentious notice thereof by other characters in the pictures.
Undressing scenes should be avoided and never used save where essential to the plot.
Indecent or undue exposure is forbidden.
Dancing costumes intended to permit undue exposure or indecent movements in the dance are forbidden.
Nudity, indecent or undue exposure and dancing costumes, shall not be interpreted to exclude authentically photographed scenes photographed in a foreign land, of natives of such foreign land, showing native life, if such scenes are a necessary and integral part of a motion picture depicting exclusively such land and native life, provided that no such scenes shall be intrinsi-

cally objectionable nor made a part of any motion picture produced in any studio; and provided further that no emphasis shall be made in any scenes of the customs or garb of such natives or in the exploitation thereof.

... the following words and phrases are obviously offensive to the patrons of motion pictures in the United States and more particularly to the patrons of motion pictures in foreign countries: Chink, Dago, Frog, Greaser, Hunkie, Kike, Nigger, Spig, Wop, Yid.

The history, institutions, prominent people and citizenry of all nations shall be represented fairly.

The treatment of bedrooms must be governed by good taste and delicacy.

The use of the Flag shall be consistently respectful.

4. Racial or nationality types shall not be shown on television in such a manner as to ridicule the race or nationality.

5. The use of locations closely associated with sexual life or with sexual sin must be governed by good taste and delicacy.

Community Responsibility

A television broadcaster and his staff occupy a position of responsibility in the community and should conscientiously endeavor to be acquainted fully with its needs and characteristics in order better to serve the welfare of its citizens.

THE TELEVISION CODE

Treatment of News and Public Events

News

1. A television station's news schedule should be adequate and well-balanced.
2. News reporting should be factual, fair and without bias.
3. Commentary and analysis should be clearly identified as such.

THE RADIO CODE

News

Radio is unique in its capacity to reach the largest number of people first with reports on current events. This competitive advantage bespeaks caution — being first is not as important as being right. The following Standards are predicated upon that viewpoint.

News Sources. Those responsible for news on radio should exercise constant professional care in the selection of sources — for the integrity of the news and consequent good reputation of radio as a dominant news medium depend largely upon the reliability of such sources.

Newscasting. News reporting should be factual and objective. . . .

Commentaries and Analyses. Special obligations devolve upon those who analyze and/or comment upon news developments, and management should be satisfied completely that the task is to be performed in the best interest of the listening public. Programs of news analysis and commentary should be clearly identified as such, distinguishing them from straight news reporting.

Editorializing. Some stations exercise their

THE MOTION-PICTURE CODE

rights to express opinions about matters of general public interest. Implicit in these efforts to provide leadership in matters of public consequence and to lend proper authority to the station's standing in the community it serves, is an equal obligation to provide opportunity for qualified divergent viewpoints.

The reputation of a station for honesty and accuracy in editorializing depends upon willingness to expose its convictions to fair rebuttal.

Station editorial comment should be clearly identified as such.

★ ★ ★

Good taste should prevail in the selection and handling of news. Morbid, sensational or alarming details not essential to factual reporting should be avoided.

News should be broadcast in such a manner as to avoid creation of panic and unnecessary alarm.

4. Good taste should prevail in the selection and handling of news:
Morbid, sensational or alarming details not essential to the factual report, especially in connection with stories of crime or sex, should be avoided. News should be telecast in such a manner as to avoid panic and unnecessary alarm.

5. At all times, pictorial and verbal material for both news and comment should conform to other sections of these standards, wherever such sections are reasonably applicable.

6. Pictorial material should be chosen with care and not presented in a misleading manner.

THE MOTION-PICTURE CODE

THE TELEVISION CODE

7. A television broadcaster should exercise due care in his supervision of content, format, and presentation of newscasts originated by his station, and in his selection of newscasters, commentators and analysts.

8. A television broadcaster should exercise particular discrimination in the acceptance, placement and presentation of advertising in news programs so that such advertising should be clearly distinguishable from the news content.

9. A television broadcaster should not present fictional events or other non-news material as authentic news telecasts or announcements nor should he permit dramatizations in any program which would give the false impression that the dramatized material constitutes news. Expletives, (presented aurally or pictorially) such as "flash" or "bulletin" and statements such as "we interrupt this program to bring you . . ." should be reserved specifically for news room use. However, a television broadcaster may properly exercise discretion in the use in non-news programs of words and phrases which do not necessarily imply that the material following is a news release.

THE RADIO CODE

Broadcasters should be diligent in their supervision of content, format, and presentation of news broadcasts. Equal diligence should be exercised in selection of editors and reporters who direct news gathering and dissemination, since the station's performance in this vital informational field depends largely upon them.

★ ★ ★

Sound effects and expressions characteristically associated with news broadcasts (such as "bulletins", "flash", etc.) should be reserved for announcement of news, and the use of any deceptive techniques in connection with fictional events and non-news programs should not be employed.

★ ★ ★

Public Events

1. A television broadcaster has an affirmative responsibility at all times to be informed of public events, and to provide coverage consonant with the ends of an informed and enlightened citizenry.

2. Because of the nature of events open to the public, the treatment of such events by a television broadcaster should be effected in a manner to provide for adequate and informed coverage as well as good taste in presentation.

Controversial Public Issues

1. Television provides a valuable forum for the expression of responsible views on public issues of a controversial nature. In keeping therewith the television broadcaster should seek out and develop with accountable individuals, groups and organizations, programs relating to controversial public issues of import to its fellow citizens; and to give fair representation to opposing sides of issues which materially affect the life or welfare of a substantial segment of the public.

2. The provision of time for this purpose should be guided by the following principles:

a) Requests by individuals, groups or organizations for time to discuss their views on controversial public issues, should be

Public Issues

A broadcaster, in allotting time for the presentation of public issues, should exert every effort to insure equality of opportunity.

Time should be allotted with due regard to all elements of balanced program schedules, and to the degree of interest on the part of the public in the questions to be presented or discussed. (To discuss is "to sift or examine by presenting considerations pro and con.") The broadcaster should limit participation in the presentation of public issues to those qualified, recognized, and properly identified groups or individuals whose opinions will assist the general public in reaching conclusions.

THE MOTION-PICTURE CODE

THE RADIO CODE

Presentation of public issues should be clearly identified.

Political Broadcasts

Political broadcasts, or the dramatization of political issues designed to influence an election, should be properly identified as such.

★   ★   ★

THE TELEVISION CODE

considered on the basis of their individual merits, and in the light of the contribution which the use requested would make to the public interest, and to a well-balanced program structure.

b) Programs devoted to the discussion of controversial public issues should be identified as such, and should not be presented in a manner which would mislead listeners or viewers to believe that the program is purely of an entertainment, news, or other character.

Political Telecasts

Political telecasts should be clearly identified as such, and should not be presented by a television broadcaster in a manner which would mislead listeners or viewers to believe that the program is of any other character.

Religious Programs

1. It is the responsibility of a television broadcaster to make available to the community as part of a well-balanced program schedule adequate opportunity for religious presentations.

2. The following principles should be followed in the treatment of such programs:

a) Telecasting which reaches men of all creeds simultaneously should avoid attacks upon religion.

b) Religious programs should be presented respectfully and accurately and without prejudice or ridicule.

c) Religious programs should be presented by responsible individuals, groups and organizations.

d) Religious programs should place emphasis on broad religious truths, excluding the presentation of controversial or partisan views not directly or necessarily related to religion or morality.

3. In the allocation of time for telecasts of religious programs it is recommended that the television station use its best efforts to apportion such time fairly among the representative faith groups of its community.

Presentation of Advertising

1. Ever mindful of the role of television as a guest in the home, a television broadcaster should exercise unceasing care to supervise the form in which advertising material is presented over his facilities. Since television is a developing medium, involving methods and techniques distinct from those of radio, it may be desirable from time to time to review and revise the presently suggested practices:

Radio broadcasting, which reaches men of all creeds simultaneously, should avoid attacks upon religion.

★ ★ ★

Religious programs should be presented respectfully and without prejudice or ridicule.

★ ★ ★

Religious programs should be presented by responsible individuals, groups, or organizations.

★ ★ ★

Religious programs should place emphasis on broad religious truths, excluding the presentation of controversial or partisan views not directly or necessarily related to religion or morality.

★ ★ ★

Presentation of Advertising

The advancing techniques of the broadcast art have shown that the *quality* and *proper integration* of advertising copy are just as important as measurement in time. The measure of a station's service to its audience is determined by its over-all performance, rather than by any individual segment of its broadcast day.

★ ★ ★

THE MOTION-PICTURE CODE

THE RADIO CODE

THE TELEVISION CODE

a) Advertising messages should be presented with courtesy and good taste; disturbing or annoying material should be avoided; every effort should be made to keep the advertising message in harmony with the content and general tone of the program in which it appears.

b) A sponsor's advertising message should be confined within the framework of the sponsor's program structure. A television broadcaster should seek to avoid the use of commercial announcements which are divorced from the program either by preceding the introduction of the program (as in the case of so-called "cow-catcher" announcements) or by following the apparent sign-off of the program (as in the case of so-called "trailer" announcements). To this end, the program itself should be announced and clearly identified, both audio and video, before the sponsor's advertising material is first used, and should be signed off, both audio and video, after the sponsor's advertising material is last used.

c) Advertising copy should contain no claims intended to disparage competitors, competing products, or other industries, professions or institutions.

d) Since advertising by television is a dynamic technique, a television broadcaster should keep under surveillance new adver-

While any number of products may be advertised by a single sponsor within the specified time standards, advertising copy for these products should be presented within the framework of the program structure. Accordingly, the use on such programs of simulated spot announcements which are divorced from the program by preceding the introduction of the program itself, or by following its *apparent* sign-off should be avoided. To this end, the program itself should be announced and clearly identified *before* the use of what have been known as "cow-catcher" announcements and the programs should be signed off *after* the use of what have been known as "hitch-hike" announcements.

★ ★ ★

tising devices so that the spirit and purpose of these standards are fulfilled.

e) Television broadcasters should exercise the utmost care and discrimination with regard to advertising material, including content, placement and presentation, near or adjacent to programs designed for children. No considerations of expediency should be permitted to impinge upon the vital responsibility towards children and adolescents, which is inherent in television, and which must be recognized and accepted by all advertisers employing television.

f) Television advertisers should be encouraged to devote portions of their allotted advertising messages and program time to the support of worthy causes in the public interest in keeping with the highest ideals of the free competitive system.

g) A charge for television time to churches and religious bodies is not recommended.

Acceptability of Advertisers and Products — General

1. A commercial television broadcaster makes his facilities available for the advertising of products and services and accepts commercial presentations for such advertising. However, a television broadcaster

The final measurement of any commercial broadcast service is quality. To this, every broadcaster should dedicate his best efforts.

Acceptability of Advertisers and Products

1. A commercial radio broadcaster makes his facilities available for the advertising of products and services and accepts commercial presentations for such advertising. However, he should, in recognition of his

THE TELEVISION CODE

should, in recognition of his responsibility to the public, refuse the facilities of his station to an advertiser where he has good reason to doubt the integrity of the advertiser, the truth of the advertising representations, or the compliance of the advertiser with the spirit and purpose of all applicable legal requirements. Moreover, in consideration of the laws and customs of the communities served, each television broadcaster should refuse his facilities to the advertisement of products and services, or the use of advertising scripts, which the station has good reason to believe would be objectionable to a substantial and responsible segment of the community. The foregoing principles should be applied with judgment and flexibility, taking into consideration the characteristics of the medium and the form and content of the particular presentation. In general, because television broadcast is designed for the home and the family, including children, the following principles should govern the business classifications listed below:

a) The advertising of hard liquor should not be accepted.

b) The advertising of beer and wines is acceptable only when presented in the best of good taste and discretion, and is acceptable subject to Federal and local laws.

THE RADIO CODE

responsibility to the public, refuse the facilities of his station to an advertiser where he has good reason to doubt the integrity of the advertiser, the truth of the advertising representations, or the compliance of the advertiser with the spirit and purpose of all applicable legal requirements. Moreover, in considerations of the laws and customs of the communities served, each radio broadcaster should refuse his facilities to the advertisement of products and services, or the use of advertising scripts, which the station has good reason to believe would be objectionable to a substantial and responsible segment of the community. The foregoing principles should be applied with judgment and flexibility, taking into consideration the characteristics of the medium and the form of the particular presentation. In general, because radio broadcasting is designed for the home and the entire family, the following principles should govern the business classifications listed below:

a) The advertising of hard liquor should not be accepted.

b) The advertising of beer and wines is acceptable only when presented in the best of good taste and discretion, and is acceptable subject to existing laws.

THE MOTION-PICTURE CODE

c) Advertising by institutions or enterprises which in their offers of instruction imply promises of employment or make exaggerated claims for the opportunities awaiting those who enroll for courses is generally unacceptable.

d) The advertising of firearms and fireworks is acceptable only subject to Federal and local laws.

e) The advertising of fortune-telling, occultism, spiritualism, astrology, phrenology, palm-reading, numerology, mind-reading, or character-reading is not acceptable.

f) Because all products of a personal nature create special problems, such products, when accepted, should be treated with especial emphasis on ethics and the canons of good taste; however, the advertising of intimately personal products which are generally regarded as unsuitable conversational topics in mixed social groups is not acceptable.

g) The advertising of tip sheets, race track publications, or organizations seeking to advertise for the purpose of giving odds or promoting betting or lotteries is unacceptable.

2. Diligence should be exercised to the end that advertising copy accepted for telecasting complies with pertinent Federal, state and local laws.

3. An advertiser who markets more than one product should not be permitted to use

c) The advertising of fortune-telling, occultism, spiritualism, astrology, phrenology, palm-reading, numerology, mind-reading or character-reading is not acceptable.

d) All advertising of products of a personal nature, when accepted, should be treated with special concern for the sensitivities of the listeners.

e) The advertising of tip sheets, publications, or organizations seeking to advertise for the purpose of giving odds or promoting betting or lotteries is unacceptable.

2. An advertiser who markets more than one product should not be permitted to use

THE TELEVISION CODE

advertising copy devoted to an acceptable product for purposes of publicizing the brand name or other identification of a product which is not acceptable.

Advertising of Medical Products

1. The advertising of medical products presents considerations of intimate and far-reaching importance to the consumer, and the following principles and procedures should apply in the advertising thereof:

a) A television broadcaster should not accept advertising material which in his opinion offensively describes or dramatizes distress or morbid situations involving ailments, by spoken word, sound or visual effects.

b) Because of the personal nature of the advertising of medical products, claims that a product will effect a cure and the indiscriminate use of such words as "safe", "without risk", "harmless", or terms of similar meaning should not be accepted in the advertising of medical products on television stations.

THE RADIO CODE

advertising copy devoted to an acceptable product for purposes of publicizing the brand name or other identification of a product which is not acceptable.

3. Care should be taken to avoid presentation of "bait-switch" advertising whereby goods or services which the advertiser has no intention of selling are offered merely to lure the customer into purchasing higher-priced substitutes.

THE MOTION-PICTURE CODE

Contests

1. Contests should offer the opportunity to all contestants to win on the basis of ability and skill, rather than chance.

2. All contest details, including rules, eligibility requirements, opening and termination dates should be clearly and completely announced and/or shown, or easily accessible to the viewing public, and the winners' names should be released and prizes awarded as soon as possible after the close of the contest.

3. When advertising is accepted which requests contestants to submit items of product identification or other evidence of purchase of product, reasonable facsimiles thereof should be made acceptable.

4. All copy pertaining to any contest (except that which is required by law) associated with the exploitation or sale of the sponsor's product or service, and all references to prizes or gifts offered in such connection should be considered a part of and included in the total time allowances as herein provided.

Premiums and Offers

1. Full details of proposed offers should be required by the television broadcaster for investigation and approval before the first

Contests

Contests should offer the opportunity to all contestants to win on the basis of ability and skill, rather than chance.

All contest details, including rules, eligibility requirements, opening and termination dates should be clearly and completely announced or easily accessible to the listening public; and the winners' names should be released as soon as possible after the close of the contest.

When contestants are required to submit items of product identification or other evidence of purchase of product, reasonable facsimiles thereof should be made acceptable.

All copy pertaining to any contest (except that which is required by law) associated with the exploitation or sale of the sponsor's product or service, and all references to prizes or gifts offered in such connection should be considered a part of and included in the total time limitations heretofore provided.

All such broadcasts should comply with pertinent Federal, State and Local laws and regulations.

Premiums and Offers

The broadcaster should require that full details of proposed offers be submitted for investigation and approval before the first

THE TELEVISION CODE

announcement of the offer is made to the public.

2. A final date for the termination of an offer should be announced as far in advance as possible.

3. Before accepting for telecast offers involving a monetary consideration, a television broadcaster should satisfy himself as to the integrity of the advertiser and the advertiser's willingness to honor complaints indicating dissatisfaction with the premium by returning the monetary consideration.

4. There should be no misleading descriptions or visual representations of any premiums or gifts which would distort or enlarge their value in the minds of the listeners.

5. Assurances should be obtained from the advertiser that premiums offered are not harmful to person or property.

6. Premiums should not be approved which appeal to superstition on the basis of "luck-bearing" powers or otherwise.

Time Standards for Advertising Copy

1. In accordance with good telecast advertising practices, the time standards for advertising copy are as follows:

THE RADIO CODE

announcement of the offer is made to the public.

A final date for the termination of an offer should be announced as far in advance as possible.

If a consideration is required, the advertiser should agree to honor complaints indicating dissatisfaction with the premium by returning the consideration.

There should be no misleading descriptions or comparisons of any premiums or gifts which will distort or enlarge their value in the minds of the listeners.

★ ★ ★

Time Standards for Advertising Copy

As a guide to the determination of good broadcast advertising practice, the time standards for advertising copy are established as follows:

THE MOTION-PICTURE CODE

Length of Program (minutes)	Length of Advertising Message (minutes and seconds)		
	News Programs Day and Night	All Other Programs Class "A" Time	All Other Hours
5	1:00	1:00	1:15
10	1:45	2:00	2:10
15	2:15	2:30	3:00
25		2:50	4:00
30		3:00	4:15
45		4:30	5:45
60		6:00	7:00

2. Reasonable and limited identification of prize and statement of the donor's name within formats wherein the presentation of contest awards or prizes is a necessary and integral part of program content shall not be included as commercial time within the meaning of paragraph 1. above; however, any oral or visual presentation concerning the product or its donor, over and beyond such identification and statement, shall be included as commercial time within the meaning of paragraph 1. above.

3. The time standards set forth above do not affect the established practice of reserving for station use the last 30 seconds of each program for station break and spot announcements.

The maximum time to be used for advertising allowable to any single sponsor, regardless of type of program, should be —

5 minute programs	1:15
10 "	2:10
15 "	3:00
25 "	4:00
30 "	4:15
45 "	5:45
60 "	7:00

The time standards allowable to a single advertiser do not affect the established practice of allowing for station breaks between programs.

★ ★ ★

THE MOTION-PICTURE CODE

THE RADIO CODE

THE TELEVISION CODE

4. Announcement programs are designed to accommodate a designated number of individual live or recorded announcements, generally one minute in length, which are carried within the body of the program and are available for sale to individual advertisers. Normally not more than 3 one-minute announcements (which should not exceed approximately 125 words if presented live) should be scheduled within a 15-minute period and not more than six such announcements should be scheduled within a 30-minute period in local announcement programs; however, fewer announcements of greater individual length may be scheduled, provided that the aggregate length of the announcements approximates three minutes in a 15-minute program or six minutes in a 30-minute program. In announcement programs other than 15 minutes or 30 minutes in length, the proportion of one minute of announcement within every five minutes of programming is normally applied. The announcements must be presented within the framework of the program period designated for their use and kept in harmony with the content of the program in which they are placed.

5. Programs presenting women's services, features, shopping guides, market information, and similar material, provide a special

Programs of multiple sponsorship presenting commercial services, features, shopping guides, marketing news, and similar service to the listening and viewing public in which advertising material is an informative and integral part of the program content. Because of these special characteristics the time standards set forth above may be waived to a reasonable extent.

6. Even though the commercial time limitations of the Code do not specifically prohibit back-to-back announcements, such a practice is not recommended for more than two announcements, either at station break or within the framework of a single program.

7. Any casual reference in a program to another's product or service under any trade name or language sufficiently descriptive to identify it, should, except for normal guest identifications, be condemned and discouraged.

8. Stationary backdrops or properties in television presentations showing the sponsor's name or product, the name of his product, his trade mark or slogan may be used only incidentally. They should not obtrude on program interest or entertainment. "On Camera" shots of such materials should be fleeting, not too frequent, and mindful of the need of maintaining a proper program balance.

Dramatized Appeals and Advertising

Appeals to help fictitious characters in television programs by purchasing the ad-

information, may include more material normally classified as "commercial" or "advertising", if it is of such nature as to serve the interests of the general public and, if properly produced and intelligently presented within the established areas of good taste.

★ ★ ★

Any reference in a sponsored program to another's product or services under any trade name, or language sufficiently descriptive to identify it, should, except for normal guest identifications, be considered as advertising copy.

★ ★ ★

THE TELEVISION CODE

ertiser's product or service or sending for a premium should not be permitted, and such fictitious characters should not be introduced into the advertising message for such purposes.

When dramatized advertising material involves statements by doctors, dentists, nurses or other professional people, the material should be presented by members of such profession reciting actual experience or it should be made apparent from the presentation itself that the portrayal is dramatized.

Sponsor Identification

Identification of sponsorship must be made in all sponsored programs in accordance with the requirements of the Communications Act of 1934, as amended, and the Rules and Regulations of the Federal Communications Commission.

THE RADIO CODE

When dramatized advertising material involves statements by doctors, dentists, nurses or other professional people, the material should be presented by members of such profession reciting actual experience or it should be made apparent from the presentation itself that the portrayal is dramatized.

In cases of programs broadcast over multiple station facilities, the originating station or network should assume responsibility for conforming such programs to these Radio Standards of Practice.

★ ★ ★

THE MOTION-PICTURE CODE

BIBLIOGRAPHICAL NOTES

Sources cited in the text are not mentioned in the following notes, which supplement the text citations without, however, attempting to provide an exhaustive bibliography.

CHAPTER 1. THE NATURE OF RADIO ENERGY

No single source combines all the material ideally desirable as background for the non-technical reader in the physical bases of broadcasting. However, the following are excellent general texts of the physical sciences which are valuable for their discussions of broader concepts.

Grant, Hector L., *et al.*, *Physics for Arts and Sciences* (Philadelphia: Blakiston, 1948).

Cheronis, Nicholas D., *et al.*, *The Study of the Physical World* (Boston: Houghton Mifflin, 1950).

CHAPTER 3. THE TELEVISION SERVICE

Ennes, Harold E., *Principles and Practices of Telecasting Operations* (Indianapolis: Howard W. Sams, 1953). Though designed for the technician, this book contains much material of interest to the layman.

Kaufman, Milton, and Thomas, Harry E., *Introduction to Color TV* (New York: John F. Rider, 1954). Also for the technician, but in language understandable to the layman.

National Television System Committee, *Television Standards and Practice* (New York: McGraw-Hill, 1943).

RCA Service Co., Inc., *Practical Color Television for the Service Industry* (Rev. ed.; New York: RCA, 1954). Excellent color diagrams.

Offenhauser, William H., *16-mm. Sound Motion Pictures* (New York: Interscience Publishers, 1949). The basic reference work on 16-mm. technology.

Spottiswoode, Raymond, *Film and Its Techniques* (Berkeley: University of California Press, 1951). The best introduction to film technology and production practices.

Read, Oliver, *The Recording and Reproduction of Sound* (2d ed.; Indianapolis: Howard W. Sams, 1952). A standard reference work.

Chapter 4. Relay and Reproducing Systems

Abramson, Albert, "A Short History of Television Recording," *Journal of the Society of Motion Picture and Television Engineers*, LXIV (February, 1955), pp. 72-76.

Chapter 5. Emergence of the Concept of Mass Communication

FCC, *Investigation of the Telephone Industry in the United States* (Washington: Government Printing Office, 1939). Said to be the most thorough exploration of a major American business ever made.

Hamilton, Walton, *Patents and Free Enterprise* (Monograph 31 of Temporary National Economic Commission — Washington: Government Printing Office, 1941). The New Deal's view of patents, and its fear of their monopolistic potentialities.

House Committee on Interstate and Foreign Commerce, *House Report 1273, Preliminary Report on Communication Companies* (Washington: Government Printing Office, 1934). Over 4,000 pages analyzing the history, practices, and status of telephone, telegraph, and broadcasting companies.

Thompson, Robert L., *Wiring a Continent* (Princeton, N.J.: Princeton University Press, 1947). Scholarly study of the foundation of the telegraph industry.

Van Deusen, Edmund L., "The Inventor in Eclipse," *Fortune* (December, 1954), pp. 132-135, 197-202. Describes the changed role of the inventor in a technological age.

Ward, Joshua J., *The United States Patent System* (Asheville, N.C.: Inland Press, 1952). Reviews the controversies concerning patent policies.

U.S. Department of Commerce, *The Story of the American Patent System, 1790-1952* (Washington: Government Printing Office, 1953). Briefly covers development of patent laws and patent statistics.

Chapter 6. Wireless Communication

Court opinions in patent cases sometimes contain interesting background material. For example, *De Forest Radio Co.* v. *General Electric Co.*, 283 U.S. 664, reviews in detail the history of the vacuum tube.

Hunt, Frederick V., *Electroacoustics: The Analysis of Transduction and Its Historical Background* (Harvard Monographs in Applied Science No. 5 — Cambridge: Harvard University Press, 1954). The first 91 pages contain unique material on the history of the microphone, the loudspeaker, and other transducers.

Chapter 7. Broadcasting: A New Communication Service

Much systematic research in the history of broadcasting remains to be done. Present materials lean heavily on the records of RCA and NBC; the history of independent stations and of non-corporate aspects of the industry has been almost completely neglected by scholars.

Columbia University Oral History Office. This office has on file over 50 recorded reminiscences of radio pioneers, gathered by Frank Ernest Hill with funds contributed by the industry through the Radio Pioneers Club. Samples of this unique material were published under the title "Music in the Air . . . and Voices on the Crystal Set" in *American Heritage* (August, 1955), pp. 64-88.

Rothafel, Samuel L., and Yates, Raymond F., *Broadcasting, Its New Day* (New York: The Century Co., 1925). Of unique interest because published at a time when the basic structure of broadcasting was still emergent. Of WEAF: "The experiment has not yet shown signs of hardening into a definite commercial proposition with a secure future" (p. 156).

(See also notes to Chapter 9.)

CHAPTER 8. ORIGIN OF GOVERNMENT REGULATION

Legislative and administrative history can be traced through the pages of the *Congressional Record,* the reports of Congressional committees, and the annual reports of the FRC. See notes to Chapters 21 and 22.

CHAPTER 9. THE RADIO ERA: 1927-1948

Anon., "Mutual Reaches Its 20th Birthday," *Broadcasting-Telecasting* (27 September 1954), pp. 90-96. Much material is available concerning the older networks, which have always had a sense of historical mission and have published freely; relatively little material is available concerning Mutual.

Chester, Giraud, "The Press–Radio War: 1933-1935," *Public Opinion Quarterly* XIII (1949), pp. 252-264. Failure of the attempt by established news media to exclude broadcasting from competition.

Hirschmann, Ira A., "The First Symphony Broadcast," *Public Opinion Quarterly* XIII (1949), pp. 683-684. Interesting example of the problems of early programming on WOR.

Kaltenborn, H. V., *Fifty Fabulous Years* (New York: Putnam, 1950). Although writing mainly about world history of the past half century, the "dean of radio commentators" tells how he introduced news commentary on the air and resisted efforts to curb his independence and to contaminate his commentary with advertising.

Lunde, Anders S., "The American Federation of Musicians and the Recording Ban," *Public Opinion Quarterly* XII (1948), pp. 45-56. An episode in the union's bitter fight against mechanization of music, which has seriously affected broadcasting, although increasing rather than decreasing the trend toward syndication.

Warner, Harry P., *Radio and Television Rights* (Albany: Matthew Bender, 1953). Contains material on the history of ASCAP's relations with broadcasting.

CHAPTER 10. THE ASCENDANCY OF TELEVISION

Bello, Francis, "Color TV: Who'll Buy a Triumph?" *Fortune* (November, 1955), pp. 136 ff. Excellent summary of the background and current status of color TV.

Hogan, John V. L., "The Early Days of Television," *Journal of the Society of Motion Picture and Television Engineers LXIII* (November, 1954), pp. 169-173. Covers briefly the period from 1875 to 1930, with emphasis on the earliest developments.

Jensen, A. G., "The Evolution of Modern Television," *Journal of the Society of Motion Picture and Television Engineers* LXIII (November, 1954), pp. 174-188. Authoritative and well-documented historical survey.

Warner, Harry P., *Radio and Television Law* (Rev. ed.; Albany: Matthew Bender, 1953). Includes a useful summary history of the regulation of commercial TV.

Chapter 11. Some Inter-Media Relationships

Caddigan, James L., and Goldsmith, Thomas E., Jr., "An Electronic-Film Combination Apparatus for Motion-Picture and Television Production," *Journal of the Society of Motion Picture and Television Engineers* LXV-1 (January, 1956), pp. 7-16. Hybrid system developed by Dumont.

Daily, Charles R., "Progress Committee Report," *Journal of the Society of Motion Picture and Television Engineers* LXIV (May, 1955), pp. 225-247. Summary of recent developments in wide-screen and other film processes.

Kellogg, Edward W., "History of Sound Motion Pictures," *Journal of the Society of Motion Picture and Television Engineers* LXIV (June, July, and August, 1955), pp. 291-302, 356-374, and 422-437. Scholarly and detailed; includes bibliography of over 400 items.

Matthews, Glenn E., and Tarkington, Raise G., "Early History of Amateur Motion-Picture Film," *Journal of the Society of Motion Picture and Television Engineers* LXIV (March, 1955), pp. 105-116. Background of the development of the now-important 16-mm. medium.

Rackett, Gerald F., "The Production of Motion Pictures in Color, 1930-1954," *Journal of the Society of Motion Picture and Television Engineers* LXIII (October, 1954), pp. 138-140.

Yorke, Dane, "The Rise and Fall of the Phonograph," *American Mercury* XXVII (September, 1932), pp. 1 ff. An interesting object lesson concerning the marketing of a mass entertainment product.

Chapter 12. Dynamics of the Advertising Market

Few of the economic theorists seem to have dealt perceptively with the role of advertising in the modern mass market. The character of the market itself has been delineated by *Fortune* in *The Changing American Market* (New York: Hanover House, 1955). *Life* magazine has produced an excellent film on the subject, also called *The Changing American Market*. The student can best gain a feeling for the character of the advertising market by observing advertising and by scanning trade journals such as *Broadcasting-Telecasting, Sponsor, Advertising Age,* and *Printer's Ink*.

Chapter 13. Integration of Advertising in the Program Service

The student can best study this subject by observing the actual practice of broadcasters and studying the trade press.

Chapter 14. The Rate Structure

See note to Chapter 13. Stations will supply rate cards on request and national rates can readily be obtained in the publications of Standard Rate and Data Service.

CHAPTER 15. MECHANISMS FOR REACHING THE ADVERTISING MARKET

See note to Chapter 13.

CHAPTER 16. THE BUSINESS OF MEASUREMENT AND EVALUATION

Most of the research organizations provide published data on their methods and services. Major research studies are reported in the trade press, and their sponsors usually supply copies.

Advertising Research Foundation, *A Short Annotated Bibliography of Marketing and Advertising Research* (New York: Advertising Research Foundation, 1953).

Bogart, Leo, "Fan Mail for the Philharmonic," *Public Opinion Quarterly* XIII (1949), pp. 423-434. Demonstrates the limitations of mail response as a research tool.

Nielsen, Arthur C., *Television Audience Research for Great Britain* (Chicago: A. C. Nielsen Co., 1955). Prepared for the newly-introduced commercial TV service in Great Britain. Of general interest as a full-dress presentation of the advantages of the automatic-recorder type of audience research.

Alfred Politz Research, Inc., *A Study of Four Media* (New York: Time, Inc., 1953). The largest inter-media research project to date, based on 36,000 interviews, two and a half years in preparation.

CHAPTER 17. ADVERTISING AGENCIES

The trade journal *Sponsor* represents the agency point of view on broadcasting. Textbooks on practical aspects of agency operation are readily available in business libraries. Frederic Wakeman's novel *The Hucksters* (New York: Rinehart, 1946) is alleged to be based on actual figures in the Madison Avenue world of advertising agencies and to reflect (with due allowances for dramatic license) the frenetic atmosphere of that world.

CHAPTER 18. FINANCIAL ORGANIZATION

Under previous administrations the FCC annually published rather full financial reports on the broadcasting industry, but in recent years the amount of information released has been radically reduced. Various estimates are compiled by Publisher's Information Bureau, *Broadcasting-Telecasting, Television Digest,* and other trade sources. The NARTB collects data on operating costs, wages, and income, but this material is not generally released.

CHAPTER 21. THE LAW OF BROADCASTING

The Communications Act can be found under Title 47 of the *United States Code* and the *United States Code Annotated,* the latter with notes on court interpretations. These publications are kept up to date with supplements. A copy of the Act can be obtained directly from the Government Printing Office for a small price. The GPO also publishes *Radio Laws of the United States* (compiled by Elmer A. Lewis), containing all radio legislation since the first act in 1910.

There are a number of books on communications law, the best being Harry

P. Warner's *Radio and Television Law* (Rev. ed.; Albany: Matthew Bender, 1953), which has provision for periodic supplements.

Most appeals from FCC decisions are made in the United States Court of Appeals for the District of Columbia, whose decisions are reported in the *Federal Reporter* (cited as *"F."* and *"F. 2d"*). Supreme Court cases are reported officially in *United States Reports* (cited as *"U.S."*).

The *Congressional Record* should be consulted for the legislative history of enactments. More general information can be obtained from *U.S. Code and Administrative News*. The published hearings of Congressional committees contain a wealth of information about broadcasting in general and about the background of enacted laws in particular. These are indexed in the official *Monthly Catalogue of U.S. Government Publications.*

In addition to the specialized field of communication law, broadcasting is particularly interested in the legal fields represented by the following:

Cross, Harold L., *The People's Right to Know* (New York: Columbia University Press, 1953). Access to the sources of news.

Warner, Harry P., *Radio and Television Rights* (Albany: Matthew Bender, 1953). Thorough treatment of copyright, trademarks, and the law of unfair competition.

Wittenberg, Philip, *Dangerous Words: A Guide to the Law of Libel* (New York: Columbia University Press, 1947).

CHAPTER 22. ADMINISTRATION OF THE LAW

FCC rules, regulations, reports, and orders are first published daily in the official *Federal Register.* Rules and regulations are cumulated as Title 47 of the official *Code of Federal Regulations,* which is brought up to date by supplements. FCC decisions are cumulated in the official *Federal Communications Commission Reports* (not to be confused with its *Annual Reports*), of which Volume 13, covering decisions for the year 1948-1949, was published in 1955.

Official sources are scattered, and are slow to publish supplements; therefore a commercial reporting service, Pike and Fischer, Inc., 1735 De Sales St., N.W., Washington, D.C., publishes *Radio Regulation* (cited as *"R.R."*), which since 1948 has provided a single up-to-date source for FCC decisions and its rules d regulations, court decisions, statutes, and Congressional committee reports.

CHAPTER 23. REGULATION: ENEMY OF FREEDOM

Emerson, Thomas I., and Haber, David, *Political and Civil Rights in the United States* (Buffalo: Dennis, 1952). A source book containing illuminating materials on the First Amendment.

CHAPTER 24. REGULATION: ALLY OF FREEDOM

Chafee, Zechariah, *Government and Mass Communications* (Chicago: University of Chicago Press, 1947). This two-volume work is one of the series published by the Commission for Freedom of the Press, other examples of which are cited at various points in the text. The Commission has provided the most systematic and complete expression to date of the responsibility theory of mass communications control.

CHAPTER 25. SELF-REGULATION

Burnett, Verne, *Self-Regulation of Advertising: A Guidebook of Major Facilities* (New York: American Association of Advertising Agencies and Association of National Advertisers, 1950, Mimeo.). Surveys the self-regulation of the various advertising media and associations.

CHAPTER 26. HIGHER EDUCATION

Broderick, Gertrude, *et al.*, "Educational Television," *Journal of the Society of Motion Picture and Television Engineers* LXV-1 (January, 1956), pp. 20-25. Papers discussing ETV in general and the JCET and ETRC in particular.

Institute for Education by Radio-Television. Although much of the material is inconsequential, the annual compilation of speeches and panel discussions heard at IERT meetings since 1929 provide a useful index to the subjects with which educational broadcasters have been concerned over the years.

Mercer, John, and Becker, Sam, "The Disenchantments of Educational TV," *Audio-Visual Communication Review* III-3 (Summer, 1955), pp. 173-182. An unusually candid caveat by ETV proponents.

National Association of Educational Broadcasters. In recent years the NAEB has been publishing a good deal of useful material; of particular value is its series of monitoring studies of television programming — the only source of detailed information on the content of the service.

United States Office of Education. Although this office is far less active than in the heyday of the FREC, one of the services it still performs is the periodic compilation of a directory of colleges and universities that offer courses in broadcasting.

CHAPTER 27. THE COMMUNICATION PROCESS AND ITS EFFECTS

Anon., "What TV Is Doing to America," *U.S. News and World Report* (2 September 1955), pp. 36-50. Popular summary of facts and opinions about the effects of television. Interesting to compare with the Gould series mentioned below.

Fearing, Franklin (ed.), *Mass Media: Content, Function, and Measurement* (entire issue of *Journal of Social Issues* III-3 [Summer, 1947]). Articles by a number of the leading scholars in the field.

Krech, David, and Crutchfield, Richard S., *Theory and Problems of Social Psychology* (New York: McGraw-Hill, 1948). Expresses the position on basic preliminary issues of social psychology which seems to have been accepted by most students of the mass media.

Gould, Jack, "What TV Is Doing to Us" (reprint by *New York Times* of seven articles originally printed June 24-July 1, 1951). Compare with the first item cited above.

Marx, H. L., *Television and Radio in American Life* (New York: H. W. Wilson, 1953). Anthology of articles from popular sources indicating scope of interest in the subject.

Mills, C. Wright, *White Collar: The American Middle Classes* (New York: Oxford University Press, 1951). An example of the broad evaluations of our society which place a good deal of emphasis on the mass media's (presumed) social influence and also on their role as a mirror of contemporary life.

Schramm, Wilbur (ed.), *The Process and Effects of Mass Communication* (Urbana: University of Illinois Press, 1954). Over 30 articles and excerpts from books by most of the scholars in the field. Its emphasis is on international propaganda (the anthology was originally prepared for the United States Information Agency), but it is valuable as an introduction in that it shows the scope and objectives of contemporary communications research.

——————— (ed.), *Communications in Modern Society* (Urbana: University of Illinois, 1948). Fifteen papers by leading scholars in the field.

Shayon, Robert Lewis, *Television and Our Children* (New York: Longmans, Green, 1951). The alarmist school of thought.

Index